QUEBEC:
Social Change and Political Crisis

Third Edition

Kenneth McRoberts

M&S

Canadian Cataloguing in Publication Data

McRoberts, Kenneth, 1942-
    Quebec: social change and political crisis

3rd ed.
Earlier eds, by Kenneth McRoberts and Dale Posgate.
Includes bibliographical references and index.
ISBN 0-7710-5515-3

1. Quebec (Province) – Social conditions.
2. Quebec (Province) – Economic conditions.
3. Quebec (Province) – Politics and government.
I. Title.

FC2911.M32 1988   971.4'04   C88-093208-2
F1052.M32 1988

Printed and bound in Canada

McClelland & Stewart Inc.
The Canadian Publishers
481 University Avenue
Toronto, Ontario
M5G 2E9

Contents

To my son,
Stéphane

Preface to Third Edition

This book emerged as a collaborative project between Dale Posgate and myself, written in the mid-1970s while Robert Bourassa was still in his second term of office and the Parti québécois held only six seats in the Assemblée nationale. Our objective was to present a fuller appreciation than was then available in English Canada of the profound changes in Quebec society and politics and, in the process, to trace the growth of the Quebec *indépendantiste* movement.

Months after publication of the book, the Parti québécois came to power and we were confronted with the challenge of comprehending and analysing the efforts of the Lévesque government to make the dream of independence a reality. Since Dale Posgate had by then become committed to other endeavours, the task fell primarily to me of preparing a revised edition. Published in the summer of 1980, it brought the analysis up to the Quebec referendum. Over the subsequent eight years developments in Quebec society and politics, and in Quebec's relations with the rest of Canada, have been such as to require yet another edition.

The 1980s have not been kind to the projects of political and economic change that so dominated Quebec's political life during the 1960s and 1970s. The campaign to establish Quebec as a sovereign state was dealt a fatal blow by the 1980 Quebec referendum, in which only 40 per cent gave the PQ government the mandate it sought. This setback for Quebec nationalism was further confirmed by the Constitution Act, 1982, with its failure to provide Québécois with any meaningful "renewal" of the federal system. More generally, the whole notion of the interventionist state, that central legacy of the Quiet Revolution, was effectively undermined by the combined challenge of prolonged economic crisis and an ascendant Francophone business class. As it coped with these developments, the second Lévesque government found itself retreating more and more from the PQ's founding ideals. Moreover, with the return to power of Robert Bourassa and the Liberal Party in 1985 the pressures to "normalize" the Quebec state assumed added momentum, sufficient to place in question not only measures of the first Lévesque government but even basic accomplishments of the Quiet Revolution.

In short, the 1980s have seen major efforts not only to halt but to reverse some of the processes of political and social change that earlier editions of this volume had sought to recount and explain.

7

We need both to understand the roots of these efforts and to determine the degree of impact they have had. To this end, much new material has been written for this volume: Chapter Ten examines the Lévesque administration's second term in office and Chapter Eleven assesses the first two years of the new Bourassa government. The final chapter takes stock of the present state of Quebec society and seeks to assess the future prospects for Quebec nationalism. As well, Chapter Nine contains a detailed analysis of the 1980 referendum campaign and its result.

Beyond these attempts to comprehend and analyse new developments in Quebec politics and society, this edition, like the second edition, addresses some of the critiques offered of the general arguments originally articulated in this book. In particular, I have sought to demonstrate more fully, through revision of earlier chapters in the book, the central role a Francophone new middle class played in initiating and leading the Quiet Revolution. And I have addressed competing interpretations that have been offered of the *indépendantiste* movement. At the same time, I have further expanded the critique of development theory and elaboration of alternative approaches introduced in the second edition.

Of course, in preparing these revised editions, I have been simply building on the foundation originally developed with Dale Posgate. Along the way I have become indebted to many scholars and political figures, who have given me needed information and materials and commented on my ideas and arguments. For their comments on this edition, I am especially indebted to André Blais of the Université de Montréal and to colleagues at York University: Reg Whitaker, Donald Smiley, Leslie Green, and Thomas Courchene, current Robarts Professor of Canadian Studies. François Vaillancourt, of the Université de Montréal, furnished important data.

Several graduate students at York University provided invaluable research assistance, including Sharon Wong, Jacqueline Wood, and, most especially, Lise Gotell. David Roseman assumed the arduous task of committing the text of the second edition to computer diskettes, thus greatly facilitating the whole revision process. Pat Cates and York University's Secretarial Services were invariably efficient and helpful. As with the second edition, Richard Tallman was a superlative editor. Michael Harrison of McClelland and Stewart helped guide the project through its various stages with care and efficiency. Finally, a grant from the Ontario Arts Council provided crucial financial assistance to the revision process.

CHAPTER ONE
Analysing Change:
Theories and Concepts

By most appearances, the dramatic and prolonged crisis into which the Quebec nationalist movement propelled Canadian politics has run its course. The Parti québécois government's proposed mandate to negotiate sovereignty-association was resoundingly defeated in the 1980 referendum. Not only is the Parti québécois no longer in power, replaced by a Liberal administration squarely committed to the federal order, but the PQ has itself retreated steadily from its goal of Quebec sovereignty, now officially committed to a vague notion of "national affirmation." The several authentically *indépendantiste* movements and parties that have sought to carry on the struggle are an exceedingly negligible force in contemporary Quebec politics. Moreover, with the Meech Lake Accord it appears that Quebec's symbolic exclusion from the Canadian constitutional order, stemming from the Constitution Act, 1982, will soon be ended. In short, it would seem that Canada's most profound political crisis, which threatened the very integrity of the Canadian political community, is over.

The predominant English-Canadian response to this turn of events has been simply to shift attention from Quebec to other matters. Yet, there are compelling reasons for reviewing and analysing Quebec's experience over the last few decades and, on this basis, seeking to understand Quebec's contemporary condition.

Appearances can be deceiving. Conceivably, the crisis has not run its course. For instance, the continuing debates over language rights within Quebec, and within other parts of Canada, might serve to resurrect nationalist grievances against the Canadian political order. Under the leadership of Jacques Parizeau, the Parti québécois not only might regain some of its past dynamism but would be much more clearly committed to Quebec independence. In any event, the history of French-Canadian nationalism is manifestly one of cycles. Even if the nationalist surge of the 1960s and

1970s is a spent force, and contemporary tensions are unable to reignite it, there is every reason to believe that at some point in the future, under different conditions and a new generation of leaders, a new nationalist movement will come to the fore. In many ways, its form and its impact will be shaped by the extent to which Quebec and the rest of Canada did, or did not, reach a meaningful reconciliation in the 1980s. In short, for English Canadians concerned with the future of their country, Quebec's past and present experience is very much a matter of importance.

Beyond that, for the student of politics in general, Quebec's recent experience is truly fascinating. Rarely within advanced capitalist societies has the territorial integrity of a state been so seriously challenged as it was by the Quebec neo-nationalist movement. During the 1960s and 1970s nationalist movements arose in various European settings – Wales, Scotland, Belgium, Brittany, and the Basque country – but none was able to mobilize, through democratic means, as broad a base of support. And none was able to assume control of a government. Thus, the case of Quebec nationalism is an especially powerful challenge to the assumptions of steady political integration and cultural homogenization that had once so dominated social science theories of economic and social development. By the same token, the experience of the Parti québécois in power is an especially striking instance of the transformations that social movements undergo if they assume office within the established order.

While there clearly are compelling reasons to seek to comprehend Quebec's experience over the last few decades, doing so is no mean task. One can document a myriad of changes in economic organization, in social practices, and in values and mores. The instances of political change are especially striking: the rise of new political parties and movements; the tensions between levels of government; the agitation for sovereignty and independence. Phrases such as "Quiet Revolution" have been invented to refer to this process of change, and they seem to carry meaning to a great many Québécois. But in merely evoking this experience of change they fail to provide any real understanding of it. A great many questions remain unanswered. Is there a common thread to all the specific instances of change? How much "real change" do they represent in the Canadian context, and is Quebec's experience any different from that of other societies? And finally, *why* have these changes occurred? In short, we need concepts and categories to summarize and describe this change, and we need theories to explain it.

The task of analysing change in Quebec would be much simpler if we could work within a single theoretical approach, confident that the factors it identifies and the relationships it highlights would be adequate to an understanding of the case of Quebec. In fact, most existing studies of Quebec have tended to rely on a single set of questions involving the relationship among classes, the conflict between language groups, or the evolution of a nationalist ideology. But we cannot afford to let our understanding be constricted and predetermined by these narrow avenues of analysis. The challenge is to identify and to keep in mind a sufficiently wide range of approaches and concepts so that an exploration of Quebec will not be prematurely narrowed. To be sure, some might object to such a rampant eclecticism, but only in this fashion can we avoid arriving at narrow, one-dimensional interpretations that, while congruent with some body of general theory, provide a partial or distorted understanding of Quebec's particular experience.

With all its defects and limitations, the developmental approach at least has the virtue of comprehensiveness. We will use it as our starting point: its general categories will provide an initial framework for assembling information on Quebec's experience over several decades. As we shall see, however, the developmental approach does not provide a satisfactory body of theory for linking together the various forms of social, economic, and political change it isolates. Accordingly, as we trace these linkages in the case of Quebec, we will call upon several different modes of analysis.

In part, the notion of economic and political dependence among regions or societies will help to explain the specific pattern of Quebec's development. But we will argue that Quebec's development also has been shaped by a "cultural division of labour" between Francophones and Anglophones, centred within Quebec. And both dependence and the cultural division of labour must be related to a class structure that straddles and subdivides geographical and cultural entities. These forces have all been mediated by the form of Canada's political institutions, especially federalism. Finally, and perhaps most importantly, we must concern ourselves with the concepts of nation and national consciousness. A French-Canadian (or, more recently, Québécois) national consciousness has closely shaped Quebec's development and mediated the specific roles that dependence, cultural division of labour, relations among classes, and federalism have played within this development.

In summary, an understanding of the Quebec experience requires a simultaneous use of a series of concepts: development, dependence, cultural division of labour, class relations, federalism, and national consciousness. The rest of this chapter will be devoted to exploring each of these concepts and to demonstrating how they can be applied to the case of Quebec.

Development and Modernization

Many social scientists use the concept of development, and the related concept of modernization, to characterize and explain broad processes of change. The criticisms of these terms, and their various applications, are numerous and often compelling, as we shall see. Nevertheless, a large body of literature in the social sciences, especially in the English language, explores these concepts and seeks to build theories around them. Moreover, they have informed in one fashion or another much of the writing on Quebec's past and present. They offer a logical place to begin our search for concepts and theories of change.

One widely used approach to the concept of development establishes two poles, "tradition" and "modernity," which are ideal types or analytical constructs and not depictions of reality, since no society will perfectly fit either side of the dichotomy. One of the earliest versions of the dichotomy was Max Weber's analysis of the different bases of authority, but numerous authors have since brought to bear a whole range of variables that attempt to cover aspects of social, economic, and political activities. As a result, there is no longer a precise or single definition of what constitutes a traditional as opposed to a modern society. Here are some of the criteria that have appeared most frequently, in one form or another: traditional society is more likely to be rural and agrarian than urban and industrial; status is more likely to be based on ascriptive ties than on achievement; values are more likely to be particularist and religious than universal and secular; social structures and social roles are more likely to be integrated with each other than differentiated.

Because it has been subjected to academic specialization, modernization is usually divided into social, economic, and political dimensions. These are simply categories, of debatable exclusiveness, under which various phenomena can be lumped for the sake of convenience and perhaps to aid analysis. A fourth category or dimension, the psychological, cuts across the others. It relies on different kinds of data (individualistic instead of aggregate), and

12

illustrates how "social mobilization" (changes in attitudes and behaviour) results from the process of modernization, or, depending on what version is followed, becomes an integral part of that process. The following paragraphs outline the contents of familiar categories of social, economic, and political change and suggest what shape the modernization process is likely to take in each case.[1]

The variables usually associated with the concept of social change include urbanization, secularization, the spread of mass education, and the growth of mass communications networks. Urbanization, measured by the demographic shift from the countryside to the city, is regarded as a social as well as an economic indicator because the city breaks down rural lifestyles and social structures identified with traditional society. The city dweller enters into new relationships in every sphere of his life and sheds the old ones. Urban anthropologists have shown that the break is not as neat and fast as was first assumed, but rural-urban migration remains a valid index of social change.

The second variable, secularization, entails the breakdown of the integrated community. In such a community, one authority (often with divine ordination) influences all activities, and individuals exist not autonomously but only in terms of their role in the community as a whole. The breakdown is not necessarily the end of religion in the individual sense but a change in the individual's relationship with his society. Separate associations for each of his activities (work, leisure, politics, education, etc.) displace the single authority of tradition, the community as a whole is no longer identifiable solely in traditional terms, and the individual comes to deal directly with forces external to the community rather than having these filtered and interpreted for him. The integrity and security of the traditional community are replaced by fragmentation and insecurity in the secular community.

The third variable, the extension of formal education to larger proportions of the population for longer periods of time, encourages the spread of skills, such as literacy, that enhance the individual's position in a modernizing society. Mass literacy is the foundation of a modern economy, and the skills of higher education are necessary to run the private and public bureaucracies of a modern society. But while mass education is widely recognized as an element of social change, the outcomes and side effects are difficult to predict and, to the distress of many, to control. Communication patterns in a traditional setting tend to be limited in scope and content and restricted to oral transmission. Modern communications reach more people with more information, and this is regarded as part of social change because the massive diffusion of information is assumed to affect the way people behave.[2] At the same time, and more significantly, much of the information transmitted in a modernized, secular society is simply irrelevant to the needs and aspirations of the people, and the bombardment of such information can confuse their decision-making faculties. In the traditional community, by contrast, most communications are germane to the problems of the day and have an integrative function.

Economic change has come to mean economic growth. Though the long search for explanations of economic growth has been inconclusive, at least there are measures of it that are relatively "hard" – quantifiable and reliable. In spite of its obviously Western origins, industrialization is a key index of economic growth and, because it depicts a shift away from the agriculture identified with traditional society, it is an index also of modernization in general. Industrialization entails structural changes and, at the individual level, a new set of economic relationships: rewards in cash instead of in kind; traditional and individual employment instead of permanent and familial; an economic hierarchy based on wealth instead of on land or ascribed status. A number of measures of industrialization are in use, such as rates of productivity, sources of the GNP, and per capita energy consumption. Measures more pertinent to the effects of industrialization on the individual include per capita income and distribution of the labour force. The former tells us, at least in aggregate terms, how well people live, and the latter, to some extent, how they spend their lives.

The final dimension, political change, is more problematic. While economic growth is a commonplace notion, there is no parallel concept of growth in the political sphere. The term political development is frequently used, but there is much disagreement over the implications of development (stability, constitutionalism, a two-party system, egalitarianism, etc.) and greater uncertainty as to how to measure it. Although any generalization about political change is prone to exceptions that arise in specific historical and cultural settings, it is possible to find sufficiently neutral and universal indicators to give a rough measure of what is meant by political modernization. The trouble with many of these is that they are too broad to be valid or reliable, or that they are very narrow and chosen only because of the availability of data. Political integration is an example of the former, and election turnout of the latter. Some more useful indicators of political modernization fall somewhere in between:[3] a growth in the proportion of the population that is politically relevant, i.e., affected by and perhaps affecting government and policy; more scope and penetration of government activities, usually through the instrument of a larger, more skilled bureaucracy; more generalized recruitment of the political elite; a style of performance and communication by the political elite that is more "open" and less tied to non-political structures; and finally, greater participation in politics, in the minimal form of voting but more importantly in the form of joining political organizations, being in touch with political communications networks, or working for political goals by legal or extra-legal means. Thus, a modern political system is generally distinguished from a traditional one by being more open and larger in the scope and scale of government, and by involving a greater proportion of the populace in activities directly related to the exercise and distribution of power. Clearly, most characterizations of political modernization can be reduced to three major dimensions: expansion of the state, popular mobilization, and popular participation.

The concept of political modernization, defined in this fashion, does contain major flaws. There are obvious links between this conception of a "modern" political system, with its stress on elections and other devices for popular participation, and the liberal democratic ideology.[4] One may seriously question whether the presence of these procedures necessarily entails any increase in real participation in political decision-making (greater, for instance, than in the traditional structures of a rural community). Many studies have suggested that election outcomes have little impact on the directions of public policy.[5] Given the possibilities of opinion being manipulated through the media, and through election campaigning, one might argue that elections do not even constitute meaningful popular choices. Also, one might ask whether political systems with elaborate formal procedures for participation (such as the United States) are, in any fundamental sense, more "modern" than such systems as that of the Soviet Union. Political change may well involve the expansion of state structures and the mobilization of larger proportions of the population to political action, but any apparent increase in popular participation may have more to do with form than substance. In fact, a detailed analysis of the history of Western Europe suggests that expansion of the state may be accompanied by a decline in the real possibility of popular participation. Frequently, state expansion was secured through force and coercion; existing political rights were abolished.[6]

For these reasons, our analysis of political change in Quebec will focus on a single dimension of political modernization: growth in the functions and structures of the state. We can anticipate that expansion of the state will induce a greater political mobilization of the population. People may see the expanded state as more salient to their daily lives; they may afford it more attention and seek to influence it more. But we will make no assumptions about change in the actual opportunities for participation in political decision-making.

The difficulties with the developmental approach to studying change go beyond the adequacy of its major concepts; they extend to the interrelationships among these concepts. The literature has yet to provide an adequate theory showing precisely how social and economic development are linked to political modernization. Several strategies have been employed. Some students have attempted to delineate a series of stages through which systems pass as they undergo development. For instance, A.F.K. Organski has differentiated four phases of political modernization: the politics of primitive unification, the politics of industrialization, the politics of national welfare, and the politics of abundance.[7] Yet, none of the sequential theories seem able to embrace the immense diversity of ways in which concrete political systems have undergone political change. They cannot handle the European experience, which has been the implicit basis of most theorizing, let alone the experience of the Third World.[8] Other students have tried to locate some general process inherent to all aspects of development – social, economic, and political – which necessitates that change in one sector be accompanied by commensurate change in the others. For instance, Phillips Cutright has focused on the complexity of organization, contending that growth in the complexity of the state is required by growth in the complexity of social and economic systems.[9] Yet, a detailed study of Western European systems indicates no clear relationship between the rise of states and the levels of social and economic complexity.[10]

Finally, some students have sought to link the character and degree of political modernization to a series of crises that all systems supposedly face at one point or another in the movement to social and economic development. The level of political modernization, and the ease with which it is attained, would be dependent on the length of time over which these crises are encountered and whether they are met one-by-one rather than several at time.[11] But, in the examination of concrete systems, it has been difficult to determine with any precision when particular crises have appeared and when they have been resolved. Moreover, in the Western European experience some of the most "successful" instances of political modernization were marked by prolonged periods of crisis, not dissimilar to the experience of Third World countries where these same crises allegedly have impeded political modernization.[12]

The development literature, then, leaves us with the plausible assumption that the broad processes of social and economic development, on the one hand, and political modernization, on the other, are somehow related. But it affords no real understanding of the dynamics of this interrelationship or any reliable means of predicting how they will present themselves in a concrete case. We will use the concepts of economic and social development, and of political modernization, simply as categories to organize our discussion of Quebec's experience with change over the past few decades. But we cannot draw from the development literature a general theory that will predict and explain how these forms of change are related; we will have to ascertain this relationship for ourselves.

In the case of Quebec, there is an additional reason to believe that the roots of political modernization, even if the term is understood simply as expansion of the state, will be complex. The Quebec state, after all, is part of a federal system; social and economic changes in Quebec might prompt expansion of the Quebec state, but the response also might come at the federal level. We could attempt to use the constitutional division of powers as a guide to predict which government might respond to a specific form or level of social and economic change, but it would not be a reliable guide. The terms of the BNA Act are too ambiguous to allow such predictions, even if we could assume that specific social or economic changes will automatically result in governmental response. As we shall see, this difficulty hinders simple application of one of the most promising theories of political modernization: the neo-Marxist thesis that the monopolization of capital imposes greater functions on the state.[13] This theory has identified a primary force for political modernization. But, in the case of Quebec, questions remain. Which "state" is to assume the new functions, Ottawa or Quebec City? We will have to examine the configurations of social and economic forces attached to each state.

Dependence

Some students contend that the developmental approach has failed to produce more than a set of useful organizing concepts because it has not properly considered the relationships among societies and political systems. Economic and political forces from other societies may indeed determine the kind of development a society undergoes, as well as the time at which it occurs. Moreover, it is argued, these interrelationships frequently are exploitative: the development of one society is based, in part, on the exploitation of another. In effect, the development of one society requires the underdevelopment of another. This underdevelopment will be manifested in a variety of ways: the weakness of secondary industry, the absence of an indigenous bourgeoisie, and the inability of the state to deploy even the limited autonomy normally available to sovereign states. Development that does occur is stunted or deformed, reflecting primarily the needs of elements in the dominant society. In reference to such a society, then, any understanding of the processes of economic and social development and of political modernization, and of their interrelationships, must be based first on an analysis of this dependence. The processes of change may be responses to the changing needs of the dominant society; in some cases, they may also reflect a determination of local forces to reduce dependence.[14]

This dependence approach has been criticized in many quarters. The tendency of dependence analysis to use societies or regions as the basic unit of analysis has been attacked by some as leading to "holistic" assumptions, which ignore powerful economic and social divisions within the unit. For orthodox Marxists, it is incorrect to base analysis on some "unequal exchange" among regions rather than on the division of labour among classes.[15] Also, it has been argued that dependence theory has not yet properly analysed precisely how external forces direct the state of a dependent society; there is no theory of political dependence.[16]

Finally, in many applications of the dependence approach (including applications to Quebec) there has been a tendency to ignore or to underestimate the intensity of movements within the society to reduce or eliminate dependence. Social, economic, and political activities are seen simply as faithful reflections of the interests of the dominant society. Yet, we know that in many dependent societies resistance to these interests has developed, which may explain some of the directions that development takes. For instance, political modernization may be shaped in part by a desire to use the state to create an indigenous bourgeoisie. Under what conditions is this likely to happen? As well as a theory of political dependence, we need a theory of political "anti-dependence."

18

In applying dependence theory to Quebec it is important to specify the precise form of dependence in question.[17] The bulk of the literature is concerned with global relations between the industrialized economic "centres" of North America and Europe and the underdeveloped, heavily agrarian economic "peripheries" of the Third World. Despite the attempts of some students to draw parallels between Quebec and these peripheral economies, Quebec in fact has more in common with the economic centres.[18] This can be seen in terms of the set of distinguishing characteristics of a periphery identified by Samir Amin, a foremost theorist of dependence. Contemporary Quebec has had some of Amin's traits of a periphery: weakness of an "indigenous" bourgeoisie (based on the Francophone majority) and an associated growth in state bureaucracy. But it does not have others: low level of industrialization and absence of a "foreign" bourgeoisie. Also, unlike the typical peripheral society, Quebec does not now have a significant "pre-capitalist" sector.[19]

Quebec's dependence can be better conceived as that of a region within an economic centre consisting of Canada, and perhaps of North America as a whole. Some students would contend that, given this degree of political and economic integration, the term "dependence" is misleading; more appropriate would be terms such as "internal colony" or *domination interieure.*"[20] Whatever the preferred terminology, Quebec's situation becomes a manifestation of a general phenomenon among industrialized societies, the uneven development of regions. Within most industrialized economies one finds that economic development tends to be concentrated, for whatever reason, in certain central regions. Technologically innovative industries are established in these areas, and both skilled labour and domestic and foreign capital are drawn to them. Frequently, when a region has established an initial preeminence in the industrialization process, it continues to enjoy a relative advantage, although Canada and other societies demonstrate how economic centres can shift over time. A multitude of explanations has been offered for these regional imbalances, from differences in cultural traits and the presence of entrepreneurial elites to the unalterable impact of such structural factors as resource base and geographical location. But such terms as "internal colony" suggest that patterns of regional dominance or disadvantage may be functionally related: the continued development of stronger regions may be based on other regions serving as sources of capital, and migrant labour, and as markets for finished products.[21]

When viewed within a Canadian or North American context, Quebec displays many of the characteristics of a dependent economy, but it is not unique in this regard: in one fashion or another, all the other Canadian regions display economic dependence. One can easily show that contemporary Quebec is disadvantaged with respect to Ontario along many dimensions, all of which denote uneven development if not domination: the size and technological sophistication of secondary industry; ownership of enterprises by residents of the other region; capital flows between the regions; levels of unemployment and per capita income.[22] But one can argue that along virtually all these dimensions Ontario displays dependence on the United States. Moreover, along some dimensions, such as foreign ownership, Ontario is even more dependent on the U.S. than is Quebec.[23] Much of the high-technology industry, which distinguishes Ontario from Quebec, is controlled by American multinational corporations. While American management may share language and other cultural traits with the bulk of Ontario's population, unlike Quebec's, economic structures are nonetheless dependent.

One particular consequence of Ontario's dependence is that, as in Quebec, there is relatively little indigenous research and development. Yet, the commonality between Quebec and Ontario of dependence on the U.S. has not served to offset regional competition. If anything, it has heightened competition as the two regions seek to attract American capital. The greater success of Ontario in securing American industrial investment, due largely to its proximity to the American economic centre, has reinforced Ontario's dominance in relations with Quebec. At the same time, it has also reinforced Ontario's dependence on the U.S.

Western Canada and the Atlantic provinces share Quebec's dependence on Ontario and the United States, but they are dependent on Quebec as well. To the extent that the National Policy of tariff protection has supported industry in Quebec (for instance, textiles and furniture) and has forced western Canada and the Atlantic provinces to purchase products of these industries, Quebec's development has been based partially on the underdevelopment of other regions. The importance of this particular manifestation of dependence should not be minimized. Among other things, it means that most Canadian provinces (although not Ontario) can argue with a certain credibility that they would have no interest in forming a common market, or even a customs union, with an independent Quebec.[24]

In short, the development of Canada as a whole, as well as each of its regions, has been shaped by various forms of economic dependence. Yet, whatever parallels one might draw between Quebec's experience and that of the rest of Canada, Quebec's experience as a region within the North American centre is different. Beyond considerable differences in the levels and forms of dependence there is the fact that for Quebec, and Quebec alone, economic dependence is parallelled by significant cultural difference. At a minimum, this means that economic dependence may be experienced differently by many residents of Quebec. The notion that a region is an "internal colony" must have a special credibility when the dominant language and culture of the other regions are different. Also, cultural differences possibly have shaped and directed Quebec's development, including its dependence on the other regions. More concretely, perhaps its cultural distinctiveness has placed Quebec at a greater disadvantage than would otherwise have been the case, thus reinforcing economic and even political dependence.

In fact, over the years many students have argued that the relatively low level of development in Quebec's economy can be traced to this cultural distinctiveness. Typically, the argument focuses on the alleged presence among Francophones of values less "appropriate" to North American capitalism than those dominant in Ontario or elsewhere. Thus, on the basis of a comparative study of manufacturing in Quebec and Ontario, University of Toronto economist John Dales argued that in the 1950s "the major part of Quebec's backwardness in manufacturing is to be explained on the basis of factors other than resources. We can reasonably refer to these 'other' factors as cultural differences. . . ."[25] Assigning a full 65 per cent of the "backwardness" to these cultural differences, he offered by way of example differences in tastes, skills, entrepreneurship, propensity to consume, and mobility.[26]

Over the last two decades, however, other students have tried to trace Quebec's economic development to factors completely independent of such cultural differences. In his effort to minimize the importance of differences in resources, Dales himself was responding to a celebrated article by Albert Faucher and Maurice Lamontagne that sought to explain Quebec's economic development in terms of the interaction between geography and changes in dominant technology.[27]

Faucher and Lamontagne noted that the economic strength Quebec displayed up to the mid-nineteenth century was based on commercial activity, as wood and foodstuffs were shipped through Montreal and Quebec City to Europe. This activity also supported the construction of wooden ships in Quebec. With the arrival of the industrial age in the mid-nineteenth century, Quebec was soon at a disadvantage to Ontario. Steel replaced wood as the basic industrial commodity, and, unlike Ontario, Quebec had no easy access to coal and iron ore, which were now essential for economic development. Thus, economic development shifted to Ontario, just as in the United States it shifted from seaboard cities to Pittsburgh, Cleveland, Detroit, and Chicago. Tariff protection enabled Ontario to draw on its privileged location to build a substantial manufacturing base. Moreover, its greater proximity to the new American economic centre meant that American firms seeking to enter the Canadian market were more likely to establish their branch plants there. Faucher and Lamontagne noted that toward the end of the nineteenth century Quebec did undergo an increase in manufacturing activity, but it was highly labour-intensive industry based on the relatively low cost of Quebec manpower. During this century, Quebec's natural resources were the basis for spectacular growth in primary industry, but Quebec never has been able to counter Ontario's pre-eminence in heavy manufacturing, a pre-eminence born of the initial advantage geographical factors gave Ontario in the mid-nineteenth century.

While specific aspects of this thesis were called into question, it continued for many years to inform most analyses of Quebec's economic development.[28] For instance, Gilles Bourque and Anne Legaré have argued that a more favourable class structure gave Ontario its initial advance in industrialization. In Quebec, "the commercialization of agriculture and the industrialization which is linked to this phenomenon"[29] were impeded by the persistence of feudal structures within Quebec agriculture and the resistance of Quebec peasants to these changes. But they did not deny the importance of Ontario's underlying geographical advantage. Ontario's class structure gave it a *"social lead* that permitted it to profit fully from comparative technological advantages such as the easier access to such important resources as iron and coal."[30]

Recently, however, John McCallum has placed this whole line of interpretation in question by demonstrating that during the nineteenth century Quebec was not disadvantaged after all in access to coal and iron ore. In the 1870s, Quebec could import coal from upstate New York and it could import pig iron from Britain at a lower cost than could Ontario from its sources of supply. On this basis, "by 1870 Montreal was the leading large-scale producer of iron and steel products, equalling the combined production of Ontario's two centers: Toronto and Hamilton."[31] Moreover, he demonstrates that the relative delay in commercialization of Quebec's agriculture (which he convincingly attributes to the declining productivity of agricultural lands) did not in any event preclude manufacturing development. During the 1850s a large number of Montreal manufacturing enterprises were able to prosper on the basis of the Ontario market.[32] Apparently, then, it was only with the beginning of this century that Quebec slipped to a secondary role in Canadian manufacturing.

The most promising route to explaining this deterioriation is to situate Quebec, and Ontario, within the international economic system. By the turn of the century Great Britain, Quebec's primary metropole, was no longer the centre of technological innovation it once was. Leadership had been lost to the United States.[33] Thus, if a region were to develop more sophisticated forms of manufacturing but was not a centre of technological innovation itself (as neither Quebec nor Ontario was), it was better to be dependent on the United States. Here, Ontario had a clear advantage, given its proximity to the U.S. industrial centres of the American Midwest. Location was all the more critical in that most U.S. investment in Canada has taken the form, not of portfolio investment as was the case with Great Britain, but of direct investment in which, in the case of manufacturing, an American enterprise would set up its own subsidiary in Canada to produce a line of products patterned after the American production. With such close integration of operations, proximity to the centre of a firm's activities in the U.S. was the key to choosing a Canadian site.[34]

Yet, it would be deterministic in the extreme to explain Quebec's industrial disdavantage simply in terms of Ontario's locational advantage in securing American branch plants. For instance, the activities of governments also need to be considered; they might have helped to redress Quebec's disadvantage. As it happens, however, through the first half of this century they tended instead to reinforce Ontario's advantage. At the provincial level, the Quebec provincial government did not actively seek to promote secondary industry, restricting its efforts to primary industry.[35] As for the federal government, many of the major federal economic policies betray a preoccupation with Ontario interests: the construction of the St. Lawrence Seaway, the concentration of research establishments in Ontario, the Canada-U.S. Auto Pact, and the 1960s ban on entry into Ontario of foreign petroleum (much of which was processed in Quebec).[36]

As we move beyond strictly geographical factors to consider such additional factors as the regional bias of the economic policies pursued by the federal government, Quebec's cultural distinctiveness once again may enter the picture. Here, the question is not the presence or absence of "appropriate" values, but the extent to which economic and political power has been organized along cultural lines. (This may account for many of the effects of cultural differences Dales claimed to have found.)

To use Stanley Ryerson's phrase, Confederation was based on an "unequal union" that involved the relative exclusion of Francophones from major economic functions: "The creation of the Canadian state was the joint work of the dominant Anglo-Canadian bourgeoisie, its French-Canadian subordinates and the semi-feudal Church."[37] This "unequal union" has closely structured the development of the Canadian Confederation. Anglophones have dominated elite positions within the Canadian economy and have monopolized economic responsibilities within the Canadian state. There are two ways this pattern of economic dominance could have served to reinforce Quebec's disadvantage – and to retard the development of policies to address it.

First, one could argue that simple cultural bias led the predominantly English-Canadian economic and political elite to favour Ontario's interests over Quebec's. This argument does have a major complication: throughout Confederation some English-Canadian economic and political power has been based in Quebec. The CPR was headquartered in Montreal. Until well into this century, Montreal-based Anglophone elites dominated financial activity within Canada. And frequently there was fierce rivalry between Montreal and Toronto elites, as they pursued their separate interests.[38] One could argue, however, that these Anglophone elites were not wedded to the development of Quebec *per se*, despite their Montreal base. Their strategies often were geared to initiating and controlling development of other areas, most notably western Canada, and in recent decades, with Ontario (and Toronto) pre-eminence clearly established, old rivalries have largely disappeared. Montreal Anglophone economic elites have steadily shifted their bases of operations to Ontario.

Second, and perhaps more compelling, is the argument that the virtual exclusion of the Quebec Francophone majority from the upper levels of the Quebec economic structure robbed the economy of much of its potential dynamism. To secure Anglophone personnel, Quebec firms often had to pay higher salaries than would have been necessary for equally qualified Francophones. Potential Francophone entrepreneurs were handicapped by the weakness of Francophone financial institutions and other factors. Indigenous economic development was heavily dependent on a small, and increasingly cautious and inbred, Anglophone elite. In other words, the human resources of Quebec were not fully and efficiently mobilized.[39] As foreign investment and technological transfer in manufacturing during this century so heavily favoured Ontario, so the weaknesses of Quebec's internal potential for entrepreneurship and technological innovation became critical.

At this point, it becomes clear that analysis of Quebec's development cannot focus simply on aggregate characteristics, as developmental approaches tend to do, nor on Quebec's relations with other regions, as most versions of dependency theory tend to do. Analysis of development must also focus on Quebec's internal structure and the forms of dependency that may exist there. This internal dependence has shaped the processes of social and economic development. Reaction against it may explain many of the forces behind political modernization and other forms of political change. Perhaps some of Quebec's dependence on other regions can be seen best as a function of these internal forms of dependence.

Cultural Division of Labour

The concept of "cultural division of labour" captures nicely the differentiation in the roles Francophones and Anglophones have played in Quebec. As developed by Michael Hechter, "a cultural division of labour occurs whenever culturally-marked groups are distributed in an occupational structure." Moreover, this distribution can take two different forms:

> The two defining parameters of the configuration of a cultural division of labour are its degree of hierarchy, and its degree of segmentation. A cultural division of labour is *hierarchical* to the extent that the . . . ethnic groups within it are differentially stratified. A cultural division of labour is *segmental* to the extent that the ethnic groups within it are highly occupationally specialized.[40]

There can be no question that both hierarchy and segmentation have long existed between the Francophones and Anglophones of Quebec.

The story of Quebec's cultural division of labour is a familiar one. It was established in the wake of the British Conquest. A clear segmentation of roles can be seen in the terms of accommodation between British colonial authorities, who retained political power, and French Canada's prevailing clerical and seigneurial elites, who were granted continued authority within Francophone society in exchange for their support of the British regime. It was reinforced with the arrival of British and American merchants who displaced the already weak French-Canadian commercial elite from any major economic role. It was evident in the failure, during the early 1800s, of the new French-Canadian liberal professional elite to secure a role in the executive of the colonial government, despite its majority position within the representative assembly established in 1791. Members of the Anglophone community continued to enjoy a privileged place within executive structures. The linguistic division among elites was dramatized during the 1820s and 1830s by the fierce struggles between French-Canadian liberal professionals and the Anglophone bourgeoisie over whether the colony would undertake major programs of economic development.

With the 1840s, there was some attenuation of the linguistic division of labour as French-Canadian liberal professionals assumed major roles within the government of the United Canadas and, in some cases, served as intermediaries on behalf of Anglophone economic elites. But within the federal political structures established after Confederation, there was a clear division of labour: Anglophones retained the important economic portfolios in the cabinet and the vast bulk of responsible positions within the public service. Similarly, when industrial structures were established in Quebec they were based on ethnic hierarchy. Positions of ownership and management were firmly in the hands of Anglophones, with Francophone participation largely limited to blue-collar positions. When a Francophone managerial class emerged in the 1950s it was housed first in the Church-related private bureaucracies and universities, and then in the provincial public sector. Only in the 1970s did the Anglophone monopoly of senior positions in private economic structures begin to decline.

For over two centuries Quebec has been marked by a clear cultural division of labour. This internal dependence has been based on the presence in Quebec of a permanent Anglophone community, which has initiated and controlled much of Quebec's economic activity. The various English-speaking external interests who have become involved in Quebec's economic development have drawn heavily on the Anglophone community for their personnel. Unlike most "foreign-language" settings, such as continental Europe, Quebec offered a large pool of established, highly qualified English-speakers; thus, there was little need for Anglo-phone corporations to turn to the Francophone majority, as long as they were prepared to pay a premium for Anglophone personnel. In this way, the internal cultural division of labour remained largely intact, despite changes in Quebec's external relations: from its British colonial status, to its role as dominant centre of Canada, to its dependence on Ontario and the United States.

A debate continues over the sources of the cultural division of labour. We will explore this debate at various points in the book. For some, the cultural division of labour can be seen as the simple function of differences in culture. It is argued that inappropriate values or work styles prevented Francophones from competing effectively with Anglophones for preferred position in the Quebec economy. Yet, a wide variety of structural factors also have been cited. The relative weakness of Francophone entrepreneurs has been traced to poor access to capital and markets and to the techniques and "know-how" necessary to economic success. As for the limited mobility of Francophones within Anglophone economic structures, many students assign the pre-eminent role to language, whether as a genuine handicap to effectiveness in work, or as a basis of outright discrimination, or simply as the boundary of informal recruitment networks.

Class and Class Relations

While the concept of cultural division of labour captures some aspects of Quebec's development that escape the notion of interregional dependence, at least one other concept is necessary. As the many critics of such terms as "ethnic class" or "internal colony" have been quick to note, power within Quebec is organized not just on cultural lines. It has always been possible to find clear class divisions within French Quebec (as well as in English Quebec, for that matter). This is true whether class is defined rigorously, in terms of economic function, or is linked loosely with such qualities as wealth, status, and prestige. These class divisions among Quebec Francophones have engendered conflicts and struggles within the Francophone collectivity. And class interests and aspirations have led many Québécois into alliances that transcend the French-English division and extend beyond the borders of Quebec, and of Canada. In short, beyond cultural division of labour and interregional dependence, Quebec's experience has been closely shaped by the relations among classes. In fact, many analysts would see class relations as the primordial factor.

27

The presence of class divisions among Quebec Francophones raises a host of questions that will pervade much of this book. As we shall see, students of Quebec society continue to be divided over the possibility of locating a distinct Francophone bourgeoisie. Since the 1950s, students of New France have vigorously argued whether or not the French colonial society spawned the nucleus of an indigenous commercial "bourgeoisie," based on trade with France. Assessments of the long-term consequences of the British Conquest have been closely tied to judgements about whether there was such a *bourgeoisie canadienne*, which the Conquest would have destroyed.[41] And with the 1970s scholars became engaged in a debate over whether there has arisen a new Francophone bourgeoisie. Some scholars claim to have located the elements of a bourgeoisie in the structures of the Quebec state and parapublic sector, or in private-sector financial institutions and manufacturing and service concerns, or in both public and private institutions.[42] Coupled with this debate about the presence of a contemporary Francophone bourgeoisie has been argument over the status of a stratum of bureaucrats, intellectuals, and white-collar workers that many have dubbed "a new middle class" or "technocratic petty bourgeoisie," but which some would prefer to incorporate within other class units. We will explore each of these debates in later chapters.

A second task in analysing class in Quebec is to trace the patterns of relations among classes. What are the primary alignments of classes among Francophones in Quebec? To what extent have there been cross-cultural alignments of Francophones with elements of their class in English Canada (as in the labour movements) or with another class (as between the Francophone clergy and Anglophone bourgeoisie at the time of Confederation)? Finally, what have been the primary sources of these various class alignments? Some analyses of class alignments among Quebec Francophones have traced them to the skilful manipulation of nationalist ideology by the dominant middle-class leaders. In effect, some lower-class Francophones were diverted from their "true" class interests. But others have argued that in some instances working-class Francophones actually may have had a clear class interest in aligning themselves with middle-class Francophones. This interest could lie in an attack on national oppression from which all Francophones suffer, or in an effort to undermine a Francophone bourgeoisie and the English-Canadian bourgeoisie to which it is wedded.

Clearly, the path of Quebec's political modernization has been closely defined by the structure of class alignments. The alignment of some lower-class Francophones with the liberal professional and clerical interests represented by Duplessis's Union nationale served to retard Quebec's political modernization. And the dreams of *indépendantistes* for the transfer of functions from the federal government to the Quebec state hinged upon whether these *indépendantistes* could forge a working coalition between "new middle-class" interests and the interests of working-class Francophones.

Nation and National Consciousness

While our variables of interregional dependence, cultural division of labour, and relations among classes may explain much of the distinctiveness of Quebec's development, even they are insufficient. They must be joined by another factor: national consciousness. After all, Quebec Francophones have long seen themselves as members of a distinct national collectivity, whether a French-Canadian nation extending to many parts of Canada or, as more recently, a Québécois nation delimited by the borders of Quebec itself.

However, social science has had only limited success in providing any real understanding of the phenomenon of national consciousness. In fact, the very concept is a matter of controversy. Among social scientists there has been little agreement as to what distinguishes a national consciousness or, more precisely, what constitutes the idea of "nation" upon which such a consciousness is based.

For some analysts, the nation simply denotes a group of people with a high degree of solidarity. Thus, American political scientist Dankwart Rustow has declared that "a nation is a self-contained group of human beings who place loyalty to the group as a whole above competing loyalties."[43] Yet, within this "subjective" approach it becomes difficult to distinguish attachment to a nation from attachment to entities not normally viewed as nations, such as tribes, classes, or even age cohorts. However, attempts to specify a universal definition of the concept of nation have been notoriously unsuccessful. Whatever criterion is used, whether language, culture, territory, religion, descent, or possession of a state, there is no single "objective" attribute that distinguishes all collectivities commonly regarded as nations and portrayed as such within ideologies typically identified as nationalist. As Alfred Cobban has noted:

> Central European nationalists have sought in vain for some invariable, positive, external symbol of the difference of their nations from one another. Language, religion, tradition, territorial congruity, natural frontiers, economic interests, race – extensive exceptions can be found to every proposed test, except the subjective one.[44]

Attempts to root nation in a more fundamental materialist base have also been unsuccessful. For instance, in an article written in the late 1960s, Quebec social scientists Gilles Bourque and Nicole Laurin-Frenette argued that "nation" refers to "certain characteristic aspects of a capitalist type of social formation." Among these "aspects" are economic unity, territorial, juridical, and political unity, linguistic and cultural unity, and an ideology defining the unity as nation.[45] In effect, the nation was equated with a "nation-state." Stanley Ryerson, in turn, attacked this approach, claiming (with reason) that it seeks to dissolve the nation into classes:

> while it is inseparable, historically, from class-structures and modes of production, the nation-community is more than just an "aspect" of any one of them. This is so because the nation-community embodies an identity, linguistic and cultural, that is not simply an "effect" of class, however closely its evolution may be interwoven with the shifting patterns of class relations and struggles. National differences both antedate and post-date the era of the capitalist mode of production.[46]

As a consequence, some scholars have proposed simply to abandon any pretence to a universal definition of "nation" and, thus, of "nationalism." A distinguished historian of nationalist movements, Hugh Seton-Watson, has written:

> What is the nation? Many people have tried to find a definition. But it seems to me, after a good deal of thought, that all we can say is that a nation exists when an active and fairly numerous section of its members are convinced that it exists. Not external objective characteristics but subjective conviction is the decisive factor.[47]

In effect, by this definition a nation would be any group of people that claims to be a nation. It is difficult to see how any meaningful analysis of nationalism can be conducted on that basis.

Probably the most fruitful way to resolve this difficulty is to avoid defining "nation" in terms of any *single* objective characteristic. In presenting his conception of nationalist ideology, Léon Dion offers a useful way of defining nation:

> By nationalist ideology, I mean a set of representations: which refer to a particular collectivity, called a people or a nation, that is defined by an amalgam of traits including among others, *but without any one of them being sufficient or necessary*, an origin, a history, a territory, a culture, institutions, and a language that are common to the members of this collectivity; which express a sense of belonging and of destiny often vis-à-vis other collectivities perceived as foreigners or enemies; and which provide projects concerning the organization of cultural, economic, and political life judged appropriate to this collectivity.[48]

By this definition of the term, a national consciousness has indeed marked Quebec's historical development. As we shall see in the next chapter, the emergence of a national consciousness can be traced back to the *Patriote* movement of the 1820s, out of which sprang the Rebellions of the 1830s. Subsequently, the national consciousness became focused on the conception of a French-Canadian nation, which extended far beyond the borders of Quebec. In more recent decades, the predominant form of national consciousness among Quebec Francophones has been defined primarily in terms of Quebec itself. None of these conceptions of the nation was able to embrace fully all the objective characteristics commonly associated with the term "nation." The nation of "French Canada" clearly possessed such characteristics as language, religion, culture, and, to a lesser degree, descent, but its territorial bases were indeterminate and there was no "national" state: the federal government did not qualify and the nation extended beyond any particular province. The notion of a Québécois nation resolves the question of territorial boundaries and clearly designates the "national" state: whether it is a fully sovereign state or simply an autonomous province. But at the same time it serves to obscure the issues of language and culture: close to 20 per cent of Quebec's population does not share these traits. Nonetheless, both conceptions clearly meet Dion's less stringent definition. And, more to the point perhaps, each depiction of the nation has been sufficiently credible in the eyes of large numbers of Quebec's

French-speaking population for them to give it their firm adherence and to adopt the term "nation" as a collective referent.

Just as social scientists have been unable to agree on the definition of "national consciousness," and of "nation," so they have favoured a wide variety of approaches to explaining the emergence and evolution of nationalist movements. Whereas some have adopted "idealist" approaches in which a national consciousness emerges and develops according to a logic of its own, others have sought to frame explanations in more structural terms. In fact, as we shall see, many analysts of neo-nationalism – the wave of nationalist movements within capitalist societies during the 1960s and 1970s – have focused on precisely the types of structural processes we have already identified as critical to the study of Quebec. They have sought to trace the emergence of nationalist movements in a wide variety of settings to the interaction between processes of economic and social development and cultural divisions of labour and to relations between regions that are marked by dependence or domination.

Canadian Political Institutions

Finally, the impact on Quebec's development of all of these factors – dependence, cultural division of labour, class relations, and national consciousness – also has been mediated by the structure of Canadian political institutions, especially federalism.

After all, it is through federalism that contemporary Quebec exists as a distinct political entity. At the time of Confederation, English-Canadian opinion, especially in Ontario (or Upper Canada), was strongly in favour of a unitary scheme. Yet, French-Canadian elites insisted that distinct French-Canadian interests could not be entrusted to a government in which English Canadians would be the overwhelming majority. These interests would be safe only with a government responsible to a predominantly French-Canadian electorate and possessing exclusive jurisdiction over the areas where these interests were at stake. Thus, not only was Quebec granted provincial status but the powers allocated to it and the other provinces were primarily those the dominant French-Canadian elites then thought necessary to protect their distinct institutions.

The new province of Quebec was, at the same time, both the only province where the majority was French-Canadian and the homeland of the vast majority of French Canadians in Canada. As Table One demonstrates, this is still the case now. The most pre-

Table One
French Origin, Mother Tongue, and Home Language by Provinces, 1981

	Nfld.	N.S.	N.B.	P.E.I.	Que.	Ont.	Man.	Sask.	Alta.	B.C.	Canada
French origin as % of pop.	2.7%	8.5%	36.4%	12.2%	80.2%	7.7%	7.3%	4.9%	5.1%	3.4%	26.7%
French mother tongue as % of pop.	0.5	4.3	33.7	4.9	82.4	5.5	5.1	2.6	2.8	1.6	25.7
French at home as % of pop.	0.3	2.9	31.4	3.1	82.5	3.9	3.1	1.1	1.3	0.1	24.6

	Nfld.	N.S.	N.B.	P.E.I.	Que.	Ont.	Man.	Sask.	Alta.	B.C.
French at home as % Canadian pop.	0.1	0.4	3.7	0.1	88.8	5.6	0.5	0.2	0.5	0.3
Total prov. pop. as % Canadian pop.	2.3	3.5	2.9	0.5	26.5	35.4	4.2	4.0	9.2	11.3

SOURCE: *Census of Canada*, 1981, 92-911, Table IV.

cise measure of Francophone presence is the primary language used at home. In 1981, over 82 per cent of Quebec residents fell into that category. New Brunswick was a distant second, with 31 per cent. Ontario had about 4 per cent. All the other provinces had 3 per cent or less. In most of Canada the Francophone presence is a marginal one indeed, despite the efforts of Ottawa and some provinces to strengthen the Francophone minorities by expanding French-language government services.

In addition, about 89 per cent of Canadians who use French at home lived in Quebec, and a comparison of the figures for French origin with the figures for use of French at home shows that Quebec is the only province where the Francophone population has not declined through assimilation. In most provinces, assimilation has been very high; demographers expect this trend to continue in the future – except in Quebec. For all these reasons, we should not be surprised to find that during the 1960s and 1970s many Quebec Francophones came to the conclusion that only in Quebec could a modern French-language society be maintained.

Even if Confederation might have been impossible otherwise, the existence of Quebec as a distinct political entity has had a great many consequences of its own. First, it has encouraged the creation of social and economic organizations on a distinctly Quebec base; this will be especially evident when we examine Quebec of the 1960s. Second, it has helped to ensure that such matters as interregional dependence, cultural division of labour, and even nationality will be perceived primarily in terms of Quebec. While each of them can be readily viewed in other ways, the Quebec-based definition has a privileged place.

For instance, with respect to patterns of economic dependence in Canada we have seen that in some respects Ontario and Quebec could be viewed as a single region: central Canada. Even if this perception should be widespread in other parts of Canada, however, the existence of separate provincial governments inhibits Quebec Francophones, and Ontarians, from seeing themselves as central Canadians. By the same token, the existence of Quebec as a single political entity hinders appreciation of the forms of disparity within the region, such as eastern Quebec's deprivation vis-à-vis Montreal. For that matter, the provincial boundary may well have inhibited some regions in Quebec from appreciating their commonality with neighbouring regions in Ontario. Without a provincial boundary separating them, for example, the Témiskamingue-Abitibi and Timmins-Sudbury areas might have been more likely to see themselves as a single economic region, dependent on resource extraction and commonly exploited by metropolitan centres, whether Montreal or Toronto. In short, political boundaries tend to focus attention on certain forms of economic dependence to the exclusion of others.

By the same token, a French-English cultural division of labour clearly exists throughout Canada, as the Royal Commission on Bilingualism and Biculturalism amply demonstrated in the 1960s through its analysis of data on incomes and occupations. And there has always been a cultural division of labour within federal institutions, as we shall see below. Nonetheless, Quebec Francophones have tended to focus on the manifestations of cultural division of labour within the boundaries of Quebec itself. These disparities seem to have greater immediacy and can be more readily addressed through political action, given the Francophone numerical majority in Quebec.

As for a national consciousness, over the decades, and centuries, Francophones have defined the territorial bases of their nation in several ways. For a few, it has existed throughout North America, wherever French-speakers have settled, as an *Amérique française*. For many, it has been a *nation canadienne-française*, stretching through much of Canada. But, reflecting the evolution of political institutions, there has been a strong tendency in recent decades to define it in terms of provincial boundaries, as *la nation québécoise*. This development, which has always been a possibility given the federal nature of Canada, has stemmed in large part from the political modernization Quebec underwent in the 1960s, leading it fully to occupy its jurisdictions as a province and even to seek to expand them. As the Quebec provincial government became more and more important in the lives of Quebec Francophones, and the federal government receded in importance, so it seemed more "natural" for them to see themselves as Québécois.

Beyond the federal character of Canada's political order, the world view of Quebec Francophones has also been shaped by the way in which central political institutions, based in Ottawa, have functioned. Simply put, within federal institutions, just as within provincial institutions, political decision-making has been heavily structured by the demographic make-up of the electorate. Within the federal electorate, Québécois, and French Canadians of all provinces, always have been very much in the minority. Thus, even if some dualistic practices, such as alternating the Governor-Generalship, might suggest a political equality between Francophones and Anglophones, the reality has been otherwise. In the instances where Francophones and Anglophones have been clearly divided over an issue, the Anglophone majority has prevailed, whether in hanging Louis Riel, contributing to the imperial effort during the Boer War, or imposing conscription for overseas service during the two world wars. By the same token, Anglophone interests have clearly prevailed in all of the provincial governments but Quebec, as with the refusal until recently to provide public education in French.

In addition, until quite recently the numerical inferiority of Francophones and Québécois within federal institutions was reinforced by a cultural division of labour, in which Francophones were restricted to certain functions. While Francophones were usually named to federal cabinets in the numbers their proportion of the Canadian electorate would warrant, they were effectively excluded from the important economic portfolios. Likewise, they were seriously underrepresented in the upper levels of the federal bureaucracy.

Thus, despite the claim of some students of "consociationalism," Canadian political life has not been organized on the basis of equality between the representatives of the Francophone and Anglophone "subcultures." In particular, there is no evidence of adherence to the "consociational" decision-making rules that require more than a simple majority in order to afford adequate protection to "subcultures." In the House of Commons, decision-making has always been on precisely that basis of a majority. In the cabinet, decision-making rules have been less explicit. But there is no evidence that Quebec members enjoyed a formal veto (an important consociational device). Nor was the alternative "consociational" device of decision-making by "grand coalition" always followed.[49]

Such a pattern of decision-making at the federal level was bound to reinforce the attachment of Quebec Francophones to "their" provincial government. In fact, starting with the government of Honoré Mercier and his Parti national, formed ostensibly in reaction to the hanging of Louis Riel, Quebec governments have often assumed the role of champion of Francophone interests in the face of federal threats. Certainly, Quebec provincial leaders have not been the only ones to defend actively provincial autonomy. At various points in time, leaders in other provinces have done so, too. Nonetheless, as we shall see, Quebec government leaders have defended control over provincial jurisdictions more consistently and over a greater range of matters than have those of other provincial governments.

In sum, both the form and the functioning of Canadian political institutions have served to reinforce the salience of Quebec as a distinct entity. In this fashion, they have ensured that the processes of social and economic development with which Quebec Francophones are most familiar will be those within Quebec itself, to the exclusion of similar processes in other parts of Canada. At the same time, they have also increased the likelihood that Quebec Francophones will be aware of forms of dependence in Quebec's relations with other regions, will be most sensitive to a cultural division of labour as it appears within Quebec itself, and most importantly, will be attracted to conceptions of nationality tied to Quebec.

Yet, if Canadian federalism, and its functioning, may have heightened attachment to Quebec, it did not create that attachment. Quebec and Quebec nationalism are not artifacts of Confederation. After all, as we have already noted, the political entity of Quebec was itself created in 1791, as Lower Canada. This was done in part so that Quebec Francophones would not be outnumbered by Anglophones in the new legislative assembly. Confederation merely restored Quebec to political existence, undoing the Act of Union of 1840. And this was done at the insistence of the Francophones of Quebec who were still unprepared to entrust their fates fully to political institutions in which they were in minority.

Over the first decades of Confederation, actions of both the federal government, such as the hanging of Riel, and the other provincial governments, such as the suppression of French-language education, could only have confirmed these suspicions. The crises these acts engendered were not themselves sufficient to spawn major separatist movements, but they must have reinforced the long-standing assumption that Québécois could best rely on their own distinct political institutions. Thus, when the Quebec government was itself transformed through the processes of political modernization and began to address so many concerns of Québécois in the 1960s, including economic dependence and the cultural division of labour, it seemed only "normal" to many that they should assume all the powers of a "national" government, and that Quebec at last should become truly sovereign. By the same token, as the Quebec government assumed this more interventionist role, the assumptions upon which the Confederation settlement had been based fell into question. The set of jurisdictions that might have been judged sufficient for the French-Canadian political elite of the 1870s, based in the liberal professions and having close links to the Church, was not adequate for the "new middle-class" political modernizers of the 1960s and their allies.

In conclusion, then, we will use the concepts of social and economic development and political modernization as a first way of organizing our exploration of change in Quebec, but they will constitute only a starting point. They will be joined by a further set of concepts to help specify the particular form and direction these broad processes of change have taken in Quebec: economic and political dependence, cultural division of labour, relations among classes, and national consciousness. Only through this broad range of concepts can we hope to capture the forces underlying Quebec's distinctive historical experience.

First, however, we need to examine the origins and early history of Quebec, and of French-Canadian society, so as to establish the backdrop to social and economic development. At the same time, we will also see how factors, both internal and external to French Quebec, served to inhibit and delay these processes of change.

CHAPTER TWO

Historical Foundations: The Roots of Tradition

To an outsider, probably the most striking feature of French-Canadian society is its very persistence, enduring over the centuries in an alien, often hostile, environment. This capacity for survival has been attributed to a number of factors, some related to time and circumstance and some to the product of conscious effort. For example, one hypothesis is that, as an agrarian society, French Canada was able to survive because it was physically and socially isolated from external influences, at least up to the time North America began to industrialize. Another explanation is the nature of the rural French-Canadian community, with its seigneurial origins and its well-integrated structure. Moreover, it is argued that the traditional French-Canadian elites, especially the clergy, succeeded in isolating the community from the North American mainstream by perpetrating an ideology and a range of social policies that kept intact French Canada's distinctive institutions and way of life.

Common to all these explanations is the premise that French Canada's survival was due to the persistence of traditional values and social structures. However, in recent decades the doctrine of *survivance* through tradition has come under attack on the grounds that it was not necessary, as well as being harmful to the social and economic well-being of French Canadians. Indeed, it is no longer as clear as it once seemed that French Canada can survive as a distinct society only by remaining faithful to the traditional mould. For many, the changes Quebec society has undergone over the past few decades have proved otherwise. In fact, we will make that argument in the coming pages. Yet, as we shall see, some observers insist that these changes necessarily carry the seeds of French Canada's ultimate assimilation. Only time can resolve this debate. There can, however, be little question of the more limited thesis that survival was *easier* for French Canada within the framework of a traditional society. As long as they remained viable, economic specialization, geographic isolation, and traditional values and institutions did indeed minimize assimilationist pressures.

There is a second problem with the thesis that French Canada owes its survival to long persistence as a traditional society. The character of French-Canadian society was never quite so simple. Throughout its history, French Canada always contained forces that challenged traditional values and institutions, whether directly or indirectly. French Canada was never as totally impervious to outside ideological influences as some analyses have maintained, such as the many applications of the Hartzian theory of "fragment cultures." And there were always social and economic contradictions in French-Canadian society itself. Typically, the challenge to traditional institutions took the form of passive resistance, as with parishioners who ignored the pronouncements of the clergy or refused to pay the tithes. But on occasion the resistance was more active, as with the liberal professionals of the early nineteenth century who openly challenged clerical authority and called for "neutral" schools. Beyond that, throughout Quebec history some French Canadians pursued with varying success endeavours, such as commerce and finance, that in effect placed them outside traditional structures. In fact, there was always a substantial number of French Canadians living in Montreal and other major cities where the hold of traditional values and authorities was much more tenuous.

Finally, of course, the thesis begs the question of *why* these elements of traditionalism persisted. Why were the clergy and other traditional elites so successful in maintaining values and institutions that contradicted so markedly those of the rest of North America and which, with time, increasingly contradicted the social and economic reality of Quebec itself? At least part of the explanation must lie in the ways "foreign" elites acted, deliberately or not, to reinforce the hold these traditional elites exercised within French Canada, whether through granting them legal privileges, as in 1774, or through suppressing their French-Canadian rivals, such as the petty bourgeoisie that led the abortive campaign against colonial rule in the 1820s and 1830s. In addition, complex ideological processes may have been involved. For instance, it has been argued that French Canadians were led by their quasi-colonial position to acquire a certain psychic investment in traditional values and institutions: through exaggerating the degree to which they differed from their "conquerors," French Canadians could make their condition more bearable. We will explore these theses in later chapters.

In short, although the framework of traditional society may have facilitated French Canada's survival, it probably was not necessary to that survival. Moreover, throughout French-Canadian history, traditional values and institutions were regularly challenged, not only from without but from within. As we undertake a rapid review of French Canada's historical development we need to bear this in mind.

New France and the Conquest

The French colonial period was crucial in distinguishing the French Canadians from the other transposed societies of North America. With some exceptional periods, the French regime displayed little interest in the development of New France. It was seventy-five years between its discovery and its founding as a colony by Samuel de Champlain in 1608. From then until the transfer of power to the British, only 10,000 French migrants came to Quebec, one-third of them military personnel who decided to stay abroad. None (in contrast to the New Englanders) came as dissenters from the regime at home.[1] The colony, again in contrast to the British settlements to the south, was a direct extension, modified by the peculiar geography of Quebec and the exigencies of distance, of the society and politics of France. Paris's lack of concern for the colony was ultimately signified by the appearance of a British invasion fleet, rather than a French relief expedition, below the besieged city of Quebec in the spring of 1759.

The social and economic life of the colony was restricted by the colonial policy on emigration – at the time of the Conquest, New France's population was at most 70,000, compared to the 1.5 million in the American colonies of Britain – and by its mercantilist approach to trade. New France was controlled and, until 1663, directly governed by the fur-trading monopolies. They did not encourage settlers, and the fur trade itself demanded expansion into the interior rather than the establishment of sedentary pursuits like agriculture. Since all other economic activity was either banned because of France's mercantilist policy or, as in the fur trade, largely controlled from France, the foundation for autonomous economic development was limited. Throughout its existence as a French colony, Quebec remained highly dependent on its European metropole.

Fur, treasure, exploration, and the Catholic mission to the Indians were the reasons for coming out to Canada; New France existed for two decades before any soil was cultivated, though the rugged land and inhospitable climate around Quebec City were undoubtedly obstacles to agricultural development. When settlement did occur, the river frontage was divided into narrow but long strips, giving each farm access to water transport and forest resources. As the river frontage was occupied, a road was built along the back of the original farms and formed the frontage for a new row, or *rang*. This pattern of settlement, which can still be detected in Quebec today, continued until the valley land gave way to the granite of the Canadian Shield.

Physical isolation from France and the common experience of facing the hardships of life in the colony led the population to develop a certain sense of identity. The terms *Canadien* and *habitant* were developed to distinguish the colony's established residents from metropolitan Frenchmen. Reinforcing this sense of difference was the emergence of a new dialect particular to New France, an amalgam of various regional dialects that immigrants had brought to the colony.[2] In addition, there was periodic resentment over the colonial practice of nominating Frenchmen to senior offices within the colony's Church and administrative structures.[3] Nonetheless, there was no fully developed sense of nationalism in opposition to France. Quebec's heavy economic dependence on France and the strength of absolutist notions of authority saw to that.

In formal terms, the colony's social structure had strong feudal elements: a privileged place was afforded both the Church and a nascent class of seigneurs. To this extent, French Canada was a "traditional society" at its outset. The Church was directly involved in governing the colony, since the Bishop was one of three figures on the ruling council and the first Bishop, Mgr. de Laval, established the bishopric as a source of political administrative power. Colonial law clearly established the Church's right to collect tithes from its faithful. Moreover, at the local level, there was no municipal structure: thus, the parish was the basic social-political, as well as religious, unit. It was governed by an elected council, or *fabrique*, of which the parish priest acted as chairman. Typically, the priest was the only person in the community with a modicum of education. Often he was drawn from one of the families of the parish.

On this basis, some writers have portrayed New France as a virtual theocracy. Among the most influential of these was the late nineteenth-century American writer, Francis Parkman. In his own mid-1950s survey of French-Canadian history, Mason Wade approvingly cites Parkman's depiction of the Church's supremacy:

> Parkman has justly stressed the fundamental importance of the Catholic Church in New France: "More even than the royal power she shaped the character and the destinies of the colony. . . . The royal government was transient; the Church was permanent. The English conquest shattered the whole apparatus of civil administration at a blow, but left her untouched."[4]

Wade himself refers to New France as a "theocracy."[5] And a 1950s account by French-Canadian sociologist Jean-Charles Falardeau declares that the parish priest was the:

> uncontested leader . . . whose role as spiritual minister and moral arbitrator of his flock developed into that of a natural protector, advisor, and, in fact, pastor in the literal sense of the word . . . [he] directly, profoundly, and inescapably influenced the temperament of the French-Canadian habitant.[6]

Yet, more recent studies have shown that the reality of New France was considerably more complex. After all, the Gallican laws, developed by the French monarch to assert his authority over the Church in temporal matters and even in some spiritual spheres, were applied integrally within the colony after Louis XIV assumed power. The Bishop and his colleagues had to struggle with secular leaders, the Intendant and the Governor, to shape colonial policy. On some matters, such as the exclusion of non-Catholics from the colony and restriction of the sale of alcohol to the native populations, the Church prevailed. On other matters, it did not. In fact, the only areas where Church involvement was not contested were education and public charity.[7]

Moreover, there is evidence that the fabled authority of the parish priest had very definite limits. Typically, the priest had great difficulty collecting tithes, despite his clear legal entitlement, and had to resort to cultivating his own fruit and vegetable garden in order to get by. Disputes with a priest over such matters as seating within the church could lead parishioners to break with the Church for several generations. In fact, a provision in New France's *fabrique* law assigned a penalty of two years in prison for anyone "who prevents a priest from saying mass or beats him when he is in the process of reading it."[8] Many parishes, too, went without a priest at all: in 1730 the ratio of priests to parishes was 20:100.[9] In the words of Colette Moreux: "It seems that ecclesiastical power was accepted to the extent that it did not inconvenience anyone, but not as an unconditional authority, as would be the case after the middle of the nineteenth century."[10]

With respect to the other "quasi-feudal" institution of New France, the seigneurial system, scholars are generally agreed that it was at best a pale imitation of its European inspiration. Peasants on the seigneuries were indeed obliged to pay rent and to undertake work details or *corvées*. And the seigneur enjoyed a monopoly over milling and other facilities. But typically the seigneur did not actually live on his seigneury, preferring city life. Nor did he personally assume charge of the military organization of his estate. And he usually was not himself of high social origins. Most importantly, even though rents were much lower than in France, he often had great difficulty collecting them. On this basis, one student has gone so far as to claim that the seigneurial regime was no more than a facade; most of the colony's population was in fact bound by a petty producer mode of production.[11] This overstates the case: the farmers did not own their land and by and large they did abide, grudgingly, their obligations under the regime, minimal as these obligations may have been.[12]

Not only were there limits to the ability of such institutions as the Church and the seigneurial regime to place a "quasi-feudal" stamp on colonial life, but according to some analyses there had emerged within the colony a class that was very much animated by capitalist values: a "colonial bourgeoisie" of merchants engaged in the fur trade. This is the thesis, in particular, of the "nationalist" school of historians identified with the Université de Montréal. According to Michel Brunet, New France had a bourgeoisie composed of "rich traders and businessmen, seigneurs, military officials and administrators."[13] In fact, the development of the colony can be understood only in terms of such a class, interested in exploiting the resources of North America. The presence of a bourgeoisie is evidenced in the incorporation of trading companies and the establishment of daily exchanges among merchants in Montreal and Quebec City. Brunet estimates that in the 1750s the colony contained at least forty millionaires.

Over the years, the thesis has incurred some vigorous critiques. Working from documents available in Paris, Jean Hamelin has sought to demonstrate that trade between Quebec and France was largely controlled within France. For instance, according to his data, in 1746, 47 per cent of the Quebec-France trade was controlled by French companies, or their agents, with only 27 per cent in the hands of long-established residents of the colony (who had arrived before 1730).[14] Hamelin argues that those few *Canadiens* who profited from the fur trade did not really have a capitalist mentality – they wasted their gains on a lavish lifestyle rather than using them to further their enterprises.[15]

Another scholar, Cameron Nish, has sought to salvage at least partially the "nationalist" thesis by reinterpreting Hamelin's evidence and qualifying the concept of "colonial bourgeoisie." When compared with the American colonies, Nish argues, New France's performance is quite respectable. New England also suffered deficits; salaries were no higher than in New France.[16] While the colony may not have contained a class of individuals devoted exclusively to capitalism, as in the classical notion of a bourgeoisie, there were throughout the colony's structures a variety of individuals who did profit well from the fur trade. Nish calls them "les bourgeois-gentilshommes de la Nouvelle-France."

However much the original notion of a "colonial bourgeoisie" needs to be qualified,[17] the fact remains that a substantial number of *Canadiens* were actively involved in commerce, based primarily on the fur trade, just as large numbers of *habitants* were themselves partially or totally engaged in securing furs, as the itinerant *coureurs de bois*. Neither activity was well regarded by the Church; they persisted nonetheless. New France did contain the bases of traditional society, with the privileged legal position of the Church and settlement of much of the population in small communities, organized under the Church and devoted to subsistence agriculture. But it contained other social elements as well; it was not a static society. Within some analyses, the merchant class in particular was a dynamic force, which with time would have overwhelmed traditional structures and brought the colony fully into capitalist relations. But this possibility was abruptly ended by the Conquest.

Post-Conquest Quebec:
Emergence of a Cultural Division of Labour

Initially, the Conquest seemed to portend the destruction of French Canada's traditional institutions and of any other form of cultural distinctiveness.[18] Under the Royal Proclamation of 1763, the Church of England was to be made the established church of the colony and the seigneuries would be abolished. English law was to be imposed and a representative assembly would be created in which English would be the official language. Catholics would need to renounce their faith to assume office within the assembly or within any other colonial structure.

However, the proclamation was never put into effect. Not only was an assimilationist strategy rendered impossible by the paucity of English-speakers within the colony, but British apprehension over rebellion in the colonies to the south fostered a new policy for Quebec. The British authorities decided to come to terms with the traditional *Canadien* elites in the belief that they could build loyalty to the British crown among the *Canadien* population as a whole. Certainly, these elites had proven themselves fully prepared to work within the new regime. Under the Quebec Act of 1774, the seigneurial system was re-established, the Church was once again empowered to collect tithes, Catholics were spared the need to renounce their faith in order to assume office, and French civil law was re-established. By the same token, in deference to the Church, a representative assembly was not established despite vigorous lobbying by British merchants. In a certain sense, after 1774 the traditional *Canadien* elites, especially the Church, were better placed to command the loyalties of the *Canadiens* than they had been in the days of New France. After all, the French-speaking secular leaders, military and administrative, had departed. Moreover, under British rule the Church was no longer bound by the Gallican laws. Thanks to British intervention, the Church had in effect emerged as the "natural leader" of the *Canadiens*.

If the transition to British rule may have reinforced the position of both the Church and the seigneurs, it very much undermined the position of the *Canadien* merchants. With the Conquest, control over the colony's trade effectively fell into British hands. For some observers, this rapid displacement of the *Canadiens* merely underlines their long-standing precariousness. Their ineffectiveness is laid once again to "inappropriate" values, including a strong individualism that allegedly prevented them from pooling their resources so as to compete effectively with the British.[19] But more profound structural processes appear to have been at work. Brunet documents how the more prosperous *Canadien* merchants returned to France. Those who stayed, if only because they could not afford to leave, soon found themselves unable to function as merchants. The British authorities prevented them from securing deliveries of goods from France, even if the goods had already been paid for, and they were unable to establish new relations with British supply houses. As would be expected, the London companies had more confidence in the fellow Britishers, and Americans, who were establishing themselves as merchants in the colony. In

45

the nature of things, the shift of the metropole from France to Britain was bound to undermine the *Canadien* merchants.[20]

By 1774, then, the British authorities had come to accept that the *Canadiens* would remain culturally distinct, at least for the foreseeable future. But it was a distinctiveness based first and foremost on traditional institutions and traditional values. Ecclesiastical and legal functions could be assumed by the *Canadiens*, at least to service their compatriots, but control of the colony's economic life was to be firmly in the hands of English-speakers. In effect, a cultural division of labour was sanctified. As we shall see, this cultural division of labour would mark Quebec for the next two centuries.

The accommodation of traditional elites was soon tested by the Americans. Quebec was offered the prospect of becoming the fourteenth colony in the new republic, with democratic assemblies and the end of tithes and seigneurial dues. The Americans successfully invaded the territory, captured Montreal, occupied a route along the river, and besieged Quebec City. They received some help from the population and even held some elections in the occupied areas. For a number of reasons (besides the military defeat of the invasion force) French Canada remained British. As the British had expected, the seigneurs and the senior clergy were staunchly loyal to the British regime and called upon the *Canadien*s to defend it – they had reason to be fearful of the Revolutionists' notions of popular sovereignty, as well as their anti-Catholic tenor. While the *habitants* showed little inclination to resist the American forces actively, neither were they inclined to join them. As the hostilities ran their course, the invaders sent captured loyalist French Canadians south of the border, failed to pay their bills, issued paper money of dubious value, and thus lost whatever popularity they had initially enjoyed.[21]

The most important effect of the American Revolution on French Canada was not, however, the brief infusion of democratic ideology nor the initial appearance of a cleavage between the layers of French-Canadian society. The influx of Anglophone Loyalists, pushed by expropriation or drawn by good farm land, changed Quebec once and for all from a homogeneous French-Canadian society to one with a prosperous and vocal English minority. The newcomers began to demand more voice in government and a removal of their minority status. Thus, the terms of Quebec's incorporation into the British Empire had to be revised once again. The resultant constitutional changes in 1791 provided a representative assembly and split the colony into Upper and Lower Canada. The latter reform pleased the Loyalists who had settled up the river and on the shores of Lake Ontario, but in Lower Canada the Anglo-Protestants of Montreal became a minority group (albeit a disproportionately powerful one) at a time when the principle of majority rule was beginning to have some effect. It meant that, although the English community continued to exert a great deal of influence, French Canadians could look to politics as one area where there numbers alone could be used as a basis for gaining and exercising power. At this stage, they were still facing many handicaps. The political institutions were alien, derived from British experience and British colonial policy, and French Canadians could not regard them as part of their own heritage and political culture. While French Canadians were able to use their electoral strength to gain a voice in the representative assembly, the assembly was dominated by the executive; the executive, in turn, was still largely the preserve of Quebec's Anglo-Canadian minority. Nonetheless, the representative assembly at least offered a forum for an emerging French-Canadian class to assert its claim to leadership of the *Canadiens*.

Quebec in the Nineteenth Century: The Rise and Defeat of the First French-Canadian Nationalist Movement

In principle, as we have seen, the Church was in a stronger position by the turn of the century than it had been in the days of New France, thanks to the elimination of its rivals through the Conquest and the re-establishment of its entitlements through the Act of 1774. In fact, in later years, Church leaders were to see the Conquest as a providential act, designed to save Catholicism from the horrors of the French Revolution. Nonetheless, it was not until the mid-1850s that the Church actually was able to assume a pre-eminent position in French-Canadian life.

In the early 1800s the Church continued to be hampered by its own organizational weakness. It simply did not have the personnel necessary to administer to a flock. Not only was this flock increasing very rapidly, thanks to a birth rate with few historical parallels, but there was an embargo on emigration of French priests to the colony and the Church's own facilities for training priests were seriously depleted. As a result, the number of faithful per priest rose from 350 in 1759 to over 1,800 in 1830. In 1790, seventy-five parishes went without a priest.[22] By the same token, without this continued clerical presence in the parish community the behaviour of the *habitants* deviated in a great many ways from the Church's ideals. As Jean-Pierre Wallot notes:

> Naturally, there were good, pious, and exemplary families. But the point is that they did not seem to be very numerous. On the contrary, the bishop was constantly admonishing, threatening or punishing parishes (by recalling the priests) for not providing enough for the subsistence and lodging of their curés; for staging "horrible" charivaris or orgies, particularly on the occasion of parish celebrations in honour of their patron saint – another occasion of feasting. . . . Finally, the bishop had to suppress most religious holidays. . . . The bishop's journal of pastoral visits mournfully lists the main sins among the population: irreligion, leaving the church during sermons, drunkenness, public disorders and scandals, dances, adultery, incest, fornication.[23]

Beyond that, the Church had to contend with a new *Canadien* elite that was challenging openly the Church's self-proclaimed status as leader of the *Canadien* people: a petty bourgeoisie composed of doctors, lawyers, and notaries, as well as some small merchants. During the first few decades of the nineteenth century the ranks of this petty bourgeoisie grew more rapidly than did the French-Canadian population itself.[24] Most of them were themselves of peasant background and thus wielded considerable influence among the *habitants*.

In fact, not only were the liberal professionals challenging the Church, they were also challenging the English-speaking merchants in the colony, who had grown to the point that they did indeed constitute a "colonial bourgeoisie." The English merchants had moved beyond the fur trade to make wood and wheat the primary bases of the colonial economy – commodities in high demand after the Napoleonic blockades led the British to establish a preferential tariff structure. This growth in trade was in turn linked to the development of a colonial banking system that worked closely with land companies in their speculative schemes.

Increasingly, the politics of the colony were dominated by the struggle of the liberal professional petty bourgeoisie with the clergy, on one hand, and the English bourgeoisie, on the other. The representative assembly became their principal forum since, even with an overrepresentation of Anglophones (in 1792, with 7 per cent of the population, Anglophones held 32 per cent of the seats), the *Canadiens* were still in the majority. Thus, the *Canadiens* used the assembly to promote such projects as a neutral school system. Even more importantly, they used the assembly to attempt to frustrate the English bourgeoisie's plans for development of the colonial economy. Within the assembly, the *Canadiens* refused to support the construction of a canal system and they advocated free trade. By the same token, they promoted taxation of commerce, rather than property, since it would fall more heavily on the British. Above all, they used their majority in the assembly to frustrate the assimilationist projects the colony's Anglophones were regularly promoting.

The structures of the colonial government reproduced with striking clarity the social divisions in the colony. Whereas the representative assembly was dominated by the *Canadien* liberal professionals, two appointive bodies, the Executive Council and Legislative Council, were composed primarily of Anglophones, plus "reliable" categories of *Canadiens* such as the seigneurs. Thus, the struggle for responsible government that soon dominated colonial politics was also a struggle between *Canadiens* and British, and among *Canadiens* themselves. Out of this struggle emerged the *Patriote* movement, grouping together *Canadien* liberal professionals and a small number of liberal-minded English-speakers around the goal of an autonomous Quebec state.

As in Upper Canada, the struggle turned into an open conflict, though there was considerably more violence in Lower Canada. The *Patriote* leader, Louis-Joseph Papineau, had pitted his strength in the assembly against some members of the Church hierarchy, the seigneurs, and the British colonial administrators. In the armed uprising of 1837 his forces, the *Patriotes*, were no match for well-armed and organized government troops. Papineau left for temporary exile in the United States, but behind him were French villages around Montreal that had been burned and looted by British soldiers. These were testimony to the ethnic antagonism that shaped the struggle for responsible rule in Quebec. When, in 1849, Governor Elgin approved compensation for French-Canadian losses sustained during the rebellion, the English in Montreal burned the assembly house.

Within some readings, the *Patriote* movement and the uprisings were really a reflection of the traditional values that had always characterized the *Canadiens*. Allegedly, their reaction was less to the British than to the capitalist values the British bore and upon which their plans for the colony's future were based. This presumed conflict of mentalities led the *Patriotes* to blame the economic difficulties of their people on the British rather than to recognize the opportunities that development of the colony's economy would represent for all.[25]

Yet, this ignores the extent to which the *Canadien* petty bourgeoise was itself the bearer of liberal values – as in its championship of liberal democratic institutions and of state control of education and hospitals.[26] To be sure, the *Patriotes* did portray the *Canadiens* as an agrarian people. And they generally defended the seigneurial system (although in 1838 the *Patriotes* finally called for its abolition). But this can be better seen as a reflection of their own economic position, and that of their people, than as a rejection of capitalism, *per se*.

Within the colonial economy, there was in fact no other role available to most *Canadiens* than farming, given British domination of commerce, and the seigneurial system did protect their land from English incursions. As the self-appointed leaders of the *Canadiens*, the *Patriotes* had to defend the seigneurial system and to frustrate projects of economic development, such as canal improvement, which would have raised the tax burden on this population. As Bourque and Legaré argue, the *Canadien* petty bourgeoisie could propose its own economic initiatives, based on this agrarian economy, as it did: improvement of techniques, development of trade relations, and even establishment of certain forms of industry based on agriculture. Some of the *Patriotes* even proposed a Bank of the People, based on the farming population. But the *Canadien* petty bourgeosie could hardly be expected to embrace the capitalist projects of the British. Caught as it was between the feudal relations of the seigneurial system and the commercial capitalism of the British, it had difficulty formulating a coherent social project of its own and vacillated between the ideals of the seigneurial system and a society of independent farmers.[27]

Rather than a culturally based reaction to capitalism, the *Patriote* movement can be better seen as a nationalist reaction to British domination of colonial government and of the economy. Within the government, the *Canadien* petty bourgeoisie was effectively limited to one part, the representative assembly; it was largely absent from the executive. *Canadiens* in general were underrepresented: even at the lowest levels of the government structures (clerks, messengers, and cleaning women) *Canadiens* held only one-third of the positions, even though they represented 90 per cent of the colony's population.[28] Within the economy, the *Canadiens* as a whole were effectively relegated to agriculture and to servicing the needs of this farming population through the liberal professions and small-scale commerce. Responsible government promised not only greater mobility for the *Canadien* petty bourgeoisie but a heightened capacity to frustrate projects of commercial development from which the *Canadiens* anticipated no benefit. Coupled with British domination of the economy was, of course, a history of periodic assimilationist projects from the English-speaking population, such as subjection of education to Anglophone officials through the Royal Institution for the Advancement of Learning, encouragement of English-speaking immigrants, and fusion of Upper and Lower Canada: ample fuel for a nationalist movement.

It is in terms of the *Patriotes'* growing nationalism that one can best understand the dilution of their anti-clericalism: as they sought to mobilize the *habitants* they had to recognize the Church's continuing influence among the *habitants*.[29] Certainly, the Church did not see the *Patriotes* as defenders of traditional values and institutions. It was badly shaken by the uprisings and resolved, in their wake, to ensure that such an attack on the established order would never happen again.

Quebec after the Rebellions: The Politics of Accommodation and the Hegemony of Traditionalist Ideology

The aftermath of the rebellions looked like a threatening time for the French Canadians. In order to find some explanations and solutions for the troubles in the colony, the British sent a royal commission to Canada under the direction of Lord Durham. Durham's famous Report was undeniably of great importance to the evolution of British colonial policy, but in the eyes of French Canadians its recommendations were a direct threat to their community and a slur on their character. Durham concluded that the way to resolve the situation of "two nations warring within the bosom of a single state" was to extinguish the French nation by means of assimilation. His rationale was that this element was inferior. He described the French Canadians as "a people with no history and no literature," and as an "uneducated and unprogressive people." While the conventional wisdom has been that personal prejudice led Durham to this conclusion, Janet Ajzenstat has recently demonstrated that his prescription can best be seen as a reflection of the liberal thought of his time, which looked to the emergence of an international political culture and saw the disappearance of national difference and sentiment as both inevitable and desirable.[30]

The second major event that ensued from the rebellions was the establishment, in 1840, of a single government for both Upper and Lower Canada. The constitution of the Union government allocated to Canada East and Canada West (the new names applied to Lower Canada and Upper Canada) an equal number of seats in the assembly. As far as the French-Canadian leaders were concerned, the purpose of the Union government was to reduce the power of the "French party" in Canadian affairs. They noted that when the government was formed, Quebec, with half the seats, had the greater population; only when Ontario grew to be larger was the principle of "representation by population" extolled by the English Canadians, who were now frustrated because the French Canadians had enough seats to block any legislation that appeared contrary to the interests of the French-Canadian community.

Although the era of Union government could have been politically disastrous for French Canadians, their more moderate leaders (i.e., those who opposed the democratic republicanism and anticlericalism of Papineau) managed to defend French Canada's interests and at the same time forge an alliance with English-Canadian reformers, like Baldwin, in the struggle for responsible government. This was achieved in 1849, largely because of a change of government in London and the installation of a sympathetic governor in Canada. The constitutional change was important, but more significant was the alliance forged to achieve it, for this marked the beginning of that dualism at the elite level that is often regarded as the key to Canada's continued existence as a nation-state. This political linkage, which by 1854 included the Anglo-Canadian merchants of Montreal and effectively excluded from power Papineau and the *rouges*, established the mode of leadership for the country for a very long time: "in general, since 1854, it is this coalition of the centre and the right which has governed Canada."[31]

In 1840, then, the French Canadians were divided and unsettled by the recent rebellion and were being told by a representative of their colonial masters that they had, and deserved to have, no future. By the 1850s they found a political solution to this gloomy impasse. They exercised political dominance in their own territory of Canada East, and, within the constraints of the Union government, had strong leaders who ensured they would play an effective role in the next stage of political evolution, the negotiations for dominion status and a federal constitution.

For French Canada, the real benefit of Confederation was the provision of a range of powers, limited but sacrosanct, over its own affairs. It meant that the province of Quebec could serve as a concrete political unit, protected by the constitution, in which the French-Canadian community could be clearly dominant and thus have a chance to survive on its own terms. Confederation also entailed a risk since, at the federal level, French Canadians were relegated to the position of a permanent minority, where their rights and powers were subject to the actions of the Anglo-Canadian majority. They were protected to some extent by the informal alliance of French and English elites in the bi-ethnic parties, and by the electoral necessity of winning some French-Canadian support in a national election, but the real protection came only from the autonomous powers that, under the aegis of the BNA Act, they could exercise in their own province. The fate of the French-Canadian communities elsewhere in Canada underlined the significance of provincial autonomy. Both in Manitoba and in New Brunswick the Francophone minorities were deprived of the rights and the powers necessary to prevent assimilation. The Riel Rebellion of 1885 seemed to demonstrate that an Anglo-Canadian federal government had little concern for French-Canadian interests and sentiments.

Nevertheless, the French-English alliance in Ottawa was maintained. After the Riel affair, it shifted away from the Conservatives, who were becoming increasingly identified with Orange elements in Ontario, to the Liberals, who managed under Laurier to shed the anti-clerical *rouge* image that had tainted them in the 1870s and 1880s. Laurier's ascendance to the federal leadership consolidated the shift.

Underlying this spirit of accommodation in Canadian politics during the mid- and late nineteenth century had been not only the failure of the 1837-38 Rebellions but the new pre-eminence of the Church. For its part, the Church had actively supported the Confederation process, just as it had always promoted loyalty to the British crown. Beyond that, it disseminated a vision of French Canada as a traditional society in which government in any event played a minimal role.

In the wake of the 1837-38 Rebellions, the Church sought to strengthen its organization. Bishop Ignace Bourget of Montreal began importing priests and expanding the religious orders, increasing the number of classical colleges for the education of the elite, and giving the Church a greater social role. With these greater resources and with the liberal professionals either discredited or largely tamed by the failure of the rebellions, the Church could at last assume its role as the "natural" leader of the French-Canadian population. The latter half of the nineteenth century and early part of the twentieth century was the period of true Church pre-eminence in French-Canadian society.

The Church developed and maintained a conservative outlook. Just as it had adamantly fought the secular-democratic force of Louis-Joseph Papineau during the 1820s and 1830s, so it largely subdued the similarly inclined *rouge* faction of the Liberal Party. The Church in Quebec gained many priests who had fled the 1848 revolution in France, and it sent troops to defend the papacy against Garibaldi. In doctrinal matters the Quebec Church contained an ultramontane faction that was more orthodox than the Pope. The conservatism extended to social and political issues, as exemplified in its opposition to the formation of trade unions, and by the latter half of the century the Church was powerful enough to have these views influence the general course of French Canada's affairs.

Critical to the Church's ability to propound its traditionalist ideology was its success in securing control over education. A conflict existed through much of this period over whether the control of education should be in secular or Church hands. The Church recognized the importance of this issue to maintaining its role as principal defender of French-Canadian culture and values; on the other side were those who wanted to Anglicize the province and who were equally aware of the importance of education in achieving this goal. The issue, then, was much more than a peda-gogical or even spiritual one. The Church emerged as the victor and was not challenged again until the 1960s, when the challenge came from within the French-Canadian community.

The issue had first been opened in 1801 when Jacob Mountain, the Anglican bishop, had a program of assimilation passed in the legislature. The reaction was so severe that it was never implemented. A mélange of the Church and state bodies were involved in education until legislation in the 1840s provided for local tax-supported school boards and put education firmly on a religious footing. This legislation did not undergo major revision for over a century. A Ministry of Education was established after Confederation but, in order to "keep politics out of education," was dropped in 1875. Control went to the Conseil de l'Instruction Publique, containing separate Catholic and Protestant committees that, after 1906, never met together. The Catholic committee was made up of all the bishops in the province and an equal number of laymen appointed by the cabinet.

Higher education was obtained at Laval, founded in 1852 on the property and revenues of the Jesuit seminary of Quebec City, and inspired partly by the concern over French Canadians having to attend McGill to get university training. Laval was Church-oriented, but at first it gave some courses in English and registered a number of Anglophone students. The Université de Montréal was a branch of Laval until 1920 when it received its own charter. The archbishop of the respective city was the rector of each university, the faculty was recruited heavily from the Church's teaching orders, and the curriculum leaned toward the subjects needed for the professions traditionally selected by French Canadians: law, medicine, and theology. Business and technical subjects received very little attention.[32] In an effort to correct this, the Quebec government established an engineering school in Montreal and a school of arts and crafts in Quebec City, both in the 1870s, and Montreal's École des hautes études commerciales, in 1907.

By the end of the century the community appeared to have developed institutions and values that were well entrenched and fully capable of defending French Canada's distinctive culture. Even if that culture – agrarian, religious, traditional – was in conflict with the trend of modernization that surrounded and penetrated it, it was not until well into the twentieth century that this conflict reached the point where French Canadians came to adopt a new identity. The demography and economy of French Canada in the nineteenth century were dominated by the establishment of French Canadians as a rural, farming population. They had not begun that way, and by the end of the century industrialization was already ensuring they would not stay that way. Still, the rural and farming way of life was surrounded by an aura of sanctity in French Canada, and it became a stereotype that persisted long after it was denied by reality. This agrarian mythology, which began to appear at the beginning of the century, served to distinguish French Canada as a separate culture and was thus an important element in the struggle for cultural survival. The nineteenth-century economy underwent significant changes, such as the switch from furs to timber as the export staple at the beginning of the century, and the coming of the railroads in the middle of the century. But for most French Canadians "farming maintained its dominant place. It was, even more than in the past, the fulcrum of French-Canadian society."[33]

There was a basic flaw in this fulcrum's structure. Under the pressure of extraordinarily high birth rates, the supply of good farm lands began to run out, and it was impossible for each son to

55

be placed on his own farm. The alternatives were to move to the more marginal lands away from the river valleys or south to the United States. Between 1851 and 1931, 700,000 chose the latter. Those who chose the former went to the Ottawa Valley and the Eastern Townships, areas that had been predominantly English since the American Revolution, or the interior of the Laurentians or Lac St. Jean. After 1850, the government and the Church ran colonization programs designed to encourage movement to the interior rather than to the blemished atmosphere of the New England mill towns or Quebec's own growing cities.

Urbanization in Quebec was dominated by Quebec City and Montreal, which were of equal size until the 1830s. As Upper Canada developed, Montreal became an important centre of trade and commerce, while Quebec City remained a much smaller centre of administration and education. Irish and British immigrants gave Quebec City a sizable non-French population (41 per cent in 1844), but gradually the city's character changed until it became, as it is today, almost purely French. Montreal, on the other hand, has always contained a large English-speaking element that included a significant group of relatively prosperous merchants and businessmen. Although class and ethnic lines did not perfectly coincide, since there were French and English among both the propertied and the workers, they were close enough to create the following impression in 1899: "In the city of Montreal . . . it is well known that, man for man, the average income of the French-Canadian is perhaps not one-fourth of that of his British neighbour."[34] When Montreal became the focus of Quebec's industrialization, it began to draw French-Canadian workers in large numbers. The city's population tripled between 1861 and 1891 to 265,000, then doubled again to 530,000 by 1913.

However, the French-Canadian population remained less urbanized than that of Quebec as a whole, and at the turn of the century the Francophones of Quebec were still 75 per cent rural. Thus, the rural parish provided the way of life that was more characteristic and supposedly more desirable than that of the cities. A monograph of the 1860s depicts the major features of such a parish, located on the North Shore: a self-sufficient economy; isolation from the influence of cities or commerce; aversion to post-elementary education as something that corrupted and unsettled accepted norms; tenacious family ties that had the family farm as a physical and symbolic focal point; a strong Catholic faith that supported the local curé with tithes and endowed him with considerable authority over local affairs.[35]

With such a self-contained rural parish as its ideal, the traditionalist ideology of the Church and its allies supported a highly truncated view of the political and economic reality in which French-Canadian society was situated. The political process was viewed essentially as a means of defending French-Canadian culture and religion. This emphasis explicitly avoided questioning the economic power of the English in Montreal or the economic consequences of cheap French-Canadian labour that was being hired by American and Anglo-Canadian enterprises. The emigration to jobs in New England was seen as a cultural rather than an economic problem, and the response was to try and perpetuate the agrarian society by opening up new parishes in the interior. It maintained that survival necessitated the rejection of industrial society and, hence, of social and economic change. But over the next few decades this change was taking root in French-Canadian society to such an extent that the ideology would be reduced to mythology, albeit a tenacious one.

Quebec in the Twentieth Century:
The Confrontation with Change

Before 1900, much of the challenge to French Canada had come from external forces and events: military defeat, economic domination, colonial policy, and constitutional manipulation. With the twentieth century, the challenge was different because it came from within the province and directly involved the mass of the French-Canadian population, not just the elite.

The society was losing its rural character, and the economy was becoming less agrarian. In spite of the colonization efforts, the population continued to move into the cities of Quebec and the United States. While western Canada was expanding into new territory with immigrants from continental Europe, Quebec was beginning to exploit its own hinterlands for hydroelectric power and for minerals. It was also building up a manufacturing base. This was largely in the form of light industries such as textiles and shoes, using the cheap labour that could still be found in Quebec but that was disappearing from New England. Cheap power, close to the population centres, was another attraction for investment. Between 1900 and 1920, with a boost from the boom years of World War I, the contribution of manufacturing to the province's economy rose from 4 per cent to 38 per cent. The agrarian economy changed in kind as well as degree. Unable to compete with western wheat producers, Quebec farmers switched to dairy production and other cash crops for the urban markets. This spelled the end of the traditional farm, and rural Quebec became tied into the urban economy.

Industrialization was accompanied by urbanization, with Montreal being the primary focus of this process. Montreal tripled in size in two decades, from 1901 to 1921, while Quebec City grew by less than 50 per cent. Three other cities, Sherbrooke, Trois-Rivières, and Hull, had doubled in size but were still only 20-25,000 (compared to Montreal's 618,500). These figures do disguise the fact that French Canadians were considerably less urbanized than Quebec's English Canadians – in 1931, 59 per cent as opposed to 82 per cent. Montreal, although it contained 36 per cent of the province's total population in 1931, was 40 per cent non-French, and only 27 per cent of Quebec's French Canadians lived there. Nonetheless, French Canadians could no longer properly be characterized as a rural people, even if their traditionalist elites continued to do so.

In other spheres, change was much less evident. The basic structure and outlook of the education system stayed the same, though schools of forestry, surveying, and chemistry were established at Laval and some of the classical colleges began teaching commerce and science. The Church resisted attempts to enlarge the government's role in education. It obstructed legislation for compulsory education, and in 1931 only 60 per cent of the 5-19 age group was attending school, the lowest rate in Canada. However, there were tendencies that indicated a change in the Church's dominant role. Urban intellectuals were beginning to question the Church's prominence in Quebec's affairs, and the Church was having to adapt to a new type of parishioner, the urban factory worker. Even in rural Quebec, the continued authority of the curé was accompanied by some signs of instability and change.[36] These influences of modernization, while noteworthy, were still peripheral, and the central institutions and structures continued to hold.

In politics, there were some upheavals but, again, the essential characteristics remained the same. Until he supported the Navy Bill in 1911, Laurier kept his leadership secure with massive support from Quebec. The Conservatives showed little concern for French-Canadian interests and, by advocating overseas service and conscription in the Boer War and World War I, went directly contrary to them. Except among British-born immigrants, there was little enthusiasm anywhere in Canada for conscription in World War I, but its implementation was met with bloody riots in Quebec. In the 1917 election Laurier, now Leader of the Opposition to the Union government, won sixty-two of Quebec's sixty-five seats, seventeen of them by acclamation. In 1921, even though Laurier had died and the Liberals were now led by Mackenzie King, all sixty-five seats went to the Liberals and the party's "safe sixty-five" was apparently becoming a permanent fixture in Canadian politics. The Liberals also dominated politics at the provincial level, staying in power, usually with huge majorities, for forty years from 1897 to 1936.

As was the case elsewhere in Canada, electoral politics was very much centred on the dispensation of patronage, and the conduct of politics in French did not affect this pattern one way or another. The parties were ruled by the caucus, not by open organizations, and at the constituency level drew on the small group of lawyers, other professionals, and proprietors of small businesses who made up the local elite and who looked after local patronage. The provincial government was similar to the federal in these respects except there was an additional form of patronage in Quebec City: the encouragement of large-scale external (i.e., non-French-Canadian) investment through incentives such as cheap rights to mineral and forest resources, monopolies over public utilities, and an unregulated and unorganized labour force. Beyond that, the scope of government concerns was limited. The Taschereau government passed some welfare legislation in the 1920s but as a rule social measures were regarded outside the government's provenance and were left to the Church.

French-Canadian nationalism remained an important part of Quebec's political life, but at this time there were some departures from its traditional modes of expression. One of the most prominent nationalists was Henri Bourassa, a grandson of Papineau and the founder of the influential Montreal daily, *Le Devoir*. Bourassa attacked the imperial connection with Great Britain and advocated a Canada that was not only independent but thoroughly bicultural. He demanded also that the province carry out reforms in the economy and in the educational system, and his demands were very similar to those that were put forward again in the 1950s. On the other hand, Bourassa's view of French Canada was essentially a conservative one, and in his later years he expressed nostalgia for the traditional way of life. Abbé Lionel Groulx provided another variation of nationalist thought. His brand, unlike Bourassa's, was more exclusively French-Canadian, and it contained the more traditional mix of patriotism and religion. Groulx wrote an influential history of French Canada from a nationalist perspective and founded the Association Catholique de la Jeunesse Canadienne-française (ACJC), at least one faction of which advocated French-Canadian separatism. Finally, there was the more progressive, secular tone of La Ligue Nationaliste, founded in 1903 by Olivar Asselin.

Inevitably, the beginnings of urbanization and industrialization in Quebec were making awareness of social and economic conditions, along with faith and language, part of the collective consciousness of French Canada. Those beginnings were on the verge of becoming sweeping and fundamental changes that would transform all aspects of French-Canadian society. What we have seen so far of French Canada was to become buried in the foundations of new structures, and would be left to play an important but unrecognizable part in Quebec's future.

CHAPTER THREE
Economic and Social Development: Quebec before the 1960s

As the twentieth century progressed, so did the transformation of Quebec's economy and society. By mid-century, if not before, Quebec had indeed become an urban, industrial society. As we shall see in the next chapter, the political response to these changes that one might expect – greater intervention by the Quebec state and modernization of its structures – lagged far behind. Not until the "Quiet Revolution" of the 1960s did the Quebec state really undertake the process of *rattrapage*, or catching up, to the profound social and economic changes Quebec had been undergoing throughout the first half of this century. Before assessing this lag in political modernization, and exploring its causes, we first need to examine the social and economic changes themselves. We will do so through the categories of economic and social development outlined in Chapter One.

Development of the Quebec Economy before 1960

Economic growth is such a powerful agent of modernization that it often seems to determine the style of social and political change. Especially with the end of World War ii, Quebec's economy achieved a notable record of growth. Although this record – which includes the pre-war Depression as well as the post-war boom – is repeated elsewhere, it contains some special characteristics that have ramifications for the accompanying processes of social and political change.

As the previous chapter suggested, French Canadians had been living, in myth and to a lesser extent in actuality, in a traditional society. Their elites not only accepted this but actively encouraged it, claiming it was a socially and morally desirable situation. Economic growth was important to Quebec's development because it not only was generating more wealth but also was shattering the foundations of this traditional society and widening the gap between the ethos of traditionalism and the day-to-day reality of most French Canadians' lives. A second distinguishing feature of economic growth in Quebec was the character of external investment and control. This meant that the theme of subordination, very familiar in Quebec, had to be reformulated in new and much more complex terms.

The Course and Components of Economic Growth Since 1920

The chronology of Quebec's economic growth more or less followed the North American pattern. The 1920s saw a heavy influx of investment capital, partly pushed by the diminishing natural resources and rising labour costs in the northeastern United States, but attracted as well by the attitude of the Taschereau government to outside investors. The Depression stopped the growth, and the decline in industrial employment was severe enough to reinstitute, with some success, a back-to-the-land movement. Then World War II prompted an economic revival. The armed forces, in spite of Quebec's political resistance to conscription, provided one type of escape from unemployment for 120,000 French Canadians. The war also opened up Quebec's interior. It contained the strategic resources to feed the industrial boom in war production, was invulnerable to attack, and was reasonably close to the industrial centres. Quebec's raw materials played an important part in the development of the continental economic structure that began to emerge in Canada during the war years. The province participated in the post-war boom by further developing its natural resources and expanding its secondary and tertiary activities. Meanwhile agriculture, although increasing its revenue and productivity, played a rapidly diminishing role in the provincial economy, especially in terms of employment.

Two factors contributed a great deal to the economic growth of these decades. The first was the impetus that came as early as the first decade of the century from Quebec's cheap and plentiful supply of hydroelectricity. Cheap power was a major factor in the growth of processing industries (pulp and paper, aluminum smelting, chemicals) as well as of manufacturing. Until the Liberals established Hydro-Québec in 1944, all the province's power, for both domestic and industrial use, was supplied by privately owned monopolies; it was not until 1963 that most hydroelectricity came under government control. The spectacular rise in hydroelectric production (see Table Two) is a good indicator of overall economic growth.

Table Two
Indicators of Economic Growth, Quebec, 1921-1971

	Hydroelectric production (millions of KWH)	Mineral production (value in dollars)
1921	1,791	$15,522,988
1931	8,066	$36,051,366
1941	17,741	$99,700,027
1951	26,690	$255,931,822
1961	50,433	$455,522,933
1971	75,274	$770,000,000

SOURCES: For hydroelectric production, 1921-61, see *Quebec Yearbook*, 1962, p. 619. For mineral production, 1921-61, see *Annuaire du Québec*, 1966-1967, p. 628. For hydro and mineral figures, 1971, see *Annuaire du Québec*, 1973, pp. 599, 571.

A second major component of growth was mining. The early mainstay of this industry was asbestos, discovered in the Eastern Townships in the nineteenth century. In the 1950s iron ore emerged as an important resource. Huge deposits of low-grade ore were discovered in the uninhabited hinterland 300 miles north of the St. Lawrence River. The increasing demand of the American steel industry, combined with the diminishing ore reserves of the Mesabi Range in Minnesota, prompted the development of these deposits. Ore was shipped by rail and the St. Lawrence Seaway (which was finally built once the American steel lobby overrode the long-standing opposition of the eastern seaboard states) to steel mills on the Great Lakes. The third contribution to the mining industry came from the copper, gold, and zinc mines in the northwest, around Rouyn-Noranda. This area was opened up in the 1920s, but major expansion came as a result of World War II.

The manufacturing sector of an economy is crucial to the notion of economic development (as distinguished from economic growth). Large-scale manufacturing in Quebec has relied to a great degree on the primary extractive industries. Pulp and paper has been the most important manufacture in terms of numbers employed and dollar value added, followed by smelting and refining. Aircraft parts and production ranks behind these. Finally there are the traditional manufactures of Quebec – textiles, clothing, tobacco products – which have their roots in the small labour-intensive operations that characterized Quebec industry before the growth of the highly capitalized resource-based industries. Unlike the primary activities, manufacturing has been concentrated in the Montreal plain, with the exception of the pulp and paper industry, which, in order to be close to the sources of supply, is concentrated around Trois-Rivières and the Saguenay region.

Although manufacturing grew after World War II, the other sectors of the economy – the resource-based primary sector and the tertiary, or services, sector – grew faster. In fact, the contribution of manufacturing to Quebec's economy slipped between 1946 and 1966 in terms of both employment (36 per cent to 31.9 per cent of the labour force) and value of production (41.2 per cent to 38.8 per cent of the provincial total).[1] Many regard this as a sign that Quebec's economy, though bigger, had not necessarily become stronger.

Table Three
Agricultural Statistics, 1941-1971

	1941	*1951*	*1961*	*1971*
Number of Farms	154,669	134,366	95,777	61,257
Population on farms as				
percentage of total population	25.2	19.5	11.1	5.6
Number of tractors	5,869	31,971	70,697	80,878
Percentage of land area in farms	5.4	5.0	4.2	3.2
Average area of farms (acres)	117	125	148	176

SOURCE: *Census of Canada*, 1971, Vol. IV, Part 2, Tables 2 and 7.

The counterpart of industrialization is the relative and even absolute decline of agriculture as an economic activity. In Quebec, this decline had particular significance, given agriculture's prominence not only in the economy but in the traditional value system of French Canada. The most striking indicator of decline is the reduction in the labour force engaged in farming, but it is also revealed in the drop in the number of farms and in the declining proportion of the population that lives on farms (see Table Three). Many of those who live on farms are not actually farmers, because they have to work at least part-time elsewhere; a study made in 1956 estimated that, even at that time, there were only 80,000 full-time resident farmers, or about 2 per cent of the population.[2] Table Three also portrays how farming became increasingly characterized by larger, more mechanized units. In the late 1950s the disappearance of the agrarian lifestyle was described by the spokesman for Quebec's farm organization, the Union Catholique des Cultivateurs, to the Royal Commission on Canada's

Economic Prospects (the Gordon Commission): "Agriculture in the province of Quebec is in the process of becoming a business and is ceasing to be a way of life."[3]

Social Effects of Economic Growth

The social dimension of economic growth can be depicted by looking at the distribution of the labour force. In the province as a whole the proportion of workers engaged in the primary sector decreased dramatically, especially after World War II. The rise in the proportion in the secondary sector was minimal; the largest increase was in the tertiary sector – utilities, commerce, public service, transport and communications, professions, etc. (See Table Four.)

Though valid in isolation, these trends are an inadequate portrayal of the effects of Quebec's industrialization because they conceal the relative position of French Canadians in the labour force. During these decades, French Canadians moved out of occupations in the primary sector into those of the secondary and tertiary sectors, as shown in Table Four, but lagged behind in this movement. Particularly in the tertiary occupations, which are usually considered part of the most advanced sector of the economy, the proportion of French Canadians was smaller than their proportion in the labour force as a whole. Before the 1960s, French Canadians as a group held a disproportionately small share of the high-status, high-paying jobs in Quebec's economy, as can be seen in a comparison of the ethnic origins of specific occupational groups (Table Five). Not only were French Canadians underrepresented in the higher occupations, but this underrepresentation held right through the post-war period of economic growth. In manufacturing jobs they moved from underrepresentation to slight overrepresentation, and they also made gains in the clerical category. French Canadians shifted into "modern" jobs but, as other studies have shown, not into the positions that control those jobs. John Porter's *The Vertical Mosaic,* written on the basis of 1951 data, found French Canadians more underrepresented in the "Professional and Financial" category than they had been in 1931; a decade later the Royal Commission on Bilingualism and Biculturalism showed French Canadians at a greater occupational disadvantage in 1961 than in 1941.[4] In effect, as Quebec's economy changed, its long-standing cultural division of labour simply took different forms. Cultural hierarchy and segmentation were as much a part of Quebec's new economy as they had been of the old one.

Table Four

Distribution of Male Labour Force and French Male Labour Force, by Industry Group, Quebec, 1931-1971

Industry Group	1931		1941		1951		1961		1971	
	Total	French	Total	French	Total	French	Total	French	Total	French
Primary	30.1%	35.2%	31.6%	36.1%	20.9%	24.0%	12.4%	14.8%	5.6%	6.7%
Secondary	29.8	27.5	36.6	34.3	41.2	40.2	38.8	37.4	35.2	34.7
Tertiary	33.8	30.6	30.2	28.0	35.9	33.8	46.0	45.0	51.2	50.9
Unspecified	6.3	6.7	1.6	1.6	2.0	2.0	2.8	2.8	8.0	7.7
	100.0	100.0	100.0	100.0	100.0	100.0	100.0	100.0	100.0	100.0

SOURCES: *Census of Canada*, 1931, Vol. VII, Table 62; *Census of Canada*, 1941, Vol. VII, Table 26; *Census of Canada*, 1951, Vol. IV, Table 20; *Census of Canada*, 1961, Vol. III.2, Table 11; *Census of Canada*, 1971, Vol. III.5, Table 4.

Table Five
Distribution of Male Labour Force, Selected Occupations, by Ethnic Group, Quebec, 1941-1971*

1941 Ethnic Group	Occupations			
	Total	Professionals	Clerical	Agriculture
French	79.1%	66.8%	59.1%	90.9%
British	14.0	26.1	34.8	7.9
Other	6.9	7.1	6.1	1.2

1961 Ethnic Group			Occupations		
	Total	Managerial	Professional & Technical	Clerical & Sales	Industrial
French	77.5%	63.8%	72.9%	72.3%	80.2%
British	11.8	19.0	22.5	17.1	8.8
Other	10.7	17.2	14.6	10.6	11.0

1971 Ethnic Group			Occupations		
	Total	Managerial	Professional & Technical	Clerical & Sales	Industrial
French	75.8%	61.9%	72.7%	79.5%	87.9%
British	11.7	22.8	14.5	8.6	7.9
Other	12.5	15.3	12.8	11.9	4.2

*Due to changes in definitions, the various occupational categories are not always comparable across censuses.
SOURCES: *Census of Canada*, 1941, Vol. VII, Table 12; *Census of Canada*, 1961, Vol. III.1, Table 22; *Census of Canada*, 1971, Vol. III.3, Table 5.

This has implications that go far beyond the problem of achieving occupational mobility in a modernizing society. The ethnic hierarchy within Quebec's occupational structure meant that the French Canadian who left the farm and the cultural homogeneity of the rural parish to work in an office or a factory became aware of both the cultural and the economic disparities of his new environment. The economic gaps were obvious enough – French Canadians made up 60 per cent of an early 1960s sample of 7,163 Quebec workers studied by the Bilingualism and Biculturalism Commission, but only 17 per cent of those earning over $12,000. More telling is the conclusion drawn by the Commission that "the present situation is highly unjust. These arrangements constitute major difficulties for Francophone employees; they have far-reaching implications with respect to work performance, career advancement, and retention of linguistic and cultural identity."[5]

The "present situation" had a feeling of permanence about it. In the 1930s, Everett Hughes's study of an industrial town in the Eastern Townships had reported that

> it is in the upper ranks of industry that one finds the English outsiders. People of local origin and French culture are in the lower ranks. The latter are, furthermore, from the lower ranks of the local society. The people of the higher ranks of French-Canadian society find little place in the industrial society.[6]

Two decades later, in the 1950s, Schefferville, a mining town, seemed to follow the same pattern: a French majority, an English minority, with the latter group holding the top jobs. It differed from Hughes's "Cantonville" in that some of the French Canadians occupied positions that were exclusively English in "Cantonville."[7] However, the old pattern of Quebec's industrial hierarchy still persisted.

The significant difference from the time of Hughes's study was the number of French-Canadian workers who were confronting this pattern of occupational stratification. The French Canadian who left the farm for industrial work within Quebec used to be the exception and was a marginal figure according to the norms of his society. By the post-war years the French Canadian who remained on the farm was in the minority, and a very small one; the rest were in the modern industrial economy, and the manner in which that economy was organized and run could no longer be ignored.

Another effect of economic growth is an increase in wealth and, as long as the wealth is distributed, rising standards of living. Even those who do not directly benefit from industrialization are affected by it: they want a higher standard of living, regardless of their capacity or opportunity to get it. Quebec's economic growth produced steadily rising incomes, and by 1960 real per capita income in the province was almost double what it had been at the beginning of the 1930s. This rise in the standard of living was indicated by a reduced rate of infant mortality, a death rate that had halved since 1931, and another ten years of life expectancy. In absolute terms the people of Quebec were better off than they were in the 1920s. Relatively, however, some of them were better off than others, and no picture of economic growth can overlook these differences. One of the differences, as the data in the preceding section suggest, was along ethnic lines. Occupational ranking was inevitably matched by income ranking, and while no economy is free of income differences, the Quebec view of these was affected by the fact that the French Canadians, as an ethnic group, ranked near the bottom of the income scale.[8]

A second disparity in the economy of mid-century Quebec existed along regional lines within the province. It was not simply a rural-urban cleavage, since the small frontier and company towns where everyone was working had very high incomes, and in a city like Montreal there were pockets of unemployment and severe poverty. On the other hand, there were strikingly poor rural areas, like *Gaspésie*, with stagnant economies and very high unemployment. The most consistent disparity in wealth was between the country and the city, especially if we look only at the farm population in the former category. In 1971 the average male urban wage-earner received $2,650 more per annum than his rural-farm counterpart. The problem of regional disparities in Quebec alerts us to the social and even cultural variety that is denied when the label "Québécois" is used to imply that all French Canadians have a similar outlook and similar problems.

Another disparity was between Quebec and the rest of the country. Except for the Maritimes, Quebec was consistently at the bottom of the rank in incomes, housing standards, unemployment rates, and so on. This difference naturally played a part in arguments on loftier themes like constitutional rights. The average annual income of Quebec males was about $300 below the national average in 1961, and almost $1,000 below that of Ontario. Although eastern Quebec is economically as well as geographically closer to the Maritimes, Quebec is invariably compared to Ontario, since the size of their populations and their degree of industrialization set them apart from the other provinces. In such a comparison (see Table Six), Quebec came a poor second on all counts: her per capita income had remained, since 1926, about 73 per cent of Ontario's; Ontario's industrial sector was more ad-

Table Six
Average Reported Annual Incomes, Males, 1971

	Quebec	Ontario	Canada
Total	$6,288	$7,250	$6,538
Urban	$6,691	$7,566	$7,050
Rural	$4,468	$5,733	$4,857
Rural-farm	$4,041	$4,955	$4,174

SOURCE: *Census of Canada*, 1971, Vol. III.1, Table 29.

vanced, more productive, paid higher wages, and mobilized a larger proportion of the population into the labour force.[9] Quebec had made substantial absolute gains, but the comparison with Ontario put those gains in a different perspective than when they are considered in isolation. Quebec looked very much like a "dependent" economy.

Economic Growth and the French Canadians

Quebec's economic growth affected the individual French Canadian in two ways: within a generation or two, it had changed the type of work he did, where he did it, and how much he got paid; also, it had made him aware that within the province a minority group held better jobs and earned more money than he did. These are obviously important keys to the understanding of mid-century Quebec, and because they are expressed in individual terms they are interesting and tangible topics. But there is a third key, the structure of the economy itself, including the relative role of the extractive and manufacturing industries and the extent to which Quebec was truly "developed" and not simply a supplier of raw materials. Another aspect was the question of ownership and control, and in Quebec this had connotations peculiar to that province. Once again, the ethnic factor gave it a special flavour.

There has been considerable debate about the reasons why French Canadians had failed to dominate the industrialization of their own province. The political ramifications of that failure prevented the debate from dying out or being restricted to historians. One explanation, often cited, is that the French-Canadian culture and value system precluded or at least discouraged economic activity that entailed anything larger than a family enterprise, or that put risk before security and growth before stability. While active as proprietors and in establishing small local firms, French-Canadian entrepreneurs did not participate in the industries that began to characterize the provincial economy at the turn of the century. And even entrepreneurship, as opposed to farming or, for the elite, the professions, was discouraged.[10] A somewhat different cultural argument is that, since capitalism was identified as an Anglo-Saxon cultural trait, French Canadians, regardless of their desire for economic growth, had to reject it in order to reaffirm their own identity and ensure their cultural survival.[11] French-Canadian institutions that transmitted and created the community's values also get the blame: the Church, because it idealized the agrarian way of life and preached against the materialism of the industrial centres; the education system, because it failed to provide the skills, let alone the motivation, for seeking economic gain. Some look behind the values of nineteenth-century French Canada to see underlying historical forces, such as the destruction of the entrepreneurial element of New France by the British Conquest (presuming that New France had a bourgeoisie for the British to destroy). There is a purely economic argument, that French Canadians did not possess the kind of capital required to invest in the large-scale expansionary enterprises, and a political-economic variation on it, that French Canadians had no power in Quebec so were never allowed access to the money and techniques that would have given them economic control. A final argument sees the anti-entrepreneurial culture as an effect, not a cause. It suggests Quebec was dominated by a set of values that rationalized the political and economic subordination of the French-Canadian community and forced it to define its virtues in other terms: its faith and its land.

Whatever the proper explanation, the fact remained that in the 1950s Quebec's economy was characterized by a predominance of non-French capital and ownership in large corporations. Even in the late 1960s only twenty-six of the 165 enterprises in the province with an annual production worth over $10 million were owned by French Canadians. The export-oriented, resource-based corporations tended to be under American or multinational control; modern light industries (electronics, etc.) tended to be owned by Anglo-Canadians; French Canadians predominated in the labour-intensive, lower productivity industries such as textiles, leather products, and food-processing.[12] The institutions that supplied and serviced investment capital – the stock market, bond and securities underwriters, banks, trusts, life insurance companies – were also predominantly Anglo-Canadian-owned, and St. James Street in Montreal was as much a stereotypical preserve of English commerce as Westmount was of English social life.

The New Urban Setting

Urbanization and industrialization are so closely related that to describe one is to know a good deal about the other. The indicators of the latter, including occupational change and rising incomes and productivity, invariably correlate highly with the indicator of the former, the migration from the countryside to cities and towns, and Quebec is no exception to this rule. But there is more to urbanization than physical movement. It is said to create a different kind of person, qualitatively distinct from the rustic who stays on the farm. An urban ethos, urbanity, is associated with a range of traits that is bewildering in its variety – tolerance, culture, decay, sin, alienation – but is always set in juxtaposition to the rural counterpart. The juxtaposition often becomes blurred: migrants import and often sustain the values and other facets of rural society in the midst of the urban milieu; also, commerce and mass communication technology have pervaded the countryside so that the villager who never leaves home has become partly urbanized. The demographic view of urbanization, of course, cannot account for these subtleties. All these generalizations apply to urbanization in Quebec, but we must add to them some special characteristics of the process that result from the province's ethnic divisions.

The myth of French Canada being a rural society survived well into the twentieth century, but the reality of French-Canadian society soon was very different. By 1921, half the population of Quebec as a whole was urban.[13] In fact, by one estimate Quebec had already reached the 50 per cent mark in 1915.[14] To be sure, among French-speakers in Quebec the level of urbanization was not quite as high. Nevertheless, by 1931, 58 per cent of the French-speaking population was classified as urban. The movement to the towns stopped, and even reversed itself, during the 1930s, thanks to the Depression. Nonetheless, in the wake of World War II urbanization began anew and accelerated rapidly. Thus, by 1951, 63 per cent of the Quebec's Francophone population was urban; in 1961, the proportion had reached 71 per cent.

Using the census, the rural population can be divided into "farm" and "non-farm" categories. The latter group lives in the countryside but not on isolated farms and as a result can safely be thought of as less attached to the rural ethos. Ringuet's novel *Trente Arpents* nicely depicts how the move to the small settlements of stores and services at the crossroads was an important initial step on the migration from farm to town. The farm/non-farm ratio in the rural population (see Table Seven) reversed itself within a decade, from 1951 to 1961, so if the absolute size of the rural population did not decline, its nature changed. By 1961, only 13 per cent of Quebec Francophones still lived on farms and, most important, the urban population had almost tripled since 1931.

Although there was a rapid decline in the French-Canadian community's farm population, Quebec's rural population is now over 90 per cent French-Canadian, since their rate of urbanization has consistently been lower than that of the province's other groups. There used to be large Anglo-Canadian populations in

Table Seven
Urban-Rural Distribution of French-Origin Population, Quebec,
1931-1971

	Rural Farm		Rural Non-Farm		Urban		Total	
1931*	945,000	42%			1,325,000	58%	2,270,000	100%
1941	1,107,000	41%	105,000	4%	1,483,000	55%	2,695,000	100%
1951	714,000	21%	522,000	16%	2,091,000	63%	3,327,000	100%
1961	533,000	13%	699,000	16%	3,009,000	71%	4,241,000	100%
1971	285,000	6%	755,000	16%	3,719,000	78%	4,759,000	100%

*The 1931 census does not distinguish between rural farm and non-farm populations.
SOURCES: *Census of Canada*, 1931, Vol. I, Table 35; *Census of Canada*, 1941, Vol. II, Table 30; *Census of Canada*, 1951, Vol. II, Table 46; *Census of Canada*, 1961, Vol. I.3, Table 121; *Census of Canada*, 1971, Vol. I.3, Table 3.

such rural areas as the Eastern Townships and Pontiac County north of Ottawa but this is no longer the case, and the British-origin population of Quebec is now only 12 per cent rural. Though it is no longer valid to call French Canada a rural society, it is possible to call rural Quebec a French-Canadian society, and the liturgy of the modern, as well as of the traditional, community still voices an attachment to the land ("Mon pays, c'est l'hiver . . .").

The whole process of urbanization in Quebec has been dominated (some would say distorted) by metropolitan Montreal, which contains almost a third of Quebec's population. It has dominated the economic and cultural life of the province to a much greater extent than Toronto has that of Ontario. But, more significantly, it has been the centre of English-speaking Quebec and the focal point of the earliest Anglo-Canadian economic interests. It maintained its place as Canada's economic metropolis until American money established Toronto as a financial centre and some of the western cities achieved autonomous economic status. Many of Canada's principal, indigenously controlled economic institutions – transportation, insurance, banking – shaped the city's commercial life and, via institutions like McGill, spread their influence to give the city a powerful and highly visible Anglophone milieu. This has survived, in spite of the fact that the British-origin population has never been more than a quarter of the total population since 1911 (see Table Eight), and in the century since the first census, when the city had only 144,000 people, the share has dropped from 38 per cent to 16 per cent.

Table Eight
Ethnic Composition of Montreal, 1871-1971

	1871	1901	1911	1931	1941	1951	1961	1971*
French	60%	64%	63%	60%	63%	64%	62%	61%
British	38	34	26	26	24	22	18	6
Jewish	–	2	5	6	6	5	4	5
Italian	–	–	1	2	2	2	6	7
Polish	–	–	1	1	1	1	1	1
Other	2	–	4	5	4	6	9	10

Total population (in thousands)

1871	1901	1911	1931	1941	1951	1961	1971
144.0	360.8	554.8	1,003.9	1,116.8	1,320.2	1,747.7	2,187.2

*1971 figures are for Montreal and Jesus Islands; the rest are for Montreal Island only.
SOURCES: N. Lacoste, *Les caractéristiques sociales de la population du Grand Montréal* (Montréal, 1958), p. 77 (for 1871-1951); *Census of Canada*, 1961, Vol. 1.2, Table 37; *Census of Canada*, 1971, Vol. 1.3, Table 7.

For many French Canadians, urbanization meant, in practice, moving to Montreal. Given the nature of the city, urbanization thus signified much more than exchanging rural for city ways. It also entailed exchanging the homogeneous French culture of the countryside for the dual culture of Montreal. The duality could not be avoided since many of the city's jobs, which attracted the migrants, were in enterprises owned or run by Anglophones. The French Canadian in Montreal associated economic and occupational mobility with the ability to speak English. Montreal was the major, perhaps the only, environment in the province where French Canadians lived side by side with a large community of Anglophones. It also has been recognized as the centre of French-Canadian nationalism.[15]

The composition of the city changed in the post-war years. One change is that the city became "more French." The proportion of the population of French origin has remained between 60 per cent and 65 per cent ever since 1871, but with the rapid growth after the 1930s a progressively larger proportion of the population spoke only French (29 per cent in 1931, 40 per cent in 1971). The other change is in the non-French portion of the city (see Table Eight). It used to be predominantly British and Jewish. In 1941 these two groups made up almost 80 per cent of the non-French population, but with the influx of other Europeans (except for French) beginning in the 1950s, their share fell to about 53 per cent in 1971. By

Table Nine
Ethnic and Linguistic Characteristics of Montreal, 1971*

1. Ethnic Origin	British Isles	French	Italian	Jewish	Other
Number	351,465	1,333,150	154,345	113,395	234,795
% of total pop.	16	61	7	5	11

2. Official	English	French	Bilingual		
Language	433,445	866,380	834,325		
% of total pop.	19.8	39.6	38.1		

3. Language Used	English	French	Other		
at Home	572,675	1,383,785	230,690		
% of total pop.	26.2	63.3	10.5		
Mother Tongue	494,950	1,382,325	309,875		
% of total pop.	22.6	63.2	14.1		

*Census division of Montreal and Jesus Islands. Total pop.: 2,187,150.
SOURCE: *Census of Canada*, 1971, Vol. 1.3, tables 4, 20, and 28.

1961 Italians had supplanted Jews as the third largest group in the city. Immigration changed the ethnic mix of the city, but the linguistic duality remained. Since immigrants showed a strong tendency to adopt English rather than French as their new language, the duality was reinforced. The new immigrants gave French Canadians another reason to regard Montreal as being, at the same time, the centre of their new urban culture and the locus of the assimilation that threatens their culture.

The other cities in the province have been not only much smaller but much more homogeneously French. As in Montreal, the ethnic make-up affects linguistic practice so that in the smaller cities, such as Trois-Rivières and Quebec City, a much higher proportion of the French population has been unilingual. This means that in Quebec the cultural and social effects of urbanization depended on which city (and especially, whether or not it was Montreal) was the target of migration.

On the other hand, it is evident that any city, or contact with the city, does have some effect on language usage. In 1961, 95 per cent of the French-origin population living on farms was unilingual, whereas the proportion for the rural non-farm French population was 86 per cent (still much higher than the 69 per cent level for the urban population). Still, those who stayed in the countryside were inevitably affected by the spread of the urban culture. This was not just a linguistic influence: as Horace Miner's study of a rural parish in the 1930s shows, it also entailed such changes as a more receptive attitude toward education. Interestingly, although Miner's parish was unilingually French, English words referring to vehicles, commerce, and politics were appearing in the parish's vocabulary.[16] The more isolated rural areas, those settled in the colonization programs of the late nineteenth and early twentieth centuries, were immune from this, but the more prosperous regions were economically and socially oriented toward the cities. The urban-rural distinction became weaker, and, as Gérald Fortin neatly illustrates, French-Canadian society was becoming homogeneous again, but urban instead of rural:

> Although, in Montreal, the urbanite of three generations responds to the songs of Gilles Vigneault, we must not forget that, in St. Rédempteur, the rustic of ten generations is responding to the music of the Beatles.[17]

Education: Renovation and Expansion

The principal features of the education system for French Canadians – mass education only through the elementary level, ecclesiastical control, emphasis on the humanities and the liberal arts – were, like the rural parish, used to differentiate French-Canadian from North American culture. The move to the cities spelled the end of agrarian life, but there was no random and uncontrolled erosion of the educational establishment, which was a powerful and well-integrated institution of French-Canadian society. Consequently, change in education came later, more suddenly, and with much more impact. Thorough review and reform of the educational system were not implemented until the 1960s. Well before that time there was an obvious need for reform in two directions: to extend free mass education beyond primary school, and to provide more scientific and technical training at the post-secondary level. Secondary education as provided by the classical colleges was very selective and, since they were affiliated with the arts faculties of the universities, produced students with neither the background nor the proclivity for higher education in anything but the liberal arts and professions. The universities were ill-equipped and understaffed in other fields, so they were unable to correct the trend. Many realized that French Canadians were at a disadvantage as their province became industrialized; only when this realization was accompanied by the conclusion that this was a deplorable situation did the quantity and quality of education for French Canadians become a target for reform.

The shortcomings of the system were clear enough. As late as 1961 only 50 per cent of the 15-19 age group were attending school. Since that was the figure for the whole province, the rate for French Canadians would have been lower still. An even more startling figure was the fact that in 1961 a full 86 per cent of Quebec's farmers and farm workers had less than nine years of education, probably a result of the absence of any compulsory education in Quebec until 1943.[18] A qualitative rather than a quantitative problem was the confusing variety of streams and programs. At one point there was considerable argument as to the exact meaning of the BA degree as a qualification, and by the 1960s there were several different ways of moving from secondary to post-secondary and to professional studies. Primary and secondary education were completely separate systems that sometimes overlapped but were not co-ordinated. In 1960 there were 500 private Catholic schools, 100 of which (the *collèges classiques*) provided the seven-year program leading to the professional faculties of the universities. Of these, sixty were for males, twenty were seminaries, and twenty for females. The latter, according to an apologist for the system writing in 1951, taught "preparation for family life, the beauty of the home, its virtues, and its unique position in society."[19] Students heading for the priesthood and for lay careers received the same curriculum, which stressed Thomist philosophy, Latin, religion, and the humanities. A final problem was the quality of teacher-training. Although three-quarters of the teachers were laity, nearly all had to be trained in normal schools run by the teaching orders. In 1956-57 only 10 per cent of the teachers had degrees, and 33 per cent had more than twelve years of schooling; in the Protestant system, the respective proportions were 30 per cent and 57 per cent.[20]

As we shall see in the next chapter, important changes had been occurring within the universities. By the 1950s, not only physical and biological sciences but *social* sciences had become institutionalized. And professional institutions the Quebec government had established long ago – l'École des hautes études commerciales and l'École polytechnique – were thriving concerns in the post-war years. But the *collèges classiques* showed little change and the public system was woefully underdeveloped. Criticism was being launched from many quarters, both in and out of the Church. In 1960 the publication of *Les Insolences du Frère Untel* ("The Impertinences of Brother Anonymous") raised considerable furore, partly because of its attack on the shoddy work done in the class-rooms, but largely because it had been written by a teaching brother (who was later sent by his order to Rome "for further studies").

In Chapter Five we will trace the processes of secularization of Quebec society. Our treatment of social change could be expanded to include other topics, such as communications patterns, but while this would broaden the concept it would not alter the conclusions we have reached. We shall instead turn to consider in the next few chapters how the changes we have recorded translate into political terms.

Finally, by way of conclusion here, it is worth noting the extent of changes that have occurred in Quebec. During his investigation of our continent in the 1830s, Alexis de Tocqueville recorded that the typical French Canadian "is tenderly attached to the land which saw his birth, to his church tower, and to his family." In *Option Québec*, the first widely distributed tract of the nascent Parti québécois, René Lévesque described his compatriots as "city dwellers, wage-earners, tenants. The standards of parish, village, and farm have been splintered." The contrast in the two observations is significant. More important are the political inferences drawn from this contrast by men like René Lévesque.

CHAPTER FOUR
The Duplessis Regime: Resistance to State-Building

In Chapter One we suggested that social and economic development are usually accompanied by changes in political life, which are often termed "political modernization." Central to the concept of "political modernization" is growth in the scope and penetration of governmental activities, usually through the instrument of a large, skilled bureaucracy. As we have seen, this relationship between social and economic development, on the one hand, and political modernization, on the other, has been presumed within a wide variety of explanatory frameworks. For example, within certain "functionalist" theories, both processes are seen as aspects of a general movement toward greater and greater structural differentiation or toward more complex communication systems. Another theory contends that industrialization leads to demands for greater equality, which in turn induce an expansion of the state at the expense of private, hierarchical structures. Finally, some theorists trace the expansion of the state to changing needs of a capitalist bourgeoisie, whose needs also are responsible for economic and social development. One can imagine these various propositions being applied even to a society strongly dependent on external political and economic forces. In addition, one can infer that dependence might itself spur local elites, with some access to the state, to seek new state initiatives intended to reduce dependence.

In the case of Quebec, for a substantial period of time the processes of political modernization lagged well behind economic and social development. Available evidence indicates that during the first half of this century the pervasive processes of industrialization and urbanization we have traced in the last chapter were not accompanied by a marked expansion of governmental activities, or by the development of a significant bureaucracy.[1] One can locate substantial growth in the financial support of private institutions by the Quebec state, but little growth in state regulation of these institutions or in direct intervention by the state. Our first task, then, is to examine this "lag" of political modernization behind economic and social change and to search for its causes.

The Limited Scope of Governmental Activities

An area in which one might expect major initiatives from the Quebec government during this period is the economy. As we have seen, both ownership and management within Quebec's industrial economy were largely in the hands of English Canadians and Americans. The Quebec government might have intervened to redress this situation through either direct ownership of economic enterprises or regulation of private enterprises. Yet, prior to the 1960s neither type of intervention was actively pursued by provincial governments. By and large, it was assumed that economic processes should remain in the hands of private interests; the economic responsibility of the provincial government was to facilitate the pursuit by private interests of their own objectives. As a result, even economic initiatives that had already been undertaken by other provinces were shunned by successive Quebec governments. As Hélène David has written:

> The Union nationale regime . . . was distinguished on the socio-economic level by a policy which excluded any thought of controlling the initiatives of private enterprise. The government avoided any responsibility for economic development, restricting itself to the creation and maintenance of conditions favouring the unfettered expansion of capitalism.[2]

Turning first to direct governmental ownership, one might most expect the nationalization of hydroelectricity. After all, the neighbouring province of Ontario (often seen as the base for comparison by many French Canadians in their evaluations of the Quebec economy) had established a public hydroelectric authority in 1906. Many other provinces had followed suit. Yet Quebec governments were highly reticent. To be sure, the Liberal government of Adélard Godbout did, in 1944, nationalize Montreal Light, Heat and Power and thus laid the basis for a Hydro-Québec. But Maurice Duplessis's Union nationale – which controlled the Quebec government for most of the period between 1936 and 1960 – actively opposed this particular move and, after returning to power, refused to bring any other hydroelectric corporations under public ownership. The vast bulk of hydroelectricity generated in

Quebec, 75 per cent in 1955, continued to come from privately owned companies.[3] Thus, even the limited initiatives of public ownership adopted in other provinces were not followed in Quebec.

As for the various regulatory powers the Quebec government held over the economy, there is no evidence (at least during the Duplessis administrations) they were seriously used to alter the behaviour of private corporate interests. It did not seem necessary or even appropriate to defend an interest of the Quebec population – or even the Quebec government – independent from that of the corporations. The administrative structures necessary for effective regulation were not developed; thus, it is difficult to see how such matters as the prices charged by public utilities could have been subject to any kind of independent check by the Quebec government. Also, numerous examples of "negotiation" between government and corporations suggest that the Quebec government was only too ready to accept corporate definitions of what was appropriate. In 1950, the Duplessis government granted concessions to an American steel company for the development of iron ore deposits in the Ungava region, based on royalty payments of approximately one cent per ton of iron ore. At about this time, the Newfoundland government established the much higher rate of thirty-three cents per ton for a similar iron ore development, close to the Quebec concession, in Labrador.[4] Evidently the Quebec government had not bargained seriously with the American firm; it had not properly assessed and exploited its position.

Various Quebec administrations passed some regulatory legislation ostensibly aimed at improving working conditions. In this area, Quebec adopted much of the same legislation as did other provinces, although typically Quebec was among the last of the provinces to adopt the legislation and its terms were often less favourable to workers. For example, British Columbia established a Ministry of Labour in 1917, as did Ontario in 1919; Quebec did so in 1931. Manitoba and B.C. legislated minimum wages for women in 1918; Quebec did so in 1919. To take an example from the Duplessis period, Ontario established a system of paid vacations in 1944; Quebec established a similar system in 1946.[5] It is unlikely that measures such as these aroused widespread opposition among business circles – especially given the ample precedents they usually had in the other provinces. (We do not even know whether these limited measures were adequately enforced.)

The Quebec government did assume an active, adversary role in one aspect of the economy: its relationship with unions. Here, the government (especially under Duplessis) actively sought to frustrate the independent action of these groups and reduce their power. Duplessis's post-World War II administration passed legislation in 1954 giving it authority to decertify unions that "tolerated Communists" or "threatened to strike public services." This legislation, which was retroactive in effect, made it possible to decertify unions seen as too aggressive – and was widely used for this purpose.[6] In addition, provincial police were used on many occasions to break up strikes that had been declared illegal. (The most notorious of these instances was, of course, the Asbestos strike in 1949.)[7] While these various measures did involve active use of the government's regulatory powers, in the last analysis the Quebec government was not really asserting itself as an autonomous actor in Quebec society. It was merely acting on its premise that initiative within the economy must lie with private corporation; unions were challenging this view and had to be suppressed. There was no pretence of asserting a distinct government view of industrial relations, of reconciling legitimate, opposing interests of labour and business. Rather, in instances such as the Asbestos strike, the corporate definition of the situation was automatically accepted by the Quebec government as its own.

The essential passivity of the Quebec government prior to 1960 is even clearer in the areas of education, health, and welfare. Whatever its nominal role, Quebec failed to play the decision-making roles which, in response to social and economic development, other provinces had assumed. We have already seen how this was the case in education. The critically important private educational sector was fully under clerical authority and outside the purview of government; even in the public sector, government officials shared authority with clerics. In 1875 an existing Ministry of Education had been disbanded, primarily to ensure clerical control over the private institutions – *collèges classiques* and universities. Also, through the Conseil de l'instruction publique, which replaced the Ministry of Education, governmental control over public education was severely restricted. This Conseil rarely met. Rather, its membership met independently as two distinct committees, one charged with Catholic schools, the other with Protestant schools. Within the Catholic committee, Quebec's bishops comprised half the membership. This Catholic committee effectively controlled all pedagogical and curricular aspects of the Catholic schools. (The Quebec government's responsibilities were limited to the provision of material facilities.) Since all public schools in Quebec were denominational – either Catholic or Protestant – the Church was able in this way to determine the content of the education received by most French Canadians in Quebec. This failure of the provincial government to take full responsibility for even public schools clearly distinguishes pre-1960 Quebec from the other provinces.

The same general arrangements existed in the areas of health and welfare as well. Here, the primary basis of state involvement had been spelled out in the Public Assistance Law of 1921. Under the provisions of this law, public funds were provided to private institutions for the health care of the needy and the housing of indigents. In this way, the application of the law reinforced the financial position of these institutions, while opening them up more fully to the public. But the role of the state was essentially a supportive one; the private institutions continued to have primary responsibility for health and welfare.[8] In 1925, clerical fears that the provincial government would actively intervene in the administration of Church institutions had even resulted in the following amendment to the law:

> In the application of these regulations, as in the functioning of this law, when the Catholic religious orders are involved, nothing will prejudice the rights of the bishop over these orders, nor their religious, moral and disciplinary interests.[9]

These fears, in any event, proved to be unfounded.

As one might expect, given the limited scope of governmental activity, administrative structures were poorly developed. Prior to 1960, the structures were quite decentralized, with weak organisms and without clear systems of operation: "despite the provincial administration's growth in administrative and operational units, during 100 years the senior structures of the central administration hardly changed."[10] Moreover, there were relatively few individuals with expertise in social science who might have commanded an independent role in decision-making. Prior to 1960 the provincial administration contained a substantial number of lawyers, engineers, and accountants but there were less than twelve economists, few statisticians or social workers, and hardly any sociologists.[11] By and large, bureaucrats were political appointees, and there was no effective merit system in operation. Thus, power over decision-making at all levels of government lay primarily with the elected officials and organizers who composed the incumbent political party. Consequently, it was relatively easy for the incumbent party to distribute services and benefits in the way it thought would best help its re-election. Patronage was open and widespread.

In summary, political modernization lagged behind social and economic development. The activities and structures of the Quebec government had not expanded to the extent that one might expect, given both the response of other provinces to similar levels of development and the type of ethnic stratification present within the Quebec economy.

The Role of Nationalist Ideology

One of the most common explanations of this lag focuses on the dominant ideology within French Canada – French-Canadian nationalism. It is argued that until the 1950s French-Canadian nationalism maintained most of its traditional assumptions about the character and needs of the "nation." As a consequence, the ideology served to inhibit the expansion of the state, whatever may have been the implications of economic and social development.[12]

A central premise of the traditional ideology was that the "nation" was essentially agrarian. The true expression of the French-Canadian identity lay in the parish community. Industrialization, and concomitant urbanization, embodied alien values and could only weaken the nation. Even after it no longer described the social reality most French Canadians faced, this agrarian myth did maintain its hold upon some nationalist intellectuals. By 1941, only 45 per cent of Quebec Francophones remained in rural areas; the forces of urbanization and industrialization were clearly irreversible. Yet, in 1943 a clerical nationalist, Richard Arès, wrote: "By tradition, vocation as well as necessity, we are a people of peasants. Everything that takes us away from the land diminishes and weakens us as a people and encourages cross-breeding, duplicity and treason."[13]

Similarly, in 1956, the report of the Tremblay Commission, a provincially appointed Commission royale d'enquête sur les problèmes constitutionnels, declared:

The consolidation and expansion of agriculture to the extreme limit imposes itself as the first article of a program of social restoration and stabilization. History shows it: all countries which let the equilibrium between agriculture and industry collapse, expose themselves to grave economic and social disorders. French Canadians must retain this lesson all the more since they owe their national survival to agriculture and rural modes of organization and life.[14]

Given such sentiment, nationalists could scarcely manage to focus adequate attention on the social and economic problems faced by the bulk of French Canadians living in cities.

More importantly, many students argue that to the extent that there did develop a concern with social problems of urban Quebec, the ideology worked against using the state to deal with these matters.[15] The traditional nationalist ideology contained a strong suspicion of the state, including the Quebec provincial government with its Anglo-Saxon, liberal democratic heritage. It was both safer and more in keeping with French-Canadian traditions to rely on autonomous French-Canadian institutions, especially the Church, to deal with social problems. Here, too, the traditional ideology maintained considerable influence. With respect to education, health, and welfare, the areas where the lag in political modernization was especially acute, it appears that many nationalist intellectuals shared this *anti-étatisme* until well into the 1960s. The report of the Tremblay Commission argued that the state should have a relatively minor, supportive role in social welfare programs. Paying tribute to "the preference which public opinion accords to private initiative, and which explains the generous and eager collaboration of the people in the construction of a private system of social institutions and services which is perhaps the most immense in North America," the Commission contended that:

The French-Canadian conception of social assistance based on the triple foundation of the family, voluntary associations and the Church has been sufficiently flexible to respond to the needs created by the successive emergence of the pioneer, rural and urban types of family and, with the aid of the State, to the new situations born of industrialization and urbanization.[16]

With respect to intervention by the Quebec government in the economy, some French-Canadian nationalists showed a greater openness toward the state. In the 1930s, a group of Catholic and lay intellectuals prepared, under the auspices of l'École sociale populaire, a document entitled *Le Programme de restauration sociale*.[17] This same program later was adopted by l'Action libérale nationale (a political movement of nationalists and dissident Liberals which, in coalition with the Conservative Party, won forty-two seats in the 1935 provincial election and subsequently was absorbed with the Conservative Party into the Union nationale).[18] The program placed first priority on the problems of rural Quebec, reflecting the persistent nationalist attachment to the agrarian society, but it was also concerned with social and economic problems faced by French Canadians in urban areas. To reduce the power of the Anglo-Saxon "trusts," the program called for a public enterprise to develop unexploited water power, for careful consideration of the nationalization of private hydroelectric firms, and for consideration of state enterprises to compete with private firms in three industries: coal, gasoline, and bread. Because the program did not explicitly demand nationalization of private enterprises, many observers tend to dismiss it as fairly inconsequential.[19] But others see it as a significant breakthrough; Herbert Quinn even dubbed it "radical" nationalism.[20] Whether or not this term is entirely appropriate, it does appear that during the 1930s some nationalists were not as fearful of using the state to defend French-Canadian interests as has often been assumed.

More significant is the program for provincial politics developed in the early 1940s by the Bloc populaire.[21] While the primary concern of the Bloc was with opposing conscription for overseas military service, the Bloc's provincial wing (under André Laurendeau) also dealt with social and economic issues. Guided by the traditional nationalist concern with the sanctity of the family, the Bloc advocated a significant increase in state intervention in the economy. It called for much stricter regulation of private industries through government-appointed independent commissions. More importantly, it explicitly called for the nationalization of all production and transmission of electricity, as well as the nationalization of telephone facilities and the importation of coal and petroleum. Moreover, the Bloc populaire national leader, Maxime Raymond, declared: *"Cette liste n'est pas necessairement restrictive."*[22]

Nevertheless, these programs for state intervention in the Quebec economy had the active support of only a minority of the nationalist intellectuals. A detailed study of nationalist newspapers and periodicals between 1934 and 1936 shows that the majority of nationalist intellectuals failed to pronounce themselves clearly in support of the Action libérale nationale or actively to help its electoral campaign.[23] This relative indifference toward the ALN and its fate may help to explain the ease with which Duplessis was able to abandon the ALN program and absorb the ALN into the Union nationale. The same *apolitisme*[24] of nationalist intellectuals may also be reflected in the failure of the Bloc populaire to contest more than one provincial election.

Apparently, then, the traditional beliefs about the character of the French-Canadian nation and the role of government continued to be a strong force among French-Canadian nationalists, even during the 1930s and 1940s. Virtually all nationalist intellectuals were unwilling to consider a greater role for the Quebec government in health, welfare, and education. Most nationalists even failed to support actively a greater role for the Quebec government in the economy, where it might help to "liberate" the French-Canadian nation from "foreign" economic domination.

This ability of traditional beliefs to hold the continued adherence of most nationalists, even in the face of pervasive social and economic change, has been interpreted in a variety of ways by students of Quebec politics. According to some, nationalists continued to propagate these beliefs simply because they served their class interests, maintaining and enhancing power and status.[25] In the case of clerical elites, agrarianism and *anti-étatisme* could indeed have served this purpose. Clerical power was unquestionably greater in rural settings and the clergy obviously had every reason to resist greater governmental intervention in such areas as education, health, and welfare. It is not as clear why lay nationalists should have been so slow in rejecting these beliefs. Their power and status were not necessarily threatened by urbanization; many of the lay protagonists of the agrarian myth were themselves lifelong urban dwellers. Expansion of the activities of the Quebec government obviously could have been to their advantage. Other factors must have underlain their continuous attachment to traditional beliefs, especially when the agrarian ideal clearly was no longer viable.

One possible explanation is that French-Canadian intellectuals simply lacked the cultural resources to develop new models of the French-Canadian nation more appropriate to the social and economic change that Quebec had undergone. Isolated by the Conquest from ideological development in France and sheltered by language from the liberal ideology dominant elsewhere in North America, French Canada was still prisoner of the belief system upon which New France was founded. Eventually, modern communication systems would allow new ideologies to penetrate the "fragment culture," but during the 1930s and 1940s most French-Canadian intellectuals still had no social model available to them other than that of New France. For André-J. Bélanger, this persistence of the "fragment culture" explains the indifference of many nationalists to concrete political action, as represented by Action libérale nationale. While aware of the ways by which urbanization and industrialization threatened traditional French-Canadian values and institutions, they were unable to see how the Quebec government, incarnating Anglo-Saxon, liberal democratic values, could be used to protect the French-Canadian nation. Within the social model inherited from New France, the only political institution through which French-Canadian needs might be met could be a pre-Absolutist monarchy. The result of this absence of legitimate political institutions was not so much an *anti-étatisme* as an *apolitisme*.[26]

Other interpretations see the traditional ideology as a direct product of the Conquest. According to Michel Brunet, agrarianism served to compensate French Canadians for their new inability to pursue economic activity, now firmly in the hands of the British:

> Because they were unable to turn to other domains of economic activity, the [French] Canadians nourished an exaggerated love of agriculture. They wished to maintain, at any cost, the old rural and communal social order which had given them refuge after the Conquest. They had acquired a diminished conception of life and the economy. Obliged to become settlers and peasants, they concluded – or rather their leaders concluded for them – they had an agricultural vocation.[27]

In the process, French Canadians ignored the potential role the Quebec provincial government might play on their behalf and succumbed to the clerical *anti-étatisme*. In a similar analysis, Pierre Harvey has argued that the Conquest produced a collective trauma, common to all conquered peoples. French Canadians sought to resolve this trauma by rejecting the value system of the British conquerors and overemphasizing all that might distinguish them from the British. It was on this basis that French Canadians became firmly attached to agriculturalism and Catholicism. With such a heavy investment in the traditional identity, French-Canadian nationalists could not easily discard it – even in the face of the urbanization and industrialization of the twentieth century. Harvey contends that even in the 1960s some French Canadians saw commerce and industry as illegitimate activities for French Canadians.[28]

In sum, there are several bases for understanding how the traditional ideology was able to maintain its influence among French-

Canadian nationalist intellectuals. But whatever may be the most appropriate explanation, this continued traditionalism cannot by itself explain the relative absence of political modernization. A first and most obvious difficulty is that nationalist doctrine was not the only influence weighing upon the governmental leaders of the day. This is true even of Maurice Duplessis, who dominated Quebec's political life for over two decades, holding power from 1936 to 1939 and from 1944 to 1959, and who sought publicly to identify himself with French-Canadian nationalism. It appears that Duplessis would merely select from nationalist thought those ideas that served his own purposes at any particular point in time. Whereas Duplessis became known in the 1940s and 1950s as a great champion of provincial autonomy, he had quite a different position when he was Leader of the Opposition in the early 1930s. At that time, he severely criticized the current premier, Alexandre Taschereau, for refusing on the basis of provincial autonomy to participate in a federal program of old age pensions.[29] More important to our interests, Duplessis associated himself in the mid-1930s with nationalists who did want an increased role for the state. During the coalition of his Conservative Party with Action libérale nationale in 1935, Duplessis was committed to the ALN program – including its plans for public enterprise in the hydro-electricity industry. Yet, as premier, Duplessis refused to establish such an enterprise – to the dismay of many of his supporters. One of these supporters, René Chaloult, quotes Duplessis as having said, "You are not a child; at your age you ought to understand that *a program is good before elections, and the election is over.*"[30] Certainly, the ambivalence of traditional nationalist intellectuals over the role of the state made it easier for Duplessis to avoid such measures. In this way, it does help to explain the "lag" in political modernization, but it cannot fully explain his refusal to act. Moreover, other elements in French-Canadian society actively sought a greater state role. Why did the Duplessis regime fail to respond to them?

Pluralism of Quebec Intelligentsia

During the latter half of the nineteenth century and into this century, traditional nationalism never completely dominated Quebec's intelligentsia: liberal assumptions about society and economy always enjoyed a certain following. For instance, a systematic analysis of the contents of *La Presse, le Canada*, and other French-language mass-circulation newspapers demonstrates that as early as the turn of the century at least some French-Canadian intellectuals, mainly editorialists and journalists, were firmly committed to economic development and the general application of modern science; they enthusiastically welcomed the industrialization of Quebec and sought to accelerate it. Many of them also subscribed to classical liberalism's laissez-faire attitude toward the state and they believed that the effectiveness of the Quebec state was compromised by patronage. But they shared none of the dismay over Quebec's social and economic transformation that was articulated by nationalist intellectuals in Action française and Action nationale. Too often it has been assumed that the "official" ideology of conservative nationalism was dominant among the whole of the Quebec intelligentsia, rather than among the clergy and other particular substrata.[31]

Moreover, with the 1940s and 1950s premises of the conservative nationalist ideology came under growing attack from a new social category – a Francophone new middle class. Many members of this new middle class strongly supported direct intervention by the state to meet Quebec's social and economic problems; by the 1950s they were actively seeking to move public opinion in this direction. Similar demands came from the leadership of Quebec's unions and, to a much lesser extent, from the Francophone business class.

The Rise of a Francophone New Middle Class

For our purposes, the new middle class can be defined as consisting of "salaried professionals." As such, it was a new element within French-Canadian society.[32] Members of the new middle class differ from the "old middle class" of lawyers, doctors, and notaries in that, while trained in a profession, they are not self-employed. (Of course, through their salaried status they also differ from the clergy, the other element of the traditional French-Canadian leadership.) Yet, even if they must rely on others for employment, the new middle class's professional qualifications put it in a fundamentally different position from the working class: "like the proletariat, members of this class lack ownership in the means of production: nevertheless, they participate in varying degrees, in the control and management of capital within the immediate process of production."[33] Thus, the new middle class enjoys much greater autonomy in its work activities, may be involved in the supervision of work by others, has much more mobility thanks to its professional qualifications, etc. In effect, professional knowledge may assume a status analogous to that of capital. Nonetheless, by definition the new middle class does not formally own capital, *per se*. Thus, in terms of Quebec society, there was bound to be a certain divergence of interests and objectives between the Francophone new middle class and a category of authentic capitalists becoming more evident with the 1950s: a French-Canadian business class. In fact, during the 1950s and 1960s the Francophone new middle class was to find substantial areas of commonality with Francophone workers.

The growth of a new middle class has in fact been a common feature of industrialized societies, especially in the wake of World War II. Whereas some scholars associate it with advances in technology, others trace it to the transition to monopoly capitalism. Typically, the new middle class assumes several discrete functions: supervising and controlling labour, as with managers and foremen; reproducing the social system, as with teachers, social workers, health professionals, and state administrators; accounting and realization of value, as with professionals in advertising, sales, accounting, and finance; and transforming the techniques of production, as with scientists and engineers.[34]

This variety of potential functions has led some analysts to contend that the category is not a distinct "class" and is at most a stratum of intermediate class positions. Nonetheless, as Val Borris has argued, a distinct class is likely to emerge when its members are distinguished in political, cultural, and ideological terms and they develop a perception of common fundamental class interests.[35] As we shall see, during the 1950s and 1960s these conditions very much applied to the Francophone new middle class. Its members came to share a common ideology of state intervention very much focused on the Quebec state. Underlying this commitment to state intervention was the structural location of the Francophone new middle class: largely absent within the private sector of the Quebec economy, it was primarily based first within French-Canadian private institutions and later within the parapublic sector of the Quebec state. In effect, during the 1950s and 1960s it was largely relegated to one of the four characteristic new-middle-class roles: reproducing the social system. To a very real extent, Quebec politics during the 1960s and 1970s was to be marked by the efforts of the Francophone new middle class to assume the other functions, largely through intervention by the Quebec state.

A first area where a new middle class was making its presence felt is French Quebec's universities. While Université Laval and Université de Montréal remained formally under the control of the

Church, the proportion of lay faculty steadily increased during the first half of this century. Not only was the economic position of these lay faculty different from that of the clerical faculty, but, more importantly, they were much more likely to be oriented in their research and teaching to secular, scientific models. Rejecting traditional authority and championing professionalism and scientific competence, many of them set about to "institutionalize" sciences within French-Canadian universities, transforming the universities themselves in the process. In some instances, lay faculty were not alone in this effort. For instance, such clerical faculty as pioneering botanist Brother Marie-Victorin were themselves firm adherents of scientific reasoning and methods of research.[36] Nonetheless, it was primarily lay faculty who sought to implant the scientific model and who bore the brunt of strong attacks from conservative clergy – at least when *social* science was involved.[37]

With respect to the physical and biological sciences, the emergence of distinct structures within French-Canadian universities can be traced to as early as 1920, when l'École supérieur de chimie was created at Université Laval and la Faculté des sciences was created at Université de Montréal. In 1930 an institute of biology was created at Laval and in 1938 Université de Montréal created a Laboratoire d'hydrobiologie et d'ichtyologie and an Institut de microbiologie et d'hygiène.[38] During these years, both universities recruited European academics to help establish and reinforce their scientific programs. But primary responsibility for research was assumed by Francophones who had gone to Europe or the United States to pursue advanced studies in the sciences, thanks in large part to a program of provincial government scholarships established in 1920.[39] While the number of students graduating in the sciences from the two universities remained relatively small during the 1920s and 1930s, it rose rapidly in the wake of World War II. For instance, by 1950 the annual number of graduates of Laval's Faculté de science had reached seventy-three.[40] Thus, Raymond Duchesne has concluded that, on the basis of such criteria as intellectual production, sources of financing, complexity of university administrative structures, and the support of social class fractions, the French-Canadian scientific community had by 1951 reached a "critical mass" allowing it to function as a distinct entity, especially in its relations with the provincial government.[41]

Especially important to our concern with the impact of the new middle class on Quebec politics is the development of the social sciences. Here, too, the efforts of individuals to establish the scientific model within French-Canadian universities can be traced back to the beginning of the century. Initially, however, this enterprise was impeded by the influence of the Church and the small number of individuals leading the effort. Nonetheless, a new impetus was received from the Depression of the 1930s, which served to raise fundamental questions about received social and economic notions. In addition, declining opportunities in the liberal professions and the growing precariousness of French-Canadian enterprises served to stimulate, among the sons of French-Canadian professionals and businessmen, an interest in careers based on knowledge of the social sciences.[42]

The earliest institutional initiative was the creation of the École des sciences sociales, économiques et politiques at Université de Montréal in 1920. The expressed purpose of the school was to meet the needs of Francophones who wished "occuper de hautes fonctions administratives," or who "choississent la carrière du journalisme."[43] The school's combined enrolment of full-time and part-time students grew steadily: ninety-three in 1920, 218 in 1930, and 370 in 1940. The annual number of graduates oscillated around fifty in the 1930s – not sufficient, to be sure, to meet the aspirations of the school's founder, Edouard Montpetit.[44] In the 1940s, Université de Montréal raised the École to the Faculté des sciences sociales (1942) and proceeded to establish more specialized schools in the social sciences: l'École des relations industrielles (1945), l'École d'hygiène and l'Institut de psychologie (1942), and l'École de service sociale (1948).

Similar institutional developments took place at Université Laval. In fact, Laval's Faculté des sciences sociales was probably the academic institution to have the greatest impact on Quebec society and politics in the 1950s and 1960s. Founded in 1932 as l'École des sciences sociales de Laval, which in turn became the École des sciences sociales, économiques et politiques in 1938, it was given the status of a Faculté in 1943. In 1955-56, la Faculté des sciences sociales contained more than fifty professors (tenured and adjunct), enrolled close to 140 students, and administered a research and teaching budget of $187,000.[45]

Initially, the École was much more heavily under clerical influence than was its counterpart at Université de Montréal. Also, unlike the Montreal institution, it was placed within the Faculté de philosophie; teaching was explictly based on Thomist philosophy. Nonetheless, with the accession to Faculté status in 1943 this institutional link was severed. Moreover, the Faculté soon came under the influence of young French-Canadian faculty who had returned to Laval after pursuing graduate studies in the social sciences at such schools as Harvard, the University of Chicago, and the University of Toronto. In fact, in 1943 University of Chicago sociologist Everett C. Hughes spent a period of time with Laval's new Département de recherches sociales, initiating students to sociological research and developing a research program.[46] The first cohort of North American-trained social scientists was later joined by others who returned from advanced study, primarily in Europe.[47] By 1950-51, the clergy represented only a third of the faculty – as opposed to 50 per cent six years earlier.[48] In fact, the Faculté came under increasing criticism from conservative clergy for the "materialist" and "socialist" teaching the professors were giving.[49] For that matter, Father George-Henri Lévesque, who founded the school and was its first dean, was succeeded in 1955 by a lay faculty member, Jean-Marie Martin.

Moreover, through producing critical assessments of the condition of Quebec society, the Faculté came to play a leading role in the movement to expand the role of the Quebec state. As sociologist Marcel Fournier has recently argued:

> This activity could be characterized as contributing, on the one hand, to the dissociation of the "social" and "religious" spheres, and thus to the autonomization of the intellectual sphere, and, on the other hand, to the elaboration of a new conception and practice of politics ("neo-liberalism" or "interventionism") primarily through training graduates who then become senior executives of ministers and also, in some cases, participate directly in the renewal of the state bureaucratic structure.[50]

In fact, Fournier goes so far as to claim that the professors and students of the Faculté constituted a genuine "social movement" that provoked the downfall of the Union nationale and was at the very origin of the Quiet Revolution.[51]

Thus, it is no surprise that Duplessis himself saw the Faculté as a threat to his regime and sought to undermine it. From the early 1940s, Duplessis had been deeply suspicious of the Faculté and of its dean, Father Lévesque, who Duplessis dubbed "the little red," despite his clerical status. After the faculty and students openly supported the Asbestos strikers in 1949, Duplessis entered into open war with the Faculté, reducing substantially its provincial grants. The following year he cut the grant completely, out of displeasure with a public address by Father Lévesque. By the same token, the government refused to provide the Faculté funds for construction of a new building, while making a grant to the university's business school for the same purpose.[52] In fact, Duplessis systematically closed the Quebec public service to graduates of the Faculté, perceiving them as socialists or Communists.[53]

Through institutionalizing the social sciences as an autonomous intellectual discipline, the Faculté was bound to have a subversive effect on the established social and political order. As Marcel Rioux has written:

> It's the Faculté des sciences sociales of Université Laval (sociologists and economists) which, in the late 1940s and during the 1950s, constituted the most coherent centre of opposition; it was then joined by periodicals, *Cité libre* is the most obvious example, and movements, for example l'Institut canadien des affaires publiques, which brought together intellectuals, professors, unionists, journalists, and Liberal politicians. Drawing on economic and sociological analyses of the Québécois milieu and knowledge of other Western democracies, these movements and individuals undertook a systematic critique of traditionalist ideology and Québécois culture.[54]

Accompanying this expansion within French-Canadian universities of the role of the various sciences, and of a new middle class, was a steady growth in the numbers of students graduating with degrees in the sciences. For instance, the combined output of undergraduate science degrees from Laval and Université de Montréal grew from fifty-two in 1926-30 to 240 in 1946-50 to 359 in 1956-60; the figures for graduate degrees are 0, 143, and 236, respectively.[55]

Beyond the growth of professional scientists, especially within French-Canadian universities, the 1940s and 1950s also saw the emergence of a second new-middle-class element within French-Canadian society: salaried practitioners who applied "modern" scientific knowledge and techniques, whether bureaucrats and administrators or technicians such as engineers and accountants. Popular impressions to the contrary, French-Canadian universities had long contained at least two institutions designed to train Francophones in modern scientific techniques: l'École polytechnique de Montréal, an engineering school created in 1873, and l'École des hautes études commerciales, a business school founded in 1907. Significantly, both were created directly by the provincial government and thus were striking exceptions to the general pattern of Church domination of higher education. The clergy had viewed the creation of the latter school with some unease. Moreover, both had been created with the express purpose of expanding the Francophone presence within careers that had been occupied largely by Anglophones. The stated objective of the business school was to provide the competence in business that was needed to assure French Canada's "conquête économique."[56]

For its first few decades the output of l'École polytechnique de Montréal was quite limited, averaging six or seven new engineers annually for the period 1877 to 1920.[57] Nonetheless, by the period 1926-30 it had reached eighty-seven, and it rose steadily during the 1930s and 1940s.[58] Moreover, in 1943 l'École polytechnique was joined by a second institution as the Godbout regime established a school of electrical engineering at Université Laval, apparently in anticipation of the pending nationalization of Montreal Light, Heat and Power.[59] By the post-World War II years, the two institutions were producing a substantial number of engineers. For the period 1946-50, they awarded a total of 460 undergraduate degrees in engineering, with twenty-one graduate degrees. By 1956-60, the figures had risen to 1,102 and sixty-three, respectively.[60]

As for l'École des hautes études commerciales, it was joined in the post-war period by l'École de commerce at Laval. In addition, a business school was founded at l'Université de Sherbrooke in the mid-1950s. In 1955, the combined enrolment of the three schools was about 650. By 1959 it was close to 1,300.[61]

Finally, the 1950s saw a very rapid growth in the training of social workers. The Université de Montréal established an École de service social in 1948; Laval created a school in 1951. In 1952, the combined enrolment of the two schools was close to 200. By 1958 it was 373.[62]

Thus, decades before the educational reforms of the 1960s, French Canada contained a certain number of institutions devoted to training Francophones for new-middle-class careers as administrators and technicians. Moreover, by the 1940s they were producing such individuals in substantial numbers. As we have already seen, however, there were only limited opportunities for this emerging Francophone new middle class.

Within the private sector of the economy, the new middle class did assume positions in the few large Francophone-owned enterprises where trained professionals clearly were needed, including the two French-Canadian banks and major retail operations. But during the 1940s and 1950s it remained seriously underrepresented in the bulk of large enterprises – the English-Canadian and American-owned ones. Thus, a survey of manufacturing firms demonstrated that as late as 1964 Francophones constituted 78 per cent of the salaried personnel of Francophone-owned firms headquartered in Quebec but only 35 per cent of the salaried personnel of the English-Canadian or British-owned counterparts, and 23 per cent of the American-owned firms.[63] Related to this, in 1963 only 26 per cent of Quebec Francophone engineers worked in the private sector, as opposed to 70 per cent of Quebec Anglophone engineers.[64] In fact, in the same year one of the biggest private hydroelectrical companies in Quebec had only twenty Francophone engineers out of 175, whereas Hydro-Québec had 190 Francophone engineers out of 243.[65] Finally, an early 1960 study found that only 40 per cent of chartered accountants employed in industry and commerce were Francophone, whereas among chartered accountants employed by the provincial and municipal governments 90 per cent were Francophone.[66]

With respect to state institutions, we have already noted the historical underrepresentation of Francophones at the federal level. As for provincial institutions, opportunities were severely limited simply by the relatively low level of development of the Quebec state. During the Duplessis regime this was compounded by a strong suspicion of social science training. There was, to be sure, the singular case of Hydro-Québec as it emerged from the nationalization of Montreal Light, Heat and Power. But it was a special case, inherited from the Godbout regime.

The one area where the knowledge and skills of the Francophone new middle class were in strong demand was within private organizations servicing the Francophone population – in particular, private bureaucracies of the Church.[67] With the flow of French Canadians into the cities, these institutions had to become more and more complex if they were to provide services to large concentrations of people at the much higher levels that urban conditions demanded. They needed administrators who had the skills necessary to cope with such complexity. This meant individuals who were trained in the social sciences, especially the "management sciences." Increasingly, the Church found it necessary to look beyond its own clerical personnel to find individuals with the requisite professional training. Lay bureaucrats came to occupy many of the administrative positions within the Church's institutions.

Beyond French-language universities, Church-related bureaucracies servicing the French-Canadian population, and the few large French-Canadian–owned enterprises, the emerging Francophone new middle class was also able to assume positions in the rapidly growing operations of Radio-Canada. For Francophone intellectuals, especially those trained in the social sciences, the introduction of television provided both new opportunities for employment and an important new vehicle for influencing French-Canadian society as a whole.

Finally, during the 1950s Francophones trained in the social sciences were beginning to assume a certain presence in the union movement. Indicative of this was Jean Marchand, a graduate of Laval's Faculté des sciences sociales, who in 1948 became secretary-general of the Confédération des travailleurs catholiques du Canada.

During the 1950s members of the new middle class, through a variety of organizations and publications, actively championed the expansion of the Quebec state. We have already noted the extent to which the activities of members of Laval's Faculté des sciences sociales served to place in question the existing political and social order and to propose new state initiatives. A similar role was played by the Institut canadien des affaires publiques. Founded in 1954, the ICAP had been born of dissatisfaction that leading French-Canadian academics felt with the traditionalist Centre des intellectuels catholiques canadiens. The ICAP staged annual conferences at which French-Canadian and foreign intellectuals were invited to explore themes that implicitly placed in question the existing political order, such as popular sovereignty, education, freedom. The proceedings were in turn broadcast over Radio-Canada and, as is suggested by the commentaries that they generated in Quebec newspapers, tended to attract large audiences.[68]

A leading force within the ICAP had been the contributors to *Cité libre*, a journal of opinion founded in 1950 that soon attracted a considerable following among the Quebec intelligentsia. One of its co-editors, Pierre Elliott Trudeau, had done graduate work in political science at Harvard, the École des sciences politiques in Paris, and the London School of Economics. Gérard Pelletier, the other editor, had been an official of student organizations and then a journalist with Radio-Canada, *Le Devoir*, and the CTCC. A central tenet of Trudeau and his fellow *Cité librists* was a profound belief in the capacity of a liberal democratic state to meet the social and economic needs of citizens. They set about attacking traditional conceptions of political authority and seeking to lead French Canadians to see the state as an agent of their will. *Cité librists* believed that once French Canadians did see government in these more enlightened liberal democratic terms, they would see its potential as an instrument of social and economic progress and would insist on and secure an expansion of the state's role. In particular, *Cité librists* sought a total reform of Quebec's educational system to make it modern, laicised, and equally available to all citizens and the creation of a Ministry of Education to secure these changes.[69] By the same token, they called for greater state intervention in the Quebec economy, especially in the resource sector.[70]

During the 1950s, *Le Devoir*, the leading newspaper of the French-Canadian intelligentsia, also took up the call for a more interventionist Quebec state. In 1947, the newspaper had come under the influence of a new generation with the appointment of Gérard Filion as director and André Laurendeau as associate editor-in-chief. Filion, a graduate of l'École des hautes études commerciales and past secretary of the Union des cultivateurs catholiques, was much preoccupied with the marginal role of Francophones in the upper levels of the Quebec economy. As for Laurendeau, through studies in France he had become familiar with the economic and political reformism of liberal Catholicism and had sought to apply these notions to Quebec through a variety of efforts. We have already seen how as provincial leader of the Bloc populaire he had campaigned for some important state initiatives. The editorialists at *Le Devoir* were not prepared to go as far as were the *Cité librists* in expanding the state's role (and reducing the Church's) in social services and health care. But they were firmly committed to greater state intervention in the economy to enable French Canadians to assume their proper role. Thus, Filion wrote in 1953:

> If, one day, the nation of Quebec wants to overcome its impediments and become master of its own destiny once again, it must start by regaining control over the natural resources which improvident governments handed to foreign capitalists.[71]

On this basis, *Le Devoir* was prepared to support nationalization of the remaining private hydroelectrical enterprises, close regulation and even nationalization if necessary of the pulp and paper industry, and creation of a provincially owned steel corporation.[72]

By the same token, through such organizations as Jeunesse étudiante catholique, young French-Canadian intellectuals were exposed to the notions of social reform, drawn from French Catholic personalism, that had inspired Laurendeau and many of the *Cité librists*.

While generally united by this commitment to greater state intervention, the emerging new middle class was divided, however, on the national question. Many of these political modernizers did not focus solely on the Quebec state and they rejected the traditional nationalist suspicion of the federal government. In fact, a large number of them rejected outright the importance of the "nation." For some modernizers, "class" was more important than "nation." For other modernizers, such as Trudeau, the individual was more important than any collectivity. Within either perspective, it was quite possible to accept that needed initiatives might come from Ottawa. The fact that post-war Ottawa was heavily engaged in major new social and economic programs, whereas Quebec was not, made Ottawa highly attractive to many of these modernizing French Canadians. But they also called on Quebec to assume more responsibilities, and much of their orientation to Ottawa was a simple function of frustration with Quebec's passivity.

A second approach, most clearly represented by three Université de Montréal historians, Maurice Séguin, Guy Frégault, and Michel Brunet, did explicitly combine the new secular conception of the state with traditional nationalist attitudes toward the federal government. For them, Quebec and only Quebec could be entrusted to act in accordance with the interests of Quebec Francophones. On this basis, they called for a rapid expansion of the Quebec state.[73] While this approach had limited influence in the 1950s, it was to become hegemonic in the 1960s, as we shall see.

The French-Canadian Business Class

Besides Quebec's emerging new middle class, there appear to have been elements among other Francophone elites that favoured a more active Quebec state. First, some members of the small, weak, French-Canadian commercial and industrial elite apparently were receptive to limited state initiatives that would have responded to their precarious situation.

Research shows that a certain Francophone business class had emerged in the last half of the nineteenth century, based on banking, manufacturing, commerce, and transportation. Paul-André Linteau's research suggests that during this period a significant number of Francophones qualified as members of a "middle bourgeoisie," although not a "big bourgeoisie." However, at the beginning of this century, with the monopolization of capital in Quebec, they were displaced by the essentially Anglophone "big bourgeoisie":

There is a structural transformation which does not eliminate

100

the middle bourgeoisie, but which weakens its hold and increases the gap between it and the big bourgeoisie. At the outbreak of the First World War, the power relations had already changed.[74]

Thus, the established Francophone business class had lost much of its force by the time the Union nationale appeared in the 1930s. In the wake of the Second World War the elements of a new Francophone business class began to emerge, but it remained weak until well after the demise of the Duplessis regime.

French-Canadian enterprises, typically small, undercapitalized, and controlled by members of a single family, were increasingly unable to compete effectively with large American and English-Canadian firms and were facing bankruptcy or takeover. Out of this state of affairs emerged several projects for state intervention. A primary difficulty of French-Canadian business was in securing capital. During the 1950s, projects were discussed in the Chambre de commerce du Québec and elsewhere through which capital would be pooled for French-Canadian enterprises. But it became clear that such an initiative could be viable only if it were orchestrated by the Quebec state.[75] Representatives of French-Canadian business thus began to call for greater planning and co-ordination of the government's economic policies. In 1957 the Chambre de commerce du Québec called on the Duplessis government to create a research council that, through co-ordinating the efforts of universities, industry, and government laboratories, would seek to develop technologies for natural resource extraction.[76] And in both 1957 and 1958, the Chambre called for the creation within the Quebec government of a council, to which business and other leaders would be named, that would advise the government on economic matters.[77] This council was, of course, a long-standing goal of nationalist intellectuals; for the struggling French-Canadian business class it offered a new direct representation in the Quebec government that could be used to promote specific policies. In 1958, the president of the Chambre declared that the Quebec government, on the basis of detailed study of Quebec's economy, should undertake the elaboration of a long-term plan of economic development.[78] By 1960, even the highly conservative Association professionnelle des industriels was calling for economic planning by the Quebec state.[79]

To be sure, the French-Canadian business community continued to be marked by a strong suspicion of state intervention in general. But, some state initiatives clearly would have been in their direct interest and, on that basis, might well have received their support. Nonetheless, the Duplessis regime was little disposed to follow such leads. One can point to certain measures, such as the selective awarding of public contracts to Quebec enterprises, but the fact remains that the Duplessis regime refused to develop more systematic means of supporting Francophone business. Despite the urgings of Francophone businessmen and intellectuals, the Duplessis government refused to establish a planning council of businessmen and other leaders. It even refused to reactivate the advisory council formed by the Godbout regime in the early 1940s. And it did little to help in the pooling of domestic sources of capital.[80] In short, as Jorge Niosi has argued: "Until 1960, the Quebec state did not play a role of promoter of a French-Canadian bourgeoisie. It did not have such a political project, and did not acquire the means."[81]

As for federal-provincial relations, which we shall soon examine, only one initiative of the Duplessis regime – the successful campaign to establish a provincial income tax – could have seriously benefited Quebec-based economic interests, and this measure was taken only after Duplessis had been subjected to a long, carefully orchestrated lobbying campaign by a broad range of Francophone elites. Even then, Duplessis was reluctant to pursue the measure. Significantly, Duplessis's decision was based on electoral considerations: he had to be persuaded that the measures would strengthen his electoral fortunes, rather than weaken them as he had feared.[82]

The Francophone Union Leadership

During the post-war years, a much more clearcut call for expansion of the Quebec state emerged within the union leadership. Leaders in two of Quebec's three labour federations argued vigorously for a variety of new governmental programs to correct the "abuses" and "inadequacies" of capitalism. The high employment conditions of the war years and general prosperity of the post-war period had encouraged a new aggressiveness on the part of the union movement in Quebec. Over the period 1945-55, union membership rose from 19.6 per cent to 28.7 per cent of Quebec's labour force.[83]

Especially striking was the new stance of the Confédération des travailleurs catholiques du Canada, where internal changes heightened the disposition to greater militancy. In the late 1940s a new generation of Francophones took over the leadership of the organization. In 1946, Alfred Charpentier, the long-time CTCC president, was defeated in his bid for re-election by Gérard Picard, a journalist. And in 1948 the position of secretary-general was assumed by Jean Marchand, a recent graduate of the Laval Faculté des sciences sociales. By 1949, more than half of the CTCC executive were newcomers.[84] Under their leadership, the CTCC gradually distanced itself from the Church. In 1948, the union had already agreed to allow its member organizations to admit non-Catholics as non-voting members. The union chaplains saw their influence steadily reduced. Not only did they lose the right to veto resolutions adopted by union executives or conventions, but two lay-controlled bodies were created: the Service d'éducation in 1949 and the Collège ouvrier in 1952.[85] Finally, in 1960 the membership agreed to deconfessionalize the organization, eliminating any reference to Catholic doctrine from its statement of principles and changing its name to Confédération des syndicats nationaux. At the same time, the CTCC's official ideology underwent important changes. Social corporatism was replaced with an emphasis on reforming capitalism through the establishment of an "industrial democracy" based on such measures as co-management, profit-sharing, and co-ownership of industrial enterprises.[86] In short, capital's prerogatives were to be considerably narrowed.[87]

As a consequence of these processes, the CTCC became the most dynamic union central in the province, as well as the fastest-growing one: its membership increased by nearly 30 per cent between 1947 and 1955.[88] It also became much more militant in its dealings with employers: its propensity to stage strikes increased significantly. The result was a series of bitter confrontations, often with multinationals. The most widely celebrated is the Asbestos strike of 1949, which pitted the CTCC against the American Johns-Manville corporation and the Asbestos Corporation. The protracted conflict became a major focus of public attention and sympathy, as not only the new-middle-class writers of *Cité libre* and *Le Devoir* but more progressive elements within the Church, led by Montreal Archbishop Charbonneau, openly sought to mobilize public support for the strikers. The Asbestos strike was followed by major strikes in other industrial towns such as Louiseville (1952) and Arvida (1957) as well as a bitter strike against a French-Canadian retail enterprise, Depuis Frères (1952) and a famous strike against Radio-Canada (1959). These episodes engendered in Quebec society both a new perception of the CTCC and a greater awareness of labour's needs. At the same time, they sharpened the tension between the more aggressive elements of the union movement and the Duplessis regime, since invariably the provincial government came down heavily on the side of the employers, most notably through deployment of often brutal provincial police units.

The CTCC was not alone in its aggressive defence of the interests of Quebec labour. Its new militancy simply brought it into line with the stance of the various locals linked to the Canadian Congress of Labour and the American CIO. In 1952, the Fédération des unions industrielles du Québec was formed to group these locals within a Quebec-based central. Strongly committed to worker solidarity and militant unionism, it supported the provincial and federal wings of the CCF. In the eyes of both the CTCC and the FUIQ, the Duplessis regime had become the implacable enemy of organized labour and they worked closely together in opposing its labour policies. For the CTCC, hostility to the Duplessis regime had become so intense that from 1956 onward it abandoned the presentation of annual briefs to the government.[89]

Not only did the CTCC and the FUIQ oppose the labour relations legislation through which the Duplessis government had sought to suppress the union movement, but they called for a major expansion of the role of the state in other areas so as to meet directly the needs of labour. The CTCC and the FUIQ regularly called for the establishment of a public health insurance system, as well as many other programs for health care and social security. Union leaders regularly criticized Quebec's educational system, arguing that only a more vigorous state intervention in education could reduce the disparity in opportunity open to Francophone children. CTCC and FUIQ leaders were especially critical of the passive role played by the Quebec government in the development of natural resources, contending that the conditions of access of American corporations to mineral deposits and timber resources were far too favourable and that, with respect to hydro power, only complete public ownership could ensure proper development. In addition, of course, the leaders called for much stricter governmental regulation of working conditions.[90]

Nonetheless, the CTCC and the FUIQ were rarely joined in these campaigns by the largest union federation in Quebec: the Fédération provinciale du travail du Québec (FPTQ), which grouped together unions affiliated with the Trades and Labour Congress.[91] In 1949 it did join with the CTCC and FUIQ in supporting the Asbestos strikers and in successfully opposing the Duplessis government's proposed revision of labour law (Bill 5), but in 1954 it refused to join the two federations in an organized march to protest the government's labour policies. Conservative and fiercely anti-Communist, the FPTQ leadership was in fact able to co-operate quite satisfactorily with the Duplessis regime. While the FPTQ leadership may not have been opposed to the projects of political modernization advanced by the other two federations, and it certainly did not try to defend the labour policies of the Duplessis regime, it did not let such concerns lead it to oppose the Duplessis regime at election time. The TLC was officially neutral in politics, but some of the leaders of the affiliated unions openly supported the re-election of the Union nationale. For that matter, within the CTCC minor leaders and the rank and file did not necessarily support the strong stand the union's leadership was taking against the Duplessis regime and its policies.[92]

In sum, during the post-war years much of the union leadership was leading a vigorous campaign for expansion of the Quebec state to meet the needs of working-class Francophones. Some union leaders and members did not join this campaign and were prepared to support the Duplessis regime despite its failure to expand the state role or even to reform its labour policies. But these attitudes can hardly *explain* the failure of the Duplessis regime to expand the state's role. They can only have helped to make it possible for the government to persist in its stance. Within the union movement the Duplessis regime had ample mandate to expand the state's role if it otherwise wished to do so.

French-Canadian Clerical and Liberal Professional Elites

To be sure, there were French-Canadian elites, most notably the clergy and traditional intellectuals, who were resolutely opposed to any greater state role in education, health, and social security. They possessed substantial moral and institutional resources to support this opposition. But the singular feature of the Duplessis regime, unlike the preceding Liberal administrations of Gouin, Taschereau, and Godbout, is that these resources did not even have to be mobilized.[93]

Duplessis had already established his credentials in this regard before becoming premier of the province. During his first tenure as Leader of the Opposition he had been quick to defend Church prerogatives in the face of alleged threats from the Taschereau government. Thus, Church leaders openly supported his election in 1936.[94] By the same token, the upper clergy was pleased with his return to power in 1944.[95] As premier, Duplessis was careful to respect the Church's sensitivities. For instance, before creating a Ministry of Youth and Social Welfare, a measure that might have been seen as infringing on the Church's established terrain, he negotiated the whole project with ecclestiastical authorities. On this basis, he incorporated within the bill formal recognition of the Church's right, through the Conseil de l'Instruction publique, to prepare the pedagogy for the schools that fell under the ministry's jurisdiction. In fact, the Conseil had the right to supervise not only the application of this pedagogy but the hiring of teachers and school inspectors.[96]

This highly favourable stance toward the Church and its place in Quebec society had its rewards: Duplessis could count on the support of most of the clergy. In fact, he further solidified this support by requiring clerical authorities to approach him directly when seeking funds for their various projects. Public funds were in effect treated as "gifts" to individual clerics and their institutions. The recipients were expected to make the faithful fully aware of their gratitude for these gifts – especially at election time. To this extent, the Duplessis government might even be seen as "dominating" the Church. In fact, Duplessis himself used to declare that "The Bishops eat from my hand."[97] In one celebrated instance, the transfer of Montreal Archbishop Charbonneau to Victoria, B.C., it has even been argued that through a Vatican visit by two of his ministers Duplessis himself secured the change, outraged as he was over the Archbishop's open support of the Asbestos strikers. However, it appears that his role was limited to encouraging and providing documentation to the more conservative elements within the Quebec Church who themselves lobbied the Vatican to reassign the liberal cleric.[98] More generally, this appears to have been Duplessis's strategy in dealing with the Church: supporting more conservative elements and exploiting to his advantage rivalries among clerical orders. As Duplessis also declared on one occasion: "There is no great difficulty in governing Quebec. All one must do is to keep the Jesuits and Dominicans fighting."[99]

In short, a kind of mutual dependence had grown between the Duplessis regime and the Church. Given its general unreadiness to expand the functions of the Quebec state in such areas as education, welfare, and health, the Duplessis regime had every reason to support the established role of the Church in these areas. For the same reason, the Church had every reason to support the Duplessis regime, even if the support had to be covert. However, if clerical attitudes made it easier for the Duplessis regime to persist in its limited conception of the role of the state, they cannot explain *why* the government held to this conception.

The Godbout regime demonstrated that with proper resolve it was possible to undertake new state initiatives even in the face of open resistance from the Church and other traditional forces. Among the many Godbout reforms, two in particular had aroused the open hostility of the Church hierarchy: the right of women to vote in provincial elections and compulsory school attendance. Nonetheless, after the government granted the vote to women despite clerical opposition, Cardinal Villeneuve called on his bishops to acquiesce to compulsory education:

> It must be done. First of all, I know well M. Godbout and M. Perrier. These men are intelligent, estimable, *stubborn*. They have promised, and promised themselves, to bring about this reform. They succeeded in introducing the vote for women despite us. They will finish by establishing compulsory education despite us, if we oppose them. It must be done. . . .[100]

The statement says a great deal about the determination of the Godbout regime to intervene in education and social affairs and about the inability of the Church to block intervention, given such determination. During the Duplessis regime, despite growing appeals for a more active state, there was no such determination.

English-Canadian and American Corporate Elites

The power and interests of English-Canadian and American economic elites have often been cited to explain the failure of the Duplessis regime to expand the role of the Quebec state. It is argued that the close symbiotic relationship the Union nationale maintained with these elites stood in the way of any governmental intervention in the economy, and perhaps even of social security and educational measures that would have increased the corporate tax burden. After all, the rationales used by Quebec politicians to oppose new plans for state intervention in the economy often were borrowed not from the conservative *anti-étatisme* of nationalist intellectuals but from the laissez-faire economic liberalism of business circles.

A close working relationship between government and business was a long-established tradition in Quebec politics. In fact, to facilitate this relationship it had been customary for the Provincial Treasurer to be a Montreal Anglophone who was a member of the Montreal financial community. Frequently, he was chosen by the

Bank of Montreal.[101] Often, provincial premiers would sit on the boards of many private companies. Especially noteworthy was Louis-Alexandre Taschereau's membership on the board of directors of Sun Life Assurance Company. One of Taschereau's major arguments against nationalization of the hydroelectric companies was that this would be detrimental to the policyholders of insurance companies who had themselves invested in the companies: "Should we allow the shareholders and bondholders to lose all their money? Surely not! Such a Hydro is not possible."[102] Sun Life was among those insurance companies that had invested in the hydroelectric companies. After narrowly winning the 1935 provincial election, the Liberal government formally forbade membership of cabinet members on boards of directors of companies doing business with the government. (Taschereau himself resigned as Prime Minister to be replaced for the remaining year of Liberal rule by Adélard Godbout.)

Nonetheless, the links with private economic interests persisted in both parties. After returning to power in 1944, Duplessis broke with practice and appointed a French Canadian to the position of Provincial Treasurer, but he maintained close links with the leaders of Montreal's Anglophone economic elite. In his book, *Duplessis*, Conrad Black documents how Duplessis enjoyed close personal friendships with J.W. McConnell, owner of the Montreal *Star* and dean of the Montreal business community, and John Bassett, owner of the Montreal *Gazette*, with whom he dined regularly. In addition, Duplessis was on good personal terms with most of the heads of the English-Canadian and American corporations operating in Quebec; they would visit or write to him regularly. These relationships were based on an acknowledged specialization of responsibilities. Duplessis was to enjoy full authority over the management of the province's political affairs (and all matters of mutual interest that lay within the French-Canadian community). In return, Anglophone business leaders were to enjoy full freedom from government intrusion in the management of their enterprises and, for that matter, from intrusion by overly aggressive union leaders. Cementing this alliance between the Union nationale and Anglophone business was a strong mutual respect for the ability of the other to control affairs firmly within its particular sphere of influence.[103]

Reinforcing the sensitivity of party leaders to the demands and needs of private companies was, of course, the dependence of both parties on these companies for campaign funds. In his study of the Union nationale, Herbert Quinn points out that the party never staged public fund-raising drives. It obtained its campaign funds primarily from the various companies given government contracts, licences, natural resource concessions, and the like. These funds were clearly instrumental to its electoral successes. The preferential distribution of government jobs and services among the electorate was not a sufficient resource. Quinn estimates the Union nationale campaigns in the 1950s involved expenditures between $3 million and $4 million; Black claims that the 1952 and 1956 campaign expenses rose to $5 million and $9 million, respectively.[104] In addition, Black documents at length how some of these funds would come directly from corporate leaders. For instance, within forty-eight hours of the announcement of the 1952 and 1956 elections, J.W. McConnell had "$50,000 to $100,000 in wads of fresh bank notes" delivered directly to Duplessis.[105] Yet, even these symbiotic links of Duplessis and the Union nationale with business interests cannot fully explain the failure to intervene seriously in the economy.

While most of the English-Canadian and American business interests predominating in Quebec may have been hostile to state intervention, *in principle*, they might well have accepted state initiatives that appeared to be to their advantage.[106] In fact, there is evidence that during the 1940s and 1950s some corporate leaders were actively advocating important measures of state intervention. To be sure, the Duplessis regime was highly popular among corporate elites for its generous concessions of timber and minerals, its determination to maintain "labour peace," and its overall subscription to a laissez-faire philosophy. But some corporations engaged in the development of Quebec's natural resources saw a clear interest in the use of public corporations to provide basic services needed for their projects.

From the mid-1940s, a Canadian-born but American-based financier, Cyrus Eaton, repeatedly sought to persuade Duplessis to continue the nationalization of private hydroelectric utilities. Eaton claimed that he could arrange for the sale of provincial bonds to raise the funds necessary to purchase all of the remaining firms. With this centralization of the development of Quebec's hydro facilities, he argued, it would then be possible to attract major energy-using projects, such as steel-processing. But Duplessis was not prepared to contemplate any further nationalization. Similarly, R.E. Powell of the Aluminum Company of Canada suggested to Duplessis that Hydro-Québec should undertake the harnessing of the Manicouagan River, thus providing the necessary energy for a much larger aluminum production facility at

Arvida. This suggestion, of course, presaged the famous "Manic" development that an enlarged Hydro-Québec undertook during the Quiet Revolution, but Duplessis was not prepared to approve such a massive state undertaking. (After Duplessis refused, Alcan went to the British Columbia government, which did accept such terms for a development at Kitimat.) Throughout his administration, Duplessis actively sought to entice private interests to undertake development projects, but he would never agree to direct involvement by the Quebec state.[107]

The Godbout government had demonstrated that under certain conditions direct state intervention in the economy was possible in Quebec even when it was strongly opposed by most if not all sectors of big business. After all, the Liberal Party was much more closely linked with Anglophone business interests than was the Union nationale, yet the wartime Godbout administration managed to nationalize Montreal Light, Heat and Power. While the circumstances of this first step in the creation of Hydro-Québec have not yet been fully studied, it appears that this was indeed a case of governmental elites asserting their powers over private interests. Montreal Light, Heat and Power was a highly profitable enterprise and fiercely opposed the nationalization. Its opposition was shared by the Anglophone financial community as a whole.[108] Nonetheless, there had been long-standing resentment among consumers over high rates and excessive profits. Apparently, mobilization of this resentment made the nationalization possible.[109] Thus, whatever may have been the constraints on governmental elites, there was a certain margin for action that an interventionist government could exploit. For their part, Duplessis and the Union nationale vigorously denounced the nationalization as "bolshevistic."[110]

Maurice Duplessis and the Union Nationale

Many observers look to the personality of Maurice Duplessis himself for clues to the resistance of his government to political modernization. They have amply demonstrated that Duplessis was a profoundly conservative man – an unlikely candidate for any kind of new government venture.[111] While he vigorously proclaimed the role of the Quebec government as protector of French-Canadian interests, he recoiled from any proposal to assert this role in concrete terms. This caution is reflected even in the two measures of his administration that did assert the nationalist role of the Quebec state: the adoption of an official Quebec flag (the *fleurdelisé*) and the establishment of a provincial income tax. The memoirs of René Chaloult, one of the key proponents of the new flag, show that Duplessis was actually opposed to the flag, fearful that it might be construed as "separatist." (To avoid any confusion about the flag, he even suggested that a crown or maple leaf be inserted in the middle.) Only when it was clear that the various French-Canadian nationalist associations were solidly behind the flag did he relent.[112]

Similarly, a study by René Durocher and Michèle Jean shows that Duplessis did not establish the provincial income tax on his own initiative. In fact, initially he was very much opposed, fearing that the resultant double tax would cost his party votes. Only under intense pressure from various voluntary associations, including the Chambre de commerce de Montréal, as well as from the members of the Tremblay Commission, did Duplessis finally agree.[113] Yet, this reluctant concession was perhaps the only measure of the Duplessis administration that gave any real content to the principle of provincial autonomy with which Duplessis had so closely associated himself.

Despite his professed attachment to French-Canadian interests, Duplessis was clearly resigned to Anglo-Saxon dominance of the Quebec economy. He appears to have seen it as normal, or at least beyond redress, that the economic initiative should lie with Anglo-Saxons – they were inherently better suited for business. According to René Chaloult:

He respected and feared them [the Anglo-Saxons] because of their economic power and also because he was victim, without reason and despite his apparent arrogance, of reflexes of inferiority, old vestiges of the Conquest. Moreover, traditionally in Quebec it is the Anglo-Saxon capitalists who feed the electoral coffers, indispensable to our pseudo-democratic government.[114]

Beyond extreme caution and a resignation to Anglophone dominance of Quebec's economy, there is a final possible explanation for Duplessis's refusal to accept a direct economic role for the Quebec state. Proposals for new state initiatives involved substantial public borrowings; Duplessis was resolutely opposed to any unnecessary borrowing. He prided himself on Quebec's low public debt and its balanced budgets. This could be seen as the normal preoccupation of an economic conservative. But the intriguing suggestions of some observers is that this attitude was the bitter fruit of Duplessis's experience in the late 1930s.

During the first Duplessis administration, which came to power in the middle of the Depression, spending programs knew little of the restraint that was to mark post-war Duplessis administrations and the Quebec government's public borrowing accelerated sharply. On a per capita basis, Quebec's total expenditures rose from $19.73 in 1934-35 to $31.87 in 1939-40.[115] Some financial institutions began to question the "fiscal responsibility" of the Duplessis administration and the government began to have difficulty selling its bonds.[116] Allegedly, these institutions suggested to Duplessis that the government should call an election to secure a new mandate before seeking additional funding.[117] To make matters worse, with the outbreak of World War II, the federal government severely restricted provincial borrowing, both within Canada and without. This financial crisis, then, led Duplessis to call the surprise election of 1939, for which the Union nationale was ill-prepared and which resulted in defeat.[118] Thus, upon his return to power, Duplessis was obsessively concerned with holding public borrowing to the strict minimum. As a consequence, over the period 1950-59 Quebec's per capita expenditures (constant dollars) on debt service fell from $10.09 to $5.99. In fact, over the period 1952-59 Quebec's annual government borrowing averaged only 48 per cent of Ontario's.[119] In his own way, Duplessis was seeking to isolate the Quebec government, and his administration, from the worst effect of Quebec's economic dependence.

While we can locate in Maurice Duplessis qualities that could have contributed to the "lag" in political modernization, this can be only part of the total picture. Duplessis was, after all, the leader of a political party. His authority within the party must have been based in part on personal qualities such as shrewdness, intelligence, and the ability to manipulate people. But it also must have had a moral dimension; there must have been at least some agreement among party members – especially the parliamentary wing – with the general policies that he espoused. To a large degree, Duplessis's beliefs about the nature and purpose of government must have been shared by the party members as well. In the 1930s, when Duplessis disavowed programs for increased governmental activity, some members of his legislative delegation denounced him in outrage and left the party.[120] But the majority stayed with him. Throughout the subsequent two decades, his position as *le chef* was not challenged.

What characteristics of the Union nationale activists as a whole might explain this apparent agreement that the role of government should remain limited? First, the Union nationale legislators were a distinctly political elite – Robert Boily's term, *"la partitoc-ratie."*[121] Having no personal involvement in elite groups that might have more positive beliefs about the role of government, such as the new middle class or the labour union leaderships, they did not carry to government the aspirations and frustrations of these groups. For them, the consuming goal of political activity was simply to gain and maintain political office. This political *métier* had been a gratifying one for them. Through it, they had been able to rise above relatively common origins to positions of considerable status and prestige. Thus, government was not primarily a tool to be used on behalf of some larger goal or interest; the mere occupancy of political office had brought its own reward. Accordingly, they had no strong personal compulsion to expand the role of government. Second, the electorates they cultivated so carefully were likely to be in the rural areas or small towns. In 1952, 90 per cent of the Union nationale legislators represented districts outside the Montreal and Quebec City areas; in 1956, the percentage was 85 per cent.[122] These populations were not as likely as were those of the metropolitan areas to be demanding new government services. Their political demands could still be adequately met (at least, for electoral purposes) through the careful distribution of the limited services and jobs then provided by the provincial government – "favours" channelled through the local legislator and which were credited by the recipients to him.

The clearest explanation for the relative "lag" in political modernization during the Duplessis years appears to lie with the Duplessis administration itself. Traditional nationalist intellectuals may have been ambivalent about state expansion and, more fundamentally, may have been quite apolitical, but new-middle-class Francophones were strongly advocating a greater state role in education, health, and social security, as well as in the economy. In this, they were joined by the union leaderships and a wide variety of voluntary and professional associations. As for the economic elites, they may have officially endorsed Duplessis's laissez-faire philosophy, but elements among both the beleaguered Francophone entrepreneurs and the powerful American and English-Canadian industrialists would have welcomed a variety of state initiatives in the Quebec economy. A margin of action open to the Quebec state was not exploited. The explanation is to be found in distinctive qualities of the Union nationale: a *partitocratie* of political entrepreneurs firmly led by a wary and aging social and economic conservative.

When this *partitocratie* held office its main concern was that the limited functions then assumed by the Quebec government should be discharged in a way that would best further its re-election. There was little interest in measures that, whatever their merit, might alienate voters through raising taxes or simply by disturbing established practices. Moreover, the electoral system's continued overrepresentation of rural areas ensured that the needs and expectations of rural party supporters would outweigh those of urban supporters when it came to formulating governmental policy. As well, there was a constant, almost obsessive concern with maintaining control over the operations of the government, and there was a fierce resistance to changes that might weaken this control, whether the change be the emergence of an independent bureaucracy within the provincial state or the subjection to private capital that comes with public borrowing. These two traits of the Duplessis regime, fear of alienating established electoral clienteles – themselves little disposed to state expansion – and the determination to maintain complete control over the state apparatus, help to explain its reticence to expand the functions of the Quebec state.

One might even argue that the Duplessis regime was less prepared to undertake new initiatives than its Liberal predecessors. According to Boily, it was through the Union nationale that the *partitocratie* came to power in Quebec politics. Previously, many occupants of political office, whether in government or in the opposition, were at the same time active members of a social and economic elite, the French-Canadian *haute bourgeoisie*. As such, politics and the affairs of state were only one of their preoccupations, and only one of their bases of power and influence. With the arrival of Duplessis and the Union nationale, the Quebec government was in the hands of a distinctly political elite composed of individuals whose positions depended entirely on electoral success and who thus were consumed with the electoral game.[123] One might infer that such an elite would be especially likely to resist new initiatives that, while welcome in some quarters, threatened to reduce their control over the governmental apparatus, whether through greater dependence on the financial institutions that supported public borrowing or through the creation of a public bureaucracy that would challenge the legislator's crucial role as intermediary between constituents and government. Similarly, they would resist any avoidable recourse to tax increases that might endanger support of the group that really counted in the *partitocratie's* consuming goal of electoral success – the rural and semi-urban electorate that was so influential within Quebec's electoral system. Thus, at the time pressures for expansion of the Quebec state were mounting, the seats of state were occupied by a political elite especially unlikely to respond to these pressures. But how did this *partitocratie* manage to keep itself in power?

The Union Nationale and Rural Quebec

The longevity of the Duplessis regime can be traced in large part to its ability to secure support in the rural and small-town areas of Quebec – areas in which, we have suggested, there would be little pressure for political modernization. Given the gross underrepresentation of Montreal and Quebec City within the Quebec electoral system, it was possible for a party to obtain a majority of seats on the basis of the non-metropolitan areas alone. The Union nationale members secured support from these non-metropolitan populations in a variety of ways. Many government services were channelled through the local member of the legislature or *député*, who distributed them in the way that seemed most likely to ensure his re-election, as "rewards" for the services (vote, campaign funds, election work, etc.) that people had rendered to him or that he hoped they would render to him.

As Vincent Lemieux demonstrates, it was important that there be a reciprocal exchange – favours bestowed by the *député* must be a response to services rendered him – and that the items exchanged be roughly commensurate by the prevailing standards of the community. *Népotisme, favoritisme,* and *graissage* were deviations from patronage and were shunned by the electorate. But "true patronage" was regarded as normal and appropriate.[124] The Union nationale was especially adept in establishing and maintaining electorally effective patron-client relations. To use the characterization of Lemieux and Raymond Hudon, the Union nationale was more *électoraliste* in its use of patronage than were the Liberals when they held power in the 1960s. Union nationale patronage was guided more by a simple concern with securing the greatest number of votes possible. It was less likely than that of the Liberals to fall into the excesses of nepotism and favouritism. By the same token, it was less restricted to members of the party and more open to the electorate as a whole (including Liberal voters).[125]

As well as the careful distribution of benefits at the level of individual electors, the Union nationale worked hard to maintain a close identification with local communities. The Union nationale candidate himself was usually an individual with roots in the constituency; his local prestige and popularity would have been essential to secure the party nomination.[126] Often he would have the open support of the mayors of municipalities within the constituency (in fact, the Union nationale would try to control election to local offices). He would arrange highly publicized personal presentations to local officials of provincial grants for construction of roads, schools, municipal buildings, and the like. At election time he would place advertisements in the local newspapers with detailed lists of funds provided by the provincial government for various categories of local public works in the county. Accompanying these lists would be statements to the effect that: this was what the Union nationale *député* (or organizer, if the incumbent should be Liberal) had done for the county over the last four years; the Union nationale was certain to form the next government so it was in the interests of the county to vote for the Union nationale candidate.[127] In addition, Vincent Lemieux contends that the Union nationale had greater respect than did the Liberals for the local community and its structures; it was less likely to favour governmental intervention in local affairs or to disrupt community life through intense partisanship.[128]

The Union Nationale and Urban Quebec

Given the style of its politics, the predominance of personnel drawn from rural or semi-rural areas, and its success among the electorates of these areas, the Union nationale has often been characterized as the party of rural Quebec. Yet, in terms of electoral support, the picture is not that simple. Union nationale victories were not restricted to the rural or semi-urban areas; they also reached into the highly urbanized French-Canadian populations. In Montreal, the Union nationale did poorly in ridings with large Anglophone populations, but it did relatively well in the ten predominantly Francophone ridings. In the three elections of 1948, 1952, and 1956, the Union nationale won an average of seven of these ten ridings.[129] Similarly, in each of these three elections the Union nationale had the majority of the votes in the cities of Chicoutimi, Hull, Sherbrooke, and Trois-Rivières. Of the six ridings in the Quebec City region, the Union nationale won an average of four.

In short, while the margins of victory may have been greater in predominantly rural ridings, the Union nationale was still able to win the majority of the urban French-Canadian ridings as well. During these three elections of 1948, 1952, and 1956, the Liberal Party had trouble establishing a strong, durable electoral base among any of the Francophone ridings of Quebec. (Of the ten districts the Liberals managed to win in both 1952 and 1956, only five were predominantly French-Canadian.) Thus, the electoral obstacle to political modernization lay not just with the rural Francophone population but with the urban Francophone population as well. Even these more "modern" populations gave greater support to the party that opposed political modernization.

To many observers, this strength of the Union nationale among urban French Canadians is surprising. The Duplessis regime seems to have been more oriented to rural Quebec, not really understanding or sympathizing with the problems of the cities: it refused to take on new responsibilities for education, health, and welfare in order to improve the level of services; it refused to intervene in the economy (e.g., through nationalization) to create new economic opportunities for French Canadians; and it actively opposed the efforts of trade unions to improve the conditions of the French-Canadian working class. Given such a record, how could it remain more popular among urban French Canadians than the Liberal Party?

The Union Nationale and French-Canadian Nationalism

One type of explanation points to French-Canadian nationalism, arguing that the Union nationale was better able than were the Liberals to exploit the concerns of French Canadians with their distinct ethnic interests. These nationalist concerns overrode the alienation that many French Canadians felt from other Union nationale policies. However more attractive may have been the Liberal Party's position on social and economic issues, French Canadians could not ignore the Liberals' failure to respond to their nationalist concerns. At the same time, these nationalist positions also contributed to the Union nationale's popularity in rural areas as well.

It is argued that the Union nationale waged a strongly nationalist campaign in 1936, attacking the power of Anglo-Saxon economic interests in Quebec and the impact that industrialization had had upon French-Canadian society. The incumbent Liberals were closely associated with these interests and had encouraged industrialization. During World War II, the Union nationale vehemently opposed the imposition by the Liberal federal government of conscription for overseas service, while the incumbent provincial Liberals were hopelessly compromised by this act of their federal counterparts. In the post-war period, the Union nationale

117

was able to define a much clearer position on the question of provincial autonomy. Claiming that the Liberal federal government was seeking to invade Quebec jurisdictions to pursue its assimilationist goals, Duplessis argued that Quebec could not afford to have a Liberal government at the provincial level as well and contended that only the Union nationale, unfettered by links to the ruling party at the federal level, could be trusted to defend Quebec's autonomy. As proof, Duplessis would point to the wartime tax agreements that the Godbout government made with the federal government.[130]

At first glance at least, this interpretation might seem compelling. After its vigorous opposition to the Liberal conscription policies, the Union nationale did indeed win the provincial election of 1944. The Liberals received a higher popular vote, but it could be argued that the nationalist vote was split between the Union nationale and the Bloc populaire, which was even more vehement in its opposition to conscription. By the same token, it could be argued that the Union nationale lost the election of 1939 because at this point the Liberals had been able to define a more effective position on the issue of conscription: the leading French-Canadian members of the federal government had threatened to resign (and thus weaken the French-Canadian influence in the federal government) unless the provincial Liberals were elected. The Union nationale did win the post-war elections of 1948, 1952, and 1956, during which it could argue that a Liberal provincial government would not be able to defend provincial autonomy in the face of a Liberal federal government. At the same time, once this argument had been undermined by the election of a Conservative government at the federal level (under Diefenbaker), the Union nationale lost the 1960 provincial election. In particular, then, the persistence of the Duplessis regime through the 1950s can be plausibly seen as a function of its exploitation of French-Canadian nationalism.

While these arguments might appear plausible, they are far from convincing. First, it must be shown that the Union nationale systematically used the issue of provincial autonomy. On the basis of an analysis of electoral campaigns (especially the content of newspaper advertisements), however, it appears that priority was given to other issues, such as the state of the economy and the support of local institutions and public works.[131] Second, it must be shown that most French Canadians actually shared the nationalists' suspicion of the federal government. However, analysis of opinion survey materials suggests that this belief was not widespread in the 1950s; only in the 1960s did this suspicion become widespread in the population.[132] Thus, while further research on the electoral processes of the Duplessis period is clearly necessary, there are good grounds for questioning the importance of nationalism, especially in the form of the provincial autonomy issue, as support for the Union nationale.

The Union Nationale and the French-Canadian Working Class

Rejecting the idea that nationalism was important to Union nationale support, Maurice Pinard suggests that its urban support can be better understood by looking at its class bases. It is the attraction of working-class French Canadians to this party that explains its urban support. For Pinard, as for many others, this is a paradox: the party whose policies are more "right-wing" (including opposition to unions) was actually preferred by working-class French Canadians. It would seem that the working class was voting against its own interests. Moreover, according to Pinard, this preference for the Union nationale was strongest among those members of the working class who identified with the working class. Through this identification, and the belief that the Union nationale was more sympathetic to this class, many French Canadians were led to vote for the Union nationale. How could this seemingly misguided identification of the working class with the Union nationale (a "right-wing" party) have developed?

For Pinard, the identification stems primarily from conditions of the Union nationale's initial rise to power. This victory was based to a large degree on an economic protest of working-class French Canadians against the hardships of the Depression. With the appearance of the Union nationale as the first credible alternative to the incumbent Liberals, the working class had a vehicle for expressing this protest. Thus, they saw the Union nationale as theirs and voted for the party out of purely economic protest – they were not attracted to or even aware of the nationalist themes articulated by the Union nationale leadership. This non-nationalist identification with the Union nationale persisted over the subsequent decades. It was primarily on this basis, not on the issue of provincial autonomy, that the Union nationale was able to do so well among working-class French Canadians.[133]

This interpretation raises questions that it does not fully resolve. For example, could there have arisen in 1936 such an enduring non-nationalist identification of the French-Canadian working class with the Union nationale if (as Pinard suggests) the

119

working class abandoned the Union nationale for the Liberals in the election of 1939? Much more data are needed about the durability of this working-class preference for the Union nationale through the 1940s and 1950s, and about the factors underlying it. Nevertheless, Pinard's analysis does provide a plausible interpretation of urban Union nationale support – an interpretation that perhaps correctly de-emphasizes the role of nationalism.

However important economic protest may have been in the initial attraction of working-class Francophones to the Union nationale in the 1930s, other factors also may have reinforced a working-class identification with the Union nationale. Several aspects of the Union nationale itself gave it a distinctly "populist" air. As the Boily study shows, the Union nationale legislators of the Duplessis regime were more highly concentrated in the middle classes than had been the Liberal legislators of the earlier Liberal regimes. With the rise to power of the Union nationale, the political role of the *haute bourgeoisie* was definitively broken; the members of what Boily calls the *class moyenne-inferieure* acquired a representation and power they had never before enjoyed.[134] In a literal sense, then, the Union nationale was "close to the people" in a way the Liberals had not been.

In addition, Duplessis himself, despite his *haute bourgeoisie* origins, was careful to cultivate the image of "a man of the people" rather than of the "snobs" – a man who spoke French in a popular vernacular and who, by his testimony, never read books. "He had a sense of the kind of language to be used with our peasants and workers: simple, direct, at times coarse."[135] This image of a party for *"les petits"* also was reinforced by the type of patronage practised by the Union nationale. Lemieux and Hudon recount how many observers told them that Union nationale patronage was more *populaire* than the Liberals' patronage, which, more *bourgeois*, favoured the *"grands amis du régime."* Their examination of political patronage suggests that these characterizations *"ne sont pas sans fondement."*[136]

We might even ask whether the position of the Liberal Party was in fact significantly more favourable to working-class interests, or sufficiently so to have offset the "populist" aspects of the Union nationale. The Liberals clearly were more "liberal" than the Union nationale on civil liberties. They also favoured a greater state role in the economy and in education, health, and welfare. But their position on such specific working-class issues as trade unionism was not as clearly differentiated. Trudeau observes that when, in 1954, the Union nationale government presented its anti-union Bills 19 and 20, the Liberal Opposition raised little protest: "as at the time of Asbestos, their watchword seemed to be: above all, no trouble with the employers."[137] While the Liberals held a majority in the upper house of the Quebec legislature they did not use it to reject these two bills.[138]

To be sure, we have seen how elements of the union leadership actively made the argument that the Union nationale was hostile to working-class interests. But as we also noted, the leadership was not united in doing so. Usually the FPTQ leadership did not join in. In fact, it generally co-operated with the Duplessis government and was rewarded for doing so. Moreover, it appears that within the CTCC, if not the FUIQ, lower-level leaders also did not always heed their leaders' call. Thus, it would not be surprising if some union members themselves remained loyal to the Union nationale.[139] Of course, since less than 30 per cent of the labour force was unionized there were real limits in any event to the ability of the union leaderships to direct the working-class vote as a whole.

In summary, the conditions of the Union nationale's rise to power, the various "populist" aspects of the party, and the contradictory position of the working-class leadership suggest quite plausibly that lower-class French Canadians could have developed and sustained the belief that the Union nationale, rather than the Liberals, was *their* party. As we shall see, this working-class suspicion of the Liberals and their programs of political modernization persisted into the 1970s. It was not dissolved in the accomplishments of the Quiet Revolution but instead was reinforced by the perception that the benefits of the Quiet Revolution programs tended to go disproportionately to the middle classes.

Any conclusions about the bases of electoral support for the Union nationale of the 1940s and 1950s must be tentative. But it does seem that the role of French-Canadian nationalism – especially in the form of the autonomy issue – was fairly limited. The electoral advantage of the Union nationale lay primarily in its abilty to politicize class divisions among urban French Canadians, at the same time maintaining a solid base among rural French Canadians through both the close integration of local social and political structures and the effective distribution of patronage. The Union nationale exploited these advantages under highly favourable conditions: the general post-war prosperity that persisted through the mid-1950s and the unity of the party under the strong hand of its founder and only leader. When these two conditions disappeared in the late 1950s, the Union nationale was to find itself vulnerable. The Liberal Party – and the forces of political modernization – were finally victorious. In the meantime, however, the Quebec government was held by a party that resisted the pressures that social and economic development generated for the expansion of the role of the state. However much such an expansion of the state might have been inhibited by the persistence of *anti-étatisme* among some French-Canadian nationalist intellectuals, and by the ability of private corporation interests to constrain government action, the primary obstacle was the persistence of these political elites in power.

Popular Participation in Politics

Beyond the scope of government activities, our concept of political modernization is also concerned with the extent of popular participation in political processes. With social and economic development, there is usually an increase in the extent to which the population as a whole will seek to affect the way government acts. Was the lag in modernization in the Quebec government parallelled by a lag in political modernization among the Quebec population as a whole? This is a more difficult question to deal with: the degree of mass involvement in the political process cannot be as readily measured as can the scope of governmental activities.

One kind of data often used to assess popular participation in politics is turnout for elections. The levels of turnout for elections in Quebec would suggest that mass involvement in politics has been quite high. Between 1900 and 1956, turnout in Quebec provincial elections averaged 72.8 per cent.[140] (Since turnout was usually lower in English-Canadian ridings, we can assume that the actual level of turnout among French Canadians was even higher.) Yet, these high levels of turnout do not appear to have been a response to social and economic development. Not only did the voter turnout for the province as a whole fail to rise with urbanization and industrialization, but there is a strong negative correlation between turnout and development (i.e., a higher percentage of the rural, agrarian population consistently went to the polls than did those in urban industrial areas).[141]

This ostensibly greater political participation in rural areas than urban areas perhaps can be better understood in terms of the style of rural politics that was discussed earlier. The systematic distribution of patronage played a central role in rural politics and explained in part the continued dominance of the Union nationale: within such patron-client politics, the incentives to vote would have been high. There was often an immediate, concrete reward for voting. These incentives could not have been as great in urban areas where favours would have to be spread much more thinly, given the much larger electorate within each district. Perhaps urban areas also contained alternative sources of help; one was not so dependent on the favours distributed by party organizations. For these reasons, electoral participation would be greater in rural areas. There would indeed be a greater interest in influencing the activities of government, at least activities that take place within the local district.

It would be risky, nevertheless, to infer from these high levels of turnout that there were high levels of awareness and involvement in the politics of Quebec as a whole. The results of opinion surveys suggest that in both rural and urban areas the levels of attention to information about provincial politics and the regular discussion of this information were both low.[142] In this sense, there *was* a lag of political modernization behind social and economic development. Prior to the 1960s, the limited scope of governmental activities was parallelled by limited popular participation in the political life of Quebec as a whole.

Quebec and the Federal System

The lag in Quebec's political modernization, or more precisely the aversion to an active, expanding Quebec state, is reflected in the Duplessis regime's relations with Ottawa. An atmosphere of tension and conflict pervaded these relations throughout Duplessis's tenure in power, but rarely did Quebec-Ottawa conflict involve a direct confrontation of power, as when two governments each seek to act within the same domain. Usually, Quebec pursued a defensive strategy with Ottawa, seeking to block federal initiatives it saw as invasions of provincial jurisdiction but not fully exploiting these jurisdictions itself. Typically, the federal initiatives were new spending programs whose implementation in a province was conditional on provincial approval or collaboration. Usually, Quebec (and Quebec alone, among the provincial governments) would refuse to approve the program. The Duplessis administration did not participate in many of the federal-provincial cost-shared programs and it forbade private institutions under its control, most notably universities, to accept federal grants. The cost of such a strategy was high: in the fiscal year 1959-60 alone Quebec lost approximately $82 million in federal funds.[143] A government equally committed to provincial autonomy but also committed to political modernization could not have countenanced such a loss of funds. The only strategy open to it would have been to challenge directly the federal programs, claiming that the funds belonged to Quebec by right and refusing to allow any federal conditions to be attached to them. As we shall see, the Lesage regime of the 1960s did adopt this strategy; the Duplessis administration, with its limited commitment to political modernization, was not driven to do so.

Another focus of the Duplessis regime's defence of provincial autonomy was the symbols of provincial authority. Thus, it was under Duplessis that the provincial government adopted an official provincial flag (after much hesitation, as we have seen). Similarly, in 1939 and 1944 Duplessis engaged Mackenzie King in little-publicized disputes over the right of the province to be consulted in the federal government's choice of a new provincial lieutenant-governor.[144] Neither issue materially involved the distribution of power between the two governments.

The only sustained direct confrontation between federal and provincial power during the Duplessis period occurred in the mid-1950s, over the collection of provincial income tax. During the war, Ottawa had secured the consent of Quebec and other provincial governments to an arrangement under which Ottawa alone would collect personal and corporate income taxes, as well as succession duties, in exchange for the payment of "tax rent" to the provinces. In 1947, Quebec and Ontario both refused to continue this arrangement for corporate taxes, and each began to impose its own provincial corporate income tax. But, in the immediate post-war period, no provincial government established its own personal income tax, even though in 1946 the federal government had introduced a provision in its tax legislation that allowed individuals to deduct from their federal tax the amount paid to a provincial income tax, up to 5 per cent of the federal tax.

During the early 1950s, French-Canadian nationalist intellectuals carefully orchestrated a campaign for a provincial income tax, enlisting the Chambre de commerce de Montréal and a wide variety of voluntary associations. As the campaign intensified, so the pressure on Duplessis grew. Finally, in 1954 he agreed to establish a provincial income tax. The bill Duplessis introduced to the Quebec legislature provided for a tax equivalent to 15 per cent of the federal tax, thus raising the possibility of a certain amount of "double taxation" for Quebec residents and provoking a struggle with Ottawa. After several months of intergovernmental wrangling, Ottawa finally agreed to increase its allowable deduction to 10 per cent of the federal taxation, and Duplessis in effect reduced the provincial tax to the same amount.[145] There is no question that by expanding the sources of provincial revenue, the tax was important to the eventual elaboration of an active, autonomous Quebec state; it is rightly hailed by Quebec nationalists as a major victory for their cause. The measure did not reflect any serious commitment on Duplessis's part to create a strong provincial state, however, and for this reason was adopted only after prolonged misgivings had been overcome. It stands in striking contrast to the other positions adopted by the Duplessis regime in its relations with Ottawa. The only clearly comparable measure, involving a direct federal-provincial confrontation of power, was provincial legislation for the creation of Radio-Quebec, thus challenging the federal pretension that radio broadcasting is an exclusively federal jurisdiction. The legislation was never implemented during the Duplessis period.

Aside from the instance of personal income tax, the Duplessis regime's basic approach to federal-provincial relations was not innovative. The basic argument Duplessis used to underpin his defence of provincial jurisdictions, the "compact theory" of Confederation, had been propounded in the 1880s by Honoré Mercier. The tactics of blunting federal programs simply by refusing to participate in them had already been deployed by Louis-Alexandre Taschereau when, citing the need to protect provincial autonomy, he refused to collaborate in federally sponsored programs for unemployment insurance and for old age pensions. Like previous governments, Duplessis's approach was conservative, calling not for the revision of the British North America Act and its divisions of powers but simply for a closer adherence to it by Ottawa. The primary difference between Duplessis and his predecessors is the regularity and energy with which he publicly proclaimed these same arguments.

Duplessis followed along in established traditions of federal-provincial relations even though his regime was free from a force that had constrained most previous provincial administrations: the presence in Ottawa of a government of the same party. Ottawa could not use party structures to influence and even control Quebec as had been the case in the nineteenth century, when federal Conservative leaders regularly chose the Quebec premier, or during this century, when Laurier imposed Simon-Napoléon Parent as premier of Quebec and Mackenzie King forced the resignation of Taschereau in 1936.[146]

The Duplessis administration approached federal-provincial relations in largely the same fashion as preceding governments because it shared the same assumptions about the role of the provincial government in Quebec's social and economic life. Like them, it gave pre-eminence to private institutions, whether the Church-related institutions that had ultimate responsibility for education and social services or the corporations that directed the economy. At most, the state was there to support these institutions, not to regulate and displace them. Within this perspective, the Quebec government did have a special mission to protect the Church-related institutions from encroachments of the Anglophone-dominated federal government. It was to act as a kind of watchdog, entrusted with the jurisdictions most closely affecting these institutions and thus pre-empting federal action. But it was not actively to occupy these jurisdictions itself.

As long as Quebec governments shared these assumptions, relations between Quebec and the federal government could be reasonably stable, whatever might be the appearances. After all, these assumptions had been the basis for the original federal bargain. The Quebec provincial government was granted the jurisdictions necessary to its watchdog function. It enjoyed exclusive jurisdiction over education, health, and welfare, and the solemnization of marriages. In addition, provincial jurisdiction over civil rights and property seemed to ensure the integrity of the Civil Code. But within the terms of the original agreement, Quebec, like other provincial governments, was limited in many respects. It had no exclusive source of revenue, unlike the federal government, which had exclusive access to indirect taxes and competed for direct taxes with the provinces. It was subject to the federal powers of disallowance and reservation. Economic responsibilities were effectively lodged with the federal government. Moreover, at the federal level French Canadians were a minority both in the House of Commons and Senate and in the cabinet. In addition, within the cabinet they had been excluded from the powerful economic portfolios. Prior to the 1960s no French Canadian had been Minister of Trade and Commerce, Minister of Finance, or Minister of Labour.[147]

These restrictions on the political role of French Canadians were tolerable only as long as it was assumed that effective power should be held by private institutions and that the essential role of the Quebec provincial government was to protect these institutions from federal interference. For these assumptions to continue to hold, two general conditions had to persist. First, it had to be credible that private institutions, protected from adverse governmental intervention, were adequate to assure the survival and development of French Canada. Second, there could be no strong

126

French-Canadian elite group with a clear incentive in the expansion of the Quebec state.

Quebec's economic and social development undermined both of these conditions. In an urban-industrial Quebec, Church-related institutions increasingly had both financial and organizational difficulty in providing education and social services. Moreover, in the urban setting, English-language influences were infinitely stronger, seeming to require new French-language institutional counterweights. In addition, as we have seen, development created a new category of French Canadians, "a new middle class," which had every reason to advocate an active Quebec state. Ultimately, these changes resulted in the dissatisfaction of many Québécois with the current federal system and, in some cases, with the very presence of Quebec in the Canadian federal system.

CHAPTER FIVE
The "Quiet Revolution": The New Ideology of the Quebec State

No period in the political life of Quebec has had a particular phrase or label as closely associated with it as has the early 1960s – the period of the "Quiet Revolution." Despite the fact that the term first appeared in the article of an English-Canadian journalist,[1] French-Canadian intellectual and political elites quickly seized on "Quiet Revolution" and made it their own. *La Révolution tranquille* became a catchword used by all to summarize the distinctive quality of Quebec politics in the 1960s, although in actuality it does not convey a great deal. Many would contend that the limited meaning the term does convey is quite inaccurate – that there were no "revolutionary" changes of any type. Certainly "Quiet Revolution" seems greatly exaggerated as a description of the concrete changes that took place in political processes during this first half of the 1960s. State activities were expanded in some areas, but these new roles were still relatively limited and in other areas there was little change at all. While some elements of the population did become more intensely involved in Quebec's political life, many others remained only marginally involved. Moreover, the changes that did take place do not seem "revolutionary" within a North American context. Where, then, was there a revolution – "quiet" or otherwise?

The popularity of this label can be better understood if one looks not to political structures but to ideologies, i.e., beliefs about the purpose and character of society and polity. Here there was indeed change so profound and far-reaching that we can see how so many would have found it "revolutionary." In the early 1960s the beliefs and assumptions that had guided most French-Canadian intellectuals for over a century were being uncompromisingly examined and, to a very large extent, abandoned. This reformulation was taking place within the mainstream of French-

Canadian thought. It was not confined just to "fringe" groups among the French-Canadian nationalist intelligentsia, nor did it deny the importance of the French-Canadian collectivity. It is this process of full liberation from a long-dominant ideology that most clearly distinguishes these first few years of the 1960s and gives them such an extraordinary quality.

The Ideology of the Quiet Revolution

At the broadest level, this ideological revolution constituted the long-avoided reconciliation with social and economic development.[2] As we have seen, the image of French-Canadian society customarily held by French-Canadian nationalists depicted French Canada in essence as rural and agrarian. Even after the bulk of French Canadians had migrated to urban areas and the traditional model no longer described the social reality, a substantial segment of nationalist intellectuals found it difficult to abandon the old ideal. However much French Canada may have become an urban society, it was only in the rural setting that the true identity of the French-Canadian nation could be expressed. Through the 1930s and 1940s many nationalists sought to restore the rural sector to something approaching its former importance. Even in the 1950s, the Tremblay Commission talked of maintaining a "balance" between the rural and urban sectors. In short, it did not seem possible to remain faithful to the national ideal and at the same time embrace fully the processes of economic and social development. With the 1960s, this traditionalism was definitively abandoned. Social and economic development was openly welcomed; rather than threatening the integrity of the nation, such development could enable it to reach new accomplishments. The new ideal of French-Canadian nationalists became a highly efficient technological society led by French Canadians and animated by a French spirit. The consuming goal of French-Canadian nationalists became *rattrapage*, catching up to social and economic development elsewhere.

Implicit in this whole-hearted espousal of social and economic development was a transformation of the perception that French Canadians held of their own capabilities. As Marcel Rioux observes, the Quiet Revolution is:

above all a reaffirmation of ourselves, the reappearance of a spirit of independence and enquiry which had been frozen during the long winter that had lasted for over a century. The Québécois became certain that they could change many things if they really wanted to.[3]

French Canadians were no longer *"né pour un petit pain"*; they could compete with other nations on their terms. Thus, the massive Manicouagan Dam in northern Quebec, constructed entirely by Francophones, became a major focus of national sentiment. The symbols of "Manic" appeared on commercial products and a popular song depicted the loneliness experienced by a "Manic" construction worker. For a few years, *all* seemed possible. Perhaps, as Léon Dion suggests, such an exaggerated self-confidence was necessary compensation for the centuries during which French Canadians had had such little faith in their capacities.[4]

This reformulation of the dominant French-Canadian ideology also involved a narrowing of the boundaries of the "nation." In the past, nationalists had been ready to see the French-Canadian nation as existing throughout much of Canada, and perhaps even extending into areas of the northeastern United States. In fact, the very term "Québécois" was not in general usage, except to refer to the residents of Quebec City. With the 1960s, nationalists became increasingly focused on Quebec alone. Whatever political arrangements were advocated, an increasing number of Québécois refused to merge the primary identity of Quebec Francophones with that of Canada as a whole. Quebec Francophones might share a Canadian identity for some political purposes, but they were first and foremost Québécois. The ambiguous compound term "French Canadian" was no longer acceptable and fell into disuse. For all intents and purposes, the "nation" and Quebec had become the same. Whereas the new beliefs about the technological society and the potentialities open to Quebec Francophones within it were to come under heavy attack over subsequent years, this redefinition of the boundaries of nation was to continue to be widely accepted.

A further thrust of the Quiet Revolution ideology was a new attitude toward the state. Now that economic and social development were to be valued rather than feared, and now that the primary goal was to create a highly developed Francophone society, the state assumed a new importance as the primary agent, *le moteur principal*, of this *rattrapage*. The old suspicions and ambivalences about the state disappeared; political modernization became the explicit goal of most French-Canadian intellectuals.[5] At the same time, this new *étatisme* was centred on one state in particular, Quebec. Only this state, under the control of Francophones, could assume the new responsibilities that Quebec's social and economic development demanded. Consequently, it was argued that the Quebec provincial government needed not only to exercise all the jurisdictions presently under its control that had not been occupied, but it must also assume responsibilities currently held by Ottawa. As well, the old strategy of thwarting federal spending programs simply by refusing to participate in them, thus forgoing massive amounts of federal funds, now appeared unbearably costly. In short, once modernization of the Quebec state, and Quebec society, became the consuming goal of the French-Canadian intelligentsia, the old "rules of the game" of Canadian federalism were no longer acceptable. The concentration of power and fiscal resources in Ottawa had to be confronted head on.

The Modernization of the Quebec State

In the previous chapter, we saw that the lag in political modernization was most evident in the areas of education, health, and welfare. Here the Quebec provincial government had allowed private institutions – primarily those of the Church – to retain a much greater degree of power and authority than was the case in the other provinces. It was in this same area that there occurred the most impressive expansion of governmental activities during the Lesage regime.

With the establishment of a provincial Ministry of Education in 1964, the Quebec government assumed full authority over all educational institutions in Quebec – public and private. In the public sector, the government no longer restricted its activities, as it had in the past, to the provision of material facilities; it now took full control of pedagogical and curricular matters. There were certain institutional measures to placate the fears of the clergy that the confessional character of Catholic schools would diminish.[6] An advisory Conseil Supérieur was established which, reminiscent of the old Conseil de l'instruction publique, was composed of "Catholic" and "Protestant" committees. Within the "Catholic" committee, the clergy were well represented. However, the authority of this committee was limited by statute to overseeing the purely confessional aspects of the Catholic schools. In addition, the groundwork was laid for the new post-secondary CEGEPs, which were to be wholly non-confessional. As well as eliminating most of the authority the clergy had long exercised over the content of public education in Quebec, the Lesage administration also reduced the role that local elites – through local school commissions –

had played in the provision of school facilities. Through "Operation 55" the new Ministry of Education forced a reorganization of the numerous local Catholic school commissions into fifty-five regional school commissions.

The same centralization of authority and power in the Quebec provincial government occurred with respect to health and welfare activities. Church-related institutions came increasingly under the dominance of provincial bureaucracies; in some cases they were fully taken over by the province. With the establishment of a provincial scheme of hospital insurance in 1961, hospitals were forced to conform to provincial norms and regulations regarding personnel qualifications, administrative procedures, standards and costs of services, etc. Private welfare organizations also were increasingly subject to governmental regulation. The provincial government became more directly involved in social welfare through expansion of its own programs and services. In 1964, a new compulsory contributory pension scheme was established by the Quebec provincial government. To a large extent, this increased provincial role in health and welfare was made possible by the transfer of existing federal programs to the Quebec government. The desires of Quebec to take over such federal programs became a major focus of Quebec-Ottawa conflict during this period.

The other focus of major new governmental initiatives under the Lesage regime was the economy. Here the primary goal was to redress the underrepresentation of French Canadians in the upper levels of Quebec's economic structures. Rather than directly seeking to change the recruitment practices of the English-Canadian and American enterprises that dominated the Quebec economy, energies were concentrated on expanding the small French-Canadian sector. Two primary strategies were pursued: the establishment of public enterprises and the strengthening of French-Canadian–owned enterprises.

In the case of public enterprises, the most notable achievement was, of course, the nationalization of the existing private electrical utility companies, which were owned and managed by English Canadians, and their incorporation into Hydro-Québec. Whatever may have been the economies gained through the integration of Quebec's hydroelectric facilities, the primary benefit was the creation of new opportunities for French Canadians in managerial and technical positions. With strong governmental support, the top management of Hydro-Québec vigorously sought to establish French as the sole working language within the new enterprise. Anglophone personnel inherited from the nationalized companies left for other positions, took early retirement, or, in some cases, acquired a working proficiency in French. Vacant positions were filled primarily by French Canadians. Hydro-Québec still remains the main instance of the successful conversion of the working language of a major economic enterprise from English to French. In addition to the regular operations of Hydro-Québec, the company's giant hydroelectric project in northern Quebec also provided new opportunity for Francophones to occupy administrative and technical positions: French was the exclusive working language in the construction of the Manicouagan Dam, the largest structure of its kind in the world. For some, there is irony in the fact that the nationalization of the private electrical utilities was financed through funds obtained on the American market, in the amount of $300 million. French Canadians were becoming *"maîtres chez nous"* at the expense of the English-Canadian bourgeoisie, but with the support of the American bourgeoisie. Nevertheless, Hydro-Québec did afford opportunities for middle-class Francophones that would not otherwise have existed. As such, it clearly was a successful initiative.

The Lesage administration's other major attempt to strengthen the Francophone presence in the Quebec economy was not as immediately successful. In 1962, Quebec created the Société générale de financement (SGF). Its purpose was to strengthen the small, often family-dominated, French-Canadian industrial and commercial enterprises that existed at the time. This was to be accomplished both through the provision of financial support, drawn from public and private funds, and through the introduction of modern management techniques. The greatest proportion of funds was tied up in Marine Industries, a large industrial firm involved in shipbuilding and other heavy industrial products, and the two associated companies of Forano Limited and Volcano Limited. SGF became the major shareholder in this complex, as well as in several smaller enterprises: manufacturing biscuits (Biscuits Stuart Limitée), knitted goods (La Salle Tricot Limitée), metal fixtures (Bonnex Inc.), and munitions (Industries Valcartier Inc.). In addition, SGF created a forest products corporation (Sogefor), a manufacturer of electrical equipment (Cegelec Industries), and, perhaps the best known, an assembly plant for Renault automobiles (SOMA, Inc.). None of these enterprises proved to be highly profitable, despite the financial and technical support of SGF. In fact, given its record, SGF experienced great difficulty in selling its shares to private investors; by 1966, it had exhausted its available capital. To be sure, none of the SGF enterprises was the total disaster experienced by some other provincial development corporations, since SGF had acquired interests in its various enterprises rather than simply lending funds. Still, SGF was not a clear success: private French-Canadian enterprises continued to remain marginal through the 1960s. Accordingly, SGF and the mixed-ownership formula fell into discredit. The only clearly successful measure to strengthen the French-Canadian presence in Quebec's economy during the Quiet Revolution remained Hydro-Québec – a public enterprise.

In addition to Hydro-Québec and SGF, one other major economic enterprise was envisaged during the Lesage administration, although it did not become a reality until the late 1960s. In 1964, the Quebec government established SIDBEC (Sidérurgie québécoise). The goal of SIDBEC was to construct a steel mill able to break Quebec's dependence on the mills of Hamilton, Ontario. Because of the enormous cost of such an operation, SIDBEC became the focus of intense controversy. To some, the project symbolized the way in which neo-nationalism had distorted governmental priorities, leading to fascination with giant projects whose economic viability was uncertain but which would bring new grandeur to the nation. For others, such a steel mill was essential for the Quebec economy to acquire sufficient autonomy to develop properly and to offer adequate opportunity to French Canadians. In any event, the cost of the project and the controversy it generated forced the Lesage administration to postpone any real implementation of it. Nevertheless, SIDBEC had played a central role in the Lesage regime's plans for intervention in the economy.

These three projects – Hydro-Québec, SGF, and SIDBEC – all reflected what the Lesage regime proclaimed as one of its primary goals: to increase the presence of French Canadians in the upper levels of the Quebec economy. In the rhetoric of the period, they were intended to make Québécois *maîtres chez nous*. Great energy was devoted to this goal, yet the impact of these and related programs was only marginal: the Anglophone dominance of the Quebec economy was not substantially reduced. The contrast between the relative failure of the Lesage regime on the economic front and its success in the other main thrust of its activities, reform of education and social welfare institutions, was striking. In the case of education, in particular, the Quebec government managed to seize full control and to impose new structures and priorities that amounted to a real transformation of the sector.

It is not surprising that the Quiet Revolution had a much more substantial effect on educational structures than on economic structures, since the task before the government was not nearly as formidable. First, whereas education was fully within the constitutional jurisdiction of the provincial government, the economy obviously was not. Some economic initiatives of the Lesage regime apparently were hampered by competing federal activities. A case in point is the Conseil d'orientation économique du Québec. Its attempts to establish a comprehensive plan for Quebec's economic development apparently ran afoul of federal priorities. Ottawa favoured a concentration on development of the Montreal region rather than the dispersal of development among several regions of Quebec that the COEQ sought to promote. Second, Anglophone corporate elites clearly had much greater resources for blunting Quebec's economic initiatives than had the clerical elites for resisting government takeover of education.

These corporate pressures may well explain the mixed results of the new public investment fund the Quebec government created in 1965 – the Caisse de dépôt et de placement du Québec. The Caisse was charged with administering the funds accumulated through Quebec's counterpart to the Canada Pension Plan and through some minor insurance schemes. The Caisse became an important purchaser of Quebec government bonds, thus reducing the government's dependence on English-Canadian and American financial institutions for the sale of its bonds. But during the 1960s the Caisse administrators apparently hesitated to concentrate its private investments in distinctly Francophone-owned enterprises. Instead it invested primarily in the major banks and other large English-Canadian institutions.

Finally, some observers contend that elements within the Quebec state itself were not yet comfortable with the notion that the state should be a direct participant in the economy. It is claimed that the government did not assume sufficient authority over the new state corporations to co-ordinate adequately their activities. And the directors of the SGF apparently allowed the novelty of their mixed enterprise to drive them to excessive caution.[7]

The relative failure, at least in the short term, of these efforts to transform the role of Francophones within the Quebec economy was to have serious consequences for Quebec's social and political stability. As the educational reforms began to have an effect, Quebec schools started to produce larger numbers of graduates who had both the qualifications for assuming white-collar positions within the economy and the aspirations to assume such positions. Given the failure of the Quiet Revolution economic policies to expand rapidly the opportunities open to them in Quebec's sector, many of these graduates were bound to be frustrated. Such frustrations could easily be generalized into attacks on the political order. There are risks for governments that accelerate development in one sector of society without being able to induce comparable development in others.

However variable may have been the successes of the new programs of the Lesage regime, they necessarily involved changes in the structures of the Quebec government. During the early 1960s, the Quebec civil service expanded rapidly. Between 1960 and 1966, six new ministries, nine consultative councils, three regulatory bodies, eight public enterprises, and one administrative tribunal were created. The total number of such institutions rose from thirty-nine to sixty-four.[8] The personnel employed in the civil service (i.e., excluding public enterprises) grew by 42.6 per cent during 1960-65, rising from 29,298 to 41,847.[9] The personnel employed in public enterprises (excluding Hydro-Québec and the Société des Alcools) grew by 93 per cent over these five years, rising from 7,468 to 14,411. In each case, these were the largest increases experienced in any five-year period between 1945 and 1970.[10]

This greatly expanded civil service began to take on the character of an independent bureaucracy – organized according to bureaucratic principles, requiring professional qualifications for appointment and promotion, and exercising considerable decision-making power. In fact, by the mid-1960s there was a widespread popular fear that the Quebec government had become a "technocracy" in which top civil servants, rather than the elected officials, were the dominant force. To be sure, these fears were not really founded: the independent power of the bureaucrats was still quite circumscribed by the elected officeholders and their immediate personnel; often, the initiatives proposed by bureaucrats were cancelled out by the opposing proposals of other bureaucrats; and the decisions that top bureaucrats did succeed in imposing were not always based solely on non-political, technical criteria. In part, this popular perception of a new "technocracy" was due to the failure of citizens to identify with the new programs the Quebec government was pursuing. But it also reflected the changing character and new importance of Quebec's civil service.

Our survey of the initiatives of the Lesage administration suggests that with the 1960s the lag of political change behind social and economic change was at last substantially reduced. Through the creation of new governmental and para-governmental institutions, the scope and penetration of governmental activities was very much expanded – political modernization had finally begun.

136

At least one observer, relying on analysis of governmental expenditures rather than on institutional change, disputes this characterization of the 1960s as a period of unprecedented change in the Quebec government. After a careful analysis of the allocation of provincial government expenditures over the period 1945-70, Daniel Latouche[11] argues that the Lesage administration did not constitute a radical departure from the past; rather, it acted on the same conception of the role of government as had previous provincial administrations. The priorities reflected in the budgets of the Lesage regime were essentially the same as those of the Duplessis administrations of the 1950s. According to Latouche, the real shift in budgetary priorities occurred over the period 1945-50, when "natural resources" was de-emphasized as an area of expenditure and "education" and "health" received new emphasis. While there was a marked increase in the overall level of expenditures during the Lesage years, the distribution of these expenditures over various categories was not significantly changed from previous years.

Latouche's analysis, with its reliance on expenditure patterns, seems to miss the essence of political modernization – the shift of power and authority to the state. In these terms, the Lesage administration was indeed acting on a different conception of the role of the state, seeking to expand its power over the ultimate use made of public funds. We found that prior to the 1960s a large part of the decision-making power within the fields of education and welfare rested not with the provincial government but with private bodies, especially those of the Church. In the case of public schools, for instance, the provincial government subsidized the construction of school facilities, but effective control over the content of the education given within these buildings lay with the clergy. It is not surprising that in the post-war years the provincial government found it necessary to devote larger and larger proportions of its revenues to supporting education and welfare activities. The needs of the growing urban populations required greater expenditures and the institutions the Church had created to serve these needs had become increasingly aggressive in seeking government financial support. Nevertheless, the Lesage administration was indeed acting on a quite different conception of its role when, with the establishment of a Ministry of Education and the expansion of its own welfare programs, it sought to place these areas directly under government control. In terms of the concentration of power and authority in the state, the Lesage administration did represent a radical departure from previous administrations and brought a significant measure of political modernization.

A more telling critique of the overall significance of the political modernization of the Quiet Revolution focuses on the comparison of these measures with the pattern of government elsewhere in North America. It is argued, with some exaggeration, that the concrete changes of the Quiet Revolution offered little in the way of originality or innovation. Moreover, these reforms did not expand the role of the state beyond what already existed elsewhere in North America.[12] In education, health, welfare, and social security the new institutions established during the six years of the Lesage regime merely brought Quebec into conformity with the North American model of what government should be doing in these areas. It was only to the extent that the new Quebec initiatives in health, welfare, and social security involved the acquisition of responsibilities previously held by the federal government, and divested the Church of power and authority, that they were "radical." Similarly, the various economic initiatives of the Lesage administration did not question the predominant North American model of a basically "free enterprise" economy. The only instance of outright nationalization was the case of Hydro-Québec; here Quebec was merely following a precedent long ago established by other provinces. Otherwise, the main thrust of Quebec's activities was to strengthen or create Francophone enterprises, usually with a mix of public and private ownership. The autonomy of American and English-Canadian corporations remained intact.

Yet, however much the content of these Quiet Revolution initiatives might have accorded with the dominant North American models of the "welfare state" and the "private enterprise" economy, these programs were to have dramatic effects on Quebec society and, indirectly, on the Canadian political system.

In terms of the structure of Quebec society, perhaps the most profound change wrought by the Quiet Revolution was the radical decline in the Church's status and influence. The Church's pre-eminent role in shaping the pedagogy and structure of Quebec's educational system was indeed broken, as was its formal control over the provision of health and social services. With the loss of its privileged role within these critical spheres of Francophone life, so the Church's general influence in French Quebec was bound to decline. So also to decline was its capacity to attract young Francophones into its orders: more attractive opportunities now existed elsewhere – especially in the structures of the Quebec state. For reasons such as these, the Church found it increasingly difficult not only to recruit new clergy but even to retain existing ones. Around 1960, there were 8,400 priests in Quebec; by 1981 the number had fallen to 4,285. Within the religious communities, total membership fell from 45,253 in 1961 to 29,173 in 1978. The communities composed of men declined by 75 per cent.[13]

These structural changes in turn helped to engender a radical change in the relationship between Quebec Francophones and their Church. Even if they remained formally Catholic, Francophones were much less inclined to pursue religious practices with the rigour that had marked the past. Attendance at mass dropped dramatically during the 1960s. Between 1961 and 1971 it fell from 61 per cent to 30 per cent in the Montreal diocese and from 65 per cent to 27 per cent in the St. Jean diocese. By the end of the 1970s it was oscillating between 37 per cent and 45 per cent for Quebec Catholics as a whole.[14]

The declining influence of the Church must also have contributed to the radical decline in Quebec's birth rate. Historically the province with the highest birth rate in Canada, Quebec soon had the lowest. In 1956, Quebec's fertility rate was still at the very high level of 3.98 children per couple. Yet, over the years 1959-72, it plummeted 56 per cent, falling below the rate of 2.1 needed to maintain the population size.[15] The decline in the Church's status and authority was not alone responsible for this trend. Its primary sources may well have been the long-term effect of conversion from the rural lifestyle and the self-sufficient family farm, with its labour needs, combined with the sudden arrival of new contraceptive techniques. But as a result of the changes of the Quiet Revolution, the Church was no longer in a position to hope to counter such influences.

The political modernization of the Quiet Revolution restructured Quebec society in other ways as well. In the next chapter, we will trace in detail how it accentuated social divisions and resulted in a new presence of these divisions in Quebec's political life. For the moment, we need to explore the immediate impact the Quiet Revolution had on the functioning of the Canadian federal system.

Quebec and the Canadian Federal System

The new Lesage administration led Quebec with a quite different set of goals in its relations with Ottawa. Its commitment to a much more active state meant that the old strategy for dealing with Ottawa was no longer acceptable. The mere exclusion of the federal government from provincial jurisdictions could no longer be the only goal. It was now important that Quebec be able to use these jurisdictions actively to institute its new programs of modernization. To do so required massive expenditure, straining the fiscal resources then available to Quebec. Moreover, as Quebec did develop new programs it found, in many instances, that it was frustrated by conflicting federal programs that might be clearly within federal jurisdiction. Thus, however conventional the initiatives of the Lesage administration might appear to be in retrospect, they called for a radically different strategy in federal-provincial relations. Because of its commitment to political modernization, Quebec was forced to challenge more and more of the established procedures of Canadian federalism.

Some of the specific demands, such as provincial primacy over direct taxation, were not unique to the Lesage regime; they had already been articulated in the 1950s by the Tremblay Commission and even by the Quebec government itself. However, this commonality between the Tremblay Commission and the Quiet Revolution should not be exaggerated.[16] In the hands of the Lesage government, the demands were linked to an interventionist conception of the role of the Quebec state, very different from that of either the Tremblay Commission or the Duplessis regime. Consequently, they acquired far greater urgency. Rather than being simple struggles over the definition of governmental jurisdiction, they were struggles over the exercise of governmental power. By the same token, leading members of the Lesage regime ultimately were led by their goals of political modernization to suggest that a new federal order was necessary. As we shall see later, other political forces were led by the same reasoning to call for even the dissolution of Canadian federalism. For its part, the Tremblay Commission had been able to retain the existing BNA Act as its frame of reference; rather than revision of the Act, the Commission had simply wanted a more "faithful" adherence to it.

The federal programs of expenditure within provincial jurisdictions became an immediate issue. At an October, 1960, federal-provincial conference, Jean Lesage declared that Quebec would now avail itself "on a temporary basis" of the federal programs in which it was not then participating. At the same time, Lesage demanded that the federal government withdraw completely from all such spending programs, with fiscal compensation to the provinces.[17] Quite simply, Quebec could no longer afford to forgo federal funds in the name of provincial autonomy; it needed the funds and demanded, in the name of provincial autonomy, to receive them without federal condition or sponsorship. The basis for the arrangement Quebec demanded – to be known as "opting-out" – had in fact already been laid during the last days of the Union nationale government when Paul Sauvé, and then Antonio Barrette, had succeeded Duplessis as Prime Minister. Under the University Finance Agreement of 1959, the federal government withdrew by 1 per cent from the corporate income tax field so that Quebec could, through its own corporate income tax, acquire revenue equivalent to what Quebec universities would have received if they had been allowed to participate in the federal program of support to universities. (Adjustments would be made each year to ensure that Quebec continued to receive an equivalent amount of funds in this fashion.)[18] The precedent had been set: a province could refuse to participate in a federal program without incurring financial loss. (According to Donald Smiley, this formula is unique among federal systems.)[19] In the hands of the aggressive Lesage regime, the precedent was used to claim a far-ranging shift of responsibilities from Ottawa to Quebec. Quebec demanded that opting-out agreements be extended to a large number of existing federal programs that touched on what it claimed to be the exclusively provincial jurisdictions of health, education, and social welfare. In cases when it became known that Ottawa was planning a new program in these areas, Quebec would immediately establish its own program to occupy the field first and then would claim compensation when the federal program was instituted.

During the early 1960s Ottawa agreed to many of these demands. The opting-out formula was applied to a large number of federal-provincial cost-shared programs as well as to programs funded elsewhere and administered exclusively by the federal government. The federal government tried hard, however, to maintain control of a proposed universal contributory pension plan. Nevertheless, at a stormy federal-provincial conference in Quebec City, Quebec succeeded in getting Ottawa to agree to still another opting-out. In the other nine provinces, the federal government would administer a Canada Pension Plan; Quebec would have its own Quebec Pension Plan.

In a sense, many of these arrangements had merely symbolic value. In each case, while disclaiming any responsibility to do so, Quebec implemented a program similar to the federal program from which it had opted out. Thus, funds were being spent for the exact purpose that Ottawa had wished. At the same time, these arrangements did afford some concrete advantages for Quebec. Opting out from exclusively federal programs helped to support the development of Quebec's bureaucratic structure. The Quebec government was able to increase the services and benefits it provided directly to the Quebec population. Beyond whatever electoral advantages this might have entailed, it also could only increase popular support for Quebec's claim that Québécois should look to it to meet their needs. In the case of the pension plan, Quebec secured a new source of funds at a time when it was having real difficulty in meeting the financial burden that political modernization had entailed. Finally, opting-out, whether from exclusively federal programs or from federal-provincial programs, helped legitimize the idea that Quebec had special needs and responsibilities beyond those of the other provinces. Even though each of these opportunities to "opt out" was made available to *all* the provinces, Quebec was the only one to take advantage of them. On a *de facto* basis, Quebec had already acquired a "special status."[20]

Beyond the widespread application of the opting-out formula, Quebec had other major demands to make on the Canadian federal system. While Quebec was less spectacularly successful in these other demands, they, too, reflected the new positive role of government embraced by the Lesage administration. Finding itself increasingly hindered by the economic costs of its new initiatives – especially in education – Quebec sought a readjustment in the share of tax revenues acquired by Ottawa and Quebec. It alleged that the federal government had occupied too large a share of the tax fields. If Quebec were to meet *its* responsibilities, the federal government would have to reduce the taxes it imposed. Also, Quebec sought to have recognition of its right to be consulted before the federal government took action within areas of recognized federal jurisdiction. Finally, Quebec sought the right to sign treaties with foreign countries on matters lying within provincial jurisdiction.

In summary, the long-standing contention of Quebec governmental elites that only Quebec could be entrusted with the distinctive interests of French Canadians came to have radically different implications for Canadian federalism when it was combined with a new positive conception of the role of government. The Lesage administration's attack on the assumptions and procedures of Canadian federalism was wide-ranging and was conducted with an energy and a purpose never before experienced. The rhetorical assaults of Taschereau and Duplessis seem very pale in comparison. In principle, there was no limit to the demands this neo-nationalism could make on Canadian federalism. In what areas of governmental activity were *no* distinct French-Canadian interests involved? If the whole of Quebec society was to undergo a *rattrapage* and if Québécois were to become *maîtres chez nous*, what responsibilities could still be left with the federal government?

The Lesage administration did not explicitly answer these questions. It appears that most of its members were still committed to a federal system, although there was uncertainty among them as to whether Quebec needed a new formal division of powers or merely "stricter" observance of the existing division of powers. The ambiguity surrounding its position on Canadian federalism, coupled with the more radical positions that other elements in Quebec had been led to adopt (partly by the Lesage regime's example), caused a deep unease in English Canada. In the short term this unease helped to foster a readiness on behalf of the federal government to accommodate Quebec's demands. But this federal accommodation did not still the demands for greater change in the system. The basic issue remained: What powers did a Quebec government need if it were to be *moteur principal* of Quebec's social and economic development? Through the ideology of political modernization it articulated and through the concrete demands it made on the federal system, the Lesage administration raised questions that went to the very heart of the Canadian political community. The continuing preoccupation of many Québécois with these questions through the 1970s was one of the major legacies of the Quiet Revolution.

Sources of the Quiet Revolution

While we can fairly readily establish the general outline of the new nationalist ideology of the Quiet Revolution and trace the expansion of the Quebec state that the ideology served to legitimize, it is much more difficult to isolate the specific factors that produced these profound changes at that particular point in time. To be sure, we can identify specific events that made political change possible: first, the death of Maurice Duplessis in 1959 and then the victory of the Liberals in 1960, under Jean Lesage. No longer was the Quebec state in the grip of a premier, and a political party, strongly adverse to state expansion and intervention. While the new Liberal cabinet did include such individuals as Bona Arsenault, a veteran of provincial politics whose political world view probably was not significantly different from Duplessis's, it also included members such as Paul-Gérin Lajoie and René Lévesque, who were deeply committed to political modernization and who were able to persuade other ministers, and the Premier, to adopt their projects.[21] Moreover, its electoral base was firmly rooted in urban Quebec, where the pressures for state expansion were the greatest. By 1962, 59 per cent of the Liberal *députés* came from districts that were more than 60 per cent urban.[22] In fact, 29 per cent of the Liberal *députés* were from Montreal or Quebec City (the comparable figure for the Union nationale in 1956 was 15 per cent).[23]

This greater openness of the Liberal regime to political and social change, however, does not tell us why the government pursued specific directions of change during the Quiet Revolution, nor does it explain the intensity with which the Lesage Liberals pursued them. In particular, it does not tell us why both the dominant ideology and the state-building of the 1960s should have been pervaded by such a strong nationalism: a distinctly *Québécois* nationalism.

We did see how during the 1950s some Francophones were actively championing a new interventionist role for the Quebec state. In publications such as *Cité libre* and *Le Devoir*, in forums such as the Institut canadien des affaires publiques, and among the leadership of the CTCC and FUIQ union federations, there had been growing demands for expansion of the role of the Quebec state.

However, these demands were not necessarily framed in nationalist terms. In fact, in many cases they were voiced in direct opposition to French-Canadian nationalism, which was quite credibly presented as tied to traditional values and social structures and bound by suspicion of state intervention. There was little to suggest that nationalism might instead become the basis for legitimizing intervention by the Quebec state. And the advocacy of state intervention did not necessarily entail the celebration of social and economic development that became the hallmark of the Quiet Revolution. How is it, then, that with the 1960s the Quebec state came to be perceived, and to present itself, not only as the essential instrument to respond to and even accelerate social and economic change, but as the central institution of a distinct Québécois nation? How is it that social and economic development became a national project?

One approach to the question would be to look to Quebec's place within the larger Canadian system. For instance, during the post-World War II years there were developments in the federal government that could have reinforced traditional Quebec concerns for provincial autonomy. As we have already seen, in the name of fostering a national culture and reducing social and economic disparities the federal government involved itself in a variety of areas assigned to the provinces under the BNA Act: health, social security, and even post-secondary education. Yet, the new

Quebec nationalism demanded more than simply an end to these measures. Unlike Duplessis and his colleagues, who had merely called upon Ottawa to respect the division of powers agreed upon at Confederation, the nationalists of the 1960s called for a radical revision of the division of powers itself.

Rather than the particular circumstances of the post-war period, one might turn to long-standing French-Canadian grievances against the federal government. Even then, however, it is difficult to understand the nationalist surge of the 1960s. For instance, one could point to the historical underrepresentation of French Canadians within federal institutions. As we have already seen, prior to the 1960s French Canadians had been largely absent from key cabinet positions, especially those with economic responsibility, and their presence in the upper levels of the federal public service had always been well below their proportion of the Canadian population as a whole. Presumably, exclusion at the federal level could have led French Canadians to focus on the provincial Quebec government and to call upon it to adopt a new interventionist role as a "national" government. Yet, precisely because this was a long-standing condition it is difficult to explain the neo-nationalism of the 1960s in terms of it. After all, the pattern had been set soon after Confederation. In fact, representation in the upper levels of the public service actually worsened after World War I, with the introduction of the merit principle. Not until the 1960s, however, did there emerge a widespread nationalist movement to expand the powers of the Quebec government.

To be sure, in the late 1950s and early 1960s, under the Progressive Conservative government of John Diefenbaker, French Canadians were relegated to an especially marginal role, but this was only an accentuation of a long-established pattern. Moreover, as we shall see, Quebec neo-nationalism continued to grow even after the return to power of the Liberals under Lester Pearson, who actively sought to expand the Francophone presence in Ottawa well above the historical norm. Apparently, more was involved than simply a reaction to underrepresentation in Ottawa.

The same type of difficulty would arise if one instead focused on grievances against the treatment that French-Canadian minorities have received from the other provincial governments. Some have argued that the historical refusal of these governments to provide French-language services, especially education, and the failure of the federal government to seek any remedy explain the new readiness of Quebec Francophones to rally to the idea of a distinct Québécois nation. Yet here, too, the pattern had been set for many decades. Provincial denial of French-language rights had begun in 1890, with the Manitoba government abolishing the use of French in the legislative assembly, the civil service, and the courts and eliminating the denominational school system under which French instruction had been possible. In 1912, Ontario enacted Regulation 17, which required that English be the sole language of instruction after the third year.[24] Some additional element to these grievances must have been necessary for the rise of neo-nationalism in the 1960s. In fact, Quebec neo-nationalism continued to flourish even after actions had been taken by both federal and provincial governments to redress these historical grievances.

Another way to explain the neo-nationalist surge would be in terms of Quebec's position within the Canadian economy. Thus, it might be argued that the neo-nationalist movement was a response to Quebec's economic disadvantage relative to Ontario, the other heavily industrialized province. As we have already seen, in the 1950s average income was markedly lower in Quebec than in Ontario and unemployment was higher. By the same token, Quebec's industrial structure was more labour-intensive than Ontario's. Once again, though, the conditions in question are long-standing ones. Compared with the rest of Canada, per capita income in Quebec has remained roughly constant since at least 1926. Quebec's share of Canadian manufacturing activity, weighted by its share of the Canadian population, has remained roughly the same since 1870; Ontario's share has grown over that period but the difference between Ontario's share and Quebec's share has been essentially the same since 1915. During this century the distribution of Quebec's labour force among industrial sectors has been transformed, but in close parallel with changes elsewhere in Canada.[25] By the same token, Ontario's ascendancy in capital-intensive, technologically sophisticated industry can be traced to the early decades of this century with the establishment of American branch plants. It is difficult, therefore, to find within Quebec's economic disadvantage the factors that triggered the neo-nationalist surge. If anything, Quebec's relative position improved in the post-war years. Only with the latter half of the 1960s did deterioration begin to set in.[26]

In sum, such factors as the treatment of Francophones within Canadian political institutions or the uneven development of the Canadian economy may well have constituted preconditions to Quebec neo-nationalism, fostering a predisposition for Francophones in Quebec to focus on their provincial institutions. But as chronic conditions of long duration they cannot themselves explain the neo-nationalist surge. And particular post-war developments such as Ottawa's centralizing thrust cannot explain the emergence of a nationalist ideology that sought not to restore a prior state of affairs but to institute a fundamentally different order. Some additional factor was necessary for the historical provincial autonomism of Quebec Francophones to be transformed into the belief that the Quebec government should be the highly interventionist state of not a province but a distinct Quebec nation.

One might try to locate this factor in the processes of decolonization sweeping Asia and Africa in the 1950s and 1960s. Conceivably, the example of these colonial societies freeing themselves from overseas imperial powers, especially Britain, might have encouraged Québécois to see their own society as a colony of the rest of Canada, if not of Britain, and to conclude that the time had come for its full liberation. As we shall see, some intellectuals, especially writers in Parti pris, did try to popularize such an analysis. For his part, René Lévesque drew upon the parallel when he portrayed Montreal Anglophones as "Westmount Rhodesians." Yet, references to the decolonization movement were not a central theme in the Quiet Revolution discourse. In fact, rather than identification with Third World colonial societies, neo-nationalist rhetoric was more concerned with the recovery of Quebec's own lost links to its original colonial metropole, France – which was, during this period, the object of so many anti-imperialist struggles. In any event, even if we should decide that the example of decolonization movements was compelling to Quebec neo-nationalists, we would still not be able to *explain* their neo-nationalism. We would still need to know *why* they found it appropriate to see their situation in these terms. In particular, we need to know which Québécois were attracted to such an analysis, and what within their own condition made it so attractive.

The New Middle Class and the Ideology of the Quiet Revolution

To explain the rise of neo-nationalism we need to turn from Quebec's place within the larger Canadian system, and from the international scene, to changes occurring within Quebec society itself.[27] We have already traced in detail how French Quebec's social structure and economy underwent profound changes during the first half of this century. We identified a variety of ways these changes could have led to a re-examination of established conceptions of political life and the role of the state. Beyond that we saw how, during the 1940s and 1950s, there arose within French Quebec a new social category, a new middle class, which was actively calling for greater state intervention. According to many analysts, this class in turn became the bearers of the neo-nationalist ideology of the Quiet Revolution.

It is not difficult to see why the Francophone new middle class should have strongly subscribed to the Quiet Revolution belief in the desirability of social and economic development and in the interventionist state. They had trained themselves in sciences that promised the capacity to understand and manipulate these processes of development. Moreover, their claim to status and power was based on superior qualifications to occupy executive positions within the institutions that accompanied economic and social development.

At first glance, the new middle class's attraction to an intense Québécois nationalism might seem less readily understandable. One might expect that their training would have undermined any identification with French Canada. After all, the new knowledge and technique were to a considerable extent "imported" from other societies. On this basis, the new middle class might have been oriented primarily to the sources of this new knowledge, especially the United States. They might even have been ill at ease within French-Canadian society; to some extent their professions would have made them "marginal men" among their own people. Nonetheless, several aspects of the condition of this new middle class explain its attraction to a new Québécois nationalism.

Perhaps the most obvious is language. For most elements of the new middle class, work activity consists largely of communication, whether of ideas and information, as with the intellectuals, or of policies and directives, as with administrators. There is every reason to believe that in the 1960s, as in the 1980s, most new-middle-class Québécois were not only predisposed to use French when expressing ideas and disseminating information but, by any reasonable standard, were in fact better able to do so in French. It was the language of their general education, and probably of their professional training as well. And it is the language in which most other aspects of their lives were conducted. On this basis, then, effectiveness in their professions was contingent on being able to deal with other Francophones, whether students in a classroom, viewers of television, or colleagues in an organization. Thus, they would have an especially strong preoccupation with the strength and persistence of French-Canadian society and of the quality of the French language. They would be especially likely to identify with the primary site of this society: Quebec.

Second, given their commitment to social and economic development, the new middle class naturally sought major social and economic reforms for this society. As we have seen, by many standards French Canada fell short. It was only natural that they would look to the Quebec government, rather than Ottawa, to bring about these changes:

> Leaders of socio-economic movements, journalists, academics formed an alliance which sought to promote a perspective that was collectivist and nationalist, seeking to conserve society as a whole and concerned with its central institutions and cultural identity.[28]

Beyond these general features of its condition as a new middle class, more specific ones related to its conflicts with other classes: namely, the Church and the Anglophone business community. In both cases, these conflicts would have been conducive to support for a neo-nationalist ideology, centred on intervention by the Quebec state.

First, the new middle class was caught up in struggles with the clergy. In Chapter Four we saw how within universities there was a growing struggle between lay intellectuals and Church authorities. There is every reason to believe that antagonisms were also developing within Church-controlled bureaucracies. While the Church provided a first opportunity for this class by opening up administrative positions in its various institutions, the clergy still sought to maintain ultimate control over the institutions. Lay bureaucrats were to work on behalf of clerical interests, modernizing institutions so that the Church could continue to hold ultimate authority over such matters as education, health, and welfare. Over the short term this strategy worked; the position of the traditional elites was reinforced by the activities of the new middle class. Over the long run, however, it was doomed. Given the middle class's superior qualifications for administering large organizations and, in general, adapting French-Canadian institutions to social and economic development, the new middle class was increasingly impatient with any clerical authority. At the same time, as the institutions of the Church became more bureaucratized and were led to a greater extent by lay personnel, the spiritual authority of the Church among French Canadians in general could only decline.[29]

Thus, the new middle class had every incentive to seek total public control over health, education, and welfare institutions. Nationalism could be a useful tool in this struggle. Through the new model of the nation as a secular, technological society, the new middle class could use nationalism to legitimize its own aspirations. The seizure by the middle class of French-Canadian social institutions was no longer simply a projection of class aspirations; it was necessary to the *l'épanouissement* of a national collectivity.

The same struggle for power also wedded new-middle-class aspirations to the Quebec provincial government. First, these Church-related institutions were largely dependent on public revenue; certainly the resources of the Church were not adequate to the kind of institutional development the new middle class had in mind. As the primary responsibility for health, welfare, and education lay with the provincial government, it would be only natural for the new middle class to champion a stronger Quebec government with, in particular, a greater share of fiscal resources. Second, as the Quebec provincial government held nominal authority over the Church-related institutions, it was a logical tool in the middle class's strategy for securing control of these institutions. As bureaucrats within the provincial government, the new middle class could use the authority of the Quebec provincial government to displace the clergy and bring these institutions directly under its control. These actions could be presented as a process of "democratization" in which "privately held" institutions would be made responsible to the people through their elected representatives in government.

The class appears to have had other aspirations that would have led even more directly to a strong Quebec nationalism. The professional qualifications of the new middle class also constituted a claim to managerial positions within economic enterprises. But it appeared that French Canadians were barred from entering the upper levels of Anglophone-owned corporations, which represented the vast bulk of managerial positions within Quebec's economy. Through nationalism, the new middle class could legitimize various governmental programs that would create new opportunity for Francophones to assume managerial positions. Programs such as the nationalization of the Anglophone-owned electrical utility companies could be presented as necessary to the advancement of the Quebec nation, giving it control over industries that are critical in the construction of a technological society.

The Francophone new middle class thus appears to have had strong motivations for adopting the Quiet Revolution neo-nationalist ideology and being its primary advocate. Firmly committed to economic and social development, and to state intervention to ensure that development, the new middle class was at the same time singularly bound to French-language institutions. Moreover, its struggles with other classes, whether the clergy or the Anglophone business class, led it inexorably to the belief that the functions of the Quebec government must be vastly expanded. Only in this way could Quebec's cultural division of labour be broken. For the new middle class, then, the struggle to raise the economic and social welfare of Quebec Francophones became a national project. The instrument through which this was to be achieved could only be the *national* state of Quebec.

The members of this class did not *create* Quebec nationalism. French-Canadian nationalism, after all, can be traced back to the 1820s. All the new middle class did was to recast this national consciousness into a more "modern" and more explicitly Québécois mould. Nor should this class be seen as motivated solely by the rational calculation of class interest. Through training and professional experience they simply had come to acquire a new conception of Francophone society and its needs. The entrenched position of clerical and Anglophone business elites was not just an obstacle to class mobility, it was an affront to the vision of the Quebec nation that stemmed from new-middle-class values.[30]

Over recent years this line of explanation, focusing on a new middle class as bearers of the neo-nationalist Quiet Revolution ideology and instigators of the expansion of the Quebec state, has been seriously questioned. Some of these "revisionists" have even gone so far as to deny any role for the new middle class in instigating the Quiet Revolution.

In the most sweeping of these revisionist critiques, William Coleman claims that "during the critical period of this explanation, 1959 to 1965, it is very doubtful that these circumstances existed." First, Coleman denies outright that the Francophone new middle class even existed prior to the Quiet Revolution: "If one examines closely Quebec's institutions at the end of the 1950s, one finds little evidence of individuals having a position in society that would form the structural base of a new middle class."[31] The new middle class, he contends, should be seen as a product of the Quiet Revolution rather than an instigator of it:

In some sense, it is more sensibly argued that the new middle class was a product of the reforms of the 1960s than their instigator. The provincial state, in rationalizing the education and social service systems and in founding a series of public corporations during the 1960s, may have created this class in its wake.[32]

Yet, this claim is based on a serious underestimation of the degree of social and ideological change Quebec underwent in the 1940s and 1950s and even earlier.[33] After all, in the previous chapter we saw ample evidence of Francophones assuming a variety of new-middle-class positions during the 1950s and earlier – whether as intellectuals, administrators, or technicians – outside the structures of the Quebec state. Coleman wonders how such a Francophone new middle class could have obtained their "modern social science knowledge" since they had been trained under "the traditional classics-oriented educational system."[34] We saw, however, that during the 1940s and 1950s substantial numbers of individuals were indeed being trained in modern social science by institutions such as Laval's Faculté des sciences sociales. Moreover, we saw that by the early 1950s a viable community of Francophone biological and chemical scientists had emerged, the result of concerted efforts by both Laval and Université de Montréal that date back to the 1920s. Beyond that, we noted that for decades l'École des hautes commerciales had been training Francophones in administrative techniques and l'École polytechnique had been training Francophones as engineers.

For that matter, the entry of large numbers of new-middle-class Francophones into the Quebec state can be traced from the very beginning of the Quiet Revolution. The Quebec public service had contained only nine trained social science professionals before 1955; between 1955 and 1959 it had acquired only seven more. Yet, between 1960 and 1962, thirty-eight social science professionals were recruited. In 1963, eighty-five more were added. And in 1965, an additional 185 were recruited, of which sixty-nine were economists and forty had degrees in industrial relations.[35] Clearly, the new middle class was not a product of the Quiet Revolution reforms, although it certainly was strengthened and expanded by them. A Francophone new middle class had already taken form well before the Quiet Revolution; in fact, only through the rapid entry of a Francophone new middle class into the Quebec state could the reforms have been possible.[36]

Coleman doubts also that a new middle class could have acted as "a conscious political agent" during the period 1959 to 1965. Yet, in the last chapter we saw evidence of new-middle-class Francophones doing precisely that, campaigning for a wide variety of state initiatives through essentially new-middle-class forums: university institutes like Laval's Faculté des sciences sociales, periodicals such as *Cité libre,* and voluntary associations such as the Institut public des affaires canadiens. As for the new-middle-class administrators housed within Church bureaucracies, Guindon points to a common widespread resentment against the Duplessis regime, reflecting their structural position. Along with their clerical overlords, "the salaried professionals of the clerical bureaucracies" were offended by the old Duplessis style of personalist, patronage politics:

> Though completely unaware of the structural reasons that linked them to the new deal [with the Sauvé regime] they responded in unison. From sheer structural location, and bureaucratic socialization, they felt that the proper ways were the ways of bureaucracy. They felt uneasy with the old rural game of politics. They felt that it brought shame to the province. The leader of the government was depicted as a dictator, a tyrant having a corrupting influence on political mores.[37]

Apparently, despite Coleman's contention, the fragmentation of these institutions among different religious orders did not inhibit the development of such a common reaction.

However, Coleman bases his contention primarily on the notion that "individuals tend to be mobilized as a class only in opposition to other classes"; he claims that there is little evidence of a new middle class struggling against "a traditional middle class of clerics, farmers, doctors and lawyers."[38] To that effect, Coleman notes that in 1959 Guindon portrayed the new middle class working in harmony with their clerical superiors, enabling the Church to maintain formal control over key social institutions. Yet, we have just noted how this harmony had been eroding over the 1950s. Also, in the last chapter we noted the conflicts between lay professors, especially social scientists, and clerics, as at Laval's Faculté des sciences sociales.

Moreover, once the Lesage regime was in power, conflict between new-middle-class Francophones and the clergy quickly became manifest and displayed all the earmarks of a "class struggle." For this to happen, new-middle-class resentment of the clergy must have existed for some time. Especially striking is the instance of educational reform, where there is ample evidence of bitter conflict between clerics and the new-middle-class intellectuals. In fact, Coleman's own study presents the Francophone new middle class as one of three classes campaigning for educational reform.[39] The structural existence of a Francophone new middle class with a clear political consciousness emerges very clearly from his account of the struggle for reform in this area. The Mouvement laïque de langue française, which was founded in April, 1961 – *at the beginning* of the Quiet Revolution – became a vehicle for new-middle-class attacks on clerical control of education:

> Although it is difficult to gauge accurately, the MLF probably drew most heavily from what might be termed a new middle class. It included professors in the social sciences, authors of less established rank, and journalists. . . . The attacks by the MLF on the church's ideology and on church-controlled institutions helped lift the debate involved into a wider public forum. They also elicited a vigorous response from the church and from traditional nationalists, who interpreted them as attacks on the foundations of French-Canadian civilization.[40]

Growing pressures on the Quebec state to displace the clergy from its positions of authority can be seen in another component of the Francophone new middle class: the social work profession. In the words of one close student of the emergence of the Quebec welfare state, Frédéric Lesemann, "a new wave of university-trained social workers arrived in the field during the 1950s and was soon to attempt to overthrow the tutelage of the Church over institutions of public assistance."[41] Considerable detail is available on the experiences of this particular new-middle-class category.

As Gilbert Renaud demonstrates in *l'Éclatement de la profession en service social*,[42] the emergence of lay social workers in social welfare institutions can be traced back to the 1930s. When, in 1938, the Church's Conseil des oeuvres de Montréal established its Bureau d'assistance aux familles in Montreal it hired on a part-time basis individuals who were taking courses at McGill's Montreal School of Social Work. This was the first time that salaried personnel were hired for Church-related social institutions. At the same time, the Church sought to establish its own institutions for training social workers, culminating in the creation of an École de service social at the Université de Montréal and another one at Université Laval. With the 1940s, there was a "massive" entry of lay social workers into the Church's social institutions. The role of social workers in Quebec was greatly strengthened by a 1947 amendment to the federal family allowance law, which specified that allowances to children in institutions must be recommended and administered by professional social workers.[43] And professional social workers assumed central roles in the Cours du Bien-être social (Social Welfare Court) and the Écoles de protection de la jeunesse (Schools for Youth Protection), which the Quebec government created in 1950.[44]

Even if the Church had been able to assume direction over the training of many of these Francophone social workers, by the 1950s they had become well aware of the extent to which clerical control of social welfare institutions in Quebec restricted their professional autonomy. In 1957, an article in *Service social*, their professional journal, declared that:

> the members of boards of directors of our agencies are not necessarily social workers, but men and women chosen for the most part outside the profession. Here, as in most places, social workers are considered as employees of an agency and not those with primary responsibility.[45]

In effect, Renaud argues, the 1950s were:

> a period of conflict over control of social services: on one side the Church, even if it supports the development of social service professionals, is no less committed to keeping this organization under its tutelage; on the other side, the transformations in the operations of these agencies weaken clerical control and favour the rise of members of the new petty bourgeoisie [social workers] who in one way or another succeed in imposing themselves.[46]

Finally, in February, 1960, Quebec social workers formed a professional organization, la Corporation des travailleurs sociaux professionnels de la province de Québec, as part of their effort to "professionalize" social work and to free it from the influence of religious ideology and from clerical institutional control.

The leaders of the social work profession clearly saw state intervention as the essential means through which they could secure this autonomy. Thus, they welcomed greater state involvement in social services. The previously cited 1957 article in *Service social* also declared:

In our society, the institutions and social services charged with social welfare have always remained private to the greatest extent possible. It was presumed that the communitarian solution to the problems which individuals and families face is more adequate, and much more humane, than that provided by state enterprises. However, growing needs and social dependence caused by economic conditions make it indisputable that support and even intervention by the state have become more and more necessary and will have to be more and more substantial.[47]

And a year later, Claude Morin (who, with the Quiet Revolution, would become a leading mandarin in the Quebec state) wrote in the same journal: "[the social worker] sees a new stabilizing and constructive dimension to the role of the state and is able to appreciate the effectiveness of social, spending, and taxation measures, adopted or proposed."[48]

In their efforts, the social workers were strongly supported by a committee of inquiry (the Boucher Committee, of which Morin himself was a member) established by the Quebec state in 1961 to study the rising costs of state support for Quebec's social welfare institutions (which remained in private hands). The report, tabled in 1963, went well beyond its original mandate to champion the notion of social work as a profession, requiring formal, "scientific" training. Not only did it insist that the Ministry of Family and Social Work equip itself with social service professionals, but it argued that the rising costs of social assistance could be controlled only by going to the "root of the problem." This entailed expansion of the programs of prevention and rehabilitation that only social workers were equipped to undertake. Beyond that, the committee challenged clerical control of social service institutions by recommending that the state assume direct responsibility for the management of public assistance funds. The Lesage government implemented these recommendations over the next two years.[49]

Beyond the new-middle-class opposition to the clergy, there is considerable evidence as well of its mobilization against another class: Anglophone business. After all, attacks on English-Canadian and American capital were a central thrust of le Rassemblement pour l'indépendance nationale, founded in September, 1960. For instance, it organized a mass demonstration against Canadian National Railways president Donald Gordon, who had suggested that no qualified French Canadian could be found to assume the vice-presidency of the enterprise. In most analyses, the RIN is seen as based primarily within the Francophone new middle class.[50]

Similarly, we will see below how new-middle-class Francophones, both within and without the Quebec state, were leaders in the campaign to nationalize the Anglophone-owned private hydro-electrical firms.

In short, there is ample evidence that not only did the new middle class become an important social category in the post-war years but that in the course of the 1950s important elements of it were actively seeking to secure an expansion of the Quebec state. In large part they were propelled in this campaign by their growing conflicts with the Church, as well as with the Anglophone business class. As such, they displayed a substantial degree of political consciousness – equivalent at least to what must have existed at the time among other "class actors" such as the French-Canadian business class or the union movement.[51]

The Role of the New Middle Class in Expansion of the Quebec State

There is ample evidence that new-middle-class Francophones based within the state itself played critical roles in promoting the initiatives. As Marcel Fournier has argued, the effect of the arrival of new social science specialists (primarily economists) in the Quebec state is all the more evident in that "it's in the ministries where they worked that were conceived and implemented the most important reforms to which the government committed itself and which typify the Quiet Revolution."[52]

The impact of the new middle class within the Quebec state can be demonstrated in concrete terms. For instance, in his account of the Conseil d'orientation économique, Dale Thomson documents how the inability of the Conseil itself to formulate policies resulted in:

> the appearance of an informal power group that moved into the vacuum and used it [the Conseil] for its own purposes. Its members, bright, well-trained, newly recruited civil servants or advisers, identified with the government's goal of using the state as a lever for economic development and with the concept of using the council for that purpose. Among them were Michel Bélanger and André Marier from the Department of Natural Resources, Claude Morin and Jacques Parizeau. They looked to René Lévesque, who shared their views, as their *de facto* leader. . . . The council, and particularly its committees, became their

primary vehicle, but their influence extended throughout the government. *They became perhaps the most dynamic force behind the Quiet Revolution.*[53]

These and other newly hired Francophone technocrats were central players in the Quiet Revolution initiatives. For instance, the studies supporting nationalization of the private hydroelectrical enterprises were prepared primarily by André Marier, an economist who had just joined the Ministry of Natural Resources.[54] A fervent nationalist long committed to the project of nationalization, Marier had in fact been one of the founders of the separatist Rassemblement pour l'indépendance nationale.[55] The committee formulating the actual nationalization proposal was headed by Michel Bélanger, a Laval-trained economist René Lévesque had hired away from the federal Department of Finance.[56] Jean Lessard, the new chairman of Hydro-Québec, also had been recruited from the federal bureaucracy.[57]

Moreover, there is every reason to believe pressures for nationalization came from within Hydro-Québec itself. Even as it existed in 1960 Hydro-Québec was a substantial enterprise, constituting the one instance where the Francophone new middle class did have a base within the structures of the Quebec state. (Before the nationalization of the other hydroelectrical enterprises, Hydro-Québec already employed 190 Francophone engineers.)[58] One can presume that expansionist tendencies would arise from Hydro-Québec's competitive advantage over the private hydroelectrical enterprises, given among other things its control of the dynamic Montreal market.[59] In fact, even before René Lévesque assumed office as Minister of Natural Resources, a Hydro-Québec official met with him to express concern that a power plant was to be awarded to an American firm rather than a Quebec firm, depriving Hydro of expertise that it would need for its upcoming Manicouagan project.[60] Similarly, when Shawinigan president J.A. Fuller indicated plans for a thermal installation below Montreal, Hydro-Québec chairman Jean Lessard was quick to express concern that his enterprise's interests might be threatened, just as he objected to granting Shawinigan new hydro concessions in the St. Maurice Valley.[61]

In the case of SIDBEC, Dale Thomson's study details how Francophone economists, based mostly within the government, led a vigorous campaign to ensure that the enterprise should be partially or wholly owned by the Quebec state, countering those in the Anglophone and Francophone business communities (and Lesage himself) who favoured a wholly private enterprise.[62] By the same token, André Marier, Jacques Parizeau, and Claude Morin, along with Claude Castonguay, a newly hired actuary, were responsible for the Quebec government's 1964 pension plan proposal, which was so markedly superior to Ottawa's.[63] Clearly, the presence of members of the Francophone new middle class within the Quebec state created a powerful new force for expansion of the state's role.

Beyond that, in the case of at least one major reform, education, it can be shown that new-middle-class Francophones outside the state structures were, through effective mobilization, a critical force for state expansion. As we have seen, new-middle-class intellectuals and professors formed the Mouvement laïque de la langue française, to further their campaign for a total laicization of Quebec's educational system. The organization was to become one of the leading forces for educational reform. In this, it greatly strengthened the hand of new-middle-class Francophones within the Quebec state such as Arthur Tremblay, Paris and Harvard-trained professor of education at Université Laval, who was named special assistant to the Minister of Youth in 1960 and became deputy minister of education upon the ministry's creation in 1964.

In the final analysis, it is difficult to understand the rapid political modernization of the early 1960s without reference to a distinct Francophone new middle class. This class was effectively excluded from the upper echelons of the Quebec economy, as well as from the federal public service. Its members correctly saw that their personal and collective mobility was closely linked to the expansion of the Quebec state. This class was not created by Quebec's political modernization; it initiated these changes and was vastly strengthened in the process.

Organized Labour and the Quiet Revolution

In promoting its various projects of political modernization, the new middle class almost always was joined by a second social force: organized labour. In the case of nationalization of hydroelectricity, the CSN's predecessor, the CTCC, had called for state control of production and distribution of electricity at various points during the 1950s. For its part, the FTQ began calling for the measure in 1960.[64] Once it became evident that René Lévesque supported nationalization, the CSN and FTQ acted quickly to build up pressure behind it. For instance, just prior to the famous Lac-à-l'épaule cabinet meeting where the nationalization question was to be discussed, the two organizations sent Jean Lesage a joint statement:

"The Fédération des travailleurs du Québec and the Confédération des syndicats nationaux, which represent 345,000 unionized workers, wish to reiterate their total support for the cause of nationalizing electricity."[65] Similarly, the unions were in the forefront of the campaign for reform of Quebec's educational system. With respect to SIDBEC, the unions not only were among the original supporters of the creation of a steel complex but kept pressuring the government to abandon the mixed-corporation format it favoured for a fully publicly owned enterprise.[66] In short, the union movement shared the same unwavering commitment to state intervention as did the new middle class.[67] Testimony to the firm pressure for political modernization the union movement exerted on the Lesage regime is the almost apologetic tone Lesage adopted in a 1962 Labour Day address to the union leaderships. While claiming that the government wanted to improve the living standard of all the population "to the greatest extent possible," he in effect pleaded for patience:

It is easy to set an objective, but it is not always easy to attain it because difficulties emerge just when one is about to take the necessary steps. What counts is to not lose sight of the objective and, in particular, to not renounce it under a false pretext. Just as with the traveller who wishes to go from one point to another, governments – and this is especially true of the Quebec government – often must follow a route which is full of detours and may contain pitfalls.[68]

The clearest demonstration of organized labour's place within the configuration of forces supporting the Quiet Revolution, and the Lesage Liberal Party, is the 1964 reform of labour law. Under a comprehensive revision of Quebec's Labour Code, the right to strike was granted to all public employees, with the exception of police and fire fighters. It was an important victory for labour; in fact, Quebec was the first government in North America to grant this right to public-sector workers. Over the next few years, the federal government, five provincial governments, and two American state governments adopted similar legislation.[69]

It appears that the reform was the direct result of strong pressure the unions exerted on the Quebec government, thanks to a high degree of militancy among their members. Under the previous regime, public employees were denied the right to affiliate with a union; workers in both public and parapublic sectors were bound by compulsory arbitration. Nonetheless, in 1962 and 1963 hospital workers had threatened and, in one case, actually staged illegal strikes. As a result, the government decided to participate directly in negotiations with hospital unions. By the same token, in 1961 a small number of public employees had formed their own union organization and secured the services of the CSN, while not formally adhering to the CSN. The CSN had in fact called for unionization of all government employees in its first brief to the new Liberal government, in November, 1960. Here, the government remained firm, refusing to grant civil servants the right to organize. In a highly celebrated phrase, Jean Lesage declared that "the Queen does not negotiate with her subjects." The 1960 Liberal Party program had called for reform of the Labour Code and he was prepared to honour the commitment, but not to that extent. Nonetheless, membership in two public employee unions continued to grow, reaching 15,000 by the end of 1964.[70]

When, in June, 1963, the government presented a first version of its proposed revision of the Labour Code, it left intact the existing provisions regarding public and parapublic employees. Despite protests from the labour movement, the same was true of a second version the government proceeded to have adopted by the Quebec legislature on second reading. However, after a series of union protests – the CSN organized a mass rally and the FTQ even threatened to call a general strike – the government withdrew the bill. CSN leader Jean Marchand had declared that "a law like that will set the Province on fire."[71] Even the Union nationale joined in supporting the right to strike for all unionized persons.[72] Nonetheless, in April the government presented yet a third version of the bill that still left intact the provisions regarding public and parapublic employees. Meanwhile, tensions increased with illegal work stoppages becoming commonplace; ministers complained that the operations of their departments were suffering as a consequence.[73] Finally, in July, 1964, the government presented a fourth version of the bill granting the right to strike to employees of hospitals, school boards, and municipalities. The following year, it extended the right to teachers and civil servants.[74]

Clearly, the unions' success in securing this objective derived in large part from the militancy of the public-sector workers, who demonstrated their readiness to undertake illegal strike action. However, it also reflected the firm desire of the Lesage government to maintain a working relationship with the union leadership. The government knew that to undertake its ambitious plans for economic and social modernization it had to have the collaboration of the union movement. Labour, along with capital, was to participate directly in the elaboration of the state's economic strategy.[75] Thus, labour had been included in the Conseil d'orientation économique, just as it had members on the Conseil supérieur de travail, which the government re-established in 1960 to prepare the projected revision of the Labour Code. In the case of the CSN, moreover, there were close personal bonds between its leader, Jean Marchand, and Premier Lesage. Ultimately, given the firmness with which the union movement advanced its demands, the government was constrained to come to terms. Organized labour was very much a part of the Quiet Revolution coalition.

The Francophone Business Class and State Intervention

Nonetheless, several recent analyses of the forces behind the Quiet Revolution have assigned primary weight to another Francophone class: an emerging Francophone business class. Allegedly, this class was a leading, if not *the* leading, force for state intervention in the economy.[76]

As we have seen, French-Canadian business was in a precarious position prior to the Quiet Revolution. A few enterprises had made important gains in the post-war period, such as Joseph Simard's Marine Industries, which had been favoured by federal government contracts. The French-Canadian banks, Banque provinciale and Banque canadienne nationale, had survived, as had retailing firms such as Depuis frères. But, typically, French-Canadian firms were facing difficult times. Small, family-owned enterprises with antiquated technology and insufficient capital, they were seriously threatened by the American and English-Canadian competition. Speaking on their behalf, the Chambre de commerce du Québec had called on the Quebec government to undertake such measures as making new sources of capital available and creating an advisory council on economic matters. These entreaties had met with no serious response from the Duplessis regime.

It can be readily demonstrated that some Quiet Revolution initiatives were indeed responses to a Francophone business lobby. With the Société générale de financement, French-Canadian business finally received the new capital fund it had been seeking for so long. The SGF clearly was geared to the needs of *Francophone* business. The first chairman of the SGF board was René Paré, pillar of the French-Canadian business class and past president of the Montreal Chambre de commerce, which had campaigned for such a fund. And its first sizable investments were to purchase in whole or part several existing French-Canadian family-owned enterprises, most in financial difficulty, rather than to support new enterprises.[77]

This was also the case with the Conseil d'orientation économique. Charged with both advising the government on economic matters and formulating a comprehesive economic development plan, the Conseil was based on the legislation through which the Godbout regime had created its advisory body.[78] French-Canadian business was well-represented in the Conseil; the chairman was René Paré, prior to his becoming president of the SGF board.[79] But it is not at all clear that the French-Canadian business class was able to use the Conseil to promote new measures of its own device. In fact, the opposite appears to have been the case. Apparently, given their many other preccupations, the Conseil members:

> found it difficult to do more than attend the meetings. In the circumstances, the Economic Council was to find that, rather then initiating projects, it was easier to endorse recommendations put forward, with the necessary documentation, by government departments, particularly those represented by a deputy minister.[80]

In fact, some of the government's economic initiatives clearly did not have the approval of French-Canadian business. In the case of the nationalization of the hydroelectrical firms, there is every indication that French-Canadian business was just as fiercely opposed to the measure as was English-Canadian business. Both the provincial Chambre de commerce and the Chambre de commerce de Montréal firmly denounced the project,[81] as did the Chambre de commerce of Quebec City.[82] In addition, French-Canadian businessmen were apparently the most vociferous in denouncing the creation of the Caisse de dépôt et de placement, branding it as "galloping socialism."[83]

As for the SIDBEC project, there can be little doubt that French-Canadian business wanted a steel complex to be created in Quebec. In 1961 the Quebec Chambre de commerce had reiterated its support for a primary iron and steel complex.[84] And when the Conseil d'orientation économique was convened, one of its first decisions was to appoint a committee to explore the possibility of such a project. In 1961, the Conseil endorsed the committee's recommendation that an integrated steel complex be built at a cost of $109 million, to be provided in whole or in part by the government. However, there are indications that Francophone business was apprehensive about the role the government was to play in the enterprise.[85] Creation of a state-owned steel complex did not entail the nationalization of an established industry, as with the expansion of Hydro-Québec. Still, for Francophone business such a state role was at best a measure of last resort.

Thus, the Francophone business class cannot really provide a satisfactory explanation of the Quiet Revolution economic initiatives. Francophone businessmen readily welcomed reforms that promised to give business greater influence over economic policy or to make available additional sources of capital, but they had little apparent enthusiasm for direct state intervention.

Monopoly Capital and the Quiet Revolution

Similar difficulties arise with revisionist analyses that seek to explain the growth of the Quebec state as a direct response to the changing needs of monopoly capital (i.e., English-Canadian and American capital). One of the earliest and most straightforward developments of this perspective is in a major study by Luc Racine and Roch Denis.[86] Racine and Denis contend that the transformation to monopoly capitalism necessitated and explains most of the new initiatives of the Quebec state. First, the monopolization of Quebec industry entailed, as elsewhere, an augmentation of "the organic composition of capital." Rather than the poorly educated, unskilled, "cheap labour" of the past, Quebec industry, at least its monopolistic component, now required well-educated, highly skilled labour. In addition, it required much higher levels of capital investment and research and development. As elsewhere, the state was now expected to meet a variety of new functions: to administer aid to the unskilled labourers displaced through this change; to raise the level of education of those entering the labour market; to establish income security programs; and, in particular, to underwrite much of the escalating costs of capital investment and research and development. Since the Canadian constitution places these functions largely within provincial jurisdictions, so the Quebec provincial government was required to assume them.

This general thesis, establishing a direct link between the monopolization of capital and the Quiet Revolution's expansion of the Quebec state, also structures a study by Gilles Bourque and Anne Legaré.[87] They modify considerably the specification of the roles played by different classes as suggested by Racine and Denis. Rejecting abstract analyses "which would make these reforms a simple adaptation of the Quebec state to the external pressures of imperialism,"[88] Bourque and Legaré tie their analysis to specifically English-Canadian monopoly capital. The transfer of power from the Union nationale to the Lesage Liberals established the hegemony of the Canadian bourgeoisie over the Quebec state; its interests were dominant in the state reforms. Nevertheless, their underlying interpretation of the Quiet Revolution is the same as that of Racine and Denis, focusing as it does on the presumed political effects of the monopolization of capital.

These applications of the thesis of monopolization of capital are suggestive, placing the Quebec experience within a much broader perspective than had previously been the case. Yet, the monopolization of capital is not alone sufficient to explain the political modernization of the Quiet Revolution. It can be readily argued that in most capitalist systems the growth of the monopolistic sector has placed pressures on the state to assume new and expanded functions. Most students would agree that Quebec has been no exception in this respect. Still, it is not clear why the Quebec state, rather than the federal state, should have responded to these pressures. The claims of some observers notwithstanding, the constitutional division of powers did not always require this. Through the general spending power and other devices, the federal government was in a position to assume most of these functions and had already done so, *in close collaboration with the English-Canadian bourgeoisie*. During the post-war years, Ottawa had established a wide variety of new programs: support for industrial research and development, subsidies and tax rebates for capital investment, retraining of poorly skilled manpower, relocation programs for displaced workers, etc.[89] Through financial support to universities, the federal government was active even in the exclusively provincial jurisdiction of education – everywhere, that is, except in Quebec. The issue raised during the Quiet Revolution was not whether these functions should be assumed by the state, but by which state, Quebec City or Ottawa? From the early 1960s, the two governments were locked in sometimes bitter struggles over control of many of these functions. Competition with Ottawa was much more intense and all-encompassing in Quebec's case than in that of other provinces, including Ontario, which also had undergone the transition to monopoly capitalism. If at times other provinces adopted similar grievances against Ottawa, it was usually Quebec that first articulated them.

In addition, the reforms of the Quiet Revolution cannot be adequately understood in terms of the particular class interests Racine and Denis and Bourque and Legaré emphasize. With respect to the English-Canadian bourgeoisie, allegedly the dominant force during the Quiet Revolution, we have seen that many of the measures Quebec sought to undertake in the 1960s had already been established at the federal level. This bourgeoisie had no strong interest in the transfer of these functions to Quebec City, or in their duplication by Quebec. But even in areas where the constitution clearly restricted responsibility to the provincial level, many of the measures undertaken in the 1960s can be best understood in terms of factors other than the interests of the English-Canadian bourgeoisie.

This argument applies even to the measure revisionist students of the Quiet Revolution have most emphatically linked to the interests of English-Canadian monopoly capital: the nationalization of the remaining private hydroelectrical firms. Despite the affirmations of some students, there is no indication that monopoly capital in fact favoured nationalization of the hydroelectrical industry, let alone lobbied for it. If anything, it was actively opposed. While some businessmen may have promoted the exploitation by Hydro-Québec of unused hydro sites, as we saw in the last chapter, it would be quite a different matter to promote the forced takeover of private firms by Hydro-Québec.

To be sure, one can demonstrate that monopoly capital ultimately benefited from the expansion of Hydro-Québec, since it provided Quebec businesses with electrical energy at a lower cost and with greater security than would otherwise have been the case.[90] Apparently, the private hydroelectrical firms were not in a position to undertake the massive expansion of hydro production capacity that the needs of monopoly capital required.[91] Moreover, nationalization served to rationalize and consolidate the market for electricity.[92] Thus, ten years later, a survey of Quebec businessmen and corporate executives found that the vast majority expressed approval of the nationalization.[93] Nonetheless, satisfaction with the measure well after the fact is not proof that business supported the measure at the time.

In assessing the attitude of monopoly capitalists to nationalization in 1962, it is important to distinguish Canadian (essentially English-Canadian) capitalists from their American counterparts. With respect to Canadian business, there is evidence that the owners of one or two of the enterprises in question did welcome nationalization.[94] However, it was strongly opposed by the three largest firms: Shawinigan Water and Power, Quebec Power, and Southern Canada Power. In fact, J.A. Fuller, who was president of

166

Shawinigan, by far the largest firm, undertook a series of public addresses to make his case.[95] More importantly, it is clear that, *as a class*, Canadian business was bitterly opposed to the measure. For instance, the Quebec division of the Canadian Manufacturers' Association sent a telegram to the Lesage cabinet declaring its total support for the principle that "the province's economy has the greatest chance of experiencing the growth which one has every right to expect under a system of open competition which ensures that the means of production are neither controlled nor placed in its hands."[96] In fact, so fierce was the opposition within English-Canadian financial circles that the Quebec government clearly would have been unable to sell on the Canadian market the bonds necessary to finance the measure.[97] It was obliged to turn to American capital markets where, without difficulty, it was able to arrange financing. Yet, if American capital was ready to underwrite the project, it in no sense precipitated the move.

One cannot satisfactorily explain the state intervention of the 1960s in terms of the needs of monopoly capital. First, the initiatives did not always respond to the needs of monopoly capital. Often, they entailed seeking to institute or recuperate programs already established at the federal level. In other cases, other classes were the essential beneficiaries of Quiet Revolution *étatisme* and were the primary forces calling for them. Beyond that, what was perhaps the most important initiative of the Quiet Revolution, the nationalization of hydroelectrical enterprises (and perhaps the creation of SIDBEC as well), was actively opposed by Canadian capital. For its part, American capital simply facilitated the project. The needs of monopoly capital may well have provided useful rationales for some of the Quiet Revolution initiatives. But they cannot provide an explanation of the measures.

The Quiet Revolution Coalition: The New Middle Class and Labour

During the early 1960s at least, there was a loose coalition of support for expansion of the Quebec state.[98] At its centre were the new middle class and organized labour, who shared a firm commitment to expansion of the Quebec state. More ambivalent in its support for political modernization was the French-Canadian business class, which was eager to be involved in policy-making, as through the Conseil d'orientation économique, and apparently welcomed the SGF as a new source of investment capital, but whose

167

fundamental mistrust of the state made it very much opposed to the Quebec state becoming itself an economic actor, as with Hydro-Québec or the Caisse.

This abiding mistrust of the state and consequent diffidence toward the initiatives of the Quiet Revolution also marked what William Coleman refers to as a "traditional middle class" of liberal professionals. Coleman presents this class as an integral part of the Quiet Revolution coalition. Nonetheless, it apparently was split on the economic initiatives of the Quiet Revolution – even if its primary spokesman, the Société Saint-Jean Baptiste, was clearly in favour of the nationalization of electricity.[99] Beyond that, it was opposed to much of the greater state involvement in education, including the creation of a Ministry of Education.[100] In general, it resisted the secular thrust that was so integral to the Quiet Revolution ideology, and its participation in the Quiet Revolution coalition was at best circumstantial.

For its part, monopoly capital could be looked to for support of some Quiet Revolution initiatives, although not of the neo-nationalist ideology that underlay them. Improvement in the qualification of manpower obviously was desirable, as was the assumption by the state of some of the costs of capital investment and research and development. To the extent that these functions already were being discharged at the federal level, English-Canadian and U.S. capital had no strong interest in the Quebec government doing the same. But it had no reason to object if the Quebec state, for its own reasons, should undertake to do so. In fact, the duplication of efforts might lead to an increase in the overall level of government support for corporate needs. Given the role the state was assuming elsewhere under monopoly capitalism, the Quiet Revolution political modernizers could readily argue that the measures they were proposing were quite "normal" in a modern capitalist system. Still, there were real limits to the readiness of at least *English-Canadian* capital to accept an enhanced economic role for the *Quebec* state. For instance, as we have seen, the vast majority of Anglophone businessmen were staunchly opposed to nationalization of the hydroelectrical firms' counterparts.[101] Similarly, there is evidence that the English-Canadian business community was so uneasy about the creation of the Société générale de financement that Jean Lesage had to meet with its leaders to reassure them about his government's intentions.[102] Moreover, their opposition to the creation of the Caisse de dépôt et de placement was personally expressed in cabinet by George Marler, their representative.[103]

For that matter, Marler had been the leading antagonist of the nationalization of the hydro firms.[104]

In short, the constellation of support for the Quiet Revolution was an uneasy one based on quite different interests; it was a *very* loose coalition. All parties, including the Francophone new middle class, shared a commitment to the established capitalist system, but they had quite different conceptions of the role of the Quebec state within that system. English-Canadian and American economic elites could scarcely share the new-middle-class project of making Québécois *maîtres chez nous* by expanding the role of Francophone managers, both in a vastly enlarged public sector and in all areas of the private sector. Even the French-Canadian business class was not prepared to support sustained state intervention in the Quebec economy. Consequently, by the mid-1960s the key Quiet Revolution political modernizers, the new middle class and organized labour, had difficulty securing support among other elites for their projects.

The Limited Popular Support for the Quiet Revolution

The early 1960s were clearly a period of widespread, far-reaching change in Quebec's political life. First and foremost, it was a period of ideological change as long-dominant assumptions about the character of the state and the French-Canadian nation were abandoned. The new Quiet Revolution ideology gained strong support in influential sectors of Quebec society and helped to provoke the Lesage administration to a major expansion of the activities of the Quebec government. These new activities, and the ideology that justified them, had a significant, unstabilizing effect on the functioning of the Canadian federal system, leading to the transfer of a considerable amount of authority and fiscal resources. These new roles the Quebec government assumed in both Quebec society and the Canadian federal system acted, in turn, to legitimize and to further strengthen support for the central beliefs of the Quiet Revolution ideology. Yet, it would be an error to assume that *all* French Canadians had been converted to the new ideology or had welcomed the policies it rationalized. The loose coalition of support for the Quiet Revolution that had emerged at the level of elites did not necessarily extend through the whole of Quebec society.

The initial victory of the Liberals in 1960 cannot be read as a widespread desire among French Canadians for major expansion of the role of government.[105] In fact, considering the overwhelming support that English Canadians customarily have given to the Liberals since the 1930s, the 52 per cent of the popular vote gained by the Liberals in 1960 probably represents less than a majority of the French-Canadian voters. To be sure, the Liberals – with their campaign slogan of *C'est le temps que ça change* – did articulate a certain commitment to change. But this commitment did not extend even to a Ministry of Education. During the election campaign, Lesage personally assured voters that a Ministry of Education would never be established under his administration. Moreover, the Liberal gains must have been at least partly due to the failure of the Union nationale to wage as coherent a campaign as it had done in the days of Duplessis. With the sudden death of Paul Sauvé, Duplessis's successor, the Union nationale had been deeply divided over the choice of a new leader. The new leader, Antonio Barrette, had not been able to heal these wounds; major party figures did not even participate in the 1960 campaign. The 1960 Liberal victory, the product of circumstances, was hardly a mandate for major political modernization.

By 1962, the Liberals had increased their popularity and perhaps did get the votes of a majority of French Canadians.[106] Yet, as Maurice Pinard suggests, the Liberal victory may not have been tied specifically to support for the Quiet Revolution program – at least not support for the nationalization of hydroelectric facilities.[107] More significantly, the Liberals had still failed to break down the suspicion that working-class French Canadians had long harboured. According to Pinard, working-class French Canadians who identified with their class and its interests were especially resistant to the Liberal appeals for support.[108] If the union leaderships, especially the CSN, were solidly in the Liberal camp, they apparently had not been able to bring the working class with them. In that sense, nothing had changed from the Duplessis period. However, among *public-sector* workers, Liberal support may well have been higher.

The stunning defeat of the Liberals in 1966 was not due solely to popular rejection of the Quiet Revolution; it was the result of many factors. Primarily, the defeat was a function of the workings of the single-member, plurality electoral system. With 40 per cent of the popular vote (seven percentage points less than the Liberals), the Union nationale secured a majority of the seats. The Union nationale had a smaller popular vote (one per cent less) in 1966 than it had received in 1962 – Union nationale support had been sliding steadily since 1956. Nevertheless, the Union nationale's ability to retain the support it did receive was at least partially due to its exploitation of popular resentments against changes that the Lesage regime had introduced. In rural areas the Union nationale had mobilized opposition to the regionalization of the secondary school system (viewed by many as a threat to family and community solidarity) and had exploited fears that the Liberals would de-confessionalize public schools. By 1966, substantial elements of French-Canadian society were claiming that the Quiet Revolution had already gone too far in its reform of French-Canadian institutions.[109]

In a perceptive analysis written in the mid-1960s,[110] Léon Dion noted the persistence of these conservative elements in Quebec society and the failure of some analysts to be sufficiently aware of their persistence. For Dion, this overestimation of the penetration of the Quiet Revolution ideology is merely one instance of a common error among analysts of ideologies in any society. With the Lesage regime, as with most political regimes, political authorities seek to create the illusion of societal convergence around the values with which they identify and distinguish their regime. It is clearly in their political interest to do so. Dion argues that analysts frequently fall for this illusion themselves and thus ignore the presence of ideological oppositions within the society. This error is all the more likely when the analysts themselves identify with the official ideology expounded by the authorities. This was the case with the Lesage regime. Yet, just as there were elements in Quebec of the 1950s who strongly opposed the conservatism with which the Duplessis regime associated itself, so there continued to be elements in Quebec of the mid-1960s who opposed the new values propounded by the Lesage regime. To some extent, they may have been intimidated into relative silence by the aggressive advocates of the Quiet Revolution (as Jean-Marc Leger suggests).[111] Nevertheless, this conservatism was evident in the opposition of various voluntary associations to the establishment of a Ministry of Education. With the 1966 provincial election, the persistence of conservatism within the general public was also evident.

The Union nationale electoral support in 1966 also appears to have drawn on the continued suspicion of working-class French Canadians that the Liberal Party and its programs of political modernization did not really serve their interest. Once again, the Liberals were substantially less successful among working-class French Canadians than among middle-class French Canadians.[112] We can plausibly infer that the situation Pinard found present in

1962 – an association between identification with the working class and identification with the Union nationale – was also operative in the 1966 election.

At the same time, the Liberals also suffered at the hands of those who felt that the Quiet Revolution had not gone far enough, especially in constitutional matters. For the first time in a Quebec election, two separatist parties participated: the Rassemblement pour l'indépendance nationale (RIN) and the Ralliement national (RN). The former received 6 per cent of the votes and the latter 3 per cent. In some Montreal French-Canadian districts, support for the RIN plus the increased alienation of working-class French Canadians from the Liberals were sufficient to give the Union nationale the plurality.

The rhetoric and programs of the Quiet Revolution had helped to provoke two quite different reactions: resistance to change and an appetite for greater change. The Liberals were unable to satisfy both tendencies. Once again, they were rejected by the majority of French Canadians. To an extent, the Liberal Party was the victim of its own actions. The process of political modernization that the Lesage administration had launched was creating divisions and antagonisms within French-Canadian society that would prove difficult for any political party to conciliate.

CHAPTER SIX
Quebec in the Wake of the Quiet Revolution: Politicization of Language and Class

The most enduring legacy of the Lesage administration was the new importance that many Québécois were led to attach to the Quebec state. The leading personalities of the Lesage regime had worked to convert Quebec Francophones to the belief that the Quebec state should be an active, dynamic force within Quebec society, that it should be (in René Lévesque's words) "one of us, the best among us." However limited may seem the structures and programs established under the Liberals, they did enable the Quebec state to play a much more substantial role than ever before. Largely as a result of the efforts of these erstwhile political modernizers, Quebec Francophones came to view the Quebec state as a powerful instrument capable of improving their social and economic condition and, moreover, obligated to do so. Here lay the seeds of political discontent. Many French Canadians were encouraged to make demands for change that government leaders were unable or unwilling to undertake. In the process, not only particular leaders and parties came under attack, but the structures of the Quebec state and the Canadian federal order itself were found wanting.

Some felt that the programs of the Quiet Revolution needed to be pursued with even more vigour and that the powers and resources of the Quebec state had to be expanded accordingly. We examined the roots of this sentiment in the last chapter. But for others the Quiet Revolution was no longer an adequate model: new kinds of policies and programs were necessary. Concern over the place of Francophones relative to non-Francophones within Quebec was one source of the new criticism of the Quiet Revolution. Concern over the position of working-class Francophones, relative to upper-class Anglophones and Francophones, was another. We now need to explore in some detail how these demands for new kinds of government programs arose.

Anglophone Domination of the Quebec Economy

Resentment over Anglophone domination of Quebec's economy and demands for state action to break this domination had been encouraged by many of the actions of the Lesage regime. Leading Liberal personalities, after all, had declared it a primary responsibility of the Quebec state to place control of Quebec's economy in the hands of French Canadians. During the 1962 provincial election campaign, as on many other occasions, Liberals had proclaimed that their goal was to make French Canadians no less than *maîtres chez nous*. And the Lesage regime undertook a series of measures it claimed would make this goal a reality.

The most direct strategy for strengthening the Francophone presence in the Quebec economy was to create and expand state enterprises. As we have seen, a plethora of enterprises was created in the 1960s, but only one had become a major actor in the Quebec economy: Hydro-Québec. This remained the case through the 1970s as well. Hydro-Québec continued to grow, becoming the largest employer within Quebec. In fact, by 1977 it had become the second largest public utility enterprise in North America. Without question, it carved out a new space within the Quebec economy for the Francophone new middle class. But all the other state enterprises continued to play only marginal roles. Even SIDBEC, which had been the source of such great expectations in the 1960s, failed to establish itself as a major force.[1]

A second direction of the Quiet Revolution reforms was to reinforce Francophone-owned enterprises. Here, too, results had been disappointing during the 1960s. The major initiative in this direction, the Société générale de financement, largely failed in its task. The several French-Canadian family firms it acquired continued to fare poorly, even with the injection of new funds and the reorganization of their structures. As for the Caisse de dépôt et de placement, the bulk of its funds were absorbed by the purchase of provincial government bonds; the funds that remained for investment in private enterprises were not channelled into specifically Francophone firms.

By the mid-1970s, however, it became clear that state support of Francophone private enterprises was having a certain impact. The SGF and the Caisse de dépôt had begun to play more effective roles. When the SGF was converted into a fully state-owned enterprise in 1972, its capital was increased to $25 million. It began to sponsor the creation of new industrial complexes, such as the integrated forestry complex at St. Felicien in the Saguenay-Lac St. Jean region. And it started to finance the continued expansion of existing major enterprises. In 1975, the SGF came to the aid of Bombardier by investing $6.8 million in MLW, Bombardier's heavy industry complex. As for the Caisse de dépôt, several of its investments gave critical support to the Francophone business class. During the 1970s, the Caisse de dépôt helped to finance the development of the Provigo grocery chain, and it sponsored the purchase of National Cablevision from the American-owned CBS by Francophone interests. Also, during the 1970s a new state institution, the Société de dévelopement industriel, undertook to subsidize small and medium-sized enterprises in Quebec, most of which were Francophone-owned. Finally, the political modernization of the Quiet Revolution entailed a vast increase in the volume of public-sector purchases, which heavily benefited Francophone-owned enterprises. In fact, Hydro-Québec established a formal policy of favouring submissions from Quebec-based firms. Thanks in large part to these and other forms of assistance from the Quebec state, the 1970s saw a marked strengthening of Francophone enterprises. Several of them acquired quite impressive dimensions. Bombardier-MLW emerged as a major manufacturer of transportation equipment, with 7,000 employees and assets of over $400 million. In 1977, almost $14 billion had been amassed in the combined assets of three Francophone banks: la Banque canadienne nationale, la Banque provinciale, and la Banque d'épargne.

Finally, a third form of Francophone economic power became much more visible and influential in the 1970s: the co-operative movement. During the early decades of this century, locally based credit unions, including the parish-based *caisses populaires*, and producers' co-operatives were established throughout French Quebec. Historically, the individual credit unions had enjoyed a high degree of autonomy, recirculating to the local community most of the savings they collect. With the 1970s, however, the Quebec-wide federation of *caisses populaires* began to channel a certain proportion of these savings into major economic ventures. Commonly known as the Mouvement Desjardins, it acquired a controlling interest in Culinar, Inc. (which, in turn, controls Vachon Cakes) and secured 23 per cent of the shares of the Banque provinciale. In addition, it assumed a 51 per cent interest in a major development in downtown Montreal, le Complex Desjardins. Collectively, the co-operative movement controlled a major share of savings in Quebec, exceeding that of any individual bank. Linked to the co-operative movement are several substantial insurance companies.

Yet, if Francophone ownership in the Quebec economy grew

markedly during the 1960s and especially the 1970s, it remained very much in a minority position. English-Canadian and American interests continued to dominate the private sector and, consequently, the whole of Quebec's economy. In the mid-1970s, there were still only twenty Francophone-controlled enterprises (including state corporations) among the 100 largest employers in Quebec.[2] Within the manufacturing industry, the proportion of the labour force employed by Francophone-owned firms remained relatively small, growing from 21.7 per cent in 1961 to 28.4 per cent in 1974.[3] And, within Canada as a whole, Francophone economic control continued to be marginal. In 1975, Francophone-controlled firms represented only 11 per cent of the 136 largest corporations in Canada under the control of Canadians.[4] In short, if the Quiet Revolution goal of *maîtres chez nous* is understood to mean Francophone ownership of the Quebec economy, then clearly it had not been realized by the mid-1970s. Many did not expect it to happen in the near future, either, and were increasingly impatient.

There still remained, however, the possibility that Francophones might become predominant in the management positions of Quebec firms, whatever may be the ownership of the firms. To the extent that inadequate or inappropriate education had prevented Francophones from acceding to the upper levels of English-Canadian and American enterprises, then the Quiet Revolution bore considerable promise. As we have seen, a central objective of the Quiet Revolution educational reforms had been to increase the number of Francophones with the technical knowledge and managerial skills requisite for assuming direction of Quebec's economy.

Some observers had assumed that a movement of Francophones into the upper echelons of Anglophone corporations would indeed follow upon the educational reforms; the historical absence of Francophones was laid simply to the lack of academically qualified French-Canadian candidates. Yet, even in the 1960s analyses had already suggested that academic qualifications were not the only obstacle to French-Canadian mobility. In an unpublished research report to the Royal Commission on Bilingualism and Biculturalism, three Université de Montréal economists showed through a detailed analysis of 1961 census data that only 33 per cent of the difference in income between English-Canadian and French-Canadian Montrealers was due to the lower educational level of French Canadians (an additional 6 per cent resulted from the different age structures of the two populations). They contended that the remaining 60 per cent of the income differential was due to a clear preference of Anglophone employers for English-Canadian candidates (*"une segregation économique"*), a preference that forced them to pay substantially higher salaries for managerial personnel than if they had been ready to draw more fully from the available academically qualified French Canadians.[5] (In its report, the B & B Commission presented some of these data, but sought to downplay the importance of discrimination or other correlates of ethnicity, labelling them "secondary" factors. It did not acknowledge this radical difference in interpretation.)[6]

By the early 1970s many Francophones concluded that the Quiet Revolution programs of educational reform and support for Francophone corporations had indeed failed to increase substantially the presence of Francophones in the upper echelons of Quebec's economy. Available evidence indicates that this conclusion was largely correct; while some improvement had been made, representation of Francophones was still weak. In a replication of John Porter's analysis of Canadian economic elites, Wallace Clement showed that the presence of French Canadians in this elite had increased only slightly over the period 1951-1972. Porter had shown that in 1951 only 6.7 per cent of the Canadian economic elite was French-Canadian; Clement found that in 1972 this figure had grown to only 8.4 per cent.[7] Similarly, in a survey of 12,741 names of executives from some 2,400 companies operating in Canada, listed in the 1971 Directory of Directors, Robert Presthus found that only 9.5 per cent were French-Canadian.[8] For Clement, the Presthus data show that French Canadians had not made gains even in the medium-sized and smaller corporations.[9]

Two studies for the Gendron Commission, conducted in 1971, demonstrate how the presence of Francophones within key sectors of the Quebec economy continued to decline markedly as one ascended corporate hierarchies. In a sample of corporate headquarters in Quebec, Francophones constituted 35 per cent of the employees receiving less than $10,000, but the comparable figures for higher income brackets were: $10,000-15,000 – 23 per cent; $15,000-22,000 – 18 per cent; and over $22,000 – 15 per cent.[10] A survey of 2,000 managerial personnel (including foremen), primarily within Quebec's manufacturing industry, showed that Francophones represented 55 per cent of the managers receiving less than $15,000 but only 30 per cent of the managers earning over $15,000.[11] The Commission also found that Francophones were relatively absent at all levels within the finance and public utility sectors. Thus, in 1974, a major report of the Quebec Ministry of Industry and Commerce concluded that "it is impossible to affirm that the relative participation of French Canadians in economic life is clearly progressing."[12]

The specific failure of educational reform to improve French-Canadian participation in the private sector of the Quebec economy was demonstrated more directly by the apparently small proportion of recent university graduates who actually entered that sector. An analysis of graduates from the Université de Montréal showed that over the period 1965-1969, only 22.5 per cent of the graduates had taken their first job in the private sector and that only 12.7 per cent of the graduates were presently working in the private sector. (Participation in the private sector was only slightly greater for students graduating during 1970-1973).[13]

Some observers ascribed this apparent failure of educational reform to a long-standing antipathy of Francophones to business activities. Training in technology and management, they contended, was insufficient to eliminate this attitude; thus, the clear preference for the public sector.[14] Many Francophones argued, however, that practices of Anglophone corporations were to blame. Discrimination, whether stemming from personal prejudice or taking subtler institutional forms, was often cited.[15] But by the 1970s, attention increasingly turned to the working-language practices of English-Canadian and American corporations. It was argued that by requiring Francophones to perform their responsibilities primarily in English, corporations were necessarily placing Francophones at a disadvantage. In white-collar and managerial positions, which involve extensive reading and writing in English, Francophones would never be able to compete equally with Anglophones. The argument had considerable merit. As sociologist Nathan Keyfitz had written several years earlier, on the basis of long service in the federal bureaucracy, a French candidate:

is genuinely unable to do the work as well as the English candidate wherever that work consists in large part in the manipulation of symbols in English. To say otherwise would be to assert that French Canadians are capable of learning to speak and think in English as well as the English themselves.[16]

The major extensive analysis of working-language practices in Quebec appears in the report of the Gendron Commission, published in late 1972. The report showed that in some sectors of the Quebec economy, Francophones, even at the highest levels of responsibility, were able to work primarily in French. This was true of public administration, personal and social services, commerce, and primary industry. But in other sectors the opportunities were much more limited. In finance and public utilities the usage of French was limited at all levels.[17] In the manufacturing sector, where opportunities to use French were also quite limited at all levels, the relationship between language practices and mobility was suggested quite clearly. Despite the need to use English extensively, Francophones were quite well represented at the levels of foreman and worker (the ratio of Francophones to Anglophones was 11:1). But they were poorly represented at the higher levels (the ratio for administrators and professionals was 1.1:1),[18] even though the usage of French by Francophones was substantially greater at this level.[19] Apparently, the high level of sophistication in English required to conduct managerial activities, as opposed to blue-collar activities, was an effective obstacle to Francophone mobility. Obstacles to mobility in the secondary sector alone would have constituted a serious challenge to Québécois aspirations of *maîtres chez nous*. Not only did secondary industry represent approximately 28 per cent of the jobs in Quebec,[20] it clearly was central to Quebec's economic development. But language may well have been an obstacle to Francophone participation in other sectors of the economy as well, such as finance and public utilities.[21]

As the Gendron Commission acknowledged, a primary source of pressure to use English in some areas of the Quebec economy arises from the close integration of enterprises with the North American economy, especially in the branch plants of American corporations.[22] This integration strengthens the role of English as a technical language; manuals, documentation, corporate memoranda, and so on are available only in English. Also, the location of head offices and other decision-making centres in the U.S. necessitates a substantial amount of written communication in English. But the Commission argued that the role of French within these operations nevertheless could be substantially increased. It was the presence of large numbers of Anglophones within the enterprises that prevented a greater use of French. Drawing on the experience of European branches of American corporations, the Commission contended that French could become the language of internal communication within U.S.-owned enterprises in Quebec. Within Quebec, according to studies conducted for the Commission, for enterprises of most types, and at all levels, the great bulk of communication is internal. Thus, if French were to become the language of internal communication of these firms it would be, effectively, the language of work. Only 10-15 per cent of the personnel at the highest levels would be required, by the necessity of communicating with an American head office, to have a strong proficiency in English. In the process, then, the competitive disadvantage of Francophones would be largely eliminated. Most Francophones would need little working knowledge of English; if some Francophones would need a knowledge of English for external communications, all Anglophones would need a working knowledge of French for internal communications.

It was difficult to see how such an extensive change in internal language practices could occur without a major change in corporate recruitment practices. The Commission contended that the conversion of language practices could not be accomplished simply through intensive language-training programs for existing Anglophone executives. Not only do these programs often fail to produce real fluency in French, they will not ensure that French will become the effective language of exchange between Anglophones and Francophones. In many companies, the use of English was such an established practice that even if the majority of workers within a unit were Francophone, the primary language of communication would remain English. Only when Francophones numbered 80 per cent of the members of a work unit was French likely to be used as frequently as English in verbal communications between the two groups. Thus, the conversion of language practices necessarily implied a massive infusion of Francophones into managerial and executive levels. The Gendron Commission called for the Quebec government to institute with private corporations "a recruitment policy in which Francophones will be clearly favoured."[23]

The rhetoric of the Quiet Revolution thus had clearly established the goal of making Quebec Francophones *maîtres chez nous*. But by the early 1970s the reforms introduced during the Quiet Revolution, and over subsequent years, had not yet succeeded in making this goal a reality. The Quebec economy continued to be dominated by English-Canadian and American-owned corporations, and within these operations Anglophones continued to predominate in managerial positions. At the same time, the educational reforms of the Quiet Revolution were enormously successful in creating a new body of Francophones who were fully qualified to assume managerial positions, and who could be a major source of political discontent if their ambitions were not met. Over the short term the rapidly growing public sector could absorb many of these Francophones, but this could only be a stopgap. With the 1970s, attention turned to the one governmental strategy not attempted during the Quiet Revolution: direct intervention in the operations of English-Canadian and American corporations to ensure greater mobility for Francophones. For many Quebec Francophones, the key to this improved mobility was to make French the primary language of work. They began to pressure the Quebec government to do so.

The Anglicization of Immigrant Populations

By the late 1960s, the attention of many French Canadians was also directed to immigrant groups in Quebec and how they affected the position of the Francophone collectivity. Once again, it was argued by a growing number of French Canadians that the Quebec state had a responsibility to intervene on behalf of French Canadians. The vast majority of new immigrants to Quebec were sending their children to English-language schools rather than to French-language schools, out of recognition that economic opportunities were greater in the English language. Many French Canadians contended that if present trends were to continue, Francophones would find themselves in a minority in Montreal. If this were to happen, the pressures for assimilation of French Canadians would be irresistible. The old obsession with survival that had dominated French-Canadian nationalism until the heady days of the Quiet Revolution now reappeared. In the name of *la survivance*, the Quebec government was called on to force the integration of the immigrant population with the Francophone community by requiring that the children of immigrants attend only French-language schools.

The greater attraction of immigrants to the Anglophone community is not new to Quebec; it was true of previous waves of immigrants as well. This can be seen in data on immigrants' children who, from birth, were already part of one of the two language communities. According to the 1971 census, among Quebec residents of neither British nor French ethnic origin, 27.4 per cent had English as their mother tongue but only 15.7 per cent had French as their mother tongue.[24] Despite this long-standing pattern, the Francophone proportion of Quebec's population remained constant, oscillating around 80 per cent. This stability was due largely to a much higher birth rate among French Canadians than among English Canadians, sufficiently higher to compensate for the greater attracting power of the Anglophone community.

In Quebec of the 1960s, however, conditions were not as favourable to the Francophone population. There was no longer a signifi-

cant difference in birth rates; the relative strength of the Francophone community depended primarily on its ability to attract
immigrants. To make matters worse, the already weak attracting
power of the Francophone community had declined even further.
The most striking change was among Italian immigrants. In the
early decades of this century, Italians had been more attracted to
the Francophone community than had any other immigrant
group. According to the 1971 census, more than twice as many
individuals of Italian origin had acquired French as their mother
tongue (14,762) than had acquired English (6,387).[25] This pattern
was reversed after World War II: only 25 per cent of the Italian
children registered with the Montreal Catholic school system were
attending French-language schools; the rest were in English-language schools. In addition, a certain number of Italian children
attended the English-only Protestant schools.[26]

Clearly, demographic trends were working against the Francophone population. For the first time its position was being weakened by the influx of immigrants. Nevertheless, it appears that
these trends were not as great a threat to ethnic survival as some
French Canadians contended. A widely publicized analysis made
in 1969 by the leading French-Canadian demographer, Jacques
Henripin, and two colleagues indicated that in 2001 the Francophone population would be between 79.2 per cent and 71.6 per
cent of the total Quebec population and between 52.7 per cent and
60.0 per cent of the Montreal population.[27] Five years later, drawing on 1971 census data, Henripin made more precise estimates for
the year 2001: 77.1 per cent for all of Quebec and 59 per cent for
Montreal.[28] Thus, the predilection of immigrants for the Anglophone community would indeed mean a decline in the demographic position of Francophones. In the case of Montreal, where
Francophones constituted about 66 per cent of the population, the
decline would be substantial. (Henripin himself saw this as a
cause for concern and recommended strong governmental intervention.)[29] Nevertheless, the analysis of Henripin, and other
demographers as well, showed that Francophones would remain
the majority not only in Quebec as a whole but in the Montreal
area as well. Apparently, the attraction of immigrants to the Anglophone community did not directly endanger the survival of a
Francophone Quebec.

Given these conclusions, some observers argue that the continuing, intense preoccupation of many French-Canadian nationalists
with the immigrant population must have had other sources than
simply a fear for ethnic survival. Some accused French Canadians

182

of responding to a deep-rooted xenophobia or even racism. Allegedly, cultural homogeneity, close kinship links, enforced isolation from France, and other factors had made French Canada a "closed society"; the influx of "foreigners" to Quebec was a provocation.[30] Yet, this argument is belied by the fact that, in the past, immigrants were successfully assimilated into French-Canadian society. Any xenophobia was not sufficiently strong to impede acceptance of Italian immigrants, who became the primary focus of nationalist agitation.

The most extensive analysis of 1960s Francophone attitudes toward immigrants appeared in a book-length study of ethnic relations in Montreal by Paul Cappon.[31] Cappon argued that Francophone antagonism to immigrants can be understood only with reference to the North American economic system and Francophone attitudes toward it. Cappon observed that many Francophones deeply resented the position Anglophones had maintained within Quebec's economic structures, but few were ready to attack the economic system *per se* Impressed with the economic benefits of participation in the continental economic system, Francophones merely wished to improve their position within the existing economic structures. They were not prepared to risk their standard of living by disengaging Quebec from this system. (Thus, such formulae as "political independence with economic association" were popular.)[32] Cappon contended that French Canadians are doomed to experience continued, deep frustration as long as they accept capitalism and the continental economic system and their demands are limited to only improved mobility within it.[33] Since the immigrants were viewed by the Francophones as economic competitors, they became the logical object upon which to displace this frustration and thus they met a strong aggressivity: the immigrants served as "scapegoats."[34] In making this analysis, Cappon was echoing the findings of Everett Hughes's study of a Quebec industrial town in the 1930s.[35]

Another possible source of the continued nationalist preoccupation with the immigrant population may have been the symbolism represented by immigrant integration with the Anglophone community. Unlike the English-Canadian population, which has always spoken in English, the immigrant population was making a conscious choice against the Francophone population. In the aftermath of the Quiet Revolution, such rejection may have been especially offensive to many Francophones. The Quiet Revolution established the idea that French Canada and Quebec are virtually identical. By choosing the Anglophone community within Quebec, the immigrant population implicitly was rejecting this identity of Quebec as a Francophone society. It was also rejecting the Quiet Revolution conviction that French Canadians are a dynamic, aggressive people fully capable of building a modern, technological society.

A final aspect of the "immigrant" issue surfaced from time to time in the statements of some nationalist leaders and may be present in the concerns of many other French Canadians: the fear that French Canadians themselves could be influenced by the example of the immigrants.[36] Having heard the repeated contention of immigrants that English is the language of social mobility, French Canadians, too, might decide to send their children to English-language schools. In this regard, French-Canadian fears for ethnic survival perhaps were not as exaggerated as was suggested by Henripin's projections, which concentrated on the immigrant population and assumed little assimilation of the Francophone population.

Obviously, one can cite a number of factors that contributed to making the assimilation of immigrants to the Anglophone community a major political issue. Most important among these was the fear that the Anglicization of immigrants threatened the survival of a Francophone Quebec. This fear for ethnic survival was a powerful force able to mobilize French Canadians who might have been indifferent to such other linguistic issues as working language (e.g., public employees and blue-collar workers in the private sector, who face little need to use English). Within the terms of the projections of professional demographers, the fear for ethnic survival may have been exaggerated. Yet, all the projections, even the most optimistic ones, did anticipate some decline in the Francophone proportion of the Quebec population. Such a decline would have been unprecedented in Quebec. However slight, it could have easily triggered fears for ethnic survival within a population that has always been in a minority within the North American continent and which, in all provinces but Quebec, has already been declining very rapidly. If, contrary to the demographic projections, substantial numbers of Francophones should have followed the example of the immigrants, then fears for survival would indeed have been well-founded.

The Focus of Language Demands on the Government of Quebec

In seeking governmental action with respect to both Anglophone domination of the Quebec economy and the Anglicization of Quebec immigrant populations, Québécois looked primarily to the government of Quebec rather than to the federal government. To some extent, this was a function of the jurisdictions held by the Quebec government. For instance, most constitutional experts agreed that the question of language of instruction lay within the exclusive provincial jurisdiction over education (the provision in the BNA Act for educational rights of religious minorities notwithstanding). But many of the jurisdictions held by the federal government also could be important in effecting governmental action on these issues. The federal government's primacy over immigration and its many powers to regulate economic activities are obvious examples. Thus, the concentration of political demands on the Quebec government must have been due primarily to the belief that only the Quebec government, with a predominantly Francophone electorate, can be induced to intervene directly on behalf of Quebec Francophones, in opposition to other groups in Quebec.

Such a conclusion can only have been reinforced by the position the federal government adopted on language matters, even under a Quebec Francophone prime minister. Refusing to recognize any prior status for French within Quebec, the federal government championed the equality of linguistic rights between Anglophones and Francophones throughout Canada. Federal leaders argued that their policies offered new opportunities to Quebec Francophones. They said that programs of bilingualism within the federal civil service promised to increase the possibility for Quebec Francophones to enter managerial and executive positions. They also argued that their programs of assistance to Francophone minorities outside Quebec promised to reinforce the demographic position of French Canada as a whole within Canada, as well as providing Quebec Francophones with the opportunity to lead satisfying lives in French elsewhere in Canada.

These programs, however, did not seem to arrest the preoccupation of many Quebec Francophones with the position of their ethnic group within Quebec, and with securing strong policies from the Quebec government to improve that position. The continued preoccupation with action within Quebec stemmed in large part from the greater rewards it promised. Improved mobility in the federal civil service could not open nearly as many positions to Quebec Francophones as could improved mobility within the private structures of the Quebec economy. Also, the viability of Francophone minorities outside Quebec did not have the same immediate visibility to Quebec Francophones as did the declining demographic position of Francophones within Quebec. But the relative indifference of many Quebec Francophones to the federal programs can only have been strengthened by the general failure of these programs to advance their stated goals.

Widespread impressions in English Canada to the contrary, the much-publicized reforms of the federal civil service were slow to have an impact on the representation of Quebec Francophones in the executive levels. In 1972, *Le Devoir* published confidential reports prepared for the federal Treasury Board that showed the proportion of Francophones holding executive positions in the federal civil service in 1971 was 14.4 per cent, only marginally higher than the 1966 figure of 13 per cent. Over the period 1966-71, Francophones had figured poorly in recruitment to executive positions, both from within the civil service itself (16 per cent) and from outside the civil service (19 per cent).[37] In the fall of 1975, Laval political scientist Léon Dion proclaimed the reforms of the civil service still ineffective and the federal civil service "just about as English" in 1975 as it was in 1963 or 1965. He noted that not only had the presence of Francophones in the upper levels of the civil service risen by only a few percentage points but that among Francophones who had been recruited to the civil service, Québécois were vastly underrepresented.

Dion's analysis was confirmed by data collected by Colin Campbell and George Szablowski in their study of senior officials in five federal central agencies.[38] Their data show that in the mid-1970s among federal "superbureaucrats" of whom one or both parents were Francophone (25 per cent of their sample), only 39.1 per cent were raised in Quebec. For "superbureaucrats" of whom both parents were Francophone (18.5 per cent of sample), 47.1 per cent were raised in Quebec.[39]

In his 1978 annual report, the Official Languages Commissioner offered this bleak diagnosis:

Briefly, the problem is much the same as it has always been. The overall proportion of Francophones in the Public Service is about on par with the national ratio – around 26% – but their geographic, hierarchic and sectorial distribution is still very uneven. . . . The problem is essentially a human one which is not amenable to organizational solutions as they are usually understood in government circles. In simple terms, it will be found that people know where they are wanted and go where they are wanted. But, by the same token, they readily discover where they are not wanted and make their arrangements accord-

186

ingly. And Francophones have yet to be persuaded – deep down – that they are welcome in Ottawa.

The report showed that despite overall improvement at the executive level, Francophones were still poorly represented in the upper levels of many departments, especially those with economic functions.[40]

As for the federal programs to strengthen Francophone communities outside Quebec, it is difficult to see how they could have checked the overwhelming pressures to assimilation that exist in most parts of Canada. The strength of these assimilationist forces was underlined by the 1971 census, which for the first time measured the language that respondents used regularly in their home. Outside Quebec, only 45 per cent of the Canadians of French origin used French regularly at home. The French-users for particular provinces were: Newfoundland – 13 per cent; P.E.I. – 28 per cent; Nova Scotia – 32 per cent; New Brunswick – 82 per cent; Ontario – 45 per cent; Manitoba – 43 per cent; Saskatchewan – 26 per cent; Alberta – 22 per cent; and B.C. – 10 per cent.[41] In fact, according to the census, outside Quebec among Canadians of all origins only 4.3 per cent used French regularly at home.[42] Demographers expect this assimilation to continue over future decades; only in northern New Brunswick and eastern Ontario will substantial Francophone communities persist. In 1974, demographer Jacques Henripin wrote that:

It seems incontestable that the Francophone population outside Quebec is going to diminish in the future. One can predict that by the year 2,000, 92% to 95% of Canada's Francophones will live in the province of Quebec. In the other provinces, their proportion of the population will be less than 4% or perhaps even 3%, except in New Brunswick where it probably will be between 25% and 30%.[43]

In fact, Table One in the first chapter demonstrates that by 1981 the proportions of provincial populations that spoke French at home were already 3 per cent or less except in Quebec, Ontario, and New Brunswick.

The language policies of the federal government appeared unable to weaken the conviction of many Quebec Francophones that not only improvement of career opportunities, but the very possibility of a large, viable Francophone society lie within Quebec alone. With this conclusion that government programs outside Quebec offered little promise and the conviction that only the government of Quebec could be induced to favour the interests of Francophones in Quebec, the linguistic concerns of Quebec Francophones created strong demands on the Quebec government. As we have seen, effective response to these demands seemed to require major state intervention in the Quebec economy to change the recruitment practices and internal operations of private corporations. To the extent that such policies were not forthcoming, Quebec independence, with its promise of a state with the powers and the will necessary for such intervention, had a ready base of support.

Class Divisions among Quebec Francophones

At the same time that many Francophones were becoming increasingly concerned over the position of their linguistic group within Quebec and were demanding government measures to strengthen the position of the Francophone collectivity, some working-class and lower-middle-class Francophones were also reacting to the position of their economic class. Pointing to the wide differences in economic and social benefit that separated them not only from most Anglophones but from upper-class Francophones as well, these lower-class Francophones called for a Quebec government that would be guided by their needs and interests. Class divisions joined ethnic divisions as a growing source of discontent with particular parties and, indeed, with the political order itself.

As with agitation over the position of Francophones within Quebec, the development of these lower-class grievances can be traced back to the Lesage regime and its impact on Quebec society. Through its rhetoric and programs, the Lesage regime encouraged many Francophones to believe that their social and economic needs would be met by the Quebec government. Yet, by and large, the Liberal programs spoke to the needs and preoccupations of middle-class Francophones, echoing the bias of the Quiet Revolution ideology. The benefits to lower-class French Canadians were less direct and palpable, especially if they remained employed in the private sector. When it nationalized the private hydroelectric enterprises and established the Société générale de financement, the Lesage government had declared that it was striving for the *libération économique* of French Canadians. But to the extent that new economic opportunities were created through these measures, they acted primarily at the white-collar and professional levels.

Similarly, the greatest beneficiaries of reform of the educational, health, and welfare institutions were the members of the bureaucratic middle class who were now freed from clerical domination.

To be sure, lower-class French Canadians might hope for greater mobility through improved educational opportunity. They might also receive more adequate health and welfare services. But these changes in their personal conditions were less dramatic than those experienced by members of the new middle class. For the most part, their economic position remained the same, as is borne out by Vincent Lemieux's comparison of income levels in 1960 and 1968. Lemieux established an index showing the relationship of the mean income of different occupational groups to the mean income of the total population. According to this index, over the period 1960 to 1968, the already favoured position of "liberal professions" increased from 269 to 332. Teachers also benefited, moving from 87 to 108. Other employees of private enterprise, the bulk of the French-Canadian working class, experienced virtually no improvement at all (95 to 97). Farmers actually experienced a decline in this index (107 to 72) and even a decline in their absolute level of income.[44]

Only if they were public-sector employees did lower-class Francophones see their economic condition directly improved by the political modernization of the 1960s. This emerges clearly from Marc Renaud's comparison of the incomes of state workers with those of private-sector workers. Whereas the declared incomes of state-sector workers increased by at least one and a half times (in constant dollars) over the 1960s, those of private-sector workers increased only very slightly. In fact, data on specific occupational categories demonstrate that as they entered the state sector (employees of institutions in 1961 for the most part, teachers in 1964, and physicians and surgeons in 1970) they underwent a considerable increase in their relative income status.[45]

The political modernization of the Quiet Revolution had proven that the Quebec state could be a much more important source of social and economic benefits for large numbers of Québécois than it had ever been in the past. At the same time, it also had demonstrated that political modernization can be far from neutral in the distribution of its benefits among different classes. Increasingly, during the late 1960s, Quebec Francophones drew these lessons and sought to make the Quebec state work more fully on behalf of specifically working-class interests.

The activities of the Lesage administration also contributed in a more direct manner to demands that the Quebec state be used on behalf of working-class interests. In the course of its program of political modernization, the Quebec government became, in one way or another, the employer of a large proportion of the Quebec Francophone labour force, about 200,000 in 1970. The number of civil servants had grown to 53,700 in 1970.[46] Public enterprises (such as Hydro-Québec) represented another 16,366 employees.[47] Also, through its assumption of authority over education, health, and welfare institutions, the Quebec government was in effect the employer of an additional large sector of the labour force. Thus, for many Québécois the Quebec state became the focus of the tensions arising from relations with an employer. The chances were correspondingly greater that they would see the state elites as hostile to their interests and to those of their class. In addition, by the late 1960s labour relations in the public sector had become charged with conflict.

On coming to power, the Liberals had enjoyed the support of Quebec's union leadership and had been anxious to maintain it. Thus, as we have seen, they facilitated the union membership of not only government employees but also the employees of the hospitals and other private institutions that were now brought under governmental authority. As a result, by 1970 the public sector contained 40 per cent of the unionized workers of Quebec.[48] The Confédération des syndicats nationaux (CSN) was especially successful in the recruitment of the public-sector workers. As a Quebec-based union, the CSN could exploit Québécois nationalism at the expense of its rival, the Fédération des travailleurs du Québec (FTQ), which was composed of Quebec branches of international unions. Over the period 1960-70, CSN members in the civil service grew by 30,000 and members in the hospitals grew by 40,000. Thus, by 1970, about half of the CSN membership was in the public sector; only 15 per cent of the FTQ membership was in the public sector.[49] Thanks to the success of the CSN in the public sector, the total memberships of the CSN and FTQ were now about the same, around 200,000 in 1970. A third major union, the teachers' union, was wholly within the public sector; the Corporation des enseignants du Québec (CEQ) grew from 14,000 members in 1959-60 to 71,360 in 1968-69.[50] Beyond facilitating the unionization of workers in the public sector, the Liberal regime gave new powers to unions in the public sector. In particular, as we have already seen, it granted public employees the right not only to bargain collectively but to strike.

By the mid-1960s, relations between the Quebec government and the public-sector unions had changed from the harmony of the initial "honeymoon" to a growing conflict. As bargaining broke down, unions exercised their newly granted rights in a rash of strikes. Frequently, the Quebec government drew on its legislative powers to end the strikes and impose its own settlement. In effect, on an *ad hoc* basis it was retracting the right to strike that the unions had secured from the Lesage regime through such struggle. In the process, union leaders began to see the Quebec government as no more accommodating than private employers. In fact, the government appeared to be an even more powerful foe since it could break a strike by rendering it illegal. Private employers could not do that. Also, in the eyes of many, the Quebec government was very much at the service of private employers, resisting demands for higher wages largely in deference to the private employers' fear such an increase would generate pressure on them to grant similar increases.

Jean-Marc Piotte contends that these frustrations experienced by the unions in their dealings with the Quebec government led the leadership of the entire Quebec union movement to conclude that the Quebec state was inevitably hostile to working-class interests, whichever of the "old-line" parties was in power.

> Faced with an employer who is also legislator and who can use the State's apparatus of repression against the unions, the public-sector unions induce the radicalization and politicization of the union federations, realizing that the Government, whether it be Liberal or Union nationale, can act only within the norms fixed by private enterprise.[51]

The CSN appeared to progress further in this "radicalization" than did the FTQ. Not only did the CSN have the majority of its membership concentrated in the public sector, but its leadership had been developing, over the 1960s, an increasingly severe critique of capitalist society.[52]

This "political radicalization" of union leaders was reflected in the tactics and rhetoric they adopted in their dealings with the Quebec government in the 1970s. In 1970, mainly at the instigation of the CSN, the CEQ and FTQ joined with the CSN in laying the groundwork for a "Common Front" of public-sector employees. The unions hoped that through forcing the provincial government to negotiate a collective agreement with a single body representing all the public-sector employees, rather than with each of the different unions as had been the case in the past, they would be able to force from the Quebec government a more generous settle-

191

ment that would be applied on a uniform basis throughout the public sector.

In 1972, after the collapse of negotiations with the Quebec government, this Common Front staged a general strike that involved most public-sector employees and lasted two weeks. The strike was finally ended with the passage of special provincial legislation suspending the right to strike in the public sector. Initially, a large segment of the union leadership (including the presidents of the CSN, FTQ, and CEQ) advised their membership to disobey the law. A referendum was held among the membership on this question. While a majority of those voting in the referendum supported disobedience of the law, the Common Front leadership judged both the size of the majorities and the proportion of members actually voting in the referendum to be too small to justify their policy of disobedience. Only at this point did they advise their members to return to work. Thus, through the Common Front strike, the top union leadership had been led to challenge openly the authority of the Quebec state in the name of the distinctive interests of working-class Québécois. Subsequently, the three union presidents were successfully prosecuted by the provincial government for inciting disobedience of the special back-to-work legislation and were each sentenced to one-year imprisonment. This conviction of the union leaders spurred a further general strike that extended beyond the public-sector employees and led to the occupation of television and radio stations and public buildings in numerous small towns.[53]

The confrontation between the union movement and the Quebec government was further accentuated by broad ideological documents[54] the union leadership had circulated to the membership and that they frequently echoed in such slogans as "Il faut casser le systeme." In particular, the CSN document, Ne comptons que sur nos propres moyens, argued vigorously that the Quebec government was the prisoner of Canadian and American economic elites and that, as a consequence, "We can rely only on our own means."

Strangled on the one side by the Anglo-Canadian bourgeoisie, which claims its share of services to fight against American competition, and on the other hand by the American monopolies that demand more and more raw materials and energy, the Quebec state has become a service state. . . . Meanwhile, the major decisions continue to be made on Bay Street and Wall Street.[55]

192

The document was especially vigorous in its detailed attack on "The Mistakes of the Quiet Revolution," contending that during the 1960s French-Canadian capitalists and technocrats simply used the Quebec state to further their own interests.

In the aftermath of the Common Front episode, it became clear that the union movement as a whole was far from united in any radical critique of the Quebec government. In reaction to the ideology and strategy adopted during the Common Front strike, a dissident element in the CSN broke to form the *Centrale des syndicats démocratiques* (CSD). It became known through the Cliche Commission hearings of 1974-75 that elements within the FTQ leadership had maintained close links with the Liberal government, securing governmental support in their struggles with the CSN over new members. At the time of the Common Front it was clear that a substantial segment of the public-sector employees did not support the tactics adopted by the leadership. It was also clear, moreover, that majority Quebec public opinion was opposed to the Common Front general strike. Nevertheless, the Common Front episode does demonstrate that a significant degree of alienation from the Quebec state existed among the Quebec workers, white-collar as well as blue-collar. The readiness of many public-sector workers to disobey the back-to-work legislation, plus the widespread general strike in opposition to the imprisonment of the three union presidents, show that large numbers of Québécois workers were ready to accept the contention of their "radicalized" leaders that the Quebec state was, by nature, hostile to working-class interests and that, as a consequence, they were not bound to respect its authority.

The Class Struggle and Canadian Political Integration

Accompanying this class-based alienation from the Quebec government was an increased antagonism against the French-Canadian upper classes in general. As we have already seen, such antagonism was not new to Quebec; it can be seen in the treatment received by religious, social, and political elites at various points in French-Canadian history. In New France and during the first decades after the Conquest, the clergy often experienced great difficulty in extracting from the French-Canadian *habitants* the tithes to which it was legally entitled. (Only after the 1840s was the clergy able to impose itself on the French-Canadian mass, thanks to increased personnel and a strengthened organization.)[56] The independently minded *habitants* never granted the seigneurial class the status it sought.

During the 1940s and 1950s some of the most bitter strikes involved the small French-Canadian family firms. Often this resentment seemed even greater than that reserved for Anglophones. The depth of this lower-class resentment is vividly portrayed in such writings as Pierre Vallières's autobiography, *Nègres blancs d'Amérique*.[57] As Vallières recounts his life, little mention is made of Quebec Anglophones; he appears to have had little contact with them. The strongest invective is reserved for upper-class French Canadians. Vallières relates his experiences as a clerk in a French-Canadian brokerage house, L.G. Beaubien and Co., in this fashion:

> At New Year's Madame de Gaspé-Beaubien, spouse of the deceased founder of the enterprise, would come in her wheelchair to offer us chocolates and her sanctimonious old smile! She was president of the Hôpital Sainte-Justine (Justine was her first name), and all the nurses detested her. The brokerage house L.G. Beaubien looked after the investments of the nuns, and the Cardinal-of-the-Poor (Paul-Émile Léger) presented the pontifical Cross to the great Christian lady whose fortune had been made out of the exploitation and alienation of the people. Ah! the remains of our 'national' bourgeoisie! To be incinerated, comrades, to be incinerated![58]

With the 1960s, this long-standing resentment against the French-Canadian upper class became much more open and intense. In part, this stemmed from the frustrations that lower-class Francophones experienced in their treatment by the Quebec government. The Quebec government was, after all, staffed almost exclusively by Francophones. Yet unless they had become part of the public sector, the lower classes had gained relatively few direct benefits from the Quiet Revolution programs these governmental elites had established in the name of the Québécois collectivity. Moreover, those Francophones who were in the public sector experienced just as much conflict and frustration in dealings with their employers as did their counterparts in private Anglophone corporations. In fact, the government elites seemed to be aligning themselves with Anglophone corporate elites, resisting demands for higher public-sector salaries out of respect for their wishes. It was here, in the public sector, that the most dramatic confrontation between Francophone workers and their employers had occurred –

a confrontation that pitted Francophone against Francophone. Thus, the expansion of the Quebec state had brought out more clearly than ever before the contradiction of class interests that divides Francophones. The struggle was no longer primarily over status and prestige, as in the days when the clerical and liberal professional elites were dominant. It was now a struggle over power and wealth, acquired primarily through control of the Quebec state.

One might expect that Francophones who identified strongly with the working class, and who perceived that they had distinct class interests directly opposed to those of upper-class Francophones, would have become increasingly oriented to working classes elsewhere in Canada. Considering the new importance that these Francophones attached to class, the differences in language and culture that distinguished them from other workers in Canada would not assume the same importance they had in the past. There would have been a much greater readiness to collaborate with Anglophone workers in pan-Canadian working-class organizations. At the same time, linguistic and cultural similarities shared by all classes of French Canadians would no longer seem as meaningful. In the process, the Francophone collectivity and the borders of Quebec would have lost much of their salience to working-class Francophones.

Many social scientists assumed that exactly such a process will take place in "multinational" countries; they predicted that the increased stress on class that comes through economic development will cause a decline of cultural and regional "particularisms" in favour of a close social and political integration. Yet, by and large, this has not been the case in Canada. Rather than collaborating with English-Canadian working-class leaders in the transformation of the Canadian system as a whole, most working-class leaders in Quebec concentrated their energies on independent action designed to bring about economic change *within* Quebec alone. In many instances, the demands for change in the Quebec government extended, tacitly or explicitly, to the disengagement of Quebec from the federal system, and the growth of working-class militancy in Quebec served to weaken support for the system.

"Class" and "Nation" in the Quebec Left

The tendency for working-class militancy to concentrate on economic and political change within Quebec can be traced most clearly among Quebec's leftist and Marxist intellectuals. In general, during the 1960s and 1970s they agreed that past French-Canadian ideologies had reflected the preoccupations of upper-class Francophones and, through manipulation of "national" symbols, served to obscure the extent to which these upper-class preoccupations were in direct opposition to the needs and interests of working-class Francophones. But they were not as unanimous regarding the ideology that should be adopted in its place. In particular, they were not be able to agree on the character and importance of what was the central issue of past ideologies, the "nation." What was to be the place of the "nation" in an ideology resolutely committed to Quebec working-class needs and interests? Despite this continuing disagreement over the "national question," most left-wing intellectuals stressed strategies for social and economic change and, typically, argued for the independence of Quebec. Even among those who dismissed the "nation" as insignificant to the needs of Francophone workers, many agreed that, for one reason or another, the emancipation of this class involved the emancipation of Quebec from Canada.

For many of the early left-wing writers, Quebec independence was necessary to Francophone workers partly because this class had *cultural* needs that could be met only through *national* liberation. Usually this argument portrayed Quebec as a colony; Francophone workers were suffering the cultural effects of colonization. In presenting Quebec as a colony, these writers were echoing as well an argument widely used by right-wing nationalists who did not recognize any class contradictions within the Francophone collectivity. They, too, argued that Quebec is a colony of both English Canada and the United States and thus is in essentially the same situation as many nations of the Third World. The logic of self-determination that was bringing independence to these peoples, they argued, should also be applied to Quebec. However, the analysis of the leftists went much further. Drawing on such writers as Franz Fanon and Jacques Berque, the new "class-oriented" intellectuals turned the colonial model into a justification not only for the liberation of Quebec from its colonial masters but also for the liberation of Francophone workers from Francophone upper classes.

A striking example of this "radicalization" of the argument for national self-determination is found in the writings of Paul Chamberland.[59] Chamberland portrayed decolonization as the emancipation of distinctive national cultures from the debilitating and destructive effects of imperialism. Such a cultural liberation would have been very much in the interests of Québécois as well.

Québécois, like all other colonized peoples, suffered from the "depossession" and "depersonalization" that were the inevitable result of "the present universalization, which is only a uniformization, dehumanization and cosmopolitanism."[60] However, he implied, upper-class Francophones have too long collaborated with English Canadians and Americans to participate in the national culture; they would always act to undermine it. Thus, the true national culture rests only with the lower classes: "only the social and economic liberation of the popular classes can bring about the emancipation of the nation and the construction of a new society, authentically Québécois."[61]

The Francophone working class, whatever economic interests it may have shared with other workers, therefore also had an interest in acquiring a coherent national identity. This could be gained only through emancipation from both Anglophones and the Francophone collaborators. A merely economic liberation of Francophone workers from capitalist forces would be insufficient for cultural liberation. There had to be a *national* liberation.

While the stress on distinct cultural interests of Francophone workers and the consequent necessity of "national liberation" were widespread in leftist writings during the 1960s, there was little agreement among leftist intellectuals over the precise content of the culture of working-class Francophones, the "authentic" culture of the Québécois collectivity. In particular, they were not able to agree on the true working-class language. For some, it was the creole-like mixture of French grammar and syntax with extensive English vocabulary that was prevalent among the lower classes in east Montreal, the famous *joual*. During the 1960s, many young Québécois writers wrote novels, plays, and poetry in *joual*, arguing that it was the true language of the Quebec people and should be recognized and appreciated as such. Yet, for others, this popular vernacular, with its heavy adoption of English, was merely a symptom of Quebec's national oppression. Rather than being celebrated, the vernacular had harmful intellectual and emotional effects and should be eliminated. This would be a primary benefit of independence. As the Parti pris manifesto of 1965-66 declared:

> the Québécois worker is divided, torn between two languages and two cultures; there are vast domains of reality that he can no longer name in his mother tongue (including technical terms, belonging as they do to the other group); as his language atrophies, his possibilities for expression being reduced, he reaches "joual," a language in the process of decomposition. Forced to

live in a world that does not belong to him, he is no longer able even to name this world. This induces a sentiment of humiliation, of inferiority, which is too well known that we should need to dwell upon it. Colonialism, as we have often explained, leads to the disintegration of the personality of the colonized.[62]

This confusion among left-wing writers over the "authentic" working-class language and culture persisted into the 1970s. In a 1975 article in a Quebec Marxist periodical of which he was co-editor, Léandre Bergeron came out squarely in favour of *joual* as the language of the Québécois; French is merely the tool of an old imperialist power. Bergeron attacked those who support the replacement of *joual* by a correct French (a position he associated with the "petty bourgeois" leadership of the Parti québécois):

If the new PQ elite arrives in power, the Québécois language will find itself violently attacked by a [new-middle-class] elite, which will cry out that we should speak French, that Quebec must be French, that the Québécois language is the oral excrement of ignorance and that we must speak the "French" of Jacques-Yvan Morin, just as this old-fashioned elite will tell us that we must develop a Québécois capitalism in order for our people to enter the world.[63]

However, the other co-editors of the periodical refused to attach their names to the article, contending that the language question is *extrêmement complexe*. They hoped, nevertheless, that publication of the article would stimulate debate.[64]

Given such confusion over the precise character of the authentic working-class language and culture, it is not surprising that by the early 1970s many attempts to define "the national question" rested simply upon how the status of the French language results in the economic deprivation of Francophone workers. *Travailleurs québécois et lutte nationale*, published in 1974, contends that:

Many Québécois workers are nationalist because they see and live every day the effects of national oppression such as the use of English as the principal working language in Quebec, favouritism toward Anglophones in promotions, and the differences in wages between Quebec and Ontario.[65]

Unlike the Parti pris literature, there is no discussion of how, through colonization, Francophone workers experience cultural alienation, loss of identity, or masochistic self-degradation. National oppression is seen in essentially material terms. (In fact, the colonial model is not used; rather, Quebec is seen as a "nation" within a large multinational state.)[66] Nevertheless, the authors argue that the "national question" is of critical importance to Quebec workers and come out squarely for the independence of Quebec.[67]

The writers of Parti pris and other intellectuals who argued that independence is necessary to liberate Francophone workers from cultural oppression always advanced a second (and, for many, more important) reason for Quebec independence: economic oppression. Quebec's colonial status had resulted not merely in cultural alienation but in underdevelopment of Quebec's economy and in discrimination against Francophone workers. For these reasons Quebec workers had a common interest in freeing Quebec from the control of foreign bourgeoisies, whether English-Canadian or American, and from the federal government that serves their will:

This situation of underdevelopment in relation to the rest of North America, and the rest of Canada, is explained by the fact that Quebec's economy is controlled from the outside: more than three quarters of the capital which is invested in Quebec and upon which its economy is based are foreign to Quebec, controlled by Canadians ["Canadians" in the French] or by Americans. The Quebec nation lives in a country which does not belong to it, of which it has been dispossessed. . . . The Quebec nation, because of Confederation, controls neither its political life nor its economic life. This a primordial fact, and it must be recognized that Confederation is the framework within which operate all the forms of domination from which Quebec suffers.[68]

During the mid-1960s, as in the document just cited, the "internal colony" thesis was dominant: foreign economic domination was seen essentially in terms of the English-Canadian bourgeoisie and Ottawa. But by the late 1960s, attention had shifted to North America as a whole, and Quebec was placed within a system of external domination centred in American imperialism.[69]

At the same time, this stress on the essentially economic exploitation of Quebec workers served to highlight the fact that exploitation was not simply the product of external agents. It existed within the nation itself. Even in the 1960s, few Francophone leftists would subscribe fully to the notion of a wholly working-class Francophone nation, whether an "ethnic class" or a *nation prolétaire*. From the beginning, the Parti pris writers noted the growing strength of a Francophone new middle class, rooted in the Quebec state of the Quiet Revolution. Quebec independence would be a hollow victory for Quebec workers if it were simply to replace the "foreign" bourgeoisie with a vastly reinforced Francophone bourgeoisie. Just as the full expression of the authentic identity of Quebec workers required freedom from the quasi-assimilated Francophone upper classes, so economic emancipation of Quebec workers had to mean the end even of Francophone economic and political domination. Quebec independence had to entail a "democratic national revolution accomplished under the impetus of the working classes."[70]

The Front de Libération du Québec

With its forthright use of political violence, the Front de libération du Québec was a highly marginal phenomenon, directly involving perhaps no more than 100 people in its various waves of bombings and vandalism during the 1960s. Nonetheless, the FLQ rhetoric also demonstrated this juxtaposition of national and social concerns.[71] This is most evident in the FLQ's actions in 1970, during what has become known as the October Crisis.

The Liberation Cell of the FLQ initiated the crisis on October 5, 1970, by kidnapping James Cross, British trade commissioner, who was a ready symbol of British colonialism. Allegedly, the cell had previously attempted to kidnap the symbol of another form of "imperialist oppression," the Montreal consul of the United States. But, apparently with no consultation of the Liberation Cell, the Chenier Cell proceeded to kidnap a French Canadian, provincial cabinet minister Pierre Laporte. Apparently, Laporte was to be seen as a representative of the Francophone dominant class. Moreover, the Liberation Cell's widely disseminated manifesto, written in a popular language clearly intended for the Francophone working class, forthrightly called for a Quebec independence that would be "total," freeing Francophone workers of their specific exploitation:

> The Front de libération du Québec is not a messiah, nor a modern-day Robin Hood. It is a movement of Quebec workers who are determined to make every effort so that the Quebec people take full control of their destiny.

The Front de libération du Québec seeks total independence for Québécois, united in a society which is free and is forever purged of the clique of voracious sharks, of domineering "big bosses" and their lackeys who have made Quebec their private preserve of cheap labour and unscrupulous exploitation.[72]

After depicting at length the deprivations of the Francophone working class, the manifesto proceeded to name both Anglophones and Francophones as this class's exploiters.

The federal government took the matter very seriously. Refusing to accede to most of the two cells' demands for release of their respective prisoners, the government proceeded to impose the War Measures Act. On this basis, membership in the FLQ was made illegal and police were given the authority to detain suspected members for up to twenty-one days without being charged and up to ninety days without a trial. Laporte was discovered murdered shortly after the Act had been imposed. However, several weeks passed before police discovered Cross's location. In exchange for his release, Cross's kidnappers were allowed to leave the country.

At the same time, popular response to the FLQ's actions demonstrated that there was little support for genuine revolutionary action, whether it was rationalized in national terms or in social terms. Initially, there were some expressions of support for the FLQ, most notably at a student rally. However, what sympathy the FLQ may have generated was quickly extinguished by the assassination of Laporte and, more generally, by the claims of the federal authorities that the FLQ posed a grave threat to the very maintenance of the existing political order.

In hindsight, it is clear that there was no genuine danger during the October Crisis. On this basis, federal imposition of the War Measures Act is difficult to defend. (In fact, it did not even contribute materially to the apprehension of the members of the two FLQ cells.)[73] In the short term, federal actions such as the detention of over 500 persons may have shaken popular readiness to use even legal means, such as the election of the Parti québécois, to secure social and political change.[74] But the actions also served to reinforce alienation from the federal order among many of the activists within law-abiding opposition groups, whether the Parti québécois or the various union movements. For some, the October Crisis demonstrated that the federal government was prepared to defend the economically powerful and to subordinate Quebec to its will. The October Crisis did not, however, lead to a new solidarity within the Quebec left as a whole. Leftist intellectuals continued to be divided over the relative importance of social and national objectives and over the appropriate strategies for securing them.

Ambivalence over the National Question: The Quebec Left in the 1970s

During the 1960s, the debate had remained open with respect to the precise role the working class should play in the movement of independence.[75] Some leftists were prepared to see alliances between Quebec workers and those of the Francophone petty bourgeoisie who advocated independence. Once the national revolution was achieved, then Quebec workers could undertake the second stage, a social revolution. Others, however, were fearful that such alliances could only result in the permanent hegemony of the Francophone petty bourgeoisie. If there were ever to be a social revolution, Quebec workers must dominate the process from the beginning. The national and social revolutions must be one and the same.

In fact, by the early 1970s, apprehension among Quebec leftists over the dangers of working-class alliances with Francophone middle classes had become so strong that the very objective of Quebec independence began to recede from attention. Increasingly, they directed their attention to underlining the profound differences of interest separating Quebec workers from other Francophones and to reorganizing along the lines of the envisaged perspective. Class, rather than nation, became the guiding concept. Nonetheless, the chief centre of attention remained securing change within Quebec itself. If there was a new ambivalence about the goal of Quebec independence, there was still the same disposition to see Quebec as the essential base of action.

Several factors explain this new tendency to concentrate on "social" issues at the expense of the national question. First, the escalating conflict between Quebec unions and the Quebec government served to exemplify the presence of class differences among Quebec Francophones. Even if the personnel of the Quebec state were Francophone, they were (according to many leftists) locked in close alliance with English-Canadian and American capital, whose bidding they followed in dealings with public-sector unions. Second, by the early 1970s the Parti québécois had been able to establish itself as the pre-eminent spokesman for Quebec nationalism. In effect, it had secured a monopoly of the national question. Quebec leftists who were dissatisfied with the social and economic program of the PQ tended to abandon the whole perspective of the national question in favour of the firmer ground of class issues.

202

Finally, the 1970s saw a new influence on younger Quebec intellectuals of contemporary European Marxism and a corresponding unease with the whole idea of nation. While the working-class sympathies of the Parti pris writers of the 1960s had led them to proclaim themselves Marxists, in point of fact most of them did not adhere closely to a Marxist framework.[76] (Jean-Marc Piotte admits that he had never made his way all through *Das Kapital*.)[77] With the 1970s, this all changed. Attention shifted from the model Parti pris had adopted from the Third World studies of Fanon and Memmi, which saw Quebec locked in a colonial relationship with English Canada. Instead, younger intellectuals sought to place Quebec within theories of advanced capitalism, which stressed the commonality of Quebec's experience with other areas that have undergone the transition to monopoly capitalism. Often, these theories were applied in a mechanical, resolutely orthodox fashion that could allow little importance to Quebec national specificity or to the national question.[78]

The 1976 election of the Parti québécois, however, appears to have induced a new determination even among orthodox Marxist intellectuals to come to grips with the national question. With the Parti québécois in power, formally committed to Quebec sovereignty and intending to mobilize the Quebec population around membership in a nation collectivity, Quebec Marxists could no longer remain indifferent to the power of national sentiment and its capacity as a force for social change – or reaction. To be sure, some Quebec Marxists remained faithful to the highly orthodox class-oriented perspective they had acquired over the decade preceding the PQ victory. Organizations such as En lutte or La ligue communiste (M-L) continued to attack national sentiment as being a bourgeois construct that can only hurt working-class solidarity by sapping pan-Canadian worker solidarity. But other Marxists sought once again to situate working-class interests within a struggle for Quebec independence. In some cases, they even returned to some of the 1960s premises of Parti pris, stressing the impact of national oppression on working-class Francophones and suggesting the potential value of strategic alliances with the Francophone petty bourgeoisie.[79]

The Centrality of Quebec to the Union Movement

The tendency to emphasize economic and political change within Quebec, rather than within the full Canadian political system, was not restricted to the more radical of the working-class spokesmen. It was true of the Quebec union movement as well. This can be seen in the attitudes the unions adopted on Quebec's relations with the rest of Canada. Over the 1960s and 1970s, the leaders of the three major unions came to advocate greater and greater autonomy for the government of Quebec. In addition, the unions were prepared to support directly or indirectly the Parti québécois in its efforts to displace the Bourassa regime. None of the unions was ready to endorse Quebec sovereignty outright and, as we shall see, the CSN and CEQ were to become critical of the Parti québécois once it had assumed power. Nevertheless, the unions maintained a firm commitment to the expansion of the Quebec state, at Ottawa's expense.

The Québécois orientation of the unions is even more clearly revealed in their attitude toward pan-Canadian union structures. Here the preference for independent action within Quebec is clear. The most forthright exponent of the importance of class, the CSN, continued to remain outside the Canadian Labour Congress, as did the CEQ. As for the FTQ, its growing militancy was accompanied by attempts to weaken its links with the CLC and strengthen its identity as a Québécois union federation. In 1979, FTQ leader Louis Laberge observed that the Québécois often feel frustrated within Canadian unions "because they can never obtain the majority in order to respond to their aspirations."[80]

The unions' focus on Quebec as the central base of action can be attributed partly to the patterns of class relations within Quebec: the Francophone new middle class had a special interest in cultivating working-class support. As Marcel Fournier observed in 1977:

> One of the principal obstacles to the realization of unity of action within the Canadian working class is the advantage that the Quebec working class seems to draw from reforms proposed by the (nationalist) Québécois petty bourgeoisie: in effect, this class was able to carry out certain reforms of the "Quiet Revolution" only on the condition that it secured the support of elements of the working movement and paid the price for it (easier access to education and health care, establishment of a better pension system, the unionization of the public service, modification of the Labour Code, increase in minimum wages, etc.).[81]

In the case of the CSN and CEQ, the Quebec political arena has had a special significance. The determination of the CSN to remain an independent Quebec-based union can be traced in part to the concentration of over half of its membership in the public sector of

204

the Quebec provincial government. The fortune of these employees, and thus of the CSN, was closely tied to that of Quebec and the success of its struggles with the federal government. The CSN could be a more credible defender of the members' interests if it was an exclusively Quebec-based union and thus could articulate a certain Quebec nationalism. (The CSN's initial success in recruiting these public employees, in competition with the CLC-FTQ, was based to a large extent on these factors.) This same reasoning applies even more to the Corporation des enseignants du Québec, whose membership is wholly concentrated within the Quebec public sector. One cannot as easily explain in these terms the desire of the FTQ to increase the distance between itself and the Canadian Labour Congress; the FTQ does not have a high concentration of public employees among its membership, but it may have been seeking to increase its attractiveness to Quebec public-sector workers.

The preference of unions in Quebec to concentrate their activities within Quebec alone may also have been a reaction to the relative conservatism of labour unions in English Canada.[82] During the 1960s and 1970s, the Canadian Labour Congress was still clearly tied to the conventional "trade unionism" Quebec union leaders have decried. The CSN and the CEQ, in particular, concerned themselves with much more than the normal objective of collective bargaining and, consequently, advanced broad-based critiques of capitalist society. Some of the tension between the FTQ and other units within the CLC stemmed from the greater radicalism of the FTQ leaders. The tactics and, especially, the rhetoric used in the Common Front strike of 1972 alarmed many English-Canadian labour leaders.

The focus of Quebec unions on action in Quebec seems to be more than just a reaction against the relative conservatism of the English-speaking union leaderships. It was also a response to distinctive features of their clientele, a Francophone labour force. In certain respects, the interests of Francophone and Anglophone workers diverged. For instance, it was in the interest of each group that its language should be the principal language of work, thus giving it an advantage in the competition for jobs. Not all Quebec Francophone workers were affected by the language question. In the public sector, which accounted for over 40 per cent of the unionized labour in Quebec, there was little need to use English at all. Even in the private sector, the need to use English, and the consequent disadvantage to Francophones, lay mainly at the white-collar level.[83] In Anglophone corporations, however, many blue-collar workers did have to master some English technical terms. They may have had to rely on English-language manuals and other documents, and they may have had to serve Anglophone customers. Moreover, capacity in English often was used in the past as a cover for simple ethnic discrimination. After all, French Canadians were relative latecomers to Quebec's industrial structures. Blue-collar positions often were already occupied by English-speakers, whether native Anglophones or immigrants who were integrating themselves with the Anglophone community. French Canadians were relegated to inferior positions. English-speaking workers had every reason to seek to perpetuate this ethnic stratification among blue-collar positions, and they could usually count on the support of Anglophone foremen and managers in this. Differences such as these may well have reinforced Francophone union leaders and militants in the belief that the interests of Francophone workers can be served best through distinctly Québécois unions.

Another area where the interests of Anglophone and Francophone workers diverged and the Quebec unions were led to support the interest of Francophones is the linguistic group to which immigrants will be integrated. Here, the pressures on union leaders in Quebec to identify their organizations with the Francophones of Quebec were very evident. In both the csn and ftq, the leadership had sought to prevent union involvement in the struggle over the right of immigrant parents to choose the language of instruction of their children.[84] The csn president, Marcel Pepin, contended that this issue did not really involve the unions: "We are not here principally as a group of French Canadians but as a group of workers."[85] But, under pressures from militants, both the csn and the ftq finally declared their opposition to parental choice of language of instruction among immigrants and their general support for a unilingual Quebec.

The degree to which Francophone workers are immersed in the Francophone collectivity should be borne in mind. Language and culture do circumscribe the people and places with whom one has contact and about whom one has knowledge. However much there may be similarities in the condition of Francophone and Anglophone workers, union leaders and militants have experienced these conditions in French, in Quebec. It is normal that they should interpret these experiences in Québécois terms, seeking both enemies and allies within the world they are most familiar with. Moreover, to the extent that Francophone workers have regular contact with Anglophone employers, grievances arising from relations with these employers (working conditions, salary, etc.) can easily become generalized to an ethnic antagonism against Anglophones in general, making it even harder to recognize any commonality of interest with workers elsewhere in Canada.

To summarize: economic development and political modernization led a substantial number of Quebec Francophones to identify with working-class interests and to see these interests as directly opposed both by Anglophone owners and managers and by upper-class Francophones as well. Yet, during the 1960s and 1970s this new class militancy did not serve to integrate the Canadian political system in the way one might expect. It did not lead to a new interest in collaborating with working-class organizations in English Canada nor did it undermine the salience of Quebec nationalism and the Francophone collectivity for working-class Francophones. Associated with the differences in language and culture that distinguish Francophone workers from other workers in Canada were differences in economic interest, identity, and world view, with the result that both radical and moderate elements within the working-class leadership sought to resolve class problems through independent action in Quebec. In many instances, these strategies for economic and political change extended to the disengagement of Quebec from the Canadian political system, so as to secure a Quebec government responsible only to Francophone working-class interests.

Business Response to the New Class Militancy

The measures Quebec business undertook to contend more effectively with the Quebec working class are testimony both to the radicalization of the working-class movement during the late 1960s and early 1970s and to the unions' tendency to focus on change within Quebec. In the late 1960s, a comprehensive employers' organization, le Conseil de patronat, was formed to bring together the various business associations existing in the province.[86] While it has had a broad membership, by the mid-1970s reaching 130 associations, which represented 80 per cent of Quebec's manpower, the Conseil has tended to be dominated by the multinational corporations that provide most of its funding.[87]

The only other province where business has formed such a comprehensive organization is British Columbia, which also has been marked by open class conflict.[88] Indeed, in the words of one business leader, the organization arose out of "the need for a common business point of view in face of a more militant labour movement and the various common fronts."[89] During the first few years of its existence, the organization focused primarily on labour legislation, but it then branched out into other areas, including the production of literature defending Canadian federalism and the free enterprise system. Nonetheless, labour relations continue to be a pre-eminent preoccupation: the Conseil has a research director on labour relations and has two industrial relations specialists on its sixteen-person staff.[90]

The Quiet Revolution modernization of the Quebec state had a highly destabilizing impact on Quebec's political life. Not only did the new dynamism of the Quebec state lead many Francophones to attach a new importance to the activities of the Quebec state, it led to a vastly heightened impact on political life of both ethnic and class divisions within Quebec society. The halting initiatives of the Lesage regime to make Quebec Francophones *maîtres chez nous* encouraged many Francophones to demand much greater intervention on behalf of their group, with respect to both Anglophone economic elites and Anglicizing immigrants. The new role of the Quebec state as employer and distributor of major material benefits to different categories of Québécois helped to make many lower-class Québécois much more aware of the differences in class interest that separated them from other Québécois. Through this politicization of ethnic and class cleavages, the reforms of the Quiet Revolution engendered not only a wider participation in Quebec political life but a greater perception of the state as a focus of inter-group struggle. For groups whose demands were not satisfied, whether Francophone nationalists or working-class militants, there was a growing tendency to see the Quebec state as the prisoner of an opposing group. Accordingly, the only solution envisaged was a major change in the political order so that the state would become more responsive. For many, the political independence of Quebec seemed to be an essential condition for this "liberation" of the Quebec state. Thus, as the case of Quebec demonstrates, one of the results of political modernization can be the intensification of conflict within not only the political system but society as a whole. This intensification of conflict may well have consequences that the initiators of political modernization neither foresaw nor welcomed.

CHAPTER SEVEN
The Politics of Discontent: Government Policies and the Rise of the Parti Québecois

As we have seen, the late 1960s and the 1970s were marked by a steady rise in political discontent and alienation among Quebec Francophones. The sources and forms of this discontent were varied, but to a large extent they can be traced to the modernizing reforms of the Quiet Revolution in the early 1960s, with their massive growth in public spending and the proliferation of new structures of authority. Through its rhetoric and actions, the Lesage regime had led many Québécois to the firm conviction that the Quebec state had both the capacity and the obligation to bring about major change: in particular, to give Francophones the pre-eminent position within the Quebec economy and to ensure that all Québécois, regardless of class position, would enjoy satisfactory levels of services in a wide variety of areas, such as education, health, welfare, and housing.

In many cases, these new expectations were not met. The forms of the Quiet Revolution served to expand and strengthen social categories that were especially likely to view the existing order with ambivalence or suspicion. These social categories included new-middle-class technocrats who argued that only concerted action of a strong Quebec state could ensure proper economic and social development; university graduates who saw little possibility of integrating themselves into Quebec's Anglophone-dominated enterprises and therefore looked to the Quebec public sector; white-collar and blue-collar public-sector employees who depended on the Quebec government for their livelihood; union leaders who increasingly saw the Quebec government as hostile to themselves and the interests of their constituents.

The various forms of political discontent devolved primarily on the Quebec rather than the federal state. It was the Quebec state, rather than Ottawa, that had engendered these new political discontents, through creating expectations of state policies and services that were not met or through becoming the state-employer to whom personal fates were tied. For the same reasons, the strategy for the discontented became the search for further change in the Quebec state, in its policies and its structures. Ottawa, for its part, appeared to be either hostile to their aspirations or, perhaps more typically, was considered irrelevant. For these further reasons, most programs for social, economic, or political change implicitly or explicitly involved the further transfer of powers or resources from Ottawa to Quebec City. In the limiting case, they involved the accession of Quebec to independence.

Many Francophones, especially among the new middle class, looked to the Quebec state to continue the basic thrust of the Quiet Revolution: to use its powers and fiscal resources to transform Francophone institutions, thus enabling Francophones to participate in the highest levels of modern, technological society. This meant a continuing reorientation and expansion of Quebec's educational system. It also meant further strengthening Francophone economic enterprises, whether through the establishment of public enterprises or through financial support of Francophone-owned private enterprises.

By the late 1960s, these pressures to continue the Quiet Revolution were not the only challenge facing the Quebec government. The two broad critiques of the Quiet Revolution we have examined had also become influential among Quebec Francophones. While sharing the Quiet Revolution belief in the potential of the Quebec state to improve the condition of Quebec Francophones, they rejected some of the Lesage government's assumptions about how the Quebec state should go about this task. First, many Francophones, concerned over the position of their group relative to other ethnic groups in Quebec, rejected the Quiet Revolution assumption that the position of Francophones could be advanced essentially through strengthening Francophone institutions. Now it was argued that the interests of Francophones demanded direct state intervention in the activities of the non-Francophone population. The language practices of Anglophone-owned enterprises would have to be changed through government action; the strengthening of Francophone corporations was insufficient. Also, the parents of immigrant children would have to be required to send their children to French-language schools. Second, Francophones who identified with working-class interests argued that the types of social and economic programs introduced by the Lesage government could have only marginal benefits for them. The Quebec state now had to develop programs especially designed to meet lower-class needs, even at the expense of the interests of upper-class Francophones and Anglophones. Similarly, in its treatment of public employees, it should be prepared to set new standards for private corporations to emulate.

The powers held by the Quebec state and the way in which these powers were deployed would have to undergo substantial change if such broad-based demands were to be satisfied. Yet, during the Union nationale administrations of Daniel Johnson (1966-68) and Jean-Jacques Bertrand (1968-70) and the Liberal administration of Robert Bourassa (1970-76), this was not the case. Not only did the transfer of powers from Ottawa to Quebec decline radically from the time of the Lesage government, but most often these administrations refused to deploy the powers they did hold in the way that the post-Quiet Revolution critiques demanded. Both the Union nationale and the Liberals sought to temporize the language issue, searching for policies acceptable to both sides. Both parties also failed to meet class-based demands. In particular, as we have seen, they failed to meet the demands of Quebec unions, resorting increasingly to direct confrontation with union leaders and to the imposition of settlements in the public sector. As a consequence of this failure to meet demands for change, the appeal of independence for Quebec grew for many Francophones.

The Union Nationale Administrations of Johnson and Bertrand

The Union nationale administration did not constitute as clean a break with the Lesage regime's program of political modernization as many observers had expected, nor as Daniel Johnson had promised during the 1966 election campaign. Reform of Quebec's educational system was continued. The concept of a two-year post-secondary "junior college," elaborated in the Parent Report and adopted in principle by the Lesage regime, was finally implemented with the establishment in 1967 of the first CEGEP. By the time the Union nationale fell from power, in 1970, thirty CEGEPs had been established in Quebec. The Union nationale government took the first steps in creating a new province-wide university system, l'Université du Québec. Also, the Union nationale realized the Liberal plans for a Quebec steel complex. In 1968, the operations of the Dominion Steel Corporation were purchased by the Quebec government and turned over to SIDBEC, a public corporation with a five-year subsidy of $60 million.

Nevertheless, despite the implementation of these particular Quiet Revolution programs, the overall level of political modernization achieved under the Union nationale was not comparable to that of the Lesage regime. Not all programs inherited from the Liberals were continued: the massive program to reorganize Quebec municipalities was dropped entirely. Moreover, few new programs were developed under the Union nationale. The rate of increase in governmental expenditures was markedly lower. During the early 1960s, the total expenditures of the Quebec government had risen steadily, culminating in a massive increase of 29.6 per cent (in constant dollars) in 1965. In the following year – the first year of Union nationale government – expenditures increased by only 9.6 per cent. The rate of increase did rise in 1967 to 13.8 per cent, but over each of the successive years it was below 10 per cent. In 1970, governmental expenditures actually decreased by 0.3 per cent (in constant dollars).[1] The rate of increase in government employees was also lower. Over the Quiet Revolution years of 1960-65, government employees had increased in number by 53 per cent; over the subsequent five-year period they increased by only 24 per cent.[2] In short, the period of Union nationale rule was a disappointment to those who had been converted to the Quiet Revolution belief in a strong, active Quebec government.

This failure of the Johnson and Bertrand administration to carry on the Quiet Revolution with the vigour of the Lesage administration can be understood in terms of the origin of the Union nationale leadership and the sources of its electoral support. The Union nationale did not have nearly as close a link as did the Liberals to the urban population, especially the new middle class, the driving force behind the Quiet Revolution. It drew most of its strength from the same elements that had dominated the Union nationale in the 1950s. Rural liberal professionals and small businessmen continued to be strongly represented among the party leadership. The Union nationale caucus in the legislature was weighted against urban Quebec. Although redistribution had substantially increased the number of urban ridings, in 1966 only 47 per cent of the successful Union nationale candidates came from areas that were over 60 per cent urban and only 15 per cent came from Montreal or Quebec City.[3] (After the 1962 election, the figures for the Liberals were 59 per cent from urban areas and 29 per cent from Montreal and Quebec City.) In urban areas, Union nationale support was greater among working-class French Canadians than among middle-class French Canadians.[4] In short, the Union nationale was still closely tied to the elements of Quebec society least attached to the beliefs and policies of the Quiet Revolution. Some of the Union nationale leadership were concerned about the relative weakness of their party among youth and the urban middle classes. Daniel Johnson succeeded in bringing some young "technocrats" into the party. His espousal of many of the slogans and goals of separatists represented an attempt to widen the bases of Union nationale support. Nevertheless, the centre of gravity within the party remained with the more traditional elements of French-Canadian society. With the death of Johnson and accession of Jean-Jacques Bertrand to power, these elements fully regained their dominance.

The weakened financial position of the Quebec government, due to the Liberal escalation of public borrowing, restricted the possibilities for government activism.[5] By 1965, the Lesage administration had already found it necessary to postpone and curtail some of its projects. But the relative absence of a commitment to political modernization among the party leadership was a greater determinant than these financial constraints. As Vincent Lemieux notes, the Quiet Revolution programs that were continued during the Union nationale administration (such as reform of the educational system) reflected less the commitments of the Union nationale leadership than those of senior civil servants. In some ministries, particularly education, civil servants had been able to acquire critical policy-making roles during the Lesage administration and maintained these positions under the Union nationale. In other ministries, such as municipal affairs, senior civil servants had not acquired such positions. There, the attitudes of the party leadership prevailed; programs established under the Lesage administration were not carried through (e.g., municipal reorganization).[6]

According to many analysts, a marked decline in the growth of government after a period of sudden and very rapid growth has produced deep political alienation in many political systems. This appears to have been the case in Quebec in the late 1960s. Those who benefited from the Quiet Revolution programs had come to expect a continued steady growth in governmental capacities and in governmental benefits; these expectations were severely frustrated by the period of Union nationale government. The alienation resulting from this "frustration of expectations" spread not only to the Union nationale but also to the structures of government themselves.[7] Many concluded that the federal system itself was to blame; it would not permit the Quebec state to assume the role it had come to expect, therefore, only through independence could the Quebec government play its "proper" role in Quebec society.

Indépendantiste logic was reinforced by the fact that during the last half of the 1960s there was not nearly the same degree of transfer of powers and responsibilities to Quebec as had occurred during the Lesage period. In federal-provincial relations, as well, the momentum of the Quiet Revolution had been broken. In part, this stemmed from the type of demands the Union nationale government, lacking a strong commitment to political modernization, made on the federal government. The demands of the Lesage regime had grown directly out of involvement in many costly programs; the Union nationale did not have such a heavy investment in new programs and, thus, its position did not have the same concrete basis. By and large, demands of the Union nationale government were general and quite vague, revolving around broad outlines of a new Canadian constitution that would be developed over the coming years. They were not firmly directed, as were those of the Lesage administration, to the immediate transfer of specific responsibilities and fiscal resources. They consisted of goals that were to be pursued over a series of federal-provincial and constitutional conferences. They were oriented to the future rather than to the present.

The one area in which Quebec did directly attack specific aspects of Canadian federalism and demand immediate change was the role that Quebec was allowed to play in international affairs. Foreign relations comprised one of the few aspects of the federal system in which a government not committed to major expansion of the role of the state and anxious to avoid new expenditures might be led to conduct a sustained campaign for change. Quebec demanded that it be able to participate in international conferences dealing with matters within provincial jurisdiction and, more importantly, that it should be allowed to sign agreements with foreign governments on these matters. The debates between Quebec and Ottawa over this issue were often very tense, leading to "comic opera" struggles over the height of flagpoles and the seating of delegations. In purely symbolic terms Quebec's demands seemed very significant; Quebec was seeking to assume what many regarded as the trappings of sovereignty. Yet, whatever the symbolism, these demands did not directly attack the real distribution of power and responsibilities within the Canadian federal system to the extent that various Lesage demands, such as a separate Quebec Pension Plan, had.

The demands of the Union nationale administration during the incumbency of Daniel Johnson for overall constitutional change, as opposed to specific immediate change, were sweeping in their

214

scope. Starting from the premise that Quebec represented one of "two nations" within the Canadian political system, the Quebec government sought a massive transfer of powers and resources to Quebec. According to Johnson, the only alternative to radical revision of the constitution was the separation of Quebec from Canada. This ultimatum was dramatically expressed in the title of Johnson's book, *Égalité ou indépendance*.[8] However, with the accession of Bertrand as prime minister and the dominance of the more traditional elements of the party, at the expense of Johnson's young "technocrats," Quebec's demands for long-term change in the federal system lost much of their force. Without any clear commitment to the goals of political modernization, sweeping attacks on the federal system and demands for radical change could have only limited credibility. The Union nationale seemed to have returned to the rhetorical posturing of the 1950s. It also became increasingly clear that Bertrand and the dominant Union nationale leadership were fully committed to Quebec's remaining within the federal system. The demands of Johnson, and even of Jean Lesage, had carried greater weight among many English Canadians because of the fear, however unfounded, that if frustrated these leaders might lead Quebec out of Canada. Frustration of Bertrand's demands did not carry the same danger; they could be more safely ignored or postponed for discussion at some future date.

The failure of Quebec to make new, concrete gains in its relations with Ottawa, and the consequent frustration of Quiet Revolution adherents, also stemmed from a new opposition within the federal government to further "concessions" to Quebec. Now, under Pierre Elliott Trudeau, the federal government was much more rigid in its attitude toward Quebec's place within the federal system. Without a strong federal presence in Quebec, Trudeau argued, the drift toward separatism was irreversible. Accordingly, the federal government refused to entertain any notions of "Associate States," or even the *statut particulier* that sometimes had been advocated by the Lesage regime. Quebec was to be simply a province like the others. The lack of a firm commitment by the Union nationale to expand the role of the Quebec government, and thus its failure to make precise demands for the immediate transfer of specific powers, made it easier for the federal government to maintain this new rigidity.

To recapitulate, during the last half of the 1960s not only did the Quebec state lose much of its modernizing momentum, but also it no longer was as successful in acquiring new powers and resources from Ottawa. In the face of this growing stalemate in federal-provincial relations, it appeared to many that the limits of major change within the federal system had been reached. Some of the adherents to the Quiet Revolution ideology concluded that in order to resume its modernizing role and become the *moteur principal* of Quebec's development, acquiring the requisite powers and resources, the Quebec state would have to leave the federal system. Others resisted this conclusion. The battle was joined within the provincial Liberal Party. The vigorous leadership of Jean Lesage and Eric Kierans carried the day: the party formally committed itself to the continued participation of Quebec within the federal system and dissociated itself from the principle of *statut particulier*. Many Liberals, such as Pierre Laporte, Robert Bourassa, and Paul Gérin-Lajoie, who had advanced programs of major constitutional reform in the past, accepted this new position. Others, most notably René Lévesque, who perhaps best embodied the spirit of the Quiet Revolution, left the party. Declaring themselves in favour of the political disengagement of Quebec from Canada, they formed the new Mouvement souveraineté-association, which the following year drew most members of the two existing separatist political parties (the RIN and the RN) into a new party, the Parti québécois.

The Union nationale administration was also disappointing for the critics of the Quiet Revolution who wanted new kinds of state policy to further ethnic and class interests. First, the Union nationale government resisted pressures to intervene in the linguistic choice of immigrants. When in 1967 the St. Leonard Catholic School Commission forced immigrant children to attend French-language schools, the provincial Minister of Education, Jean-Guy Cardinal, initially refused to take a stand on the issue and establish a general policy for all local school commissions to follow. However, in 1968, Jean-Jacques Bertrand introduced legislation to establish formally the right of all parents to choose the language in which their children would be educated. The opposition among various Francophone groups was so intense that Bertrand temporarily yielded and the bill was shelved. (The surprise of Bertrand and other Union nationale leaders over the strength of the opposition betrayed their insensitivity to the character of linguistic conflict in Quebec.) Nevertheless, Bertrand persisted and, after his confirmation as party leader in the summer of 1969, a second bill to guarantee the choice of language of instruction, Bill 63, was introduced. This time, although opposition was even more intense (on one occasion 50,000 people demonstrated before the Quebec legislative buildings), the legislation was passed, with the concurrence of all but two Union nationale legislators and one Liberal legislator. In a vain attempt to appease Francophone opponents to the measure, the Bertrand government included provisions in the legislation requiring graduates of English-language schools to have a certain competence in French and established a commission, under linguist Jean-Denis Gendron, to investigate the state of the French language in Quebec. In the eyes of Francophone activists, these "concessions" were of little consequence. The language issue was not subject to compromise. To allow immigrant children to attend English-language schools was to forsake the interests of the Francophone community in favour of the Anglophone community. The fact that the Liberal opposition had supported Bill 63 only added to the frustration, and to a general alienation from the established political order.

During the Union nationale administration, relations between the Quebec government and the Quebec trade unions (especially those in the public sector) came into increasing conflict. In 1967, the Union nationale government suspended *de facto* the right of members of the teachers' union (the CEQ) to strike. In the same year, it passed special legislation to force back to work the Montreal public transportation employees. In 1968, government prosecution of the leaders of a second teachers' union (Syndicat des professeurs de l'État du Québec) for ignoring a 1966 back-to-work injunction led to the imprisonment of thirteen of them for a twenty-day period.[9] Nor did the Union nationale correct the bias toward middle-class needs and aspirations that characterized much of the provincial government programs in the wake of the Quiet Revolution. It was even unable to restore much of the patronage through which, in the days of Duplessis, the Union nationale benefited lower-class French Canadians.

This failure of the Union nationale administration to meet the grievances of those who wanted new policies to promote ethnic and class interests reinforced the appeal of Quebec independence. For those who wanted the Quebec government to embrace openly the interests of Francophones, at the expense of Anglophone interests, Quebec independence at least offered a "more favourable" definition of the situation. Quebec Francophones would be clearly *the* majority group. For those concerned with the position of working-class Francophones, independence at least promised to reduce the strength of English-Canadian corporate interests and offered the potential of *all* the powers of government being used on behalf of Francophone working-class interests.

217

Thus, the last half of the 1960s saw a broadening of the bases of support for Quebec independence. Disappointment with the failure of the Union nationale to continue the modernizing momentum of the Lesage regime and frustration with the growing rigidity of the federal government led many adherents to the neo-nationalism of the Quiet Revolution to see Quebec independence as a necessity. In addition, with the increasing political salience of linguistic conflict and class conflict, separatism gained solid bases of support beyond this essentially new-middle-class core. Analysis of a 1968 survey demonstrates that economic grievances and left-wing beliefs had produced among working-class Francophones a level of support for independence comparable to that of the middle class.[10] We can also conclude that the quickening of linguistic conflict of the late 1960s, and the frustration with Union nationale policies regarding immigrants, provided a further attraction to independence among working-class Francophones.[11]

The Liberal Administration of Robert Bourassa

One might have expected that with the return to power of the Liberals in 1970, many grievances against the Quebec government would have been better accommodated. Presumably, as the party of the Quiet Revolution, the Liberals would have been more sympathetic to demands for an active, dynamic Quebec state, championing the interests of Quebec Francophones. It soon became apparent, however, that the Liberal Party of the 1970s was quite different from that of the early 1960s, with its *équipe du tonnerre* and its abiding commitment to political modernization. Bourassa and his colleagues were not as prepared to accept the central Quiet Revolution contention that Quebec's social and economic development necessitated a continuing expansion of the powers and activities of the Quebec state. In particular, they professed a much greater faith in the ability of private economic forces to serve the interests of Quebec Francophones without governmental intervention.

This absence within the Bourassa regime of a strong impulse to political modernization can be traced, in large part, to the major change that the Liberal leadership had undergone in the last half of the 1960s. Most of the dynamic figures of the Quiet Revolution were no longer present. Some had simply left Quebec political life: Georges-Émile Lapalme, Eric Kierans, Paul Gérin-Lajoie, and at least officially, Jean Lesage. But, more significantly, René Lévesque and other neo-nationalist political modernizers had abandoned the Liberal Party for le Mouvement souveraineté-association and its successor, the *indépendantiste* Parti québécois.

By the mid-1960s, Lévesque and his "technocratic" faction had found it increasingly difficult to get support for their programs of political modernization from other segments of the Liberal leadership more closely tied to private Francophone and Anglophone economic elites. In addition, the growing rigidity in Quebec-Ottawa relations had led them to conclude that their programs of political modernization could never be implemented within the present federal system; Quebec would never acquire the necessary powers. This same conclusion was subsequently drawn by several bureaucratic leaders of the Quiet Revolution who had been intimately involved in Quebec-Ottawa relations: Claude Morin, Louis Bernard, and Jacques Parizeau. Increasingly, then, the goal of political modernization was being linked to radical constitutional change. As Quebec political elites realigned themselves accordingly, the modernizing influences within the Liberal Party weakened. The Bourassa regime became much more fully identified than had been the Lesage regime with private economic elites and the restricted role they assigned to the state.

Economic Policies of the Bourassa Regime

Rejection of the *étatisme* of the Lesage regime was most evident with respect to Quebec's economy. From the beginning, the primary assumption of Bourassa and his colleagues was that Quebec's economic development can be accomplished best through private initiative; there was little of the Quiet Revolution rhetoric about the Quebec state being the *moteur principal* of Quebec's development. First and foremost, this meant that governmental energies should be concentrated on encouraging the investment of private capital in Quebec, especially American capital, which was seen as the primary available source. On this basis, Bourassa vigorously opposed federal legislation to screen foreign investment in Canada, warning that "this law places in question one of the fundamental principles of the traditional economic policy of Quebec, namely inciting the implantation of new enterprises, whether they be of Canadian or foreign origin."[12]

The Bourassa style of government was pervaded by a concern with creating a social, economic, and political climate that would attract U.S. investment. For Bourassa, the most telling argument against Quebec independence, and also against greater intervention of the present Quebec government in such areas as language policy, was the possibility that U.S. investment might be discouraged. The Bourassa regime's rejection of *étatisme* was especially evident in its attitude toward public corporations; private enterprise was seen as more efficient and, for this reason, preferable. There was little serious interest in spectacular new public ventures such as Hydro-Québec or SIDBEC. Whereas the Lesage government confided in Hydro-Québec total responsibility for its major hydro-electricity development, the Manicouagan Dam, the Bourassa government turned the administration of its giant James Bay hydro-electric development over to a private corporation, even though it guaranteed the sale of Hydro-Québec bonds to finance the project. In the early years of the Bourassa administration, confidence in the ability of private initiative, especially that of American corporations, to develop Quebec's economy was accompanied by a reticence even to continue financial support for privately owned Francophone firms in Quebec. The disappointing performance of the Société générale de financement during the 1960s was cited as proof that this strategy could bring little real economic development. (Implicitly, Francophone participation in the upper levels of Quebec's economic structures had a lower priority than aggregate economic growth.)

The Bourassa Liberals could not persist in this formal retreat from the *étatiste* assumptions and policies of the 1960s without antagonizing elements within the Quebec bureaucracy. If the Liberal Party had undergone a change in its official doctrines, Quebec's technocrats had not. Many of the pioneers of political modernization during the Quiet Revolution remained within the bureaucracy or were highly influential upon it. As a consequence, the bureaucracy continued to produce policy proposals and position papers calling for new state initiatives in the Quebec economy, such as nationalization in the asbestos industry. For some Liberals this stubborn *étatisme* was infuriating, leading them to suspect (at times with reason) that some public servants were PQ sympathizers. The depth of the technocratic adherence to statist economic policies by Quebec bureaucrats is reflected in two major studies prepared within the Quebec government that directly contradict key assumptions of the Bourassa regime's official economic doctrines.

The first of these is a study of U.S. investment in Quebec, prepared under the supervision of a cabinet subcommittee and known as the Tetley Report; it concluded that Quebec is not as dependent on American capital as some had assumed. In normal periods, it asserted, savings freed by the Quebec economy would be sufficient to finance internal investments. Moreover, it contended that U.S. investment had not been as uniformly beneficial to Quebec as had been assumed. Echoing the conclusions of such English-Canadian studies as the Gray Report[13] and Kari Levitt's *Silent Surrender*,[14] it documented how U.S. investment in Quebec had often meant the takeover of existing Quebec firms without benefit of new capital or technological know-how, leaving the remaining Quebec enterprises at a disadvantage in the process. It also argued that U.S. enterprises frequently were not adequately integrated with the *circuit économique du Québec* and had restricted the opportunities for Francophones to assume managerial positions within the Quebec economy: "The management gap [in English in original] of the Québécois does not stem, first and foremost, from deficiencies at the level of academic preparation but more from the isolation which large enterprises have always maintained."[15] Accordingly, the report recommended a series of measures designed to ensure a greater use of capital generated in Quebec and to strengthen the Québécois presence in foreign-owned organizations. Obviously ill at ease with the results of the study, the cabinet delayed publication of it for a considerable period of time, even after large extracts had been leaked through *Le Devoir*. Finally, it was released, but without its ninety-six recommendations. William Tetley, Minister of Financial Institutions, explained that the recommendations might be "misinterpreted." In addition, he reaffirmed that "all investors in Quebec should be treated on the same footing and the same rules should apply to everyone."[16]

A second study, prepared by economists in the Quebec Ministry of Industry and Commerce and known as the Descoteaux Report, examined the same pattern of overall investment in Quebec and reached these same conclusions, with even greater emphasis. It argued that the level of overall investment in Quebec had been seriously deficient and would remain so without a greater level of governmental intervention. In particular, the manufacturing industry had not undergone an adequate degree of modernization and growth. In a ringing call for a new exploitation of the powers of the Quebec government to stimulate and guide Quebec's economic development, it declared: "It remains . . . that the private sector has proven that it has not managed to use fully the available resources and that the government of Quebec represents, for Quebec Francophones as a whole, the principal instrument able to permit them to achieve their aspirations."[17]

In the later years of the Bourassa administration, some major steps were taken in the direction of greater governmental support for Quebec enterprises. The Société générale de financement acquired virtually complete ownership of Marine Industries, at a cost of $4 million. At the same time, as we have seen, it invested $6.8 million in the heavy transportation division of Bombardier Corporation (which now included the Montreal Locomotive Works). Also, Lucien Saulnier, president of the Société de développement industriel, a sister organization to the SGF, forthrightly declared that the funds of the SDI would be used to support Francophone enterprises. The SDI lent funds to some small Francophone corporations that would not otherwise have been able to secure funds.[18] But the Bourassa government resisted pressures to create completely public enterprises, for example, in the asbestos industry. Nor was it ready to modify its belief in Quebec's dependence on American investment, as indicated by its treatment of the Tetley Report.

Social Policies of the Bourassa Regime

The Bourassa administration showed a closer continuity with the Liberal government of the Quiet Revolution in areas of policy not directly involved with private economic interests: education and, more notably, health and welfare. The expansion of educational facilities, especially at the post-secondary level, continued under the Liberals. But it was tempered by a certain discomfort with the social and political "radicalism" that university education seemed to have induced among many young Francophones and by an open disenchantment with the quality of education within the new mass educational institutions. Minister of Education François Cloutier was heard to remark that Francophone African countries would be ill-advised to adopt the Quebec system of CEGEPS; in particular, he was not at all convinced that the combination of vocational and academic education within the same institution had been wise.[19] In addition, the Bourassa regime appeared to be untroubled by the substantial number of students educated outside the public system. In 1973, 51,000 students attended private schools. In fact, it supported this trend by providing high levels of financial assistance to private institutions. In 1973, the provincial government paid 80 per cent of the costs of 181 private schools and 60 per cent of the costs of another thirty-six private schools.[20]

It is mainly in health and welfare that the Bourassa government acted vigorously to expand its authority, under the aggressive leadership of Claude Castonguay, who was himself a young technocrat in the Lesage administration. In implementing the provincial health insurance scheme, Castonguay imposed substantially tougher conditions on the medical profession than those in most other provinces. Doctors were required to adhere to the fee scale set by the plan. Even in the face of strike action by some doctors, the government's resolve did not weaken. This open confrontation with the primarily Francophone medical profession contrasted sharply with the Bourassa regime's dealings with Anglophone economic elites. It also dramatized the extent to which, within French-Canadian society, power had passed from the old middle class of liberal professions to the state technocrats of the new middle class.

Quebec-Ottawa Relations in the 1970s

The Bourassa government's belief in the dependence of Quebec's economy on private initiative and capital was faithfully reflected in its approach to Canadian federalism. For Bourassa and his colleagues, the disengagement of Quebec from the federal system meant a sharp drop in private investment, especially from American sources. For this reason, separatism was a "dangerous adventure" to be avoided at all costs. There was no ringing call for national solidarity of Quebec Francophones with their fellow Canadians. Nor, for that matter, was there the liberal advocacy of the multinational state elaborated by Trudeau and the other anti-nationalists of his generation. The Canadian system was presented simply as a practical arrangement that makes economic sense, *un fédéralisme rentable*; whatever the merits of the status quo, the dangers of the separatist alternative are totally unsupportable.

Also, in an attempt to undermine support for the ideas of *indépendantisme*, Bourassa and his colleagues were led to adopt some of the Parti québécois slogans, in the process obscuring their commitment to the Canadian system. On one notable occasion, Bourassa even described the existing status of Quebec as that of a "French state within the Canadian common market," as if the program of the Parti québécois had already been achieved. (Trudeau and other French-Canadian federal figures testily pointed out that the Canadian federal system represented much more than a "common market.") The Bourassa government sought to associate itself with the goal of sovereignty by stating that in its dealings with Ottawa it, too, was seeking to achieve sovereignty, *"cultural sovereignty."* In practice, this ill-defined "cultural sovereignty" seemed to embrace little more than jurisdiction over communications and culture and pre-eminence within the already concurrent jurisdiction of immigration. Despite the rhetoric, the Liberal commitment to the federal system was firm and unequivocal.

The Bourassa administration did not succeed in securing any major transfer of powers and resources from Ottawa to Quebec. Those who had been led during the period of Union nationale rule to conclude that the limits to further growth of Quebec's position within the federal system had been reached, found confirmation in the record of the Bourassa regime as well. The Bourassa government's relative failure in federal-provincial relations stemmed partly from its clear commitment to federalism. Some of the tactical ploys used by past Quebec governments were no longer available to it. It could not support its demands with vague evocations of separation, as did Daniel Johnson and some members of the Lesage regime. Such threats would not be credible. Moreover, within the Bourassa regime's perspective, they might undermine the all-important confidence of private investors. Also, it could not even afford to show too great a dissatisfaction with Quebec's treatment by the federal system; committed to the system, it had to demonstrate that the system works for Quebec. To contend too emphatically that Ottawa or the other provincial governments are unsympathetic to Quebec's needs and not giving its demands the consideration they deserve would be to confirm the separatist arguments of the Liberal's main electoral threat, the Parti québécois. Finally, the Bourassa government had to face a federal government firmly convinced that the erosion of power to Quebec (and the other provinces, for that matter) had gone far enough and vigorously opposed to any further shifts to Quebec.

Federal-provincial negotiations over income security demonstrate the extent to which the Bourassa government was constrained to accept arrangements that fell far short of its demands and to present them as "successes" for Quebec. Quebec went to the Victoria federal-provincial conference of June, 1971, demanding no less than the "legislative primacy" of Quebec over the entire sector of social security. In Quebec's proposal, federal programs of family allowances, manpower training allowances, and old-age supplements would have effect within a province only if the provincial government approved; otherwise, the provincial government would receive full compensation from the federal government. With respect to youth and social allowances, unemployment insurance, and old-age pensions and survivors' benefits, any federal law could not affect the operation of provincial programs; the provinces would have paramount authority.

Quebec contended that this demand for overall primacy within the area of social security was merely the logical completion of the piecemeal shift of responsibilities from Ottawa to Quebec that had occurred during the 1960s.[21] The federal government rejected Quebec's demands and, in concert with all provinces but Quebec, approved the terms of a new constitution (the Victoria Charter) with no specification of fields in which provincial governments might be able to block federal programs and receive compensation. It merely stated that in the case of old-age pensions, family, youth, and occupational allowance, federal programs "should not affect the operation of provincial laws" and that provinces should be consulted before any new federal programs are put into effect.[22] Quebec refused to approve the Victoria Charter; dissatisfaction with the terms of the social provisions was a primary motivation.

After this failure to secure Quebec's goals through formal constitutional revision, Bourassa declared in a newspaper interview that Quebec was adopting a new strategy. Henceforth, Quebec would focus on negotiating with Ottawa the terms of legislative and administrative arrangements to deal with specific programs:

> In a federal regime, one cannot expect to win everything, to negotiate nothing, to make no concession. This is why I say that in the area of social security we must find concrete solutions away from the constitutional path. With this done, it will be very much simpler to agree on a new constitution.[23]

In this new strategy, the first goal of Quebec was new arrangements with respect to family allowances. At Victoria, Quebec had demanded the right to occupy fully the family allowance field, with full federal compensation for federal programs. Now, Quebec merely asked that, while maintaining its family allowance programs, Ottawa should allow the provinces to determine the criteria for payment of the allowances to their citizens, within certain national norms. According to Bourassa, "If Ottawa should reject this proposition, you might as well conclude that we have unitary federalism, a rigid federalism."[24] Yet, in effect, the federal government did reject Quebec's proposition. New federal legislation modified the federal family allowance system such that there could be some provincial determination of the criteria for payment. But, the "national" norms set by Ottawa were so high that this provincial prerogative was restricted to only 40 per cent of the total funds.[25] Nevertheless, Quebec called this arrangement a major victory; Claude Castonguay declared that having accomplished his primary goals in federal-provincial relations, he was soon leaving his cabinet position.

Subsequently, Quebec and the other provinces began negotiating with the federal government the terms of a new integrated social security program. In the working papers presented by the federal government for a system of income guarantees and supplements, the provinces clearly would have only a secondary role, similar to what Quebec acquired in the revised family allowance scheme. The provinces would be able to establish criteria for some federal payments to their citizens, but within norms and constraints established by the federal government.[26] In sum, neither strategy, formal constitutional revision or piecemeal negotiation, brought Quebec substantially closer to its goal of "legislative primacy" within the field of social security. In fact, Claude Ryan, then editor of *Le Devoir* and later the Liberal Party leader in Quebec, contended in 1975 that the federal proposals regarding income security would *reduce* Quebec's position: "Not only would Ottawa conserve its present fiscal preponderance, but tax points laboriously acquired by Quebec under Messieurs Pearson and Lesage eventually would be seen returning to Ottawa."[27]

The Bourassa administration met with even less success in the second area where it sought major change in the federal system: communications. Under the aggressive leadership of Communications Minister Jean-Paul L'Allier, widely regarded as the most "nationalist" of the Bourassa cabinet members, Quebec staked a claim over a wide area of communications. Contending that this jurisdiction has an intimate relationship with the cultural integrity of Quebec, L'Allier argued it could be entrusted only to the Quebec government; Quebec had to become the *"maître d'oeuvre de la politique des communications sur son territoire."*[28] In more concrete terms, Quebec demanded complete jurisdiction over radio-television, ground installations (such as telephones), and cable systems. At first, it appeared that Quebec might be successful on this constitutional front: this issue seemed to enjoy much more support among the other provinces than had been the case with other issues. Through a series of interprovincial conferences, L'Allier carefully developed a coalition of all provincial governments behind his demands. However, in the face of firm federal opposition, this provincial alliance crumbled. Virtually all the provinces but Quebec accepted the federal offer of participation in a new federal regulatory agency. In the eyes of L'Allier, acceptance of such participation could only mean betrayal of Quebec's goals;

and he declared that he was returning the communications dossier to his prime minister and suggested that the Quebec government should seriously reconsider its goal of "cultural sovereignty."[29] Soon after, he was transferred to another portfolio.

In sum, the 1970s witnessed the repeated failure of Quebec's offensives in federal-provincial relations. The long series of federal-provincial sessions on formal constitutional revision finally produced a document containing little concession to Quebec's stated demands on social security and offering no expansion of provincial jurisdiction in other areas. Quebec was forced to veto the proposed revision, frustrating the will of all other provinces, as well as that of the federal government. Negotiation of specific programs with Ottawa, as in social security, resulted in the virtual abandonment of Quebec's goals. Attempts to force the hand of the federal government through a coalition of the provinces, as in communications, failed. If at times other provinces embraced some of Quebec's demands they did so without the preoccupations with cultural survival and development that animated Quebec's demands; their commitment to the demands was not sufficient to withstand the strategies of an aggressive federal government. Given the hostility of the federal government to any further concessions to Quebec, there is little that the Bourassa government, with its firm commitment to Quebec's continued participation in the federal system, could do to secure additional powers and resources. Thus, the experience of the Bourassa years only reinforced the judgement of some Quebec Francophones that political modernization of Quebec could no longer be achieved within the federal system: only through political independence could the Quebec state resume the role it set for itself during the Quiet Revolution of an active, dynamic actor within Quebec society.

The Bourassa Regime and Language: Bill 22

Many Francophones looking to the Quebec government for support in their struggles with other ethnic groups in Quebec were also disappointed during the Bourassa administration and found the appeal of Quebec independence correspondingly stronger. Strong dissatisfaction among Francophones might seem rather puzzling. The Bourassa government was the first Quebec government to pass legislation comprehensively defining the status of French within Quebec: Bill 22. The opening provision of Bill 22 declared French alone to be the "official language" of Quebec, thus upsetting the coequal status that English had always enjoyed in Quebec. This and many other provisions of Bill 22 were fiercely opposed by members of the English-Canadian and immigrant populations in Quebec, some even accusing the Bourassa regime of "Nazi-like tactics" and "cultural genocide." Anglophone groups sought (in vain) to have Bill 22 disallowed by the federal government and undertook court action to have Bill 22 declared unconstitutional.[30] Yet, many Francophones contended that, despite appearances, Bill 22 would do little to change the relative position of their group within Quebec. Francophone dissatisfaction centred on the sections of Bill 22 that cover what we found to be the two central points of conflict between Francophones and Anglophones: the access to English-language schools of the children of non-Anglophone immigrants and the status of French as the language of work in the private sector of the Quebec economy. In each case, Francophone nationalists contended that Bill 22 did not deploy in a clear and unambiguous fashion the full powers of government on behalf of the Francophone group.

The provisions of Bill 22 dealing with access to English-language schools were indeed ambiguous. The Bourassa government was anxious to avoid explicitly adopting the goal of Francophone nationalists: to force the children of non-Anglophone immigrants to go to Francophone schools. Thus, it resisted Francophone demands that English-language schools be restricted exclusively to children whose mother tongue is English. Instead, it sought to pursue this goal through procedures ostensibly concerned with the effectiveness of education. Henceforth, to be admitted to English-language schools children would have to demonstrate that they have a "sufficient knowledge" of English "to receive their instruction in that language."[31] In this fashion, the issue of language of instruction was presented as a technical question rather than the inherently political question that it is.

On the surface, the provincial government was not siding with the Francophone community, imposing its interests over the economic self-interest of immigrant children, but was merely ensuring that children had the linguistic capacity necessary for effective education. In principle, the right of parents to choose the language of instruction of their children was preserved. This procedure offered little satisfaction to Francophone nationalists who correctly feared that, especially with private tutoring, most immigrant children would manage to pass the tests. Nationalist dissatisfaction was not mollified by a second provision of Bill 22 that required approval of the Minister of Education for any change in the size of English-language facilities offered by a school commission and specified that this approval should be given only if warranted by the number of students whose mother tongue is English.[32] A zealous Minister of Education might have used this provision to restrict access of immigrant children (this was the very purpose for which Jérôme Choquette had this provision inserted as an amendment to the original bill), but there was no certainty that he or she would do so.

Subsequently, the Quebec government was led to abandon its initial strategy of using language tests as the sole device for restricting access to English-language schools. In April, 1975, the Minister of Education declared that enrolment in English-language schools would not be allowed to grow beyond certain limits, except to accommodate children whose mother tongue is English.[33] On this basis, in some school districts immigrant children who did pass tests demonstrating they had acquired competence in English would still be refused access to English-language schools. By administrative decree, then, the Quebec government did abrogate the right of some parents to choose the language of instruction of their children. It had finally adopted the procedure Francophone nationalists had demanded in the first place and that the government had sought to avoid: overt discrimination on the basis of mother tongue rather than of acquired competence in English. Nevertheless, use of the administrative device could offer only limited satisfaction to Francophone nationalists, dependent as it was on the disposition of the Minister of Education. Only legislation requiring English as a mother tongue for access to English-language schools could meet nationalist demands.

The Bourassa government had avoided such legislation in the hope that through stress on language tests Bill 22 could be made acceptable to both Anglophones and Francophones. In fact, given its dependence on both language groups for electoral support, the Bourassa Liberals had little choice but to search for some formula its Anglophone and Francophone adherents would find mutually acceptable. But this hope proved unrealistic. Without a clear statement of the intent of Bill 22's educational provisions, *both* groups were merely confirmed in the fear that their respective interests were not being served.

The provisions of Bill 22 regarding the use of French in the private sector of the Quebec economy also were quite ambiguous. Any change in the status of French as a working language was relegated to a system of *"francisation"* certificates that private firms would be required to obtain in order to receive Quebec government premiums, subsidies, or benefits and to conduct business with the Quebec government.[34] Yet, while Bill 22 listed several aspects of a firm's operations to be considered, all bearing directly on language practices, it did not indicate how rigorously the Régie de la langue française should judge these points. In fact, Bill 22 explicitly gave the Régie wide latitude with the phrase: "while taking account of the situation and structure of each firm, of its head office and of its subsidiaries and branches."[35] (Significantly, this phrase was inserted at the prodding of the Minister of Trade and Commerce, Guy St. Pierre, reflecting his desire to create and maintain a favourable climate for private investment.) Thus, the effect of the bill on working-language practices was ultimately dependent on how the Régie, and the government that appointed it, should decide that it be implemented. The close ties between the Bourassa regime and Anglophone capital gave reason to believe that the provisions would not be firmly enforced. To be sure, the Régie might itself have decided to enforce the bill rigorously, but it had no clear mandate to do so. Such ambiguity could only confirm the suspicions of some Francophones that, as in the case of access to English-language schools, the Bourassa regime was not prepared to deploy fully the powers of the Quebec state to strengthen the French presence in Quebec.

Finally, we have already seen how the Bourassa administration engaged in dramatic confrontations with the Francophone working-class leadership, especially the unions. The Bourassa government did not retreat from the strong position it took during the 1972 strike of the public sector, when it not only passed special legislation to end the strike but secured the imprisonment of the three union leaders. During the 1973 provincial election campaign, Bourassa repeatedly invoked the events of the strike, congratulating his government for the courage it displayed in standing up to the union leaders and maintaining social order: "Those who abide by the law will support the Quebec government in this election. As for those who are against law and order, we don't want their votes."[36] Similarly, in 1975 the Bourassa government seized on the Cliche Commission revelations of corruption and violence within the construction unions to place these unions under government tutelage so as to maintain *la paix sociale*. The Bourassa administration was quite ready to present itself as a fierce adversary of Quebec unions, in the process furthering the political alienation of those who identified strongly with working-class interests.

Our analysis shows that government policy under the Bourassa administration was similar in many ways to that of its Union nationale predecessor. The Bourassa administration did not resume the wide-scale political modernization of the Quiet Revolution; it was especially reticent to intervene in new ways within the Quebec economy. It resisted demands of Francophone nationalists for the forthright restriction of immigrant children to French-language schools and for active intervention in the private sector to force a major change in working-language practices. In playing a strongly adversarial role with unions it reinforced the contention of working-class militants that the Quebec government was fundamentally hostile to their interests. To a certain extent, these broad lines of policy had been dictated by the refusal of the federal government to allow the further transfer of powers and resources to Quebec. But they also reflected a strong identification on the part of the Bourassa regime with private economic initiative and its need for a favourable climate for investment. This commitment seemed to restrain the Bourassa government from using more aggressively the powers it did have in such matters as the language of instruction of immigrants and private-sector working language. Also, its refusal to accept such Common Front demands as a minimum $100-a-week wage stemmed not so much from the fiscal resources available to it as from the entreaties of private corporations.

The Specificity of Political Alienation in Quebec

It would have been difficult for any administration to resolve the deepening political alienation that had marked many people in Quebec since the mid-1960s. To a certain extent, Quebec's experience was parallelled elsewhere in North America and Europe. There, too, governments were beset with a rapid increase in the variety and intensity of demands made upon them, demands they had often engendered through their own actions and promises. In addition, growing resource scarcity and international economic recession drained the capacity of many Western states even to maintain existing levels of public services and economic well-being. It became fashionable to speak of a universal problem of "ungovernability," of "demand overload," of the "fiscal crisis of the state," and of the "politics of scarcity."[37]

Particular aspects of Quebec's experience, nevertheless, made the prospect of political alienation especially strong. Political modernization was rapid, causing commensurately greater strains in the conversion of private institutions to public ones, constricting the time period for defining relations between new public-sector employees and their state employer, and swiftly transforming popular expectations of government. Moreover, political modernization occurred in a setting marked not only by dependence on external political and economic forces but by an internal "cultural division of labour." Thus, it strengthened and expanded social categories likely to view the existing social and political order with ambivalence or suspicion: new-middle-class technocrats with a strong investment in expansion of the state's capacities and young university graduates who saw little possibility of integrating themselves into existing economic structures. Finally, it occurred in a collectivity that sees itself as a nation. Therefore, the Quebec state was looked to as the primary, if not the exclusive, source for change; limitations on Quebec's jurisdiction and resources were especially provocative. In short, political alienation had a particular form and intensity in Quebec, and the challenge it posed for governmental elites was correspondingly greater.

As we have seen, the two brief Union nationale administrations and the Bourassa regime adopted positions and policies that, in many instances, were likely to reinforce rather than to reduce this alienation. The firm commitment of these governments to private initiative, often with an explicit acceptance of dependence on American and English-Canadian capital, could only frustrate the new-middle-class advocates of an interventionist state. The open engagement of the Bertrand and Bourassa administrations to Quebec's continued presence in the federal system seriously undercut the possibility of securing new powers for Quebec. Their attempts to temporize the language issue, with Bills 63 and 22, only deepened the resentments of Francophone linguistic nationalists. And, of course, the Bourassa regime's ready confrontation with public-sector unions only hardened the hostility of union leaderships and of some of their clientele.

The Strategy of the Bourassa Regime

While the Bertrand administration rapidly succumbed to growing alienation, the Bourassa regime was more successful. Until the mid-1970s it was able to maintain a strong electoral base, despite its failure to reduce alienation. In fact, to a large extent, Liberal support was based precisely on the regime's refusal to acknowledge the grievances of the politically alienated. Whether on the issues of language, economic policy, labour relations, or Quebec's connection with the rest of Canada, the Bourassa regime presented itself as the champion of the existing order and the only party able to hold in check the forces of social and political turmoil.

This strategy was especially important in the election of 1973, in which the Liberals secured 55 per cent of the popular vote and, through the workings of the electoral system, received 102 seats in the 110-seat National Assembly, the largest parliamentary majority in Quebec's history. Throughout the campaign, the Liberals claimed that the Parti québécois would take Quebec on a "dangerous adventure" through state intervention in the economy, radical language policies, submission to unions, and, most notably, through the separation of Quebec from Canada. There was widespread popular apprehension over Parti québécois objectives, and the Liberals campaigned skilfully on these fears. Thus, in their analysis of a survey administered during the campaign, Hamilton and Pinard show that even the unemployed, who normally would be expected to vote against the government party, voted mainly (63 per cent) for the Liberals if they were opposed to independence.[38] Similarly, a post-election survey showed that 49 per cent of respondents who were dissatisfied with the Liberals, but opposed to independence, voted Liberal.[39] Also revealing is the Hamilton and Pinard finding that even among voters who thought the Parti québécois had the best program, 60 per cent voted for the Liberals if they rejected independence.[40] The argument that the Liberals were the only party able to defeat the PQ had a devastating effect on other opposition parties; 49 per cent of respondents who had supported other parties in 1970, but were opposed to independence, switched to the Liberals in 1973.[41]

Over the short run at least, it may have made good electoral sense for the Bourassa regime to postpone or limit major new initiatives, whether in the economy, in language affairs, or in its relations with Ottawa, and to present itself as the only barrier against the chaos of separatism and radical unions. This reflected closely the needs and preoccupations of the party's most reliable bases of support: Francophone business elites and liberal professionals, the Quebec Anglophone population, and English-Canadian and American capital.[42] But in the long run this stance served to reinforce the pressures for political change.

First, the Bourassa strategy strengthened the hand of those who argued that the failings in government performance stemmed not from the particular incumbents in office but from a deeper source: the established economic and political order. After all, the change in incumbents with the election of the Liberals in 1970 had not materially affected the direction of Quebec government. In many areas, policies followed lines that had been established during the Bertrand administration. The Liberals of the 1970s in effect had abandoned their legacy of the Quiet Revolution, with its aggressive and often progressive state intervention. Accordingly, it was said, some external force must be preventing the Quebec government from assuming its proper responsibilities. As we have seen, left-wing intellectuals saw this force as pre-eminently economic: the Quebec government was the prisoner of the capitalist system and its American imperialist centre. (It is striking that in 1973 a full 59 per cent of Francophones believed that the Liberal Party was controlled by high finance.)[43] For others, the problem lay with the existing political order: a rigid and centralized federal system prevented Quebec from assuming the additional powers it needed. Whatever the diagnosis, the continuity in image and policy between the Union nationale and the Liberal regime was a telling argument for those who claimed that only a restructuring of the existing order would be sufficient.

The Bourassa strategy imperilled the established political order in a second, more indirect manner. By emphasizing that the election of the Parti québécois would thrust Quebec into economic and social chaos, and by insisting that they were the only force able to prevent a PQ victory, the Liberals had undermined the electoral position of third parties such as the Union nationale and the Ralliement créditiste. As the 1973 election results showed, the Quebec party system had been polarized between a Liberal government party and the Parti québécois opposition party. The Liberals had received 55 per cent of the popular vote, with 102 seats; the Parti québécois had secured only six seats, but had received 30 per cent of the popular vote. On the other hand, the Union nationale (temporarily renamed Unité-Québec) had received only 4 per cent of the popular vote, with no seats; and the Ralliement créditiste had two seats, with only 6 per cent of the popular vote. Moreover, most of the support these parties did receive was concentrated in semi-urban rural areas. Thus, especially in Montreal and other urban centres, voters who sought an electorally viable alternative to the Liberals were left with only the Parti québécois.[44]

The Parti québécois had many attractions for voters disaffected with the Liberals. It was new, with no clear links to existing parties. (The ex-Liberals in the party had been virtually expelled from Liberals ranks.) Its ability to raise impressive funds through membership drives meant that it could credibly claim not to be beholden to corporate interests. Its leader had a long-standing reputation for candour and personal independence. It had a "social-democrat" or at least "populist" social program. It enjoyed the sympathy of most of Quebec's journalists and intellectuals (although not the growing ranks of Marxist-oriented academics and intellectuals). The one PQ difficulty, which the Liberals exploited to the hilt, was the party's commitment to Quebec independence, which precluded the support of voters whose political disaffection did not extend to the Canadian political order itself. This was corrected in the fall of 1974 when the party formally committed itself to hold a referendum on Quebec independence, if it should be elected to power. A party convention ratified a new position according to which a PQ government would have to secure approval of independence in a referendum before taking Quebec into independence.[45] Accordingly, voters dissatisfied with the Bourassa regime could vote for the Parti québécois without at the same time endorsing Quebec independence. In this fashion, a party formally committed to a radical restructuring of the political order, and mobilizing extensive support on that basis, also became a vehicle for expressing the myriad of discontents that normally accumulate against any government party.

The Decline of the Bourassa Regime

The continued Parti québécois monopoly of the role of opposition guaranteed that at some point, with the inevitable Liberal defeat, the political order would be directly challenged and the Canadian political system would be thrown into crisis. But this eventuality was hastened by the drift of political events in the mid-1970s. First, the Liberals had growing difficulty maintaining an internal consensus on major issues; divisions that in the past separated the Liberals from the Parti québécois began to appear within the Liberal Party itself. Attempts to devise formulae for a new consensus failed; frequently, they merely intensified the internal conflict. Bill 22, with its failure to provide clear guidelines on access to English-language schools, did not satisfy many Liberal Francophones; Education Minister Jérôme Choquette cited the inadequacies of Bill 22 to justify his resignation from the party. But the bill was sufficiently strong to alienate Anglophone Liberals, including members of the Liberal parliamentary caucus (two of whom voted against the bill). Attempts to win over Quebec nationalists by adopting slogans such as cultural sovereignty or by referring to

Quebec as a "French state within the Canadian common market" served only to enrage Liberal hard-line federalists while, at the same time, legitimizing the *souverainiste* cause.

Also, by the mid-1970s the Bourassa regime and, most notably, Bourassa himself experienced difficulty simply in presenting themselves as able to carry on the normal tasks of government. Rising unemployment and inflation undermined its pretensions to a special competence in economic management; recurrent allegations of scandal and corruption extended to the cabinet itself. Henry Milner holds that widespread patronage and political favouritism sprang from the Bourassa Liberals' well-founded distrust of the new-middle-class state bureaucrats, who resented the Liberal disavowal of state intervention. Through these devices the Bourassa regime sought to regain control over the state apparatus and to secure the execution of its policies.[46] But the regime's carefully cultivated image of managerial competence was also hurt by the tensions within the party itself, over language and constitution, and Bourassa's inability to cope with them. The open contempt of Ottawa Liberals for Bourassa, as seen in Trudeau's public ridicule of Bourassa's stand on repatriation, could only weaken Bourassa's stature as leader of the government.

All these factors played against the Bourassa regime during the 1976 campaign. The Parti québécois resolutely maintained its stance as party of *all* the oppositions, refusing to engage in extended discussions of independence. The divisions among the Liberal clientele, and within the party, rapidly surfaced: Liberal candidates openly attacked Bill 22 as being either too weak or too strong; three leading Ottawa figures, Jean Marchand, Bryce Mackasey, and André Raynauld, presented themselves as candidates, reviving old charges that the Liberals are run from Ottawa. These charges were given some credibility when Mackasey and Marchand proceeded to deliver public letters to Bourassa in which they expressed unease with his language and constitutional policies.

Association with the federal Liberals must have been especially costly in the wake of the much-publicized decision of the federal government to delay granting Francophone pilots the right to use French when communicating with traffic controllers in the major Quebec airports. Unlike virtually all other federal language policies, concerned with the role of French in the civil service or the provision of French-language services outside Quebec, this policy dealt with language practices within Quebec itself. Ottawa was restricting the use of French rather than extending it. Most significantly, Ottawa appeared to have responded to pressure from English-speaking Canadians. Thus, even though the number of individuals directly affected by the decision was minuscule, it acquired a high symbolic status for many Québécois.[47]

The 1976 Election: The Broad Bases of PQ Support

In part, the magnitude of the Parti québécois victory – seventy-one seats – was due to a resurgence of the Union nationale. This resurgence was greatest in Anglophone West Montreal, where all but one seat nonetheless remained in the Liberal fold. But it also occurred in Francophone ridings, primarily outside Montreal. In some of these ridings, as many as twenty-eight by one estimate, the Union nationale's drain of past Liberals supporters was sufficient to deliver the victory to the Parti québécois.[48]

Nevertheless, the most important factor in the PQ victory was the impressive growth in its popular support. The PQ rose from 30 per cent of the popular vote in 1973 to 41 per cent in 1976. (The Liberals were reduced to 34 per cent of the popular vote, with twenty-six seats; the Union nationale received 18 per cent of the vote and eleven seats; the Ralliement créditiste garnered 5 per cent and one seat; and the Parti national populaire one per cent and one seat.)

In a very real sense, the Parti québécois emerged from the election as *the* party of French Quebec. It clearly had the support of a majority of Francophones; a mid-campaign survey had given the following party choices for Quebec Francophones: 54 per cent for the PQ, 26 per cent for the Liberals, 14 per cent for the Union nationale.[49] In virtually all regions of Quebec except Anglophone-dominated West Montreal the PQ had the largest proportions of voters.[50] Finally, a mid-campaign survey showed that 50 per cent or more respondents favoured the PQ in all occupational categories but "farmer" and "administrator and owner of enterprise" (these percentages include both Francophone and Anglophone respondents). The PQ was particularly strong in one middle-class category, "professional and semi-professional," where it received 64 per cent of the survey respondents. This percentage is substantially higher than those given by any other occupational category, including working-class categories. This particular result might be seen to confirm the argument of some that the Parti québécois was a middle-class party, although this would hold for only one segment of the middle class considering the relatively weak support among the "administrator and owner of enterprise" category. But

Parti québécois working-class support was simply too strong to let such a characterization stand: the mid-campaign survey gave the PQ 49 per cent among skilled workers and 51 per cent among unskilled workers, twice the Liberal support in each category. The percentages were even higher among Francophones. Rather than being specifically middle-class, support for the PQ constituted a broad coalition that crossed most class lines. This coalition can be more clearly defined in terms of age: the PQ was much more popular among young Francophones.[51]

Support for the PQ and the Question of Quebec Independence

Given this heterogeneity of PQ support and the multitude of factors that conceivably could have mobilized it, there naturally arises the question of whether supporters for the PQ were necessarily in favour of independence. This issue had a special pertinence in the wake of the 1976 election. During the campaign, the PQ had taken great pains to convince voters it was not seeking a mandate for Quebec independence; such a mandate would be sought only after the PQ assumed office, in a referendum intended solely for that purpose. Yet, the point should not be overemphasized. While other concerns than Quebec independence may well have led voters to reject the Liberals and support the Parti québécois, these voters could not have been fiercely antagonistic to the idea of Quebec independence. There could have been no confusion in the minds of Quebec voters that the PQ was formally committed to independence: the Liberal campaigns of the previous elections (as well as that of 1976) were sufficient to establish that. And the PQ had openly acknowledged that if it should secure the government it would seek to demonstrate to Québécois that independence is both desirable and possible, in order to win the referendum it was committed to hold.

Ideally, it should be possible to resolve this debate through the analysis of opinion surveys. Ever since the founding of the Parti québécois a steady stream of survey analyses sought to determine precisely to what extent support for the PQ constituted support for Quebec independence.[52] But they often reached quite divergent conclusions, some arguing it was essentially an *indépendantiste* vote while others argued it was a protest vote that happened to be registered through an *indépendantiste* party. To a large extent, these various conclusions are associated with differences in the question posed in the survey. In a questionnaire the use of "separation" rather than "independence" can affect the response.[53] Particularly important is whether the question evoked the prospect of some form of economic association between an independent Quebec and the rest of Canada. This was revealed early in the history of the Parti québécois, during the 1970 election campaign, when a survey used two differently formulated questions to measure support for independence. First, respondents were asked whether they supported *"une séparation politique et économique du Québec avec le Canada."* Within the full sample of respondents, only 14 per cent were in favour, with 76 per cent opposed; even among respondents supporting the PQ only 39 per cent were in favour, with 50 per cent opposed. The second question asked whether respondents were in favour of *"une séparation politique du Québec moyennant une association économique avec le Canada."* This time, a full 35 per cent of all respondents were in favour, with 55 per cent opposed, and among PQ supporters a majority of 70 per cent were in favour, with 24 per cent opposed.[54] In short, most supporters of the Parti québécois did indeed favour Quebec independence, but only in an economic association with the rest of Canada.

In the case of the 1973 election, polarization of the campaign around the independence question apparently limited PQ support to only those who had an unconditional commitment to independence, with or without an economic association. In two different surveys, neither of which referred to economic association, the majority of PQ supporters appear to be *indépendantiste*. In one survey, respondents were asked whether they favoured the separation of Quebec from Canada: 71 per cent of the Francophone PQ supporters answered positively, with only 16 per cent opposed.[55] In the other survey, which referred simply to the "independence of Quebec," 77 per cent of the PQ supporters were in favour, with 13 per cent opposed.[56]

As we have seen, the 1976 campaign was not polarized around the independence question. With the PQ commitment to a referendum, non-*indépendantistes* could more easily join the ranks of the Parti québécois. A survey administered during the campaign seemed to confirm that this had indeed happened. It found that among those intending to support the PQ, only 49 per cent were in favour of independence, with 26 per cent opposed. But the question referred to the "separation of Quebec from Canada"; apparently, the survey contained no question evoking the possibility of an economic association.[57] A survey administered in October, 1977, did pose a question in which independence was linked to an economic association; the results of this survey suggest that in

1976 the vast majority of PQ supporters favoured independence. Respondents were asked whether they were in favour of: *"La souveraineté-association, c'est-à-dire l'indépendance politique du Québec accompagnée d'une association économique avec le Canada."* Among respondents who had voted for the Parti québécois in 1973 *or* 1976, 60 per cent said that they were in favour; among those who had voted for the PQ in *both* 1973 and 1976, 80 per cent were in favour.[58] There is, of course, the possibility that some of these individuals were not in favour of independence at the time they voted for the PQ but subsequently were converted, perhaps through their new-found identification with the PQ. It should be noted, moreover, that the Parti québécois was much more successful in attracting voters who were "undecided" about sovereignty-association (59 per cent by one estimate) than those who were actually opposed to sovereignty-association (27 per cent).[59]

Whatever the role of non-*indépendantistes* in the 1976 electoral victory of the Parti québécois, a 1978 survey confirmed that the vast majority of those continuing to support the PQ favoured independence. This time 78 per cent of the respondents who declared that they would vote for the PQ said they favoured independence with an economic association. Only 35 per cent of PQ supporters were prepared to support *"l'indépendance du Québec, c'est-à-dire, l'indépendance politique et économique complète."*[60] At the same time, the survey revealed that among PQ supporters there was considerable confusion or disagreement over the precise form that sovereignty might take. For many, it did not imply as complete a *political* disengagement as the PQ leadership had normally maintained: 47 per cent indicated that under sovereignty-association Quebec would continue to elect *députés* to sit in Ottawa. Moreover, many PQ supporters apparently did not regard political sovereignty as an irrevocable goal: 68 per cent of PQ supporters also said they would be favourable to *"un fédéralisme renouvelé par lequel le Québec et les autres provinces obtiendraient plus de pouvoirs au sein de la Confédération Canadienne."*[61]

Thus, during the 1970s PQ supporters always shared a general sympathy for the goal of Quebec sovereignty, with the possible exception of the 1976 election. But there were limitations to this support for independence. The majority of PQ supporters favoured independence only if accompanied by an economic association. Also, as the 1978 survey suggests, there was no clear consensus about even the political relations between a sovereign Quebec and the rest of Canada. Some PQ supporters apparently preferred the maintenance of some political links. Moreover, one cannot explain attraction to the Parti québécois simply in terms of independence. Support for independence was not always a sufficient condition, hence, other factors must also have been necessary. In 1970, a sizable proportion of adherents to sovereignty-association supported other parties: 41 per cent of the Union nationale supporters came from this group.[62] According to a study of the 1973 election, support for independence was a sufficient condition for a PQ vote in Montreal (it had not been in 1970), but not in the rest of the province.[63] Nevertheless, most PQ supporters did stand as supporters of Quebec independence.

The Parti québécois and the idea of Quebec independence could have attracted such a large following only through tapping a wide variety of grievances and aspirations. Within the Quebec electorate they must have become symbols of a great many different visions of social and political change. As long as the PQ had not secured power and had not begun its campaign to win the referendum, both the party and Quebec independence could continue to symbolize different things to different people. But, as the PQ tenure in office was to show, it would be no easy task for a government to implement policies corresponding to all these expectations. Similarly, it would be a major challenge to transform the PQ clientele's general sympathy for Quebec independence into support in a referendum for a particular conception of independence, and of an independent Quebec. Compounding this challenge was the fact that to win the referendum the PQ needed to present a conception of independence that could also secure support of Québécois who had resisted the electoral movement to the Parti québécois, perhaps out of unease with the idea of independence.

Characterizing the Parti Québécois: Social Bases and Ideology

Before directly examining how the Parti québécois, once in power, sought to implement this highly diverse mandate for change, we first need to examine the PQ's development during its first eight years of existence. In particular, we need to assess the social and ideological forces that guided the PQ during these years. What configuration of class interests did the party reflect? What were the ideals and objectives around which the party was united? With this information, we may better understand the goals the party leaders brought to office in 1976 and the expectations party militants had of "their" new government. And we will have a standard for measuring the extent to which the inevitable constraints of holding power forced a redefinition of goals and a revision of strategies.

While observers often disagree over how to characterize the class bases or ideology of a political party, in the case of the Parti québécois the disagreements have been especially profound. For some, during its first eight years the PQ was a "bourgeois" party guided by the interests of a Francophone capitalist class; for others, it was a fundamentally "social democratic" movement; still others contend that it was little more than a party of "intellectuals." In part, these different assessments reflect differences in the indicators or criteria used. Whereas some analysts have focused on the social characteristics of party members, others have been concerned with the relationship of the party to external forces or with the party program and discourse and the class interests reflected therein. Accordingly, as we examine the PQ we will need to pay attention to all three: social composition, relationship to external forces, and party program and discourse. On this basis, we will argue that the Parti québécois, at least before it assumed office, can best be characterized as a broadly based coalition of social forces, dominated by elements of the new middle class, which was united by the goal of Quebec independence along with an ideology combining belief in the technocratic state with a populist social program.

Social Composition of the PQ: A Coalition under New-Middle-Class Dominance

The most straightforward way to characterize a party is in terms of the social characteristics of its members. As with other political parties in Quebec and elsewhere, the Parti québécois membership has always been heavily weighted in favour of middle-class elements. This was confirmed by the party itself when in 1971 it released the following data on the occupations of its members: professions (including teachers and administrators): 37.2 per cent; white-collar: 22.1 per cent; blue-collar: 12.6 per cent; students: 14 per cent; and housewives: 8.9 per cent.[64]

What has distinguished the Parti québécois from other Quebec parties is the particular categories of the middle class from which, at least until recent years, it has drawn so many of its members – the Francophone "new middle class" of salaried professionals based primarily in the public sector: administrators and bureaucrats, intellectuals and teachers, social scientists, and mass media specialists. The weight of these new-middle-class elements and the relative absence of businessmen and traditional liberal professionals (such as law and medicine) were reflected in the occupations of PQ candidates in the 1970, 1973, and 1976 elections. New-middle-class elements (salary-earners, university graduates, and teachers) constituted 47 per cent of the PQ candidates, with liberal professionals and businessmen making up 19 per cent and 21 per cent, respectively. In the case of the Liberal Party, new-middle-class occupations accounted for only 23 per cent of the candidates, while 26 per cent were in the liberal professions and a full 39 per cent were businessmen.[65]

Several students of the Parti québécois have called attention to a specific category within the Francophone new middle class: "intellectuals," or creators and disseminators of culture and knowledge. The category includes artists, performers, journalists, and, above all, professors and teachers. Clearly, this element of the new middle class has played a critical role in the Parti québécois. For example, of 218 PQ candidates in 1970 and 1973, forty-seven were teachers compared with nine in the Liberal Party, ten in the Ralliement créditiste, and thirteen in the Union nationale.[66] In 1976, teachers were the largest single category among PQ candidates.[67] As Marcel Fournier has argued, these *travailleurs du langage* possess *"un fort capital cultural"* that can be best exploited in French.[68] Thus, they have a strong interest in the strength of French-language institutions in Quebec and, more generally, in the pre-eminence of French as the language of Quebec residents. In an urban, industrialized Quebec these concerns provide compelling arguments for state intervention: to strengthen French-language schools and to ensure, by coercion if need be, that the children of Francophones (and immigrants) be educated there rather than in English-language schools; to support French-language publishing, broadcasting, and film production; to reinforce the status of French as the primary language of work in Quebec; and to eliminate Anglicizing tendencies in the French used in Quebec. For all these reasons, one would expect Francophone intellectuals and teachers to have a strong attraction to Quebec neo-nationalism and to play a critical role within the Parti québécois.

Nonetheless, it would be an error to see teachers and other intellectuals as dominating the party, as have Pinard and Hamilton, who characterize it as a "party of intellectuals."[69] As the essential vehicle of Quebec nationalism, the Parti québécois should have drawn activists from most components of the new middle class. A particular case in point would be Francophone managers and administrators. We have already seen how Francophones historically were severely underrepresented in managerial positions in the Quebec economy and the federal bureaucracy. It was mainly within the Quebec state, and public sector, that aspiring Francophone managers could look for opportunity. We saw how this component of the new middle class was instrumental to the political modernization of the Quiet Revolution; they were bearers of the neo-nationalist ideology through which it was legitimized. There is every reason to believe that Francophone managers and administrators based within the Quebec state would be strongly supportive of the PQ effort to transform the Quebec state into a sovereign one. By the same token, we can expect that the professionals and semi-professionals who had become lodged within the Quebec public sector during the 1960s and 1970s – economists, engineers, social workers, public health specialists, etc. – would be similarly attracted to the promise of a sovereign Quebec state with vastly strengthened powers and resources.

The role the new middle class as a whole, rather than just intellectuals, played in the upper levels of the Parti québécois can be readily demonstrated. Probably the best indicator of the effective leadership of the party is the membership of the first PQ cabinet, formed after the 1976 election. Here, intellectuals were indeed strongly represented. By our calculations, eight or 33 per cent of the members of the cabinet were intellectuals (six professors and two journalists).[70] However, ten or 42 per cent came from other elements of the new middle class. Primarily, this group consisted of administrators or economic advisers.[71] As we would expect, moreover, none of the administrators had been based within the corporate sector. Rather, they had made their careers in government or in such parapublic institutions as hospitals and universities.[72] These additional new-middle-class members of the cabinet also included two individuals who, while trained in a liberal profession (law), had made their careers as salaried employees – of the CSN in one case, and of the co-operative movement in the other.[73] Taken together, of course, new-middle-class members represented the overwhelming majority of the PQ cabinet: 75 per cent. By way of contrast, only nine members or 35 per cent of the previous Bourassa cabinet were from the new middle class.[74]

By the same token, the first Parti québécois government caucus cannot be reduced to intellectuals either. By our calculations, teachers represented 30 per cent of the PQ candidates who were successful in 1976; the addition of other categories of intellectuals brings the proportion to 38 per cent. Nonetheless, another 32 per cent of the caucus members came from "other" new-middle-class occupations. On this basis, a total of 70 per cent of the caucus members were "new middle class."[75]

The party, however, cannot be reduced even to these various elements of the new middle class and their preoccupations. After all, the party was formed through the merger of three quite distinct organizations. The strongest of the three, le Mouvement souveraineté-association, was closely related to the technocratic vision of the neo-nationalist politicians and bureaucrats who had abandoned the Liberal Party after its refusal to adopt their plan for the political disengagement of Quebec from Canada, with the maintenance of close economic ties. However, the Rassemblement pour l'indépendance nationale reflected a different nationalist tradition, with its advocacy of complete disengagement of Quebec from Canada, with its forthright commitment to the full pre-eminence of French within Quebec, and with a rather demagogic style of leadership that offended the liberal-democratic norms of the Quiet Revolution political modernizers.[76] The Ralliement national, for its part, was closely linked with the Créditiste movement, and shared much of its populism, anti-statism, and social conservatism. On some issues, such as the treatment of the Anglophone minority, the definition of independence, and the commitment to a referendum on independence, the ex-members of the RIN and RN, most notably the former, severely tested the authority of Lévesque and his new-middle-class colleagues.

Also, while relations between the PQ and many union leaders were often strained, the party nonetheless contained many union militants. Some of these militants fall into the new middle class, as with the CEQ and, in large part, the CSN members. But private-sector and blue-collar militants also have been present. In fact, Jean Gérin-Lajoie, head of the Syndicat des métallurgistes unis d'Amérique, and Michel Bourdon, head of the construction federation of the CSN, were long-standing PQ activists. Officials of the FTQ were among PQ candidates; in the 1976 election, the FTQ formally supported the PQ.[77] These union militants regularly sought to move the party to a closer relationship with the union movement than the PQ leadership was ready to accept. Some of them also advanced proposals for social measures and decentralization of public and private authority with which the PQ technocrats were very much ill at ease. Finally, the party was closely allied to traditional nationalist groups, such as la Société Saint-Jean Baptiste, with their preponderantly liberal professional and socially conservative bases.

The one element of French Quebec society virtually absent from the leaders and militants of the Parti québécois has been the emerging capitalist class. We have seen how during the 1970s Francophone businessmen were relatively underrepresented among PQ candidates (21 per cent), compared with their strong presence among Liberal candidates (39 per cent). (Moreover, the businessmen who were PQ candidates were mainly owners of small businesses.) The same pattern is even more pronounced at the cabinet level: only one member of the first Lévesque cabinet (Guy Joron) was a businessman whereas five members of the preceding Bourassa cabinet had been businessmen. As we shall see, some analysts have insisted that the party was intimately linked to the Francophone business class. However, their argument rests on the interests served by the party rather than on the pattern of representation within it.

In sum, during the 1970s Parti québécois activists constituted a broad-based coalition. The most important single element was the Francophone new middle class, coming primarily from the Quebec public sector: technocrats and administrators, intellectuals and teachers, and other categories of salaried professionals and semi-professionals. However, the coalition extended to others: public-sector clerical and blue-collar workers; even private-sector workers and their union organizers; liberal professionals still imbued with traditional nationalism; and perhaps even some owners of small and medium-sized enterprises. Uniting such a diverse and potentially divisive coalition was the vision of an independent Quebec.

PQ Structures: Formal and Financial Autonomy

Some analysts have argued that the key to locating the class interests served by a party lies less in the social characteristics of its members than in the relationships between the party and external forces. In particular, they point to the sources of party financing. After all, a party may have few important business people among its militants, or even its leaders, and yet effectively be bound by corporate interests if it is dependent on them for campaign funding. By the same token, a "social democratic" party may be closely tied to the interests of union organizations and their leaderships if it is dependent on them for much of its funding. Beyond that, it may be formally linked to unions, as with such social democratic parties as the New Democratic Party or the British Labour Party.

For its part, the Parti québécois could credibly claim to be free of such constraints. From the beginning the party had relied for its

finances on membership fees and the results of skilfully orchestrated annual funding campaigns. By the mid-1970s, the annual
campaigns were securing over 50,000 individual contributions.[78]
In fact, on this basis, the party was able to raise $1,200,000 in the
spring of 1976 – sufficient to match the Liberal's saturation media
exposure during the subsequent election campaign.[79]

As for formal links with the organized working class, the PQ had
none. After all, the Parti québécois had not originated within
working-class movements or organizations. And party leaders had
successfully opposed the several attempts by some party militants
to establish a formal relationship with the union movement.[80]

In short, the hallmark of the Parti québécois was autonomy
from all external forces, whether business or labour. With its highly perfected system of internal financing the PQ could make such a
claim with far greater credibility than can most political parties.
Accordingly, the party should have reflected more faithfully its
internal configuration of social and ideological forces than do
most parties.

The PQ Program: A National Bourgeoisie, Social Democracy, and Nationalist Populism

A final basis for characterizing a political party is its general discourse and program. In the case of the PQ, we have ample materials
available. During the eight years before its accession to power, the
Parti québécois detailed many aspects of the social, economic, and
political organization of an independent Quebec, both in the party
program and in a series of special documents.[81] Resulting from
extensive debates within the party, this vision of an independent
Quebec offers an invaluable guide to the party's ideology.

In PQ publications, the greatest attention was given to reorganization of the Quebec economy. The persistence of a capitalist system was presumed, along with a continued presence of American
capital and initiative. But it was argued that through the transition of Quebec to sovereignty many of the worst effects of Quebec's
economic dependence could be eliminated: the economy would be
made more dynamic and more evenly developed, and Francophones would play a greater role in its direction and management.
The key to this transformation was to lie in the new capacities
sovereignty would bring to the Quebec state, which would have
full legal authority to plan and regulate economic activity and
would have the fiscal resources for more effective direct intervention and for support of private enterprises.

The program's basic economic model was state capitalism, despite the addition over time of pronouncements about the dangers of concentration of power in political and economic elites. These elements in party documents continued to be overshadowed by a strongly technocratic perspective, with its concern for economic efficiency and rationality, and its seemingly boundless confidence in the capacity of state action to produce desired change. Typical of this perspective is a passage from the 1972 document *Quand nous serons vraiment chez nous*, which provides the essential background to the party program:

On the condition that a firm and clear political will prevails, we are convinced for our part that truly miraculous changes could result [from sovereignty], that numerous obstacles which are presently insurmountable would become perfectly solvable technical problems. . . .[82]

Quebec's economic dependence was usually traced to an improper organization of capital. Time and again, the Parti québécois argued that the Quebec economy had always generated sufficient capital to meet the needs of economic development but that much of this capital had left the province, turning the province into a net exporter of capital. With independence this would change. First, state institutions would have a radically different impact. The federal government would no longer be withdrawing revenue from Quebec and, allegedly, returning only part of these funds to Quebec through its expenditures. The Caisse de dépôt et de placement, which manages pension funds generated in the provincial public sector, would expand its activities to include the parapublic sector as a whole, as well as private firms whose employees request that their pension funds be lodged with the Caisse. Also, a Banque du Québec would be constituted to oversee Quebec's financial institutions, to act as financial agent for the government, and perhaps to create and regulate a Quebec currency.

Second, private financial institutions would no longer be in the hands of non-Quebec interests. Here the PQ plans for reorganization of the Quebec economy were most dramatic, and most likely to meet fierce resistance. According to the PQ program, all banks, trust companies, and insurance companies operating in an independent Quebec not only would have to be chartered in Quebec but no more than 25 per cent of their shares could be in the hands of non-Québécois. Reflecting the "social democratic" influences in the party, the program also required that no single individual or group own more than 10 per cent of the shares in a financial institution. One or perhaps two banks would come under direct state ownership. Most other shares needing to be transferred to conform to these regulations would be purchased by savings and credit co-operatives. In addition, financial institutions would be expected, and perhaps legally required, to reinvest in Quebec the savings they acquire from Québécois.[83]

Another thrust in this strategy to reduce economic dependence was to be an expansion of the role of the Quebec state as planner and initiator of Quebec-based development. A comprehensive plan of economic development would be produced jointly by "representatives, in equal number, of workers and other parts of the population, of enterprises and of public powers."[84] Existing public corporations would be strengthened and new ones created: the program committed the party to "favour as the preferred form of economic intervention a sustained extension of the public sector (state and mixed enterprises), particularly in sectors which have a major impact on the pattern of economic development."[85] Preferential purchasing policies would be adopted for the public sector as a whole. A Société de Réorganisation industrielle, financed fully by public funds, would go about the task of creating viable economic complexes by acquiring majority ownership in weak enterprises, modernizing them, and integrating them with other enterprises, some of which it would create itself. Once the new complexes became viable, they would be sold – primarily to co-operative bodies, with some participation of the Caisse de dépôt et de placement.[86]

With these structural changes in place, Quebec presumably would be able to escape economic dependence. To use a frequently employed phrase, it would have repatriated the "centres of decision." There were only limited plans for further transfer of ownership of firms from non-Quebec interests. Through accession to sovereignty, the Quebec government would acquire ownership of public enterprises presently attached to the federal government, most notably in communications and transportation. These enterprises would then become the nuclei for unified Quebec-wide operations. Ownership was to be *majoritairement public*; Canadian Pacific would lose control over its railway facilities in Quebec and Bell Canada would lose control over its exchanges.[87] Beyond these changes in transportation and communications, however, the party was explicitly committed to a transfer of ownership of private enterprises from non-Quebec interests only in the financial sector. Any other changes in the pattern of ownership would come through the need to conform to an investment code, which in very broad terms distinguished among several economic sectors and prescribed limits to foreign ownership within each.

All foreign ownership would be excluded from sectors considered "vital," essentially cultural activities where the non-Quebec presence is already limited, and from "industrial sectors where the behaviour of enterprises should be modified to bring it into conformity with the public interest." (The steel-refining industry, already occupied by a public corporation, SIDBEC, was specifically cited.)[88] Only minority ownership (up to 49 per cent) would be permitted in manufacturing when "available technical personnel and acquired experience allow the creation of primarily Québécois units."[89] Elsewhere, up to 99 per cent foreign ownership would be permitted. Moreover, while the code would be applied immediately to enterprises not yet established in Quebec, its application to existing firms "would be subject . . . to transition periods that take account both of the concern to proceed in an orderly fashion and of the financial means available to us without endangering the financing of new programs and of new projects."[90] In principle, foreign-owned firms would be constrained by a provision that dividends paid by these firms represent no more than half of after-tax profits, but it would be a difficult measure to enforce effectively.[91]

Some of the measures envisaged did not require sovereignty: e.g., the extension of the Caisse de dépôt et de placement to the parapublic sector; the creation of a Société de réorganisation industrielle; and the development of a more comprehensive preferential purchasing policy for the public sector. But the regulation of ownership in most sectors of the economy does presume sovereignty. As we have seen, the changes would be greatest in three areas: financial institutions, transportation, and communication. What is striking about the first two areas, in which the change would be greatest, is that the main interests affected are English-Canadian, not American. Unlike primary and secondary industry, finance and transportation are domains in which historically the English-Canadian bourgeoisie has been able to prevent American domination, with the support of various federal policies. Some observers have concluded from this that the Parti québécois was concerned in fact merely with eliminating English-Canadian economic domination and was quite prepared for greater subordination to American interests in order to accomplish this. But this would be a misreading of the intent of the PQ proposals and of their probable effect. The desire for greater autonomy from "foreign" capital, Canadian or American, was authentic, and some of the measures would indeed have expanded the overall autonomy of Québécois institutions, if only marginally. But whether Quebec could escape economic dependence without going beyond the financial sector to change patterns of ownership in other, American-dominated sectors is quite a different matter.

On the basis of these measures there can be no question that the PQ vision of a sovereign Quebec entailed a major expansion of the state's role within the Quebec economy. A major purpose of this intervention would be to strengthen Francophone ownership within the Quebec economy. For some observers, this is proof that the party operated under the hegemony of the emerging Francophone business class, even if, as we have seen, representatives of the class were largely absent within the party itself and it has not been a significant source of party funds. Yet, even framed in these terms the argument is not compelling. It is difficult to see how the PQ's essential goal of Quebec sovereignty could have been in the interest of this class, at least that part of it based in the private sector. In effect, there were very good reasons why Quebec businessmen could not be found among PQ members or financial supporters.

It is not at all clear that the large Francophone manufacturing, agricultural-food, and financial firms had an affinity with the Parti québécois or its project of sovereignty. If anything, their interests would seem more closely aligned with maintenance of the existing Canadian political order. In general, once their activity within Quebec reaches a certain level, these Francophone-owned firms start to look to the Canadian market as a whole. Often, they acquire establishments in other provinces. For instance, the highly successful food chain of Provigo, Inc. in Montreal bought out the Ottawa-based M. Locb Ltd. In the process, it acquired control of Horne and Pitfield Foods of Edmonton, as well as Market Wholesale Grocery of California. Similarly, prior to their merger to form la Banque nationale, the two largest Francophone-owned banks, la Banque provinciale and la Banque canadienne nationale, both had been actively seeking to establish a presence in the rest of Canada. La Banque provinciale had already acquired control of both the Toronto-based Unity Bank of Canada and the Laurentide Financial Corporation of Vancouver. And the merger itself sprang in large part from the desire of both banks to strengthen these operations in the other provinces. As Niosi argues: "for the French-Canadian bourgeoisie, the separation of Quebec could only truncate its principal market, force it to reorganize its enterprises and weaken its position on the Canadian and international scene."[92] By this same token, Niosi may well be correct in treating Francophone capitalists not as a Quebec bourgeoisie but as simply a component of the Canadian bourgeoisie: a French-Canadian bourgeoisie.

To be sure, the Parti québécois argued that it did not seek "separation"; it would try to link sovereignty to an economic association with the rest of Canada. But it could not promise such an association. And there is always the possibility that, once under way, the movement to sovereignty could acquire such a momentum that Quebec would accede to sovereignty even without an association. Given the strong interest they had in the maintenance of the Canadian economic and political system, one would expect that large Francophone firms were apprehensive about the whole notion of Quebec sovereignty. As we shall see, at the time of the 1980 referendum most major Francophone businessmen openly advocated a "No" vote and gave financial support to the campaign organization for such a vote.

There remain the smaller Francophone enterprises, which, if only because of their size, have bases of action clearly restricted to Quebec. For them, sovereignty might have appeared less threatening. In fact, those highly dependent on Quebec government contracts might have seen real advantages in a radical expansion of the resources of the Quebec state. But it also is clear that many of these small enterprises were deeply suspicious of the *étatiste* tendencies of the PQ. These suspicions likely spilled over into the PQ's project of sovereignty as well. In any event, whatever their attitude, this element of the Francophone business class was too weak to be regarded as a "hegemonic" force within the Parti québécois.

Conceivably, one might attempt to salvage the thesis of bourgeois hegemony of the Parti québécois by turning to the heads of Quebec state enterprises and the Quebec co-operative movement. Both Gilles Bourque and Pierre Fournier are careful to include them within their notions of a distinct "Quebec bourgeoisie." They can indeed be seen as falling within, to use Fournier's formulation, a distinctly Quebec-based "financial circuit." By and large, their sources of capital do lie within Quebec (although Hydro-Québec has become heavily dependent on foreign capital markets). And their markets are similarly concentrated in Quebec (although, once again, Hydro Québec has become heavily involved in American markets). Finally, the state enterprises obviously are closely linked to the Quebec state; the Mouvement Desjardins has received extensive state support.

Perhaps there was support for Quebec independence among the

heads of state enterprises and the co-operative movement, although there is no clear evidence to that effect. But if the thesis of bourgeois hegemony were to rest on them alone, it would be heavily qualified indeed. In effect, it would have to ignore what Bourque and Fournier themselves see as an integral part of the Quebec bourgeoisie.[93]

In sum, the *péquiste* state technocrats may well have had a vision of private capital joining public enterprises and the co-operative movement to construct a distinctly Quebec capitalism under the guidance of a sovereign Quebec state. But it is not at all clear that this vision was shared by private Francophone businessmen. Quebec Marxist Nicole Laurin-Frenette has disposed of this question in an especially trenchant fashion:

> The myth of the national bourgeoisie (complete or fragmented) acceding to power through independence has been hard to destroy but one can only wonder how much longer it can stand in face of the facts. The notorious personal, family, and professional ties between members of the previous government [the Bourassa regime] and the business and financial communities do indeed serve to shore up the argument upon which rests the thesis of an intentional complicity between the State and the dominant class, and its application to the Québécois context. [But] one must admit that the professors, poets, curés and communicators newly promoted to the rank of statesman do not make very convincing flunkeys of the bourgeoisie.[94]

In direct contradiction of the thesis that the PQ was guided by the interests of a Quebec bourgeoisie, other analysts, as well as activists within the PQ, have seen in the PQ plans for state intervention confirmation that the party is "social democratic."

The term "social democracy" did not actually appear in the original versions of the PQ program, although terms such as "social justice" were featured prominently.[95] However, when it came to identifying the type of economic and social system a sovereign Quebec would create, typically leaders and militants alike would point to Sweden, the quintessential "social democratic" state. Thus, soon after the PQ accession to power Lévesque characterized the party as "an *indépendantiste* party which would at the same time be in the current of a social democracy, Scandinavian-style (which is the maximum of 'progressivism' possible within the North American context)."[96] And, evoking the PQ commitment to social democratic ideals, during the late seventies and the early eighties the leadership regularly sought without success to secure the party's admission into the Socialist International.

As a term of analysis "social democratic" does not lend itself to a precise definition, given the multitude of ways in which it has been used over the years. However, at its most general level, social democracy can be taken to mean a commitment not only to strengthen political democracy but to apply democratic principles to economic life.[97] Typically this has entailed a concern with state intervention to arrange "a better deal" for organized labour and lower income groups, and more generally to manage more effectively the economy.[98] Several policy thrusts can be identified within the programs of social democratic parties in Western Europe and Canada: reduction of disparities in income and living conditions; extension of state ownership and control of the economy; state economic planning; and broadened participation in decision-making, whether through tripartite decision-making structures and popular consultation by the state or through worker control within private enterprises.[99] On this basis social democratic regimes have sought to institutionalize "compromises" between organizations of workers and of capitalists. This notion of a labour-capital compromise, or "social contract," has most clearly distinguished social democratic programs in recent decades.[100]

Some of these typically "social democratic" policies have indeed emerged in our examination of the Parti québécois program. The program was very much concerned with increasing state intervention in the Quebec economy, especially in the form of state enterprises. Beyond that, it called for a substantial degree of indicative economic planning.

Other aspects of the PQ program, which we have not yet noted, reflect a concern with reducing economic and social disparities. In the name of *"la justice sociale"* the program envisaged a host of new social services and redistributive measures: a guaranteed minimum income, complete public health care system, free day-care centres, the right to early retirement, four-week annual holidays, close public regulation of the pharmaceutical industry, protection of consumers, improvement in housing, etc. Finally, the program called for the expansion of co-operative organizations through many sectors of Quebec society.[101]

In addition, the PQ program contained measures specifically concerned with workers. It called for greater worker participation in the management of enterprises. In fact, it went so far as to commit the party "to establish an economic system eliminating all form of exploitation of workers and responding to the real needs of

Québécois as a whole rather than to the requirements of a privileged economic minority."[102] And it contained measures to facilitate union organization and to strengthen the strike weapon.

On the basis of these specific measures in its program, the Parti québécois might well be classified as "social democratic." Certainly, they undermine the notion that the PQ was tied to "bourgeois" interests. Nonetheless, the party cannot be properly understood in terms of its formal program alone. Before classifying the party as "social democratic" it is important to examine directly its relationship to the Quebec labour movement. After all, unlike most social democratic parties, the Parti québécois did not originate within working-class movements or organizations. Moreover, as we have seen, it did not establish a formal link with the union movement, despite repeated efforts of some party militants to establish such a linkage, nor, for that matter, did it look to the union movement for funding. In fact, the PQ leadership had made its position clear early in the party's history when the Conseil exécutif secured approval by the Conseil national of the following definition of relations between the PQ and the unions:

> With the unions and their organs, we share a fundamental objective of changing and humanizing the social and economic situation. In each case of activities clearly tied to this goal, we must try to collaborate as closely as possible. But we must never forget – and the unions must not forget it – that our deadlines are not the same, nor our means; that their approach remains essentially one of making demands whereas ours is essentially persuasive; and, above all, that union action is most often fragmented and sectoral whereas ours must necessarily be as global as possible.[103]

As the statement indicates, the PQ defined itself first and foremost as the party of the Québécois national collectivity as a whole rather than of any element within it – its approach was "global" rather than "sectoral." The general ideology of the party effectively denied the salience of class relations, at most recognizing within the national collectivity a wide variety of social and economic differentiations. The various social measures the party advocated were viewed simply as part of the collectivity's responsibility to its members or as conditions necessary to the dignity or *l'épanouissement* of the individual. Thus, when it came to specifying the process through which a comprehensive economic plan was to be developed, the program was careful to refer not just to organized labour, business, and state officials, as in most tripartite schemes, but to "representatives, in equal number, of workers *and other parts of the population,* of enterprises and of public powers."[104] The leaders of organized labour would be just one of various sets of representatives of "the population."

In short, despite many of the provisions in the PQ program, the party's historical origins, its relationship with organized labour, and its general discourse all suggest that the party has not assigned the Quebec working class the privileged position that one would expect of a social democratic party. For these reasons, most analysts in fact have always resisted granting the Parti québécois "social democratic" status.

The Parti québécois more closely fits the normal understanding of a "populist" party. Typically, the concept of a populist party entails three distinguishing characteristics: an ideology that focuses on a notion of "the people" and attacks the concentration of political or economic power at their expense; a discourse that draws on elements of an indigenous popular culture; and a very broad and well-mobilized base of support.[105] Clearly, the Parti québécois displayed all three characteristics. It articulated the notion of a Québécois people transcending class divisions and subjugated by a highly centralized federal system and by Anglophone corporate power. Its message was very much framed within an indigenous popular culture, although it generally excluded the working-class *joual* variety. And, while the leadership was predominantly from the new middle class, the party had indeed succeeded in mobilizing a wide base of support that extended to most classes within Francophone Quebec. It was limited primarily by age.

Within the Parti québécois world view the national collectivity took precedence over all social divisions. Thus, the program called for improving the lot of a variety of categories of Québécois: the old, the young, the handicapped, the poor, and the unemployed. However, the party leadership, if not the militants, remained suspicious of unions or any other large-scale organization claiming to speak on the behalf a particular category of Québécois – they were "sectoral" in nature. To be sure, the PQ was committed to forums designed to bring together business, union organizations, and representatives of "other parts of the population" to address the problems of the day. But this reflected less the "social democratic" objective of a "social contract," let alone a "class compromise," than the quite different nationalist project of drawing together the parts of the national collectivity to create a national consensus and solidarity. As such, its roots were as much in the "social corporatism" of traditional French-Canadian nationalism as in the contemporary notions of "neo-corporatism" enshrined in Western European social democratic regimes. In short, the Parti québécois ideology can be best characterized as "nationalist populist," as has argued Raymond Laliberté:

a *populist nationalism*, rooted in culture and politics but with a program sufficiently ambiguous as both to deny social classes and to integrate firmly class interests, all in the name, naturally, of the nation as a whole, indivisible in principle, fragmented in practice.[106]

Such an ideology, with its suspicion of both capital and organized labour, translated especially well the contradictory position of the party's new-middle-class leadership. Intellectuals and senior administrators stood midway in the class structure, belonging fully to neither capital nor labour, and could not identify easily with either big business or the union movement. In addition, state technocrats had a special interest in expanding the autonomy of the Quebec state from both capital and organized labour. The Quebec state was the primary institution in which they had been able to secure opportunity and mobility, given the long-standing obstacles to entry into the Quebec corporate world. Thus, they had every reason to defend the power and authority of the state and its institutions, assigning them a mandate and a role that transcended those of business, the unions, or any other "pressure group."

At the same time, the "nationalist populist" ideology could effectively accommodate the other elements of the PQ coalition. Even if the PQ's working-class and lower-middle-class supporters could not be certain of the status of their union organizations within the PQ firmament, they could look forward to state programs of social and economic redistribution. For their part, some liberal professionals may well have found an affinity in the PQ's populist unease about "big business" and "big labour." The same would have been true of the owners of small and medium-sized businesses, to the extent they were present in the PQ coalition.

To be sure, a highly active minority in the Parti québécois did articulate an authentically "social democratic" or even "socialist" project, as with Robert Burns and other activists from the public-sector unions. This project was integral to their commitment to Quebec sovereignty, and to the PQ. But they never quite succeeded in converting the party as a whole to it. In the last analysis, the PQ coalition was united by the idea of the Quebec nation, and the necessity of its accession to independence, rather than by social ideology.

Securing Quebec Sovereignty

Despite this common ground within the party, there often was intense disagreement over the exact process through which Quebec should accede to independence, as well as the form of independence itself. Through the early 1970s, Parti québécois leaders, most notably Lévesque and Claude Morin, sought to commit the party to the principle that independence could only follow upon popular approval of the idea in a referendum and took various steps to move the party in that direction. The party was at first committed to hold a referendum only on the constitution of an independent Quebec. During the 1973 electoral campaign, however, party advertisements declared that the referendum would focus on independence itself. At a subsequent party congress Morin finally secured the addition to the program of a commitment to hold a referendum on independence, but this commitment was conditional: it would apply only if negotiations with Ottawa over Quebec's accession to independence broke down, and then Quebec would be free to declare independence unilaterally.[107]

Nonetheless, as we have seen, during the 1976 campaign the PQ leadership presented this as an unconditional commitment to hold a referendum. In effect, the leadership had repeatedly sought a closer commitment to a referendum than much of the membership had been ready to accept. While the electoral advantages of a formal, unconditional commitment to a referendum had always been clear (and were confirmed by the 1976 election), such a commitment carried risks that some party members were quick to point out. Beyond the real possibility that victory on a referendum might simply be unattainable, activists assailed the long-term implications of dissociating the election of the PQ to power and the accession of Quebec to independence. With considerable foresight, as we shall see, they argued that the party's overall commitment to independence could be diluted.

The precise relationship between an independent Quebec and the rest of Canada was also a centre of dispute. The party program specified that a PQ government would seek an agreement with Canada creating a customs union and, "if possible, the harmonization and co-ordination of a larger number of economic policies as well as the establishment of a number of common services, including monetary mechanisms."[108] However, there was considerable dispute within the party over the desirability of collaboration beyond a simple customs union. In particular, the idea of a monetary union drew heavy fire. This was evident in the 1972 document *Quand nous serons vraiment chez nous*, which declared that a monetary union "remains highly problematic"[109] and that "coordination of economic or fiscal policies can wait. . . . Once various major reorganizations are undertaken in Quebec, once economic activity is under way again and certain modernization programs are completed, it will be time to think about it."[110]

The lack of consensus in the party may help to explain why the provisions of the program regarding Quebec-Canada relations were both ambiguous and brief. They contrasted sharply with the elaborate detail surrounding the internal economic policies an independent Quebec might implement. In the absence of consensus, it may have been necessary to cultivate ambiguity. But other factors also may have been operative. It may have been thought unwise to reveal full details of Quebec's proposals before entering negotiation with Canada, although it is difficult to see how the PQ could have hoped to win a referendum on independence without first revealing considerable detail about its option. But there is also the possibility that, for whatever reason, the party simply had failed to explore in full detail the issues raised by Quebec-Canada relations and thus may not have been prepared to develop a clear position. This particular interpretation was given some credibility by the decision, after the PQ had been elected to power, to commission a series of studies into the various forms that Quebec-Canada relations might take.

Conclusion

The program the Parti québécois developed during its eight years in opposition closely reflected the prevailing assumptions of the Quiet Revolution, when many of the party's leaders first entered active political life. As in the 1960s, there was a deeply rooted faith in the capacity of the Quebec state to bring about change. The weakness of Quebec's industrial sectors, its continuing dependence on Ontario, the absence of Francophones in the upper levels of much of Quebec's economy, the declining demographic position of Francophones within Quebec – all these continuing problems stemmed from the failure of the Quebec state to assume its proper responsibilities. But for the Quebec state to realize this potential it had to acquire most if not all of the functions Ottawa continued to exert within Quebec. In short, there had to be a radical redefinition of the Canadian political order. Only then could the essential promise of the Quiet Revolution, the creation of a modern Quebec state, finally be fulfilled.

To be sure, over the late 1960s and into the 1970s, apprehensions had emerged about the rigidities and excesses of state power and about the danger that the state's new-found capacities might be used to the advantage of a few, rather than the citizenry as a whole. Thus, the Parti québécois program acquired a certain commitment to "decentralization" and "participation." Yet, the technocratic belief in a strong, dynamic state continued to pervade the program. And, however much *péquistes* might differ over the uses to which the Quebec state should be put, they were united by their conviction that the Quebec state had to be liberated from the shackles of the federal order.

Thus, one finds within the Parti québécois discourse little of the reaction to the state reforms of the Quiet Revolution that one scholar has recently detected within the *indépendantiste* movement.[111] Rather than reflecting a sense of loss over traditional solidarities and institutions destroyed through state intervention, the PQ program was pervaded by a confidence that Quebec will at last be able to achieve its potential through more coherent and broadly based intervention, by a *sovereign* state. Rather than the act of desperation of a people threatened by cultural extinction, accession to sovereignty appeared as simply the "normal" culmination of the processes of political change launched by the Quiet Revolution.

With November 15, 1976, only eight years after the founding of the party, the Parti québécois leaders found themselves assuming office, much even to their own surprise. For them, the time had come to put the program into practice, to transform a provincial government into a sovereign state.

The party clearly had a popular mandate for change. But the terms of this mandate were confused; they hardly constituted a complete endorsement of the PQ program. First, some Québécois certainly did not view their vote for the Parti québécois as an endorsement of the party's objective of sovereignty. They took the PQ leadership at its word; they would not have to make up their minds on the sovereignty question until another occasion. This time around, they were giving the PQ a mandate simply to fulfil its promise to provide a "good" provincial government, free of the scandals that had tarnished the Bourassa regime and better equipped to manage the Quebec economy. Second, even among the PQ voters, probably the majority, who did endorse the ideal of Quebec sovereignty there was no clear consensus as to the precise form Quebec sovereignty should take. Some of these voters, probably a minority, wanted full political and economic independence and expected a PQ government to secure it. But for others, Quebec sovereignty was acceptable only if coupled with continued economic integration. If sovereignty could not be secured on these terms, then they favoured not outright independence but some form of "renewed federalism."

To a certain extent, this lack of a common perception of Quebec sovereignty within the PQ's electoral clientele reflected the failure of the PQ leadership to articulate fully its own model of Quebec sovereignty. As we have seen, the various versions of the PQ program gave little attention to the all-important question of a sovereign Quebec's relations with Canada. But it also reflected the wide variety in the considerations that apparently had led Québécois to sympathy for the objective of sovereignty. For some Québécois, support for sovereignty clearly was tied to a firm notion of the powers and resources a sovereign state would enjoy and of how they could be used to secure social and economic change. For many Québécois, however, adoption of the goal of sovereignty seems to have sprung less from attraction to the institutions of sovereignty themselves than from dissatisfaction with the status quo, whether that was the functioning of the federal system or the particular policies adopted by Ottawa or Quebec City.

During the late 1960s and into the 1970s, dissatisfaction had arisen over the new rigidities in Ottawa's relations with Quebec City and with the failure of the Quebec government to carry on the intense state-building of the Quiet Revolution. There was resentment over the refusal of the two Union nationale administrations and the Bourassa Liberals to champion aggressively the pre-eminence of French in Quebec and with the stance they adopted toward public-sector unions and lower-income groups in general. In each of these cases, Quebec sovereignty had come to stand as the necessary precondition to change. The failure of constitutional review seemed to confirm the growing impression that the federal system could no longer accommodate Quebec state-building. In critical areas the similarity in policies between the Bourassa administration and its Union nationale predecessors reinforced the notion that the obstacle to change lay not with the particular incumbents in office but with the political order itself. Moreover, by monopolizing the federalist mantle within Quebec, the Bourassa Liberals virtually ensured that a wide variety of opposition forces would coalesce behind the Parti québécois and, as a consequence, its goal of sovereignty. In short, Quebec sovereignty had become an all-encompassing symbol for change, whether change in state structures or change in major areas of policy. While this may have broadened the appeal of sovereignty, it also served to dilute and diffuse its meaning.

The challenges that suddenly faced the Parti québécois leadership on its surprise election to power were monumental. In the next chapter, we will examine the actions of the first Lévesque administration. We will explore how it went about providing "good government" within the structures of a provincial government, and how it dealt with the challenge of building support for Quebec sovereignty. Also, we will examine the way in which the PQ leadership sought to spell out a proposal for sovereignty and will assess the response this proposal elicited from English Canada. Finally, we will turn to the Quebec referendum, seeking to locate the factors that led to the government's defeat.

CHAPTER EIGHT
The Parti Québécois in Power: Policies and Strategies of the First Lévesque Administration

The election of the Parti québécois to power was widely viewed as the portent of unprecedented political and social change. Many in Quebec welcomed this promise of change, anticipating that the new administration would transform the functioning of the Quebec state and would lead the Quebec nation into its long awaited political and economic emancipation. Others in Quebec and in English Canada were traumatized by this prospect of change, fearing social upheaval within Quebec and the dissolution of the Canadian state. Either way, it appeared that the Canadian political system had been plunged into its most serious crisis. Never before had its integrity been so directly challenged.

Yet, the dominant posture of the PQ government during its first term in office was one of prudence and restraint. First, in its administration of the provincial government, the Lévesque administration displayed care both for the presumed aversion of Québécois to radical change in government policies and for the desire of financial and corporate elites (most notably in the United States) for fiscal responsibility and continuity in economic policies. Second, the PQ government's strategy for securing popular support for sovereignty was avowedly *étapiste*, seeking to build this support through gradual, step-by-step change. Finally, in elaborating a concept of Quebec sovereignty the PQ government sought to minimize popular fear of transitional costs by linking sovereignty to a close economic association with the rest of Canada.

In each of these areas the Lévesque government's approach carried important costs. Restraint in new policy initiatives meant the postponement of major aspects of the PQ program. The *étapiste* strategy for securing sovereignty carried internal contradictions that, over time, could undermine its very effectiveness. Linking political sovereignty to a close economic association with Canada meant the forfeiture of many of the potential advantages of national sovereignty.

Public Policy under the Lévesque Administration

With the election of the Parti québécois, one might have expected a new period of growth in the structures of the Quebec state and in the scope of state intervention, comparable to the political modernization of the 1960s. After all, the credo of the Parti québécois derived from an abiding faith in the capacity of the Quebec state to change the condition of Quebec Francophones; this was the essential promise of Quebec sovereignty. And, over the years, the PQ leadership had roundly denounced the Bourassa regime for failing to exploit this state capacity. In place of the passivity and indecision of the Liberals, it was argued, Québécois needed *un vrai gouvernement*.

Moreover, as we have seen, the PQ cabinet was solidly rooted in the Francophone new middle class, the agents of the Quiet Revolution. Teachers, professors, and administrators composed more than 75 per cent of the new cabinet, whereas they had constituted only 35 per cent of the pre-election Bourassa cabinet. The PQ cabinet had a singularly low proportion of liberal professionals. Self-employed professionals had accounted for almost half (46 per cent) of the Bourassa cabinet, but they represented only 21 per cent of the Lévesque cabinet. The Bourassa cabinet had contained five businessmen; in the Lévesque cabinet there was only Guy Joron. And, for the first time in Quebec history, the cabinet contained no Anglophones.[1]

Despite this change in government elites, the PQ's first term in power was not marked by an overall expansion in state intervention. As we shall see, by such measures of state expansion as growth in public spending or the creation of state enterprises, change under the PQ government was quite limited. There were some significant innovations, but they were fewer than one might have expected on the basis of the party program. By the same token, the scope of specifically "social democratic" measures was limited. Moreover, the case of social policy suggests that whatever commitment to "social democratic" objectives the PQ leadership may have brought to office was very much weakened by the end of the first Lévesque government.

Public Finances

One commonly used measure of the extent of state intervention is the level of public spending. Certainly, government spending has been a critical element of most social democratic administrations. With the strong commitment of the Parti québécois to state action and public-sector expansion, one would have expected public spending to rise rapidly under the Lévesque government. Yet, rather than increasing spending growth, the Lévesque administration committed itself to curtailing it.

Thanks primarily to high levels of inflation, spending growth had in fact been exceptionally high during the final years in office of the PQ's Liberal predecessors. In the last fiscal year for which the Bourassa regime was fully responsible, 1975-76, spending had grown by 22.72 per cent (down only slightly from the previous year's 25.58 per cent).[2] Liberal Finance Minister Raymond Garneau had expressed serious concern about this trend in his 1976-77 budget speech.[3] Upon assuming office, Jacques Parizeau had been quick to make this concern that of the Lévesque administration as well. In his first budget speech he declared that putting Quebec's public finances in order had to be the first priority of the PQ government.

> The high cost of public services, the heavy tax burden and Quebec's considerable debt all constitute a burdensome inheritance for the new government. How can the new programs, such as the job creation program, required for the well-being of Quebeckers be carried out without making the tax burden and Quebec's debt yet heavier? There are no two ways about it: in order to obtain a manoeuvring margin, we must slash into existing programs and reform the rate systems of certain public services so that they give a truer reflection of the expenditures incurred by the Quebec community.[4]

Parizeau reiterated this objective in each of his subsequent budget speeches. Moreover, the PQ did bring the growth rate down from the high levels of the mid-1970s. Over the four fiscal years that fall fully within the first Lévesque administration, the spending growth averaged 14.01 per cent.

To be sure, spending growth remained substantial over these years. In fact, by the last fiscal year, 1980-81, it had risen to 18.22 per cent, and it remained higher than in most other provinces, where governments had also declared an intention to cut spending growth. One might see this failure of the PQ government to curtail spending growth as fully as other provincial governments as evidence that the Lévesque administration was in fact more wedded to state intervention than were government parties elsewhere. Alternatively, however, one might simply trace this to the PQ preparations for the frequently postponed referendum. No government is inclined to reduce public services when it is about to seek a popular mandate. If this is true of elections, it is even more true for a referendum such as the one the PQ was committed to.[5]

Yet, even if the PQ government was less rigorous than other governments in curtailing spending growth, it is surprising that the PQ pursued this objective at all. Given the party's abiding commitment to the interventionist state, one might have expected continued if not accelerated growth, at least during the early phase of the new Lévesque government.

State Enterprises

A second major measure of state intervention is the creation and reinforcement of state enterprises. It is a form of intervention especially favoured by social democratic regimes. As we have seen, the Parti québécois had long been the champion of Quebec's state enterprises. In fact, the PQ program had declared the public sector to be the "preferred" form of state intervention in the economy and had called for the creation of a variety of new state enterprises.

Yet, apart from the Regie de l'assurance automobile, which was a social measure rather than an attempt to strengthen French economic power, only one major state enterprise, la Société nationale de l'amiante, was created during the first Lévesque government. It was to take over the Thetford Mines operations of the Asbestos Corporation, a Quebec-based subsidiary of the U.S. firm, General Dynamics. Through it the Quebec state was to gain a direct presence in the mining and transformation of asbestos. But even this measure represented a retreat from the pre-election program of the Parti québécois, which had called for majority ownership of the entire asbestos industry in Quebec, and it was accompanied by the repeated assurances of the PQ leaders that they would undertake no other nationalizations.[6]

As to the existing state enterprises, they were not able to draw on any particular favouritism from the PQ government. In fact, they were subjected to rigorous critiques of their management and performance that went far beyond the rebukes of the Bourassa years. In his 1978 budget speech, Parizeau openly admitted that many of the enterprises had not lived up to expectations:

If certain state enterprises by their very nature will never be profit-making, it must be recognized that, in the case of most of the enterprises that are intended to be profit-making, hopes have not been translated into reality. Some enterprises, of a clearly commercial character, several years after their creation are unable to borrow at the bank without the guarantee of the state and cannot balance their books at the end of the year without the aid of the Consolidated Funds.

In certain cases, recourse to the state, which ought to be exceptional, has become a practice that is no longer questioned.

One is beginning to see the emergence within the public sector of a centre of commercial and industrial miracles, which is costly for taxpayer and unjust for the private sector that must compete with it.[7]

Economic and Social Redistribution and Well-Being

As we noted in the previous chapter, a specific form of state intervention that has always been central to social democratic ideals is the redistribution of income and the provision of social services. In these terms, during its first few years in power the Lévesque government compared quite well with "social democratic" regimes elsewhere in Canada. By the end of the first administration, however, the government's ardour for social reform had diminished considerably.

Soon after assuming power, it raised the minimum wage to three dollars an hour, the highest level in North America. Moreover, it indexed the minimum wage to the cost of living. Given the inherent regressiveness of sales tax, earners of lower incomes gained the most from the abolition of tax on clothing, furniture, and shoes. (To be sure, this measure was spurred by the constitutional struggle rather than by a concern to redistribute income.) In 1979, the government introduced a limited program of income supplementation for the working poor. Those on middle and lower incomes were advantaged by the 1978 decision of the PQ government to index income taxes to the cost of living only for those whose salaries are under $30,000.[8] Finance Minister Parizeau was quite ready to wrap the Lévesque regime in a "social democratic" banner as he rejected the pretence of high-income corporate executives. Denouncing "the sort of revolt of the well-off we have witnessed over the last year," Parizeau declared:

The curve of the tax on personal income in Quebec is going to remain very progressive. It corresponds to the objectives of a social democratic government, and it is astonishing to see how, in certain milieux, one is surprised not to find the objectives of a rightist government.[9]

The Lévesque government introduced other measures more generally aimed at the economically and socially disadvantaged, including free medication for people over sixty-five, free dental care to children under sixteen, a ban on advertising aimed at children, guarantees of the rights of the handicapped, and, most important, establishment of a public system of automobile insurance against personal injury (although not damage to property).

By the end of its first term, however, the PQ had backed away considerably from its initial social reformism. In the case of the minimum wage, for instance, the government ceased in 1978 to index the minimum wage: in 1979 the minimum wage was increased by only a third of the inflation rate; in 1980 it was increased by one half of the rate.[10] For that matter, sociologist Yves Vaillancourt contends that the benefits made available under the guaranteed income scheme were quite marginal. In fact, during 1979-80, the first year of the scheme's operation, there were insufficient claimants to exhaust the funds set aside for the scheme: almost half remained unspent. In 1980-81, and again in 1981-82, the budget was substantially reduced.[11]

Labour Relations

A critical test of a government's claim to social democratic status is the way it seeks to regulate labour relations. As we saw in the previous chapter, arranging "a better deal" for organized labour is the fundamental goal of social democratic parties. One would expect a social democratic regime to seek actively to reinforce the position of organized labour vis-à-vis private employers. Likewise, one would expect it to respect and even strengthen the rights of public-sector unions.

We have already noted that while the PQ had always claimed a strong commitment to social democratic measures of social services and economic redistribution, its attitude toward organized labour was less straightforward. The party program had contained measures to facilitate union organization, but there had always been tension between the party leadership and the union leadership, especially of the public-sector unions. It was here that the PQ claim to "social democratic" status was most problematic.

In its initial months, the Lévesque administration did make several gestures that met with universal union approval. It dismissed the charges against the three union leaders that had been laid under the Bourassa regime. Also, it terminated participation in the federal government's price and incomes control program, which had been vigorously denounced by union leaders. However, the Lévesque government's most important initiative was a major reform of the Labour Code, contained in Bill 45.[12]

The new law contained several important provisions. It established procedures for the compulsory arbitration of first contracts, so as to prevent employers' delaying tactics. It facilitated union certification, by reducing to 35 per cent the proportion of workers in a bargaining unit who must be signed up for a representation election to be authorized. By eliminating an existing requirement that conciliation take place before a strike can be undertaken, the law eliminated all restriction on the right to strike in the private sector. It obliged employers to deduct union dues from all employees in a bargaining union, whether or not they are union members. It contained provisions designed to increase "union democracy." However, the most significant provision was an "anti-scab" law – the first of its kind in North America – that precludes employers from using other individuals to do the work of employees who are in a legal strike or lockout. The employer cannot hire new employees for this purpose nor can it use existing non-striking ones.[13]

In its initial form this part of the bill had met with the approval of all union organizations, but in the face of intense business opposition it was amended to allow employers to hire personnel to prevent the destruction or deterioration of property. The FTQ, which had a good working relationship with the PQ government, continued to support the bill despite this amendment. But the CSN and CEQ did not. In fact, not only did they decry this amendment but they denounced the provisions of the bill dealing with "union democracy," branding them anti-union intrusions into their internal affairs. The CSN and CEQ concluded that it would be better simply to withdraw the legislation. Nonetheless, the PQ government proceeded to enact the bill, as amended.[14]

Despite the criticisms of the bill from the CSN and CEQ, most observers agree that it constitutes a significant reinforcement of the position of organized labour, at least in Quebec's private sector. In fact, some students of labour relations have expressed fear that the anti-scab law goes too far. Gérard Dion, veteran member of Laval's Department of Industrial Relations, declared this provision, and others in the bill, to be "une folle aventure" that would create a "syndicarchie," or government by unions.[15] D.D. Carter, professor at Queen's University and former chairman of the Ontario Labour Relations Board, has declared that "such provisions may substantially alter the balance of power between trade unions and employers and in this respect Quebec is out of step with the other Canadian jurisdictions."[16] Indeed, the bill did have the potential of greatly increasing the ability of strike action to bring production to a halt.[17]

The CSN and CEQ hostility to provisions of Bill 45's revision of private-sector labour relations, and to the PQ government in general, can largely be traced to suspicion of the government's intentions regarding *public-sector* employees. During its period as the primary opposition party the Parti québécois had tried to appear as an ally of the CSN and CEQ, vigorously attacking their treatment by the Bourassa government. At the same time, however, the PQ had been careful to maintain a certain distance from the unions, refusing to participate in several major union-sponsored demonstrations.

With its assumption of power, the PQ was necessarily cast in a different role. And any likelihood that the PQ government could maintain harmonious relations with the public-sector unions was eliminated by its decision to reduce the growth in public spending. In fact, the PQ government began to echo the argument of the Bourassa government that private-sector salaries should be the reference for the public sector. Whereas Bourassa had argued that the increases in public-sector salaries demanded by the unions would create unsupportable pressures on the private sector, Parizeau and other PQ leaders began to argue that simple equity required that the public-sector salaries should not exceed private-sector salaries.[18] Moreover, the PQ government proceeded to restructure public-sector collective bargaining, notably through Bills 50, 55, and 59, in ways that were bitterly denounced by both the CSN and CEQ. In the course of the 1979 round of bargaining the PQ government was led to adopt a special law, Bill 62, which, while not revoking the right to strike as had special laws of the Bourassa regime, did put a two-week moratorium on strike activity. Moreover, the bill enabled the government to by-pass the union leaders by requiring that the membership vote by secret ballot on the government offer.[19] The government was able to secure a settlement without resorting to more draconian measures. Its success in doing so, however, was due in large part to the relatively "generous" terms it was prepared to offer. The government's "generosity," and general avoidance of repressive measures, in turn can be best explained by the rapid approach of the referendum on sovereignty-association.[20]

In sum, the relationship between the first PQ government and the CSN and CEQ leaderships, if not all of the union militants, was openly adversarial. It did not display the type of working relationship that one would expect under a social democratic regime. Both the CEQ and the CSN regularly denounced government policies, especially those dealing with labour relations. Only the FTQ and the minuscule Centrale des syndicats démocratiques (CSD) regularly approved the actions of the Lévesque government. The CEQ and the CSN both postponed taking a position on the "national question," given the fear of some elements that any clear position would be construed as support for the PQ's project of sovereignty-association.[21] Ultimately, the CSN did officially endorse a "Yes" vote in the referendum; the CEQ remained officially neutral, along with the CSD and the Union des producteurs agricoles.

For their part, the government leaders were prepared to challenge outright the pretension of union leaders to represent the aspirations of Quebec workers. Soon after the PQ accession to power, Lévesque declared:

Very often, I have the impression that we are closer to this base of workers, in our political action, than those who, officially, speak in their name. That was very clear in the results of the 1976 elections. And our government must maintain a favourable prejudice toward workers.[22]

In other words, the PQ government's "favourable prejudice" to Quebec workers was to be expressed directly, through state social programs and income measures. It was not necessarily to be mediated through the working-class organizations. The Lévesque government, like the Parti québécois, was not to be fettered by any special relationship to the union movement.

This public disavowal of special, preferential links with any private group or organization was, in fact, typical of the PQ government. The Quebec state was to be an autonomous agent, free to respond to the needs and aspirations of all Québécois. Thus, the Lévesque administration took particular pride in its measures to eradicate political patronage. Public contracts, they claimed, were awarded without reference to party affiliation. Through Bill 2, the financing of political parties was to be carefully regulated. Only individual citizens can contribute to parties, and only to the amount of $3,000 per year; corporations and (it should be noted) unions are prohibited from doing so. Moreover, parties must regularly publish the names of their contributors.[23]

Finally, as we have seen, the hallmark of social democratic regimes in recent decades has been the commitment to state-sponsored collaboration between business and labour. In full-fledged "liberal corporatist" regimes this collaboration can entail the joint determination of broad social and economic policy. Class representatives, under the aegis of the state, reach agreements that are then binding on business and labour as a whole.[24] For its part, as we have seen, the PQ program had placed considerable emphasis on joint production of comprehensive economic plans. But it did not restrict participation to organized labour and business alone; "other parts of the population" were also to be represented.

Unlike the Bourassa regime, the Lévesque government did sponsor a series of public forums on economic questions. In its pursuit of *concertation*, the government had convened eighteen socio-economic conferences by the end of its first term in office. Two consisted of comprehensive *sommets économiques*, intended to examine Quebec's general economic condition. Fifteen were geared to specific sectors of the economy: the "soft" sectors (textiles, clothing, footwear, and furniture); agriculture and food industries; fishing; co-operativism; tourism; and cultural industries. One conference addressed the problems of Montreal's economy.[25]

Yet, the objectives of this exercise were quite limited, falling far short of any social democratic "liberal corporatism." The goal of the PQ government's *concertation* was simply to bring together representatives of the various sectors of society to promote dialogue and mutual understanding, in the belief that such an experience would lead to greater social and economic harmony. There was no expectation that binding agreements would emerge from these discussions. Moreover, strictly speaking, the sessions were not "tripartite": beyond business and labour other societal interests, such as women's groups and consumer groups, were also invited.

Thus, the PQ government took on the aura of a social democratic government in some aspects of its activities, such as nationalizing Asbestos Corporation, creating a public automobile insurance scheme, and reforming private-sector labour relations law. But its social policy, its relationship with the public-sector unions, and its modest tripartite experiments all fall short of the social democratic model. Instead, the government's actions more clearly evoke the nationalist-populist label we developed in the previous chapter. By the same token, the overall stance of the government, with its push to curtail spending growth and its critical treatment of state enterprises, is much less interventionist than the party's program had seemed to promise.

The PQ Government and the Creation of a "National Bourgeoisie"

While the PQ government did not demonstrate clearly social democratic credentials, it demonstrated even less the commitment to reinforcement of the Francophone business class that some observers had predicted.[26] Guided by its project of creating a national bourgeoisie, these observers had claimed, the PQ leadership was seeking to reinforce each of the three forms of Francophone economic power: private enterprise, the co-operative movement, and state corporations. We have already seen how support for these various institutions figured heavily in the documents the Parti québécois had prepared in the years before its accession to power. Yet, the actions of the first PQ government do not clearly reveal such a strategy.

This can be seen in the pattern of expenditures.[27] Among the four global "missions" (as defined by the Quebec government) – economic, education and culture, social, and governmental and administrative – the economic mission came fourth in the rate of expenditure growth during each budget year between 1976 and 1980.[28] Within more narrowly defined missions, called "domains," the economic domains tended to show the slowest growth, with transportation the slowest of all domains and, interestingly enough, secondary industry the third slowest.[29] Finally, the expenditures of the ministry most clearly charged with strengthening the Francophone business class, Industry and Commerce, showed one of the slowest rates of growth of any ministry during 1976-80, 25.5 per cent; expenditures actually declined in 1979-80 by 2.6 per cent.[30] As for the tax structure, the government did introduce in March, 1979, its Régime d'épargne-actions or Quebec Stock Savings Plan. While the scheme of personal income tax writeoffs for new stock issues of Quebec firms promised to provide new sources of capital, during the first few years of operations it was not designed to favour smaller, and thus Francophone, enterprises. The primary motivation appears to have been the provision of relief to upper-income taxpayers. This pattern would suggest that reinforcement of the Francophone economic presence was not the central priority of the PQ administration. The same pattern can be seen by examining the specific initiatives of the Lévesque government.

The PQ government did provide considerable support for small and medium-sized enterprises. Soon after its election, the PQ administration declared a new policy under which Quebec firms would be favoured in all purchases within the public and para-public sector.[31] It also created an "industrial recovery fund" of $30 million to support small and medium-sized enterprises.[32] The Société de développement industriel, charged with supporting small and medium-sized Francophone firms, began to play an increasingly active role. In particular, the SDI increased its support for small enterprises of less than twenty employees; in 1978-79 SDI grants to these firms tripled those of the previous years, reaching $8.6 million.[33] And a Société de développement de l'entreprise was created to provide risk capital to small and medium-sized firms.[34]

Nevertheless, the government was not as solicitous when it came to the large Francophone enterprises. First, when the Quebec government awarded a contract for 1,200 buses in 1977, it chose a bid from General Motors over one from Bombardier-MLW, explaining that expansion of GM's operations in Quebec induced by the contract would lead to a higher level of long-term exports than would have arisen from granting the contract to Bombardier. In an open letter responding to a public protest from the Bombardier president, René Lévesque declared:

> even if it is a multinational, General Motors nevertheless has an important establishment at Sainte-Thérèse, to which it has just added $36 million in new investments. Especially in this period of economic sluggishness, the purchasing policy does not allow us therefore to consider General Motors as an external competitor, unless one establishes a criterion of pure "cultural" preference, which would soon lead us to the creation of a genuine economic ghetto.[35]

In other words, the overriding concern of the Lévesque administration was with stimulating a sagging economy, and this stimulus could come just as well, if not more, from a multinational as from a Francophone firm. The PQ government may also have been seeking to counter American business's evident mistrust of it.

Second, when the Lévesque administration responded to pressure from the participationist forces within the party by establishing a public automobile insurance scheme, it deprived Francophone insurance companies, and agents, of a major source of revenue. By so doing, it incurred the wrath of much of the Francophone (as well as Anglophone) business community. The minister in charge, Lise Payette, felt led to denounce the "shameful blackmail" of business leaders. As Jorge Niosi has noted, if "the PQ administration wanted to represent the Francophone bourgeoisie, it missed yet another occasion to do so."[36]

As one might expect, given the importance the Parti québécois had always attached to the co-operative movement, the Lévesque administration was supportive of the Mouvement Desjardins and other Francophone co-operative organizations. It created a new organism, la Société de développpment coopératif, but the budget afforded the SDC, $1.4 million a year, was at best symbolic.[37] Also, it vigorously championed the efforts of the *caisses populaires* to escape federal jurisdiction and subjection to federal requirements that they deposit reserves with the Bank of Canada.[38] However, the PQ government's general preoccupation with preserving and expanding provincial autonomy in any event would have led it to take a strong stand. Finally, with respect to the state enterprises, we have already seen that they enjoyed no particular favour with the PQ government.

In other words, the PQ government's dealings with Francophone-owned firms, state enterprises, and even the co-operative movement did not reflect a concerted, overriding effort to strengthen the Francophone economic presence, to create the triple bases of a "national bourgeoisie." The economic programs were not the primary focus of additional government spending. Support for Francophone enterprises was heavily conditioned by other priorities, whether simple job creation (as with rejection of the Bombardier bid) or social measures (as with the nationalization of automobile insurance) or the reduction of growth in public expenditures (as with state enterprises). The overriding concern of the PQ administration with simple growth in the Quebec economy, whatever the form of ownership involved, was most clearly demonstrated by its determined effort to persuade a U.S. automobile producer to establish a new plant in Quebec. The government was prepared to compete with Ontario, plus several American states, in offering the most favourable terms to Ford Motors. When this effort failed, it turned, again in vain, to General Motors. In short, the PQ administration allowed itself to become embroiled in the kind of competition for multinational investment for which it had so vigorously criticized the Bourassa regime.

Bill 101: The Constraints on Policy Change

The one major initiative of the PQ government we have not yet examined, Bill 101, clearly reflects the defining features of the Parti québécois: the mobilization of the movement around an essentially nationalist logic and the predominance of a new-middle-class perspective among the party leadership. It was natural that, in its first year of office, the PQ government should become consumed with initiating a comprehensive policy to affirm the pre-eminence of French in Quebec. And the thrust of this policy closely reflected the preoccupations of the new-middle-class *travailleurs du langage*: the strength and vitality of the French-language school system; the role of the French language, and of Francophones, within the upper levels of the Quebec economy; the symbolic status of French within Quebec, etc.[39] At the same time, Bill 101 is perhaps the most dramatic illustration of the extent to which in pursuing its objectives the PQ found itself under heavy constraints, especially from the business community. Despite the widespread assumption that Bill 101 constituted a radical departure, the changes it introduced are in fact largely incremental in nature.

Basically, the final version of Bill 101 departed completely from the principles and procedures of its predecessor, Bill 22, in only two ways. Both of these departures clearly bear the stamp of the Parti québécois. One is its requirement that all public signs and other forms of commercial advertising should be in French only.[40] While the various regulations implementing the measure aroused the wrath of Quebec's Anglophone community, in most cases they constitute irritants more than anything else. Nevertheless, the measure reflects a concern with the symbolic definition of everyday life that could have emerged only from a party forthrightly committed to the French presence. Second, in determining access to English-language schools, Bill 101 used the boundaries of Quebec as the point of reference, in effect denying access to children from other parts of Canada, even if English should be their mother tongue.[41] The effect of this particular measure can be mediated by provisions allowing officials to issue temporary authorizations to attend English-language schools. Also, if the other provincial governments should ever accept Quebec's plan for reciprocal access to second-language schools, then the measure would disappear completely. Still, it reflects a determination that Quebec, not Canada, should be the pre-eminent community. Such a rigid distinction between Quebec and the rest of Canada could not have come from any previous Quebec government. In fact, some of the leaders of the PQ government were themselves uneasy with it.[42] (This is the one aspect of the bill that did not meet popular approval among Quebec Francophones.)[43] Also, in restricting so carefully the conditions of access to English-language schools, Bill 101 reflects the preoccupations of a major force among the *travailleurs péquistes du langage*: Francophone school teachers. They shared not only an institutional loyalty to the French-language school system but an anxiety over the dwindling numbers of incoming students.

Otherwise, the changes Bill 101 made over Bill 22 are essentially incremental, adapting and building on principles and measures already established by Bill 22. Bill 22, for example, established the principle that French is the official language of Quebec. Bill 101 vastly extended the application of this principle: by making French the only language in which legislation is written, presented, and adopted in the National Assembly; by reinforcing its role within the public administration; and by making French the language of the judicial system, including court proceedings involving corporations (unless they should agree to use English).[44] In addition, unlike its predecessor, Bill 101 sought to apply this same principle to municipal and parapublic institutions as well, requiring that all official texts and external commmunication (other than to individuals) be in French, that "appropriate" knowledge of French be a condition for appointment and promotion, and that in the case of municipal institutions French be the language of internal communication.[45] Bill 22 had already breached the principle of free parental choice of language of instruction, reserving this choice to parents whose children have a "sufficient knowledge" of English. Bill 101 is more restrictive, reserving the choice of language of instruction to children whose mother tongue is English (thus openly embracing what many had presumed was the unstated intent of Bill 22).[46]

With respect to the role of French in the workplace, Bill 101 did innovate over Bill 22 by declaring, in its proclamation of fundamental language rights, that workers have the right to work in French and in stipulating that an employee cannot be fired because he knows only French. Otherwise, Bill 101 carried on the same basic procedures for *francisation* of major enterprises that Bill 22 had laid out.[47] It, too, has a program of *francisation* certificates, although the program is compulsory for enterprises with fifty or more employees rather than optional as was the case with Bill 22. Bill 101 also allows head office operations to be treated differently from Quebec-centred operations, although firms need to secure this special treatment by individual negotiations with l'Office de la langue française rather than qualifying for this treatment automatically, as was the case with Bill 22. But the regulations governing treatment of head offices under this provision are virtually identical to those adopted under Bill 22.[48] Taken as a whole, these provisions share Bill 22's focus on expanding the use of French as a working language rather than attempting to increase the presence of people whose principal language is French.

This concentration on the role of French as a working language apparently constituted a major shift from the original intent of those who drafted Bill 101. Soon after assuming office, Cultural Development Minister Camille Laurin declared that henceforth the Quebec government would seek not only the *francisation* of firms, as had been the stated purpose of Bill 22, but their *"francophonisation."*[49] This goal was evoked in the White Paper on language when it sought to clarify the sense in which the term *"la presence francophone"* (which, interestingly, was translated as "presence of French-speaking personnel") should be applied to the business world:

> The expression is without ambiguity when viewed in its social context. However, when it is maintained in a business that the physical environment (manuals, forms, and typewriters equipped with accents) should be identified with the presence of French-speaking personnel, the phrase becomes obscure and the interpretations given multiply and make it even less clear. To avoid becoming embroiled in quarrels over words, business firms could set themselves the following definite objective: to reflect, at every level and in every function of their personnel, the ethnic make-up of the population of Quebec. There is nothing revolutionary about this; it is such an elementary principle of social justice that the United States, that paradise of private enterprise, has adopted it as the basis of its social hiring policy.[50]

Moreover, the PQ government's first version of a new language law, Bill 1, faithfully reflected this concern with *francophonisation*. Thus, the bill proclaimed the objective of increasing the *"nombre du Québécois"* at all levels within the enterprise so as "to assure generalization of the use of French."[51] Clearly, the term Québécois was intended to denote Francophones. For that matter, the preamble to the bill began with the statement that "the National Assembly recognizes that the French language has always been the language of the Quebec people."[52]

However, under pressure from business leaders and the Anglophone community in general, Laurin and other government leaders subsequently began to emphasize Bill 101's role as an instrument of "linguistic promotion" rather than an instrument of "social promotion."[53] In the final version of Bill 101, the specification of the elements of the *francisation* of enterprises calls "for the increase in the number of persons having a good knowledge of the French language so as to ensure its generalized utilization."[54] (There is no reference to ethnic origin, let alone quotas.) L'Office de la langue française, created by Bill 101, declared that this description can apply to people whose principal language is not French but who have a good knowledge of French. (To the stupefaction of Maurice Sauvé, vice-president of Consolidated-Bathurst, a representative of l'Office agreed that even Queen Elizabeth could meet this description!)[55] This interpretation conforms to the operational definition of "Francophone" the now-defunct Régie de la langue française had developed to apply to Bill 22 – and to which Camille Laurin had taken exception.[56] The president of l'Office de la langue française himself declared that the bill is concerned with the promotion of the French language rather than French Canadians *per se*.[57] And the questionnaire through which l'Office administered its program of *francisation* certificates was virtually identical to that which the Régie de la langue française had used.[58]

In short, as Quebec business school professors Yvan Allaire and Roger E. Miller concluded about Bill 101:

> The Act's objective is strictly linguistic. It does not seek directly to promote social mobility. It mentions neither francophone (or Quebec) presence nor balanced participation. The ambiguity that had existed concerning efforts to pursue simultaneously the use of French and the promotion of the French presence has been totally eliminated. Knowledge of French is a general target, and pursuit of that target is viewed as a means of ensuring the use of French at work.[59]

In addition to the redefinition of objectives, Bill 1 had gone well beyond Bill 22 in the procedures it established for securing change in the workplace. Here, too, given intense opposition from business circles, the bill was modified to bring it more in line with Bill 22. Bill 1 not only stipulated that firms of fifty or more employees must have *francisation* certifications, but declared that a firm without a certificate would not have a right to government subsidies, premiums, or even permits. This provision does not appear in Bill 101. In addition, Bill 1 introduced a powerful Commission de surveillance to regulate *francisation*. Bill 101 modified considerably its powers. Bill 1 had provided that within an enterprise *francisation* was to be supervised not by management but by a committee, one-third of the members to be workers, which would report directly to l'Office de la langue française. Bill 101 stipulated that the committee instead would report to management, which would in turn report to l'Office. Finally, in introducing the possibility that head offices could negotiate special agreements exempting them totally from *francisation* programs, Bill 101 in fact introduced greater flexibility than had been available not only in Bill 1, but in Bill 22 as well. Also, unlike Bill 22, the requirement in Bill 1 that members of a profession have a working knowledge of French did not exempt professionals working for a single employer or having no direct contact with the public. Bill 101 restored the exemption.[60]

As a result of these various modifications, Bill 101 became less and less objectionable to the Anglophone business community. Thus, in a January, 1978, article entitled "Give Quebec's language law yet another long, cool look," *The Financial Post*'s Quebec correspondent reported that:

> It is daily more evident, especially given Sun Life's desire to depart Quebec, that it is the implied thrust of the province's Charter of French that is heightening emotions, provoking backlash and generating widespread apprehension. Its actual implementation, at least in the initial stages, will produce only relatively minor specific change. . . . The "generalized use" of French is a far cry from what the legislators once envisioned. . . . Now everybody can get by – even though unhappily for a few – provided there is *some* knowledge of French. Whatever the spirit of the law, in other words, its technical demands are really not as onerous as many people think or fear.[61]

And by the late spring of 1978 attention of Anglophone executives had shifted from Bill 101 to the new increase in provincial income tax on upper incomes. Pointing to the effect this measure would have on corporate executives, companies advised their shareholders that the impact of this measure would be "worse than the impact of Bill 101."[62]

On the surface, then, the PQ government was led to abandon its original intent to induce *francophonisation* of firms, contenting itself with *francisation*. To be sure, the sponsors of Bill 101 and most of its supporters may have expected that *francisation* in turn would induce *francophonisation*. Perhaps with the greater possibility to use French, Francophone candidates would be able to rise more easily within corporate structures. Also, perhaps some firms simply would decide that the most effective way to increase the use of French is to increase the presence of French-speakers. But there was no guarantee this would be the case. The only certain means of improving the presence of Francophones would have been a system of quotas, as the government's White Paper on language had proposed. In fact, even the Gendron Commission of the early 1970s had advocated a system of recruitment that would favour Francophone candidates.[63]

Over the late 1970s, Francophones apparently did enter in greater numbers into the upper levels of English-Canadian and American-owned corporate structures in Quebec. It is not clear, however, that Bill 101 (let alone Bill 22) was directly responsible for this. In their 1979 study, Bernard *et al.* explain this primarily in terms not of language legislation but of the substantial net outmigration of Anglophones during the 1970s:

> that Francophones almost totally monopolized the new positions . . . created was not the result of political intervention on the language question; instead it resulted directly from the fact that Francophones constituted the only new pool of new workers available on the Quebec market from 1971 to 1978.[64]

In sum, the constraints were such that the new government was forced to moderate its policy goals even in the area of clearest consensus within the Parti québécois that the Quebec government should undertake new, aggressive action. At the same time, the government did not retreat on *all* aspects of its initiative. With respect to the language of public administration, including local and parapublic institutions, and of education the alterations of Bill 1 were rather slight. It is mainly with respect to the work world that the PQ government reverted to the provisions of Bill 22.

As William Coleman has argued, the fact that the government conceded primarily in this realm to opposition demands may well reflect the degree to which these provisions of the bill dealt directly with business's own prerogatives and thus were more immediate to the "accumulation process."[65] Under capitalism, the strength and very viability of state structures are in turn dependent on the strength and viability of private enterprises. Thus, state officials must heed the complaints of business when they argue that proposed state policies will seriously undermine profitability or might lead them to curtail their operations. This may not be the whole explanation of the treatment of Bill 1, however. After all, Quebec business had been very much opposed to Bill 1's restrictions on access to English-language schools, claiming that they would severely handicap enterprises in attracting executive personnel; yet, the government refused to act in this area. Given the centrality of the Quebec state and its potential within the PQ's own ideology, one would naturally expect PQ leaders to give highest priority to the role of French within institutions that are themselves part of the state or closely related to it, as with health and education. One would also expect this because of the extent to which the PQ was itself based within the Quebec public sector. For instance, with such a strong presence of teachers in the party it could hardly afford to back down on the attempt to channel more students to French-language schools.

The Lévesque Government: Change within Constraints

Two general conclusions emerge from our survey of policy initiatives under the Lévesque regime. First, while difficult to characterize in simple terms, the overall direction of policy change conformed more clearly to a type of "nationalist populism" than to either an attempt to implement a "social democracy," despite several important initiatives, or a concerted drive to create a "national bourgeoisie," which was manifestly not the case. The focus of a "nationalist populist" world view is not on class but on a national collectivity that transcends all social divisions; the primary objective is not to secure a "better deal" for labour, let alone establish a better "labour-capital compromise," but to emancipate the national collectivity, and thus the "people," from external domination. Thus, the government could establish several new programs to benefit various disadvantaged social categories and it could proclaim a "favourable prejudice" toward workers. Yet, it also could openly challenge the pretension of labour leaders to speak for their members, pass legislation that prohibited unions (and corporations) from contributing to political parties, and broaden participation at its socio-economic forums beyond labour and business to include other elements of the national collectivity.

Second, the scope of new policy initiatives was quite limited. As even the instance of language policy suggests, the PQ government appears to have been constrained from pursuing the kind of intensive, global change associated with the Quiet Revolution, when many of the present PQ leaders first occupied positions in the Quebec government. The language of "constraints" in fact became a central theme in Parti québécois rhetoric once it assumed power. A series of constraints were openly acknowledged, and the limits of policy change were rationalized in terms of them. In the name of these constraints, major elements of the PQ program were not fully implemented by the Lévesque government, even though they did not presume Quebec's accession to sovereignty. For example, only one major operation within the asbestos industry was slated to be nationalized, rather than the industry as a whole; the new program of automobile insurance covered only personal injury, not damage to the automobile; state support for private schools was not substantially reduced; support for day-care centres remained minimal and few measures in general were adopted to improve the position of women; and only limited additions were made to the scope of public health-care coverage.

Some of the constraints regularly identified by the PQ government were essentially "external." Certain of these, at least in principle, were temporary. Thus, Ottawa's fiscal capacity and legislative authority were cited to explain the limits of the PQ government's economic initiatives; with sovereignty this constraint would disappear and the ability of the Quebec state to spur economic revival would be correspondingly greater. But other external constraints were viewed, at least tacitly, as more long-term. One of these is dependence on American (or European) capital markets, especially for financing public-sector bonds. The PQ government clearly was concerned that Quebec should maintain a good rating on foreign capital markets. It contended that Quebec's rating had been endangered by the rapid increase in public borrowing under the Bourassa regime. But it obviously was aware that some foreign investors were leery of the Parti québécois and its plans for sovereignty. Thus, in his first budget speech, Parizeau forthrightly declared, "The government has decided to put the public finances in order first of all and to reduce deficits before going any further. The road to independence rests on healthy finances."[66]

Consequently, the Lévesque administration found itself unable to initiate major spending programs and sought to restrict spending in some ongoing programs. Concern over the attitude of American economic elites led Lévesque and his colleagues frequently to assure American audiences that their government was forgoing any nationalization of American firms other than a single enterprise in the asbestos industry, Asbestos Corporation.

Other constraints cited by the Lévesque administration were essentially internal to Quebec itself. In the very process of elaborating new policies and transforming them into concrete action, the government found its capacity for change limited by the weight of past commitments, the resistance of existing structures, and the attachment of civil servants to established practice. But Lévesque, in particular, repeatedly cited a second constraint: the refusal of the Quebec population to accept radical forms of change or even a heavy concentration of moderate changes. In fact, this had been a long-standing Lévesque theme. In 1974 he declared to a PQ National Congress:

> As we work on the party program during the coming two days, we must try to bear in mind that, over the last seven years, we have already carried the program about as far in the direction of change as our Québécois society, such as it is, has need as well as the capacity.[67]

The PQ government's commitment to securing Quebec sovereignty perhaps made it even more sensitive to these constraints on policy-making than it would have been otherwise. Thus, the need to curtail expenditures to impress foreign capital markets stemmed as much from the desire to persuade investors that the government of a sovereign Quebec would be "responsible" and reliable as from a concern with the credit rating of the provincial government and other public institutions. And in carefully restricting its policy reforms to the degree of change it perceived most Québécois were prepared to accept, the PQ government was not just concerned with its re-election. It was also responding to the overriding necessity of winning a large majority vote in the referendum on sovereignty. To do this, it had to build popular support far beyond its established electoral clientele. Presumably, popular decisions about the referendum would be heavily influenced by perceptions of the Parti québécois as a government and of its capacity to lead Quebec. Given the certain opposition of most Quebec Anglophones to independence and their high turnout for a referendum, any majority vote in a referendum would have to draw on the vast majority of Francophones. The PQ government could not pursue policies that would alienate any sizable segment of the Quebec Francophone population, even if these measures could reinforce its popularity with the PQ electoral clientele. In some instances, much to the resentment of some long-term PQ supporters, concern with winning the referendum led the PQ government to focus heavily on Francophone groups not strongly present within the party's electoral base, such as old-age categories and small businessmen, in the hope that they might be brought into the fold.[68] As Lévesque acknowledged:

> One must take into account . . . the holding of the referendum, and of Quebec society's capacity to absorb the reforms which have high priority. It's not easy to carry on our work as social democrats, good administrators, and reformers in a host of sectors, without risking to compromise the central moment, the democratic decision about the future.[69]

At the same time, the impact of these constraints on the Parti québécois and its government was not restricted just to the formulation of public policy. They also affected the way the leadership of the Parti québécois defined its ultimate objective, sovereignty, and the procedures through which this objective was to be achieved. Awareness of external dependence and a sense that Québécois would accept only gradual change spawned both the strategy of *étapisme* and the objective of sovereignty-association.

The Logic of Étapisme: Contradictions and Ambiguities

Given the primordial role the idea of Quebec sovereignty has always played within the Parti québécois, one might have expected that the new PQ government would move quickly to secure sovereignty for Quebec. After all, within its first six months of power the PQ government had already elaborated a comprehensive new policy for another long-standing preoccupation of *péquistes*: the status of the French language within Quebec. Moreover, during the first few months after its victory, the PQ government clearly enjoyed extraordinary popular support in Quebec: the election of an *indépendantiste* party had constituted an act of national affirmation from which even Québécois who had voted against the party took sudden pride. Surveys did suggest that the majority of Québécois still had apprehensions about the idea of Quebec sovereignty. But the new government nevertheless might have seized the moment to launch a concerted campaign to overcome these fears. At this point, there were not yet any of the highly publicized corporate decisions to defer investment or to move facilities out of the province, decisions that opponents of the PQ government were to blame on its commitment to sovereignty. In addition, the forces of federalism, within and without Quebec, were in serious disarray and would have been hard put to launch an effective referendum campaign.

Instead, the PQ leadership chose to defer action on the sovereignty question. The referendum was to take place at a time when Québécois could reflect more "serenely" on the question, well after an impending federal election. Of course, the federal election was finally held only after the Parti québécois had been in power for over two and a half years, and elements of a model of Quebec independence did not begin to emerge until after the Parti québécois had been in power for over two years. In the fall of 1978 an unofficial model of sovereignty-association appeared in *l'Option*,[70] a lengthy book written by two Parti québécois backbenchers. And in June, 1979, the Parti québécois Congrès national ratified the document, *D'egal à egal*,[71] which outlined the basic components of a new Quebec-Canada association.

This cautious deliberation of the PQ government carried some real risks. Rightly or wrongly, observers began to characterize the government as fearful of pursuing Quebec sovereignty. The refusal of the PQ to debate publicly Quebec sovereignty during its first serious electoral test, the by-elections of spring, 1979, may well have alienated some potential voters. Accordingly, one can wonder what considerations might have led the PQ leadership to incur such risks.

Several factors may have been at work. It is clear that the leadership of the Parti québécois had not expected to win the 1976 election and was not fully prepared to assume office. In particular, it had not yet developed a comprehensive plan for sovereignty-association. The fact that the new government felt obliged to commission a large number of studies on Quebec's actual and potential external relations suggests that the full range of possible relationships had not been systematically explored.[72] In addition, as we have seen, there had long been disagreement within the Parti québécois over the desirability of continued economic integration with the rest of Canada. In particular, there had been a long-standing debate over the question of a monetary union. Thus, the party needed time to resolve this internal debate. Finally, as we have noted, there was a sense that it would be "strategically" wise to wait until after the federal election.

However, if these and other factors explain the length of the delay between assuming power and staging the referendum on Quebec sovereignty, they do not explain the fact of delay. The PQ leadership had always intended that a PQ government should occupy office for a substantial period of time before holding a referendum. This intention, in turn, formed part of the overall strategy for securing sovereignty: *étapisme* or step-by-step change.

As we have already seen in our examination of the policy activities of the PQ administration, Lévesque and his closest colleagues had long insisted that the Quebec population would accept only gradual change, that it would recoil from the prospect of radical change. Change must come in stages, or steps, preserving existing advantages while correcting what is disadvantageous. This *étapisme* had its critics within the party, but Lévesque had steadfastly held to it. Thus, at the 1979 PQ Congrès national he declared:

> The stages which we have completed, I know here and there some people do not like this word, stages. But frankly, I have always asked myself why – since that is the way life is – social life, like that of each one of us, is composed of stages which are linked one to the other. Life does not consist of "flea jumps," even in Ancient Times you know, you remember, they had already discovered that nature does not accept leaps which are too abrupt. . . .[73]

The idea of a referendum had been central to this *étapiste* strategy. As we have seen, during the eight years prior to the 1976 victory, René Lévesque and his colleague, Claude Morin, had fought with considerable success to commit the party to holding a referendum on sovereignty, if it were elected. They were able to reinforce this commitment even further once the party was in power. The 1977 Congrès national ratified a change in the program that eliminated all remaining ambiguity about the necessity of a referendum. The PQ government would demand full repatriation of powers to Quebec only after it had first secured approval of sovereignty in a referendum; the referendum was no longer limited only to the eventuality that the rest of Canada should refuse Quebec's project of economic association.[74] Finally, at the 1979 Congrès national the party committed itself to still a further step, specifically linked to a refusal of association. In such a case, the Quebec government could not unilaterally declare Quebec sovereignty without first securing approval in a popular "consultation."[75] In presenting this resolution, Jacques Parizeau had taken pains to emphasize that this consultation could take the form of either an election or a referendum.[76]

The primary purpose (and effect) of such a clear-cut commitment to a referendum was to dissociate the election to power (and even the re-election to power) of the Parti québécois and the accession of Quebec to independence. They were to constitute distinct stages in a long march. While this distinction had obvious value to the electoral fortunes of the PQ, Morin and others argued that it also would help the PQ to achieve its fundamental objective: the sovereignty of Quebec. With control of the Quebec government, it was contended, the PQ would have enormous new resources at its disposal to persuade Québécois of the necessity of sovereignty. First, through simply providing "good government" within the context of a provincial government, the PQ would be able to demonstrate its inherent competence to govern Quebec. Independence or sovereignty would seem less risky if it were to be secured through the same proven leadership that had already efficiently directed the Quebec provincial government. Second, through special studies, carefully calculated policy moves, and appropriate speeches and publicity, a PQ government would be able to demonstrate to Québécois, in a way not before possible, that the federal system is inadequate to meet the needs of Québécois and that major (although not "radical"!) change is necessary. Thus, as the government of Quebec, the Parti québécois would be able to resolve the hesitations and doubts that many Québécois continued to hold about sovereignty. And, once a solid popular majority for sovereignty had been created and its existence clearly demonstrated through a referendum, then no external force would be able or willing to block Quebec's accession to sovereignty. For its part, English Canada would finally recognize the inevitability of Quebec sovereignty and proceed to negotiate the creation of a new Quebec-Canada economic association.

Many of these *étapiste* premises can be found in the following lengthy extract from a document Claude Morin prepared prior to the 1974 PQ Congrès national, in which he argued for a formal commitment to a referendum on sovereignty:

> in practice, our sovereignty can come only through the transfer of powers from Ottawa to Quebec. . . . But, what are in fact Quebec's strengths with respect to Ottawa? What might make the federal government act?
>
> Do we intend to undertake an armed struggle in order to obtain through force what is refused to us otherwise? No.
>
> What, then, do we have available to push things forward? The political will of our government and the will of the people. It is political will which will make our elected representatives show firmness toward Ottawa and place pressure upon it. But it is the will of the people which gives our politicians their strength. Our lever will be public opinion, nothing else.
>
> The question, then, is to know how a péquiste government

will be able to assure itself of the constant and decisive support of Québécois public opinion.

It goes without saying that first it must administer the Quebec state in a satisfactory manner. But, beyond this entirely normal requirement, it will be indispensable for it [the PQ government] to associate itself immediately with the population, from the moment of taking power. Experience shows that when the Quebec population is informed, it naturally takes the side of the Quebec government. (Examples: "provincial autonomy" with M. Duplessis, fiscal arrangements and the pension plan under M. Lesage, constitutional revision with MM. Johnson and Bertrand, the "No" at Victoria with M. Bourassa.) This is why, in all discussions with Ottawa, a PQ administration would need to explain to the citizens what it is doing, and to do so on a scale never before attained.[77]

Within this *étapiste* logic, it made eminent sense for the Parti québécois to defer holding its referendum on sovereignty. Now that the Québécois had taken the critical, but difficult, step of putting the PQ in power, they had to be carefully prepared for the next step of formally approving sovereignty. To do this, the PQ would exploit the many advantages now available to it as the government of Quebec. But, as we have seen, the Lévesque administration was slow to do so. During the first two and half years, virtually all energies appeared to be focused on only one thrust of the post-election strategy, providing "good government." There was little in the way of a concerted effort to mobilize opinion around sovereignty. Even the broad outline of sovereignty-association did not become official until June, 1979. Yet, "good government" alone was not sufficient to persuade Québécois to the cause of sovereignty. Surveys show that the proportion of Québécois supporting sovereignty-association remained unchanged during the first two and a half years of PQ government; it was markedly lower than the proportion who said they were satisfied with the PQ's administration of the province. In fact, in a 1979 survey barely half of the respondents who were "satisfied" with the PQ administration said they were in favour of sovereignty-association.[78]

The delay in initiating the campaign for sovereignty served to reveal, and even amplify, the inherent contradictions of the *étapiste* strategy. The longer the PQ continued to function as a provincial government without acceding to sovereignty, the more powerful these contradictions became – perhaps foreclosing the possibility of Quebec ever acceding to sovereignty. These contradictions are the dilemmas faced by any party that seeks to secure global change while holding power within liberal democratic institutions.

First, there was a contradiction between the goal of independence and the concrete benefits that flowed to the PQ simply from occupying the structures of the Quebec government. As Bill 101 demonstrated, it was possible for the nationalist impulse of *péquiste* militants to be gratified through even the policy initiatives of a provincial government. And the "participationist" forces within the party must have felt at least some satisfaction in such limited social measures as public automobile insurance and guaranteed income schemes. In addition, of course, there was always the possibility that "opportunist" elements among leaders and militants in the party should see personal payoffs in the PQ remaining in power, whatever its policy initiatives. Continued apprehensions among the Quebec population about independence may have led some *péquistes* to conclude that the party should redefine the idea of independence into a more generally acceptable form. After all, one analysis of survey data had suggested that some Québécois (as much as 14 per cent of the electorate) who were satisfied with the PQ's administration of the province would hesitate even to vote for its re-election, simply because of their unease over the goal of sovereignty.[79] Some *péquistes* may well have concluded that it was better to conserve power within a provincial government, and perhaps secure new jurisdictions for it within the federal system, than to risk all in favour of the goal of independence. In Canada and other liberal democratic systems, the rewards of office have led some movements to postpone indefinitely implementation of some of their most important original goals. The longer the PQ remained in power without securing its fundamental goal of independence, the more difficult it became for the party to escape the fate of the CCF or Social Credit.

A second contradiction flowing from the *étapiste* strategy of the PQ leadership involves the relationship between party leaders and party militants. When political parties first secure control of a government, relations between the leadership and militants are redefined. As party leaders assume positions within government structures they are no longer as dependent on party militants for power and status. Moreover, they become subject to a whole host of new pressures. The plethora of social and economic interests that normally seek to influence the day-to-day functioning of any liberal democratic state now become directly fastened on them. The militants, for their part, no longer have a privileged relationship to the leaders. The other interests with which they must now compete may well have more important resources at their immediate disposal than do the militants, who will become important, if ever, only with the next election. Typically, then, the leadership acquires a certain independence from the militants, and the structures of the party atrophy.

There is no question that these processes occurred within the Parti québécois after the 1976 electoral victory. In fact, upon assuming office the PQ leaders were quite open in declaring that they now saw themselves as members of a government and did not feel exclusively bound by their status as leaders within a party. René Lévesque flatly warned the party militants that the party "must not take itself for the government."[80] And there is considerable evidence that the party lost much of its dynamism over the first two years of PQ administration. In November, 1978, one close observer of both party and the PQ government wrote:

Directed by an executive that is timid, unobtrusive, and essentially submitted to the wishes of René Lévesque, ill-at-ease in the face of a government that dominates everything and tolerates little criticism, haunted by the fear that any public discord could hurt the chances of success in the referendum, the Parti québécois is no more than a shadow of itself.

Largely turned in on itself since the victory of November, 1976, it has deliberately chosen to avoid any open challenge of governmental power and to take refuge in the safer and more discreet backstage of political pressure and lobbying.[81]

Similarly, in May, 1979, prior to the PQ Congrès national, Robert Barberis, a longtime PQ militant, declared that there had been a demobilization of the party and blamed this on *"les arrogances de pouvoir"* of the PQ government and its attempt to " 'technocratize' the movement to sovereignty-association."[82] At the congress itself, party vice-presidential candidate Louise Harel evoked a certain disenchantment with the party leadership when she warned that it must not become "the trustees or managers of the national question" and declared that "we will gain nothing by dissimulating our ideas." These remarks were greeted with strong applause and Harel was elected to the vice-presidency by a sweeping majority, despite the declared opposition of Lévesque and other leaders to her candidacy.[83]

Finally, the *étapiste* strategy posed a contradiction between the established role of a provincial government, which the PQ had to pursue given its commitment to provide "good government," and the PQ's abiding contention that this role is inadequate; only as a sovereign state can the Quebec state hope to meet its responsibilities. First, the PQ's *indépendantiste* position hampered its efforts to discharge the normal responsibilities of a provincial government. The motives behind particular policy initiatives were widely questioned, and the initiatives sometimes had a different impact than had been intended. This difficulty was apparent in the government's implementation of new language policy. Despite the protestations of Camille Laurin and other government spokesmen that Bill 101 was concerned solely with resolving problems in language policy, offsetting the deficiencies of Bill 22, many observers persisted in claiming the legislation really was intended to serve the larger end of mobilizing support for independence, whether through pitting Anglophones against Francophones or through making Quebec a linguistically "separate" state. The provisions of Bill 101 would have drawn fierce opposition from corporate elites and Quebec's Anglophone population in general (as had Bill 22) whatever party had introduced it. But the fact that the bill was presented by a government committed to independence certainly heightened resentment and apprehension, making it more difficult to secure compliance.

The contradiction worked in the opposite direction as well: by occupying the functions of a provincial government and even achieving new successes in certain areas, the PQ government may in fact have restored a certain credibility to the federal system, undermining support for sovereignty. An especially striking case of this is Bill 101. Over the years some of the provisions of the law have been declared unconstitutional. The Supreme Court declared, late in 1979, that it was unconstitutional under Section 133 of the British North America Act for Bill 101 to eliminate the use of English in legislative (and regulatory) documents and in judicial proceedings and within municipal institutions.[84] Subsequently, the Charter of Rights and Freedoms in the Constitution Act, 1982, has been the basis for judicial decisions declaring unconstitutional the requirement that public advertising be in French only and the ban on access to English-language schools by children whose parents were educated in English elsewhere in Canada. Nonetheless, most of the law still stands. The provisions to "francisize" the Quebec economy remain standing. The judicial extension of access to English-language schools is relatively slight: all children of non-Anglophones and even children of Anglophones born outside Canada remain excluded from English-language schools. To the extent, then, that Bill 101 was the major new initiative its authors claimed it to be, the PQ government demonstrated not the need for independence but the possibilities for meaningful change even within the existing federal structure.

Intergovernmental Relations within an Étapiste Strategy

These contradictions between seeking to discharge the "normal" responsibilities of a provincial government, on the one hand, and seeking to transform Quebec into a sovereign state, on the other, were most clearly present when the PQ government was involved in intergovernmental relations. If Quebec were to pursue and achieve new agreements with the other Canadian governments, whether federal or provincial, then this would give some ammunition to those who contended that an aggressive Quebec government can still meet the needs of Quebec within the federal system. Yet, if the PQ government was to provide "good government," it could not do otherwise. Some measure of collaboration was necessitated by the high degree of fusion between federal and provincial responsibilities and the proliferation of federal-provincial and interprovincial accords. Thus, despite the rhetoric and the prearranged walkouts from federal-provincial conferences, the PQ government found itself constrained to collaborate with Ottawa on a large number of programs; in fact, some major new agreements were reached. This was especially the case in areas involving major governmental services, which affected large numbers of people and about which there were well-defined public expectations of governmental performance. Through such collaboration the PQ government could not help but give some credibility to the very system it was seeking to change.

The most striking instance of this pressure to collaborate, and hence to avoid public confrontation, lay in the management of the economy. From the beginning, Quebec City had denounced federal economic policies and the federal system in which they are applied, seeking to show through its analysis of the national accounts that the federal government had drained funds out of Quebec. In this fashion, it had tried to saddle Ottawa with the blame for the deterioration of Quebec's economy. For its part, Ottawa had just as regularly denounced Quebec's policies, claiming that the PQ government's *indépendantiste* option had undermined the Quebec economy. Yet, while both governments had developed clear rationales for pinning the other with the full blame for economic decline, by the end of 1977 they felt strong popular pressure to collaborate. Thus, after a meeting in Quebec City, Trudeau and Lévesque declared that, while continuing to differ on constitutional matters, they had decided to make every effort to collaborate in economic matters, in order to reduce inflation and stimulate economic recovery.[85]

In the first six months of 1978 alone, the two governments jointly announced seven new spending programs; each program was lauded as a major stimulus to economic activity. Impressive amounts of money were involved in the Quebec-Ottawa agreements: $77 million for industrial infrastructures;[86] $200 million for the purification of water in the Montreal region;[87] $50 million for the construction of a freeway to the Mirabel airport;[88] $76 million for tourism, cultural sites (such as museums), and leisure activities;[89] $35 million for municipal improvements in northeast Quebec;[90] $35 million for local improvements in seventeen selected municipalities;[91] and $47 million (the 1978 instalment) for general support of municipal improvements.[92] In each case, Ottawa undertook to cover 60 per cent or more of the projected expenditures.

The same pressures for federal-provincial collaboration appear to have operated with respect to social policy. The PQ government regularly had denounced federal programs in social affairs, as well as education and health, as unacceptable intrusions into provincial jurisdiction, and had called for Ottawa's immediate and complete withdrawal. Yet, when it came to negotiating new federal-provincial agreements for federal support of social services programs, Quebec City demonstrated considerable flexibility, agreeing to arrangements that fell far short of complete withdrawal. The federal proposal consisted of a "block payment" arrangement, as under the arrangement for federal support of hospital insurance and medicare, which the PQ government had already signed in 1977. This time, however, Ottawa adamantly refused to agree to the formula of tax point concessions. Rather, it proposed simply to furnish regular payments to the provincial governments, providing that certain minimal conditions should be met. Quebec declared it would have preferred tax point concessions: this would have more closely approximated a federal withdrawal. But, by a sense of "realism" and "solidarity" (with the other provinces), it felt obligated to accept the arrangement that was offered.[93]

Finally, in the area of municipal affairs, the two governments regularly sparred over Ottawa's relations with Quebec municipal governments. Quebec even released a *dossier noir* to support its contention that Ottawa was systematically intruding into the provincial jurisdiction over municipalities and that serious inefficiencies and wastes resulted. Quebec took strong exception to a proposed federal program to support a vast range of municipal services, contending that any direct federal payments to the municipal governments constituted invasions of provincial autonomy. Yet, in June of 1978 Quebec agreed to an arrangement under which, in effect, it would serve as an intermediary in the distribution of federal support for the municipalities. The federal funds were to be forwarded directly to the provincial governments. But it was clearly understood that the money was to be used for allocations to the municipalities; the provinces were free to determine the precise allocations, within federally set norms. Quebec and the other provinces agreed that when announcing the grants to their municipalities they would do so in the company of federal representatives and would even mount a publicity campaign to indicate clearly that the money had originated with the federal government. Also, Quebec and the other provinces agreed to furnish Ottawa with an annual accounting of the disbursement of funds.[94]

Beyond continued collaboration or the semblance of collaboration in many areas, federal-provincial relations under the Lévesque regime were marked by at least one new comprehensive agreement, in the area of immigration. Under the Cullen-Couture agreement signed by the two governments on February 20, 1978, Quebec was delegated the right to select candidates for the status of independent immigrants who intend to settle in Quebec. Also, procedures are spelled out for Quebec's participation in (but not control of) the selection of other categories of immigrants. As in the past, immigrants would still need formal federal approval for such statutory concerns as health and security. To be sure, individuals admitted to other provinces would still be able to move to Quebec subsequently, without approval of the provincial government, just as individuals admitted to Quebec could subsequently move to another province. Nonetheless, the Quebec government clearly secured a very substantial control over immigration into its territory – in fact, the fullest extent of control that would seem possible within a federal system. In effect, it could be argued that in signing this agreement Quebec was proving the "virtues" of the existing federal system, showing that even without constitutional change, let alone sovereignty, an essential need of Quebec could be met. As with its Bill 101, the PQ government may have undercut the case for sovereignty simply through exploiting vigorously the jurisdictions of a provincial government.[95]

In one area, however, Quebec did see an advantage in confrontation with Ottawa rather than collaboration: the federal proposal for a reduction in provincial sales tax. In the spring of 1978, Ottawa announced a new program under which provinces that reduced their sales taxes by specified percentages would receive reimbursement in part or in full (depending on the province) by Ottawa. Quebec alone among the provinces refused to participate. Soon thereafter, the provincial government declared a total and immediate abolition of sales taxes on several items important to Quebec's economy: textiles, clothing, furniture, shoes, and hotel rooms. It called on Ottawa to provide full compensation for the funds lost through this move. In this fashion, Quebec sought to demonstrate how it was much better able than Ottawa to recognize and pursue the particular interests of Québécois.[96] Especially with the refusal of Ottawa to provide full compensation, Quebec was able to mobilize widespread support for its position not only in Quebec but elsewhere in Canada.

Yet, if Quebec was successful in rallying support in this vigorous defence of provincial autonomy, it was less clear that it had advanced its ultimate objective, building support for the idea of Quebec independence. Support was so broadly based, extending beyond Quebec to other provincial capitals and to all the federal opposition parties, precisely because Quebec was defending no more than a long-established principle of Quebec provincial governments that it should have pre-eminence in such fields of direct taxation as retail sales taxes. At most, Quebec was demonstrating that the federal system could function more effectively if there were to be a more flexible partner in Ottawa. In making this contention, the PQ government shared the position of federalists in many quarters throughout Canada.

The contradiction between providing good provincial government and mobilizing support for sovereignty might have been clearly posed in the federal-provincial discussion of constitutional revision. If Ottawa and the nine other provinces had been able to agree to a new constitutional package that effectively met the established demands of previous Quebec provincial governments but included repatriation of the constitution, a PQ government might have felt strong pressure to agree to repatriation. In doing so, however, it would in effect be giving its blessings to the federal system, implying that the system had been sufficiently adapted to meet Quebec's needs that the Quebec government could afford to drop its primary bargaining weapon, agreement to repatriation. Fortunately for the PQ government, it was not caught in this dilemma. The round of federal-provincial discussions on constitutional revision, culminating in the conference of February, 1979, did not produce consensus on a comprehensive package of constitutional reform. Ottawa and the provinces could agree on only a few relatively minor revisions. Quebec alone was not responsible for the outcome; in virtually every other instance, proposed reforms were opposed by another provincial government. Thus, Quebec had no difficulty in arguing that the package was so small that a *good* provincial government of Quebec could not accept repatriation.

In sum, the decision of the PQ government to defer the debate on independence and to pursue its *étapiste* goal of providing good provincial government required that it pursue essentially the same strategies in its federal-provincial relations as had previous provincial governments. In effect, the Parti québécois had become a conventional actor within a system that, ostensibly at least, it had set out to destroy. Even the most dramatic confrontation with Ottawa, over the provincial sales tax, was framed in terms of a vigorous defence of provincial jurisdiction and adherence to the Canadian constitution. Maurice Duplessis would have acted no differently.

In the course of the referendum campaign, the Parti québécois would argue that these various arrangements to which it agreed were inadequate; that, despite its best efforts, the PQ government could not secure a sufficient share of powers and fiscal resources for Quebec. Yet, the various instances provided major ammunition to those who would argue that Quebec can secure its interests within the federal system, especially through a more flexible "renewed" federal system. More importantly, by tacitly accepting the logic of federalism and playing by the established "rules of the game" for three years, the PQ government may have helped to ensure that for most Québécois the basic frame of reference remained a federalist one. If even the Parti québécois could work within the federal system for several years, providing what most Quebec Francophones perceived to be good government, then many of these same Francophones may have found it difficult to believe that the system was beyond reform. In giving the Parti québécois a mandate to negotiate sovereignty-association, they may well have expected that the "new deal" to emerge would lie within a federal framework. They may have been even less disposed than before to follow a different logic, that of the accession of Quebec to sovereignty.

Conclusion

The first Lévesque administration did not quite fit with the vision of a Parti québécois government that emerged from the many documents the party had produced over the eight years before it took power. As we have seen, these documents were pervaded by a firm technocratic commitment to deploy to the maximum the capacities of the Quebec state for economic and social intervention and by the determination to liberate Quebec from the shackles of the federal order. Time was passing and Québécois had to move quickly to regain lost opportunities and to prevent Quebec's further decline – before it was too late. On this basis, one would not have anticipated the degree of deliberation and restraint that characterized the Lévesque government's approach both to administering a provincial government and to securing its professed goal of Quebec sovereignty.

To be sure, there were numerous policy initiatives under the Lévesque administration, but they did not constitute the radical departure one would have expected from a group of committed technocrats. Typically, the changes were essentially incremental, working within approaches already established under the Bourassa regime, as with language policy. In the instances of genuinely new initiatives they usually fell considerably short of their potential scope, as with the decisions to nationalize only a single enterprise in Quebec's asbestos industry and to restrict the new public automobile insurance to coverage of personal injury. Most significantly, there was little disposition to establish major new state enterprises, and existing enterprises were subjected to severe critiques. Apparently, major constraints prevented the Lévesque administration from fully implementing the *étatiste* assumptions that had so pervaded the PQ's pre-election documents and its critiques of the Bourassa regime. In the process, of course, many elements of the PQ program simply were not implemented. Thus, the PQ government ran the risk of alienating and disillusioning party militants.

To a large extent, the relative moderation of the Lévesque administration's policy initiatives can be traced to fiscal constraints facing all governments in North America: the mounting pressures against increased taxation and the spiralling costs of public borrowing. But this moderation can also be traced to the same concerns that shaped the PQ's *étapiste* approach to securing sovereignty. The Quebec population, it was regularly maintained, simply will not accept abrupt change. Moreover, it was argued, external actors, most notably American economic and political elites, would accept Quebec sovereignty more easily if they were confident that the government of a sovereign Quebec would be "responsible," content to "civilize" foreign capital rather than to seize it or to alter seriously its rate of return. The best way to create such a confidence would be for the Parti québécois to demonstrate its "responsibility" before sovereignty, in the structures of a provincial government.

As we shall see in the next chapter, these same assumptions about the disposition of both Québécois and external actors toward change also affected the way the party came to define its ultimate goal of sovereignty and the strategy it adopted to pursue the goal. Change was to be wrapped in continuity: Quebec would become politically sovereign but remain linked to the rest of Canada in an economic association. As Lévesque assured the members of New York's Economic Club, Quebec's accession to independence would be *"une indépendance tranquille."*

CHAPTER NINE

The Roots of Defeat: Sovereignty-Association and the Referendum

The election to the Quebec government of a party formally committed to Quebec sovereignty had a dramatic impact on the rest of Canada. Never before had the integrity of the Canadian state been so directly challenged. A sense of crisis pervaded Canadian politics as, at countless meetings and conferences, politicians, pundits, academics, and concerned citizens debated what were the "real" intentions of the PQ government and what was the best way to rally Québécois support for the Canadian political order. Yet, the debate had an artificiality about it as long as the Quebec government had not actually elaborated its *souverainiste* option. The PQ leadership had, through assuming office, initiated a political crisis, but it seemed hesitant to take the next step.

In fact, over two years passed before, in the spring of 1979, the leadership of the Parti québécois finally produced an outline of its proposed association between a sovereign Quebec and the rest of Canada. Entitled *D'égal à égal*, this document was ratified (with some minor changes) at the Congrès national of the party in June.[1] Five months later, the Quebec government released a lengthy White Paper, *Quebec-Canada: A New Deal*, with the subtitle, *The Quebec Government's Proposal for a New Partnership between Equals: Sovereignty-Association*.[2] The White Paper reiterated (with some modification) the model of economic association outlined in *D'égal à égal*, while describing in greater detail the institutions of the proposed association.[3]

As it appeared in these two documents, the proposed association closely reflected the conviction of the PQ leadership that Quebec's accession to independence should not constitute radical change or "rupture." In fact, the preamble of *D'égal à égal* declared that the good of Quebec, as well as the interest of Canada, doubtlessly necessitates that "in the measure compatible with our collective

300

interests, the nation accede to sovereignty in a perspective of economic continuity."[4] Thus, Quebec would formally assume the powers of a state and it would acquire its share of federal assets and debts. But it would maintain a relatively high level of economic integration with the rest of Canada.

Linking Political Sovereignty to Close Economic Association

Several different forms of economic collaboration were outlined in the Quebec government's White Paper. First, there was to be a customs union, based on the agreement of the two parties not to erect barriers to commerce between Canada and Quebec and to establish a common set of tariffs with other countries. Second, there was to be a free movement of capital and persons between the two units. Third, the two states were to retain the dollar as the sole currency but could maintain separate central banks. Given this retention of a common currency, the two parties were to undertake to co-ordinate "policies inspired by current trends." Fourth, there was the possibility of collaboration in railway and air transportation, including co-management of Air Canada and the Canadian National. Finally, to assure continuity in international relations, a sovereign Quebec was to join Canada as a member of both NATO and NORAD.

In effect, these provisions would amount to both a common market and elements of a monetary union. As such, they exceeded the current level of integration in the European Economic Community and vastly exceed the level of integration of the Scandinavian States' Nordic Council, the two bodies regularly cited as possible parallels with Quebec-Canada sovereignty-association.[5] The government White Paper did not call for any restrictions on the movement of labour and, surprisingly, contained a provision that appeared to eliminate the possibility of state preferential purchasing policies: "The two states will take the necessary steps to guarantee free competition within their market and will abstain from any discriminatory fiscal measure towards each other's products."[6] If this latter provision were to be in effect, the Quebec-Canada economic association would in fact be closer to a "complete" customs union than is the present Canadian system.

It is mainly in the movement of capital that new restrictions were to appear. Under the White Paper, states would have the opportunity to establish investment codes and to regulate "certain" financial institutions. Although some provincial govern-

301

ments have acted to influence the movement of capital, they do not have the power to restrict its movement outright (as is entailed in the notion of "investment codes").

While this new association would have kept intact many of the current forms of economic integration between Quebec and the rest of Canada, it would have restructured the political institutions through which they are governed. There would be no federal government exercising autonomy within a set of jurisdictions exclusively its own: all institutions of the Quebec-Canada association would be creatures of the Quebec and Canadian governments. These institutions would depend on direct financial support by the two governments or revenue generated through activities the two governments have approved; they would have no independent authority to secure these funds. They would be composed of individuals appointed by the two governments; no individuals would be directly elected to these institutions by the populations of the two states. Finally, reflecting the principle of parity, Quebec and Canadian representatives would have an equal number of votes in these various institutions.

Nevertheless, with respect to the final principle, parity between Quebec and Canada, the White Paper suggested that considerable flexibility was possible. Apparently, not all organisms of the association had to be organized on the basis of parity. The White Paper declared:

> In an association between two partners, some fundamental subjects must naturally be subjected to parity, otherwise one of the parties would be at the mercy of the other. That does not mean, however, that in everyday practice everything will be subject to a double veto.[7]

Two of the bodies spelled out in the document were indeed to be based on parity. The decision-making body of the association, the Community Council, was to be composed of teams of delegates from each of the two states, with each team disposing of one vote: decision-making had to be based on unanimity. The White Paper was careful, however, to restrict the authority of the Community Council to matters that would have been defined as "fundamental" by the treaty of the association. The second body based on parity, the Court of Justice, was to be formed of an equal number of judges named by each state, plus a president whose nomination needed the approval of both states. The Court was to be charged with interpreting the agreements upon which the Quebec-Canada association would be constituted and through which it would function.

Two additional organisms were not explicitly organized on a parity basis. A Commission of Experts or general secretariat was to be composed of specialists nominated by the two governments; there was no specification of the proportion of members to be nominated by each state. And a monetary authority, which was to see to the day-to-day administration of the money supply and exchange rates, would have only minority Québécois representation: "the number of seats allocated to each party on the board of directors of the monetary authority will be proportional to the relative size of each economy."[8] Finally, the White Paper raised the possibility that representation in other organisms would be determined by the particular importance they have to each of the states:

It is perfectly possible, indeed, to provide for special cases where the predominant interest of one of the parties would be recognized; Canada would have a decisive voice insofar as wheat is concerned, and Quebec in the area of asbestos.[9]

Thus, the Quebec government's White Paper evoked the possibility that Quebec might content itself with securing formal equality in only some of the key institutions of the association.

In opening up this possibility, the White Paper, of course, was responding to the vast disproportion in economic and demographic weight between the two parties of the proposed association. As the White Paper acknowledged, "the fact that there are only two partners, unequal demographically and economically, will certainly raise some difficulties in the course of negotiations."[10] In fact, there is every reason to believe that Canada's vastly greater economic and demographic weight would command a more than "equal" influence in the policy-making even if Quebec were to enjoy full formal parity in all the organisms of the association.[11] In offering to relax application of the parity principle, the White Paper was merely acknowledging the underlying reality of collaboration between two partners of markedly different strength. Moreover, within the terms of association outlined by the Parti québécois leadership, this "balancing" of Quebec's interests with those of Canada was to extend over much of economic policy. It would include both commercial policy and monetary policy, with its role in economic stabilization. If the new association were to incorporate such common services as an airline and a railway, then Quebec's transportation policy would also be constrained. Thus, under sovereignty-association many aspects of the current political order would have continued. Major areas of economic policy would have remained under pan-Canadian bodies in which Quebec would have less influence than the rest of Canada.

To be sure, such an arrangement would still provide the Quebec state with major gains over its present position. It would have the symbols and perquisites of formal political sovereignty, including membership in the United Nations. It would have exclusive authority to pass laws within the territory of Quebec. It would enjoy complete control over taxation and public expenditures (although the monetary union might necessitate some co-ordination of fiscal policy with Canada). It could elaborate comprehensive industrial policies, secure in the knowledge that contrary policies would not be applied in Quebec by a federal government. And it would secure many areas of economic regulation that are presently in the hands of Ottawa, such as supervision of the operations of banks and related financial institutions or restriction on foreign ownership of major enterprises.[12] Its control over economic policy, however, would fall considerably short of the aspirations of many *indépendantistes*.

As we have seen, during the 1970s the Parti québécois appeared to be moving away from the notion of close economic collaboration between an independent Quebec and Canada; there was a "cooling off in enthusiasm for the idea of a close economic association with Canada."[13] In the minds of many *péquistes*, economic association was no longer a necessary condition for Quebec sovereignty; it was merely desirable. By 1977, the section of the PQ program on external economic relations merely stated that a customs union with Canada would be desirable, if the two parties should find it to be advantageous. In the wake of the PQ electoral victory, *péquiste* economist Jean-P. Vezina wrote that "Quebec controls neither commercial policy nor monetary policy. . . . These tools are indispensable for realizing a host of commitments made by the PQ."[14] And, in the summer of 1978, Jacques Parizeau let it be known that, while he felt a customs union to be essential, a monetary union "is far from indispensable to the economic survival of an independent Quebec." Moreover, he claimed, a monetary union would constitute a very important constraint on political sovereignty, given the co-ordination of fiscal and other economic policies it requires.[15]

Nonetheless, René Lévesque and other elements in the PQ leadership had stoutly resisted this trend.[16] Their thinking remained much the same as in the mid-1960s, when Lévesque founded his

Mouvement souveraineté-association and wrote *Option Quebec*.[17] If other elements in the PQ, especially former members of the RIN, had become aroused about the implications of a formal commitment to association, fearing it would compromise the very possibility of securing a meaningful independence, Lévesque and his colleagues had not.

This determination of the PQ leadership to link Quebec sovereignty to a comprehensive Quebec-Canada economic association was, in turn, rooted in their underlying belief that Québécois will not accept abrupt or radical change. It was important that the PQ should be able to present Quebec's accession to sovereignty as an orderly process through which Québécois can only improve their relative position. Thus, any transitional costs involved in becoming sovereign had to be minimized to the greatest extent possible.

As we shall see, some experts have argued that Quebec could gain some important new economic levers by acceding to full independence, unfettered by an economic association. Over the *long term*, the benefits of Quebec maintaining a distinct Quebec money or a separate commercial policy might well outweigh the losses incurred by dropping the economic link with Canada. But there clearly would be major short-term, transitional costs to acceding to full independence. Within the perspective of the PQ leadership the short-term costs had precedence over potential long-term gains; they had to be avoided, whatever their probable magnitude.[18] There could be no talk of making short-term sacrifices in order to draw long-term gains: this rhetoric belonged to an earlier day, that of Pierre Bourgault and his followers in the RIN whom Lévesque ridiculed as *"les purs et les durs."* The maintenance of a Quebec-Canada economic association would at least help to reduce the short-term costs. If some of the potential advantages of sovereignty should be lost in the process, then this had to be accepted as a necessary concession to "realism" and "responsibility."

The Costs and Benefits of Sovereignty without Association

A sovereign Quebec, over the long term, could draw substantial advantages, as well as disadvantages, from an independent commercial policy, unfettered by a Quebec-Canada customs union.[19] The long-term disadvantages have been well documented. Quebec would have less bargaining power in negotiating tariffs with other countries if it were to do so alone rather than in tandem with Canada. Thus, its weakly competitive, labour-intensive industries would be less able to withstand the international pressures toward the liberalization of trade.[20] With a much smaller protected market, there could be losses in economies of scale (production methods would be less efficient) and efficacy of internal competition. Access to low-cost producers would also suffer.[21] (Of course, a sovereign Quebec could overcome these factors if it were to join in a customs union with some other economic unit, such as the U.S. or the European Economic Community.) Quebec would lose secure access to Canadian fossil energy reserves.[22] And it would lose unrestricted access to Canadian markets for its manufactured goods. As repeated studies have demonstrated, the Canadian market is important to Quebec manufacturers: in 1973, the rest of Canada received 55.6 per cent of Quebec's manufacturing exports, which represented 18.3 per cent of Quebec's national product.[23] Moreover, most of these exports to the rest of Canada draw on such labour-intensive industries as textiles and clothing and depend heavily on tariff protection.

Nonetheless, a sovereign Quebec would also derive major advantages from an independent commercial policy. Using tariff structures, Quebec would be better able to promote a reorganization of its industries and make them more efficient and internationally competitive.[24] As an important element of a comprehensive industrial strategy, an independent commercial policy could be part of a positive response to the pressures for liberalization of world trade. Also, Quebec would be free of the pressures often exerted on partners in a customs union to evolve toward much closer economic integration.[25]

In addition, some economists have contended that the direct costs of withdrawal from the present Canadian customs union would be quite limited and could be overcome relatively easily over the long term. Some Quebec products would be able to continue to compete on the Canadian market. Others might become competitive as Quebec producers respond to the challenge. While abolition of the free flow of goods between Quebec and Canada would eliminate some of the trade created by Confederation, it would also eliminate the "trade diversion" that stems from Confederation: Quebec would be free to secure goods from suppliers in other countries who can provide them more cheaply than can Canadian sources. In fact, Clarence Barber has calculated that the combined effects of economies of scale, increased competition, and trade diversion and creation (the effects of "the customs union implicit in confederation") make a contribution in the order of only "1.5 per cent or more to the income of Quebec."[26]

In short, it can be plausibly argued that over the long term Quebec would gain by withdrawal from the Canadian customs union, or at least would not be worse off. These arguments have their limits. They deal only with the "static" effects of no longer belonging to the Canadian union; the process of disengagement may itself produce long-term "dynamic" effects, both positive and negative, which are difficult to foresee. Even arguments about "static" effects can be only "plausible"; they cannot be proven beforehand. But the existence of arguments such as these should have been sufficient to reassure fervent *indépendantistes* about the feasibility of their project. If these *indépendantistes* were led to opt for close economic association rather than full independence, it cannot be because evidence about the long-term costs of independence made them do so. No such evidence exists. As Queen's University economist, Richard Lipsey, declared in 1978: "The case for Canada is political, social and cultural. We do this strong case a disservice if we try to pretend that persuasive evidence exists that the economic case is strong as well."[27]

Over the short term, however, Quebec (as well as Canada) clearly would undergo the "transitional" costs of adjusting to the new trade structure. Quebec would be immediately confronted with the displacement of workers from its tariff-protected industries. According to a 1978 estimate, there would be 41,000 additional unemployed workers in Quebec, if Quebec and Canada were to erect tariffs on a "tit-for-tat" basis.[28] But a 1979 estimate puts this figure at 149,000 (a 6.5 per cent decline in employment).[29] This initial unemployment might well be absorbed over time, as Quebec producers begin to exploit new economic opportunities within the Quebec market and as the government of an independent Quebec uses its new powers to make Quebec's economy more internationally competitive. But in the first few years of independence, the Quebec government would be burdened with heightened expenditures on income support and with the general discontent that unemployment can produce. A party that believed Québécois will not support abrupt, let alone costly, change could not afford to entertain a notion of sovereignty that might entail substantial adjustment strains. Even if these costs were entirely short-term in nature and were balanced by the long-term benefits of expanded economic powers, they still would be unacceptable.

This same problem of heavy short-term or transitional costs also figured in the question of an independent currency. As we have seen, some *péquistes* argued vigorously that a sovereign Quebec should have its own currency rather than enter a monetary union with Canada. They could point to several long-term advantages.[30]

Currency can constitute a tangible symbol of national status, to which citizens are daily exposed. More importantly, perhaps, control of the money supply can be an important tool in improving trade flows or in isolating Quebec from external economic fluctuations. Economist Tim Hazeldine tried to show how possession of a distinct currency could help Quebec to ease the transition to independence. If a newly independent Quebec were to devalue its currency by 9.3 per cent, it could maintain its balance of payments with a decline in employment of only 21,500 (about one per cent) and "a very small fall in wage rates." This devaluation of the Quebec currency vis-à-vis the Canadian dollar would represent a 5 per cent drop in the economic well-being ("absorption rate") of Québécois. But it would at least reduce the number of Québécois for whom Quebec's accession to independence would mean unemployment, and the drop in the absorption rate could be recovered fairly quickly. Thus, in the words of one observer, the study showed that "the impact of separation would in most respects be slight. . . . In laymen's terms, Quebec might miss a year's growth, but not all that dramatic an outcome in the light of history."[31] Finally, and perhaps most important from an *indépendantiste* perspective, Quebec would be able to avoid the extensive amount of common economic planning and management a monetary union would impose, and which Parizeau and others contended would greatly diminish the import of sovereignty.[32]

Some permanent costs are associated with an independent Quebec currency. There is the burden of maintaining international reserves and offsetting deficits in current accounts, if there should be a desire to manipulate exchange rates. As well, Quebec would no longer participate in an integrated Canadian capital market. Also, trade could be hampered by the added accounting and transaction costs posed by the use of a distinct Quebec currency.[33]

Yet, whatever the mix of costs and benefits that a distinct Quebec money would produce over the long term, the attention of *péquiste* advocates of a monetary union clearly was focused on the short term. During the first few years of independence, the new currency might be unstable, and uncertainty over the future economic performance of an independent Quebec could encourage speculation. (Such instability would undermine the ability of a Quebec currency to ease the transition to independence, as suggested by Hazeldine.) An independent Quebec could seek to stabilize the currency by formally pegging it to another currency, whether Canada's or that of the U.S. However, such a gesture may not be entirely credible: observers might still suspect that at a later point the Quebec government would draw on its power to readjust the value of the currency.[34] Thus, in his 1977 address to the New York Economic Club, Lévesque indicated that the PQ government was prepared to negotiate a monetary union between a sovereign Quebec and Canada "which obviously would allow for political change to be implemented with a real minimum of uncertainty in economic affairs."[35] During the 1973 provincial election campaign, the Bourassa Liberals vividly demonstrated the potential for exploiting popular fears over conversion to a separate Quebec money by claiming that a Quebec dollar would be worth less than the Canadian or American dollar. The PQ could hardly afford a recurrence of this theme in the pre-referendum campaign.

A final set of potential short-term costs clearly played a major role in the thinking of the PQ leadership. The mere fact of change in political institutions, whatever this change may be, is bound to induce some hesitation among economic elites.[36] Private investments may be postponed until the changes have been made and it is known how the new institutions will function. In the case of Quebec's accession to sovereignty, these hesitations and delays among economic elites could not be entirely avoided. But, by placing Quebec sovereignty within the framework of a comprehensive economic association, the scope of potential change was at least reduced. Presumably, then, an economic association, even if it should not extend as far as a common money, would help to reduce business uncertainties. The PQ government had waged an intensive campaign among American opinion leaders, emphasizing that Quebec's accession to sovereignty would mean merely the reorganization of political structures north of the American border, not a total rupture.

Quebec sovereignty as championed by the dominant elements in the Parti québécois, therefore, was closely guided by a concern for minimizing the costs involved in Quebec's accession to sovereignty. Potential costs had to be avoided even if they were short-term and transitional, and even if, as studies for the Economic Council of Canada had suggested, they could be surmounted over the long term or balanced by the advantages of a distinct Quebec money or a separate commercial policy. To avoid the spectre of major transition costs, Quebec had to become at one and the same time a sovereign state and the partner with Canada in a comprehensive economic association. Within the association, Quebec would have the formal status of parity with the rest of Canada. As we have noted, however, there is reason to believe that Canada's vastly greater economic and demographic weight would ensure that

Quebec would have a less than "equal" say in the activities of the Quebec-Canada association. If Quebec were to enjoy "real" equality in the association it would still be balancing its interests with those of Canada. It would not have the freedom to manoeuvre it might acquire if the accession to sovereignty eliminated any special relationship with Canada.

Nonetheless, at least close economic association reduces the potential "costs" of sovereignty. By maintaining a common currency with Canada, Quebec would avoid the potential instability of a new Quebec currency, especially during its early years. And by maintaining a customs unions, Quebec would avoid the necessity of suddenly reorganizing its industrial base; modernization and consolidation could be stretched over a longer period of time. Finally, the maintenance of such close economic integration promised to reduce hesitation and uncertainty among private investors, whether in Quebec, Canada, or the U.S.

Having built all these features into its conception of sovereignty, the Parti québécois was in a much better position to counter adversaries who claimed that Quebec sovereignty was a "dangerous adventure into the unknown." The alleged Québécois fear of rapid or radical change could be assuaged simply by limiting the scope of proposed change. The question remains, however, as to whether such an *indépendance tranquille* would, in fact, have been independence at all.

English Canada and Sovereignty-Association

In firmly linking Quebec sovereignty to a comprehensive economic association with the rest of Canada, the PQ government may well have made Quebec sovereignty more acceptable both to the majority of Québécois, assuaging their alleged fear of radical change, and to American political and economic elites, promising the economic continuity that facilitates decision-making and planning. But, ironically, it also eliminated the primary consideration that could have led English Canadians to accept sovereignty-association: the possibility that Quebec might accede to sovereignty without any special economic link to Canada. When compared with the federal system, even without extensive adjustment or "renewal," sovereignty-association had little appeal to English Canada. Only in the prospect of a complete rupture in the Quebec-Canada relationship, and the costs that might ensue, could sovereignty-association possibly be attractive. For English Canada, as for Quebec, economic association would be attractive essentially as a device for avoiding the long- or short-term costs of Quebec's accession to sovereignty. Unless Quebec obviously was going to accede to sovereignty in any event, agreement to sovereignty-association made little sense to English Canada.

This attitude can be seen in the results of a 1978 survey analysis of English-Canadian attitudes regarding Quebec. The vast majority of English-Canadian respondents outside Quebec opposed "making major concessions to Quebec if these will prevent separation" (in each of the four main regions of English Canada this proposition was supported by only 13 per cent or less of the respondents). But a small majority favoured negotiating an economic agreement with Quebec, "if Quebec does become independent."[37]

Of course, the PQ leadership had been careful to avoid raising the spectre of rupture when presenting its project of sovereignty to Québécois. There was the careful assurance that Quebec's accession to sovereignty would be accompanied by economic continuity. In effect, then, the PQ government's two audiences, Quebec and English Canada, required radically different visions: "change with continuity" for Québécois (and the U.S.) and "the costs of rupture" for English Canada.

Accordingly, when the PQ government issued its White Paper, with its contention that sovereignty-association would be in the interest not only of Quebec but of the rest of Canada as well, it met with resounding rejection among English-Canadian political elites and business leaders. Thus, soon after the publication of the document, the four western Canadian premiers jointly declared:

At Brandon in 1977, and at Prince George earlier this year, the Western premiers rejected the concept of Quebec independence with economic association. While recognizing that major changes in the federal system are clearly necessary, the Western premiers believe that sovereignty-association is neither in the economic interests of Western Canada nor in the broader interest of Canadians as a whole. The Western premiers agreed that there is nothing contained in the White Paper issued last week by the Quebec government that would in any way cause them to alter their views.[38]

In late November of 1979, Ontario Intergovernmental Affairs Minister Thomas Wells elaborated:

There are ten provincial premiers in Confederation, each with varying populations and economic strengths, but ten partners nonetheless. At the intergovernmental conference table, everybody has an equal voice. The White Paper would make representation 50-50. Fifty per cent Quebec and fifty per cent for all the rest of Canada. The attraction of such an arrangement to Quebec is obvious. But there is no attraction to Ontario. Nothing would compel us to accept. Yet that is exactly what the White Paper concludes. It does so because it makes two very debatable assumptions.

First, it assumes that political relationships must be based almost exclusively on linguistic or cultural communities. . . .

Secondly, the White Paper compounds this error by downplaying the real differences in economic and other interest which exist among Canadians outside Quebec. The current debate over oil and gas pricing is but one example of the significance of these differences.[39]

The declarations became even more blunt as the Quebec government's referendum on sovereignty-association approached. On April 22, 1980, at their annual conference the four western Canadian premiers jointly reiterated their refusal to negotiate sovereignty-association. In fact, Saskatchewan Premier Allan Blakeney had just returned from Montreal where, in a speech to the Montreal Board of Trade, he had declared that "A Yes vote in the referendum would lead to stalemate – a virtual pursuit of a goal which all would know is unattainable."[40] For his part, Ontario Premier William Davis appeared at the Montreal Board of Trade on May 1, declaring that:

in no way, shape, or form will sovereignty-association be negotiated with the government which I lead because to do so would be to negotiate the breakup of Canada. Quite simply we see it as a negative proposition that does nothing but close the door on the real opportunities for constitutional change, reform, and progress in this country.[41]

Definitions of Collective Identity

This resolute resistance of English Canadians to the idea of sovereignty-association can be traced to two sets of factors: (1) definitions of collective identity, and (2) calculations of economic and political interest. It goes without saying that these factors are closely interrelated and mutually reinforcing. Collectively, they seem quite able to prevent serious consideration of sovereignty-association, as outlined in *D'égal à égal* and the Quebec government's White Paper, unless English Canadians should see themselves confronted with a real prospect of rupture in the Quebec-Canada relationship.

At the level of identity, the difficulties sovereignty-association poses for English Canadians are well known. Sovereignty-association implies a misleading parallellism between Quebec and English Canada. In effect, it posits the existence of a collectivity that few English Canadians recognize: an English-Canadian nation. The lack of a firm sense of English-Canadian identity is both reflected in and explained by the fact that the English-Canadian collectivity, unlike the Quebec nation, does not have a clear institutional framework. Virtually no governmental structures are explicitly tied to English Canada; cultural organisms within the federal government stand as the essential exception. Nor are there major political and social movements organized in explicitly English-Canadian terms. English-Canadian cultural institutions and mass media do not have the popular impact of their counterparts in Quebec.

Predominant definitions of identity among English Canadians either greatly exceed any specifically English-Canadian collectivity, embracing Francophones as well as Anglophones, or fall considerably short of it, as with "regional" identities. Within some forms of pan-Canadian identity, the French-English distinction has no clear relevance at all, as with attachment to "national" political objectives and institutions (represented by Smiley's notion of "shared commitment"[42]) or with a simple attachment to the physical integrity of the Canadian territory (derided as "mappism" by Abraham Rotstein).[43] There is no rationale within these definitions for excluding Quebec, nor is there a clear basis for recognizing a distinctly English-Canadian collectivity. Of course, the notion of a bicultural nation, largely spawned by the 1960s necessity of responding to Quebec neo-nationalism, does place great emphasis on English-French cultural differences, celebrating and perhaps even exaggerating them. But, by definition, this notion of identity cannot rest on Quebec-without-Canada. In all these various notions of pan-Canadian identity, Quebec sovereignty stands as a rupture. Canada will have "failed." Of course, Quebec's accession to membership in the United Nations, as proposed in the PQ model of sovereignty-association, would only heighten the sense of rupture and deepen the feeling of failure.

In the case of more "local" English-Canadian attachments,

313

whether to a region or to a province, sovereignty-association not only demands absorption into a larger English-Canadian whole, it offers the added insult of reserving a distinct status for Quebec when, in the eyes of many English Canadians, Quebec constitutes simply one more region or province.

Calculations of Economic and Political Interest

Sovereignty-association also clashes with English-Canadian calculations of economic and political interest, at least as they appear at the elite level. For this reason as well, English-Canadian elites will see no reason to move the Quebec-Canada relationship out of the federal formula unless faced with a serious threat of rupture. English-Canadian elites are themselves divided over the proper balance between central and provincial power within the federal system. But the irony of sovereignty-association, at least as it was formulated by the PQ government, is that it can respond to the grievances and aspirations of neither camp – "centralist" or "decentralist."

It is not surprising that sovereignty-association should have little appeal to English Canadians who favour a strong role for central institutions. First, sovereignty-association would place many of the functions presently exercised by the federal government under new conjoint institutions, in which Canada and Quebec would have general parity. Not only is there the likelihood that English-Canadian interests would have diminished influence, but there is the possibility that the new institutions would be cumbersome and prone to conflict and deadlock and would lack the international leverage presently wielded by the central government.[44] (The fact that the new "Canadian" federal government would be free of Quebec influence is not sufficient compensation.) Second, there is the possibility that the devolution of major powers to the new Quebec sovereign state would intensify pressures for decentralization of powers within the remaining Canadian state.[45]

One can see, then, why sovereignty-association would be opposed not only by English-Canadian political elites lodged within federal institutions, but by the political elites of provinces where federal activity is seen as beneficial. Ontario is the most obvious instance. To the extent that Ontario has been especially advantaged by federal economic policies (starting with the National Policy) and by the smooth functioning of the Canadian economic union, then Ontario has little to gain through a restructuring of central institutions or a diminution of their power. Similarly, the

314

heavy dependence of the Atlantic provinces on federal support, whether through equalization payments or economic development programs, induces strong apprehensions among their political elites over any changes that might trigger decentralization.

Much the same kind of reasoning would hold for the dominant English-Canadian economic elites, rooted in central Canada and long dependent on close and advantageous relationships with the federal government. Most striking is the instance of English-Canadian banks and financial institutions, now centred in Ontario, which were directly menaced by the provisions in the PQ program for the transfer of ownership in a sovereign Quebec. In fact, elites in this sector made highly visible their apprehensions about the PQ and its plans for sovereignty. Two financial institutions moved their headquarters to Ontario (Sun Life to Toronto and Royal Trust to Ottawa) to escape Quebec jurisdiction. And Bill 101 was the pretext of a highly publicized, personal attack on the PQ government by the head of the Royal Bank, one of the two English-Canadian banks to maintain a nominal headquarters in Montreal.[46]

Western Canada and Sovereignty-Association

At the same time, one might have expected that the PQ project of sovereignty-association would have had a better reception among English-Canadian elites who favoured a reduction in the power of central institutions. In particular, one thinks of the political elites of the four western Canadian provinces and the regionally based businessmen who have tended to identify with them. There are close parallels between these elements and the "new-middle-class" leaders of the Parti québécois. The power and aspirations of both groups had been closely linked to the modernization of their respective provincial governments, with the concomitant increase in fiscal resources, in the scope of economic and social intervention, in bureaucratic capacity, and in general importance of the provincial state in the lives of citizens. These processes of political modernization, in turn, had reflected the same ambiguous relationship between the state and multinational capital: resource development had been initiated and directed by multinational capital and its needs, but the provincial state had sought to use this development as an opportunity to expand regional economic and political power. In this effort to increase local economic power, Alberta and Saskatchewan had initiated programs of regional economic development that strongly evoke the many projects of the Quiet Revolution attempt to be *maîtres chez nous*. And, in the process, Alberta and Saskatchewan had been drawn into fierce jurisdictional struggles with Ottawa reminiscent of those of Quebec in the 1960s. Both western Canadian and Québécois elites had felt strongly that they were not adequately represented in federal institutions and that the interests of their regions had not received adequate support from Ottawa.[47]

Yet, despite these similarities in background, position, and aspirations between western Canadian elites and the new-middle-class leadership of the Parti québécois, western Canadians showed no more interest in the PQ project of sovereignty-association than did the "centralists" of central and eastern Canada. Several factors were at work here. The PQ leadership did not make a concerted effort to build a western Canadian appeal for support, framed in terms of western Canadian interests and preoccupations. Typically, Quebec political elites had a very "Ontario-centred" view of English government. They were slow to recognize the growing autonomism of western Canadian provinces and the opportunities that this might have created for common alliances against Ottawa. The old "Ontario-Quebec Axis" was a more familiar base of action. Also, for western Canadians the whole issue of Quebec-Canada relations tended to be submerged in the long-standing question of central Canadian economic dominance. The distinction between Ontario and Quebec was inconsequential; both provinces stood as partners in the exploitation of western Canada as a source of cheap raw materials and a market for costly manufactured goods. Thus, the idea of a new Quebec-Canada link whose essential *raison d'être* was economic collaboration could have only limited appeal. Moreover, the basic mode of collaboration, a customs union, focused on tariffs, precisely the area where western Canadian grievances have always been the greatest.[48]

These factors were vastly reinforced by the institutional form of the proposed sovereignty-association. First, it offered no decentralization of power from Ottawa to the English-Canadian provinces. Only Quebec was to acquire new powers: the rest was left up to the "English-Canadian nation" to sort out. Second, and perhaps more important, it reduced the formal status of western Canada within central institutions. Since Quebec was to enjoy parity with the rest of Canada, western Canada would have had to share a single "Canadian" vote with Ontario and Atlantic Canada, and this diminution in status would have come at a time when western Canada's demographic and economic weight was greater than ever before and continuing to grow. By the late 1970s, the combined population of the four western provinces had become greater than that of Quebec, and the critical importance of Alberta and Saskatchewan energy resources had helped to give the West a new leverage on Ontario, if not on Quebec. On this basis, granting Quebec full parity with the rest of Canada could only seem a regressive step, helping to perpetuate an old National Policy economic order that otherwise would be fading fast.[49]

Through this commitment to parity, the terms of sovereignty-association betrayed the fundamental difference between alienation in western Canada and in Quebec – the role of the national question. Despite the many parallels between the economic and social bases of the two movements, the fact remains that Quebec aspirations were defined within the framework of a distinct nation and western Canadian grievances were not. Only within the logic of a nation does Quebec's demand for formal parity with the rest of Canada make sense. There have been no western Canadian demands for parity in central institutions, even though the population of western Canada is larger than that of Quebec. By the same token, there has been little interest in western Canada in accession to full sovereignty; the federal system has remained the basic frame of reference. Since the provincial state is not the embodiment of a nation, there is not the same concern that it should be sovereign and equal in status to all other states. Finally, without an internal cultural division of labour, the state did not assume the central importance it had in Quebec. The provincial state might have been important as an agent of regional economic development but it was not the primary instrument for personal mobility and opportunity that it had become for many Quebec Francophones. For this reason, as well, the dynamic of state-building in western Canada has not been the same as in Quebec: without the national question, regional sentiment does not slip as easily into the logic of sovereignty.

The model of sovereignty-association elaborated in the Quebec government's White Paper had represented a considerable retreat from the vision of Quebec sovereignty championed by many long-term *indépendantistes*. Most critical areas of economic policy were to remain under the control of pan-Canadian institutions in which Quebec would have, in practice if not in form, only a minority voice. Nevertheless, sovereignty-association remained wedded to the same assumptions about Quebec's status as a nation as did the earlier notions of independence. These assumptions closely structured the project of economic association, with its stipulation that Quebec have formal equality within at least some

317

of the association's key institutions. The sovereignty of the Quebec nation required, in turn, the existence of an English-Canadian nation that few English Canadians are prepared to recognize. And, given that the project's essential concern was with the Quebec nation and its fulfilment, it could not easily link up with the ambitions and grievances of English-Canadian elites, whether "centralists" or "decentralists."

The underlying flaw of sovereignty-association was that it sought to create institutional equality between two parties who are manifestly unequal in economic and demographic strength. This tension between the formal definition of the Quebec-Canada relationship and the actual distribution of power between the two entities was bound to pervade the operations of any Quebec-Canada economic association. It should be noted that no association of the scope proposed by the Parti québécois presently exists on a basis of only *two* sovereign states, let alone two states of markedly different strength.[50]

English Canada and the Threat of "Rupture"

English Canadians might have viewed the project differently if they had thought they faced the prospect of Quebec acceding to sovereignty without special economic links to the rest of Canada. For English Canadians (or, more precisely, English-Canadian elites) to find the second prospect credible, we have argued, they must believe that the Quebec government is in a position to declare independence unilaterally, or that it *could* place itself in such a position if it so decided.

English-Canadian elites might have been induced to reach an agreement by several essentially economic incentives. These would parallel the short-term costs we have suggested Quebec could experience in its transition to full sovereignty. First, if trade barriers were to be established between Quebec and Canada, there would be some decline in Canadian industrial exports to Quebec. A 1979 study estimated that if tariffs were erected between Quebec and the rest of Canada on a "tit-for-tat" basis, 23,000 manufacturing jobs would be lost in the rest of Canada. But another 1979 study estimated that 84,000 manufacturing jobs (or 2.6 per cent employment) would be lost in Ontario alone; the loss of employment in the rest of English Canada would be marginal (0.5 per cent).[51] These losses might well be absorbed over the long term, just as in Quebec, and there could be long-term advantages for Canada in pursuing its own commercial policy. But in the short term there would be some decline in exports, with a corresponding loss of jobs. This outcome could be avoided through a customs union. Also, a customs union would allow the movement of goods between Ontario and the Atlantic provinces to continue without impediment.

Second, the billions of dollars of English-Canadian-owned assets in Quebec might have been an incentive for agreeing to a monetary union. As Abraham Rotstein has noted, "The ongoing value of these assets will be no greater than the value of the Quebec currency in which they would be expressed."[52] A strong and stable currency in Quebec could be best achieved through a monetary union. Also, to refuse association would be to run the risk of undermining the more moderate elements within the *indépendantiste* movement with the result that the government of a sovereign Quebec (or even a continuing "province" of Quebec) would be more radical in its treatment of English-Canadian (and American) operations in Quebec and in its social measures and labour relations policies.[53] Finally, the maintenance of extensive economic integration would help to reduce the investor uncertainty accompanying Quebec's political disengagement from Canada. This uncertainty, it should be noted, could hurt English Canada as well as Quebec. Foreign investors, and even English-Canadian investors, might decide to invest in another part of the world than Canada until the new arrangements are in effect.

Thus, faced with a clear threat that Quebec would declare independence unilaterally, breaking the Quebec-Canada economic link, the major English-Canadian economic elites might have opted for sovereignty-association. In fact, a 1977 study of attitudes among a sample of Canadian elites found that "big business" elites were slightly more likely to say they were in favour of negotiating an economic association, under these conditions, than to say that they were opposed (49 per cent versus 44 per cent). Moreover, this option had clear majorities among less powerful elite categories: mass media executives (73 per cent versus 27 per cent), lawyers (52 per cent versus 41 per cent), and academics (62 per cent versus 31 per cent). In addition, it had a strong majority support among labour leaders (62 per cent versus 35 per cent).[54]

We can presume these influences would have been reinforced by U.S. economic and political elites, who would be concerned essentially with maintaining political stability and economic continuity. On the basis of interviews conducted with U.S. State Department officials shortly after the PQ victory, Louis Balthazar affirmed that if Quebec ever secured a mandate to proceed to sovereignty unilaterally, the U.S. would expect English-Canadian elites to agree to a sovereignty-association arrangement, and it probably would encourage them to do so.[55]

On the other hand, western Canadian political elites, and the regional businessmen attached to them, likely would have seen no interest at all in a Quebec-Canada association. Western Canada would escape most of the transitional costs imposed by Quebec's accession to full independence. Of the jobs lost through the imposition of tariff barriers between Canada and Quebec, less than 2 per cent would lie outside Ontario.[56] And preoccupation with the values of English-Canadian investments in Quebec is essentially an Ontario concern. Moreover, western Canada might see real advantages in the dissolution of any Quebec-Canada economic link. In the new Canada-without-Quebec, the weight of central Canada would be substantially reduced, and the West might have correspondingly better chances of securing more satisfactory federal economic policies. It would, at a minimum, be freed from the necessity of buying Quebec-produced tariff-protected goods, such as textiles. To overcome western Canadian resistance, perhaps the Ontario-based political and economic elites with an interest in maintaining economic linkage with Quebec would have to tie sovereignty-association to a larger package in which western Canadian grievances would be accommodated. It would not be an easy task.

Whatever the relative balance of economic and political interests in English Canada for and against sovereignty-association, some observers have argued that it would not in any event have been the primary determinant of English Canada's response. Allegedly, other considerations would have been more important. Donald Smiley wrote at the time:

> The Parti québécois leadership seems to perceive the Anglophone Canadian as preeminently an economic man whose conduct will be determined in the last analysis by a hard-headed calculation of material advantage. This is a misjudgement with potentially tragic consequences. . . . whether within the framework of a federal system or otherwise, it is reasonable to suppose that the future relations between Canadians and Québécois will be significantly influenced by non-economic circumstances.[57]

Yet, while the impact of questions of pride, identity, and general ethnic antagonism should not be minimized, it is difficult to believe that in the end a kind of "economic rationality" would not have prevailed. In such a pre-eminently "economic matter" as the question of economic association, the calculation of "material advantage" likely will be the decisive consideration. Moreover, if hesitations were to remain among English-Canadian political or economic elites, they would have difficulty resisting the certain U.S. pressure to reach an agreement and maintain continuity and stability. In effect, the decisive pressure for the maintenance of a link between Quebec and the rest of Canada might well be external: Canada would have been "saved" by its own dependence.

Obviously, then, one can locate a complex of forces that might have led English Canadians to accept an economic association with a sovereign Quebec. But these forces would have operated only if, in fact, there were a clear sense in English Canada that Quebec was about to move to sovereignty in any event. The common thread of these forces is an interest in maintaining continuity and stability; without the virtual certainty of Quebec sovereignty, these very same forces would be firmly attached to the existing constitutional framework. But in publishing the White Paper the PQ government was not really evoking such a prospect. It was merely proposing sovereignty-association to the rest of Canada, claiming it was in the interest of both Quebec and the rest of Canada. Thus, English-Canadian political and economic elites lost little time in declaring that they would see no appeal in such an arrangement.

Of course, the contention of PQ leaders had always been that a successful Quebec referendum would force English-Canadian leaders to change their tune. Once the Quebec people had put their support behind sovereignty-association these political and business leaders would adopt a much more positive attitude. In fact, there was good reason to believe a strong "Yes" vote would induce a new English-Canadian stance, if not approval of sovereignty-association then at least support for a major restructuring of the federal system.

The Referendum
The Campaign

Several weeks after presentation of the White Paper the Quebec government finally set the date for the referendum, May 20, 1980, and announced the terms of the referendum question:

> The Government of Quebec has made public its proposal to negotiate a new arrangement with the rest of Canada, based on the equality of nations;
> this arrangement would enable Quebec to acquire the exclu-

sive power to make its laws, administer its taxes and establish relations abroad – in other words, sovereignty – and at the same time to maintain with Canada an economic association including a common currency;

no change in political status resulting from these negotiations will be effected without approval by the people through another referendum;

on these terms, do you give the Government of Quebec the mandate to negotiate the proposed agreement between Quebec and Canada?

Yes.

No.[58]

The question was complex, infused as it was with the *étapiste* strategy the PQ government had so carefully followed up to that point.[59] Emphasis was placed on a "new arrangement" with the rest of Canada. The elements of sovereignty were carefully linked to an economic association. Most strikingly, through the third clause, the Quebec government had committed itself to yet another *étape* on the road to Quebec sovereignty: any change in Quebec's political status to emerge from the Quebec-Canada negotiations following a successful referendum would have to be submitted to a second referendum. A successful referendum simply would give the Quebec government a mandate to negotiate with the rest of Canada a "new deal" based on sovereignty-association. If these negotiations succeeded, the terms of this "new deal" would have to be submitted for popular approval. Thus, within even the PQ plans the ultimate *étape*, Quebec's accession to independence, had been deferred further into the future.

As to be expected, the Quebec government's campaign for a "Yes" vote emphasized the need for all Québécois (at least all Francophones) to rally together in an unprecedented affirmation of their national solidarity. This was necessary so as to reject once and for all the existing political order. In the words of Pierre Marois, Minister of State for Social Development:

To be masters in one's own house while showing the greatest respect for others: is this not an ideal both great and legitimate? Would the children growing up now and those who will follow them understand if, collectively, we said No to Quebec? Would they understand that in 1980 we, their parents, their grandparents, had said No to their prosperity, No to their future? How would history interpret it if in 1980, at the moment of the outcome of the most vital struggle not only for our survival as a nation, but in particular for our development and our flowering, we lacked self-confidence, we lacked solidarity, and that just when all we have to do was stand up and say Yes, we had, in a way, resigned?[60]

In making this appeal, however, the government was careful to frame it in terms of continuity rather than rupture. Québécois were to unite around an objective that Québécois political and intellectual leaders had championed for many decades: equality with the rest of Canada. If federalism had been proven to be unworkable, the common interest in maintaining mutual institutions remained. As Lévesque himself put it in his opening address to the National Assembly debate on the referendum question:

we say that instead of living in a regime which everyone . . . admits is outdated, but without casting aside a long-standing tradition of coexistence that has given birth to a whole series of exchanges, we now owe it to ourselves to enter into a new agreement between equals, with our neighbours and partners in the rest of Canada.[61]

Thus, as the government claimed in its campaign literature: "Sovereignty-association is . . . neither the status quo, nor separatism. It's a realistic formula which will enable genuine change without the need to overturn everything or to begin from zero."[62]

Underlying the case for such a new arrangement was a very positive vision of the present condition of the Quebec nation and of its future potential. In his National Assembly address Lévesque proudly reviewed Quebec's last few decades – a cultural renaissance, political and administrative competence and creativity, the ascendancy of Hydro-Québec to world leadership in its field – before declaring:

Quite simply, we are at a point where, without seeking any delusions of grandeur, we can no longer, in any major segment of our society, see ourselves as anything less than what we really are. We can no longer assume that we would not be as capable as anyone else of taking our affairs in hand; indeed, we would be better equipped than anyone else to manage our affairs.

We are now in the front ranks of what are called the developed countries. Our human resources are becoming increasingly competent and creative. We have always known how to save money, and this has enabled us to accumulate all the capital we need to ensure the essential part of our development.[63]

During the National Assembly debate itself, the Minister of State for Economic Development, Bernard Landry, was even more forthright, contending that "it is an objective truth that the economy of Quebec is at this time one of the strongest in the Western world, despite the federal handicap. Its possibilities are practically unlimited."[64]

In short, within this discourse, the Quebec nation had already achieved a great deal over recent decades. All that remained was to free Quebec from the constraints of the federal system so that with the full resources of a modern state its now manifest potential could at last be achieved. Thus, as we found in our analysis of the Parti québécois program, the tenets of Quebec sovereignty displayed little nostalgia for the traditional French-Canadian institutions and solidarities that had been undermined with the Quiet Revolution.[65] Rather than lamenting the changes of the 1960s, nationalists were celebrating them and positing sovereignty as their logical outcome. There was little sense of any collective loss of power or control, only a demand for more of it.

At the same time, the Quebec government was careful to claim that the possibility of *any* change within the existing political order, even a genuine "renewal" of the federal system, hinged upon a strong "Yes" vote in the referendum: "if the response is negative, [English Canada] would no longer need to concern itself with Quebec's demands since Quebec would no longer have any means to escape the status quo."[66]

For their part, the federalist forces in Quebec dismissed such reasoning, arguing that, whatever the wording of the referendum, the real choice was between federalism and outright independence. English Canada, they warned, would never accept the creation of an economic association, even after Quebec became sovereign. As we have seen, political and economic elites in the rest of Canada could not have been more resolute in affirming this. With this demonstration of the "impossibility" of sovereignty-association, federalist forces focused on the horrendous costs that, they contended, would surely accompany the "dangerous adventure" of separatism, the only way through which the Quebec government would be able to secure its goal of Quebec sovereignty.

The federalist case against Quebec independence was based on appeals to a sense of Canadian identity. Quebec Francophones were told that they would no longer be members of the Canadian political community and that the riches and beauties of the Canadian territory (the Rockies were a frequent point of reference) would no longer be theirs. In the process, moreover, they would be betraying their ancestors who had sought to establish a French-Canadian presence throughout Canada. Such pan-Canadian appeals were typical of Quebec Francophones based at the federal level, including Pierre Trudeau himself who declared on one occasion that "we must say no to those who wish to destroy our home, to take away our heritage, to deprive us of our territory."[67]

The primary focus of the federalist campaign, however, was on the *economic* costs Quebec Francophones would themselves suffer from Quebec independence. Federalist spokesmen contended that as a sovereign state the Quebec government would not have the fiscal resources it presently enjoys, thanks to equalization payments and other redistributive programs. Thus, basic social benefits, such as old-age pensions or family allowances, would be more limited under Quebec sovereignty. In some instances federalists even argued that there would be no old-age pensions at all under sovereignty-association or independence.[68] Similarly, it was argued that Quebec would no longer have secure access to Alberta oil at less than the world price. More generally, it was claimed the accession to independence would lead to a massive loss of investment, especially American, which would in turn lead to large-scale unemployment. Finally, federalists even evoked the spectre of authoritarianism. Claude Ryan repeatedly charged the Parti québécois with "tactics that resemble fascism" and the billboards of the Pro-Canada Federation proclaimed, "Canada, I stay – for my liberties."[69]

To reinforce their case against a "Yes" vote in the referendum, federalist forces contended that not only would sovereignty-association be an impossibility and separation a calamity, but that a "Yes" vote could not secure a renewed federalism, despite the claims of the "Yes" forces to the contrary. A mandate to negotiate sovereignty-association, they argued, would not be a propitious basis for negotiating a renewal of the federal system. Such a renewal could be better secured through a "No" vote. To demonstrate its commitment to "a renewed federalism," the Quebec Liberal Party formulated its *Une nouvelle fédération* (otherwise known as the Beige Paper). And, in the course of the referendum campaign, Pierre Trudeau made a solemn promise that if the "No" vote should win, he would personally initiate a thorough process of revision of the federal system. On May 14, in one of three highly publicized speeches made in Quebec during the campaign, Trudeau declared:

> I know because I spoke to the [Liberal] MPs this morning, I know that I can make the most solemn commitment that following a No, we will start immediately the mechanism of renewing the Constitution, and we will not stop until it is done. We are staking our heads, we Quebec MPs, because we are telling Quebeckers to vote No, and we are saying to you in other provinces that we will not accept having a No interpreted as an indication that everything is fine, and everything can stay as it was before. We want change, we are staking our seats to have change.[70]

To underline his point, Trudeau even declared that he would call a constitutional conference for the following July.

Appeals to Canadian identity were a theme in the campaign, yet it is striking that in their effort to counter the campaign for a "Yes" vote, federalist forces found themselves recognizing and appealing to the Quebec nationalist sentiment upon which the "Yes" campaign was based. Quebec Liberal leaders began to dispute the claim of PQ leaders to speak for Quebec's national interests. In the final day of National Assembly debate on the referendum question, Liberal House Leader Gérard-D. Lévesque felt obliged to proclaim: "I have no lesson of patriotism or love of Quebec to learn from the government. I have given my life to Quebec. My first love is Quebec. I have tried to serve the superior interests of Quebec. This has always been my purpose."[71] And the Liberal forces devised a slogan that depicted their quandary: *Mon non est québécois* ("My no is Québécois," which also evoked the phrase "my name is Québécois"). The slogan had a curiously defensive quality. One might have expected federalist forces to proclaim: *Mon non est canadien*. Ultimately, even Ottawa-based federalists, who had always professed a deep disdain for the narrow parochialism of Quebec nationalism, found themselves appealing to it in their attempt to secure a "No" vote. For instance, Pierre Trudeau professed a concern that a "Yes" vote would place Quebec at the mercy of English Canada, since sovereignty-association would be impossible without English Canada's consent: "They are proposing an option which puts the choice of our destiny in the hands of others." Since English Canada would certainly refuse to negotiate sovereignty-association, Trudeau claimed, the result could only be a "cul-de-sac," which would be a "grave humiliation" for the Québécois.[72]

The Quebec federalist forces recognized as well that the Quebec government's call for formal equality between Quebec and the rest of Canada tapped a long-standing aspiration of Quebec Francophones. Accordingly, they sought to reformulate the goal into terms more easily handled within a federal framework. Thus, during the National Assembly debate, Claude Ryan declared:

> When we speak of equality, we are ready to debate the government party no matter where on the concept of equality, because we defend profoundly, we too, the values of equality. But we defend them following an interpretation and applications which are infinitely more realistic and authentic than those which you propose.[73]

The Result: The Causes of Defeat

In terms of the Quebec electorate as a whole, the defeat of the Quebec government's proposition was resounding: 59.6 per cent voted "No," leaving a "Yes" vote of only 40.4 per cent. For Francophone voters alone, however, the result was less clear-cut. Initially, some analysts contended that a bare majority of Francophones, perhaps 51 per cent, had in fact voted "Yes."[74] Nonetheless, other observers were quick to challenge this contention and, drawing on superior data, prevailed in the ensuing debate.[75] Apparently, among Francophones the "Yes" vote was little more than 48 per cent. Thus, neo-nationalists were denied even the "moral victory" of a clear majority among Francophones.

The failure of the PQ government to receive significant support among non-Francophones in Quebec – the best estimates of the non-Francophone "Yes" vote place it at no more than 5 per cent – is not surprising given the traditional attitudes of non-Francophones to Quebec sovereignty and to Quebec nationalism in general.[76] But, given the government's emphasis during its referendum campaign on appealing broadly to all Quebec Francophones, one might have expected that at least it would have received a strong majority of the Francophone vote. Instead, the "Yes" vote in the referendum was largely restricted to the same categories of Francophones that had in the past supported the PQ and the option of Quebec sovereignty.[77]

The Francophone "Yes" vote was defined, first and foremost, by age. An analysis of survey data by Blais and Nadeau demonstrates that Francophones born between 1945 and 1959 were most likely to have voted "Yes," with those born slightly earlier than 1945 (1940-1944) or since 1959 being somewhat less likely to vote "Yes." Conversely, Francophones born before 1940 were much less likely to have voted "Yes." As with past support for the PQ itself, the referendum support for the PQ option was rooted in those who had reached adulthood in the 1960s or 1970s. This generation entered political life after Quebec politics had been transformed by the Quiet Revolution but before the neo-nationalist movement had begun the transition to a government party, with the election of the Parti québécois in 1976.[78] Thus, the referendum result graphically confirmed the extent to which the Quebec *souverainiste* movement had been a pre-eminently generational phenomenon: from its ability to symbolize the aspirations of a generation of Francophones sprang both the strength and the limits of Quebec *souverainisme*.

Beyond age, support for the "Yes" vote was limited by other factors that seem to reflect socialization experiences. It was much lower among Francophones who were not members of unions, and thus had not been exposed to the demands for social and economic reform and even for Quebec sovereignty, which had been widely disseminated through the union movement in the 1970s. By the same token, the "Yes" was substantially lower among Francophones who continued to practice the Catholic religion, and thus may have been reinforced in social and political conservatism. Finally, the likelihood of a "Yes" was firmly linked to education: increasing as did the level of education.[79] Education may have induced *souverainisme* not only through direct exposure to the nationalist messages of Francophone teachers and professors, who themselves were manifestly attracted to the cause, but also in more subtle ways, such as an enhanced awareness of political life or a heightened belief in a personal capacity to have an impact on politics.

However, despite the general importance of education in supporting a "Yes" vote, it is an exaggeration to claim, as have Pinard and Hamilton, that the "Yes" vote had its strongest occupational base among the most highly educated: "intellectuals."[80] Only among older voters was the "Yes" vote apparently stronger among intellectuals, and even then available data are far from satisfactory.[81] Among younger voters another category, semi-professionals, was as likely to have voted "Yes" as intellectuals.

In fact, an analysis by Blais and Nadeau demonstrates that the

"Yes" clientele was more clearly defined in terms of economic sector than occupation: it was substantially stronger in the public sector. Within the public sector the "Yes" vote drew equally from all categories: professionals, semi-professionals, and workers. This distinction between sectors, moreover, explains the surprisingly low support for the "Yes" vote among administrators that Pinard and Hamilton, in particular, have noted.[82] Among administrators in the public sector, support for the referendum proposition was as high as among all other occupations in that sector.[83]

In sum, as in the past, support for the PQ option was limited by such factors as age, education, and religiosity and was rooted in the public sector. The Quebec government had been largely unsuccessful in its effort to go beyond the established *péquiste* clientele and reach other categories of Quebec Francophones through such tactics as diluting the *souverainiste* option and minimizing the stakes of the referendum.[84]

The relative failure of this strategy is also apparent when one examines directly the perceptions that Quebec Francophones held of the PQ option and their reasons for supporting or opposing it. In fact, two different studies of survey data have demonstrated that many Québécois were considerably confused about the very terms of the referendum proposition. In particular, many misunderstood the precise nature of "sovereignty-association." For instance, Pammet *et al.* found that when asked to explain the meaning of the term only a small minority of their respondents did so in ways that approximated the Quebec government's own definition: "a relation between equals" (1.6 per cent), "more control for Quebec within an economic association" (3.9 per cent), or more control within simply "an association" (14 per cent). Respondents were more likely to link sovereignty-association to "separatism" (15.1 per cent) or "independence" (10.5 per cent). A much smaller proportion (7.4 per cent) saw sovereignty-association as simply "more control for Quebec." Finally, 9.2 per cent expressed no more than a generally negative sentiment, 6.4 per cent said the term had never been properly defined, 6.2 per cent responded in none of these terms, and 24.8 per cent gave no response at all.[85]

When presented with incorrect statements about the content of sovereignty-association, substantial proportions of survey respondents agreed with them. In a survey conducted less than a month before the referendum date, two statements that clearly exaggerated the degree of change contained in the official definition of sovereignty-association received substantial affirmative responses: "There would be customs duties between Quebec and Canada" –

yes, 41 per cent, no, 41 per cent; and "Quebec would have its own money" – yes, 32 per cent, no, 52 per cent.[86] Yet, a survey conducted by Pinard and Hamilton during the same period found substantial numbers of respondents prepared to agree to propositions that *underestimated* the change involved: "If sovereignty-association were to come into being, . . . would Quebec continue to elect MPs?" – yes, 28 per cent; no, 48 per cent; "would it remain a province of Canada?" – yes, 40 per cent; no, 44 per cent; "would the federal government continue to make laws for Quebec?" – yes, 23 per cent, no, 58 per cent.[87]

While the existence of substantial confusion is beyond doubt, it is less clear what the overall effect of this confusion was on voting decisions. For their part, Pinard and Hamilton contend that the confusion favoured the "Yes" vote. In comparing the responses to several affirmations about sovereignty-association, they found that underestimation of the change favoured a "Yes" vote more than overestimation inhibited one.[88] But such a conclusion can be only tentative at best: analysis of responses to a different set of propositions might well produce the opposite pattern. More revealing, perhaps, are the respondents' attempts to define the content of sovereignty-association. Here, the findings of the Pammet *et al*. study cited above are highly suggestive: respondents were much more likely to overestimate than to underestimate the degree of change (25.6 per cent versus 7.4 per cent). Unfortunately, Pammet *et al*. do not directly demonstrate the relationship between these responses and the actual voting decisions. Nonetheless, their data are at least sufficient to show that the Quebec government's strategy of seeking to reassure voters by linking sovereignty to economic association had only limited success.

Not only did the Quebec government fail, despite a concerted effort, to make its official option properly understood among the Quebec electorate, but the Pammet *et al*. study suggests that for many voters the precise formulation of the government's option, or even the referendum question, was in any event irrelevant to their referendum decision. When asked the grounds upon which they made their decision, only a minority of respondents (32 per cent) referred to sovereignty-association or, for that matter, change within the federal system. They were much more likely (73 per cent) to cite concerns of a higher order: the dissolution or retention of any Quebec-Canada linkage or the definition of cultural identity (whether Canadian or Québécois).[89] At this level, the "Yes" vote was clearly at a disadvantage: there was little disposition among Québécois to undertake a definitive break from the rest of Canada.

The Quebec government's position, of course, had been that sovereignty-association, let alone support for the referendum question, would entail only alteration of a continuing Quebec-Canada relationship. Yet, many voters either did not understand the position this way or simply felt that the referendum transcended the option. (In fact, 39 per cent of the respondents saw the real objective of the PQ government as not sovereignty-association but "the [complete] independence of Quebec.")[90] Pammet et al. conclude that if the Quebec government had been able to persuade Québécois that the referendum involved simply a redefinition of a continuing Quebec-Canada relationship, then it would have fared better.[91] Of course, the government's relative inability to do this must have stemmed in part from the concerted efforts of federalist politicians and economic elites to convince Québécois that sovereignty-association simply was not a viable option. By contending that sovereignty-association was impossible, and that separation was the only route available to secure Quebec sovereignty, federalist spokesmen may themselves have persuaded Québécois that the "real" question of the referendum was in fact independence.

Findings such as these raise serious questions about the PQ referendum strategy, with its *étapiste* assumptions. Efforts to maximize the referendum vote through defining both sovereignty-association and the referendum question itself in ways that minimized the degree of change presumed that voters would indeed make their decisions in these terms. It would appear, however, that despite the best of efforts on the government's part many voters persisted, in part because of the intervention of other actors, in believing that much more change was at stake than the provincial government suggested, and they voted accordingly. In effect, they voted as if the referendum question were much "harder."

Conceivably, the government might have been better placed to adopt itself a "harder" question, such as a mandate for "Quebec sovereignty," without any assurance of an economic association. By seeking to minimize the change at stake, the government was tacitly agreeing that *major* change would have a devastating effect on Quebec. By openly accepting that the issue was Quebec sovereignty, *per se*, PQ leaders could have adopted a much more aggressive discourse: for instance, extolling the strengths of the Quebec economy and showing how Quebec had the potential to compete openly on the world markets. There would no longer have been the contradiction between first portraying Quebec as dominated and shackled by the rest of Canada and then calling for the maintenance of a close economic association with the rest of Canada. The closest the government leaders came to adopting this more aggressive discourse was during the formal National Assembly debate on the referendum question. There, in a series of carefully orchestrated addresses, government members detailed the strength of different sectors of the Quebec economy and sought to demonstrate how they could be even more successful if not shackled by the structures of Canadian federalism. Frequently, it was implied that these industries could prosper even without the protection of an economic association with Canada. Surveys taken at that time revealed a surge of support for sovereignty-association. Soon after, however, the Quebec government reverted to its more cautious approach, and support for sovereignty-association fell to its previous level.[92]

In short, with a referendum defined in straightforward terms of "Quebec independence" the government could have tackled directly popular fears about profound change and might have been able to persuade at least some additional voters to support sovereignty. Moreover, even if it had made little headway, the Quebec government would at least have been able to claim that the votes it did receive all expressed a desire for fundamental change. Surveys taken at the time of the referendum suggest that about 25 per cent of the Quebec population, and at least 27 per cent of Quebec Francophones, were prepared to support Quebec independence without any economic association.[93] With a concerted campaign, the Quebec government should have been able to raise this figure, if only by a few percentage points. In terms of any bargaining with the rest of Canada, a vote of 30 per cent or more for a referendum proposition explicitly calling for Quebec sovereignty probably would have had more of an impact than even a clear majority for the kind of "soft" question the Quebec government adopted.

Also hindering the Quebec government's campaign was the extent to which popular attitudes about Quebec sovereignty (with or without association) were linked to positions on broader social and economic issues. For instance, the massive gathering of women at the Montreal Forum, "les Yvettes," was not simply an expression of patriotism for Canada. It was also a response to cabinet minister Lise Payette's slur on the more traditional role of Quebec women. More generally, as Ornstein and Stevenson demonstrated in their analysis of 1977 survey data, "In Quebec, nationalism is associated with social democratic positions on class issues."[94] Thus, the struggle over Quebec sovereignty was also a struggle over Quebec itself.

The respective organizations for a "Yes" and "No" vote clearly incarnated very different visions of how the Quebec society and economy should be organized, and especially the role the state should play within that society. It was no accident that within the "No" camp the Conseil du patronat du Québec played a leading role in denouncing sovereignty-association. In this, it was strongly supported by the Chambre de commerce du Québec. Conversely, while no significant business association supported the "Yes" vote, two of the three labour federations did so: the FTQ and the CSN. The CEQ maintained a position of official neutrality, as did the CSD and the UPA (Union des producteurs agricoles).

The fierce opposition of business groups to the Quebec government's proposition obviously reduced the likelihood of support from Québécois who fell under their influence. Among Québécois who were, in any event, more likely to take their cue from the union movement and popular organizations than business leaders, the situation was reversed, but not entirely. As we have seen, many of these groups were far from satisfied with the performance of the Parti québécois as a provincial government. This explains the failure of the CEQ even to support formally the "Yes" vote, and the decision of the CSN to wait until the very last minute to do so. In its attempt to govern the province in a way that would make it acceptable to the largest possible majority of Quebec Francophones, the Lévesque administration had run the risk of alienating the element most likely to support its option. This may well have been reflected in the referendum result.

Finally, the *souverainiste* cause may also have been weakened by the slowness with which the government approached the referendum. After all, the government allowed three years to pass before it produced a blueprint for sovereignty-association, not to mention before it began to mobilize support for a referendum vote. During those three years, attention was focused on the provision of "good government" within the existing federal system. In the process, the PQ may well have served to render the existing political order more tolerable. For instance, through such measures as Bill 101 and the Couture-Cullen agreement on immigration, the Lévesque administration may have eased some of the cultural insecurity that could otherwise have led to support for sovereignty. As a consequence, it may have been all that more difficult for the Quebec government to begin to argue, in the fall of 1979, that it was essential that Quebec abandon the federal system and accede to sovereignty. By the same token, the long delay in the referendum had given the federalist forces the time needed to recover from the disarray and confusion that the surprise PQ electoral victory had produced.

In fact, it appears that potential support for the referendum proposition actually declined over the years that the Parti québécois held office. In August, 1977, a survey showed that 50 per cent of the Quebec population would be ready to give the Quebec government a mandate to negotiate sovereignty-association. This lead was maintained until the fall of 1979, when it began to decline.[95] As for support of the PQ's option of sovereignty-association itself, it appears to have made no net gain over the three and a half years leading up to the referendum.[96] At the same time, support for outright independence – the radical change the PQ leadership consistently disavowed – appears to have increased over this period.[97]

In the end, of course, there is no way of knowing what would have been the result if the government had pursued a different, more aggressive strategy, both in defining the government's option and in conducting the referendum campaign. By the same token, there is no way of knowing for certain whether the government would have been wiser to hold the referendum earlier in its mandate, while the party was still highly mobilized and federalist forces were in serious disarray. Yet, if the consequences of these decisions are not certain, the decisions themselves form a clear pattern: almost invariably, party leaders opted for the more cautious alternative.[98]

The PQ Strategy for Change: The Discourse of Prudence and Realism

Our analysis of the ways in which the PQ defined sovereignty and staged its referendum confirms what we already found in our analysis of policy-making during the first PQ administration. In each case, the theme of change and renewal, although certainly present, was qualified through the evocation of constraints and by the need for prudence and realism. First, in its administration of the province, the Lévesque government repeatedly argued that Quebec's public finances did not permit major initiatives. Moreover, it contended, the goal of sovereignty itself required both restraint in spending ("the road to independence rests on healthy finances") and the avoidance of measures that might alienate major segments of the population (thus, Lévesque's harsh rejection of the 1977 Congrès national's resolution on abortion). These constraints had to be respected even if major elements of the PQ program had to be either postponed or implemented only partially. Second, in defining its strategy for securing sovereignty the PQ leadership pointed to the double constraints of a reticence among

Québécois to accept rapid change and the need to reassure economic elites of the inherent "reasonableness" of the Parti québécois. Thus, the PQ was wedded to pursue a strategy of *étapes*, even though the inherent contradictions of *étapisme* could undermine the very possibility of ever attaining sovereignty. Finally, in defining sovereignty itself the PQ leadership claimed that the need to minimize popular fears over the transitional costs of sovereignty dictated that it be combined with an economic association, even if many of the advantages of sovereignty would be lost in the process.

This emphasis on constraint was much greater than one might have foreseen on the basis of the Parti québécois rhetoric before it assumed power. Certainly, the open acknowledgement of constraints was greater than the last time a party promising reform was elected to the Quebec government, in 1960. Elected on the slogan *"c'est le temps que ça change"* ("it's time for a change"), the Liberals of Jean Lesage had sustained the rhetoric of change over four or five years and had undertaken a major program of reform in the functions and structures of government. They had claimed to be achieving nothing less than making Québécois *maîtres chez nous*.

To be sure, the constraints on the PQ government were indeed strong, perhaps stronger than the PQ leadership itself realized before assuming power. They emerge clearly when the Lévesque government's situation is compared with that of the Lesage regime upon its election. In the late 1970s, the government of Quebec did not have the latitude that the *équipe du tonnerre* enjoyed during the sixties. Quebec's public finances were indeed tight: whereas the 1950s had been marked by a succession of balanced budgets with limited public borrowing, the early and mid-1970s featured deficit budgets with constantly increasing public borrowing. Further, the Lesage regime assumed power after a long period of political stagnation, during which a desire for change had arisen in many different quarters. The Lévesque government, on the other hand, came to power after fifteen years of intense political change, including rapid growth in the functions of the state, secularization of key institutions, and proliferation of groups directly attacking the established social and political order. Many Québécois may well have had little capacity left for digesting further change.

By its very nature, the *péquiste* project induced oppositions and counter-movements that vastly exceeded those faced by the initiatives of the Quiet Revolution. While uneasy with the Lesage regime's neo-nationalism, English Canadians could identify with the educational and social reforms of the 1960s. They could even presume (with their customary condescension) that *rattrapage* meant conversion to the English-Canadian social and political model and entry into "the mainstream of Canadian life." By definition, the project of political sovereignty for Quebec could not support such illusions of national integration; instead, it threatened to lay to rest, for once and for all, the myth of "One Canada." For English-Canadian economic elites, the prospect of Quebec assuming full legislative authority was much more unsettling than the Quiet Revolution's limited economic initiatives. As for American political and economic elites, their customary indifference to Quebec, based on the province's decades of stability and "responsibility," could hardly be maintained in the prospect of *une indépendance tranquille*, which, in his poorly received New York address, Lévesque equated to nothing less than the American Revolution, and which also evoked memories among many Americans of their Civil War. Given the fierce antagonism Quebec sovereignty had aroused among many English-Canadian elites, if not the general population, and the alarm it had produced among some American elites, the *péquiste* project was bound to produce apprehension and fears for economic security within the Quebec population, which the Quiet Revolution did not do. Thus, the Parti québécois was indeed "constrained" by a need to overcome English-Canadian hostilities and American alarm, and to somehow resolve Québécois apprehensions. *Étapisme* and sovereignty-association flowed quite logically from these necessities.

Yet, some observers have insisted that the actions of the PQ government cannot be explained simply in terms of the nature and force of these various constraints. In the heady enthusiasm that has marked other nationalist movements, the PQ leadership might have simply refused to recognize the constraints rather than seeking to work within them. Or it might have attacked the constraints outright. By offering Québécois a program of radical change, perhaps based on the creation of a genuinely social democratic or even socialist order, the PQ could have sought to provide Québécois with a more compelling reason to cast aside their inhibitions about change. Perhaps Québécois might have been more prepared to accept short-term costs if they had been presented with the prospect of "real" independence and the promise of long-term gains. Rather than offering economic continuity, the PQ government might have offered economic liberation. And the hostility of foreign elites to Quebec sovereignty could have been used as a target for mobilizing national solidarity rather than being treated as a temporary problem, stemming from the misperception by these elites of the PQ objectives. In fact, at the time some observers contended that it was *only* on this basis that the PQ could have hoped to mobilize popular support for its project:

> For the majority of the workers . . . this support for a *souverainiste* party stems first and above all from a support for the reformist orientations and social democratic ideals articulated by the PQ program. As a consequence, the project of Quebec sovereignty has a chance of winning the stable adhesion of the Quebec worker movement only on the condition that it be coupled with a project of economic sovereignty – in other words, on condition that political sovereignty induce the implementation of an ensemble of structural reforms setting in motion the transition to a new mode of economic development and a new type of organization of social relations.[99]

There is no way of really "proving" or "disproving" such a thesis. To those who would question it by pointing to the current reaction of many union members against the "radicalism" of some union leaders, it could be countered that these leaders had not defined their objectives in sufficiently concrete terms or had not devoted enough energies to sensitizing workers to the benefits of radical change. But there must be at least some truth in the underlying thrust of this radical critique: that the PQ leadership's catalogue of constraints was essentially a projection of its own interests and preoccupations. The way in which the new-middle-class leadership defined the constraints and the extent to which it accepted them and sought to work within them require some type of explanation that goes beyond the nature of the constraints themselves.

As we have noted, the long-standing obstacles to mobility of Francophones within the private sectors of the Quebec economy meant that the new middle class, whether administrators, teachers, or other salaried professionals, had become closely linked to the Quebec state and the parapublic sector. For such a class, Quebec sovereignty might hold great promise even if it were limited by a close economic association with the rest of Canada. If nothing else, it promised the expansion of the Quebec state and, more generally, of the role of French as the language in which knowledge is acquired and applied. The primary economic gains for the Quebec state would be in fiscal powers rather than in monetary policy or commercial policy. But for Francophones dependent on the public sector, the doubling of Quebec's fiscal capacity would be an important gain. And the accession to sovereignty would eliminate any lingering doubts about the pre-eminence of French within Quebec public and private institutions.

Soon after the election of the PQ, sociologist Marcel Fournier, among others, was already developing this line of argument. After showing how the PQ was guided by the preoccupations of *les travailleurs du langage*, Fournier noted that "All nationalism which is only cultural, linguistic, or even political carries limits which cannot be easily masked." On this basis he concluded that, while it was too early to tell (he was writing in 1977), there was a possibility that the PQ might forgo the goal of independence:

> Inasmuch as the political project of the Parti québécois – the political independence of Quebec – is not based on the transformation of the relations of economic power, it is to be strongly feared that it [the PQ], on the one hand, would be constrained to reduce the national question to a simply linguistic question and, on the other, would fall into the trap of looking for a third way (renewed federalism, particular status, etc.). Equivocal nationalism would have led to the elaboration of an ambiguous solution. . . .
> . . . the *péquiste* government, preferring by prudence or realism not to attack the large economic interests, certainly would still make several explosive moves but it would maintain a relatively conservative economic policy and would move, by means of the referendum, which it might win, towards a much diluted nationalism counting more on association than sovereignty. . . . The PQ would then have offered us only a *vast collective psychoanalysis*![100]

If the accession of Quebec to independence is seen essentially as a political process, involving the transition of the Quebec state to sovereignty, rather than a transformation in the structure of economic power, then it does not constitute a "rupture." Rather, it would be merely the culmination of a long process: *l'étape finale* in the process of political modernization under way since the early 1960s. For many members of the new middle class, the goal of sovereignty had been born simply out of frustration with the way in which the federal system, especially during the Trudeau years in power, had hindered this expansion of the Quebec state. For a Francophone new middle class, rooted in the institutions of the

Quebec state, even a narrowly juridical sovereignty would be no small victory.

In fact, *l'étapisme* may have stood as more than simply a means for bringing Quebec to the essential goal of sovereignty. It may have constituted an objective in itself. Any addition to the jurisdictions of the Quebec government, even within a federal framework, constituted a gain for those dependent on the Quebec state. And, given the progress that already had been made in expanding Quebec's effective autonomy, *l'étapisme* constituted a prudent strategy, building on past gains without jeopardizing them in the name of radical change.

One might even root *étapisme* in the electoral interests of the PQ itself, since it provided a ready rationale for maintaining the PQ leadership in power. For instance, the alleged slowness of the Quebec population to accept change could justify stretching out Quebec's accession to independence over a long period of time, an accumulation of many *étapes*. As long as the final *étape* had not been reached (and PQ strategists could be counted on to always find yet another *étape*), then the Parti québécois could argue that Québécois cannot afford to entrust their fates to any other party.

> One can expect that the pre-sovereign Quebec State will count for as long as possible on *l'étapisme* . . . the ideal would be to conserve for the party in power the ideological advantage which it holds if one compares it to the others: that of being the administrator of a dull present, only in the expectation of a brilliant future.[101]

Nevertheless, as we have already argued, the Parti québécois, and its quest for sovereignty, cannot be understood simply in terms of the class composition of its leadership or its clientele nor can it be comprehended in the same terms as can a conventional political party. The PQ also stood as a social movement and a pre-eminently nationalist one, seeking to mobilize Québécois around a collective identity. It offered not just change, but change within a specifically nationalist framework. As such, it faced challenges that might have induced caution and prudence among the party leadership, whatever its particular class interests and preoccupations.

In seeking to mobilize the population around Quebec nationalism, in the unprecedented context of a referendum, the PQ leadership was obviously aware of the history of previous French-Canadian nationalist movements that failed (most notably in the 1830s) in large part because their leaders had moved too quickly for their presumed followers and had failed to articulate a nationalist project that related to popular preoccupations and aspirations. Even in the short history of the neo-nationalist wave there had been painful surprises – sufficiently painful to be a constant reminder of the fragility of the *indépendantiste* cause. As members of the Lesage regime, some PQ leaders had been personal victims of the 1966 electoral reaction against the rapidity of change under the Quiet Revolution. And the failure in both 1970 and 1973 of the Parti québécois to get even its leader elected, let alone a large number of candidates, obviously had left its mark on Lévesque and his colleagues in the "Long Trek." To cite a 1979 statement of Lévesque:

> Created ten years ago, the Parti québécois has been the very outcome of all this series of steps, which have demanded unimaginable effort, expenditure of energy, and devotion. The idea of emancipation has literally seized the guts of the people who are defending it. It would be very difficult, if all should fail, or simply be postponed, to recharge the batteries, to deploy once again energies, and to start up another movement, or even to keep alive the present movement, after a long period of depression which would follow upon a failure of the will for emancipation.[102]

Of course, such an almost obsessive fear of failure could itself produce error and miscalculation, consisting of the underestimation of strength and the overly long delay of initiatives, until the "right" moment arrives.

CHAPTER TEN

The Collapse of the Neo-Nationalist Project: Its Impact on the Parti Québécois

With the 1980s, the Parti québécois and the neo-nationalist movement in general were confronted with challenges that put in question, and ultimately overwhelmed, its very *raison d'être*. These challenges amounted to no less than the collapse of the neo-nationalist project. As we have seen, there had been two central components of this project: the necessity of Quebec sovereignty and the desirability and efficacy of an interventionist, even "social democratic" state. The 1980s were to deal hard blows to both ideals. With respect to the national question, the stunning referendum defeat had led many *souverainistes* to abandon any hope of achieving their goal, and in fact to abandon active political life altogether. This bleak prognosis was only confirmed by the 1982 constitutional revision, which, closely reflecting Quebec's diminished bargaining power, offered no concessions whatsoever to neo-nationalist aspirations. As for the goal of an interventionist state, it, too, came under heavy assault in the early 1980s: the general movement against state intervention that affected most advanced capitalist states seemed to acquire a special force in the case of Quebec, thanks in large part to the new ascendancy of a Francophone business class. This retreat from the ideal of the interventionist state was to have a devastating effect on the Quebec neo-nationalist project. Much of the force of the neo-nationalist project, especially its social democratic variant, had derived from belief in the efficacy of state intervention to solve social and economic problems. Once this premise was placed in question, let alone dismissed, the neo-nationalist project was gravely compromised.

In short, with the 1980s, the prospects of achieving the ideals upon which the Parti québécois had been founded became increasingly remote. As a consequence, the second PQ government was to have more and more difficulty governing the province in a way that was at all acceptable not only to many of the militants but even to key elements of the leadership that remained faithful to these ideals. If some *péquistes* could support and even promote the transformation of the PQ to a "government party," whose primary objective was simply to conserve power, others continued to see the PQ as a social movement and were enraged by any concessions to "reality." Out of these contradictions emerged a conflict that ultimately was to consume the government, and the party.

The 1981 Quebec Election

The surprise victory of the Parti québécois in the 1981 election might be seen as confirmation that neo-nationalism continued to hold sway over Quebec politics, given both the PQ's official commitment to Quebec sovereignty and the Lévesque government's vehement opposition to the federal government's constitutional revision plans. After all, the Parti québécois was re-elected with a commanding majority of 80 seats and a popular vote of 49.2 per cent, up eight percentage points from the 1976 level. The Liberal popular vote of 46.1 per cent did constitute a dramatic recovery (thirteen percentage points) from the rout of 1976; with it, the Liberals increased their seats from 26 to 42. Moreover, with the virtual disappearance of the Union nationale, the Liberals could monopolize the role of opposition to the Parti québécois. However, these gains were small consolation to the Liberal leadership, which had assumed, as a result of both the PQ defeat in the referendum and the string of Liberal by-election victories, that Liberal success in the provincial election was inevitable.

Yet, on close examination it becomes clear that in fact the PQ was re-elected *despite* its neo-nationalist project. It did this by carefully distancing itself from its *souverainiste* goals. The PQ electoral program stipulated that the party would fully respect the result of the 1980 referendum and would not call another referendum within a new mandate. Beyond this formal renunciation of any campaign to secure sovereignty-association, at least over the short term, the PQ leaders by and large ignored the national question. They even avoided discussion of the federal government's project of unilateral repatriation.[1]

In general, the Liberal campaign complemented this PQ strategy by also focusing on the Lévesque government's record. To be sure, the Liberal purpose was to show the existence of grave deficiencies in this record, whether mismanagement of public finances or excesses of bureaucratic power. But there was little discussion of the national question, other than to cast doubt on the PQ contention that a new Lévesque government would not actively pursue sovereignty-association. In particular, there was little sustained reference to the constitutional negotiations. Of course, given the support of their federal counterparts for unilateral repatriation, the provincial Liberals were ill-placed to make an issue of the negotiations.[2]

Analyses of opinion surveys conducted during the campaign clearly demonstrated that the voters themselves did not choose between the parties on the basis of the national question.[3] When asked what they regarded as the most important issue in the campaign, respondents to a survey administered by CROP were most likely to cite economic concerns such as inflation (38 per cent), unemployment (11 per cent), or the the economic situation in general (21 per cent). Only 8 per cent of them cited constitutional repatriation as the most important issue.[4] At the same time, both this survey and one conducted by SORECOM found a very strong level of general satisfaction with the PQ government: 60 per cent in one and 59 per cent in the other. To be sure, satisfaction with the Lévesque administration was not highest in terms of what respondents saw as the most important question: only 48 per cent were satisfied with the Lévesque government's handling of the economy. And it certainly was not based on the government's handling of the constitutional question (only 30 per cent said they were satisfied with this). Rather, satisfaction was highest in terms of such PQ initiatives as consumer protection (72 per cent), automobile insurance (57 per cent), and the status of women (57 per cent), as well as with the language question (60 per cent).[5] In fact, the high level of overall satisfaction probably had less to do with specific aspects of the Lévesque government's performance than with confidence in René Lévesque himself: 50 per cent of the SORECOM respondents found Lévesque the party leader best able to govern, with only 23 per cent opting for Ryan (the figures for the CROP survey were 45 per cent and 23 per cent).[6]

Voter satisfaction with the Lévesque government in fact had always been high, ever since its election in 1976. However, until the referendum had been held apprehension over the government's souverainiste project had prevented many voters from translating their satisfaction with the government's performance into a readiness to vote for it. With the referendum defeat, along with the PQ's careful renunciation of any effort to secure sovereignty during a new mandate, voters were no longer inhibited. For the first time since 1978, the readiness of the Quebec electorate to vote for the PQ approximated its levels of satisfaction with the Lévesque government and confidence in Lévesque himself.[7] In effect, only by renouncing, for the short term at least, its *raison d'être* could the Parti québécois make itself fully acceptable to the Quebec electorate. Electoral imperatives had hastened the transformation of a social movement into a conventional political party. Thus, rather than reversing the setback that the cause of Quebec sovereignty had suffered with the referendum result, the 1981 election merely reinforced this setback by further distancing the Parti québécois from the fundamental objective for which it had been created.

While the 1981 election campaign clearly reflected a general movement from the goal of a "national" state, it was less clearly marked by the growing attack on the other neo-nationalist tenet: the interventionist state. The Liberal campaign, especially in Claude Ryan's major addresses, did raise the spectre of a bloated, if not authoritarian, Quebec state that was intruding excessively in Quebec society. The application of Bill 101 and a law to preserve agricultural lands were cited as prime examples.[8] Nonetheless, the Liberal complaint about the state of Quebec's public finances was seriously compromised by the Liberals' own commitment to a wide variety of new programs.[9] For its part, the Parti québécois ostensibly remained committed to the interventionist state. The PQ did not propose major new state initiatives other than spending programs to stimulate economic recovery, but PQ campaigners were quick to profess alarm about a provision in the Liberal electoral program for a review of state enterprises.[10] As for the electorate itself, we have seen that the extraordinarily high level of satisfaction with the Lévesque government was based in part on such "social democratic" initiatives as automobile insurance and consumer protection. Nonetheless, as we shall see, it was not too long after the election before not only the Liberals but even the PQ government itself were vigorously seeking to dissociate themselves from the ideal of the interventionist state.

In sum, rather than reversing the referendum defeat of the neo-nationalist project, the re-election of the Parti québécois in a sense merely confirmed it: the PQ had sought to secure its re-election by further distancing itself from Quebec sovereignty, and the strategy had worked. In the process, however, the Parti québécois had taken one more step in its transformation from social movement to government party. We now need to see how this steady retreat from the party's ideals continued through the second PQ administration and how it in turn produced a reaction among veteran *péquistes* that ultimately engulfed the party as a whole.

Quebec as a "National State"

The goal of making Quebec a truly "national" state was, of course, the key component of the PQ neo-nationalist project. By and large, *péquistes* had seen sovereignty, political if not economic, as the route through which the Quebec state would at last attain national status. While they might have acknowledged the theoretical possibility of Quebec being given its "proper" status within the Canadian federal system, they had always insisted that this was a purely theoretical possibility: the rest of Canada would never agree to it. After all, English Canada had firmly resisted the many different proposals for reform of the federal system that had circulated during the 1960s and 1970s.

The goal of a sovereign Quebec state was dealt a fatal blow by the results of the 1980 referendum. After all its efforts to win Québécois to the *souverainiste* cause, the Quebec government had been unable to secure from Francophones, let alone the Quebec population as a whole, clear majority support for the most minimal of mandates: simply to negotiate sovereignty with the federal government. In despair, many nationalists seemed to abandon political action altogether. For their part, the PQ leadership determined that they should attempt to accomplish what they had always said was impossible: to achieve at least some elements of the neo-nationalist project within the federal political order, through the much promised "renewal" of the federal system. In fact, as the duly elected provincial government they had little choice but to do so, given the resounding defeat of their own option. Ultimately, however, their efforts met with total failure – and the leadership brought discredit upon itself in the process.

Initially there had been indications that some of the neo-nationalist demands might be met through renewal of the federal system. As we have seen, in an effort to secure a "No" vote in the referendum, leaders of the federalist cause had solemnly pledged that they would view a majority "No" vote as a mandate to revise the federal system.   Moreover, once the results of the referendum were known, federal politicians were quick to declare a firm commitment to make good on their pre-referendum promises of a renewed federalism. The day after the referendum, Prime Minister Trudeau himself declared to the House of Commons that:

> The majority of Quebec voters have refused to give their provincial government the mandate to negotiate the withdrawal of Quebec from the Canadian federation even though they had

been assured over and over again that that could be done while maintaining some form of economic association with the rest of the country. Those voters said no because they put their confidence in Canada. They said no because they accepted the assurance from Mr. Ryan of the Liberal Party of Quebec, and from other federalist groups in that province. They accepted the assurance from the premiers of the other regions of the country, from the Leader of the New Democratic Party, from all my colleagues in the Liberal Party of Canada and from myself that changes were not only possible within confederation but that the rejection of the option advocated by the Parti québécois would take us out of the dead end and allow us at last to renew our political system.[11]

Typically, these commitments contained little detail on the precise changes that would be sought. Nonetheless, a variety of comprehensive schemes for "renewed federalism" had been presented over the previous two or three years. Most prominent among these schemes were *A Future Together* by the federal government's Task Force on National Unity and the Quebec Liberal Party's *A New Canadian Federation*.[12] Some of the reforms they proposed responded directly to neo-nationalist demands. Moreover, in his post-referendum address to the House of Commons, Prime Minister Trudeau indicated that renewal of the federal system would have to draw on these two documents, along with other proposals for change.[13] Thus, they constitute appropriate standards for any accommodation of Quebec; we need to examine them in some detail.

Within these two proposals there were to be a significant enhancement of provincial jurisdiction and a curtailment of federal power. Under *A New Canadian Federation* all provinces were to receive exclusive jurisdiction over such matters as manpower training, family law, social insurance (including unemployment insurance), and health and social services. The provinces would be given exclusive jurisdiction over offshore resources (although this would be subject to the federal emergency power). They were to be allowed access to any means of taxation and were to be assigned the residual power. In *A Future Together* there was to be a similar transfer of jurisdictions with the proviso that provincial governments could readily delegate them to the federal government if they so wished. On this basis, Quebec could well emerge with a *de facto* special status if some of the new jurisdictions were not of interest to the other provinces. Also, both proposals altered or abolished other powers the federal government had always enjoyed: the reservation, disallowance, and declaratory powers were to be abolished; restrictions were to be placed on federal spending and emergency powers.

In addition, both proposals contained provisions for changes in federal-level institutions. A new upper chamber in the federal Parliament, composed exclusively of representatives selected by the provincial governments, would have a suspensive veto over federal legislation, with a permanent veto of bills involving the federal spending power and of proclamations of a state of emergency. As well, it would have the power to approve appointments to key federal agencies. Within this upper chamber, Quebec would be entitled to 25 per cent of the voting seats under the Quebec Liberal Party's proposal and 20 per cent under the Task Force's proposal. In addition, under the latter proposal, reform of the Supreme Court would have led to a "near equality" between the number of justices from Quebec and the number from the rest of the country. For its part, the Quebec Liberal Party's proposal would have guaranteed that constitutional disputes would be placed before a "constitutional bench" in which half of the justices would be from Quebec.

To be sure, in terms of the aspirations of Quebec neo-nationalists these proposals did have important deficiencies. Neither set of reforms involved explicit recognition of Quebec as a national collectivity, although the Task Force report did refer to Quebec as a "distinct society." Thus, all powers assigned to Quebec were to be assigned to all the other provinces as well. Also, neither document awarded Quebec parity within federal institutions. In the new upper chamber, Quebec would have no greater representation than the largest of the other provinces, namely Ontario.[14] The reforms of the Supreme Court, calling for "near equality" in membership or equality before a constitutional bench, involved the judicial interpretation of law rather than its formulation. Finally, the proposals for enhanced provincial power carefully avoid "economic" jurisdictions. In fact, both documents would have diminished provincial economic power by restricting such tools of provincial economic development policy as preferential purchasing policies and barriers to interprovincial movement of labour and capital. Taken as a whole, then, these changes would have been a far cry from sovereignty-association as it had been defined by the PQ government.

Nonetheless, both documents did presume, as a fundamental

347

premise, that a "renewal" of the federal system would necessarily involve expansion of provincial jurisdictions. To that extent, they met a central tenet of the Quebec neo-nationalists. Moreover, specific proposals such as exclusive provincial control of manpower policy and social insurance, abolition of the federal powers of reservation and disallowance, and restriction (if not abolition) of the federal spending power echoed long-standing demands of Quebec nationalists.

However, federalist leaders had themselves made no firm commitments to these specific proposals. Moreover, other proposals for a " renewed federalism" offered little, if anything at all, to Quebec neo-nationalists. For instance, the federal government's own proposals for reform, *A Time for Action*, offered no transfer of jurisdictions to the provincial governments, instead evoking the possibility of mutual exchanges of power, as well as clarification of jurisdictions and some broadening of concurrency. The essential focus was on reform to federal-level institutions. Even here, there would be no appreciable enhancement of the power of provincial governments: in the new House of the Federation only half of the members would be appointed at the provincial level, and these appointments would be made not just by the leaders of the provincial governments but by the leaders of all parties present in the provincial legislatures.[15]

Ultimately, it became clear that, at least in the case of Pierre Trudeau and his federal colleagues, "renewed federalism" did not mean an enhancement of the powers of the Quebec government. In fact, Trudeau had never actually agreed that it should. To proposals for strengthening the Quebec government he had always opposed an alternative strategy for meeting Québécois discontent: strengthening the Francophone presence in federal institutions and expanding French-language federal and provincial services to the Francophone minorities outside Quebec. Thus, just as the Official Languages Act of 1969 was one of his first accomplishments as prime minister, so the protection of language rights was the primary motivation of his proposals for an entrenched charter of rights.

Under the proposal for constitutional change the federal government presented in the fall of 1980, not only was the division of powers ignored, but even federal institutions were to remain untouched. Instead, renewal of the federal system was to consist simply of Trudeau's long-standing project of repatriation of the constitution coupled with an entrenched charter of rights.[16] It was a very slim package indeed. Certainly, it fell far short of the twelve-item agenda to which the first ministers had agreed the previous June. Only four of the items on that agenda were incorporated in the Constitution Act: resource ownership and interprovincial trade, equalization and regional disparities, the Charter, and patriation with an amendment formula. Eight items remained: communications, family law, fisheries, offshore resources, the Senate, the Supreme Court, powers over the economy, and a statement of principles.[17]

Even if federal leaders were to insist that this proposal constituted fulfilment of their pre-referendum pledge to Quebec, and that its implementation was all the more necessary for this reason, it bore little relationship to the main schemes for renewed federalism that were circulating at the time of the referendum: *A New Canadian Federation* and *A Future Together*. It fell short even of the federal government's own *A Time for Action*. And it bore no relationship at all to the long-standing aspirations of Quebec neo-nationalists. In some respects, it directly challenged these aspirations. Nonetheless, the new constitution to which Ottawa and the provincial governments (excluding Quebec) agreed in November of 1981 falls essentially within the framework of Trudeau's 1980 proposal.

Under the Constitution Act, 1982, there is no significant enhancement of the powers of the Quebec government, or of any other provincial government.[18] In fact, through the new Charter of Rights and Freedoms, there is even a curtailment of certain provincial jurisdictions. In the process, important laws of the Quebec government are affected. Provincial jurisdiction over education, the historical rallying cry of Quebec nationalists, is contravened by the new provisions governing language of education. Thus, in contradiction of the prevailing "Quebec clause" of Bill 101, Quebec is compelled to make public education in English available to all children whose parents were educated anywhere in Canada, as well as any additional children who have already received (or have a sibling who has received) education in English in Canada.[19] Also, under the mobility provision, Quebec is precluded from restricting access of non-residents to employment in Quebec. On this basis, Quebec's law to regulate the construction industry is jeopardized. For the time being, however, the law is secure since this provision of the Charter is inoperable if a province's employment rate is below the national average (a likely prospect for Quebec in the foreseeable future).[20] Unlike several provisions of the Charter, neither of these provisions is subject to the "notwithstanding" provision.

By some interpretations, the Constitution Act's amendment procedure also detracts from powers exercised in the past by the Quebec government. Under this procedure, Quebec can exercise no veto over most forms of constitutional change: approval by a combination of any seven provinces, collectively representing 50 per cent of the Canadian population, is sufficient (along with federal approval).[21] Some commentators contend that in the past Quebec had always exercised a *de facto* veto. There are strong arguments to support this interpretation, even if it was not upheld by the Canadian Supreme Court in its 1982 decision.[22] There is no question, however, that within most notions of "renewed federalism" Quebec was expected to enjoy a veto. Not only had past attempts to establish an amendment procedure provided for such a veto, but most major proposals for constitutional revision to be produced during the years leading up to the final round of constitutional negotiations had always included a Quebec veto over all amendments.[23]

In short, rather than strengthening Quebec's position, the constitution settlement weakened it. Rather than responding to the aspirations of Quebec nationalists, "renewal" of the federal system only served to confirm their long-standing belief that these aspirations could not be met within Canadian federalism. The Constitution Act was faithful to Trudeau's vision of a bilingual Canada, but this had not been their vision.

Explaining Quebec's Defeat

In large part, this outright failure of constitutional revision to address the demands of Quebec nationalists stemmed directly, and quite logically, from the referendum outcome, and the way in which it so weakened Quebec's bargaining position. With the defeat of the *souverainiste* option, Quebec nationalists lost their essential tool for influencing English Canadians and federalists in general. English-Canadian readiness to consider Quebec's constitutional demands had always hinged on the belief that some accommodation of Quebec was necessary to head off the possibility of Quebec deciding to disengage itself from Canada altogether. In the last analysis, this fear of "rupture," vastly heightened by the accession of the Parti québécois to power in 1976, had spurred the sudden interest in "renewed federalism" and had led to the preparation of such blueprints for "renewal" as *A New Canadian Federation* and *A Future Together*. With the massive rejection of sovereignty in the referendum, Quebec nationalists could no longer credibly raise the spectre of "rupture." For twenty years, Quebec nationalists had been able to claim that the forces of secession were steadily growing, requiring an urgent response on the part of the rest of Canada. Through the referendum, the Quebec government had sought to give this argument even greater strength. Instead, it did exactly the opposite. In the eyes of many English Canadians, the "Quebec problem" had simply resolved itself.

For those who were concerned, nonetheless, that there be some fulfilment of the pre-referendum commitment to "renewed federalism," the federal government offered its limited package of reform. While totally ignoring the demands of Quebec nationalists as well as most notions of "renewed federalism," the proposals were invested with the moral authority of Pierre Trudeau, who not only was himself a French Canadian but, in the eyes of many, had personally secured the strong "No" vote.

English-Canadian sentiment was perhaps best exemplified by Richard Hatfield when, during a televised discussion in the summer of 1980, he grew impatient with an elaboration of Quebec's constitutional position by Daniel Latouche, constitutional adviser to the Lévesque government. Even though Quebec's proposals for an enhancement of its powers were very much along the lines of the models of "renewed federalism" that had been circulating in the late 1970s, Hatfield declared, "We don't have to listen to this anymore – this is over. . . . There was a referendum which settled all that."[24]

Yet, beyond Quebec's weakened bargaining position, the constitutional outcome also reflects the fierce determination of the federal government to take full advantage of this and every other opportunity to assert federal power. Through the late 1970s a growing sense had developed among officials in Ottawa that federal power had declined, and provincial power increased, to such an extent that Ottawa could no longer properly discharge its responsibilities as the government of all Canadians. On this basis, they mounted a concerted attack on the pretensions of the provincial governments, in general, and the aspirations of Quebec nationalists, in particular. Once the referendum had been defeated, a result for which federal officials gave themselves full credit, this determination was given full rein.[25] In the process, the whole of intergovernmental relations between Ottawa and Quebec City came into much greater conflict than they had ever been before the referendum.

The federal government's unprecedented threat in the fall of 1980 to send its package of constitutional reforms to Westminster even without the approval of the provincial governments was, in fact, only one of several instances of a new federal disposition to act unilaterally in areas where in the past it had always sought the collaboration and consent of the provincial governments. In October of the same year, Ottawa announced the National Energy Policy through which, for the first time, it would impose a pricing and taxation regime for oil and gas without first securing the consent of the producer provinces. And in the fall of 1981 federal officials announced radical reductions in federal transfers to the provinces without allowing time for the extensive consultation of the provincial governments, which had always preceded Ottawa's determination of the five-year fiscal arrangements in the past.

By the same token, the federal government sought in several ways to provide direct services and benefits to citizens and institutions that in the past, out of deference to provincial jurisdiction, it had funnelled through the provincial governments. For instance, in June, 1983, the Ministry of Employment and Immigration established a direct job creation program through which funds were made available to a variety of recipients, including municipal governments. More significantly, in January, 1982, Prime Minister Trudeau announced a radically different approach to regional development policy through which, in some cases, the federal government would retain exclusive responsiblity for projects rather than allowing provincial management of them as had been the case in the past.[26]

Also striking are several federal initiatives that fell on Quebec alone. In 1981, the federal government amended the National Energy Act to authorize it to draw on the rarely used declaratory power to create a right-of-way across Quebec territory for the transmission to the United States of Labrador electrical power. This was intended to undermine Hydro-Québec's long-standing contract with Newfoundland – a contract Newfoundland had been seeking in vain to renegotiate.[27] In 1983, the government introduced to the Senate a bill, S-31, to restrict provincial ownership in enterprises engaged in interprovincial transportation. By all reports, the bill was aimed at Quebec's Caisse de dépôt et de placement, which was alleged to be seeking a controlling interest in Canadian Pacific.[28] Also, two major regional economic development projects were undertaken unilaterally by the federal government. In May, 1983, a massive $224 million five-year program was announced for the Gaspé and Lower St. Lawrence and in June, 1984, a $109 million project for the province as a whole was announced. Federal officials justified these unilateral moves in terms of difficulties in negotiating a new comprehensive agreement

(ERDA) with Quebec. Nonetheless, negotiations were also lagging with Ontario and British Columbia, yet no projects had been declared unilaterally for these provinces.[29]

A variety of factors could be cited to explain the rise of this extraordinary determination to assert federal power. It may have been engendered in part by institutional changes within the federal government itself. The introduction of new rationalized decision-making procedures, and concomitant concern with measuring the effectiveness of expenditures in terms of clearly defined policy objectives, may have helped to trigger the disaffection with federal-provincial collaboration. Also, with the shift of power within the federal government from line departments to the new central agencies, the alliances between federal and provincial program officials that had supported federal-provincial collaboration in the past may have been undermined.[30]

Beyond such institutional changes, one might also point to changes in the international political economy and Canada's place within it to account for the new federal assertiveness. Yet, while these changes may have provided ready rationales for federal action, it is not clear that they can explain it. For instance, the prolonged recession of the early 1980s was cited by federal officials to explain their determination to reduce federal transfers to the provinces. They contended that funds had to be diverted to reduce the spiralling federal deficit. Yet, it appears that the real purpose was to free up funds for new, highly "visible" forms of direct spending by Ottawa: in its own projections, the government's financial requirements were to fall from $10 billion in 1980-81 to $5.5 billion in 1983-84.[31] Likewise, the movement of economic activity to western Canada, in response to the soaring world price for oil, was cited as justification for the National Energy Policy. Officials argued that economic activity had to be stimulated in other parts of Canada, such as the North and offshore, in order to avoid important dislocative effects on the distribution of capital and labour. A more persuasive explanation of federal intervention, however, lies in the fact that these areas were outside provincial jurisdiction, were dubbed the "Canada Lands" by Ottawa, and thus economic activity would be taxed by the federal government alone.

In the last analysis, the new federal assertiveness was more than simply the result of the reorganization of federal institutions or an attempt to redress the problems of the Canadian economy. Its roots were fundamentally ideological. For Trudeau and for many of his colleagues, the primary purpose of political life always had been to implant a new conception of the Canadian political community and of the role the federal government should play as a "national government," the government of all Canadians. With their victory in the Quebec referendum, they had an unprecedented opportunity to put their ideas into effect. The past conventions of collaboration with the provinces could now be safely ignored.

Thus, in 1981 Trudeau declared that federal transfers to the provinces had to be radically altered so that Ottawa could undertake new projects of its own. On this basis, he declared, "We have stopped the momentum that would turn Canada into, in everything but name only, ten countries."[32] It was time, he said, to:

> reassert in our national policies that Canada is one country which must be capable of moving with unity of spirit and purpose towards shared goals. If Canada is indeed to be a nation, there must be a national will which is something more than the lowest common denominator among the desires of the provincial governments.[33]

It is clear that for Trudeau, as for many of his colleagues, the obstacle to such a Canadian "national will" lay first and foremost in Quebec and in the counter-project of a Quebec nation. Thus, it is not surprising that the new unilateral initiatives were aimed most frequently at Quebec. By the same token, it is not surprising that a primary concern of Ottawa's new initiatives was to establish a closer relationship between citizens and the federal government. Ottawa had long been preoccupied with its "visibility" in Quebec, fearing that through "opting out" and other arrangements that heightened the role of the Quebec government, Québécois had become estranged from the federal government.[34] Flush with a referendum victory based in part on media campaigns that extolled the many benefits of federal activity, federal officials were determined that this estrangement should never occur again. Any renewal of the federal system had to be compatible with this fundamental objective. The ultimate accord faithfully reflected this premise.

Finally, however, beyond the very heavy constraints that were placed on Quebec, the outcome also reflected the ineffective way the Quebec government itself handled the constitutional negotiations. The Lévesque government's position was, to be sure, an exceedingly awkward one in the post-referendum negotiations. Having sought without success to persuade Québécois that their collective aspirations could be met only if Quebec were to become a sovereign state, it now had to define and defend Quebec's interests within the Canadian federation.

Initially, it did so by turning to the positions on constitutional change articulated by previous Quebec governments. Accordingly, as negotiations got under way in the summer of 1980, Quebec insisted that repatriation must be linked to a substantial revision of the division of powers, including provincial ownership of offshore resources and control of communications. In addition, Quebec maintained, any constitutional declaration of principles must contain a recognition of Quebec's distinctiveness, there must be no entrenchment of linguistic rights (at least with respect to Quebec), and the Supreme Court should be reorganized to give Quebec justices equality within a constitutional bench or "near equality" within the Court as a whole.[35]

However, in April, 1981, apparently out of the fear that the federal government might otherwise be able to persuade the British House of Commons to approve its package of constitutional revision, thus diminishing provincial power with an entrenched charter, Quebec joined the seven other dissenting provinces in formally supporting repatriation if it were to be accompanied simply by a modified version of what had become known as "the Vancouver formula."[36] Under this formula, Quebec would not have a veto: constitutional amendment would require the support of any seven provinces, representing 50 per cent of the Canadian population. To be sure, under the formula, a dissenting province could opt out of any transfer of jurisdiction to the federal level, and still receive financial compensation. Nonetheless, never before had a Quebec government publicly endorsed an amendment formula in which Quebec did not have a veto over all forms of change in the constitution. Moreover, no previous Quebec government, at least within recent decades, had ever approved repatriation without an accompanying change in the division of powers.

In effect, through its actions the Lévesque government had itself sanctioned a "renewal" of the federal system in which the long-standing aspirations of Quebec nationalists were totally ignored. To be sure, the "common front" position to which it had subscribed had not entailed any curtailment of provincial jurisdiction through an entrenched charter. However, reflecting the priorities of the other provinces, neither had it involved an enhancement of provincial power. Having thus assimilated its position to that of the other provinces, the Quebec government was poorly placed to object when the other provinces reached their accord with the federal government. The deviations they accepted from the original interprovincial position do not seem to have transcending significance. With respect to the amending formula, the other provinces accepted that while a province could opt out of transfers of jurisdiction to the federal level, compensation would be restricted to transfers that involve "education and culture." (As it happens, transfers of any kind are unlikely in any event within the foreseeable future.) They did agree to a Charter of Rights and Freedoms, which restricts provincial governments' actions. Nonetheless, most of these provisions are subject to the "notwithstanding" clause. In the case of Quebec, many of these provisions bear restrictions that Quebec governments had already imposed on themselves through the Quebec Human Rights Act. The main exception is, of course, the provision for minority-language education. Yet, in its application to Quebec, this provision generally approximates the terms of Bill 101's "Canada clause."[37] As for the mobility provision, it will not, in any event, apply to Quebec within the foreseeable future given the exemption of provinces whose level of employment falls below the national average.

In terms of the historical aspirations of Quebec nationalists, the problem with the amendment formula is not the scope of "compensation" if Quebec opts out of transfers of jurisdiction but the absence of a Quebec veto over all forms of constitutional change: the Lévesque government had already conceded this. More generally, the failure of the constitutional revision, as "renewal" of Canadian federalism, is not so much in what it accomplished as in what it did not accomplish: to enhance the position of the Quebec government. This objective had been recognized, to varying degrees, by all previous Quebec governments in their proposals for constitutional reform just as it had been central to the Lévesque government's post-referendum proposals for a renewed federalism. But in subscribing to the "common front" position, the Lévesque government had itself renounced this goal, in the process making it easier for Ottawa and the other provinces to claim that they could fulfil "the promise" to Quebec with a constitutional revision that does nothing to enhance the status and powers of the Quebec government, let alone recognize it as a "national" state.

In the face of both the extent of its defeat and the evident contradictions of its own tactics, the Lévesque government had difficulty formulating a new strategy for defending Quebec's interests, even as a provincial government. Four years passed before, with an apparently more sympathetic government in Ottawa, the Lévesque government presented a new package for constitutional revision. There would be recognition of Quebec's existence as a people. Quebec would have exclusive jurisdiction over language, with statutory protection of English-language rights. With respect to the Charter of Rights and Freedoms, Quebec would be bound only by the "democratic rights." Quebec would have power of veto over modifications of federal institutions and the establishment of new provinces and would have a veto or receive full compensation with respect to changes in the division of powers. The federal spending power would be limited and the federal powers of disallowance and reservation eliminated. With respect to the division of powers, Quebec (and other interested provinces) would have: primary responsibility for manpower policy, economic development, and selection and settlement of immigrants; increased powers pertaining to communication; exclusive jurisdiction over marriage and divorce; and the right to international dealings on matters falling within its jurisdiction. Finally, with respect to the Supreme Court, three of the nine justices would come from Quebec, with sole authority in matters of civil law, and the Quebec government would participate in the appointment of Quebec judges. Also, the Quebec government would have authority to appoint judges to Quebec superior courts.[38]

It was hardly a radical document. By and large, Quebec was simply reintroducing notions of reform that had already surfaced in the discussions of "renewed federalism" of the late 1970s. Virtually all of Quebec's proposals could be found in either the Task Force on National Unity's *A Future Together* or the Quebec Liberal Party's *A New Canadian Federation*, or in both.[39] Nonetheless, times had changed: if English Canada had had some disposition to discuss such reforms in the late l970s, by the mid-1980s it clearly did not. The Quebec question and constitutional revision in general were viewed as closed.

In sum, during its second term in office the government of a party formally committed to Quebec independence had instead focused its efforts on trying to secure an improved position for Quebec within the existing political order. Even this reduced objective had continued to elude the PQ government, only in part because of its own ineptness. This result seemed to reinforce the conclusion that many neo-nationalists had already drawn from the referendum defeat: the dream of making Quebec a truly "national" state was effectively dead. As we shall see later, many militants began to vent their frustration on the party leadership, claiming that it had in effect traded the goal of independence for a "renewal" of the federal system. For these militants, a party founded on the ideal of Quebec sovereignty could legitimately

357

pursue nothing else, however bleak may be the immediate prospects of success. Before examining these developments within the party, however, we first need to explore how the second PQ government dealt with the other premise of the neo-nationalist project: the ideal of an interventionist, even social democratic, state.

The Interventionist State and Social Democracy

We saw in Chapter Seven how the ideal of an interventionist state had been central to the ideology of the Parti québécois, pervading the party program. At the same time, we saw how some party leaders and members had claimed that their project of state intervention was in fact "social democratic." For a good number of them, social democratic objectives were an essential condition of their support of the PQ and of the neo-nationalist project in general. To be sure, we also noted important qualifications to any PQ claim to social democratic status. The general ideology of the party effectively denied the salience of class relations, focusing on the nation as the essential collectivity and at most recognizing within that collectivity a wide variety of social and economic differentiations. By the same token, the party had no formal link with the union movement, in the manner of such social democratic parties as the New Democratic Party or the British Labour Party. In fact, Lévesque and his colleagues had repeatedly rejected such a linkage as a deviation from the party's fundamental purpose. Nor could it be said that the party had originated with working-class movements or organizations. In fact, we concluded for these reasons that the party's ideology, especially among the leadership, could be better classified as nationalist populist. Nonetheless, drawing primarily on the party program, one could at least make the argument that the PQ was a social democratic party. Thus, there was at least some reason to believe that a Parti québécois government might prove to be a social democratic one.

In Chapter Eight we found that by most measures the first PQ administration was considerably less interventionist than the party program would have suggested, though there were some significant initiatives. In fact, one could see the government's relative failure to curtail spending growth as proof of a lingering commitment to state intervention. Moreover, a good number of the initiatives could be classified as social democratic in inspiration: the nationalization of Asbestos Corporation; the establishment of public automobile insurance; social measures such as a limited guaranteed income scheme, free medication for the elderly, and free dental care for children; the anti-scab law and other provisions of Bill 45; and the convening of tripartite *sommets économiques*. Some of these measures were of quite limited scope and impact. In addition, there were serious difficulties in the administration's relations with organized labour, at least with the two public-sector unions, the CEQ and the CSN. They had bitterly denounced Bill 45 as inconsequential and had vigorously resisted Bill 59, which sought to modify public-sector labour relations. Nor did they participate with much enthusiasm in *sommets économiques,* given their fundamental suspicion of the Lévesque administration. Through considerable concessions, the government did secure a new public-sector collective agreement without being the object of major strike action. However, as we have seen, the CEQ's hostility to the PQ government was such that it refused to support the government in the referendum, even though securing this support apparently had been the primary purpose of the government's "generosity."

Nonetheless, one could at least make a case that the first Lévesque administration had provided social democratic government. By the end of the second PQ administration, it had become virtually impossible to make such a case. Indeed, there is little evidence of any interventionist thrust at all, let alone a social democratic one; in the process, the underlying nationalist populist ideology of the PQ was fully revealed.

Heightened Constraints on the PQ and the Quebec State

To a large extent this retreat from state intervention, especially of social democratic inspiration, can be understood in terms of the vastly heightened constraints on the Quebec state in the 1980s. In the early 1980s, the established notions of the neo-Keynesian welfare state came under sustained attack in most advanced capitalist societies, as a result of taxpayers' revolts and the ascendancy of neo-liberalist doctrines. At the same time, Western capitalism entered a protracted crisis that effectively narrowed the room for manoeuvre of all states; even authentically social democratic governments found themselves radically revising their policies. For instance, barely one year after its election François Mitterand's Socialist administration abandoned its strategy of state economic intervention, entailing the nationalization of major banking and industrial enterprises, and shifted to a *plan de rigeur* of austerity in public expenditures and reductions in taxation of business and high income earners.[40]

Clearly, the Quebec state was affected by these developments. By the early 1980s New York financial houses were taking a much harder look at the state of Quebec's public finances. They expressed concern about Quebec's mounting deficits and criticized the failure of the first Lévesque administration to pursue spending cuts with the same vigour as had other provinces in a similar predicament. Thus, in Quebec's case, the "fiscal crisis of the state" was especially acute. And the neo-liberal critiques of state intervention found strong echoes among Quebec intellectuals, as reflected in the appearance of new periodicals, such as *Analyste,* and in polemical essays on the state, such as Luc Bureau's *Entre l'éden et l'utopie.*[41]

More than a reflection of general trends, however, seems to have been involved: attacks on state intervention seem to have acquired a particular force in Quebec. In part this may reflect the vacuum created by defeat of the referendum. With the sudden collapse of the *souverainiste* project, the primary vehicle of state intervention in Quebec, the field was open for a new "counter-project." But the new disaffection with state intervention seems to have had a momentum of its own – already evident before the referendum. It may reflect the peculiarly high expectations of the Quebec state that marked the 1960s and 1970s – expectations that could never have been fully met even under the best of conditions. It may also be a reaction to the costs this state-building imposed as Quebec sought to create a modern, interventionist state despite a relatively weak economy. By the 1980s, this state-building project had resulted in Québécois being faced with a "tax effort" (the level to which available resources for taxation are actually exploited) that was 130 per cent of the Canadian average (in fact, 140 per cent in 1983). In 1983 it was 160 per cent of that in Ontario, the province Québécois customarily pick as the basis of comparison.[42]

In the last analysis, however, the new attack on the Quebec state must also have reflected changes within the structure of Quebec society itself. By the end of the 1970s, French Quebec clearly had acquired a viable capitalist class. One could identify a substantial number of large Francophone-owned and managed enterprises: the Banque national, Power Corporation, the Laurentian Group, and the Mouvement Desjardins in finance; Lavalin and snc in engineering; Bombardier in manufacturing; Provigo in food retailing; and Culinar in food-processing. Not only did these institutions assume first-rank positions within the Quebec economy but they were all becoming important actors on North American and even international markets.

To a very real extent, this development can be traced to the activities of the Quebec state. The various state initiatives of the 1960s to establish a Francophone presence in the Quebec economy did ultimately bear fruit, despite often disappointing initial results. The mere expansion in the state's role as a purchaser of goods and services was enormously beneficial to Francophone firms, given the general disposition of government officials to favour Francophone bids. (In the case of Hydro-Québec it was official policy to do so.) Thus, Bombardier's entry into the construction of mass transit equipment was the result of a $117 million contract it secured in the early 1970s to build cars for the Montreal subway.[43] SNC established its international credibility by building the Manic 5 dam in the 1960s; Lavalin earned an estimated $150 million through its participation in construction of the James Bay project.[44] In some instances, state officials had arranged for needed financing, as when in 1970 they induced the Mouvement Desjardins to buy most of the shares of Culinar, thus saving it from takeover by Beatrice Foods of the U.S. But in many cases, needed capital came fully or in part from the Quebec state itself. For instance, investments by the Caisse de dépôt et de placement were instrumental to the creation and growth of Provigo. The Caisse supported Bombardier's takeover of MLW-Worthington and, subsequently, the Société générale de financement secured a minority of shares in Bombardier. For that matter, the pool of capital with which Pierre Desmarais's Power Corporation launched its operations had been created through compensation to Power (then controlled by the Thomson family) for nationalization of Shawinigan Water & Power.

In fact, one can even identify among the chief officers of these and other firms individuals who had begun their careers within the Quebec state. The president of the Laurentian Group, Claude Castonguay, was a Quiet Revolution technocrat, responsible for conceiving the Quebec Pension Plan and for designing and implementing (as minister) a program of far-reaching reform of health and social services. Michel Bélanger was an assistant deputy minister of natural resources, under René Lévesque, and a deputy minister of trade and commerce before becoming president of the Montreal Stock Exchange and, ultimately, the head of the Banque nationale.

Nonetheless, despite their past close relationship with the Quebec state, Francophone businessmen became increasingly open in their criticism of the state's social and economic role. To be sure, many of them were not adverse to securing injections of capital

from such Quebec state institutions as the Caisse or Société générale de financement. But they were not dependent on such support.
Some of them, such as Lavalin and SNC, had become adept at
securing contracts from foreign governments, in many parts of the
world. And when Bombardier secured its $1 billion contract with
the New York City transit authority in 1982 it had arranged advantageous financing from an agency of the Canadian government. In
short, by the late 1970s Francophone capitalists had reached scales
of resources and operations where the Quebec state no longer had
any special importance. Not only did they not see any particular
interest of their own in an interventionist Quebec state but they
became increasingly critical of the social role the Quebec state had
assumed. In their eyes, the welfare state had become an insupport-
able burden – and they were increasingly prepared to call for its
retrenchment. As Claude Castonguay himself has declared:

> I've never believed in the idea of *l'état providence*. I believe
> wealth should be created, not just distributed. In Quebec, some
> basic steps, such as in health and education, had to be taken.
> But I think that the government went too far.[45]

Reflecting the impact of these growing pressures, the PQ government itself began to echo the new anti-statist discourse. Thus, in
his May, 1981, Inaugural Address Lévesque declared that during
his government's new term in office there would not be the rhythm
of new state initiatives that had marked the past:

> because we must keep reminding ourselves, and not only for this
> last year, that the times of unlimited growth are over. The same
> is true for automatic growth in the economy and, consequently,
> an equivalent growth in spending. Like all other societies, with-
> out exception, Quebec is now confronted by very visible limits
> from which it is absolutely impossible to escape. . . .
>   Thus, while maintaining and even accentuating the measures
> of [budgetary] reorganization and retrenchment that we have
> been pursuing since 1976, henceforth we will have to select with
> the greatest of care each of our new programs, knowing that it
> has become unthinkable to keep adding them to those which
> already exist, as was done in the past.[46]

At the same time, he made it clear that "just to the limit of the
margin of manoeuvre and the devices which are available to us,"
the permanent priority of the new mandate would be stimulation
of economic activity.[47]

In subsequent addresses, this change in attitude toward the Quebec state became more and more pronounced. More was involved than fiscal and other constraints on state action: the very efficacy of the Quebec state, as it had developed over the preceding decades, increasingly was placed in question. It needed to be regionalized and decentralized to make it more responsive to citizens. And it had to undergo a "weight loss treatment." To this end, in his 1983 address Lévesque proudly declared that two ministries were about to disappear, to be replaced by more efficient structures. Moreover, some organisms soon would be abolished outright, including the Conseil de planification et de développement du Québec (CDPQ).[48] There could be no clearer demonstration of the disaffection from *étatiste* notions of the interventionist state than the abolition of that body.[49]

With Lévesque's last Inaugural Address, in 1984, the transition was complete to a discourse in which Quebec's competitive position in the world economy is the transcending policy concern: "the complex and strongly competitive environment in which Quebec is placed and which dictates the conditions under which we can accomplish truly contemporary development." The state's role in improving Quebec's competitive position was not to intervene directly in the economy itself but to enable private enterprises to be as competitive as possible. This role involved, to be sure, state financial assistance of private enterprises, for which new programs were to be created, but it also involved a reassessment of all domains of state activity to ensure that they not weaken Quebec's competitive positions. Only in this way, in the Quebec of the 1980s, could new employment be found:

> we believe that the State has effectively reached its "cruising size" and that the creation of jobs depends primarily on the private sector. But we think that, as a consequence, we must play a more active role than ever in creating a fiscal, educational, legislative, and financial envirnonment able to liberate the private sector from certain economic and social rigidities, to promote the rapid and honourable resolution of differences between groups, and thus to heighten the competitive capacity of our enterprises, the only way in which employment can be increased on a lasting basis.[50]

The disaffection from the interventionist state, including one based on the social democratic model, could not be clearer. The change in orientation, moreover, was well reflected in the actual behaviour of the second Lévesque administration. We can trace its impact along the same dimensions of state activity with which we analysed the first PQ government.

Public Finances

With the 1980s, the Lévesque administration became firmly convinced that public expenditures could not be allowed to grow any further. If spending were to continue to increase, the government concluded, it would be forced to raise even further the level of taxation, given the inadequacies of other revenue sources. Yet, it had been coming under increasing pressure to *reduce* taxation. Thus, the consuming objective of the PQ government became one of reversing a trend that had fundamentally shaped the previous two decades of Quebec politics: the steady expansion of government spending and taxation. This objective certainly limited the possibilities for the Lévesque administration of undertaking new state initiatives of its own. But the consequences were even more profound. As we shall see, in seeking to achieve its objective the PQ government was led to adopt strategies that undermined once and for all its claim to be social democratic, and these strategies destroyed the party's primary electoral base: public-sector workers.

The PQ government had already sought to curtail spending growth during its first term in office. The government did bring the growth rate down from the mid-1970s highs, but it remained substantial. Over the four fiscal years that fall fully within the first Lévesque administration, as noted in Chapter Eight, spending growth averaged just over 14 per cent.[51] By the same token, the relative importance of public spending within Quebec's economy, as expressed as a proportion of the province's gross domestic product, had grown unabated during the first Lévesque administration, reaching an all-time high of 28 per cent in 1980-81.[52]

To finance this continued spending growth the Quebec government had been led to impose a level of taxation far exceeding that of the other provinces in order to maintain such an exceptional level of expenditure.[53] It could not draw on as high a level of provincial wealth as could such high-spending western Canadian provinces as Alberta. Nor could it rely on as high a level of per capita federal equalization payments as could such Atlantic provinces as Newfoundland. As a result, by the beginning of the PQ's second term in office, Quebec's public finances were in a quite exceptional state.

The new PQ government was convinced that this state of affairs could continue no more, that spending growth had to be cut once and for all. Thus, in his 1981-82 budget speech, after noting that during the previous fiscal year spending had risen more sharply than before, Finance Minister Parizeau stated that his government had resolved to alter this trend. "For the taxpayer," he declared, "no program is a sacred cow."[54] The following year, Parizeau reiterated his government's resolve while also declaring, ominously, that "we shall have to re-examine the collective argeements within the public sector, since after all they account for over half of the government's budget."[55]

This time around, the PQ government did indeed curtail spending growth. In 1983-84 the growth rate slipped to 8.42 per cent; in 1984-85 it fell to 3.98 per cent.[56] Moreover, for the first time since at least the 1950s, spending no longer grew as a proportion of gross domestic product: it levelled off at 30 per cent over 1982-83 and 1983-84. In 1983-84, it actually fell: to 29 per cent.[57] Ultimately, then, the PQ government had come to the same conviction as had the other provincial governments: the limits of state intervention, at least as measured by public spending and taxation, had been reached. In these terms, the second Lévesque administration was quite different from the first.

State Enterprises

Despite the prominence given state enterprises in the Parti québécois progam, we saw that during the first Lévesque administration only two major enterprises of note were created and, perhaps of more importance, the existing enterprises were subjected to a more severe evaluation than they had ever received in the past. This new, more critical stance toward state enterprises had been amply confirmed, moreover, in *Bâtir le Québec*, a comprehensive review of economic development policy published in 1979.[58]

The second Lévesque administration adhered even more closely to this new orientation. Existing state enterprises continued to be subjected to the demand that they be profitable. In his 1981-82 budget, after proudly declaring that all but one enterprise, the hapless SIDBEC, at last had achieved profitability, Parizeau went on to announce that in the future these enterprises would be expected to forward part of their profits to the Quebec treasury. Industrial or commercial enterprises that compete with private enterprises, such as Société générale de financement, Soquem, Rexfor, or Soquia, would be expected to transmit 20 per cent of their net income, along with the same taxes that are paid by private enterprises (except for the tax on profits).[59] As for Hydro-Québec, it had already been the subject of efforts by the Lévesque administration to reduce its autonomy, resulting in the passage in 1978 of Bill 41, which, among other things, gave the government power to appoint the enterprise's board of directors, along with its president.[60] In 1981, the Quebec government passed Bill 16, which was designed to force Hydro-Québec to pay annual dividends to the Minister of Finance, its sole shareholder, up to a maximum of 75 per cent of the available surplus.[61]

At the same time, the Lévesque administration sought to wind down the operations of some state enterprises or eliminate them outright. In some cases, these were enterprises that simply were not meeting the government's standards of profitability. A chronic instance was, of course, SIDBEC, which had shown a profit on only three occasions since its founding in 1968, running up total losses of over $600 million. In 1983, faced with SIDBEC's ever mounting need for additional government funds, Minister of Industry, Commerce and Tourism Rodrigue Biron declared that he would be only too pleased to act on the suggestion of the Quebec Chamber of Commerce that the enterprise be sold to private interests. But it was clear that there were no interested parties, apart from Canadian or U.S. competitors who would buy the enterprise only to phase out its operations.[62] SIDBEC was compelled to scale down its activities drastically. In October, 1984, its iron-ore mining operation, Sidbec-Normines, was closed down: the Lac Fire mine ceased operations and the Port-Cartier iron pellet operation was leased, for a symbolic dollar, to Quebec Cartier, a private firm with which Sidbec-Normines had collaborated. Henceforth, SIDBEC was to concentrate on what was left of its manufacturing facilities, whose own viability was far from assured.[63]

Another such case was of the Lévesque government's own making: la Société nationale de l'amiante and its subsidiary, la Société Asbestos. The enterprises were created through the Lévesque government's takeover of the American-controlled Asbestos Corporation, the largest asbestos producer in Quebec, and British-controlled Bell Asbestos, the smallest one.[64] Designed to give Quebec a virtual monopoly over asbestos production, the move was fatally undermined by a rapidly deteriorating international market. As a result, the SNA was registering ever increasing deficits, and some of the facilities acquired through the nationalization were closed or were left to operate well below capacity.[65]

Nonetheless, by its last year in office, the Lévesque administration was seriously contemplating the "privatization" of enterprises showing strong profits, in order to have their assets for other purposes (such as covering the provincial deficit). Finance Minister Yves Duhaime declared in his 1985-86 budget speech that:

> The strategic utility of certain government corporations has declined in recent years, to the extent that we may now ask ourselves if it is advisable to maintain the financial resources allocated to them. The government may simply recover part or all of the funds invested in order to achieve other goals. It goes without saying that these assets can only be sold provided the government obtains a fair value for them.[66]

As a case in point, he announced the government's intention to privatize la Société des alcools du Québec. For other enterprises, he proposed a partial privatization and proceeded to announce that a bill would be introduced to allow the sale to Québécois of preferred shares in Hydro-Québec. More generally, Duhaime claimed, state enterprises should be encouraged to collaborate closely with private enterprises acting in the same sphere of economic activity: "Today there are partners in the private sector capable of replacing the State, or of associating themselves with it in several sectors. A review of the objectives of government corporations will take this into account."[67]

In practice, "privatization" of state enterprises had some unforeseen complications. The declaration of the government's intention to privatize la Société des alcools du Québec engendered a strong reaction from the union representing the affected employees, despite government guarantees that their positions would be secure. As a consequence, the PQ government was unable to carry out its plan before falling from power. On the other hand, the government did pursue its "partial" privatization of Hydro-Québec. In the fall of 1985 a bill was introduced to authorize the Quebec government, Hydro-Québec's sole shareholder, to sell up to $400 million of its shares to Quebec investors.[68] For its part, la Société générale de financement announced in May, 1985, that it, too, would pursue a "partial" privatization. Its subsidiary, Dofor Inc., which had shares in some of SGF's more profitable enterprises, would soon be offering shares on the market.[69]

The second Lévesque administration was even less disposed than the first to create new state enterprises. The main instance is Québecair, which the Quebec government acquired in June, 1983, from a consortium of Francophone interests: Alfred Hamel, the Société d'Investissement Desjardins, and the Provost trucking group. But in this case the Lévesque administration appears to have created a state enterprise despite itself. The government had not actually sought ownership of the enterprise.[70] Rather, over the previous two years it had tried to make Québecair viable as a private operation under the Hamel-led consortium, investing $45 million in the process.[71] However, government leaders claimed, government takeover had become the only available alternative to Ottawa's plan of absorption of Québecair within Air Canada's operations.[72] While the initiative may have reflected the PQ government's continuing nationalism, as the opposition maintained, it did not reflect the commitment to direct state intervention that had in the past led to the creation of state enterprises, such as Hydro-Québec or even la Société nationale de l'amiante.

To be sure, beyond state enterprises, the Quebec government had available to it more subtle forms of intervention in the economy. Foremost among these was the Caisse de dépôt et de placement, whose pool of Quebec Pension Plan funds and related sources gave it assets of $25 billion (in 1986), more than any private investor in Canada. As we have seen, through most of its existence the Caisse had operated in the conventional manner for pension portfolios: making prudent investments in a wide variety of institutions but not seeking a controlling interest in any of them. To that extent it had frustrated neo-nationalists who had seen the Caisse as a vehicle for promoting Quebec's economic development, especially under Francophone leadership.[73] In 1980, Jean Campeau, the new director of the Caisse (and former assistant deputy minister of finance under Jacques Parizeau), announced that in the future his institution would indeed be "more active and quite aggressive" in promoting Quebec's economic development. Henceforth, unlike private pension funds, the Caisse would demand its full place on the boards of directors of firms in which it held considerable shares, and it would use this presence to make the operations of these firms more compatible with the interests of Quebec.[74] In addition, the Caisse appears to have decided to acquire much larger ownership shares in corporations than in the past.[75]

One object of this new strategy was Domtar. The Caisse joined forces with the la Société générale de financement with the result that between them they had secured 42 per cent of Domtar's shares in August, 1981.[76] They then requested a comparable proportion of places on Domtar's board of directors. On this basis they were able, among other things, to block Domtar's plan to move its head office to Toronto. Another target was Provigo: the Caisse increased its holdings to 30 per cent and demanded that its representation on the board of directors be increased accordingly.[77] It became the most important shareholder in Alcan, with 5.3 per cent of its ordinary shares.[78] But the Caisse's most notorious initiative involved Canadian Pacific: with 9 per cent of the shares, the Caisse became the largest single shareholder, once again demanding comparable representation on the firm's board of directors. This time, the Caisse's request was refused.[79] Claiming to speak on behalf of the heads of several large enterprises, including Stelco, Bell, the Royal Bank, the Bank of Montreal, Inco, and Dominion Textile, the president of Canadian Pacific wrote to none other than Prime Minister Pierre Trudeau to request that the Caisse be reined in.[80] The upshot was the federal government's introduction to the Canadian Senate of Bill S-31, designed to restrict provincial ownership in transportation enterprises.

While the Lévesque administration clearly encouraged the Caisse in it new aggressiveness and defended the Caisse when under attack, the government did not seek to make it a formal instrument of government policy, despite the expectations of some observers and, in fact, the positions the PQ itself had adopted in its opposition days.[81] Rather, the PQ left the Caisse formally autonomous from the Quebec government. As it happened, by the end of 1983 the Caisse had backed off from its new aggressive strategy and reverted to the customary mode of operation of a private pension fund. No longer was it seeking to secure *controlling* positions within firms or to influence their operations.[82] Apparently, by the end of the second Lévesque administration this form of state intervention in the Quebec economy had also run its course.

Economic and Social Well-Being

A key basis of the PQ's claim to social democratic status was, of course, its long-standing commitment to raise the social and economic well-being of all Québécois. As we saw in Chapter Nine, the first PQ government had introduced several such measures. However, the Lévesque administration's new determination to "restore order" to Quebec's public finances did not bode well for such concerns. Not only was the scope for new programs reduced, but there was the possibility that existing public services might be cut back. Accordingly, we need to examine in some detail where the cuts in spending tended to fall.[83]

During 1981-82, the government tended to focus on programs that had remained fairly marginal or were in decline. Thus, the cuts fell most heavily on the Ministry of Immigration and the Ministry of Consumers, Cooperatives and Financial Institutions and on such programs as: water purification, aid to farmers, road maintenance, recreation, l'Office des professions du Québec, and l'Office franco-Québécois pour la jeunesse. Conversely, there was a substantial increase in funds for industrial assistance (forestry and manufacturing), housing construction, and public works, along with Radio-Québec and the provincial police (whose contract had been renewed). For the most part, health and social services were not unduly affected.

With 1982-83, however, the government did cut spending in areas of social services. Family allowances were not indexed, the list of medications available to welfare recipients was reduced, and the surveillance of their income was increased. Dental services available to children were reduced and rents in public housing were increased. Nor did the government announce any new programs of significance in the social services area. Also, the government steadily reduced its commitment of funds to the guaranteed income scheme established in 1979. From the 1979-80 figure of $31 million the allocation had fallen in 1982-83 to $22.5 million.[84] Conversely, once again additional funds went to programs designed to promote economic development: industrial assistance, job creation, and residential construction.

In effect, then, the government's pattern of spending parallels quite closely the change in general orientation reflected in Lévesque's inaugural addresses. Social democratic objectives had indeed been traded for job creation and, in particular, for assistance to private enterprise.

This shift in priorities is even more clearly revealed when spending during the second PQ government as a whole is compared with that of the first PQ government. This can be done readily in terms of the four main "missions" defined by the Quebec government: economic; education and culture; social; and governmental and administrative. During the first PQ government, "education and culture" (96.4 per cent) had had the highest growth rate, with "social" (87 per cent) close behind. "Government and administration" (52.2 per cent) was substantially lower, with "economic" (32.4 per cent) a distant fourth. The pattern was reversed under the second PQ government. "Government and administration" experienced the highest growth rate (78.9 per cent), with the "economic" mission (73.5 per cent) a close second. The "social" mission (69.9 per cent) slipped to third place and "education and culture" fell far behind (38.6 per cent). In terms of specific programs, there were instances of substantial growth in all four missions. Nonetheless, the largest growth of all was in support for secondary industry, which rose by a remarkable 249.2 per cent during the second PQ government (it had grown by only 63 per cent during the first government).[85]

As this treatment of existing social programs would suggest, there were no major new social programs created during the second Lévesque administration other than the Corvée-habitation, a program of subsidies for first mortgages that was as much a means of stimulating economic recovery as a social measure.

This same retreat from social democratic objectives can also be seen in the Lévesque government's regulation of the minimum wage. Here, the policy in question did not involve major government expenditure. Rather than any "crisis" in Quebec's public finances, it was apparently the increasingly influential entreaties of business that swayed the government. During the first Bourassa regime, the minimum wage had been regularly indexed; in November, 1976, when the PQ assumed power, it had reached $2.87. For its part, the Quebec business milieu, especially as represented by the Conseil du patronat du Québec, had begun to argue vigorously against such use of the minimum wage as a social measure rather than as part of a general labour market policy. As we have seen, the first PQ government started out by resisting these pressures and continued to index the minimum wage. But in 1978 it abandoned this practice: henceforth, increases in the minimum wage fell well below the rate of inflation. In 1982, there was no increase at all in the minimum wage, despite inflation of 10.5 per cent.[86] In fact, the minimum wage remained frozen at $4.00 throughout the rest of the PQ's tenure in office. In June of 1985, the cabinet did agree in principle to raise the minimum wage; the government proposed to raise it by between 5 per cent and 10 per cent. But in the face of strong opposition from business groups the government left the proposal in limbo.[87]

Labour Relations

Probably the most important criterion for assessing the second PQ government's performance as a social democratic government is its treatment of organized labour. Here, the determination to reduce public spending was to have explosive consequences. Claiming that "excessive" public-sector salaries were the root cause of Quebec's continued spending growth, government leaders sought to reduce the proportion of expenditure consumed by salaries. The result was an all-out confrontation with the public-sector unions and the imposition of measures that were unprecedented in their withdrawal of the rights of union members.

According to the government's calculations, public-sector salaries represented 52 per cent of Quebec's total expenditures in 1982.[88] Officials claimed that this high proportion, higher than in other provinces, was a function of "excessive" compensation that Quebec public-sector workers were receiving, thanks to the militant tactics of their unions. As we saw, Parizeau had already evoked public-sector/private-sector compensation differences in the late 1970s. With the new drive to cut expenditures, such comparisons became the order of the day as the government published a variety of studies comparing public-sector workers with other categories of workers.

The results of the comparisons were far from conclusive. Typically, the studies compared public-sector workers, virtually all of whom were unionized, with *all* private-sector workers, many of whom were not unionized. In the nature of things, one would expect unionized workers to receive better compensation than non-unionized ones, whatever the sector of the economy in which they are employed. Other government studies sought to demonstrate that Quebec public-sector workers were being paid considerably more for the same functions than were their counterparts in other provinces. Yet, it was difficult to establish precise equivalence in functions. By the same token, attempts to show that Quebec workers were less "productive" than their counterparts were hampered by a failure to control adequately for differences in the quality of service rendered. For instance, if Quebec teachers were teaching fewer students per person than their Ontario counterparts, as government studies of teacher/student ratios seemed to demonstrate, then they may well have been teaching more effectively.[89] It became clear, though, that whatever the outcome of the vigorous debate these studies generated, government officials were firmly determined to reduce public-sector salaries as a proportion of total expenditures – by whatever means necessary.

On this basis, the Lévesque government felt warranted in taking unprecedented actions. First, citing the "crisis" in Quebec's public finances, in the fall of 1981 officials asked the public-sector unions to agree to forgo part of the pay increases they were to receive in 1982 under the existing collective agreement. In exchange the agreement would be prolonged for two years. After the unions refused to do so, the government announced that it would abide by these provisions after all. But it also declared that once the agreement had expired during the following three months it would reduce salaries by the amount necessary to recover the increases the public-sector unions had refused to forgo. At the same time, the right to strike was to be withdrawn from the public sector until April 1, 1983. In June, 1982, Bill 70 was passed to put these provisions into effect.

The government had hoped that this threat of a rollback, amounting to 25 per cent of salaries during the first three months of 1983, would induce the public-sector unions to adopt a more "reasonable" stance as, during the fall of 1982, they negotiated with the government the terms of the next three-year collective agreement.[90] Ultimately, however, dissatisfied with the pace of negotiations, the government imposed new collective agreements. Under Bill 105, passed in December, 1982, 109 collective agreements were imposed on the public-sector employees. Negotiations continued with respect to parapublic workers. By February, 1983, only the teachers, who had gone out on strike, remained without an agreement.

When the teachers overwhelmingly rejected a final government offer, the government introduced and had passed Bill 111, which was designed to force teachers back to work. As such, the statute provided that participation in illegal strikes could lead to: dismissal without possibility of recourse; reduction in salary; loss of seniority (at the rate of three years per day of unauthorized absence); and withdrawal of such union rights as dues deduction. Moreover, clause 28 stipulated that the Quebec Charter of Human Rights and Freedoms could not affect application of the law. (The Canadian Charter of Rights and Freedoms had been exempted through the PQ government's routine invocation of the notwithstanding clause.) The law was unprecedented in the scope of sanctions it introduced.[91] Section 28, with its nullification of the human rights charter, was denounced from many quarters, including the Quebec Bar Association, the president of the Quebec Human Rights Commission, the *bâtonnier* of Quebec, l'Association des avocats de la défense, and la Fédération internationale des droits de l'homme.[92] In the judgement of political scientist Gérard Bergeron, Bill 111 was "probably the harshest statute in Quebec history."[93]

In sum, in its dealings with public-sector workers the PQ government ended by adopting measures whose severity far exceeded those of any Quebec administration since the union-bashing days of Duplessis. Not only did it impose collective agreements and withdraw or restrict the right to strike, but it threatened illegal strike activity with wildly disproportionate sanctions.

Moreover, PQ leaders coupled these measures with a rhetoric that was clearly anti-union. Appealing to nationalist sentiments, Camille Laurin declared his outrage at this "assault on the Quebec state," the state "whose strength is necessary to the development of our identity."[94] For his part, René Lévesque declared that he welcomed the departure from the Parti québécois of militants who left in protest over Bill 111 and believed that they would be fully replaced by new members who are "normal people."[95] Rather than seeking to mollify the bill's critics, Lévesque went so far as to threaten to call an election over the issue.[96] Needless to say, the Lévesque administration had earned the undying opposition of the leaderships of the two public-sector unions: the CSN and the CEQ. We will argue below that while an effort to contain public-sector salaries was unavoidable given anxieties over the government's credit rating and mounting opposition in Quebec society, especially in the business community, to Quebec's exceptionally high levels of taxation, the intensity of the attack on public-sector unions can best be understood in ideological terms: it reflected the "nationalist populist" outlook of the PQ leaders.

Subsequently, the government moved to restructure public-sector industrial relations, reducing on a permanent basis the right to strike. Under Bill 37, passed in June, 1985, public and parapublic employees can use strike action to affect the determination of salaries for only the first year of an ageement. Salaries and related matters for the second and third years of an agreement (which cannot be less advantageous than those of the first year) are to be fixed by government regulation on the basis of the annual report of a government-appointed institute of research and information on remuneration. Also, the negotiation processes are substantially decentralized. Finally, requirements for essential services are strengthened, especially through granting additional powers to an Essential Services Council.[97]

With respect to the regulation of private-sector labour relations, the second Lévesque administration adopted quite a different stance. In 1983, the government passed Bill 17 to amend several aspects of the Quebec Labour Code despite the fierce opposition of Quebec businesses, some of which threatened to leave the province. Safeguards were strengthened against discrimination or reprisals by employers against employees exercising Labour Code rights, and union certification was facilitated. But the most important part of Bill 17, which was the focus of business hostility, was designed to strengthen the anti-scab law, which the PQ had itself established in 1977 as part of its Bill 45 reforms. Under Bill 17, during a legal strike employers are forbidden from substituting non-striking employees for strikers or from contracting out the work of strikers.[98] Also, in the same year, the PQ government established, through Bill 192, le Fonds de solidarité des travailleurs du Québec. Developed at the suggestion of the FTQ, the measure created a risk capital pool for investment in Quebec firms. The pool was to be created through salary deductions from FTQ members. For its part, the FTQ is entitled to appoint thirteen directors to le Fonds.[99]

Nonetheless, in any overall assessment of the extent to which the Lévesque administration was social democratic in its treatment of organized labour, primary weight has to be assigned to its public-sector dealings. There, the extraordinarily repressive measures and the open ideological attack on union leaderships clearly disqualify the PQ government from such a label.

Concertation

A final earmark of social democratic regimes is the commitment to state-sponsored collaboration between business and labour. As we saw in the previous chapter, the PQ government was indeed very active in its pursuit of *concertation*, organizing a large number of conferences to address aspects of the Quebec economy.

This effort continued during the second Lévesque government as well. Over the PQ's second term in office, the Quebec government organized twenty such conferences, including the third *sommet* conference on the state of the Quebec economy as a whole in 1982. Eleven conferences dealt with specific industries. One conference dealt with Quebec's international trade. Other conferences dealt with the economic condition of Quebec women, the problems of the handicapped, and the government's budgetary restraints in education and social affairs. Finally, four conferences addressed the problems of specific regions within Quebec.[100]

Yet, if the extent of this activity is impressive, the results, in terms of concrete accomplishments, are not. According to one close observer of the process, where these conferences have reached agreements "on the whole these have been of a rather pedestrian nature."[101] Certainly, they did not bring Quebec any closer to the "liberal corporatist" systems of European social democratic states.

Several factors explain this result. As elsewhere in Canada, the key actors in such an enterprise, business and labour, do not themselves have the degree of central organization that would allow representatives to speak with any authority on their behalf. Ideologically, business and labour groups are not prepared to accept the constraints upon their action that serious collaboration would entail. Nor is business fully prepared to recognize labour as an equal partner in any such enterprise. But the factor that ultimately impeded even the limited objective of *concertation* was the fundamental suspicion the two public-sector unions, the CSN and the CEQ, bore toward both class collaboration and the PQ government itself. Of course, this suspicion was transformed into outright confrontation in the wake of the 1983 public-sector crisis. These were hardly propitious conditions for the Quebec state to assume the mantle of a neutral intermediary among social actors. In fact, no *sommet économique* was called during the final three years of the PQ government.

Thus we can see that the tendencies already evident in the first PQ government became dominant with the second PQ government. The second government bore little resemblance at all to the model of state intervention the Parti québécois had championed so vigorously before its accession to power. Rather than expanding state activity the PQ government sought to contract it, whether through expenditure cutbacks or privatization of state enterprises. And it adopted a discourse that effectively removed the state from its privileged position within the PQ project as the central instrument of Quebec's economic and social development.

By the same token, there was little place within this new orientation for a specifically social democratic project. The cutbacks in spending for social and health programs and the virulence of the government's dealings with the public-sector unions effectively destroyed any remaining pretension to social democratic government. As it happened, the PQ government's measures to cut spending fell most heavily on what had always been the leading element among the Parti québécois militants and the most loyal component of the PQ's electoral clientele, the public-sector new middle class.[102] This was not forgotten, moreover, in subsequent by-elections, such as the one in Louis-Hébert where public-sector workers apparently were responsible for the stunning reversal of the PQ's standing, or in the general election of 1985, as we soon shall see. It is unusual, to say the least, for a government party to pursue policies so certain to alienate long-standing supporters.

Direct Support for Francophone Business

Not only did the second Lévesque administration effectively complete the retreat from social democratic pretensions that was already evident by the end of the first administration, but it was much more fully committed than was the first administration to reinforcing the position of business, especially Francophone business. In the words of one informed observer, "the Parti québécois became, after the referendum, the most business-oriented or market-oriented government in Canada."[103] We have already examined the much more aggressive actions of the Caisse de dépôt et de placement during the early 1980s. Two other developments need to be noted.

The PQ government had already introduced, in March, 1979, a new scheme to encourage investment in Quebec enterprises: the Régime d'épargne-action or REA (known in English as the Quebec Stock Savings Plan). The scheme allows payers of Quebec personal income tax to deduct the amount of purchases in new equity issues of Quebec-based companies. Initially, purchases in all such companies were treated equally. However, in 1983 the scheme was modified to favour smaller (thus, more likely Francophone) corporations. On this basis, it became a powerful tool for generating capital for Francophone enterprises. Between 1979 and 1987, it triggered about $5 billion in first-issue share purchases.[104] Thanks to this scheme, the number of new public companies listed on the Montreal Stock Exchange tripled between 1983 and 1987. By the same token, a number of major Francophone enterprises financed takeovers and expansion through the plan: SNC, Bombardier, Unigesco (which controls Provigo), and Quebecor (a publishing and newspaper conglomerate).[105]

One sector of Francophone business, the insurance industry, also received a powerful boost from another PQ innovation. Under Bill 75, introduced by Jacques Parizeau in June, 1984, Quebec was the first government in Canada to relax existing regulations to allow insurance companies to diversify into other areas, such as property management, mutual insurance companies, pension funds, and stock savings plans, and, through holding companies, into non-financial investments. Insurance companies are also allowed to take deposits from the public and make commercial loans. As a result, the Laurentian Group was able to acquire Eaton Financial Services of Toronto as well as Trident Life Assurance in England, three American insurance companies, and, indirectly, shares in Provigo.[106]

Explaining the PQ's Transformation

The steady retreat from the goal of Quebec sovereignty that marked the second Lévesque administration was parallelled by an even more drastic retreat from the second component of the neo-nationalist project: the ideal of an interventionist, even "social democratic" state. There was indeed little remaining of the PQ's neo-nationalist project. What forces could have led to such a dramatic departure from the party's founding ideals?

In large part, as we have already noted, this retreat from the neo-nationalist project can be explained in terms of the severe constraints with which the PQ government was confronted during its second term in office. With the referendum defeat, not only was the goal of Quebec sovereignty effectively shelved but Quebec's ability to secure any meaningful renewal of the federal political order was drastically reduced. By the same token, the crisis in the international capitalist economy clearly undercut the ability of most states to pursue interventionist policies, as the experience of the French Socialist government dramatically demonstrated. Nonetheless, it is not clear that these constraints required as radical a retreat as the PQ government undertook. After all, the referendum defeat did not require the PQ government to take the step we will see below: to collaborate openly with the Mulroney government and relegate sovereignty to no more than an "insurance policy." Nor did the economic crisis necessarily require such a concerted attack on the Quebec public sector. It is not at all clear that the pressures from financial circles warranted as drastic a measure as the 1983 rollback in public-sector salaries. In fact, according to some informed observers, the events surrounding the rollback precipitated the revision of the Quebec government's credit rating from AA to A.[107] Finally, it is not clear that the Quebec government's spending cutback had to fall so heavily on social services while sparing assistance to business, which in fact increased dramatically.

To explain fully the evolution of the second Lévesque government we need to go beyond the external constraints playing upon the government to examine the nature of the Parti québécois itself. As we have already noted, there was always a fundamental ambiguity surrounding the party's objectives. First, while declaring that Quebec needed the powers and resources of a sovereign state, the PQ linked sovereignty to a comprehensive economic association with the rest of Canada. Moreover, even this limited objective was pursued through an *étapiste* strategy in which Québécois could

378

avoid taking a position on Quebec sovereignty, *per se*, whether in electing a PQ government or in voting in the referendum. Second, while the party claimed to be social democratic, there were major qualifications to the claim. The party program contained a large number of specific provisions generally associated with social democratic parties. But the PQ did not emerge from working-class organizations, nor did it have a formal linkage with the union movement, through which it might be held accountable to working-class concerns. And the world view articulated by the party leadership refused to assign any privileged place to the working class, incorporating workers and all other social categories within the national collectivity. In the last analysis, it was more nationalist populist than social democratic.

These pervasive ambiguities can perhaps best be traced to the new-middle-class character of the party leadership and of so many of its militants. As we argued in Chapter Nine, the party's *étapiste* approach to Quebec sovereignty can be seen as the appropriate stance for a class that has already managed to secure an important position for itself under the existing political order. While the new middle class had every reason to welcome further incremental improvements in Quebec's status, it had no reason to risk the uncertainties of radical change. Likewise, the party's ambivalence toward organized labour is quite typical of new middle classes – at least the more privileged elements within them. As salaried professionals, they are not part of the capitalist class and, especially if they are based in the public sector, may be unlikely to identify closely with capital. But neither are they clearly part of the working class. As professionals, they can secure not only better income, but greater security and substantial personal autonomy.

As it happens, in the case of the PQ leadership, the ambiguities inherent to the structural position of the new middle class may well have been reinforced by the traits of such individuals as Claude Morin or René Lévesque. Of Lévesque, one associate has commented:

René Lévesque seems to me to have understood and empathized with the contradictions facing every Québécois which compel him to strive for liberation and at the same time prevent him from achieving it. This is why he himself oscillates between the light and the dark, impatience and confidence, tenderness and severity, scolding and the call to self-betterment, whenever he thinks to himself or talks to others. . . . This is why he is a symbol of contradiction in everyone's eyes, and an object of recognition, hatred, and love.[108]

In these terms, Lévesque was perhaps the ideal leader for a new-middle-class movement, as well as for a "colonized" people.

For these reasons, there may have been little disposition within the PQ leadership to resist aggressively the constraints that increasingly weighed on its neo-nationalist project. As well, whatever disposition might have existed must have been weakened by the cumulative impact on the party of the successive defeats the project encountered. Clearly, the referendum defeat led a good number of fervent *indépendantiste* militants simply to withdraw from the party and to abandon political action in general. Then, too, the government's inability to meet the expectations of committed social democrats led to their gradual marginalization within the party. This was certainly the case among social democratic party militants who, as we have seen, felt marginalized from the beginning of the party's assumption of power. It can even be seen within the leadership of the party. Robert Burns, the leader of social democratic forces, was the first to go: in 1979. Frustrated from the outset with his appointment as House Leader, an assignment apparently intended to neutralize his left-wing commitments, Burns was discouraged by what he perceived as a shift to the right in the government's policies.[109] Jacques Couture, who as the first PQ Minister of Labour had initiated the labour law reform of Bill 45, soon left the government, too. Pierre Marois resigned his position as Minister of Labour in November, 1983, exhausted by his years in office but apparently also discouraged by the welfare reform program the cabinet had imposed on him.[110] Denis Lazure remained in the government but saw his role steadily diminished from Minister of Social Affairs in 1976 to Minister of State for Social Development in 1981, to Minister Responsible for Citizen Relations in 1982.

This progressive marginalization of social democratic influences within the party leadership may in turn explain how the government was able to adopt such a repressive set of measures during the 1983 public-sector labour crisis. Social democrats who remained in the PQ caucus could do little else than try to disassociate themselves from the laws, whether by abstaining or by absenting themselves altogether from the National Assembly.[111] Of course, the crisis served to undermine even further what remained of a social democratic presence in the party.

For some observers, the PQ's loss of its social democratic veneer simply revealed its real nature as a party of the Francophone business class. While perhaps acknowledging that the most powerful elements in this class, fiercely federalist and increasingly *anti-étatiste*, see the Liberal Party as the logical defender of their interests, these observers point to the middle and lower ranges of this class: the famous *"petits et moyennes entreprises."* Clearly, the PQ government did initiate a variety of policies that benefited these enterprises, such as freezing the minimum wage and, in particular, vastly expanding industrial assistance programs, during the second Lévesque administration. Yet, in other areas, especially labour relations, the PQ government seemed to be responding to quite different interests. The reinforcement of the "anti-scab" law was bitterly opposed by Quebec business, small and medium-sized enterprises included. In vain, Charles Langlois, president of the Chambre de commerce du Québec, called on the Quebec government to give enterprises the means "to resist the unions" rather than reinforcing their powers under the Labour Code.[112] In a survey of participants at the 1984 annual congress of the Chambre de commerce de Montréal, 51 per cent declared that if they were to establish a new plant they would prefer to do so outside Quebec. This sentiment was based primarily on opposition to Quebec's labour laws.

Despite the departure of social democratic elements, especially those linked to the public-sector unions, the Parti québécois remained a multi-class coalition. The middle and lower levels of the Quebec business class may well have exercised influence, especially with the early 1980s, but they were not alone. The strengthening of the "anti-scab" law and such measures as the Fonds de solidarité speak to the influence of the private-sector unions, especially the FTQ, within the party. Also, despite the loss of public-sector workers, the PQ continued to reflect the aspirations and preoccupations of the highest levels of the Quebec state structure: the state technocrats, for lack of a better term. In seeking to reduce the proportion of Quebec expenditures locked into public-sector salaries, the PQ government was at the same time seeking to strengthen the ability of state officials to themselves shape the pattern of spending. Moreover, by its second term in office the PQ had attracted new elements to its coalition among small-town and rural voters.

This revised PQ coalition was even more congruent with the nationalist populist ideology that characterized the PQ leadership's general outlook. Quebec nationalism, albeit in a diluted form, was reflected in many of the government's preoccupations, such as the defence of Quebec's provincial autonomy, however inept it may have been, or the staging of *sommets économiques* designed to uncover, if not create, a national consensus. If it is more difficult to find populist reforms during the second Lévesque administration, populist assumptions certainly underpinned the government's attack on the public-sector unions. Government leaders regularly declared that the public-sector unions had fallen under the control of radical self-perpetuating elites that not only were out of touch with their own members but were totally oblivious to the needs of the "average" Québécois. By the same token, there was a strongly nationalist thrust to this attack: no force was to be allowed to challenge the authority of the Quebec state, the central institution of the Quebec nation. In fact, Bill 111, concerned as it was with striking teachers, may even have reflected lingering resentment over the failure of the CEQ to call for a "Yes" vote in the 1980 referendum.

Finally, beyond ambiguities in the party's basic commitment to the neo-nationalist project, the government's steady retreat from the project also can be traced to the normal effects of holding political office. As we argued earlier, moderation of policies and objectives is in fact typical of most movements for radical change once they have assumed office within the established order. Party leaders become accustomed to the privileges of office, the gulf between leaders and militants widens, and disillusioned activists drift away to be replaced by newcomers who are more attracted by the rewards of holding office than by the movement's founding ideals. With time, the party's agenda narrows to a preoccupation primarily with securing re-election.

Revolt within the Parti Québécois

What is rather remarkable about the Parti québécois is the extent to which, despite the normal moderating effects of holding office coupled with the heavy constraints weighing on its overriding project, important elements in the party were still bound to its founding objectives. If during the early 1980s substantial numbers of militants, and even some leaders, left the party out of frustration with the PQ government's failure to achieve any form of "national" status for Quebec and with its gradual renunciation of the interventionist state, especially a social democratic one, others were not yet prepared to abandon the PQ. However, loyal as they were to the party's founding ideals, their frustration steadily mounted with each new disappointment. Contradiction between the ideals of a social movement and the exigencies of routine electoral politics produced a crisis that convulsed the party.

Parti québécois conventions had, in fact, always been marked by open conflicts, between militants on one side and Lévesque and his colleagues on the other, over questions such as English-language school rights, access to abortion, or even the strategy to be pursued in securing sovereignty. Each time, Lévesque ultimately had prevailed, often by threatening to resign, and the militants had more or less rallied around his leadership. The December, 1981, convention ended differently. Rage over the referendum defeat and Quebec's fate in the constitutional negotiations was such that Lévesque lost control of the delegates. Determined to renounce once and for all the *étapiste* strategy the government had been pursuing, militants passed a resolution declaring that Quebec's accession to sovereignty would no longer be conditional on first securing an economic association with the rest of Canada. Moreover, they passed another resolution declaring that in the future a parliamentary majority would constitute a sufficient mandate to declare Quebec sovereign; a majority of the popular vote would not be necessary nor, for that matter, would a referendum. To undo these measures, the party leadership had to circumvent the party convention by organizing a special referendum of the full party membership which, by 95 per cent, reaffirmed the principles: accession to sovereignty by democratic means, the desirability (although not necessity) of an economic association with the rest of Canada, and respect for cultural and ethnic minorities within Quebec.[113] Nonetheless, two years later at the next party convention, the delegates overwhelmingly approved a resolution declaring that in the next election "a vote for a Parti québécois candidate will mean a vote for Quebec sovereignty." Once again, Lévesque had been unable to prevail over convention delegates.

However, fully aware of survey findings that the PQ could substantially reduce the gap separating it from the Liberals if it were to distance itself from the goal of sovereignty, Lévesque seized on the September, 1984, election of the Mulroney Conservative government in Ottawa. Citing Mulroney's professed determination to replace the federal-provincial acrimony of the Trudeau years with a national "reconciliation," Lévesque announced at a PQ national council meeting on September 22 that his government was prepared to enter negotiations with Ottawa and the other provinces over Quebec's adherence to the new Canadian constitution. Lévesque candidly acknowledged if it were to be successful such a stance could undermine the PQ's fundamental cause of Quebec sovereignty. But he was not deterred by the prospect:

> And if the Conservative government's collaboration should improve, would that not run the risk of stifling our fundamental option and relegating sovereignty to oblivion? Obviously, there's an element of risk. But it's a beautiful risk.[114]

Lévesque reiterated his government's intent in his October Inaugural Address.

While he did not say as much, Lévesque's new stance seemed to contradict the party's formal commitment to fight the next election on the question of Quebec sovereignty. By the end of October, open debate erupted within the party over precisely that question. In mid-November Lévesque declared that a special party convention would be necessary to adopt a new strategy for the next election. Under this new strategy sovereignty would not be at stake in any manner, directly or indirectly. In fact, his statement relegated sovereignty, which would remain the party's ideal, to the status of an insurance policy, *"la suprême police d'assurance"* – something to be held in reserve for an emergency rather than to be pursued for itself.[115]

Not surprisingly, Lévesque's declarations engendered bitter opposition among militants, who viewed them as yet another deviation from the pursuit of Quebec independence. What is surprising, perhaps, is the extent to which Lévesque's position aroused opposition within the very leadership of the party. After all, Lévesque's interventions could be seen as a normal response to the electoral pressures with which the party found itself confronted. Most other movements that have assumed office within ongoing democratic structures ultimately have sought to distance themselves, in one fashion or another, from their founding ideology. Party leaders who are themselves ensconced within cabinet usually have every reason to encourage such departures. In the case of the Parti québécois, more recent comers to the caucus and cabinet did indeed support Lévesque's stance: for them it stood to reason that the party's position should be revised in order to improve the party's desperate electoral situation. But many of the founding leaders of the party had no patience for such electorally motivated revisionism. For them, it was better to risk electoral defeat than to renounce the party's *raison d'être*. Ultimately, seven members of the cabinet, including two of the most powerful, resigned their positions: Jacques Parizeau, Camille Laurin, Gilbert Paquette,

Jacques Léonard, Denise Leblanc-Bantey, Louise Harel, and Denis Lazure. Four of them resigned either from the PQ caucus or from the National Assembly altogether. At a special party convention the following January, Lévesque's new position was indeed adopted. But the exodus of party militants continued, and Lévesque's own sometimes bizarre behaviour mirrored the steady disintegration the party had undergone.[116]

The episode demonstrated that even after eight years in power the Parti québécois had not yet completed the transition from social movement to political party, and government party, at least with respect to the fundamental goal of sovereignty if not the objective of "social democracy." In that, the experience of the PQ is quite remarkable. Nonetheless, redefinition of party position is the usual outcome of the contradictions faced by any social movement once in power. By December, 1985, when the Parti québécois finally faced the electorate under its new leader, Pierre-Marc Johnson, the son of former Union nationale leader and premier, Daniel Johnson, the transition had indeed been completed.

1985 Election

The party conceived an electoral strategy with the basic objective of dissociating the PQ from the Lévesque administration, and especially from its earlier phase as a social movement committed to Quebec sovereignty. Accordingly, primary stress was placed on the personality of the new leader and the implication that the Liberals, under Bourassa, offered an old, already discredited leadership. In the process, even the party name and logo were reduced to marginal status in campaign publicity. By the same token, other party figures were left only limited roles to play.[117]

Thus, the PQ campaign bore little trace of the ideological traditions of the party. No attention at all was given to the goal of sovereignty other than to cite the official party position that a referendum would not be held during a new PQ administration.

Nor was there much discussion of the PQ government's proposals for constitutional reform. In fact, the PQ campaign devoted little attention to any issues of real substance. When Pierre-Marc Johnson did address issues in his campaign appearances, as in his debate with Robert Bourassa, it was difficult to discern real differences between the PQ positions and those of the Liberals. Not surprisingly, then, a survey analysis of the attitudes of PQ and Liberal supporters found no major difference in their positions on such matters as government assistance of public enterprise, social assistance for youth, users' fees for public services, or free trade with the United States.[118]

Similarly, differences in the characteristics of voters for the two parties were less pronounced than in the past. Among Francophones, PQ voters remained differentiated by higher levels of education and lower levels of religious practice but they were not as sharply differentiated by age as they had been at the time of the 1981 election. Other past differences disappeared completely. In particular, this was true of both unionization and the sector of employment: public vs. private. Clearly, the party had lost its strongest electoral base: public-sector workers.[119]

This development had in fact been augured by events during the campaign itself. When Manpower Minister Pauline Marois attempted to explain the government's behaviour during a Quebec City election meeting, she was met with a vigorous round of boos. For its part, le Syndicat des professionels de l'État went to the length of publishing during the campaign a manifesto accusing the PQ government of betraying civil servants and constituting nothing less than a menace to the public service.[120] Not surprisingly, when, during the campaign, public-sector workers were asked their opinion on the government's 1982-83 measures, 68 per cent declared that they were opposed. More surprising perhaps is the extent to which this attitude was shared in the general population: 57 per cent were opposed. At the same time, private-sector workers were somewhat less likely to be critical (half were opposed), a reflection perhaps of the extent to which the PQ government had actively cultivated links with the FTQ and, in general, sought to capitalize on the inevitable tensions between private- and public-sector workers.[121]

In purely electoral terms, the strategy was a "rational" one. Johnson was indeed a popular leader: when asked in which leader they had greater overall confidence, 58 per cent of respondents to one survey cited Johnson, with 42 per cent citing Bourassa.[122] To a certain degree, moreover, the strategy worked. The personal popularity of Johnson alone could not have kept the PQ in power, given both the accumulation of voter dissatisfaction with the Lévesque administration and the deterioration of the PQ's party organization after so many internal conflicts. But it at least saved the PQ from the total disaster that might have occurred if the election had been held a year earlier. With a popular vote of 38 per cent, the Parti québécois secured twenty-four of the 122 National Assembly seats. For their part, the Liberals received 56 per cent of the popular vote and a commanding majority of ninety-eight seats.

Nonetheless, whatever may have been its electoral efficacy, the campaign strategy carried a price: the final abandonment of the party's ideological roots. The party had reached the ultimate logic of the strategy of *étapisme*, with its concern to dissociate assuming office from Quebec's accession to independence.

The Legacy of Parti Québécois Government: Rehabilitating the Existing Political Order

In terms of the fundamental objectives the Parti québécois had set for itself prior to assuming office, the record of nine years of PQ government is a mixed one at best. Clearly, the PQ government failed in what had always been viewed as the party's fundamental purpose: to make Quebec a fully sovereign state. In fact, during the PQ tenure even Quebec's position within the federal system was weakened, thanks to the Constitution Act, 1982. The PQ administration was the first Quebec government to have this distinction since the Godbout regime of the early 1940s, which had subscribed to the federal government's wartime tax arrangements.

Also, despite the long-standing commitment to a strongly interventionist state with a social democratic thrust that had underpinned the PQ's *souverainiste* project, there were relatively few initiatives during the PQ regime that seriously expanded the economic or social role of the Quebec state. Especially striking is the case of state enterprises, that dramatic form of state intervention which had so marked the Quiet Revolution. Not only did the PQ government create very few new enterprises, but by the second term in office its primary concern was with identifying which of the existing ones might be candidates for privatization.

Nonetheless, the PQ government did undertake some important reforms of Quebec's political institutions. While they may not have constituted central objectives of the party, the measures have had major effects on Quebec society. One such reform is Bill 2, passed in 1977, which sought to reform party financing through major new regulations. Another is the reform of municipal finances. By the same token, we have seen how Bill 45 introduced groundbreaking changes to the regulation of Quebec's private-sector labour relations. In addition, the PQ government introduced some limited programs of social reform, such as public automobile insurance and income supplementation for the working poor.

However, the single reform probably most clearly identified with the PQ government is Bill 101, the revision of Quebec's language legislation. We have argued that in most respects Bill 101 merely tightened up or reinforced provisions the Bourassa regime had already established through its Bill 22: the privileged status of French within government institutions, as the sole official language, was vastly reinforced; access to English-language schools was to be based on mother tongue rather than on language tests; and private-sector *francisation* programs were to be compulsory rather than voluntary. Nonetheless, beyond these added "teeth," Quebec's language law acquired a new credibility simply because the PQ was itself clearly committed to French priority within Quebec. In addition, as we have noted, Bill 101 did differ from Bill 22 in certain respects that were bound to have great importance to Quebec nationalists. First, in determining access to English-language schools, the law used the boundaries of Quebec rather than Canada as the reference point. Second, it imposed French-language obligations on municipal and parapublic institutions that Bill 22 had spared out of deference to the English-Canadian community. Finally, through requiring that all public signs and commercial advertising be in French only, Bill 101 sought to alter the images Québécois saw in their everyday life.

In the course of the second PQ administration, some of Bill 101's innovations were eliminated. In one instance, the PQ government itself modified the law. In 1983 Gérald Godin, Minister of Cultural Communities and Immigration, secured changes in Bill 101 to allow for institutional bilingualism in English-language schools, hospitals, and social services agencies. In other cases, modifications were imposed by the courts, thanks in part to the new Charter of Rights and Freedoms. Confirming previous judgements of Quebec's Superior Court and Court of Appeal, the Canadian Supreme Court declared in July, 1984, that under the Charter access to Quebec's English-language schools had to be extended to children of whom a parent was educated in English in any part of Canada, not just Quebec. And in December, 1986, the Quebec Court of Appeal confirmed a 1984 decision of the Quebec Superior Court by declaring that Bill 101's requirement that public advertising, as well as company names, be exclusively in French contravened not only the Charter but even Quebec's own Charter of Human Rights and Freedoms. While the Quebec legislature could require that French be used in public advertising, it could not prohibit use of English. In 1979, the Supreme Court had already declared unconstitutional the bill's restriction on English in legislative documents and in judicial proceedings.

Many of the changes introduced by Bill 101 remained in force, however, and have affected Quebec society in fundamental ways.

Most important perhaps is the bill's regulation of access to English-language schools on the basis of mother tongue rather than the results of language tests, as under Bill 22. The efficacy of this provision is reflected in the radical drop in the proportion of first-grade students in Montreal schools who are in English-language institutions: from 40 per cent in 1977 to 26.5 per cent in 1985.[123] In fact, it has been estimated that by the early 1990s Montreal English-language schools will contain only 24 per cent of Montreal Island's school population.[124] The Charter of Rights and Freedoms will have little concrete effect on this part of Bill 101 since the Charter guarantees access to English-language schools only for children of whom a parent was educated in English in Canada; it provides no such access to Quebec's "allophone" population.

In a sense, it is ironic that Bill 101 should stand as perhaps the greatest accomplishment of the PQ government. As we have seen, René Lévesque and others in the cabinet had always been ill at ease with legislation to regulate language use in Quebec and had sought to weaken such provisions as the restriction of access to English-language schooling to children of parents who were educated in English in Quebec alone, as opposed to the whole of Canada. Lévesque and others had insisted that the proper route to resolving Quebec's language problems was Quebec sovereignty; these problems, they contended, would largely disappear with Quebec's transition to sovereignty.

To further compound the irony, Bill 101 may well have served to reduce the likelihood of Quebec ever achieving sovereignty. We have argued that by appearing to resolve the language question through provincial legislation, Bill 101 may have served to rehabilitate the federal system in the eyes of some Québécois.

In fact, Bill 101 is not the only feature of the PQ tenure in office that may have had that effect. For instance, through the Cullen-Couture Accord, the PQ secured for Quebec nothing less than the right to select immigrants. Moreover, the very fact that a party formally dedicated to Quebec independence was nonetheless allowed to secure office through democratic processes may have made the existing political order appear a little less hostile to the distinctive aspirations of Québécois. Likewise, the fact that committed *indépendantistes* were prepared to devote so much of their energies simply to pursuing the normal responsibilities of a provincial government may have helped to demonstrate that within the existing federal system provincial powers and resources are no small matter.

As we have already noted, the Parti québécois is only one of many movements which, upon assuming power within an order they are ostensibly committed to alter radically, instead have served through their actions to give that order a new legitimacy. In fact, rather than transforming the existing system, the movement is itself transformed by the constraints and rewards of holding office. Thus, a party created to secure Quebec sovereignty ultimately becomes committed to collaborating with the federal government, because it detects a certain openness in a newly elected Prime Minister. And a party committed to creating "social democracy" through state intervention finds itself devoted to creating the climate needed to "liberate" private business.

CHAPTER ELEVEN

The "Normalization" of the Quebec State? The New Bourassa Regime

With the return to power of the Bourassa Liberals, there were strong reasons to expect that the Quebec state, and its role in Quebec society, would undergo fundamental changes. After all, the new government was based on a very different configuration of social forces than had been its Parti québécois predecessor. Most obviously, it had a strong link to English-speaking Quebec. Beyond that, it had close links with the Anglophone business community and much firmer links with Francophone business than the PQ had ever been able to establish. In recent years, moreover, Francophone business had itself become a much stronger force in Quebec society. Uniting these various forces was the expectation that "their" new government would act to "normalize" the Quebec state, both in its relations with the rest of Canada and in the role it played within Quebec economy and society. In effect, the new Quebec government was expected to reverse some of the major accomplishments of its PQ predecessors. In some quarters there was even pressure on the Bourassa government to dismantle some of the main achievements of the Quiet Revolution. Quebec was to become much more of a province like the others.

There were at least three different ways in which Liberal supporters expected the Quebec state to be "normalized." First, it meant normalizing Quebec's position within the federal system. Toward the end of its tenure, the PQ government had already re-established a working relationship with the federal government, under the Mulroney Progressive Conservatives, but the question of Quebec's constitutional status remained unresolved. Second, normalizing the Quebec state meant reducing the role it played in the Quebec society and economy so as to approximate the role played by other provincial states, most notably Ontario. To be sure, the PQ government had begun to reduce this role, but substantial differences remained, whether in levels of spending and taxation, in the importance of state enterprises, or in the relative advantages of the union movement under labour relations law. Finally, especially for Quebec Anglophones, normalization meant relaxing if not eliminating outright Bill 101's regulation of language practices in the province.

The different social bases of the Bourassa Liberals were evident in the patterns of electoral support. Whereas the Liberals split the Francophone vote almost evenly with the Parti québécois, they received the overwhelming majority of Anglophone votes (about 90 per cent) and allophone votes (about 80 per cent). Supporters of the two parties also differed in terms of religious practice, with the more faithful Francophones supporting the Liberals, and occupation, with the Liberal Party drawing less well than the PQ among working-class Francophones. The two clienteles were less well differentiated along some other variables than they had been in the past: thanks to the PQ's alienation of public-sector workers, the public sector/private sector split was not as pronounced as it had been in the past nor were the voters clearly differentiated in terms of age.[1] Nonetheless, the pronounced role of non-Francophones within the Liberal clientele, coupled with the role of more traditional Francophones, should have been sufficient to generate quite different pressures on the Quebec government than had been the case under the Parti québécois.

The difference in social bases was also revealed in the composition of the Bourassa government itself. Compared with its PQ predecessors, the new Liberal cabinet was, of course, especially striking for the relatively high number of Anglophones: four. However, even more significant are the differences in the previous occupational and institutional bases of the cabinet members. Whereas new-middle-class categories had constituted the overwhelming majority of PQ cabinets, especially the first one, they were in the minority in the new Liberal cabinet: 44 per cent. Instead, the majority of cabinet members were from old-middle-class careers such as law or notary (30 per cent) or the business world (26 per cent). Especially striking are the past positions as senior corporate executives: vice-president of Power Corporation, vice-president of Provigo, vice-president of the Bank of Montreal, and president of an engineering firm.[2] As for the new-middle-class members, most of their backgrounds are markedly different from those of their *péquiste* counterparts. For instance, of three university professors the only social scientist specializes in business administration; the other two are in law.[3] Of two economists, one is a former vice-president of the Chambre de commerce de Montréal;[4] the other is Bourassa himself.[5]

Yet, while these social forces supporting and composing the Liberal government may have been committed to the project of "normalizing" the Quebec state, there were major obstacles facing each aspect of it. With respect to Quebec's constitutional status, not only did the question arouse little interest in the rest of the country but Quebec's bargaining position was at an all-time low. As for any concerted attempt to roll back the economic and social role of the Quebec state, the fact remained that through the 1960s and 1970s many Québécois, especially Francophones, had become strongly committed to intervention by the Quebec state; many of them were heavily dependent on it. They could be expected to defend vigorously the role the Quebec state had assumed. By the same token, Bill 101 had acquired a high legitimacy among many Francophones; any attempt to alter it would be bound to encounter strong, organized resistance. Thus, if the Bourassa government may have had a clear mandate from its supporters to normalize the Quebec state, there were genuine constraints on any serious attempt to pursue the mandate. If the Parti québécois government had found itself heavily constrained in its efforts to expand the role of the Quebec state to that of national state, so the Bourassa regime was to find itself constrained in its effort to contract the Quebec state's role to that of a province.

In the early days, the new government did commit itself fully to these various goals. Soon after the election Bourassa proclaimed that "Henceforth it is to the state as a catalyst, not an entrepreneur, that will fall the responsibility to create a favourable climate for entrepreneurship." By the same token, he expressed a desire that Quebec's constitutional limbo be resolved within his government's mandate: "This is without doubt a question that will have to be addressed quite rapidly."[6] Days later, in his Inaugural Address, Bourassa reiterated the constitutional commitment while elaborating a strategy of economic revival centred on private enterprise. Declaring that "[private] enterprise is the crucible of technological change," the address outlined a series of measures designed to strengthen private enterprises, including a more stable political climate, tax reform, infrastructure investment, and support for export development and research. For the same reason, the government committed itself to programs of deregulation, privatization of state enterprises, and the "rationalization" of public spending. The government declared that through this host of measures to enable private enterprise to assume its proper role, 400,000 new jobs would be created by 1990. While the Inaugural Address did close with a commitment to improve the quality of health and social services and even to improve support for the arts, its conception of the economic role of the state could not have adhered more closely to neo-liberal tenets.[7]

Nonetheless, even if the new government were committed to these objectives, the question still remained as to how aggressively it would pursue them, especially if they should engender serious opposition. Bourassa and his colleagues were also very much committed to remaining in office, now that it had finally been recovered.

Quebec and the Constitution

The most dramatic way in which Quebec was in an "abnormal" position relative to the other provinces was, of course, with respect to the constitution. Throughout its second term in office the Lévesque government had persisted in its initial refusal to sign the constitutional accord reached between Ottawa and all the other provinces in 1981. To be sure, legally Quebec was bound by the Constitution Act, 1982. The Supreme Court had established that fact when, in the spring of 1982, it had rejected Quebec's claim that, by convention, it had to be signatory to any constitutional revision. But the absence of Quebec's formal adherence to the constitution was a continuing embarrassment. Moreover, there was fear in some quarters that with time it could have much worse consequences, serving to stimulate a revival of *indépendantiste* sentiment in Quebec. For its part, the Trudeau government had been quite ready to live with this state of affairs, claiming that one could not in any event hope to reach a reasonable accommodation with a "separatist" government. With the election of the Bourassa government, of course, this argument could no longer be made.

Upon the Bourassa Liberals' assumption of power, conditions still were not very favourable to a meaningful accommodation of Quebec's historical conditions for signing a new constitution. Quebec's bargaining position continued to be weak. The consistent position of Quebec governments in the 1960s and 1970s had always been that repatriation had to be accompanied by a substantial enlargement of Quebec's powers, if not those of all the provinces. But the Lévesque government's subscription to the interprovincial "common front" constitutional proposals of April, 1981, had undermined any such claim. In effect, Quebec had been ready to accept a constitutional repatriation in which the division of powers would be unchanged. While four years later the Lévesque government did return to the traditional Quebec position, linking adherence to the constitution with substantial additional powers, the damage had been done. If even a PQ government had been prepared to dissociate adherence to the constitution from a major expansion in Quebec's powers, it would be exceedingly difficult for a Liberal government to insist that the two be linked. Even more importantly, with the 1980 referendum defeat Quebec governments could no longer employ what had been during the 1960s and 1970s their ultimate argument for serious change in the federal order: the need to undercut the movement for Quebec independence.

Nonetheless, Quebec's formal constitutional status was an obvious piece of unfinished business and the Bourassa government was generally committed to discharging it. There was the hope, moreover, that English Canada might be more accommodating to a Quebec government squarely committed to Canadian federalism. Therefore, soon after its election the Bourassa government sought to signal this commitment by abandoning the PQ government's practice of automatically attaching to all legislation an invocation of the notwithstanding clause of the Charter of Rights and Freedoms. It continued, however, the Lévesque government's policy of refusing to participate in all first ministers conferences focusing on constitutional revision.

More importantly, the Bourassa government produced its own proposal for constitutional revision. The proposal was rather modest in scope, reflecting the government's desire to reach an accord despite Quebec's weak bargaining position. Basically, the government set out five conditions for its formal adhesion to the constitution: a Quebec veto over constitutional change; formal recognition of Quebec's status as a distinct society; limitation of the federal government's use of its spending power in provincial jurisdictions; participation in nominations to the Supreme Court; and recognition of Quebec's existing role in immigration. None of the provisions would involve the transfer of jurisdiction from Ottawa to Quebec, or to the other provinces. Compared with the proposals of previous Quebec governments, it was a slim package indeed.

Despite the Bourassa regime's effort to initiate constitutional discussions there was little evident interest among English-Canadian elites in the matter. To be sure, there was some desire to reward the Bourassa government, and Quebec, for its formal commitment to Canadian federalism. In some quarters, there was also a recognition that Bourassa's proposals were indeed relatively modest and that Quebec's bargaining position was weak. In these terms, then, there could not be a better time to secure Quebec's adhesion to the constitution. But the matter clearly was not a major priority with the other provincial governments.

However, for the federal government, accommodating Quebec had acquired a certain urgency with the arrival of the Mulroney Conservatives in power. Eager to dissociate itself from the "rigid" approach to federalism of the Trudeau years and anxious to solidify support among Québécois for the Canadian federal order, as well as for the federal Conservative Party, Mulroney and his colleagues were determined to secure Quebec's official inclusion in the constitution and had made an election commitment to that effect. To this end, the new Prime Minister actively sought to persuade the provincial premiers to accept an ageement and even sought, to the extent necessary, to accommodate their demands as well in the process.

The result of these efforts was the Meech Lake Accord, reached among the first ministers on April 30, 1987. Subsequently, on June 4, the ministers agreed to a somewhat revised specification of the Accord in formal legal language (generally known as the Langevin accord).[8]

The Meech Lake Accord clearly reflects the conditions we have just outlined. In keeping with Quebec's weak bargaining position and the Bourassa government's correspondingly limited set of proposals, the Accord is quite modest in scope, despite some claims to the contrary. At the same time, it also reflects the need to accommodate at least minimally some of the concerns of the other provinces in order for them to accept Quebec's proposals.

Basically, the Accord reduces to six measures. Each is quite limited in substance; some are carefully circumscribed within the text itself. Probably the most important provision in terms of any accommodation of Quebec is the declaration that Quebec constitutes a "distinct society." The Accord declares that the constitution should be interpreted in a manner consistent with "the recognition that Quebec constitutes within Canada a distinct society." Moreover, it then affirms that "the role of the Legislature and Government of Quebec is to preserve and promote the distinct identity of Quebec" referred to in the above section. However, recognition of a distinct Quebec society is carefully qualified by invocation of a linguistic duality that transcends Quebec's boundaries. The preceding provision declares that the constitution is to be interpreted in a manner consistent with "The recognition that the existence of French-speaking Canadians, centred in Quebec but also present elsewhere in Canada, and English-speaking Canadians, concentrated outside Quebec but also present in Quebec, constitutes a fundamental characteristic of Canada." Moreover, Parliament and the provincial legislatures are given the role of preserving this "fundamental characteristic."[9]

Beyond that, these various statements are followed by the declaration that they are not to diminish the powers of either the federal government or the provincial governments.[10] On this basis, it is difficult to see how the "distinct society" provision could enable the Quebec government to assume any jurisdictions exclusively held by the federal government. A more likely possibility is that the provision could limit the degree to which Quebec's existing jurisdictions can be restricted through application of the Charter.

In instances such as Bill 101 this could be quite significant. Conceivably, the "distinct society" clause might lead the courts to accept restrictions as reasonable that otherwise would have been seen to violate provisions of the Charter (although the courts would also need to weigh the import of a clause referring to the presence of English-speaking Canadians in Quebec). A case in point would be Bill 101's restriction of public advertising to French only – a provision Quebec courts have found to be in violation of the Charter's protection of freedom of speech. To be sure, Quebec could also avoid such a judgement by resorting to its notwithstanding clause: the main provision of the Charter from which Quebec cannot otherwise escape through the notwithstanding clause, other than the "democratic" rights and the "equality" clause, is the provision regarding access to English-language schools.[11] But this could be a politically awkward route to follow.

A second area of the Accord has to do with immigration. The preamble of the Accord declares that the federal government and Quebec should conclude an ageement that would "incorporate the principles of the Cullen-Couture agreement" on the selection of independent immigrants and a variety of other categories of candidates for admission to the country. In effect, then, the Meech Lake document simply recognizes intergovernmental arrangements that have already developed (during the Trudeau regime, in fact) within the existing federal order. Immigration is a jurisdiction that, under the terms of Confederation, Ottawa must share in any event with the provinces. As with the Cullen-Couture arrangements, the candidates for admission that Quebec selects would still need to meet standards set by the federal government in such matters as health and security. Unlike the Cullen-Couture agreement, the new agreement also would assign Quebec the right to assume responsibility for the "integration" of immigrants. But it would still leave intact Ottawa's exclusive responsibility for awarding citizenship. The new agreement also would add the guarantee that Quebec would receive a proportion of the annual totals for immigrants set by Ottawa that would be equivalent to its share of the Canadian population, with the right to exceed that amount by 5 per cent. But the Accord places no restriction on the movement of immigrants to another province once they have arrived.[12]

A third area is the federal government's use of its spending power within provincial jurisdictions. Here, the Accord declares that if a provincial government should decide not to participate in a shared-cost program the federal government establishes within exclusive provincial jurisdiction, then the province should be given "reasonable compensation" by Ottawa. Nonetheless, the Accord carefully stipulates that to be entitled to such compensation the province would need to maintain a "program or initiative" of its own which is "compatible with the national objectives."[13] These national objectives are to be specified by the federal government. An example of such a "national objective" that provinces would have to meet to receive federal funds would be the Canada Health Act's ban on extra-billing. Thus, Ottawa would still be in a position to structure significantly how provincial governments act within exclusive provincial jurisdictions. By the same token, under the Accord Ottawa would still be free to establish on its own any spending program that it wishes within exclusive provincial jurisdictions.

The Accord also deals with the Supreme Court. First, it stipulates that three of the nine justices must be from Quebec. But this simply recognizes a standing provision of the Supreme Court Act. Second, the Accord specifies that provincial governments may be allowed to draw up lists of candidates for appointment to the Supreme Court. But the actual appointment is to be made by the federal government, which is bound to choose among names submitted by the provinces. In the case of the three justices from Quebec, the choice must be made from among names submitted by the Quebec government. Nonetheless, there is nothing in the Accord that obliges Ottawa to choose from the first list submitted to it. If dissatisfied with those names, it could insist on further lists until a satisfactory name emerges. In effect, rather than handing over Supreme Court appointments to Quebec and the other provinces, as some observers have alleged, the Accord creates a double-veto system. Since the justices are appointed for life (until age seventy-five), the provincial governments and the federal government can have no direct influence over how justices actually adjudicate the cases before them. Thus it is incorrect to declare, as has one leading opponent, that the Accord "transfers supreme judicial power to the provinces."[14]

With respect to the Senate the Accord gives provincial governments the right to present Ottawa with lists of candidates for appointment. Once again, a double-veto system is created. Moreover, as with Supreme Court justices, senators are appointed for life (to age seventy-five) rather than for fixed terms. Thus, they would be no more beholden to the provincial government that included them in its list than, for that matter, to the federal government that selected them from the list.[15]

Finally, the Accord alters the amending formula so that amendments involving several very specific matters (certain aspects of Parliament and the Supreme Court, plus the creation of new provinces or extension of existing ones) would require the support of all provinces rather than seven provinces representing 50 per cent of the population, as is presently the case. In addition, "reasonable compensation" to provinces not agreeing to transfers of jurisdiction to the federal level will no longer be restricted to matters involving education and culture, as it is under the 1982 agreement.[16]

Also, in explicit recognition of the concerns of provinces other than Quebec, the Accord calls for a constitutional conference at least once each year. The Accord stipulates that the agenda of these conferences shall include Senate reform, an Alberta demand, and jurisdiction over fisheries, a Newfoundland demand.[17] For that matter, the provision for provincial participation in the appointment of members of the present Senate is itself a response to the demands of other provinces. It did not figure in the Quebec government's original proposal.

The Meech Lake Accord does respond, to be sure, to each of the five issues raised in the Bourassa government's proposal, although in some cases the responses are highly circumscribed. But, as we have seen, the Bourassa proposal was itself highly modest relative to past Quebec proposals. In fact, the Meech Lake Accord falls within the same general limits as did the 1971 Victoria Charter, which Bourassa ultimately rejected as inadequate.[18] Therefore, the Accord reflects quite faithfully Quebec's weakened position since the 1980 referendum. Moreover, it can be seen as the logical outcome of the PQ's 1981 adoption of the common front accord.

Given its limited scope, it is surprising that the Accord has aroused such virulent opposition. In a dramatic public statement, former Prime Minister Pierre Trudeau declared that the measure "will render the Canadian state totally impotent," destined "to eventually be governed by eunuchs." In fact, he claimed that the Accord places Canada on the "fast track" to sovereignty-association.[19] Similar cries came from Toronto academics. One claimed that the Accord would usher in the "deconfederation" of Canada and would "emasculate" the Canadian state. Another declared the Accord to be no less than a "subversion" of the Canadian nation. A third warned that the Accord could lead to a day when Ottawa would be left with little more than responsibility for defence and the post office. A Toronto publisher, Robert Fulford, denounced Mulroney for "surrendering Canada."[20] Not to be outdone, a western Canadian political scientist, president of the Canada West Foundation, denounced the Accord's provisions as "the political equivalent of the AIDS virus," in that its implications are initially innocuous but eventually will be debilitating for Canada.[21]

The explanation of such apocalyptic reaction lies not in the measures themselves, which certainly do not warrant it, but in the premises underlying them. Modest as it may be, the Accord is very clearly rooted in the notion that Canada is an inherently federal political order. In addition, of course, one of its provisions declares Quebec to be a distinct society.

As such, the Accord explicitly denies an alternative vision of Canada: a *national* community, in which only the federal state is the legitimate expression of a national will. This is a vision of Canada which, as the reaction to the Meech Lake Acord demonstrates, has had a surprising degree of tenacity. Only within this essentially unitary perspective might one conclude that the alleged shift of power to the provinces could "render the Canadian state totally impotent" – as if the provinces and their premiers were not themselves part of the Canadian political order. By the same token, only if the Supreme Court should be seen as the possession of the "national" government might it seem so totally unacceptable that the provincial governments be involved in the selection of its members. Within a federalist perspective, it might seem quite appropriate that the members of a body charged with adjudicating disputes between governments should be named by both of the parties to the disputes rather than one of them alone. And only if Ottawa is seen as the true "national" government might it seem "subversive" to limit the extent to which Ottawa can prescribe how provincial governments spend money within their exclusive jurisdictions. Finally, and most importantly, only if one sees Canada as a supremely national collectivity could it be so offensive to recognize the obvious fact of Quebec's distinctness.

An opinion survey taken three weeks after the Meech Lake meeting suggests that while most English-speaking Canadians shared a strong attachment to national political institutions, their attachment was not so extreme as to preclude acceptance of the Accord. The majority of respondents declared they were prepared to accept the Accord even though they apparently thought that Mulroney had given up too much to the provinces.[22] Evidently, their approval of the Accord was motivated not by a desire to see the provinces strengthened but by a wish to see resolved at last Quebec's adhesion to the constitution. When asked whether they would prefer "a strong national government" or "strong provincial governments and not as strong a national government," in each of the predominantly Anglophone regions overwhelming majorities opted for a strong national government: B.C. – 67.8 per cent; Prairies – 64.2 per cent; Ontario – 75.4 per cent; and Atlantic Canada – 66.9 per cent. Thus, even in western Canada there is a strong attachment to the federal government, despite all the apparent manifestations of "western alienation."

At the same time, in a graphic demonstration of the extent to which English-speaking Canadians and Quebec Francophones remain divided in their primary political allegiances, 57 per cent of Quebec respondents opted for a strong provincial government while only 40 per cent opted for a strong national government. (One can presume that among Francophone respondents alone, support for the provincial government was even higher.) Thus, after all the events of recent years, including the collapse of Quebec neo-nationalism, this fundamental feature of Canadian political life is as present as ever.

Not surprisingly, among the specific provisions of the Meech Lake Accord, the one to receive the lowest level of support among all respondents (46.3 per cent) is the recognition of Quebec as a distinct society. Similarly, in a survey taken shortly after the Langevin version of the Accord was reached, 56 per cent of respondents outside Quebec disapproved of the provision. In fact, close to a majority of respondents in both the West (47 per cent) and Ontario (46 per cent) and 38 per cent of respondents in Atlantic Canada agreed that the Accord gave too much to Quebec.[23]

Given the demonstrated persistence among Quebec Francophones of a strong attachment to their provincial government, one

401

might have expected the Accord to be poorly received in Quebec. Certainly, its provisions fall far short of the proposals for a "renewed federalism" that circulated in Quebec and Canada during the late 1970s and which had been the basis for the pre-referendum promises that a "No" vote would be rewarded with major changes in the federal order. No major figure in Quebec provincial politics would have dared make such a modest proposal then.

Central to the 1970s proposals, and to all proposals from Quebec governments in recent decades, had been a substantial transfer of jurisdictions to the provincial level. The Meech Lake Accord transfers none. Moreover, proposals such as the Quebec Liberal Party's Beige Paper would have gone much further in the areas where the Meech Lake Accord does introduce change.[24] For example, with the Beige Paper proposals for the Supreme Court, constitutional matters would, upon request, have been adjudicated by a special bench, half of whose members would be Quebec justices. And the Senate would have been replaced by a new Federal Council whose members are appointed exclusively by the provinces and who would be expected to act as instructed delegates of the governments that appointed them. Among other things, the Council would be charged with ratifying Supreme Court appointments. Federal use of the spending power would have been radically circumscribed: consent of two-thirds of the members of the Federal Council would have been necessary for any program and even then a dissenting province could opt out with compensation. For that matter, the report of the federal government's own Pépin-Robarts Task Force on National Unity would have gone much further still.[25] Quebec (and all the other provinces) would have been free of any constitutional requirements whatsoever regarding its linguistic minority. It would have had near-equality (five out of eleven) in the number of Supreme Court justices. Compared to proposals such as these, the Meech Lake Accord seems rather tame.

As one would expect, the Accord did receive harsh judgements from some long-standing *indépendantiste* elements in Quebec. Jacques-Yvan Morin, a major figure in Lévesque's cabinets, denounced the Accord as a "trap." Quebec would secure no additional powers (he cited as proof a federal official's reassurances to English Canada to that effect) and would be sacrificing its bargaining power in the process.[26] And Jacques Parizeau pronounced the Accord unacceptable, constituting a major setback to Quebec's traditional demands.[27] By the same token, the Accord was denounced by the Société Saint-Jean Baptiste and the Mouvement national québécois, which sought to rally public support for their position. PQ leader Pierre-Marc Johnson, too, bitterly denounced the Accord, claiming that Bourassa had "sold the house" at well below the market value. On this basis, he was able to rally the party's Conseil national behind his leadership.[28] In this case, however, the attack was not entirely credible since there was little evident distance between the Meech Lake Accord and the PQ's emerging policy of "national affirmation."

However, most elements in French Quebec were generally satisfied with the measure. For instance, in a survey taken just after the Langevin version had been reached, 61 per cent of the Quebec respondents declared that they approved the agreement, and only 16 per cent said that they disapproved.[29] This general satisfaction was true not just of federalists who were prepared to overlook the obvious shortcomings of the Accord when compared with the models of "renewed federalism" they had championed in the late 1970s.[30] It was even true of individuals who had played key roles in the PQ government. Louis Bernard, who had been the senior civil servant under Lévesque, and Jean-K. Samson, who had been a constitutional adviser to Lévesque, both served on a committee of the Bourassa government charged with preparing a legal version of the Accord.

In fact, René Lévesque himself was ambiguous in his assessment of the Accord. Initially, he declared that the Accord was "neither very good nor catastrophic," noting in particular that progress had been made with respect to immigration.[31] It was only days before the first ministers reconvened to settle on the legal version of the Accord that Lévesque declared that the Accord should not be signed unless certain ambiguities were to be resolved. Even then the issue for Lévesque was the inadequacy of certain measures that appear in the Accord rather than all the other matters which, although they had been part of Quebec's historical position, the Accord ignores completely.[32] Apparently, even for Lévesque, the general framework of the Accord was a satisfactory basis for Quebec's adhesion to the constitution. This appears also to have been the sentiment of his Intergovernmental Affairs Minister, Claude Morin.[33]

The apparent receptiveness to the Meech Lake Accord among even some elements of the past *péquiste* leadership could be interpreted in two ways. It could be seen as a reflection of the degree to which expectations of any accommodation of Quebec had been severely battered by the referendum defeat and the 1981 constitutional fiasco. In such a context, such provisions of the Accord as the declaration that Quebec is a "distinct society," however devoid of any real significance, may have come as a welcome surprise. However, the apparent readiness of such leaders as Lévesque and Morin, but not Jacques Parizeau or Jacques-Yvan Morin, to reconcile themselves to such a limited accommodation of Quebec may also betray the extent to which their advocacy of Quebec sovereignty in the 1970s may have reflected less a commitment to sovereignty itself, as an objective, than a reaction to the intransigence of the federal government, under Trudeau, to *any* serious accommodation of the Quebec government within the federal system. The virulence of Trudeau's denunciation of the Meech Lake Accord gave a clear intimation of what Quebec leaders must have been up against in the 1970s.

Economic and Social Role of the Quebec State: Rolling Back the Quiet Revolution

Beyond normalizing Quebec's status within the Canadian constitution, the new Bourassa regime was under strong pressure to normalize the role the Quebec state played in the economy and social affairs of Quebec. We know that business leaders in Quebec, both Francophone and Anglophone, were regularly denouncing such distinctive aspects of the Quebec state as its network of state enterprises, greater than that of any other province, its labour legislation, which in some instances was more progressive than anywhere else in North America, and its singularly high level of taxation. In addition, many elements within Anglophone Quebec clearly had a particular grievance against aspects of Bill 101, if not against the very notion of protecting French through regulation. Not only were business leaders, and Quebec Anglophones in general, strong supporters of the Liberal Party but, as we have seen, they were very much present within the Bourassa government itself, both in the caucus and in the cabinet. In fact, Bourassa had signalled his commitment to reducing the role of the state by creating a Minister of Privatization, Pierre Fortier, and by giving his parliamentary assistant, Reed Scowen, special responsibility for deregulation.

In the summer of 1986, seven months after the election of the Bourassa government, the pressures to "roll back" the Quebec state took very palpable form with the release of three reports the government had commissioned in the wake of its election. Each dealt with a central aspect of the Quebec state: its functions and structures; its network of state enterprises; and its regulatory role. The committees that prepared the reports were composed essentially of business leaders and private-sector professionals, such as accountants and lawyers, to the total exclusion of representatives of other economic and social interests, such as organized labour, consumers, cultural groups, or social service beneficiaries. There was none of the pretension to balanced representation or *concertation*, which had been so important to the PQ. Not surprisingly, then, each of the committees took its cue entirely from the private sector, seeking to apply business notions of efficiency and viability to the state and to free the private sector from the "dead hand" of state intervention. Thatcher's Britain and Reagan's United States were freely cited as the models Quebec should follow in these unabashed applications of neo-liberal logic. The result was a truly remarkable agenda for radically altering the role of the Quebec state. If the reports were to be implemented, then Quebec's role would indeed be reduced to that of the other provinces. In fact, it would be considerably less than that of some provinces. In the process many, if not all, of the most significant initiatives of the Quiet Revolution, and of succeeding Quebec governments, would disappear.

The task force on government functions and structures, headed by Treasury Board President Paul Gobeil and drawing on the Board's technical support, contained leading members of the Francophone business class, who in the past also held important positions in the Quebec bureaucracy: Michel Bélanger, chairman of the board of the Banque national; Pierre Lortie, former president of the Montreal Stock Exchange and current president of Quebec's largest food retail enterprise (Provigo); and Yvon Marcoux, vice-president of the Montreal City and District Savings Bank. An additional member was Jean-Claude Rivest, political adviser to Robert Bourassa.

Generally known as the Gobeil Report, the document called for a sweeping reduction in state structures. Up to 100 agencies would be abolished or merged with other bodies. Among those to be abolished outright would be Radio-Québec; two of the organisms that oversee language matters under Bill 101; and a large number of research institutes. Quebec would revert to the practice of the other provinces and allow Ottawa to collect its personal income tax, renouncing in the process the most important nationalist achievement of the 1950s. Many cultural institutions would be transferred to public or private entities at the local level. All medium and small hospitals, and some larger ones, would be turned over to the private sector. If their use of medical and hospital services in a given year should exceed $2,000, individuals would pay a tax or user fee. A voucher system would be introduced to primary and secondary education and university fees would be raised by 20 to 25 per cent. At the same time, faithful to its theme of paring down the state, the report also called for the abolition of subsidies to large corporations and the revision of subsidies to smaller businesses. The state bureaucracy would itself be pared down through the elimination by 25 per cent of senior executive positions.[34] Finally, over twenty consultative organisms attached to various government branches would be abolished. The committee thought it sufficient for a department to rely on surveys and *ad hoc* measures of its own device to determine public attitudes toward its activities. Nothing reveals more clearly the attitude of the committee toward the political process than this summary dismissal of the elaborate structures for balanced popular "participation" in government that previous administrations, especially the PQ, had so carefully developed.[35]

For its part, the advisory committee on privatization was no less sweeping in its proposals, going so far as to declare the Quiet Revolution to be dead. Under the chairmanship of lawyer Roger Beaulieu, the committee included business leaders Claude Castonguay, president of The Laurentian Group insurance companies (and former Quebec senior civil servant and Minister of Social Affairs), J.V. Raymond Cyr, president of Bell Canada, and Diane Marcellin-Laurin of Steinberg's, as well as accountants Marcel Bélanger and Herbert E. Siblin. The committee proposed that no less than ten of the Quebec state's large commercial and industrial enterprises should be privatized, including: la Société générale de financement, SIDBEC, SOQUEM (which promotes mining exploration), SOQUIP (petroleum exploration and development), Québec-air, and SNA (the asbestos operations the PQ had nationalized). Beyond that, the committee proposed that state enterprises based on "natural monopolies" should be thoroughly re-examined with a view to modifying their structures, although not necessarily privatizing them. Among these enterprises the committee included: la Caisse de dépôt et de placement, Loto-Québec, la Société des alcools, and even Hydro-Québec. Finally, with respect to thirty enterprises dependent on state subsidization, such as Radio-Québec, Office du crédit agricole, and the Régie des installations olympiques, the committee suggested that many should be privatized or transformed into non-profit corporations. In short, the committee sought to reduce drastically the network of state enterprises that had emerged over the last twenty-five years. In fact, it was quite explicit in contending that with the emergence of a strong base of

Francophone entrepreneurs and managers, many of the state enterprises had outlived their usefulness:

> It is clear to us that between now and the year 2000 the dynamism of Québécois enterprises and entrepreneurs will be the principal determining element of Quebec's economic development. The Quiet Revolution has done its job: it has bequeathed us a strong and dynamic private sector. Now it is time to turn the page.[36]

The committee did think that as a general rule the enterprises should pass into Quebec hands, although this should not be an absolute objective. In fact, it declared that "A certain degree of external control is normal in Quebec," as long as Quebec interests are themselves securing a similar presence outside Quebec. In some cases, the committee acknowledged, privatization would lead to the elimination of jobs. But such is the price for making enterprises competitive and profitable. Ultimately, the committee reasoned, employment would be created.[37]

As for the committee on deregulation, its report was explicitly derived from the premise that Quebec's state role must be no greater than that which exists elsewhere. The proper functioning of the Quebec economy, they argued, demands this: "Economic progress and job creation demand that the impact of our social regulation be comparable to what prevails among our Canadian and foreign competitors."[38]

Needless to say, given this approach to state regulation, the committee was itself dominated by business leaders: Sébastien Allard, past president of the Conseil du patronat du Québec; Pierre Clément, president of the Quebec section of the Canadian Federation of Independent Businesses; Serge Racine, president of Shermag; and Anne-Lise Brien, an administrator of small and medium-sized businesses. In addition, the committee contained two lawyers, Reynold Langlois and René Dussault (also a professor), and economist Jean-Luc Migué, the leading promoter of neo-liberal public choice theory in French Quebec. Clearly, with such a committee there was little likelihood that state regulation would be assessed in terms of social or cultural objectives. All that mattered was its presumed impact on private investment.

Thus, the committee went about identifying areas in which regulation was more onerous for Quebec business than was regulation in other jurisdictions. The key comparison was with Ontario. In fact, the committee's mandate from Premier Bourassa had explicitly called for this: "to formulate recommendations designed to place Quebec enterprises in a position which is at least as advantageous as that of Ontario" with respect to the impact of regulations on their productivity.[39] On this basis, they produced ninety-three recommendations. In particular, they called for a major overhaul of regulations concerned with occupational health and safety, claiming that these regulations were perceived by business as the most costly and restrictive of all. And they pointed to labour relations legislation, attacking in particular the restrictions on use of strikebreakers and on contracting out during a strike – regulations they claimed alter the balance between employers and unions. Quebec's regime, they argued, should be made to conform with that of the other provinces. Also, the committee called for abolition of the other major distinguishing feature of Quebec's labour law: judicial extensions of collective agreements to industrial sectors. And it sought to eliminate Quebec's elaborate system for regulating labour relations in the construction industry. Finally, the report called for gradual deregulation of the housing construction industry and of trucking and inter-city bus transportation and for the abolition of the power of professional corporations to set fees for such groups as surveyors and notaries. These reforms, they contended, would constitute the strongest job creation program proposed in Quebec in many years.[40]

In short, the three reports clearly reflected the thinking of Quebec's now ascendant Francophone business class. In the past, Francophone business had always been ambivalent about the economic initiatives of the Quebec state, supporting some, such as la Société générale de financement, but opposing others, such as the 1963 expansion of Hydro-Québec. There is no trace of ambivalence now. Large Francophone businesses may have needed the Quebec state's intervention on their behalf in the 1960s and even the 1970s, but they see no such need now. If only for this reason, Francophone business no longer needs to tolerate many of the forms of state support for other social categories that have emerged over the last two decades. Thus, it could give the Bourassa Liberals a firm mandate for the radical rollback of the Quebec state.

Nonetheless, however desirous Bourassa and his colleagues may have been to act on this mandate, there were potential hazards in doing so. After all, Francophone business had not been the only beneficiary of the expansion of the Quebec state. Nor had it been the primary force calling for that expansion, some recent analyses to the contrary. Other elements in Quebec, which played critical roles in the 1960s movement for political modernization, continued to rely heavily on state intervention. For new-middle-class and working-class Francophones based in the public sector, for Francophone intellectuals in general, for private-sector workers, and for the variety of people dependent on state social services, the Quebec state's intervention remained as essential as ever. Under a serious threat, these forces might be mobilized and the anti-Liberal coalition of the 1970s resuscitated, even without the leadership of the Parti québécois.

In fact, the potential for mobilizing opposition against the contraction of the Quebec state was demonstrated in mid-December of 1986 when the three union federations organized a massive demonstration. Close to 20,000 union members gathered in downtown Montreal chanting such slogans as "Bourassa destroys, he must be stopped." Yvon Charbonneau, head of the CEQ, declared they had gathered to denounce "the vandalism of the Quebec state which the Bourassa government is undertaking. No, to putting our collective patrimony up for sale. No, to the shrunken Quebec [state] which has been promoted ever since Bourassa's arrival."[41]

Moreover, analysis of public opinion suggests that most Québécois did not share business's urgency to roll back the state. Although few Québécois supported further expansion of the Quebec state, apparently most of them were reasonably supportive of the present scale of state activity. In a December, 1985, survey, when asked whether the government should increase, decrease, or leave unchanged its level of services and taxes, 60 per cent chose the last option, with 7 per cent opting for an increase and 33 per cent choosing a reduction. Moreover, 57 per cent of the respondents declared that they disapproved of the reductions in public-sector salaries the Lévesque government imposed in 1982. Even among respondents who were themselves based in the private sector this sentiment was widespread, with 49 per cent disapproving the actions and 51 per cent approving them.[42] By the same token, a survey administered in 1986 found that 73 per cent of Québécois favoured the maintenance or expansion of the state's role in the economy and 61 per cent agreed that the number of state enterprises should be maintained or increased.[43]

Not surprisingly, then, Premier Bourassa avoided taking a public position on the recommendations, simply indicating that the three reports would be examined by the cabinet, "serenely, lucidly, and without prejudice." In doing so, he said, the cabinet would apply the criterion of the majority interest rather than that of administrative efficiency "important as it might appear to be."[44] The government must "balance the need for efficient administration and the state's social and cultural goals."[45]

In fact, in late September, 1986, the president of the Quebec Chamber of Commerce felt obliged not only to endorse the three reports but to express his organization's disappointment that thus far the Bourassa administration had not acted with sufficient vigour on the matters addressed by the report, especially regarding deregulation. For him, the Liberals were not meeting their electoral commitments.[46] A year later, the Bourassa government's record in normalizing the Quebec state still was uneven.

Public Finances

Upon its assumption of office, the Bourassa government acted rapidly to place its own stamp on the structure of Quebec's spending and taxation. In fact, the nomination of Paul Gobeil to the Treasury Board was itself designed to help secure a contraction in public spending since Gobeil, a former executive of Provigo, had already established a reputation for budget slashing at that firm.

Thus, when Finance Minister Gérard-D. Lévesque presented a special mini-budget on December 19, 1985, he announced that the government intended to cut spending by $50 million in the coming months.[47] This was reinforced, moreover, by such measures as the abolition of 1,600 vacant positions in the civil service and by a 25 per cent reduction in funds available to ministers for hiring their personal staff.[48] In its 1986-87 budget the government projected a spending growth rate of 4.6 per cent;[49] the 1987-88 budget projected a rate of 5.6 per cent.[50] On this basis, spending growth would be far below that of the early and middle years of the PQ government. Nonetheless, it was higher than were the rates of the final PQ years, when the PQ's draconian cutback measures had their full impact.

As for taxation, the government acted as one might have expected given its close links with the business community, both reducing the income tax burden on high incomes and encouraging investment in Quebec enterprises. The primary purpose of the December, 1985, mini-budget was to honour some election promises by making three important changes to the tax structure. An insurance tax was reduced and a gasoline surtax was eliminated for some regions. Most importantly, the government revised downward the rate structure of the personal income tax. The greatest benefit went to the highest income groups: taxpayers with taxable

410

incomes of $100,000 profited by $1,301 whereas those with incomes of $20,000 profited by only $120. In the process, the progressivity of the tax was considerably reduced: only four percentage points remained between incomes as disparate as $15,000 and $200,000.[51] The action constituted the advancement by one year of a measure contained in the last PQ budget (although without, the opposition noted, projected increases in child exemptions).[52] As a result of these measures, the government could claim that Quebec no longer was the Canadian province with the highest rate of taxation: that distinction had fallen to Manitoba.[53] As for Quebec businesses, in his 1986-87 budget Finance Minister Lévesque announced a measure to incite workers to invest in the enterprises where they are employed. Also, to stimulate the creation of new enterprises, he announced that for their first three years they would be spared from the provincial tax on paid-up capital. At the same time, he did announce slight increases in the taxes on corporate profits and capital and in the employer contributions for health services – blaming them on the federal government's cutback in transfer payments to Quebec.[54] Moreover, as we shall see later, the government did introduce some measures favouring low-income families.

In sum, the Bourassa government approached Quebec public finances in the expected manner: reducing the tax burden on upper-income groups, encouraging investment, and seeking to curtail expenditure growth. Nonetheless, the government was not totally consumed by neo-liberal objectives: it was prepared to allow spending to rise above the record low set in the latter years of the PQ and its support for the business community did not preclude some limited measures to assist low-income groups.

State Enterprises

The area in which the Bourassa government acted most dramatically to reduce the state's role is the privatization of state enterprises. As we have seen, the second PQ administration had already attempted to identify candidates for privatization but had made little progress in actually selling them off. With the Bourassa regime, the process began in earnest. In his 1986-87 budget address Finance Minister Lévesque made it clear why his government believed the state enterprises had outlived their usefulness:

In Quebec, we have made great use of this instrument [state enterprises] during the last twenty-five years. It was, in particular, a means by which Francophones could rapidly establish themselves in a domain that history has led them to neglect, that of large enterprises.

It is clear today that the role of state enterprises in Quebec's economic development no longer needs to be as important. There now exists a class of extremely dynamic and competent Francophone entrepreneurs who are able to take over from the state and who aspire to assume more and more responsibility. Moreover, the pressing need of our enterprises to be more and more competitive should lead us to count more on the private sector.[55]

At about the same time, Pierre Fortier, the cabinet minister in charge of privatization, released a document outlining how the government intended to conduct its privatization program.[56]

First to go was le Raffinerie du sucre: it was sold in March, 1986, to Lantic, which promptly closed the enterprise. Then, in July, 1986, the Doyon and Niobec mines, the most profitable holdings of SOQUEM, were sold to Cambior, Inc.[57] Also in July, 1986, the government sold two subsidiaries of the Société nationale de l'amiante and declared its intention to sell seven more SNA subsidiaries over the next two years.[58] As well, the government sold Manoir Richelieu, a former summer resort of the wealthy on the North Shore, to hotel and motel magnate Raymond Malenfant.

Soon it was Québecair's turn. As we have seen, the PQ government had secured control of the enterprise largely by default. With a debt of $60 million, Québecair had been losing $12 million per year. In midsummer, 1986, the government sold it to Nordair-Métro for the sum of $10 million. Nordair-Métro was in turn linked to Canadian Pacific, which owned 35 per cent of its shares.[59]

The government then proceeded to sell Madelipêche, a fishery complex on the Îles-de la-Madeleine. The PQ government had created the enterprise in 1977 through purchasing some old plants. As a result of an extensive modernization of the operation, in 1986 the firm was employing 1,100 of the island's residents, thus accounting for 90 per cent of the island's economy. Nonetheless, for 1986 it had a projected deficit of $2 million.[60] In February, 1987, it was sold in two sections, each to a different group of local businessmen.[61]

Most of these enterprises had been clear money-losers. Thus, the government could readily argue that, especially in times of financial constraint, it could not afford to subsidize them any further:

privatization was the only answer. This meant the sacrifice of whatever social or political objectives the enterprises may have served. In strictly financial terms, though, the enterprises were logical candidates for privatization. As the process continued, however, the government turned to enterprises with strong profit records. Here, then, the objective was not to stem a drain on public finances but to secure new funds. In fact, according to one analysis, it was precisely through privatizing viable firms, which could fetch strong prices, that the Bourassa government sought to locate the sources of revenue needed to meet its electoral promises. Since the $400-600 million margin evoked during the 1985 election campaign had not materialized, and increases in taxation or borrowing of that scale clearly were out of the question, the government turned to the sale of its most attractive enterprises.[62]

The most dramatic case in point was Dofor Inc. A holding company of the Société générale de financement, Dofor had a controlling interest in two large and highly profitable enterprises: Domtar Inc. and Donohue Inc. Together, Domtar and Donohue had registered sales of $1.7 billion in 1985, which represented 20 per cent of the sales of forest products by Quebec firms;[63] they had employed 20,000 Québécois in 1985, equivalent to Hydro-Québec's work force, and had made a net profit of $34 million.[64] In February, 1987, the government accomplished its goal, selling its shares in Donohue for $320 million to a consortium composed of Québecor, owned by Québécois newspaper magnate Pierre Peladeau, and British financier Robert Maxwell. Under the terms of the sale Québecor acquired 51 per cent of Donohue, with Maxwell getting 49 per cent.[65] Selling the Domtar shares turned out to be more difficult. After the government had announced its intention to sell its interests in Domtar and Donohue, speculation on Domtar was so intense that the market value of the government's shares in the firm soared from $400 million to $550 million. This was sufficient to discourage any would-be buyer. Nonetheless, the government was determined to try again on another occasion.[66]

The Bourassa government was to discover that however attractive privatization may be as a source of revenue, it also carried major hazards. The announcement in September, 1986, of the intention to sell Dofor's holdings engendered strong criticism in a variety of quarters. Not only the PQ opposition in the National Assembly, but editorialists and even some Francophone businessmen questioned the wisdom of selling such highly profitable and important enterprises. Domtar and Donohue had become known as the "crown jewels" of the SGF holdings. In fact, with the sale of

Dofor, SGF would lose two-thirds of its assets. For that matter, the government had declared on September 30 that SGF would no longer be a holding company: its role would be simply one of promoting new projects as a minority partner with private enterprises. Moreover, SGF was to pursue this redefined role under a new president, Yvon Marcoux, the bank vice-president who had helped to prepare the Gobeil Report.[67]

In a widely discussed speech, Jacques Parizeau declared that while it made good sense to discharge demonstrably unviable enterprises, it made no sense at all to sell such enterprises as Dofor just to reduce the deficit: "it appears that [the government's] criterion for privatizing the state enterprises is the ease with which it can divest itself of the portfolio of shares which it holds."[68]

At the same time, questions also began to arise about the sale of such money-losers as Québecair. While privatization may have stemmed a drain on public funds, it had other consequences as well. In the case of Québecair, with the change in ownership substantial numbers of employees were laid off and service to some regions of Quebec deteriorated markedly. In addition, it became evident that the reorganization of Québecair's assets was being guided by the interests of Canadian Pacific, which controlled Nordair-Métro. For instance, the best of Québecair's jet fleet was sold to Canadian Pacific at what many regarded as an unusually low price.[69] Even Francophone businessmen, who had strongly supported the government's privatization drive, expressed concern that the enterprises remain in Quebec hands.[70] After all, Margaret Thatcher's British government had retained an interest in the enterprises it placed on the market, so as to have some ability to oversee the operations of the firms and prevent undesirable takeovers.

To further underline the hazards of privatization, the sale of Manoir Richelieu triggered a bitter labour dispute that had repercussions on labour peace throughout the province. The new owner, Raymond Malenfant, refused to honour the existing arrangements with the hotel's unionized personnel and proceeded to replace them with workers prepared to accept his terms. A long series of union demonstrations culminated in the death of one picketer, allegedly at the hands of provincial police officers. Later, after spectacular raids on CSN offices in Montreal and Quebec City, the provincial police charged three union officials with conspiring to dynamite Malenfant's property in Chicoutimi. In the process, evidence emerged that a long-time CSN official had in fact been an undercover agent of the RCMP and the federal government's Canadian Security and Intelligence Service. Thus, long-standing charges by union leaders that they have been regularly persecuted by federal and provincial police acquired a new vigour.[71]

Editorialists, the union movement, and a variety of other groups echoed the PQ's call for a moratorium on privatization and a public inquiry on the matter.[72] In fact, opposition to the privatization of Quebec's state enterprises was the primary theme of the mass rally staged by the union movement in December, 1986.

Nonetheless, apparently driven by the promise of new revenue, the Bourassa administration persisted in its plans to privatize Quebec's state enterprises. By the summer of 1987, still remaining on the list were such firms as SOQUIA, SOQUEM, SIDBEC, and SOQUIP.

Social Policy

In the case of social policy, the Bourassa government acted with much more deliberation. Soon after its election, the government did launch a highly publicized campaign to uncover instances of cheating and fraud among social assistance recipients. But by and large, existing social policies were left in place.

In its 1987-88 budget the government announced measures to help families with low or moderate incomes. The floor for the imposition of income tax was raised from $13,004 to $20,082 for a two-parent family with two children. As a result, 45,000 additional families were spared income taxation. In addition, the government announced that the existing program of supplements to income from work would be replaced by a new program of assistance to parents. Called APPORT, the program would assume 50 per cent of the cost of day care and leave the families with a larger proportion of earnings from work (reflecting a government concern to strengthen the work incentive).[73]

It was known that Pierre Paradis, the minister responsible for reform of social assistance, was preparing a comprehensive reform of the system, but he repeatedly delayed presenting it, apparently at the request of Bourassa himself.[74] It was not until May of 1987 that Paradis finally divulged the elements of his proposed reform. As to be expected, the reform was pervaded by a concern that social assistance should not undermine the incentive to work. Thus, it involved a clear distinction between those capable of working and those not. Those able to work would benefit from the fiscal reforms to assist the working poor, which we have alluded to earlier. They were designed both to maximize the incentive to work, by allowing workers to retain a greater proportion of their earnings, and to increase the feasibility of working, through contributing to day-care costs. Also, to help social assistance recipients to equip themselves for the labour market there would be programs covering such matters as education upgrading and job training. As for those who meet the government's definition of being unable to work, a restructured program of assistance would be created.[75]

While the proposed reform clearly reflected the preoccupation of the Bourassa government with the smooth functioning of the labour market, it was not as draconian as the measures pursued in such areas as the state enterprises. In effect, it entailed more a restructuring of state intervention than a contraction of it.

By the same token, the government did not heed the Gobeil Report's recommendation that it abolish outright the Centres locaux de services communautaires (CLSC), community health and social service centres created in the 1970s. Instead, the Minister of Health and Social Services, Thérèse Lavoie-Roux, adopted the recommendations of a committee she had herself created to the effect that the network of CLSC be completed and the system receive proper funding.[76]

Finally, in the case of the minimum wage, which the Lévesque government froze in 1981, the Bourassa government raised it to $4.55 per hour.

With respect to education, Education Minister Claude Ryan managed to avoid the radical restructuring of Quebec universities that the Gobeil Report had advocated. The report had called for the dismantling of the Université du Québec system, under which six different campuses and four specialized institutes are co-ordinated through a central corporation based in Quebec City. They wanted the market principle to be applied to higher education: university campuses would be given full autonomy and allowed to compete among themselves for students and resources. After first staging parliamentary hearings on the proposals, Ryan then appointed his own commission. Not surprisingly, since it was headed by a former Université du Québec president and composed entirely of individuals associated with Quebec higher education, the committee repudiated the Gobeil recommendations: the Université du Québec system was to be maintained and the free market model avoided.[77]

Labour Relations

The new Bourassa government was similarly slow to initiate changes in Quebec's labour relations law. Few laws have aroused as much opposition among Quebec business circles as the "anti-scab" provisions of Bill 45, reinforced in 1983 through Bill 17. The Scowen Report had made a particular point of decrying this measure, along with the decades-old regime of judicial extension of contracts throughout a sector. Yet, by the summer of 1987, the government had yet to outline any proposals for reform of the general labour relations law. Only with respect to the construction industry did it act on business demands and proceed, through Bill 119, to dismantle the elaborate regulatory scheme the Bourassa government had itself helped to create in the mid-1970s. Thus, in July, 1987, Ghislain Dufour, president of Conseil du patronat du Québec, indicated that while business was satisfied with the Bourassa government's reduction of the provincial deficit and apparent resolution of the constitutional question, and with its general image of integrity, it was keenly disappointed with the government's continued failure to revise the laws governing labour relations and occupational health and safety.[78]

Nonetheless, the government proceeded to secure the passage in December, 1987, of Bill 30, which the business community had firmly denounced. Rather than revising the substance of the labour relations law, Bill 30 reorganizes its administration. The existing regulatory bodies are fused into a single body to be appointed directly by the government. The Conseil du patronat opposed the bill, as did two of the union federations, the CSN and the CEQ. In effect, the government appeared to be skirting the whole question of labour law reform by focusing on administrative machinery. In doing so, it managed to alienate all the interested parties.[79]

As for its own labour relations in the public sector, in December, 1986, the Bourassa government succeeded in negotiating a new three-year contract. Not only the government but the public sector unions as well were clearly satisfied with the result. Moreover, it was accomplished without any major work stoppage. To be sure, this latter good fortune was largely the result of the government's Bill 160 (supported by the PQ opposition), which imposed very severe penalties on illegal strikers. Nonetheless, at least the Bourassa government avoided the bitter conflict and even violence that had marked the public-sector collective bargaining three years before under the Lévesque government.

Language Policy

As we have already noted, language policy was one area in which the Bourassa government was under intense pressure to revise radically the existing policy. Most non-Francophones continued to

417

find totally unacceptable key features of Bill 101, such as unilingual advertising, or the restrictions on access to English-language schools, or the imposition of French within parapublic institutions with Anglophone clienteles. For many businesses, including some large Francophone enterprises, the *francisation* program entailed an excessive degree of state intervention into their internal operations. Not only had Quebec Anglophones and allophones, along with most categories of business people, massively supported the Liberals in the 1985 election, but they were strongly represented within the Liberal caucus and the Bourassa cabinet. Clearly, the Bourassa government had to act. Yet, the prospect of Bill 101 being revised was sufficient to mobilize strong opposition among the law's Francophone supporters. In fact, so strong was the rallying of nationalist forces around Bill 101 that the Bourassa government found itself obliged to abandon plans for one set of changes in the law and and was unable even to agree on proposed changes for another part of the law. In the process, many of the social divisions that had marked past debates over language law in Quebec were fully revived.

In November, 1986, the government introduced Bill 140, which would have seriously modified the structures under which Bill 101 is administered. In particular, the Commission de la protection de la langue française was to be merged with the Office de la langue française, the Conseil de la langue française was to be replaced by an advisory committee of the Minister of Cultural Affairs, and appeals of decisions regarding *francisation* certificates would go to the Provincial Court rather than to an existing appeal board, which would be abolished. Critics contended that Bill 101 would be severely weakened in the process: the Office would lose its autonomy, registering complaints about infractions of the law would be much more difficult, and the new advisory committee would not play the same role in informing the public as had the Conseil.[80]

In the same month, the Bourassa government introduced Bill 142, which was designed to enshrine the right to English-language services in public health and social services facilities. Significantly, the bill afforded this right to all individuals "who express themselves in English."[81] As such it could have extended throughout the entire Quebec social affairs system a right that, under Bill 101, had been restricted just to those institutions the Office de la langue française had designated as "Anglophone" because of the presence of Anglophones within their clienteles.[82] Given the reaction of nationalist forces, the government was obliged to amend the bill so as to restrict its impact. The right to

English-language services was to be dependent on the linguistic composition of a region. Nonetheless, opposition forces still insisted that the bill could undermine the role of French as a working language within the parapublic sector.

Both bills were vigorously attacked not only by the PQ opposition in the National Assembly but by nationalist forces in general. The Société Saint-Jean Baptiste and the Mouvement Québec français sought to mobilize public opinion around the slogan, "Ne touchez pas à la loi 101." Leading intellectuals registered their alarm in a variety of public statements. These efforts culminated in a mid-December rally, where 5,000 people heard denunciations by leading nationalist figures, including Jacques Parizeau. Defence of Bill 101 was also a theme of the 20,000-person demonstration the union movement organized on the same weekend. Ultimately, the government yielded to the opposition and abandoned Bill 140, although it suggested the possibility of introducing a new version of the bill at a later date. As for Bill 142, the government finally had to use closure to end the PQ opposition's efforts to prevent passage of the bill.

Another aspect of Bill 101 to become the focus of intense debate was the requirement that public advertising be in French only. The Liberal program called for revising the law to allow for public advertising in another language, as long as French was given priority. However, the Liberal caucus was seriously divided on the question. While Anglophone members were keen to proceed with the change, many Francophone members felt compelled to oppose it. In fact, in January, 1987, the Liberal Party's General Council passed a resolution calling not for the relaxation of the provision but for its reinforcement.

The debate was joined within the public at large, as Anglophone groups campaigned vigorously for application of the Liberal program and nationalist forces campaigned just as vigorously against any modification of Bill 101. Ultimately, the Montreal Chamber of Commerce felt obliged to intervene, alarmed by the intensity of the debate and convinced that it endangered "la paix sociale" and economic prosperity of Montreal. The Chamber called on the Bourassa government to state its intentions clearly and reminded the government that a new *modus vivendi* had emerged in Montreal "based upon recognition of Montreal's distinctive identity, a French city in North America." The Chamber insisted that the public advertising provisions of Bill 101 be properly enforced as long as they have the force of law.[83]

For their part, Bourassa and his immediate colleagues acted in a way that, through self-contradiction if not outright confusion, quite closely reflected these opposing pressures. Initially, Bourassa intimated that the government might avoid any formal amendment to the Bill 101 by simply modifying regulations to allow for bilingual advertising under some conditions. Nonetheless, he did not come forward with any specific proposal. In December, 1986, the Quebec Appeal Court appeared to have resolved the matter for the government by declaring that the provisions of Bill 101 regarding public advertising were in any event unconstitutional, since they violated the Charter of Rights and Freedoms (as well as Quebec's own Charter of Human Rights and Freedoms). Nonetheless, three months later Quebec Attorney-General Herbert Marx announced that Quebec was appealing this decision to the Supreme Court. He claimed the decision was based on "technical matters" rather than defence of the provision itself.[84]

With the matter under appeal, the government at least had a pretext to postpone any attempt to formulate a new policy with respect to public advertising. But when the Appeal Court decision was announced Bourassa declared that the government could still proceed to implement the party program, even if an appeal should be launched, and that it fully intended to do so.[85] In February, 1987, a special two-day session of the Liberal caucus debated the matter at length but failed to produce a consensus. Accordingly, Bourassa declared that the government would not be taking any action on the matter until the fall, at the earliest. In the meantime, a special cabinet committee would seek to formulate a set of proposals. Also, Bourassa declared, until the public advertising provision of Bill 101 should be amended or the Supreme Court should pronounce on its constitutionality, the Quebec government would enforce it. In fact, the government had recently laid some new charges. Finally, Bourasssa felt obliged to assure Québécois that "there is no question of retracting the essence of this law." He insisted on the necessity to assure "the progress, flourishing, and security of French in Quebec." His concern was one of reconciling this objective with fundamental democratic principles, in particular freedom of speech.[86]

Three months later, Bourassa intimated that his government would not be undertaking any amendment of the public advertising provision until the Supreme Court pronounced on its constitutionality. Observers expected that a judgement would be several months, if not a few years, in coming.[87] In effect, then, the government had fallen back on a pretext to avoid an issue over which the party was badly divided.

Clearly, the issue of public advertising had proven to be much more intractable than the Liberal leadership had anticipated. Yet, the conflict within the Liberal Party mirrored a conflict within Quebec society as a whole. On the face of it, the matter hardly seemed to warrant such intense debate. The question of public advertising was an essentially symbolic one. For Anglophones, the absence of English in public advertising was at most an inconvenience that could be readily remedied through learning a few French words. For Francophones, the language of advertising had little material impact on their ability to live and work in French. Nonetheless, it was a symbolic question of high importance. For Anglophones and Francophones alike, the debate over whether Montreal was to have a "French face" really was a debate about the very nature of Quebec society. Once that debate had been opened, it was very difficult to bring it to a conclusion.

Conclusion

In short, there was a major effort during the first two years of the new Bourassa government to "normalize" Quebec's status relative to the other provinces, in effect reversing the predominant trend of Quebec politics over the previous two decades. However, there were major obstacles and constraints to such an effort. Important elements within Quebec society were strongly committed to the social and economic roles the Quebec state had assumed over the last twenty-five years. Thus, the "normalization" of the Quebec state proceeded much further in some areas than in others.

The clearest instance of "normalization" had to do, of course, with Quebec's status within the federal political order. The Meech Lake Accord promised to resolve the symbolic exclusion of Quebec arising from the 1982 repatriation; Quebec would be formally integrated within the Canadian constitution. On the face of it, the Bourassa government had secured an important victory: the Accord responded to each of the demands Quebec had raised. Yet, this merely reflected the extent to which the Bourassa government had had to "normalize" Quebec's demands, making them much closer to the demands that might emanate from the other provinces. In the process, it had had to discard most of the demands of previous Quebec governments. Nonetheless, at least the Bourassa government was able to achieve its objective.

With respect to "normalizing" the role of the state within Quebec itself, the record was uneven. The government tended to focus more on some areas than others – and its level of success was highly variable, too. In some cases, such as the privatization of state enterprises, the government did act with great vigour; in other cases it was much more circumspect. For instance, with respect to governmental organisms the Gobeil Report wanted to abolish, the government announced in some instances that it would maintain them instead but then froze or even reduced financing, as with Radio-Québec or l'Institut québécois de recherche sur la culture.[88] There are other instances, however, where the government decided not only to maintain the organisms but to expand them and raise their financing, as with the network of CLSC. Typically, this came about through ministers establishing their own, more sympathetic commissions of inquiry, as with the committees on the CLSC and the Université du Québec. In important areas such as labour relations and social welfare policy, the government proceeded with extreme deliberation, postponing outright major policy shifts. Finally, in some instances, such as relaxation of Bill 101, the government actually backed off positions it had originally staked out for itself.

Clearly, some ministers, such as Claude Ryan and Thérèse Lavoie-Roux, did not share the anti-statist zeal of Gobeil and company – at least not when it came to their own ministries. Beyond that the government and, especially, Premier Bourassa appear to have been quite concerned about the degree to which potential initiatives would face well-mobilized opposition. If Bourassa and many of his colleagues claimed a desire to contract the Quebec state, they also professed a commitment to "restoring political and social stability" and thus apparently had little interest in open confrontation. For that matter, Bourassa in particular clearly had little disposition to pursue policies that might prove to be politically damaging. Having regained power after an extraordinary political comeback, he showed little readiness to jeopardize it by persisting with widely unpopular initiatives.

Thus, despite its electoral promise to Quebec Anglophones to end the ban on English-language commercial advertising, the government was not prepared to override the organized opposition of Francophone nationalists to do so. Likewise, despite its penchant for neo-liberal rhetoric, the Bourassa regime hesitated to confront *directly* the labour movement. The government was ready to risk incurring labour's wrath over the privatization of state enterprises. After all, privatization offered major injections of revenue, which among other things could be used to facilitate a public-sector settlement. But it hesitated to redefine labour's legal position through altering the labour relations laws in the ways that business so urgently sought. Instead, it limited itself to changing the administrative machinery of labour relations, in the process incurring the dissatisfaction of both business and labour.

As it turned out, even this more selective approach had its problems. Transferring ownership of state enterprises to private hands could have unanticipated consequences, seriously antagonizing labour – as with Québecair's layoffs and the protracted and violent conflict surrounding Manoir Richelieu. By the same token, it was not always possible to anticipate the degree of opposition an initiative might face. Thus, Bill 140's projected reform of the administrative structures of Bill 101 had to be shelved when it engendered such an articulate and well-orchestrated opposition.

In short, the experience of the new Bourassa regime served to demonstrate the extent to which the political modernization of the 1960s and 1970s had greatly expanded and strengthened social categories who have substantial resources to defend their position and for whom intervention by the Quebec state has a critical importance. Undoing the Quiet Revolution would be no easy task. At the midpoint of the Bourassa administration it appeared that the government was not prepared to take the next step and launch the direct attack on organized labour and its allies that would be necessary to normalize fully the social and economic role of the Quebec state. By the same token, it appeared that the government had no intention to roll back the single most important legacy of the campaign to make Quebec a "national" state: Bill 101.

CHAPTER TWELVE
Conclusions

In the course of this century, Quebec has indeed undergone the kinds of changes identified by the theories of development outlined in Chapter One. Its economy has been transformed: a predominantly agrarian base has given way to an industrial structure, with heavy concentration in resource-based primary industry and in light manufacturing. In the process, French Quebec has experienced the many social changes usually attendant upon industrialization: urbanization, secularization, the spread of mass education, and the growth of mass communication networks. Finally, conversion to an urban, industrial society was joined by a late but rapid modernization of Quebec's political life. This political modernization involved both state-building, i.e., growth in the functions and structures of the Quebec state, and politicization, i.e., the mobilization of a much greater proportion of the population to political action.

The Specificity of Quebec's Development

Yet, if the categories of development theory can identify the broad contours of change in Quebec, they nevertheless miss a great deal of what is involved. The direction that economic and social development took in Quebec can be understood only in terms of factors that have closely shaped Quebec's experience: economic and political dependence on both Ontario and the United States; a cultural division of labour between Francophone and Anglophones; a skewed class structure within French Quebec; a federal political order in Canada; and the long-standing presence of a national consciousness among Quebec Francophones. In the absence of these conditions, the processes of economic and social development and political modernization would have taken different shapes and the results would not have been the same. For instance, the political modernization of Quebec resulted in the state assuming a significantly greater economic and social role than was the case in neighbouring Ontario, even though the two provinces are similar along such broad indicators of development as urbanization and industrialization. In 1976, 34 per cent of Quebec's gross provincial product was spent by the province and by municipal and hospital institutions (which fall under provincial jurisdiction), compared to only 25 per cent in Ontario.[1] And, in 1975, the public sector assumed 39.8 per cent of capital expenditure in Quebec but only 30 per cent in Ontario; by 1978, the spread was even greater: the figures for Quebec and Ontario were 45.2 and 25.7 per cent, respectively.[2]

Dependence on external initiative and control clearly has shaped Quebec's economic development, with its stress on extraction of resources for export to foreign markets and the relative absence of technologically sophisticated industry. By the same token, the desire to reduce this dependence, vis-à-vis Ontario if not the United States, was a powerful force behind the political modernization of the 1960s. A modern Quebec state bore the promise of reinforcing local sources of capital, as with the Société générale de financement, and creating new industrial enterprises able to break Ontario's dominance, as with the SIDBEC steel-refining complex.

The cultural division of labour closely shaped economic and political change in Quebec. Not only may it have skewed the distribution of the benefits of economic development, but it may even have influenced the form economic development took. Without an active Francophone entrepreneurial class, the stimulus for Quebec-based industrial development may have been less and the dependence on external initiative correspondingly greater. In addition, the cultural division of labour clearly provided a compelling incentive for the expansion of the Quebec state: to carve out new space for Francophones within the upper levels of the Quebec economy. Thus, Quebec's private hydroelectric firms had to be nationalized, even though the controlling interests (such as Peter Nesbitt Thomson and his Power Corporation) were largely based in Quebec. These interests were Anglophone. Therefore, only through nationalization could Francophones accede to the upper levels of these firms – and only then could Québécois be *maîtres chez nous*.

As for French Quebec's class structure, we have noted how Quebec's economic development was closely shaped by the absence of a strong Francophone economic elite. And the conflicts within this class structure clearly contributed to the drive for political mod-

425

ernization. By placing education, health, and welfare institutions directly under the state, this new middle class could free itself from the dominance of clerical elites. But to do so, the new middle class had to forge an alliance with lower-class Francophones. One palpable result of this alliance in the 1960s was the reinforcement of union organizations, most notably the CSN and CEQ.

In addition, the presence of a national consciousness in Quebec clearly has directed and channelled the processes of economic, social, and political change. For instance, the union organizations that emerged in response to industrialization have been closely bound by the national identity; they either have tied themselves exclusively to the membership of the nation (as with the Confédération des syndicats nationaux and the Centrale des enseignants du Québec) or have maintained only tenuous links with "pan-Canadian" bodies (as is the case with the Fédération des travailleurs du Québec).

The transformed system of public education also has been marked by the national consciousness. Formal instruction in the national heritage may have lost much of the impact it enjoyed in the days of the *collèges classiques*, but curricula and pedagogy have been influenced in countless more subtle ways by the assumption that Quebec is a national collectivity. This influence extends from the selection of flags and other symbols of political authority to the priority given to acquisition of English as a "second language" – matters of continuing debate within Quebec's educational system. Belief in Quebec's nationhood also underlies the contention of many Québécois that the school system should be used to integrate into the Francophone population the children of immigrants, whether these "immigrants" be from other countries or from elsewhere in Canada.

The impact of national consciousness is, of course, most evident in Quebec's processes of political modernization. It ensured that for most Quebec Francophones these processes would be centred on the government in Quebec City rather than the one in Ottawa. The persistence of a French-Canadian identity meant that when most Québécois sought to advance their interests and objectives within the political process, they looked to the governmental institutions manned by fellow Francophones in Quebec, just as in the past they had looked to the institutions of the Church. In fact, many of the political demands Quebec Francophones articulated in the 1960s and 1970s could be better dealt with in Quebec City than in Ottawa; Ottawa appeared to be hostile to them or, more typically, simply irrelevant. This was especially the case with demands involving the position of Francophones in Quebec, relative to Anglophones, or the reinforcement of the provincial public sector, to which many Quebec Francophones had linked their careers.

The presence of a national consciousness also meant that the symbolism of Quebec's political modernization bore an enormous importance. The Quebec provincial government became *l'État du Québec* with its *Assemblée nationale*. And it was important to many Québécois that the newly modernized Quebec state be clearly differentiated from all other provincial governments, whether through a *statut particulier* or through accession to some form of sovereignty. It was similarly important that the Quebec government be able to deal directly with the sovereign states of *la Francophonie*. As a result of all these factors, Québécois were led to make demands for changes in the federal system far exceeding those articulated in the rest of Canada.

Finally, of course, basic features of the Canadian political order shaped the way Francophones in Quebec experienced all these processes. Anglophone dominance of central political institutions and the existence of an autonomous Quebec provincial government combined to ensure that many Francophones would see Quebec as the arena in which to address the problems created by economic and social development; they would be most oriented to forms of French-English inequality that existed in Quebec. By the same token, as the role of the Quebec state grew, they would see themselves as members of a distinctly Québécois nation.

The Contemporary State of Quebec

In contemporary Quebec, not only are the processes of economic and social development and political modernization largely complete but the several factors, specific to Quebec, that so heavily conditioned their course have themselves undergone important change in recent years.

The most striking change is in French Quebec's class structure: for the first time it contains a dynamic business class. If the notion of French Canada as an "ethnic class" ever had any validity, it certainly does not now. As we have seen, a major objective of the Quebec state's initiatives during the 1960s and 1970s had been to provide increased support for Francophone business, whether through subsidies, investment funds, or preferential purchasing policies. Initially, many of these efforts had had disappointing results, as with the mixed record of the Société génerale de financement's ventures and the general timidity of the Caisse to support actively Francophone enterprises. Even in the early 1970s, Francophone capitalists still seemed to be a negligible force. Nonetheless, by the end of the 1970s it was clear that the Quebec state's efforts had had an important cumulative effect. In fact, Francophone capitalists had reached the stage where they were moving beyond Quebec to Canadian and international markets; state support of their initiatives, if it were needed, could come as easily from the federal state as from the Quebec state. Typically, they saw themselves as dependent on no state.

Providing an added boost to Francophone ownership in the Quebec economy was the major exodus of Anglophone business elites in the 1970s, creating a vacuum that Francophone entrepreneurs began to fill. For its part, the PQ government helped them to do so. As we have seen, the PQ government's Régime d'épargne-action du Québec greatly increased the availability of investment funds for Quebec firms. In addition, by deregulating the insurance industry, through Bill 75, the PQ government allowed such institutions as the Laurentian Group to move into other sectors of finance and into the economy as a whole. And, during the early 1980s, the Caisse de dépôt et de placement aggressively promoted a greater Francophone economic presence.[3]

As a result, in the Quebec of the late 1980s one can readily identify a large number of important Francophone-owned and managed corporations that have both secured dominant positions within the Quebec economy and established themselves elsewhere as well. Their presence is most evident in finance and insurance: by the mid-1980s Francophone firms represented ten of the fifty largest financial institutions in Canada and five of the twenty-five largest insurance companies. In engineering, the two largest firms in Canada are Francophone. However, only three of the fifty largest industrial firms are Francophone-owned.

Leading the field is Paul Desmarais's Power Corporation, a holding company whose $50 billion assets include controlling interests in Consolidated-Bathurst, Great-West Life, Montreal Trustco, and *La Presse*.[4] Desmarais's ambitions and financial resources have been sufficient even to frighten the management of that pillar of English-Canadian capitalism, Canadian Pacific. Another financial giant is the Laurentian Group, with assets of close to $10 billion that include insurance companies in Great Britain and the United States as well as Toronto-based Eaton Financial Services.[5] The Banque nationale, which has absorbed both the Toronto-based Unity Bank and the American-owned Mercantile Bank, stands sixth among Canadian banks. And the Mouvement Desjardins, the largest credit union in North America, controls over $30 billion in assets.[6]

In retailing, Provigo, which absorbed Dominion Stores' Quebec operations in 1981, now accounts for 35 per cent of Quebec's food retailing market and has major operations in Ontario, Alberta, and California. In addition, it controls Consumers Distributing, a catalogue warehouse network with over 200 stores in Canada and the eastern United States.[7] The Jean Coutu group of pharmacies controls 43 per cent of the Quebec market, has been slowly establishing itself in the northeastern United States, and is presently seeking to purchase the ninety-two-unit Big V Pharmacies chain in Ontario.[8]

In manufacturing, Bombardier has emerged as a world leader in mass transit equipment, with sales of $656 million in 1985.[9] Recently it purchased Canadair, an airplane manufacturer, from the federal government. Cascades, Inc., a pulp-and-paper enterprise, reached $19.1 million in earnings by 1985, thanks in large part to a highly successful issue of public shares under the REA.[10] Lavalin stands as one of the world's largest engineering firms, with more than 7,000 employees, $1 billion in revenues, and operations in more than ninety countries.[11] Its rival, SNC, with nearly $400 million in annual revenue, recently outbid it to purchase the Ontario government's Urban Transit Development Corporation. As a final confirmation of the new role of Francophone business, two cherished institutions of the Montreal English-Canadian community, Ogilvy's and the Windsor Hotel, have fallen under Francophone control.

Not only does French Quebec now have a dynamic business class, but the structural bases of its new middle class have been altered. Now it is the private sector that offers mobility, rather than the state sector as in the 1960s and early 1970s. In 1970, 90 per cent of the graduates of the École des hautes études commerciales went into government positions, but by 1985 the figure had fallen to only 5 per cent.[12] Thus, in the Quebec of the future the Francophone new middle class may not have the strong commitment to state expansion, which had been so important to the neo-nationalism of the 1960s and 1970s. And, for the first time, it will have a dynamic business class whose involvement in Canadian and American markets will make it a strong and influential opponent of Quebec sovereignty.

Coupled with these changes in French Quebec's class structure has been an attenuation of the historical cultural division of labour in Quebec's economy. The cultural segmentation of economic activity has declined as Francophone business has moved beyond its traditional peripheral specializations into such formerly Anglophone domains as heavy industry and engineering. Initially, of course, this breakthrough was based on such state initiatives as Hydro-Québec and SIDBEC. More recently, however, it has come about through the expansion of private Francophone firms. Beyond this decline in cultural segmentation, cultural hierarchy has also declined as English-Canadian and American-owned enterprises have introduced much higher proportions of Francophones to managerial levels. As we saw in Chapter Eight, it is unclear whether this stemmed directly from Quebec's language laws or whether it reflected the vacuum created by the migration of young Quebec Anglophones. Whatever its cause, the change is indisputable. As a result of this decline in Quebec's cultural division of labour, the historical income differences between Anglophones and Francophones have largely disappeared.[13]

As for the Canadian federal order, much more limited but nonetheless significant changes have occurred here, too. Most dramatic perhaps is the Meech Lake Accord, with its promise that Quebec will be formally integrated within the Canadian constitution. This integration is to be accompanied, moreover, by the formal recognition of Quebec's status as a distinct society. Even if this provision should be no more than a symbolic gesture, it and other provisions of the Accord would have been unthinkable under the Trudeau regime just a few years before. Beyond that, the linguistic reforms in the federal government have had at least some success. The Francophone presence within the upper levels of the federal bureaucracy has increased, even if Québécois may be seriously underrepresented and opportunities to work in French may remain limited. Moreover, in recent decades Francophones, primarily from Quebec, clearly have assumed a more important role in the federal cabinet than was ever the case before. If nothing else, these measures at least have served to give the federal state a bilingual "face," making it appear less alien to Quebec Francophones. Finally, French-language services have been greatly expanded in some provinces, most notably the neighbouring provinces of New Brunswick and Ontario. These changes may have little direct meaning to Quebec Francophones, and there is little likelihood that they will be able to arrest the steady demographic decline of French-speakers in most parts of Canada. Nonetheless, they, too, may make the existing order appear less hostile. In short, while it appears unlikely these various changes could alter the allegiances of Quebec nationalists, they may at least make it easier for Quebec nationalists to reconcile themselves to the Canadian political order, given their failure to achieve their own objectives.

Quebec's economic relations with Ontario and the United States continue to reflect the historical patterns of dependence. The industrial economy still has a much lower share of high-technology, capital-intensive activity than does that of Ontario. American, European, and Japanese multinationals continue to favour Ontario over Quebec for locating their branch plants. SID-BEC is still unable to break Ontario's dominance of steel production. Toronto now has clearly usurped Montreal's historical role as financial metropolis of Canada. If the aggressive activities of the Montreal Stock Exchange and the plans to make Montreal an international banking centre may attenuate Toronto's superiority, they cannot hope to eliminate it.

Despite these constrictions, there have been important instances of essentially Francophone Quebec firms breaking into new areas of activity, as with Bombardier's entry into the production of mass transportation equipment and the emergence of important Francophone engineering firms such as Lavalin. Moreover, the most important of these successes are based not just on the Quebec market, or even the Canadian market, but on American and international markets. Just as Bombardier has secured contracts in major American cities such as New York City, so food-processing and retail firms, such as Culinar and St. Hubert, have been greatly concerned with establishing themselves in the American market. As a consequence, leading Francophone businessmen have become a force, not for state intervention to protect Quebec firms from Canadian or American competition on the Quebec market as some of them may have sought in the past, but for the dissolution of state-created barriers to trade – both within Canada and between Canada and the United States. Thus, they have been highly supportive of a free-trade arrangement with the United States. If Quebec's economic dependence is unlikely to fade, at least its terms are being altered somewhat.

As for the role of a Quebec national consciousness, some of its most basic premises continue to shape Quebec profoundly. It is now an accepted fact of life that Quebec is a pre-eminently Francophone province. No Francophone political figures, and few Anglophone ones, are advocating a return to official bilingualism. And Quebec Francophones continue to demonstrate in a multitude of ways the vastly heightened pride and sense of personal capacity that arose with the Quiet Revolution, when their leaders

431

banished forever the notion that French Canadians were *"né pour un petit pain."* However, as a political movement, Quebec nationalism clearly does not have the mobilizing capacity it demonstrated in the 1960s and 1970s. This is reflected not only in the fate of the Parti québécois, which in any event had come to distance itself from much of the neo-nationalist project. It can be seen in the failure to make any impact on the political firmament on the part of the several new movements formed to carry on the *indépendantiste* struggle. Nonetheless, as we shall argue below, this apparent decline in the role of nationalism within Quebec political life need not mean a decline in national identity itself.

The Rise and Decline of Quebec Neo-nationalism

The apparent decline of nationalism in contemporary Quebec can be traced to several factors. In part, it reflects the sheer impact of the fate that has befallen the neo-nationalist movement: the overwhelming defeat in the Quebec referendum, followed by the constitutional debacle, followed by the steady retreat of the Parti québécois from the national question. In addition, it reflects the inroads into Quebec of neo-liberal sentiment, which, through its attack on the desirability or efficacy of state intervention, has served to undermine a central premise of the neo-nationalist argument for Quebec sovereignty. However, the decline of Quebec nationalism also reflects the changes we have outlined above. As a result of these changes, Quebec neo-nationalism is no longer favoured by the remarkable complex of factors that gave rise to it in the first place.

During the 1960s, Quebec was not the only setting in which nationalism acquired a new and more dynamic force. In many parts of Western Europe, where cultural differences and a related sense of identity also had persisted despite the presumed homogenizing and integrating effects of economic and social change, significant neo-nationalist movements also arose during the 1960s: Wales, Scotland, the Basque country and Catalonia, Brittany, and Wallonia and Flanders.[14] Yet, the Quebec neo-nationalist movement was much more successful than its Western European counterparts. Nowhere else did a political party committed to neo-nationalist objectives secure such a high proportion of the popular vote as in Quebec. And, of course, nowhere else did a neo-nationalist movement actually assume power. This may reflect the extent to which Quebec neo-nationalism stemmed not only from external conditions but from profound processes of change within

432

the "national" collectivity itself.

In many settings, the neo-nationalist revival has been satisfactorily explained in terms of the structure of relations between regions. For instance, within the "internal colony" model, nationalism is understood as the reaction of a peripheral region, such as Wales and Brittany, to economic domination by a core region.[15] In other instances, nationalism may arise from the frustrations of a region that is more dynamic than the political centre, and stands as a "middle class enclave in a more backward country."[16] Examples might be Catalonia, the Basque country, and Croatia. Yet, if Quebec hardly fits this latter pattern, it does not clearly fit the former one either. After all, as we have seen, Quebec has been bound in a complex of relations, standing along with Ontario as a central Canadian core to Atlantic and western Canada yet displaying some of the traits of a periphery with respect to Ontario. Even if one were to focus simply on Quebec's relationship with Ontario, it is difficult to find in that alone an explanation of the neo-nationalist surge. As we have seen, by most measures of economic performance Quebec's relative position improved rather than declined over the post-war years. It was only in the last half of the 1960s, when the neo-nationalist movement was well under way, that indicators began to reveal a new deterioration in Quebec's position relative to Ontario. This new economic decline may have given added force to the neo-nationalist movement, but it cannot have triggered the movement's creation. In any event, disadvantage relative to Ontario was only one theme of the neo-nationalists: while such initiatives as SIDBEC were clearly designed to reduce Ontario's advantage, other measures, such as expansion of Hydro-Québec or the creation of the Société générale de financement, were more concerned with strengthening the role of Francophones within the Quebec economy.

Thus, beyond interregional relations, a satisfactory understanding of the Quebec neo-nationalist movement requires an assessment of the cultural division of labour within Quebec itself. Here, too, there was no evident change during the post-war years in the underrepresentation of Francophones within the upper levels of the Quebec economy, just as there was no evident deterioration in Quebec's economic position relative to Ontario. However, there were some long-term processes at work that could have supported a neo-nationalist surge. Even if most aggregate measures of Quebec's economic performance may have been strong in the post-war years, English-Canadian and American corporations were steadily shifting their head office operations from Montreal to Toronto. In the process, Anglophone executives in Quebec were increasingly reduced to the status of regional managers, following the instructions of head offices in Toronto. This change may, in turn, have undermined the prestige Quebec Anglophones had always enjoyed within the Francophone population, making them more vulnerable to a challenge.[17]

Nonetheless, as we have seen, the key to understanding Quebec neo-nationalism lies in the change in French Quebec's class structure: namely, the emergence of a new middle class. For the Francophone new middle class that arose in post-war Quebec, both regional disadvantage and an internal cultural division of labour became increasingly intolerable. Also intolerable was the continued pre-eminence of the clergy and Church-related institutions within Francophone society itself. The key to addressing all these matters was state intervention: thanks to Canadian federalism the structures of a state were available for this purpose. Neo-nationalism provided all the legitimation that was needed for the wide-ranging deployment of these structures. Thus, the roots of neo-nationalism lay in the efforts of the new middle class, and its allies in the labour movement and to a much lesser extent in Francophone business, to use the powers and resources of the Quebec state not only to "modernize" French Quebec society but to attack the twin obstacles of regional disadvantage and a cultural division of labour. This combination of factors provided an unusually powerful base for a neo-nationalist movement. And nowhere else did neo-nationalists have the opportunity to use such powerful state institutions to remake their "nation" and free it from its constraints. In the process, most of a whole generation of Quebec Francophones came to see Quebec as their nation and the Quebec state as the primary instrumentality of that nation.

By the same token, the decline in Quebec's neo-nationalist movement can be understood in terms of a decline in these very same conditions. Thanks to vigorous state intervention the transformation of Francophone society has been largely completed and Quebec's cultural division of labour has been considerably attenuated. And the Francophone business class, which has been spawned in the process, is projecting a very different view of Quebec's relations with other regions. Their widely trumpeted successes in Ontario and American markets have served to downplay the pessimistic analyses of Quebec's regional position that were so current in the 1970s.[18] Finally, of course, the whole notion of the interventionist state has fallen into disrepute, the result of both these trends and international ones.

In effect, our reading of the rise, and decline, of Quebec neo-nationalism sees it as the reflection of a desire to use the state to accentuate Quebec's economic and social development, and to overcome the conditions that frustrated or "distorted" this development. On this basis, we reject an alternative interpretation of the most recent wave of Quebec nationalism, or *indépendantisme*, which sees it as a response to the processes of development and political modernization themselves. According to William Coleman, the various groups supporting Quebec independence were moved primarily by a reaction *against* the reforms of the Quiet Revolution, such as the transformation of the educational system, since they diluted Quebec's cultural distinctiveness, rooted in the Catholic religion, and promoted integration into North American capitalism: "changes which have fundamentally shaken the culture of French Canada, that have left the traditional bases of that culture almost in ruins, and that hold no promise, not even a conception, of putting anything in their place."[19] Thus, according to Coleman, the *indépendantisme* movement is:

> based upon more than the frustration of the francophone middle classes arising from their inability to hold economic power, more than the anger of intellectuals who find it increasingly difficult to find values sufficiently shared to constitute a community, and more than the despair of workers who know only of the instability of economic recession. It is also a cry of fright from the people of which these groups are part, a people that remembers having some sense of self and of being a community and that feels that both are now virtually gone.[20]

A first difficulty with this thesis is that the leadership of the *indépendantiste* movement itself gave little indication of having been moved by the sense of loss of a tradition-based solidarity or in fact of being fundamentally uncomfortable with North American capitalism. As we saw in our analysis of the Parti québécois program, rather than seeking to arrest capitalist development, let alone restore earlier values and institutions, the PQ leadership was concerned with accelerating the processes so as to better advantage the Quebec economy. More generally, during the 1960s and 1970s, as in the referendum campaign, the *indépendantiste* leadership projected not a preoccupation with the survival of the Québec nation but a determination that the nation be able to achieve its full potential; rather than defensive and fearful, the dominant discourse was aggressive and self-confident. To be sure, some of the conservative nationalists clustered around the Société Saint-Jean Baptiste may have evoked a nostalgia for traditional values and solidarities. Conversely, as we have seen, some intellectuals and union activists did articulate a well-developed critique of North American capitalism. In particular, the CEQ was highly critical of the extent to which, within its analysis, the Quiet Revolution educational reforms have been geared to the needs of monopoly capital – although it had been equally critical of the traditional institutions the Quiet Revolution had destroyed. However, as we have seen, these were not the themes the mainstream of the *indépendantiste* leadership used to make its case. In fact, Quebec independence was presented as the logical continuation of the Quiet Revolution: the Quebec state would finally have all the resources and powers needed to fulfil the promise first evoked in the 1960s.

In addition, the alleged sense of loss seems to be belied by the clear commitment of the *indépendantiste* movement to cultural pluralism. As Coleman rightly recognizes, the *indépendantiste* leadership fully supported integration into the Quebec *nation* of non-French Canadians, whether immigrants or English-speaking residents of Quebec, as long as they accepted the pre-eminence of French within Quebec and equipped themselves to participate in Francophone society. One would expect a movement based on reaction to modernization and the loss of cultural solidarity to be highly exclusivist.[21]

There is a final difficulty in viewing the movement as one of a people who remember "having some sense of self and of being a community" and who are bemoaning their loss. So much of the movement's membership could not have known the solidarity of traditional society. It is an error to presume that the supporters of Quebec independence had *themselves* experienced the transformations that Quebec society underwent in the post-war years. We found in Chapter Seven that the "Yes" vote in the 1980 referendum was strongest among Francophones who were born between 1945 and 1959. Not only were traditional institutions already in decline during the years of this cohort's early existence, the 1950s and early 1960s, but by the time these Francophones entered active political life and acquired their political allegiances the Quiet Revolution had already taken place. It is precisely because they had *not* been socialized by more traditional institutions that they were available for mobilization into the *indépendantiste* movement. In fact, we found a close correlation between infrequency of religious practice and support for Quebec independence. If anything, then, *indépendantisme* was part of a *rejection* of traditional French-Canadian civilization rather than an angst over its loss.

The Future of Quebec Nationalism

Within our interpretation we would not presume that the Quebec nationalist movement "may itself die."[22] First, we see a continuing basis for a distinct Quebec identity – even if contemporary Quebec is fundamentally different from what it was two or three decades ago. There is no inherent reason why a viable Quebec identity must be based on the myth, let alone the reality, of a traditional society. The extent of cultural difference is not the sole factor determining whether a sense of identity will persist. If it were, groups in many parts of the world would have lost their solidarity years ago.

Few people would disagree with the contention that the changes Quebec society has undergone over the last few decades have reduced its difference from surrounding North American capitalist society and from its values of consumerism and individualism. The economic policies of successive Quebec governments over the 1960s and 1970s have indeed served to integrate Quebec with the North American market and to spur collaboration between Quebec and American firms. Education policy has been focused on the needs of capitalism, with stress on technical and occupational training. It may even be correct to argue that the Quebec state's language policies have caused the incorporation into the French spoken by Québécois of "new and foreign words," many derived from France.

Yet, to infer that these processes have undermined the basis for a distinct Quebec identity is to presume that such an identity can be based only on a society that is in fact *fundamentally* different from others. It is as if a viable sense of Quebec identity can exist only within the pre-revolutionary Catholic civilization the Tremblay Commission idealized and *thought* was the basis of French-Canadian society, or *perhaps* in a "humanist" society, which would somehow transcend North American capitalist values. Leaving aside the question of whether either alternative is genuinely feasible, it is not at all clear that either one is really necessary for a viable Québécois identity.

First, a sense of identity, and distinctiveness, can rest as much on separateness as on difference. Even if language should be the primary remaining cultural difference in Quebec, which is far from certain, it alone could be the basis of a powerful sense of identity. Language serves to structure most aspects of the lives of Quebec Francophones. Even if their knowledge of English should be sufficient to permit personal contacts with Anglophones and exposure to English-language media, the vast bulk of their normal day-today interaction – whether it involves work, family, or leisure – will be with fellow Francophones, just as the most efficient source of information will be Francophone media. Thus, language alone is bound to maintain a strong sense of separateness and distinctiveness. Beyond that, the knowledge that so many generations of Francophones fought so hard to maintain the viability of French-language institutions within Quebec and, with so much less success, elsewhere in Canada is bound to support a strong normative commitment to defence of the pre-eminence of French within Quebec. The widespread opposition to the Bourassa government's plans to restructure Bill 101's administrative structures, and the government's retreat in face of this opposition, is strong testimony to the continuing commitment of Quebec Francophones to defence of their language, as is the continuing debate over the language of commercial advertising and over the proper role in French-language schools of initiation to English.

In these terms, rather than being a threat to a sense of Québécois identity, standardization of the French spoken in Quebec with that spoken in other Francophone countries should in fact be highly supportive. Through government programs to encourage contact with other French-speaking countries and to disseminate information about International French, the vocabulary of French Quebec has been greatly enriched: Anglicisms have been reduced and vast numbers of new terms have been introduced that denote recent technological and intellectual developments. On this basis, Québécois are better able to apply and advance technology in their own language and to participate in a larger French-speaking world. In the last analysis, it is only on this basis that French-language institutions can hope to survive within contemporary North America. Accordingly, it is all to the good if the French language in Quebec is moving from its "traditional roots and becoming more like the language of advanced capitalism in North America, English."[23] At the same time, it is also becoming more closely integrated with one of the languages of advanced capitalism in Europe: French. In short, through greater integration with the rest of the French-speaking world, Quebec Francophones have greater resources to maintain French-language institutions in North America and increased resolve to maintain them. Beyond that, it is not at all clear that subtle cultural differences have disappeared. They may not be rooted in distinctive institutions, such as the Church, but they clearly persist.

Finally, as Léon Dion has demonstrated in a recent study, national identities ultimately are based in the realm of the imaginary.[24] Rather than simple reflections of sociological reality, they are constructions that combine myths about the past with visions of the future. This process of constructing and reconstructing a Québécois national identity is bound to continue.

In short, there clearly remains the basis of a Québécois identity that will continue to have stronger appeal to most Quebec Francophones than do the available alternatives, such as a pan-Canadian identity. In a sense, to deny this possibility, and to set the impossible condition that a viable Québécois identity must be based on a cultural and social reality unique within North America, is simply to perpetuate an old English-Canadian habit of denying French Canadians the right to see themselves as a distinct collectivity. It is as if Québécois must, as keepers of a museum, confine themselves to the traditional "backward" society that in the past English Canadians had always been so quick to decry.

The future strength of nationalist movements based on the Québécois identity will not depend simply on the degree of cultural difference between Québécois and other North Americans. As elsewhere, the primary dynamic lies in the variety of structural relationships in which members of the "nation" find themselves. In the case of Quebec, long-term structural factors could well support a resurgence of nationalism – even if it were to be based on no more than defence of the French language.

Demographers agree that in the coming years in Canada the Francophone presence outside Quebec will continue its steady decline. By the year 2000, close to 95 per cent of Canada's Francophone population will live in Quebec.[25] By the same token, Quebec itself is expected to become even more heavily Francophone, perhaps by over 84 per cent in the year 2000.[26] Thus, if the nation should continue to be defined primarily in terms of language, it will become more and more congruent with the boundaries of Quebec. However, Quebec's total population is expected to grow very slowly during the 1990s and actually to decline in the first decade of the next century, given both a continued low birthrate and unfavourable net migration. As a result, its demographic weight within Canada as a whole is bound to decline, perhaps falling below 24 per cent by the year 2006.[27] In the process, Quebec's weight within Canadian political institutions is bound to decline as well. These trends could well serve to reinforce an attachment to Quebec.

Also, the implementation of a free trade agreement between Canada and the United States could create new opportunities for Quebec *indépendantistes*. With assured access to the American

439

markets, Québécois might be more prepared to risk moving to Quebec independence. No longer would they need the assurance of an economic association with the rest of Canada. To be sure, American officials would have to accept Quebec as a separate signatory to the agreement. But they would have strong incentives to do so, especially if free trade had further strengthened economic integration between Quebec and the U.S. A free trade agreement with the United Staes might place heavy constraints on the political independence a sovereign Quebec might expect to enjoy. Conceivably, through heightening exposure to American cultural influences, closer economic integration with the United States might weaken a Québécois sense of identity and thus attraction to the goal of Quebec sovereignty. But we have already argued that the strength of this identity is not in any event a simple function of the degree of cultural difference. At least, with an established Canada-U.S. free trade agreement the economic uncertainties of Quebec sovereignty, which were largely responsible for the 1980 referendum defeat, could be greatly minimized.

Thus, one can readily imagine conditions under which Quebec *indépendantisme* could once again become an important political force. In fact, Québécois apparently have not closed their minds on the question of Quebec sovereignty: in a recent survey over 44 per cent of respondents indicated that they preferred sovereignty-association to not only complete separation from Canada but even a federalism "renewed" through the Meech Lake Accord.[28] Whether a renewed Parti québécois, under Jacques Parizeau, would be able to mobilize support for Quebec sovereignty is another matter. Given the union movement's deep alienation from the PQ, borne from the Lévesque government's treatment of public-sector unions, it is difficult to see how the *péquiste* coalition of the 1970s could be resurrected.[29] Yet the Francophone business leaders, with their neo-liberal antipathy to state intervention, are improbable converts to the *indépendantiste* cause, however favourably they were treated by the Lévesque government and Finance Minister Parizeau. They have no more an interest in Quebec sovereignty now than they did during the 1980 referendum, when they supported a "Non" vote with virtual unanimity.

For the moment, however, Quebec nationalism is quiescent. Canada's most serious political crisis, which originated in the political modernization of the Quiet Revolution and saw the election of a Quebec government formally committed to Quebec sovereignty, appears to have run its course.

Notes

Chapter One

1. The dimensions of change are discussed in C.E. Black, *The Dynamics of Modernization* (New York: Harper, 1967). The psychological dimension of "social mobilization" is analysed by Karl Deutsch, "Social Mobilization and Political Development," *American Political Science Review*, 55 (September, 1961), 493-514. For a concise and critical review of the various treatments of the tradition/modernity type of analysis, see J.A. Bill and Robert Hardgrave, Jr., *Comparative Politics: The Quest for Theory* (Columbus, Ohio: Charles E. Merrill, 1973), 50-57. A useful critique of the numerous and disparate versions of political development is L.C. Mayer, *Comparative Political Inquiry* (Homewood, Ill.: Dorsey Press, 1972), Chapter Twelve. Also, a very good review of the political development literature, with advocacy of dependence theory for interpreting Quebec, is contained in Gérald Bernier, "Le cas québécois et les théories de développement et la dépendance," in Edmond Orban (ed.), *La Modernisation politique du Québec* (Sillery, Québec: Boréal Express, 1976), 19-54.

2. One example of this argument is Daniel Lerner, "Towards a Communication Theory of Modernization: A Set of Considerations," in Lucian Pye (ed.), *Communications and Political Development* (Princeton, N.J.: Princeton University Press, 1963).

3. These are adapted from Deutsch, "Social Mobilization and Political Development," but they arise in one form or another throughout the literature on political change.

4. Bernier, "Le cas québécois," 29-35.

5. See Richard Rose (ed.), *The Dynamics of Public Policy: A Comparative Analysis* (Beverly Hills: Sage, 1976); Leon Lindberg (ed.), *Stress and Contradiction in Modern Capitalism* (Lexington, Mass: Heath, 1975). For Canada, see Conrad Winn and John McMenemy (eds.), *Political Parties in Canada* (Toronto: McGraw-Hill Ryerson, 1976).

6. Charles Tilly, "Western State-Making and Theories of Political Transformation," in Tilly (ed.), *The Formation of National States in Western Europe* (Princeton, N.J.: Princeton University Press, 1975), 601-38.

7. A.F.K. Organski, *The Stages of Political Development* (New York: Alfred Knopf, 1965).

8. Tilly, "Western State-Making," 607; Bernier, "Le cas québécois," 21-25.

9. Phillips Cutright, "National Political Development: Measurement and Analysis," *American Sociological Review*, 28 (1963), 253-64.

10. Tilly, "Western State-Making," 613.

11. Leonard Binder *et al. Crises and Sequences in Political Development* (Princeton, N.J.: Princeton University Press, 1971).

12. Tilly, "Western State-Making," 608-11.

13. See James O'Connor, *The Fiscal Crisis of the State* (New York: St. Martin's Press, 1973).

14. Discussions of dependence theory, with applications to Quebec, appear in Maurice Saint-Germain, *Une économie à libérer: le Québec analysé dans ses structures économiques* (Montréal: Les Presses de l'Université de Montréal, 1973); Bernier, "Le cas québécois"; Jules Savaria, "Le Québec est-il une société périphérique?" *Sociologie et sociétés*, 7 (novembre, 1975), 115-28.

15. For instance, see Henry Veltmeyer, "Dependency and Underdevelopment," *Canadian Journal of Political and Social Theory*, 2 (Spring, 1978), 55; and William K. Carroll, "Dependency, Imperialism, and the Capitalist Class in Canada," in Robert J. Prym, *The Structure of the Canadian Capitalist Class* (Toronto: Garamond Press, 1985), 21-52.

16. Tilly, "Western State-Making," 628.

17. Savaria, "Le Québec est-il une société périphérique?" is especially pertinent in this regard. He calls for a theory of dependence, appropriate for the analysis of regions within an economic centre, which is concerned with the articulation of different modes of production.

18. For a detailed elaboration of Quebec's status as a region within an economic centre, and an especially vigorous attack on the characterization of Quebec as underdeveloped or peripheral, see Michel Van Schendel, "Impérialisme et classe ouvrière au Québec," *Socialisme québécois*, Nos. 21-22 (avril, 1971), 156-209.

19. See Samir Amin, *Le développement inégal* (Paris: Éditions de Minuit, 1973), especially 292, 301-08.

20. For instance, see Gilles Bourque, *L'État capitaliste et la question nationale* (Montréal: Les Presses de l'Université de Montréal, 1977), Chapter v; Michael Hechter, *Internal Colonialism: The Celtic Fringe in British National Development, 1536-1966* (Berkeley: University of California Press, 1975).

21. For a brief outline of some modes of explanation of uneven development, see Economic Council of Canada, *Living Together* (Ottawa, 1977).

22. See Saint-Germain, *Une économie à libérer*; Savaria, "Le Québec est-il une société périphérique?"; Bernard Bonin et Mario Polèse, *À propos de l'association Canada-Québec* (Québec: École nationale d'administration publique, 1980).

23. With respect to foreign ownership this pattern holds for all industrial sectors except transportation and, to a very limited extent, services. See Government of Canada, *Foreign Direct Investment in Canada* (Ottawa, 1972), 23. Also, see Kari Levitt, *Silent Surrender* (Toronto: Macmillan, 1970); John Hutcheson, *Dominance and Dependency: Liberalism and National Policies in the North Atlantic Triangle* (Toronto: McClelland and Stewart, 1978); R.M. Laxer (ed.), *Canada (Ltd): The Political Economy of Dependency* (Toronto: McClelland and Stewart, 1973); Jorge Niosi, *La bourgeoisie canadienne: La formation et le développement d'une classe dominante* (Montréal: Boréal Express, 1980).

24. For an exploration of the relationship of western and Atlantic Canada to Ontario and Quebec, see David Jay Bercuson, *The Burden of Unity* (Toronto: Macmillan, 1977). See also Harold Chorney, "Regional Underdevelopment and Cultural Decay," in Marxist Institute of Toronto, *Imperialism, Nationalism, and Canada* (Toronto: New Hogtown Press, 1977), 108-41.

25. John H. Dales, "A Comparison of Manufacturing Industry in Quebec and Ontario, 1952," in Mason Wade (ed.), *Canadian Dualism/La dualité canadienne* (Québec: Les Presses de l'Université Laval, 1960), 220.

26. *Ibid.*

27. Albert Faucher and Maurice Lamontagne, "History of Industrial Development," in Marcel Rioux and Yves Martin (eds.), *French-Canadian Society* (Toronto: McClelland and Stewart, 1964), I, 257-71.

28. In 1977, three Quebec economists wrote: "No one has better expressed than Albert Faucher the importance of technology and of geography in the economic experience of Quebec in America." Pierre Fortin, Gilles Paquet et Yves Rabeau, "Coûts et bénéfices de l'appartenance du Québec à la Confédération canadienne: analyse préliminaire," préparée à la demande de Radio-Canada pour l'émission *l'Économothèque* du 21 mai 1977, p. 14 (our translation).

29. Gilles Bourque et Anne Legaré, *Le Québec: la question nationale* (Paris: Maspero, 1979), 121 (our translation).

30. *Ibid.*

31. John McCallum, *Unequal Beginnings: agriculture and economic development in Quebec and Ontario until 1870* (Toronto: University of Toronto Press, 1980), 104.

32. *Ibid.*, Chapter Seven.

33. Glen Williams, "The National Policy Tariffs," *Canadian Journal of Political Science*, XII, 2 (1979), 333-68.

34. D.M. Ray, "The Location of American Subsidiaries in Canada," *Economic Geography*, 47, 3 ((1971), 389-400. This general interpretation is presented more fully in Kenneth McRoberts, "The Sources of Neo-nationalism in Quebec," *Ethnic and Racial Studies*, 7, 1 (January, 1984), 62-68.

35. Fortin *et al.*, "Coûts et bénéfices," 14-15.

36. See Pierre Frechette, "L'économie de la Confédération: un point de vue québécois," *Canadian Public Policy* (Autumn, 1977), 431-40; Yves Rabeau, "Les relations économiques Québec-Ontario," background paper presented to colloquium on Quebec-Ontario relations, Toronto, January, 1978.

37. Stanley B. Ryerson, *Unequal Union* (Toronto: Progress Books, 1968).

38. Donald Kerr, "Metropolitan Dominance in Canada," in W.E. Mann (ed.), *Canada: A Sociological Profile* (Toronto: Copp Clark, 1968), 225-43.

39. Evidence of the premium paid to Anglophones appears in André Raynauld, Gérald Marion et Richard Béland, "La répartition des revenus selon les groupes ethniques au Canada," Research Report submitted to the Royal Commission on Bilingualism and Biculturalism. A summary of the findings appeared in Gilles Racine, "Les québécois gagnent peu à cause de la ségrégation économique pratiquée par les anglophones à leur endroit," *La Presse*, November 14, 1970. On the consequences for regional growth of the limits on Francophone economic participation, see Saint-Germain, *Une économie à libérer*. Also, see Pierre Harvey, "Pourquoi le Québec et les Canadiens français occupent-ils une place inférieure sur le plan économique?" in René Durocher et Paul-André Linteau (eds.), *Le "Retard" du Québec et l'infériorité économique des canadiens français* (Montréal: Boréal Express, 1971), 113-27.

40. The quotations are from Michael Hechter, "Group Formation and the Cultural Division of Labor," *American Journal of Sociology*, 84 (September, 1978), 6, 29. Hechter originally developed the concept in *Internal Colonialism: The Celtic Fringe in British National Development, 1536-1966*. For a discussion of the applicability to Quebec of cultural division of labour and of Hechter's

theory of internal colonialism, see Kenneth McRoberts, "Internal Colonialism: The Case of Quebec," *Ethnic and Racial Studies*, 2 (July, 1979), 293-318.

41. The major studies of this question are Jean Hamelin, *Économie et société en Nouvelle-France* (Québec: Les Presses de l'Université Laval, 1960); Cameron Nish, *Les bourgeois gentilshommes de la Nouvelle-France, 1729-1748* (Montréal: Fides, 1968); Michel Brunet, "La conquête anglaise et la déchéance de la bourgeoisie canadienne, 1760-1793," in Brunet, *La présence anglaise et les Canadiens* (Montréal: Beauchemin, 1964); Louise Dechêne, *Habitants et marchands de Montréal au XVIIe siècle* (Paris: Plon, 1974). Useful surveys of the whole debate are Serge Gagnon, "The Historiography of New France, 1960-1974," *Journal of Canadian Studies*, 13 (Spring, 1978), 80-99: Ramsay Cook, "French-Canadian Interpretations of Canadian History," *Journal of Canadian Studies*, 2 (May, 1967), 3-18.

42. In particular, see Bourque et Legaré, *Le Québec*, 156-59, 194-99.

43. Dankwart Rustow, *A World of Nations* (Washington, D.C.: Brookings Institution, 1967), 15. See also Chong-Do Hah and Jeffrey Martin, "Toward a Synthesis of Conflict and Integration Theories of Nationalism," *World Politics*, 27 (April, 1975), 361-88.

44. Alfred Cobban, *The Nation State and National Self-Determination* (London: Collins, 1969), 107.

45. Gilles Bourque et Nicole Laurin-Frenette, "Classes sociales et idéologies nationalistes au Québec (1760-1970), *Socialisme québécois*, No. 20 (avril-mai-juin, 1970), 18-20 (our translation).

46. Stanley B. Ryerson, "Quebec: Concepts of Class and Nation," in Gary Teeple (ed.), *Capitalism and the National Question in Canada* (Toronto: University of Toronto Press, 1972), 224.

47. Hugh Seton-Watson, *Nationalism Old and New* (Sydney: Sydney University Press, 1964), 5.

48. Léon Dion, *Nationalismes et politique au Québec* (Montréal: Hurtubise HMH, 1975), 16 (our translation, emphasis added). In a similar vein, Anthony D. Smith defines a nation as: "a large, vertically integrated and territorially mobile group featuring common citizenship rights and collective sentiment together with one (or more) common characteristic(s) which differentiate its members from those of similar groups with whom they stand in relations of alliance or conflict." (Anthony D. Smith, *Theories of Nationalism* [New York: Harper & Row, 1972], 175.)

49. The best known development of the "consociational" model is in the work of Arend Lijphart (*The Politics of Accommodation* [Berkeley: University of California Press, 1968] and *Democracy in Plural Societies: a comparative exploration* [New Haven: Yale University Press, 1977]). Discussions, both favourable and critical, of the applicability of the model to Canada appear in: S.J.R. Noel, "Political Parties and Elite Accommodation: interpretations of Canadian federalism," in J. Peter Meekison (ed.), *Canadian Federalism: Myth or Reality*, second edition (Toronto: Methuen, 1971), 121-40; Robert Presthus, *Elite Accommodation in Canadian Politics* (Cambridge: Cambridge University Press, 1973); Kenneth McRae, "Consociationalism and the Canadian Political System," in McRae (ed.), *Consociational Democracy: political accommodation in segmented societies* (Toronto: McClelland and Stewart, 1974), 238-61; Donald V. Smiley, "French-English Relations and Consociational Democracy," in Milton J. Esman (ed.), *Ethnic Conflict in the Western World* (Ithaca: Cornell University Press, 1977),

179-203; and Kenneth McRoberts, "The Study of English-French Relations in Canada," unpublished paper.

Chapter Two

1. Kenneth McRae, "The Structure of Canadian History," in Louis Hartz *et al., The Founding of New Societies* (New York: Harcourt Brace & World, 1964), 222-26.

2. For discussions of this emergence of a *Canadien* dialect, see Gilles-R. Lefebvre, "L'étude de la culture: la linguistique," in Fernand Dumont et Yves Martin, *Situation de la recherche sur le Canada français* (Québec: Les Presses de l'Université Laval, 1965), 233-49; Pierre Harvey, "Nous sommes tous des sous-développés," *Interprétation*, IV, 3 (July-September, 1970), 85-96.

3. For evidence of this friction between *Canadien* elites and metropolitan Frenchmen, see Michel Brunet, *La présence anglaise et les Canadiens* (Montréal: Beauchemin, 1964), 58; and Denis Monière, *Le développement des idéologies au Québec des origines à nos jours* (Montréal: Éditions Québec/Amérique, 1977), 71-72. See also Marcel Rioux, *La question du Québec* (Paris: Seghers, 1969), Chapter Two.

4. Mason Wade, *The French Canadians, 1760-1976*, revised edition, vol. I (Toronto: Macmillan, 1968), 37.

5. *Ibid.*, 23-25.

6. Jean-Charles Falardeau, "The Role and Importance of the Church in French Canada," in Rioux and Martin (eds.), *French-Canadian Society*, 346.

7. See Colette Moreux, *Fin d'une religion?: monographie d'une paroisse canadienne-française* (Montréal: Presses de l'Université de Montréal, 1969), 8.

8. *Ibid.*, 11 (our translation). This paragraph is drawn primarily from the same source.

9. Monière, *Le développement des idéologies*, 67.

10. Moreux, *Fin d'une religion?*, 11 (our translation).

11. Monière, *Le développement des idéologies*, 54-65.

12. See the critique in Gilles Bourque et Anne Legaré, *Le Québec: la question nationale* (Paris: François Maspero, 1979), 12-18.

13. Brunet, *La présence anglaise*, 55 (our translation).

14. Jean Hamelin, *Économie et société en Nouvelle-France* (Québec: Les presses de l'Université Laval, n.d.), 129. The remaining 14 per cent was held by Frenchmen who had established themselves in the colony after 1730.

15. *Ibid.*, 135.

16. Nish, *Les bourgeois-gentilshommes*.

17. For their part, Bourque and Legaré prefer to term these merchants "une couche sociale" of the metropolitan merchant bourgeoisie. Bourque et Legaré, *Le Québec*, 22.

18. Among the major treatments of the post-Conquest period are: Fernand Ouellet, *Histoire économique et sociale du Québec, 1760-1859* (Montréal: Fides, 1971); Jean-Pierre Wallot, *Un Québec qui bougeait* (Montréal: Boréal Express, 1973); Gilles Bourque, *Classes sociales et question nationale au Québec, 1760-1840* (Montréal: Parti pris, 1970).

19. Ouellet, *Histoire économique et sociale*, 567.

20. Brunet, *La présence anglaise*, 54-85.

21. The prevailing conclusion among historians is that while one-third of the

Canadien population did favour the British cause, another third supported the Americans and the final third remained neutral or indifferent. See Richard J. Ossenberg, "The Conquest Revisited: Another Look at Canadian Dualism," *Canadian Review of Sociology and Anthropology*, IV (August, 1967), 213; Bourque, *Classes sociales et question nationale*, 144; Wade, *The French Canadians*, 70. Ossenberg takes this mass indifference to the fate of the British regime, plus resistance to the payment of tithes, as evidence of an assimilationist desire and, in particular, support for "the ideology of the American Revolution" (p. 213). But his analysis is not persuasive. These patterns of behaviour can be better seen as simple reflections of the long-standing, stubborn independence of the rural population vis-à-vis any form of authority.

22. Jean-Pierre Wallot, "Religion and French-Canadian Mores in the Early Nineteenth Century," *Canadian Historical Review*, 52, 1 (March, 1971), 51-94.

23. *Ibid.*, 63, 81.

24. During the first decade of the nineteenth century, the French-Canadian population increased by 32 per cent, but the number of liberal professionals increased by 58 per cent (Ouellet, *Histoire économique et sociale*, 202).

25. See, for instance, Ouellet, *Histoire économique et sociale*, 567. See also Dominique Clift et Sheila McLeod Arnopolous, *Le Fait anglais au Québec* (Montréal: Libre expression, 1979); David V.J. Bell and Louis Balthazar, "Nation and Non-nation: ideological persistence in Canadian history: the early nineteenth century," paper presented to Canadian Political Science Association, June 5, 1969.

26. See Monière, *Le développement des idéologies*, 138.

27. This paragraph is based essentially on Bourque et Legaré, *Le Québec: la question nationale*, 70. See also Monière, *Le développement des idéologies*, 136.

28. Gilles Paquet et Jean-Pierre Wallot, *Patronage et pouvoir dans le Bas-Canada (1794-1812)* (Montréal: Presses de l'Université du Québec, 1973), 90, as cited by Bourque et Legaré, *Le Québec: la question nationale*, 66. As Bourque and Legaré point out, within all colonies the local population is bound to be underrepresented within the upper governmental structures, given the tendency to appoint officials from the metropole. But even where this should not have been a factor, the *Canadiens* were seriously underrepresented.

29. This ambivalence of the *Patriotes* toward the Church is well developed in Fernand Dumont, "Idéologie et conscience historique," in Jean-Paul Bernard (ed.), *Les Idéologies québécoises au 19ᵉ siècle* (Montréal: Boréal Express, 1973), 69; Fernand Ouellet, "Nationalisme et laicisme au XIXᵉ siècle," *ibid.*, 50.

30. Janet Ajzenstat, "Liberalism and Nationality," *Canadian Journal of Political Science*, XIV, 3 (September, 1981), 588-609. Ajzenstat may well be correct in criticizing our suggestion, in previous editions of this volume, that Durham was acting simply on the basis of racial bias. But we can hardly agree with her equation of our analysis of Quebec neo-nationalism to Durham's analysis of the nationalism of the *Patriotes*. It is not our position that "nationalism of the 1960s and after was the product of elites and existed *simply* because it was in the interests of the individuals involved" (p. 594, emphasis added). In fact, Ajzenstat seems to confirm this in her footnote 16.

31. Jean Hamelin *et al.*, *Aperçu de la politique canadienne au XIXᵉ siècle* (Québec: Culture, 1965), 11 (our translation).

32. In fact, the interest in technical education was on the decline at the turn of the century, according to a study of educational journals cited in Ramsay Cook,

Canada and the French-Canadian Question (Toronto: Macmillan, 1967), 51. For a summary of education in Quebec, see *Report* of the Royal Commission of Inquiry on Education in the Province of Quebec (The Parent Commission), Vol. I (Quebec, 1963), Chapter 1; or Louis-Philip Audet, *Histoire de l'enseignement au Québec 1840-1971* (Montréal: Holt, Rinehart & Winston, 1971).

33. Ouellet, *Histoire économique et sociale*, 241 (our translation).

34. From the *Montreal Herald*, quoted in Jean Hamelin et Yves Roby, "L'évolution économique et sociale du Québec 1851-1896," *Recherches Sociographiques*, 10 (mai-décembre, 1969), 167. See also C.J. Cooper, "The social structure of Montreal in the 1850s," *Canadian Historical Association Annual Report* (1956), 66-72.

35. Léon Gérin, "The French-Canadian Family – its Strengths and Weaknesses," in Rioux and Martin (eds.), *French-Canadian Society*.

36. Gérin, "The French-Canadian Family"; also see the discussion of Gérin's work by Gerald Fortin, "L'Étude du milieu rural," in F. Dumont (ed.), *Situation de la recherche sur le Canada français* (Québec: Presses de l'Université Laval, 1962), 106-09.

Chapter Three

1. The share of the tertiary sector of the value of production went from 41.2 to 54.6 per cent, and of employment from 37.2 to 59.7 per cent. Saint-Germain, *Une économie à libérer*, 87.

2. Quoted in P. Dagenais, "Le mythe de la vocation agricole du Québec," in *Mélanges géographiques canadiens offerts à Raoul Blanchard* (Québec: Presses de l'Université Laval, 1959), 195.

3. *Ibid.*

4. John Porter, *The Vertical Mosaic* (Toronto: University of Toronto Press, 1965), 83-89, 93-94; *Report of the Royal Commission on Bilingualism and Biculturalism*, Vol. III B, 447-69.

5. *Report of the Royal Commission on Bilingualism and Biculturalism*, Vol. III B, 469.

6. Everett Hughes, *French Canada in Transition* (Chicago: University of Chicago Press, 1963), 61.

7. Philip Garigue, "Une enquête sur l'industrialisation de la Province de Québec: Schefferville," *L'Actualité économique*, 33 (octobre-décembre, 1957), 419-36; E. Derbyshire, "Notes on the Social Structure of a Canadian Pioneer Town," *Sociological Review*, 8 (July, 1960), 63-75.

8. *Report of the Royal Commission on Bilingualism and Biculturalism*, Vol. III B, 23.

9. A. Raynauld, *Croissance et structure économique de la Province de Québec* (Québec: Ministre de l'industrie et du commerce, 1961). For a comparison in the 1960s, see Bernard Guermond, "Évolution des investissements du Québec de 1961 à 1970," *L'Actualité économique*, 47 (avril-juin, 1971), 162-75.

10. N.W. Taylor, "The Effects of Industrialization, its Opportunities and Consequences, Upon French-Canadian Society," *Journal of Economic History*, 20 (December, 1960), 638-47.

11. P. Harvey, "La perception du capitalisme chez les Canadiens français: une hypothèse pour la recherche," in J.-L. Migué, *Le Québec d'aujourd'hui* (Montréal: Éditions Hurtubise HMH, 1971).

12. Saint-Germain, *Une économie à libérer*, 109ff.

13. See the data in Paul-André Linteau, René Durocher et Jean-Claude Robert, *Histoire du Québec contemporain: de la Confédération à la crise (1867-1929)* (Montréal: Boréal Express, 1979), 410.

14. This was William Ryan's estimate (*ibid.*).

15. This can be gleaned from a wide variety of sources and events. Some examples: the Montreal Regional Council of the CSN takes more nationalist stands than the provincial organization; the University of Montreal has a reputation for its "nationalist school" of historians; a survey of attitudes among high school students in Quebec City and Montreal found the latter more nationalistic regardless of socio-economic status, sex, or age. (H.D. Forbes, "Some Correlates of Nationalism among Quebec Youth in 1968," paper presented to the Canadian Political Science Association, McGill University, June, 1972, pp. 20-21.)

16. H. Miner, "Changes in French-Canadian Rural Culture," in Rioux and Martin (eds.), *French-Canadian Society*, 64-70.

17. G. Fortin, "Le Québec: une ville à inventer," *Recherches sociographiques*, 9 (janvier-août, 1968), 17 (our translation). For the variation that the urban-rural dichotomy disguises, see the same author's "Une classification socio-économique des municipalités agricoles du Québec," *Recherches sociographiques*, 1 (avril-juin, 1960), 207-16.

18. M.A. Tremblay and W.J. Anderson (eds.), *Rural Canada in Transition* (Agricultural Economics Research Council of Canada, Publication No. 6), 65.

19. J.C. Bilodeau, "Canada: Quebec," *Yearbook of Education 1951* (London, 1951), 401.

20. Quebec Royal Commission of Enquiry on Education (The Parent Commission), *Report*, Vol. I, 49. See also Paul Nash, "Quality and Inequality in Canadian Education," *Comparative Education Review*, 5 (October, 1961), 127.

Chapter Four

1. Among the published analyses of the activities of the Quebec provincial governments over this period are: Jean-Guy Genest, "Aspects de l'administration Duplessis," *Revue d'histoire de l'Amérique française*, 25 (décembre, 1971), 389-91; Herbert Quinn, *The Union Nationale: A Study in Quebec Nationalism* (Toronto: University of Toronto Press, 1963), Chapter V; Pierre Elliott Trudeau, "La Province de Québec au moment de la grève," in Trudeau (ed.), *La Grève de l'amiante* (Montréal: Cité libre, 1956), Chapter I; Antonin Dupont, "Louis-Alexandre Taschereau et la législation sociale au Québec, 1920-1936," *Revue d'histoire de l'Amérique française*, 26 (décembre, 1972), 397-426. Gérard Boismenu, *le Duplessisme: politique économique et rapports de force, 1944-1960* (Montréal: Presses de l'Université de Montréal, 1981); James Iain Gow, *Histoire de l'administration publique québécoise, 1867-1970* (Montréal: Presses de l'Université de Montréal, 1986); and Bernard L. Vigod, *Quebec Before Duplessis; the political career of Louis-Alexandre Taschereau* (Kingston and Montreal: McGill-Queen's University Press, 1986).

2. Hélène David, "La grève et le bon Dieu: la grève de l'amiante au Québec," *Sociologie et sociétés*, 1 (novembre, 1969), 258 (our translation).

3. Dominion Bureau of Statistics, *Canada Year Book*, 1957-58, 574-75.

4. D. Vaugeois et J. Lacoursière (eds.), *Histoire 1534-1968* (Montréal: Éditions du renouveau pédagogique, 1968), 539. This common interpretation of the Ungava deal is vigorously disputed in Conrad Black, *Duplessis* (Toronto:

McClelland and Stewart, 1976), 587-88. But see the analysis in Gow, *Histoire de l'administration publique*, 201.

5. Trudeau, "La Province de Québec," 73-76.

6. This legislation is described in detail in Quinn, *The Union Nationale*, 91-94.

7. See, in particular, Trudeau, "La Province de Québec"; and David, "La grève et le bon Dieu."

8. Quebec, Rapport de la commission d'enquête sur la santé et le bien-être social, *Le développement*, Vol. III, Tome I, 143.

9. *Statuts du Québec*, 15 George v (1925), Chap. 55:167, as cited in Dupont, "Taschereau," 407.

10. James I. Gow, "Modernisation et administration publique," in Orban (ed.), *La modernisation politique du Québec*, 163 (our translation). See also Gow, "L'histoire de l'administration publique québécoise," *Recherches sociographiques*, 16 (septembre-décembre, 1975), 385-412.

11. R. Bolduc, "Le recrutement et la sélection dans la fonction publique au Québec," *Administration publique du Canada*, 7 (1964), 207.

12. See, for instance, Michel Brunet, "Trois dominantes de la pensée canadienne-française: l'agriculturisme, l'anti-étatisme et le messianisme," in Brunet, *La présence anglaise et les Canadiens: études sur l'histoire et la pensée des deux Canadas* (Montréal: Beauchemin, 1964), 113-66.

13. Richard Arès, S.J., *Notre question nationale* (Montréal: Éditions de l'Action nationale, 1943), 225 (quoted in Fernand Dumont and Guy Rocher, "An Introduction to a Sociology of French Canada," in Rioux and Martin [eds.], *French-Canadian Society*, 346).

14. Québec, *Commission royale d'enquête sur les problèmes constitutionnels*, 1956, Vol. III, 40.

15. See Brunet, "Trois dominantes de la pensée canadienne-française," 140-66; Trudeau, "La Province de Québec," 1-90.

16. Québec, *Commission royale*, Vol. III, Tome I, 66.

17. L'École sociale populaire, *Pour la restauration sociale au Canada* (Montréal: L'École sociale populaire, 1933).

18. The text of this program appears in Quinn, *The Union Nationale*, Appendix B.

19. Thus, André-J. Bélanger observes that the program "ne reconnait que timidement le droit d'intervention par voie de nationalisation auprès des entreprises fautives." André-J. Bélanger, *L'apolitisme des idéologies québécoises: le grand tournant de 1934-36* (Québec: Les Presses de l'Université Laval, 1974), 312.

20. Quinn, *The Union Nationale*, 61.

21. Maxime Raymond, *Program fédéral du Bloc*, Document No. 10 (Montréal: Imprimerie populaire, 1943).

22. *Ibid.*

23. Bélanger, *L'apolitisme*, 359-68.

24. Bélanger applies this term to the nationalist intellectuals of the 1930s.

25. See Gérald Fortin, "Le nationalisme canadien-français et les classes sociales," *Revue d'histoire de l'Amérique française*, 22 (mars, 1969), 525-34.

26. Bélanger, *L'apolitisme*, 359-68.

27. Brunet, "Trois dominantes de la pensée canadienne-française," 124 (our translation).

28. Harvey, "Pourquoi le Québec et les Canadiens français occupent-ils une place inférieure sur le plan économique?" in Durocher et Linteau, *Le "retard"*

du Québec, 113-27. Harvey's analysis evokes Albert Memmi's thesis of the colonized's attempt to assert himself by forthrightly glorifying the negative image the colonizer imposes on him (an image which is the mirror opposite of the colonizer's self-image). See Albert Memmi, *Portrait du colonisé* (Montréal: Les Éditions l'Etincelle, 1972). This edition includes Memmi's essay, "Les Canadiens français sont-ils des colonisés?"

29. René Durocher, "Maurice Duplessis et sa conception de l'autonomie provinciale au début de sa carrière politique," *Revue d'histoire de l'Amérique française*, 23 (juin, 1969), 21.

30. René Chaloult, *Mémoires politiques* (Montréal: Éditions du Jour, 1969), 67. See also the analysis of Duplessis's personal ideology in Denis Monière, *Le développement des idéologies au Québec: des origines à nos jours* (Montréal: Éditions Québec/Amérique, 1977), 296-308.

31. See Ralph R. Heintzman, "The Struggle for Life: The French Daily Press of Montreal and the Problem of Economic Growth in the Age of Laurier, 1896-1911" (Ph.D. dissertation, York University, 1977). For a detailed description of the writings of *Action française* and *Action nationale*, see Susan Mann Trofimenkoff, *Action française: French-Canadian Nationalism in the Twenties* (Toronto: University of Toronto Press, 1975).

32. As Marcel Fournier documents, the notion of a "new middle class" has figured very prominently in analyses by Québécois social scientists of Quebec's post-World War II history (Marcel Fournier, *L'entrée dans la modernité: science, culture et société au Québec* [Montréal: Éditions Saint-Martin, 1986], 39, note 22]. Probably the first analyst to refer explicitly to a Francophone new middle class was Hubert Guindon ("The Social Evolution of Quebec Reconsidered," in Rioux and Martin [eds.], *French-Canadian Society*, 157-61). Some more recent analyses employing the term have been Louis Maheu, "La conjoncture des luttes nationales au Québec: mode d'intervention étatique des classes moyennes et enjeux d'un mouvement social de rupture," *Sociologie et sociétés*, 11, 2 (1979), 125-44; Marc Renaud, "Quebec New Middle Class in the Search of Local Hegemony," *International Review of Community Development*, 39-40 (1978), 1-36; Gilbert Renaud, *A l'ombre du rationalisme: La société québécoise, de sa dépendance à sa quotidienneté* (Montréal: Editions Saint-Martin, 1984).

33. Val Borris, "Capital Accumulation and the Rise of the New Middle Class," *The Review of Radical Political Economics*, 12, 1 (Spring, 1980), 17-34.

34. This discussion of the new middle class, as a general concept, is drawn essentially from Borris, "Capital Accumulation." See also George Ross, "Marxism and the New Middle Classes," *Theory and Society*, 5, 2 (1978), 163-90; George Ross and Jane Jenson, "Post-War Class Struggles and the Crisis of Left Politics," in Ralph Miliband *et al.* (eds.), *Socialist Register, 1985-86* (London: Merlin, 1986), 28-29; G. Cardechi, "On the Economic Identification of the New Middle Class," *Economy and Society*, 4, 4 (1975); Anthony Giddens, *The Class Structure of Advanced Societies*, second edition (London: Hutchinson, 1981), 107, 177; and Erik Olin Wright, *Class, Crisis and the State* (London: Verso, 1979).

35. Borris, "Capital Accumulation," 19.

36. See Marcel Fournier, "La frère Marie-Victorin et les 'petites sciences,'" in Marcel Fournier, *L'entrée dans la modernité: science, culture et société au Québec* (Montréal: Éditions Saint-Martin, 1986), 74-113.

37. Raymond Duchesne demonstrates that there was little opposition among the clergy to the development of physical and biological sciences in French-Canadian universities. The initiatives were supported at the highest levels of the

Church. Raymond Duchesne, "D'intérêt public et d'intérêt privé: l'institution-nalisation de l'enseignement et de la recherche scientifiques au Québec (1920-1940)," in Yvan Lamonde et Esther Trépanier, *L'avènement de la modernité culturelle au Québec* (Québec: Institut québécois de recherche sur la culture, 1986), 195-202.

38. Raymond Duchesne, *La science et le pouvoir au Québec (1920-1965)*, La documentation québécoise (Québec: Éditeur officiel du Québec, 1978), 113-16.

39. *Ibid.*, 207-15.

40. Duchesne, "D'intérêt public et d'intérêt privé," 192, Table One.

41. *Ibid.*, 49.

42. See Fournier, *L'entrée dans la modernité*, 29-37.

43. *Annuaire de l'École des sciences sociales, économiques et politiques, 1920-1921*, Université de Montréal, 2 (as cited in Marcel Fournier, *L'entrée dans la modernité*, 70).

44. *Ibid.*, 62.

45. *Ibid.*, 143. See also Alain G. Gagnon, "The Development and Nationaliza-tion of Social Sciences in Quebec," *Quebec Studies*, 1, 4 (1986), 71-89.

46. Marcel Fournier, "L'institutionnalisation des sciences sociales au Québec," *Sociologie et sociétés*, v, 1 (mai, 1973), 38.

47. Georges-Henri Lévesque, "La première décennie de la Faculté des sciences sociales à l'Université Laval," in Georges-Henri Lévesque *et al.* (eds.), *Continu-ité et rupture: les sciences sociales au Québec* (Montréal: Presses de l'Université de Montréal, 1984), 56.

48. Fournier, *L'entrée dans la modernité*, 132

49. *Ibid.*, 137; Lévesque, "La première décennie," 60.

50. Fournier, *L'entrée dans la modernité*, 143-44 (our translation).

51. *Ibid.*, 138. The term "social movement" was in fact adopted by one of the Faculté's leading professors, Jean-Charles Falardeau, in 1959. It is striking that on the basis of his own careful analysis of the period, Fournier, a younger scholar, should echo Falardeau's claim, even seeing the school as at the origin of the Quiet Revolution. After all, during the 1970s it had become distinctly unfa-shionable to ascribe such historical significance to the liberal intellectuals of the Faculté.

52. Fournier, *L'entrée dans la modernité*, 140-41.

53. Duchesne, *La science et le pouvoir*, 64. See also Fournier, "L'institution-nalisation," 50.

54. Marcel Rioux, "Sur l'évolution des idéologies au Québec," *Revue de l'In-stitut de sociologie*, No. 1 (1968), 113-14, as approvingly quoted by Fournier, *L'entrée dans la modernité*, 139 (our translation).

55. Duchesne, *La science et le pouvoir*, 102.

56. Fournier, *L'entrée dans la modernité*, 6.

57. Laval University had refused the subsidy in 1871, allegedly for fear that it would entail political interference. (Duchesne, *La science et le pouvoir*, 2.)

58. *Ibid.*, 103.

59. *Ibid.*, 44.

60. *Ibid.*, 103. To be sure, these figures were far below McGill's: 2,350, 247, and 45, respectively.

61. Dominion Bureau of Statistics, *Fall Enrollment in Universities and Col-leges*, Series 81-204. By way of comparison, the enrolments for McGill were 420 in 1955 and 315 in 1959. In fact, enrolment *decreased* at McGill during the 1950s.

62. *Ibid.* The figures for McGill were 58 in 1952 and 53 in 1958.

63. *Report of the Royal Commission on Bilingualism and Biculturalism,* Book III: *The Work World,* 451.

64. *Ibid.,* 474.

65. Pierre-Paul Gagné, "L'Hydro et les Québécois: l'histoire d'amour achève," *La Presse,* June 13, 1975, A-8 (as cited in Marc Renaud, "Quebec New Middle Class," 24).

66. Royal Commission, *The Work World,* 474.

67. Hubert Guindon, "Two Cultures: an essay on nationalism, class and ethnic tension," in Richard H. Leach (ed.), *Contemporary Canada* (Durham, N.C.: Duke University Press, 1967), 33-59. See also Guindon's earlier essay, "The Social Evolution of Quebec Reconsidered," in Rioux and Martin (eds.), *French-Canadian Society,* 137-61.

68. Michael B. Behiels, *Prelude to Quebec's Quiet Revolution* (Kingston and Montreal: McGill-Queen's Unversity Press, 1985), 80, 236.

69. *Ibid.,* Chapter Eight.

70. *Ibid.,* p. 119. For commentaries on *Cité libre,* see André-J. Bélanger, *Ruptures et constantes: idéologies du Québec en éclatement, La Relève, La JEC, Cité libre, Parti pris* (Montreal: Hurtubise HMH, 1977); André Carrier, "L'idéologie politique de la révue Cité libre," *Canadian Journal of Political Science,* 1 (December, 1968), 414-28; Monière, *Le développement des idéologies,* 311-18. Also, see the analyses of Trudeau and *Cité libre* in Ramsay Cook, *The Maple Leaf Forever* (Toronto: Macmillan, 1971), 23-45; and the introduction by Cook to Pierre Elliott Trudeau, *Approaches to Politics* (Toronto: Oxford University Press, 1970). See also Reg Whitaker, "Reason, Passion and Interest: Pierre Trudeau's Eternal Liberal Triangle," *Canadian Journal of Political and Social Theory,* 4, 1 (Winter, 1980), 5-31. For a less sympathetic analysis of Trudeau's political philosophy, see in particular Henry David Rempel, "The Practice and Theory of the Fragile State: Trudeau's Conception of Authority," *Journal of Canadian Studies,* 10 (November, 1976), 24-38.

71. Gérard Filion, "La reprise de nos richesses naturelles," *Le Devoir,* November 25, 1953 (as quoted in Behiels, *Prelude to Quebec's Quiet Revolution,* 112).

72. Behiels, *Prelude to Quebec's Quiet Revolution,* 111-14.

73. See, for instance, Brunet, *La présence anglaise et les Canadiens.*

74. Paul-André Linteau, "Quelques réflexions autour de la bourgeoisie québécoise 1950-1914," *Revue d'histoire de l'Amérique française,* 30 (juin, 1976), 64 (our translation).

75. See Dorval Brunelle, *La désillusion tranquille* (Montréal: Hurtubise HMH, 1978), 107. Also, see Luc Racine et Roch Denis, "La conjoncture politique québécoise depuis 1960," *Socialisme québécois,* nos. 21-22 (avril, 1971), 17.

76. Coleman, *The Independence Movement,* 96.

77. See Brunelle, *La désillusion tranquille,* 104.

78. Boismenu, *Le duplessisme,* 344.

79. Roy, *La marche des Québécois,* 174.

80. See Gow, *Histoire de l'administration publique,* 270.

81. Jorge Niosi, "La nouvelle bourgeoisie canadienne-française," *Les Cahiers du socialisme,* No. 1 (printemps, 1978), 8 (our translation; emphasis in original deleted). See also, Boismenu, *Le duplessisme,* 121.

82. See René Durocher et Michèle Jean, "Duplessis et la Commission royale d'enquête sur les problèmes constitutionnels, 1953-1956," *Revue d'histoire de l'Amérique français,* 25 (décembre, 1971), 337-64.

83. Hélène David, "L'état des rapports de classe au Québec de 1945 à 1967," *Sociologie et sociétés*, 7 (novembre, 1975), 47, table 1, 63 (as cited in Behiels, *Prelude to Quebec's Quiet Revolution*, 122).

84. Jacques Rouillard, *Histoire de la CSN, 1921-1981* (Montréal: Boréal Express and CSN, 1981), 169.

85. Behiels, *Prelude to Quebec's Quiet Revolution*, 132.

86. *Ibid.*, 133.

87. See Rouillard, *Histoire de la CSN*, 174-77; Behiels, *Prelude to Quebec's Quiet Revolution*, 133-38.

88. Behiels, *Prelude to Quebec's Quiet Revolution*, 124.

89. *Ibid.*, Chapter Eight; Rouillard, *Histoire de la CSN*, 193.

90. Behiels, *Prelude to Quebec's Quiet Revolution*, Chapters One and Two.

91. On the FPTQ's stance toward the Duplessis regime, see Quinn, *The Union nationale*, 97, 121-22.

92. *Ibid.*, 122.

93. As we have already noted, the Gouin administration had created the École des hautes études commerciales despite clerical opposition. For a detailed examination of Church-state tensions during the Taschereau period, see Antonin Dupont, *Les Relations entre l'Église et l'État sous Louis-Alexandre Taschereau, 1920-1936* (Montréal: Guerin, 1973). Also, see Gow, *Histoire de l'administration publique*, 263.

94. Boismenu, *Le duplessisme*, 337.

95. Black, *Duplessis*, 499.

96. Robert Rumilly, *Maurice Duplessis et son temps* (Montréal: Fides, 1973), II, 117-18, as cited in Boismenu, *Le duplessisme*, 338.

97. Black, *Duplessis*, 497.

98. See Black, *Duplessis*, 528-39. As well, see the assessment and references in Gow, *Histoire de l'administration publique*, 264.

99. Black, *Duplessis*, 549.

100. Robert Rumilly, *Histoire de la Province de Québec* (Montréal: Fides, 1969), XL, 102-03 (our translation).

101. See Jean Hamelin et Louis Beaudoin, "Les cabinets provinciaux, 1867-1967," *Recherches sociographiques*, 8 (septembre-décembre, 1967), 299-318.

102. *L'Information*, 18 mai 1935, as cited in Albert Faucher, "Pouvoir politique et pouvoir économique dans l'évolution du Canada français," in Fernand Dumont et Jean-Paul Montminy, *Le pouvoir dans la société canadienne-française* (Québec: Les presses de l'Université Laval, 1966), 69.

103. Black, *Duplessis*, Chapter 18. Also see Porter, *The Vertical Mosaic*, 92, 311, 546-48.

104. Quinn, *The Union Nationale*, 142, note 27; Black, *Duplessis*, 304.

105. Black, *Duplessis*, 606.

106. Gérard Boismenu contends that the economic policies of the Duplessis regime can be understood by situating them within the interests of Canadian capital, which presumably in the case of Quebec was primarily anti-Keynesian, and American capital, which was the hegemonic interest (Boismenu, *Le duplessisme*, 115-27, 325-27, 393). But it is not entirely clear that these interests dictated the passive state role of the Duplessis years. Canadian capital's attitude was changing: Boismenu acknowledges that Keynesianism already had become the majority position with Canadian capital as a whole (*ibid.*, 115). As we shall see, American capital (which is portrayed as the predominant force) was not at all hostile to the vigorous state expansion of the Quiet Revolution, including such

state inroads on Canadian capital as the nationalization of hydroelectrical enterprises. The instances we cite suggest that during the 1950s Canadian and American capital in Quebec might well have supported important forms of state intervention – if the Quebec government was resolved to pursue them.

107. Black, *Duplessis*, 585-87.

108. See the brief account in Rumilly, *Histoire de la Province de Québec*, 253-56.

109. See Christopher Armstrong and H.V. Nelles, "Contrasting Development of the Hydro-Electric Industry in the Montreal and Toronto Regions, 1900-1930," *Journal of Canadian Studies*, 18, 1 (Spring, 1983), 5-27.

110. Montreal *Gazette*, December 11, 1944 (as cited in Quinn, *The Union nationale*, 83). See also Rumilly, *Histoire de la Province de Québec*, XL, 257.

111. According to Pierre Laporte: "Duplessis was horrified at the thought of change – not only in his immediate circle but in the provincial administration as well. Born in the last quarter of the 19th century, he apparently lived through the tremendous industrial changes of the past fifty years without being influenced by them in any way. He did adopt a timid program of social welfare, but his odd manner of striving to make it as ineffectual as possible clearly indicates that he moved forward in this field against his true wishes." Pierre Laporte, *The True Face of Duplessis* (Montreal: Harvest House, 1960), 119.

112. Chaloult, *Mémoires politiques*, 281-95.

113. Durocher et Jean, "Duplessis et la Commission royale."

114. Chaloult, *Mémoires politiques*, 42.

115. In comparison, under the Liberal regime of Mitchell Hepburn, Ontario's expenditures also increased over this period but not by quite the same extent. Quebec's spending was 73.6 per cent of that of Ontario in 1934-35 but had risen to 84.3 per cent in 1949-50. These figures are drawn from André Blais and Kenneth McRoberts, "Public Expenditure in Ontario and Quebec, 1950-1980: explaining the differences," *Journal of Canadian Studies*, 18, 1 (Spring, 1983), Table One.

116. Black, *Duplessis*, 199-204. See also Boismenu, *Le duplessisme*, 262-63. See also Gow, *Histoire de l'administration publique*, 267.

117. See Dominique Clift, Montreal *Star*, March 5, 1977.

118. Black, *Duplessis*, 204.

119. These data are drawn from Blais and McRoberts, "Public Expenditure in Ontario and Quebec," note 8.

120. See the account of the fate of these dissidents in Rumilly, *Histoire de la Province de Québec*, XXXVI (Montréal: Fides, 1966), Chapter VI.

121. Robert Boily, "Les hommes politiques du Québec, 1867-1967," *Revue d'histoire de l'Amérique française*, 21 (décembre, 1967), 626.

122. The districts designated for the purposes of this calculation as parts of the Montreal and Quebec City regions include all districts designated with "Montreal" or "Quebec" plus Chambly, Jacques-Cartier, Laval, Levis, Maisonneuve, and St. Sauveur. Calculated from data in Québec, *Annuaire du Québec, 1966-67* (Québec: Ministere de l'Industrie et du commerce, 1967), 158, Table 6. In 1951, these districts collectively represented about 42 percent of the total Quebec population.

123. Boily, "Les hommes politiques," 614-16.

124. Vincent Lemieux, *Parenté et politique: l'organisation sociale dans l'Île d'Orléans* (Québec: Les Presses de l'Université Laval, 1971), Appendice C.

125. Vincent Lemieux et Raymond Hudon, *Patronage et politique au Québec*,

1944-1972 (Sillery, Québec: Les Éditions du Boréal Express, 1975), Chapter v.

126. Boily, "Les hommes politiques," 621, note 46.

127. An analysis of this aspect of Union nationale electoral campaigns is contained in Kenneth McRoberts, "Mass Acquisition of a Nationalist Ideology: Quebec Prior to the Quiet Revolution" (Ph.D. dissertation, University of Chicago, 1975), Chapter x.

128. Lemieux, *Parenté et politique*, Chapters ii and iii.

129. This demarcation of the districts of the Montreal and Quebec City areas follows note 122. To be sure, we should not exaggerate this picture of Union nationale omnipotence in Quebec. Even in rural areas, substantial proportions of electors voted for the Liberals. In the counties outside Montreal and Quebec City, the Liberals received 36 per cent of the vote in 1948 and 42 per cent in 1952 and 1956 (the figures for the Union nationale are 54, 55, and 56 per cent). Given the single-member plurality electoral system, most of these Liberal votes were not translated into seats. Among the ten French-Canadian districts of Montreal the Union nationale percentages were somewhat lower: the Union nationale received 56 per cent of the votes in 1948, 49 per cent in 1952, and 52 per cent in 1956.

130. The argument is most explicitly made in Quinn, *The Union Nationale*, Chapter vi.

131. See McRoberts, "Mass Acquisition," Chapter x.

132. This analysis of survey data appears in *ibid.*, Chapter vii.

133. Maurice Pinard, "Working Class Politics: An Interpretation of the Quebec Case," *Canadian Review of Sociology and Anthropology*, 7 (1970), 87-109. The primary empirical support that Pinard offers for his interpretation of the Union nationale strength is his analysis of 1962 electoral survey data, which shows that class identification explains most of the difference between working-class and middle-class French Canadians in support for the Union nationale. He also finds that Union nationale support is positively associated with traditionalism and authoritarianism but, as this is true for both classes, these variables do not explain the disproportionate working-class support for the Union nationale. On the other hand, by having different effects in the two classes, religiosity and conservatism do help to interpret part of the class differential in Union nationale support. Ethnic consciousness has no association with support for the Union nationale. Beyond the 1962 survey data, Pinard also refers to ecological analysis of the 1936 and 1939 elections, which suggests that whereas working-class French Canadians had been strong supporters of Union nationale in 1936 they abandoned it in 1939. To Pinard, this suggests that initial Union nationale working-class support had been based on purely economic grievances, which were not satisfied by the first Duplessis administration, rather than adherence to the distinctive nationalist ideology of the Union nationale.

134. Boily shows that from this *"classe moyenne-inférieure" – "le commerçant, le marchand, le petit industriel"* – were drawn twelve of the thirty-four ministers of the Duplessis period. Only two ministers of the Taschereau cabinets had been drawn from this commercial middle class. Thus, not only was the power of the *haute-bourgeoisie* definitively broken during the Duplessis period, even the liberal professional middle class had to make room for others. (Boily, "Les hommes politiques," 621, note 47.) This major change in the social origins of the political elite, with the Union nationale, is just one more indication that the coming to power of the Duplessis regime was a much greater turning point in Quebec history than has generally been acknowledged.

135. Chaloult, *Mémoires politiques*, 55. Léon Dion has also stressed the extent

to which the Duplessis regime had few close links to the intellectuals and Duplessis had no interest in developing such links. He preferred simply to neutralize the influence of intellectuals by discrediting them. Léon Dion, *La prochaine révolution* (Québec: Éditions Leméac, 1973), 16.

136. Lemieux et Hudon, *Patronage et politique*, 81.

137. Trudeau, *La grève de l'amiante*, 397. It should be noted, however, that the Liberals did promise to rescind these laws during their 1956 election campaign.

138. *Ibid.*

139. See Quinn, *The Union Nationale*, 157. See also Hélène David, "L'état des rapports de classe au Québec de 1945 à 1967," *Sociologie et sociétés*, 7 (novembre, 1975), 44-47. Quinn's analysis of voting patterns in industrial towns does show that support for the Union nationale was significantly lower in towns where CTCC affiliation was high (Quinn, *The Union Nationale*, 101).

140. Calculated from tables in Jean Hamelin, Jacques Letarte et Marcel Hamelin, "Les élections provinciales dans le Québec," *Cahiers de géographie de Québec*, 4 (octobre, 1959-mars, 1960), Première partie.

141. See W. Dale Posgate, "Social Mobilization and Political Change in Quebec" (Ph.D. dissertation, State University of New York at Buffalo, 1972).

142. See McRoberts, "Mass Acquisition," Chapter IX.

143. See Donald V. Smiley, "Constitutional Adaptation and Canadian Federalism since 1945," *Documents of the Royal Commission on Bilingualism and Biculturalism*, No. 4 (Ottawa: Queen's Printer, 1970), 72. See also Gow, *Histoire de l'administration publique*, 266.

144. Black, *Duplessis*, 449-55.

145. See the accounts in Durocher et Jean, "Duplessis et la Commission royale," and in Black, *Duplessis*, Chapter 14. See also Kenneth McRoberts, "Unilateralism, Bilateralism and Multilateralism: approaches to Canadian federalism," in Richard Simeon (ed.), *Intergovernmental Relations*, Collected Research Studies of the Royal Commission on the Economic Union and Development Prospects for Canada (Ottawa: Supply and Services Canada, 1985), 83.

146. Hamelin et Beaudoin, "Les cabinets provinciaux."

147. There is even evidence that French-Canadian federal politicians were not particularly interested in securing the economic portfolios. Reflecting their own backgrounds in the liberal professions and the relative weakness of business elites within their French-Canadian clientele, they appear to have placed top priority on posts commanding the greatest amount of prestige among liberal professional circles – in particular, Minister of Justice – or on those providing access to patronage that would secure electoral support, e.g., the post office. They apparently demonstrated a "repeated indifference . . . to the disposition of the principal economic and finance portfolios." Frederick W. Gibson (ed.), "Cabinet Formation and Bicultural Relations," *Studies of the Royal Commission on Bilingualism and Biculturalism*, No. 6 (Ottawa: Queen's Printer, 1970), 169.

Chapter Five

1. There is in fact a continuing minor debate over the precise origins of the term. Léon Dion claims that the term first appeared in an anonymous article in the Toronto *Globe and Mail* (Dion, *La prochaine revolution ou le Québec en crise* [Montréal: Leméac, 1973], 11). But Evelyn Dumas has recently credited Peter Gzowski, who was not writing for the *Globe and Mail* (Evelyn Dumas, "The Two Faces of the Revolution," *Canadian Forum* [December, 1984], 31).

However, Dumas's claim in turn led Montreal journalist Jean-V. Dufresne to write to the *Canadian Forum* to establish that the journalist in question really was Brian Upton of the *Toronto Telegram* (*Canadian Forum*, [February, 1985], 5). Nonetheless, there is at least agreement that the term was coined by a Toronto-based, Anglophone journalist.

2. For descriptions and analyses of the Quiet Revolution ideology, see Richard Jones, *Community in Crisis: French-Canadian Nationalism in Perspective*, Carleton Library No. 59 (Toronto: McClelland and Stewart, 1972); Léon Dion, "Genèse et caractères du nationalisme de croissance," in Congrès des affaires canadiennes, *Les nouveaux Québécois* (Québec: Les Presses de l'Université Laval, 1964), 59-76; Jean-Marc Léger, "Le néo-nationalisme, où conduit-il?," *ibid.*, 41-48; Marcel Rioux, "Sur l'évolution des idéologies au Québec," *Revue de l'Institut de sociologie*, 1 (1968), 95-124; Gérard Bergeron, *Le Canada Français: après deux siècles de patience* (Paris: Éditions du seuil, 1967), Chapter VI; Louis Balthazar, *Bilan du nationalisme au Québec* (Montréal: Hexagone, 1986), Chapter VII.

3. Marcel Rioux, *La question du Québec* (Paris: Seghers, 1969), 104 (our translation).

4. Dion, "Genèse et caractères," 68.

5. Institut canadien des affaires publiques, *Le rôle de l'État* (Montréal: Éditions du jour, 1962).

6. See the analysis of the controversy surrounding the establishment of a Ministry of Education in Léon Dion, *Le Bill 60 et la société québécoise* (Montréal: Éditions Hurtubise HMH, 1967).

7. For discussion of federal-provincial conflict over economic development, see Roland Parenteau, "L'expérience de la planification au Québec (1960-1969)," *L'Actualité économique*, No. 4 (janvier-février, 1970), 679-96; Bourque et Legaré, *Le Québec: la question nationale*, 186-87; and Claude Morin, *Le pouvoir québécois . . . en négociation* (Montréal: Boréal Express, 1972), 120-22. The experience of the Caisse is discussed in Bourque et Legaré, *Le Québec*, 88. For a discussion of the alleged hesitations within the Quebec state, see Jacques Parizeau, "Le Québec remet-il en cause le rôle même du secteur public?" *Le Devoir*, December 30, 1970.

8. J.I. Gow, "L'évolution de l'administration publique au Québec," as cited in Daniel Latouche, "La vraie nature de . . . La Révolution tranquille," *Canadian Journal of Political Science*, 7 (September, 1974), 533.

9. Latouche, "La vraie nature," 533.

10. *Ibid.* These data seem to disprove William Coleman's claim that "The provincial bureaucracy actually grew more in the 1950s than it did in the early 1960s." (Coleman, *The Independence Movement in Quebec*, 11.)

11. Latouche, "La vraie nature." See the comments in Gow, *Histoire de l'administration publique*, 298.

12. This point is made in an especially incisive fashion by Jean-Marc Léger in "Commentaire: paradoxes d'une révolution ou le temps des illusions," in Dumont et Montminy (eds.), *Le pouvoir dans la société canadienne-française*, 39-53.

13. Paul-André Linteau, René Durocher, Jean-Claude Robert et François Ricard, *Le Québec depuis 1930* (Montréal: Boréal Express, 1986), 592.

14. *Ibid.*

15. Georges Matthews, *Le choc démographique* (Montréal: Boréal Express, 1984), 17-18, 32. The rate cited is the Indice synthetique de fécondité.

16. On this basis, we would heavily qualify William Coleman's assertion that:

"the political program of the Tremblay Commission became the basis, the cornerstone, of political strategy of Quebec throughout the 1960s and into the 1970s. It may be argued that the various movements for independence and for renewed federalism that have emerged since are all variations on the Tremblay theme." (Coleman, *The Independence Movement*, 17-18.) If they may have shared with the Tremblay Commission some common jurisdictional grievances against the federal government, the political movements of the 1960s and 1970s were based on a fundamentally different conception of the role of the Quebec state. The movements for independence and for renewed federalism can be better seen as variations on *this* theme of the interventionist state. In fact, it is because they were rooted in a different conception of the state's role that they could so far exceed the Tremblay Commission's "political program" of demands on the federal government. On this fundamental disjunction between the Tremblay Commission and the Quiet Revolution, see Gilles Bourque, "À propos du mouvement indépendantiste," *Canadian Journal of Political and Social Theory*, x, 3 (Fall, 1986), 157.

17. A detailed description and analysis of Quebec-Ottawa relations over this period appears in Smiley, "Constitutional Adaptation and Canadian Federalism since 1945." The next few pages draw quite extensively on this document.

18. *Ibid.*, Chapter VI.

19. *Ibid.*, 69.

20. For a more detailed discussion of these arrangements and their implications for Canadian federalism, see Kenneth McRoberts, "Unilateralism, Bilateralism and Multilateralism: approaches to Canadian federalism," in Richard Simeon (ed.), *Intergovernmental Relations*, Collected Research Studies of the Royal Commission on the Economic Union and Development Prospects for Canada, No. 63 (Ottawa: Supply and Services, 1985), 80-87.

21. While Lesage would claim personal credit for the new initiatives of his administration, they often originated with others who had had to fight hard to overcome his misgivings (see Bergeron, *le Canada français*, 144). In the election of 1960, Lesage had personally assured the electorate that his administration would never establish a provincial Ministry of Education. Only after Paul Gérin-Lajoie had waged a long and intensive campaign to get the idea of a Ministry of Education accepted within the party did Lesage finally agree to change his position. Similarly, the nationalization of Hydro-Québec in 1963 was largely due to the indefatigable efforts of René Lévesque. Without the approval of the cabinet, Lévesque launched a personal campaign on behalf of nationalization, speaking throughout the province and arousing considerable public support. Then, in a famous cabinet session at the Lac-à-l'épaule wilderness retreat, Lévesque finally managed to overcome the hesitations of his colleagues. Throughout this process, Lévesque met the active opposition of Lesage. In the words of Georges-Émile Lapalme, former Liberal leader and major minister within the Lesage cabinet, "the Prime Minister remained an unyielding opponent of nationalization right to the last minute" (Georges Émile Lapalme, *Le paradis du pouvoir* [Montréal: Lémeac, 1973], 196, our translation). Without the presence of Gérin-Lajoie and Lévesque, the accomplishments of the Lesage administration would have been much less substantial. Nevertheless, they were present, constituting a force that was virtually absent from the Duplessis cabinet.

22. Calculated from data in Vincent Lemieux, *Le quotient politique vrai: le vote provincial et fédéral au Québec* (Québec: Les Presses de l'Université Laval, 1973), 24.

23. The 1962 figure is based on the same set of districts as were used in the 1956 calculation.

24. See *Report of the Royal Commission on Bilingualism and Biculturalism*, Book II: Education (Ottawa: Queen's Printer, 1968).

25. These results are drawn from Bernard Bonin and Mario Polèse, "À propos de l'association économique Canada-Québec," École nationale d'administration publique, mars, 1980, 13-25.

26. See the data in Pierre Frechette, "L'économie de la Confédération: un point de vue québécois," *Canadian Public Policy*, 3, 4 (1977), 431-39.

27. The point that the dynamic of the Quiet Revolution and its neo-nationalism came from within Quebec was energetically made in a speech by Claude Charron, a Parti québécois member of the National Assembly: "I will never agree with those who portray this moment in Quebec history as a measure imposed from the outside. One must agree with them that, led in those times as it is today by the foreign investor, Quebec's economic development risked losing its attractiveness to foreign investors if our level of qualified manpower did not 'catch up' to some mean. But one must have very little knowledge of our history to ignore how much it [the Quiet Revolution] was from the interior, it must be said, from our soul and our head, this taste to learn which thrust on the public scene the most dynamic and devoted men of our epoch." (Text of speech delivered in the National Assembly by Claude Charron, March 25, 1975 – as reproduced in *Le Jour*, March 27, 1975 [our translation].)

28. Jean-Jacques Simard, *La longue marche des technocrates* (Montréal: Éditions coopératives Albert Saint-Martin, 1979), 28 (our translation).

29. Guindon, "The Social Evolution of Quebec Reconsidered," 157-61.

30. See Charles Taylor, "Nationalism and the Political Intelligentsia: A Case Study," *Queen's Quarterly*, 72, 1 (Spring, 1965), 150-68.

31. Coleman, *The Independence Movement*, 7.

32. *Ibid.*

33. See, for instance, the account of new-middle-class growth over the post-war years in Linteau *et al.*, *Le Québec depuis 1930*, 281.

34. Coleman, *The Independence Movement*, 7.

35. P. Gervais, "Les diplomés en science sociales dans la fonction publique du Québec" (thèse de maîtrise en sciences politiques, Université de Montréal, 1970), as cited in Simard, *La longue marche*, 38.

36. Coleman notes that during the 1950s the civil service drew primarily from individuals having twelve years of education or less (Coleman, *The Independence Movement*, 8). Yet, this is beside the point. The issue should be whether new-middle-class Francophones were available when in fact they were seriously sought. After all, Duplessis had banned graduates of Laval's Faculté des sciences sociales from the Quebec civil service. In the 1960s, when new-middle-class Francophones were recruited for the Quebec public service they clearly were available.

37. Guindon, "The Social Evolution of Quebec Reconsidered," 159.

38. Coleman, *The Independence Movement*, 8.

39. In his chapter on educational reform, Coleman declares that "the changes were supported by the French-Canadian business class, organized labour and nationalists drawn from the new middle class" (*ibid.*, 180).

40. Coleman, *The Independence Movement*, 162.

41. Frédéric Lesemann, *Services and Circuses: community and the welfare state* (Montreal: Black Rose Books, 1984 [translation of *Du pain et des services*]), 58.

42. Gilbert Renaud, *L'éclatement de la profession en service social* (Montréal: Éditions coopératives Albert Saint-Martin, 1978), 21. This paragraph is drawn entirely from Renaud's study.

43. Gow, *Histoire de l'administration publique*, 234. A source cited in Renaud presents the measure as the result of an administrative decision (Renaud, *L'éclatement de la profession*).

44. Gow, *Histoire de l'administration publique*, 234. Renaud notes the earlier impact of the Cour des jeunes délinquants established in Montreal and Quebec City between 1936 and 1940 (Renaud, *L'éclatement de la profession*, 23).

45. Alphonse Giroux, "Le Conseil des oeuvres et l'intégration de la profession de service social dans la communauté," *Service social* (printemps, 1957), 11 (as cited in Renaud, *L'éclatement de la profession*, 21; our translation).

46. Renaud, *L'éclatement de la profession*, 31 (our translation).

47. Giroux, "Le Conseil des oeuvres," 13 (our translation).

48. Claude Morin, "Économique et Service social ou 'Les étrangers dans la maison,'" *Service social* (hiver, 1958), 161 (as cited in Renaud, *L'éclatement de la profession*, 25; our translation).

49. Gow, *Histoire de l'administration publique*, 236.

50. See, for instance, Gilles Bourque, "Class, Nation and the Parti québécois," in Alain G. Gagnon (ed.), *Quebec: State and Society* (Toronto: Methuen, 1984), 127.

51. Coleman sees these classes as "conscious political agents."

52. Fournier, *L'entrée dans la modernité*, 144 (our translation).

53. Thomson, *Jean Lesage*, 199 (emphasis added).

54. *Ibid.*, 234-39.

55. *Ibid.*, 185.

56. Graham Fraser, *PQ: René Lévesque and the Parti Québécois in Power* (Toronto: Macmillan of Canada, 1984), 27.

57. Thomson, *Jean Lesage*, 234.

58. Gagné, "L'Hydro et les Québécois: l'histoire d'amour achève," *La Presse* (June, 13, 1975), A-8, as cited in Marc Renaud, "Quebec New Middle Class in Search of Social Hegemony," *International Review of Community Development*, 39-40 (1978), 1-36.

59. André Blais and Philippe Faucher, Review of Jobin, *Les enjeux économiques de la nationalisation de l'électricité*, in *Canadian Journal of Political Science*, 12 (December, 1979). In addition, Blais and Faucher suggest that the relatively low profit rates of the private firms were themselves partly a function of the treatment they had received from Quebec's Régie de l'électricité. Beyond having monopoly over the most important market, apparently Hydro-Québec was also advantaged by state regulatory policies. In fact, soon after the Liberals' accession to power Shawinigan president J.A. Fuller documented his firm's relative disadvantage in a letter to Jean Lesage. In the letter he claimed that his firm's own sources of power were largely developed, called for a new understanding about how the Quebec market was to be shared, and complained that Hydro-Québec's exemption from federal taxation gave it an unfair advantage (Thomson, *Jean Lesage*, 234).

60. Fraser, *P.Q.*, 26.

61. Thomson, *Jean Lesage*, 234.

62. According to Thomson's account, economists René Tremblay and Jacques Parizeau, along with Montreal investment broker Roland Giroux, were ap-

pointed to the original Conseil committee that recommended the creation of a fully or partially publicly owned steel complex. He describes the committee's resistance to proposals for private enterprises from two Anglophone industrialists and a Francophone financier. After approval of the report, a Steel Plant Committee of civil servants was formed to oversee the preparations. Seconded by Claude Morin and Jacques Parizeau, the Committee intervened with Jean Lesage to ensure that the possibility of its publicly funded scheme would not be preempted by DOSCO's plans to establish its own plant at Contrecoeur. In 1964 it proposed that a mixed corporation should be created to begin construction of an integrated steel complex. The government would appoint the administrators and make an initial contribution of $40 million. The committee members apparently opposed a subsequent proposal from Francophone financier, Paul Desmarais, that he create a complex, with government financial support. (Thomson, *Jean Lesage*, 212-16.)

63. Thomson, *Jean Lesage*, 185-87.

64. Coleman, *The Independence Movement*, 121.

65. *Le Devoir*, September 1, 1962 (our translation). See also Niosi, *La Bourgeoisie canadienne*, 132.

66. Coleman, *The Independence Movement*, 112.

67. The apparently close working relationship between new middle-class Francophones within the Quebec state and the leaders of organized labour evokes Fred Block's notion of "state managers" who draw upon working-class support to pursue programs of state expansion to which business is hostile. The state managers can only go so far in this direction for fear of undermining "business confidence," as expressed in levels of investment. As we shall see below, this confidence was very much an issue for the Lesage regime. Fred Block, "The Ruling Class Does Not Rule," *Socialist Revolution*, 7 (1977), 3, 6-28.

68. *Le Devoir*, September 4, 1962 (our translation).

69. Jean Boivin, "Labour Relations in Quebec," in Hugh Anderson and Morley Gunderson (eds.), *Union-Management Relations in Canada* (Don Mills, Ont.: Addison-Wesley, 1982), 438.

70. CSN, *Procès-verbal du congrès* (1964), 70, as cited in Rouillard, *Histoire de la CSN*, 278.

71. Thomson, *Jean Lesage*, 169.

72. *Ibid.*

73. *Ibid.*

74. This account draws primarily on Rouillard, *Histoire de la CSN*; and Roch Denis, *Luttes de classes et question nationale au Québec, 1948-1968* (Montréal: Presses socialistes internationales, 1979), 267-72.

75. See Carla Lipsig-Mummé, "The Web of Dependence: Quebec unions in politics before 1976," in Gagnon (ed.), *Quebec: Society and Politics* (Toronto: Methuen, 1984), 300; Thomson, *Jean Lesage*, 168.

76. In Coleman's analysis, the "francophone business class" stands as one of three elements of "the Quiet Revolution" coalition, along with organized labour and the "traditional middle class," in the case of economic reforms, or "the new middle class," in the case of educational reform. For Jorge Niosi, the creation of state enterprises during the Quiet Revolution "a une explication fondamentale: la formation d'une bourgeoisie canadienne-française au cours de l'après-guerre, et sa prise du pouvoir politique en 1960 sous la Révolution tranquille au moyen du Parti libéral" (Niosi, *La Bourgeoisie canadienne* [Montréal: Boréal Express,

1980], 126). In the analyses of Racine and Denis, on one hand, and Bourque and Legaré, on the other, reinforcement of the position of this class plays a secondary role in the Quiet Revolution reforms.

77. Thomson, *Jean Lesage*, 210; Fournier, *The Quebec Establishment*, 183. See the analysis of the linkages between the SGF and Francophone capital in Brunelle, *La désillusion tranquille*, 108-13.

78. Thomson, *Jean Lesage*, 196.

79. *Ibid.* Jorge Niosi even claims that the Conseil was "dirigé par des membres de la Chambre de commerce de la Province du Québec" (Niosi, *La bourgeoisie canadienne*, 137). Brunelle traces in detail the role of Francophone businessmen within the COEQ (Brunelle, *La désillusion tranquille*, 108-09).

80. Thomson, *Jean Lesage*, 199. See also Gow, *Histoire de l'administration publique*, 306.

81. See Niosi, *La bourgeoisie canadienne*, 132. Also, Coleman cites a July, 1961, brief to Lévesque articulating the Chamber's opposition and an April, 1962, editorial to this effect in the Chamber's journal, *Faits et tendances* (Coleman, *The Independence Movement*, 121). Incorrectly in our view, Niosi sees both chambers as spokesmen for English-Canadian and American interests.

82. *Le Devoir*, September 6, 1962.

83. In the words of Jacques Parizeau, "L'ouverture de cette caisse de placements industriels faisait en outre ressurgir chez l'homme d'affaires canadien-français en particulier des craintes tenaces à l'égard d'un socialisme envahissant" (Parizeau, "De certaines manoeuvres").

84. Coleman, *The Independence Movement*, 111; Thomson, *Jean Lesage*, 213.

85. For instance, the Conseil d'orientation économique gave somewhat guarded support to proposals for direct government involvement in SIDBEC. Approval of a state enterprise came only after it was clear that private funding was unavailable. (Thomson, *Jean Lesage*, 218-20.) In a speech to the Chambre de commerce de Montréal in favour of a state enterprise, Daniel Johnson was careful to argue that the private sector was "deficient," unlike the case of hydro-electricity. He also noted how the federal corporation tax could be avoided. (*Le Devoir*, February 17, 1965.)

86. Racine et Denis, "La conjoncture politique québécoise," 17-79.

87. Bourque et Legaré, *Le Québec*, Chapter Seven. For other applications of the monopolization of capital thesis to the Quiet Revolution, see Brunelle, *La désillusion tranquille*; Henry Milner, *Politics in the New Quebec* (Toronto: McClelland and Stewart, 1978), Chapters III, IV.

88. Bourque et Legaré, *Le Québec*, 171 (our translation).

89. See Rianne Mahon, "Canadian Public Policy: The Unequal Structure of Representation," in Leo Panitch (ed.), *The Canadian State: Political Economy and Political Power* (Toronto: University of Toronto Press, 1977), 167-98.

90. Carol Jobin, *Les enjeux économiques de la nationalisation de l'électricité (1962-1963)* (Montréal: Éditions coopératives Albert Saint-Martin, 1978).

91. *Ibid.*

92. Pierre Fournier, *The Quebec Establishment* (Montreal: Black Rose Books, 1976), 181. See also the discussion of the "economic" arguments for nationalization of Hydro-Québec by Douglas H. Fullerton, an Ottawa Anglophone and financial consultant who worked closely with the Lesage regime: Fullerton, *The Dangerous Delusion* (Toronto: McClelland and Stewart, 1978), Chapter Four.

93. *Ibid.*

94. Apparently of the eleven companies the Lesage government proposed to

nationalize, two small firms, Northern Quebec Power and la Compagnie de Pouvoir du Bas Saint-Laurent, did welcome the prospect. (Pierre Godin, *Daniel Johnson: 1946-1964, la passion du pouvoir* (Montréal: Éditions de l'homme, 1980), 304-20.

95. Dale C. Thomson, *Jean Lesage and the Quiet Revolution* (Toronto: Macmillan, 1984), 242. In fact, Fuller made the nationalization issue the essential theme of an address to Shawinigan's annual stockholders' meeting. The text of the address was reproduced, at the company's expense, in Montreal newspapers. See *Le Devoir*, March 23, 1962; René Lévesque, *Memoirs* (Toronto: McClelland and Stewart, 1986), 171.

Well prior to the Lesage cabinet's approval of the project, Peter Nesbitt Thomson, owner of Power Corporation, the principal shareholder in Shawinigan, did indicate to René Lévesque his preference to negotiate a sale of the firm's assets rather than undergo expropriation. But it is not clear that this constituted an encouragement of the project itself. (Thomson, *Jean Lesage and the Quiet Revolution*, 242.)

96. "le 'concile' du Lac à l'épaule," *Le Devoir*, September 5, 1962 (our translation). See also Coleman, *The Independence Movement*, 244, note 88.

97. According to Jacques Parizeau, the syndicate that for decades had always underwritten the Quebec government's borrowing, headed by the Bank of Montreal and Ames, was highly sympathetic to Shawinigan and Power Corporation. On this basis, there was no possibility of arranging financing on the Canadian market. Only after Parizeau, René Lévesque, Michel Bélanger, and Roland Giroux (then of the financial house Lévesque-Beaubien) had met with New York firm Halsey-Stuart and secured its agreement to arrange financing in the U.S. did the Bank of Montreal-Ames syndicate agree to secure the financing, on the U.S. market, through its associate, First Boston Bank. This is recounted in Jacques Parizeau, "De certaines manoeuvres d'un syndicat financier en vue de conserver son empire au Québec," *Le Devoir*, February 2, 1970; Gagné, "L'Hydro et les Québécois: l'histoire d'amour achève." See also Richard Brunelle et Pierre Papineau, "Le Gouvernement du Capital," *Socialisme québécois*, no. 23 (1972), 106ff. Also see Ted Gerrard, "Quebec/Ontario Access to Capital Markets, 1867-1980," unpublished paper, York University, 37; Ian Rodger, "Politics or Finance First in Bond Sales?" *Financial Post*, October 16, 1971.

98. At the same time, beyond carefully specifying the coalition of class forces supporting the Quiet Revolution state initiatives, we also need to recognize the role other influences played in generating these measures. For instance, there is good reason to believe that purely political considerations precipitated the Liberal government's decision to nationalize the hydroelectrical enterprises. The nationalization question gave the government a pretext to call a snap election to secure a mandate to carry out the project. By defining the election in these terms, the Liberals could hope to preclude Union nationale attacks on parts of their two-year record in office where they clearly were quite vulnerable. In addition, for Lesage, an election battle offered a way to rally his disintegrating cabinet. See Godin, *Daniel Johnson*, 314; Thomson, *Jean Lesage*, 244; Lévesque, *Memoirs*, 176-77.

99. Coleman, *The Independence Movement*, 213.

100. *Ibid.*, 163.

101. To be sure, at least one Anglophone financier did support the measure. See the "economic" arguments for nationalization of Hydro-Québec recalled by Douglas H. Fullerton in Fullerton, *The Dangerous Delusion*.

102. According to Jacques Parizeau: "La création de la Société de financement avait été marquée de tractations pénibles avec les milieux d'affaires qui avaient atteint leur point culminant lors d'une rencontre tenue avec quelques dizaines d'hommes d'affaires dont plusieurs des membres les plus puissants du syndicat [which underwrote Quebec government's borrowing] à l'hotel Le Reine Elizabeth." (Parizeau, "De certaines manoeuvres.")

103. Matthew Fraser, *Quebec Inc.* (Toronto: Key Porter Books, 1987), 79.

104. Thomson, *Jean Lesage*, 117; Lévesque, *Attendez que je me rappelle*, 236.

105. This line of argument has been reiterated by Gingras and Nevitte, who also seek to demonstrate the limits to the secularization of the 1960s. (François-Pierre Gingras et Neil Nevitte, "la Révolution en plan et le paradigme en cause," *Canadian Journal of Political Science*, xvi, 4 (December, 1983), 691-716. For the record, it might also be noted that this final section of our chapter, reproduced virtually intact from the previous editions of this volume, would seem to belie the claim of Gingras and Nevitte that McRoberts and Posgate have declared that the traditional ideology "was in large part abandoned by the whole of the population." *Ibid.*, 692 (our translation).

106. A survey administered prior to the 1962 provincial election campaign by the Groupe de recherches sociales found that 58 per cent of the Francophones of Montreal declared themselves ready to vote Liberal and 53 per cent of the Francophones in the rest of Quebec declared the same intention. See Lemieux, "Les partis et le pouvoir politique," 28.

107. Maurice Pinard, "La rationalité de l'électorat: le cas de 1962," in Vincent Lemieux (ed.), *Quatre élections provinciales au Québec: 1956-1966* (Québec: Les Presses de l'Université Laval, 1969), 179-96.

108. Pinard, "Working Class Politics: An Interpretation of the Quebec Case," 87-109.

109. See Vincent Lemieux, "Les partis et leurs contradictions," in Jean-Luc Migué (ed.), *Le Québec d'aujourd'hui* (Montréal: нмн Hurtubise, 1971), 153-72.

110. Léon Dion, "La polarité des idéologies: conservatisme et progressisme," in Dumont et Montminy (eds.), *Le pouvoir dans la société canadienne-française*, 25-35.

111. Léger, "Commentaire."

112. According to a 1966 pre-election survey – which overestimated the level of Liberal support – 75 per cent of the white-collar respondents were ready to vote Liberal, as opposed to only 50 per cent of the working-class respondents. (Lemieux, *Le quotient politique vraie*, 29.) See also Robert Boily, "Montréal, une forteresse libérale," *Socialisme*, 66 (1966), 138-60.

Chapter Six

1. For general treatments of the contemporary Francophone presence in the Quebec economy, see Pierre Fournier, "Les nouveaux paramètres de la bourgeoisie québécois," in Pierre Fournier (ed.), *Le capitalisme au Québec* (Montréal: Éditions Coopératives Albert Saint-Martin, 1978), 135-83; Niosi, "La nouvelle bourgeoisie canadienne-française," 5-50; Arnaud Sales, *La bourgeoisie industrielle au Québec* (Montréal: Les Presses de l'Université de Montréal, 1979); and François Vaillancourt, "La situation démographique et socio-économique des Francophones du Québec: une revue," Cahier 7940, Département de science politique, Université de Montréal (mai, 1979).

2. Pierre Fournier, "Vers une grande bourgeoisie canadienne-française?"

Département de science politique, Université du Québec a Montréal (juin, 1976), 4.

3. Vaillancourt, "La situation démographique," 12, Table III.

4. Niosi, "La nouvelle bourgeoisie," 10.

5. Raynauld, Marion et Béland, "La répartition des revenus selon les groupes ethniques au Canada." A summary of the report appeared in Racine, "Les québécois gagnent peu." See Chapter One, note 39.

6. The Commission restricts the possible impact of discrimination to the unexplained variance that remains after the effects of age, industry, schooling, occupation, and unemployment have been measured. On this basis, it can account for no more than 40 per cent of the difference in incomes between Canadians of French and British origin in Montreal. (*Report of the Royal Commission on Bilingualism and Biculturalism*, Book III: *The Work World* [Ottawa: Queen's Printer, 1969], 68-71.) However, Raynauld *et al.* explicitly state that only age and education can be properly seen as independent of discrimination; industry, occupation, and unemployment "sont des effets plutôt que des causes de la ségrégation ou discrimination" (as quoted in Racine, "Les Québécois gagnent peu").

7. Wallace Clement, *The Canadian Corporate Elite: An Analysis of Economic Power*, Carleton Library No. 89 (Toronto: McClelland and Stewart, 1975), 232, Table 34.

8. Robert Presthus, *Elite Accommodation in Canadian Politics* (Toronto: Macmillan, 1973), 56.

9. Clement, *Canadian Corporate Elite*, 233.

10. Rapport de la Commission d'enquête sur la situation de la langue française et sur les droits linguistiques au Québec, *Livre I: Langue de travail* (Québec: Gouvernement du Québec, 1972), 124, Table I.67. (Cited henceforth as Gendron Report.)

11. *Ibid.*, 123, Table I.66.

12. Québec, Ministère de l'Industrie et du Commerce, *Une politique économique québécoise* (Québec, 1974), 30 (our translation).

13. Report of the Centre de Recherches en développement économique de l'Université de Montréal, cited by Quebec Conseil du patronat, *Le Devoir*, January 24, 1975. The study excluded graduates in medicine, dentistry, and optometry and from *l'École Polytechnique* (engineering) and *l'École des Hautes Études commerciales* (administration).

14. See Harvey, "Pourquoi le Québec et les Canadiens français occupent-ils une place inférieure sur le plan économique?" in Durocher et Linteau, *Le "retard" du Québec*, 113-27.

15. Raynauld *et al.*, "La répartition."

16. Nathan Keyfitz, "Canadians and Canadiens," *Queen's Quarterly*, 70 (Winter, 1963), 171. See the detailed exploration of this hypothesis, drawing on extensive data gathered in the federal civil service, by Christopher Beattie, *Minority Men in a Majority Setting: Middle-level Francophones in the Canadian Public Service* (Toronto: McClelland and Stewart, 1975). The overall importance of language to work opportunities is well elaborated in an early article by Jacques Brazeau, "Language Differences and Occupational Experience," *Canadian Journal of Economics and Political Science*, 24 (November, 1958), 532-40.

17. This was especially true in Montreal. See Gendron Report, 121, Table I.64.

18. *Ibid.*, 119, Table I.63.

19. See *ibid.*, 47, Table I.23.

20. Calculated from *ibid.*, 77, Table I.38.

21. See *ibid.*, 114-26, for the general discussion of language practices and ethnic stratification.

22. *Ibid.*, Part I, Chapter 2.

23. *Ibid.*, 164-70 (our translation).

24. As shown in Jacques Henripin, *L'immigration et le déséquilibre linguistique* (Ottawa: Main-d'oeuvre et immigration, 1974), 31, Table 4.7.

25. Presented in *Report of the Royal Commission on Bilingualism and Biculturalism*, Book I: *The Official Language*, 32, Table 6.

26. Paul Cappon, *Conflit entre les Néo-Canadians et les francophones de Montréal* (Québec: Presses de l'Université Laval, 1974), 31.

27. Hubert Charbonneau, Jacques Henripin et Jacques Légaré, "L'avenir démographique des francophones au Québec et à Montréal en l'absence de politiques adéquates," *Revue de géographie de Montréal*, 24 (1974), 199-202.

28. Henripin *L'immigration*, 33.

29. Henripin declared: "Le Québec doit imposer les règles du jeu en matière d'immigration et la loi 22 réprésente à cet égard plus un symbole qu'un instrument efficace." (*Le Devoir*, April 23, 1975.)

30. See Cappon, *Conflit*, 35-37.

31. Cappon, *Conflit*.

32. *Ibid.*, 118-22.

33. *Ibid.*, 148.

34. *Ibid.*, 124ff.

35. Everett Hughes suggested such a process in his pioneering study of Drummondville in the 1930s, *French Canada in Transition* (1963). His concern was with the presence of anti-Semitism among French Canadians during that period. "Observation throughout the period leads me to conclude that the symbolic Jew receives the more bitter of the attacks which the French Canadians would like to make upon the English or perhaps even upon some of their own leaders and institutions. When French Canadians attack the English, they pull their punches. Long association on fairly good terms had led to a good deal of honest mutual respect between French and English of Quebec. . . . The English are also powerful. Against the Jew, however, attack may proceed without fear either of retaliation or of a bad conscience." (pp. 215-16)

36. Nationalists repeatedly draw attention to a small number of French-Canadian children who had been enrolled in English-language schools.

37. *Le Devoir*, October 18, 20, 1972. In a follow-up to his 1965 study of a sample of middle-level civil servants in Ottawa, Christopher Beattie found that in 1973 Francophone salaries were just as far below Anglophone salaries as they had been in 1965. Beattie traces this salary differential primarily to the difficulty Francophones experience in meeting the necessity of performing their work in English with predominantly Anglophone co-workers. See Beattie, *Minority Men in a Majority Setting*, Carleton Library No. 92 (Toronto: McClelland and Stewart, 1975).

38. Colin Campbell and George Szablowski, *The Superbureaucrats* (Toronto: Macmillan, 1979). Dion's assertions appear in *Le Devoir*, September 22, 1975.

39. I am indebted to Professor Campbell for making this information available to me. For its part, the federal government claims it is "unable" to provide data on the province of origin of Francophones within the public service. See Kenneth Kernaghan, "Representative Bureaucracy: the Canadian perspective," *Canadian Public Administration*, 21, 4 (Winter, 1978), 501.

40. Canada, *Annual Report 1978: Commissioner of Official Languages* (Ottawa: Supply and Services, 1979), 17.

41. The data are analysed in Richard Arès, *Les positions ethniques, linguistiques et religieuses des Canadiens français à la suite du recensement de 1971* (Montréal: Éditions Bellarmin, 1975), Chapter XIII. Also see Richard J. Joy, *Languages in Conflict* (Toronto: McClelland and Stewart, 1972). Joy analysed the results of the 1971 census in "Les groupes linguistiques et le recensement de 1971," *Le Devoir*, July 19, 1973.

42. Joy, "Les groupes linguistiques."

43. Henripin, *L'immigration*, 22 (our translation).

44. Lemieux, "Les partis et leurs contradictions," 163-65.

45. Marc Renaud, "Quebec New Middle Class in Search of Social Hegemony," *International Review of Community Development*, 39-40 (1978), 25.

46. Latouche, "La vraie nature," 533, Table IV.

47. *Ibid.*

48. Gérard Dion, "Les relations patronales-ouvrières sous la 'révolution tranquille'," *Relations*, No. 344 (décembre, 1969), 334.

49. *Ibid.*

50. *Ibid.*

51. Jean-Marc Piotte, "Le syndicalisme au Québec depuis 1960," in Diane Ethier, Jean-Marc Piotte et Jean Reynolds, *Les travailleurs contre l'État bourgeois* (Montréal: L'Aurore, 1975), 27 (our translation).

52. See Louis-Marie Tremblay, *Idéologies de la C.S.N. et de la F.T.Q.: 1940-1970* (Montréal: Presses de l'Université de Montréal, 1972).

53. The events of the Common Front strike are analysed in detail in Ethier, Piotte et Reynolds, *Les travailleurs*. Also see the descriptions in Sheilagh Hodgins Milner and Henry Milner, *The Decolonization of Quebec* (Toronto: McClelland and Stewart, 1973), Chapter 9; Robert Chodos and Nick Auf der Maur (eds.), *Quebec: A Chronicle 1968-1972* (Toronto: James Lewis and Samuel, 1972).

54. The three CSN, FTQ, and CEQ documents are available in English translation in Daniel Drache (ed.), *Quebec – Only the Beginning: The Manifestoes of the Common Front* (Toronto: New Press, 1972).

55. *Ne comptons que sur nos propres moyens*, document de travail présenté aux membres du Conseil confédéral de la CSN le 6 octobre 1971, 22 (our translation).

56. See the accounts in the Introduction in Moreux, *Fin d'une religion?*; Jean-Pierre Wallot, "Religion and French-Canadian Mores in the Early Nineteenth Century," *Canadian Historical Review*, 51 (March, 1971), 51-94.

57. Pierre Vallières, *Nègres blancs d'Amérique* (Montréal: Éditions parti pris, 1969).

58. Pierre Vallières, *White Niggers of America*, trans. Joan Pinkham (Toronto: McClelland and Stewart, 1971), 143-44.

59. Paul Chamberland, "De la damnation à la liberté," in Parti pris, *Les Québécois* (Paris: Maspero, 1967), 75-113.

60. *Ibid.*, 104 (our translation).

61. *Ibid.*, 109-10.

62. Parti pris, "Manifeste 1965-1966," in Parti pris, *Les Québécois*, 259 (our translation).

63. Léandre Bergeron, "Pour une langue québécoise," *Chroniques*, 1 (mars, 1975), 1 (as quoted in *Le Jour*, April 19, 1975; our translation).

64. *Le Jour,* April 19, 1975.

65. *Travailleurs québécois et lutte nationale* (Montréal, 1974), 23 (our translation).

66. *Ibid.,* Appendix III.

67. *Ibid.,* Introduction.

68. Parti pris, *Les Québécois,* 250 (our translation).

69. Bélanger, *Ruptures et constantes,* 172.

70. Parti pris, *Les Québécois,* 264 (our translation).

71. In Appendix II of his comprehensive study of political violence in Quebec, Marc Laurendeau lists the names of ninety-five people who were suspected of terrorism (Marc Laurendeau, *Les Québécois violents* [Montréal: Boréal Express, 1974], 222-24). For his part, Gérard Pelletier suggests that at the time of the October Crisis the FLQ consisted of "a core of 40 to 50 extremists (perhaps 100) ready to set off bombs and to stage kidnappings, even to commit murder." In addition, he suggests, there may have been a smaller group of propagandists, plus "200 to 300 active sympathizers" and "a periphery of more or less passive sympathizers" that may have numbered between 2,000 and 3,000. (Gérard Pelletier, *La Crise d'octobre* [Montréal: Éditions du jour, 1971], 55-57.)

72. As reproduced in *Octobre 70: un an . . . après*: French adaptation by Jean-V. Dufresne *et al.* of Ron Haggart and Aubrey E. Golden, *Rumors of War* (Montreal: Éditions Hurtubise HMH, 1971), 251 (our translation). The initial mass reaction to the FLQ manifesto is discussed in Laurendeau, *Les Québécois violents,* 189, and Marcel Rioux, *La Question du Québec,* Édition revue et augmenté (Paris: Éditions seghers, 1971), 224. A narrative of pronouncements by public figures during the October Crisis appears in John Saywell, *Quebec 70: A Documentary Narrative* (Toronto: University of Toronto Press, 1971). A strongly critical history of the FLQ itself, based on interviews with members of the various FLQ cells, is Mustave Morf, *Le terrorisme québécois* (Montréal: Éditions de l'homme, 1970).

73. This point is made in *Octobre 70: un an . . . après,* 250. Other works in the debate over the appropriateness of the governmental response to the FLQ kidnappings are Denis Smith, *Bleeding Hearts . . . Bleeding Country* (Edmonton: Hurtig, 1971); Pelletier, *La crise d'octobre.* See also Sandra Djwa, *The Politics of the Imagination: A Life of F.R. Scott* (Toronto: McClelland and Stewart, 1987), 404-18; Lévesque, *Memoirs,* 242-51.

74. *Octobre 70: un an . . . après,* 242.

75. See the discussion in Monière, *Le développement des idéologies au Québec,* 350-51.

76. Bélanger, *Ruptures et constantes,* 192-93.

77. *Ibid.,* 165.

78. Typical of this development is Bourque, *L'État capitaliste et la question nationale,* especially 134, 294.

79. For instance, see Bourque et Legaré, *Le Québec: la question nationale;* Jacques Mascotto et Pierre-Yves Soucy, *Sociologie politique de la question nationale* (Montréal: Éditions coopératives Albert Saint-Martin, 1979).

80. *Le Devoir,* August 2, 1979 (our translation).

81. Marcel Fournier, "La question nationale," *Possible,* 1 (hiver, 1977), 15 (our translation).

82. For a provocative comparison of the labour movements in English Canada and Quebec, see Robert Cox, "Employment, Labour and Future Political Struc-

tures," in R.B. Byers and Robert W. Reford (eds.), *Canada Challenged* (Toronto: Canadian Institute for International Affairs, 1979), 262-92.

83. See the data in Gendron Report, 85-90.

84. See the description of debates over this issue in Milner and Milner, *The Decolonization of Quebec*, 197-98.

85. Communiqué de presse de la CSN, Montréal, January 26, 1979 (as cited in Tremblay, *Idéologies de la C.S.N. et de la F.T.Q.*, 42; our translation).

86. The organization is described in Pierre Fournier, *The Quebec Establishment* (Montreal: Black Rose Books, 1976), 63-65; and William D. Coleman, "Quebec Nationalism and the Organization of Business Interests," unpublished paper, 29-30. Whereas Coleman dates the Conseil from 1966, although he says that it did not become active until 1969, Fournier claims that it was not founded until January, 1969.

87. Fournier, *The Quebec Establishment*, 63.

88. Coleman, "Quebec Nationalism and the Organization of Business Interests," 27. He notes that the Business Council of British Columbia has both direct members and association members.

89. Fournier, *The Quebec Establishment*, 64.

90. Coleman, "Quebec Nationalism and the Organization of Business Interests," 30.

Chapter Seven

1. Latouche, "La vraie nature," 529, Table I.

2. *Ibid.*, 533, Table IV.

3. The classification of districts according to levels of urbanization is based on the 1961 census and is contained in unpublished materials prepared by Vincent Lemieux. Our calculations were drawn from these materials and the official 1961 election results: Quebec, Report of the Chief Returning Officer, *Elections: 1966*.

4. See p. 171.

5. Over the period 1959-69, Quebec's per capita bond indebtedness rose from $248 to $863, almost equalling Ontario's $877. Douglas Fullerton, *Quebec's Access to Financial Markets*, Understanding Canada Series (Ottawa: Supply and Services, 1979), 21.

6. Vincent Lemieux, "Quebec: Heaven is Blue and Hell is Red," in Martin Robin (ed.), *Canadian Provincial Politics: The Party Systems of the Ten Provinces* (Scarborough: Prentice-Hall, 1972), 269.

7. Daniel Latouche hypothesizes that, until 1960, the needs of Québécois and the capacity of the system to meet these needs were in a state of equilibrium. During the first few years of the 1960s the capacities of the Quebec system grew so prodigiously that they exceeded the wants expressed by the population. By the mid-1960s, wants grew rapidly; frustration intensified with the stabilization of governmental capacities during the Union nationale administration. Latouche hypothesizes that growing frustration, combined with an anticipation of continued frustration as a result of the meagre number of seats gained by the PQ in 1970, encouraged the use of political violence. See Daniel Latouche, "Violence, politique et crise dans la société québécoise," in Laurier LaPierre *et al.* (eds.), *Essays on the Left* (Toronto: McClelland and Stewart, 1971), 77-99. These ideas are also developed in Marc Laurendeau, *Les Québécois violents* (Montréal: Boréal Express, 1974), 157-67.

8. Daniel Johnson, *Égalité ou indépendance* (Montréal: Éditions de l'Homme, 1965).

9. See Piotte, "Le syndicalisme au Québec depuis 1960," 32ff.

10. See Carl J. Cuneo and James E. Curtis, "Quebec Separatism: An Analysis of Determinants within Social-Class Levels," *Canadian Review of Sociology and Anthropology*, 2 (1974), 1-29.

11. See the statements of working-class participants in inter-ethnic discussions of the immigrant and linguistic questions in *Conflit entre les Néo-Canadiens et les francophones de Montréal*, Appendix A, 241-68.

12. *Le Devoir*, August 7, 1974 (our translation).

13. Canada, *Foreign Direct Investment in Canada* (Ottawa: Information Canada, 1972).

14. Levitt, *Silent Surrender* (Toronto: Macmillan, 1970).

15. Québec, *Le cadre et les moyens d'une politique québécoise concernant les investissements étrangers*, Rapport du Comité interministériel sur les investissements étrangers, Québec, septembre, 1973 (texte revisé de mars à juin, 1974; Québec: Éditeur officiel du Québec), 49.

16. *Le Devoir*, January 10, 1976 (our translation). Also, see a general discussion of the Tetley Report and its treatment in Pierre Lamonde, "Le contrôle étranger, ou la difficulté d'être maîtres chez nous," in Daniel Latouche (ed.), *Premier mandat* (Montréal: L'Aurore, 1977), Chapter One.

17. Québec, Ministère de l'Industrie et du commerce, *Une politique économique québécoise* (Québec, 1974), 34.

18. *Le Jour*, May 5, 1975.

19. *Le Devoir*, May 15, 1975.

20. Hélène Pelletier-Baillargeon, "L'exode vers les collèges privés," *Maintenant*, No. 123 (février, 1973), 11.

21. The Quebec position paper was reproduced in *Le Devoir*, June 19, 1971.

22. The Victoria Charter is reproduced in *La Presse*, June 18, 1971.

23. *Le Devoir*, September 15, 1971 (our translation).

24. *Ibid.* (our translation)

25. See the analyses by Claude Ryan in *Le Devoir*, September 4, 6, 1973.

26. Canada, *Working Paper on Social Security in Canada* (April 18, 1973), 36-39.

27. *Le Devoir*, May 2, 1975 (our translation).

28. See *Le Québec: maître d'oeuvre de la politique des communications sur son territoire* (Québec: Éditeur officiel, n.d.).

29. *Le Devoir*, July 19, 1975.

30. See the analysis of Anglophone reaction to Bill 22 in Michael Stein, "Le Bill 22 et la population non-francophone au Québec: une étude de cas sur les attitudes du groupe minoritaire face à la législation de la langue," *Choix*, No. 7 (1975), 127-59. See also Djwa, *The Politics of the Imagination*, 423-28.

31. Quebec, *Official Language Act*, Bill No. 22 (1974), sec. 41.

32. *Ibid.*, sec. 43.

33. *Le Devoir*, April 8, 1975.

34. Quebec, *Official Language Act*. The other provisions touching upon language practices in the work world (sections 24, 25, 30-35) cover: general notices to personnel, language of labour relations, official name of firm, and the language of contracts, product labels, and public signs. Section 29 outlines the points to be considered in awarding *francisation* certificates: "(a) the knowledge that the management and the personnel must have of the official language; (b) the Franco-

phone presence in management; (c) the language in which the manuals, catalogues, written instructions and other documents distributed to the personnel must be drawn up; (d) the provisions that the business firms must have for communication in French by the members of their personnel, in their work, among themselves and with their superior officers; (e) the terminology employed."

35. *Ibid.*, first paragraph of section 29.

36. *Toronto Star*, October 6, 1973.

37. For a very useful discussion of the "ungovernability" and "overload" theses and the applicability to Canada, see Richard E.B. Simeon, "The 'Overload' Thesis and Canadian Government," *Canadian Public Policy* (Autumn, 1976), 541-52. Also, see the articles by H.I. Macdonald, John Meisel, and Claude Ryan in the same issue. The classic statement of the "fiscal crisis of the state" thesis is James O'Connor, *The Fiscal Crisis of the State*.

38. Maurice Pinard and Richard Hamilton, "The Independence Issue and the Polarization of the Electorate: The 1973 Quebec Election," *Canadian Journal of Political Science*, 10, 2 (June, 1977), Table 6.

39. Serge Carlos, Édouard Cloutier et Daniel Latouche, "Le choix des électeurs en 1973: caractéristiques sociales et orientation nationale," in Daniel Latouche, Guy Lord et Jean-Guy Vaillancourt (cds.), *Le processus électoral au Québec: les élections provinciales de 1970 et 1973* (Montréal: Hurtubise HMH, 1976), Tableau IX.

40. Pinard and Hamilton, "The Independence Issue," 251.

41. *Ibid.*, Table 2.

42. See Vincent Lemieux's characterization of the socio-economic bases of the Liberal Party of the 1970s: Vincent Lemieux, "Les partis provinciaux du Québec," in Réjean Pelletier (ed.), *Partis politiques au Québec* (Montréal: Hurtubise HMH, Cahiers du Québec, 1976), 67.

43. Pinard and Hamilton, "The Independence Issue," 253.

44. *Ibid.*, 254.

45. Technically, such a referendum would be necessary only if negotiations with Ottawa over the conditions of Quebec's accession to independence should break down. But the PQ leadership presented this commitment to the general public as an unconditional commitment to stage a referendum. See Vera Murray, *Le Parti québécois* (Montréal: Hurtubise HMH, 1977), 191-95.

46. Henry Milner, "The Decline and Fall of the Quebec Liberal Regime: Contradictions in the Modern Quebec State," in Panitch (ed.), *The Canadian State: Political Economy and Political Power*, 116-22.

47. For an excellent account of the whole dispute, see Sanford F. Borins, *Language of the Skies: the bilingual air traffic control conflict in Canada* (Montreal: McGill-Queen's Press, 1983).

48. André Bernard claims that the resurgence of the Union nationale may have been responsible for PQ victories in twenty-eight seats. See Bernard, *Québec: élections 1976* (Montréal: Hurtubise HMH, 1976), 137. On the basis of a survey conducted during the 1976 election campaign, Maurice Pinard and Richard Hamilton explain the Liberal defeat in these terms: "The specific components of dissatisfaction with the Liberal government involved its inaction, weakness and indecision in many areas (for example, the economy, labour conflicts in the public sector, public morality), its inability to forge a consensus, even among its following, on the language issue, and, coupled with all of this, its weak leadership." Maurice Pinard and Richard Hamilton, "The Parti Québécois Comes to

Power: the 1976 Election," *Canadian Journal of Political Science*, 11 (December, 1978), 751.

49. John Saywell, *The Rise of the Parti québécois, 1967-1976* (Toronto: University of Toronto Press, 1977), 167.

50. *Ibid.*, 168.

51. These data appear in Bernard, *Québec: élections 1976*, 51, Table 9.

52. A listing of most of the surveys up to 1976 appears in Pinard and Hamilton, "The Independence Issue," 247. In addition, see: Société Radio-Canada, "Le gouvernement Lévesque, un an après," unpublished paper, 1977; "What Quebec Really Wants" [the Goldfarb study], *Toronto Star*, May 14-20, 1977; Sorecom, "Opinions et attitudes des Québécois au sujet de la situation politique au Québec," unpublished paper, 1977; CBC-90 Minutes Live, "Hamilton-Pinard Study," unpublished paper, October, 1977; Société Radio-Canada, "Les Québécois et la dualité fédérale-provinciale," unpublished paper, June, 1978; and Société Radio-Canada, "Confédération/Référendum," unpublished paper, March, 1979.

53. See the discussion of this point in Maurice Pinard, "La dualité des loyautés et les options constitutionnelles des Québécois francophones," in *le Nationalisme québécois à la croisée des chemins* (Québec: Centre québécois de relations internationales, La Collection Choix, 1975), 81-87.

54. *Le Devoir*, April 25, 1970.

55. Pinard and Hamilton, "The Independence Issue," 252.

56. Daniel Latouche, "Le Québec et l'Amérique du Nord: une comparaison à partir d'un scénario," in *le Nationalisme québécois à la croisée des chemins*, 101, Table IV.

57. These results of the Pinard-Hamilton survey appeared in *Le Devoir*, November 10, 1976.

58. Société Radio-Canada, "Le gouvernement Lévesque, un an après," 37-38

59. Pinard and Hamilton, "The Parti Québécois Comes to Power," 745.

60. Société Radio-Canada, "Les Québécois et la dualité fédérale-provinciale," Annexe D, Q. 20.

61. *Ibid.*, Q. 25 and Q. 20.

62. *Le Devoir*, April 25, 1970.

63. Serge Carlos et Daniel Latouche, "La composition de l'électorat péquiste," in Latouche, Lord et Vaillancourt (eds.), *Le processus électoral*, Chapter 8.

64. Cited in Murray, *Le Parti québécois*, 31.

65. Calculated from data presented in Bernard, *Québec: élections 1976*, 82, Table 15.

66. Calculated from Quebec, *Official Election Returns*, 1970 and 1973.

67. Calculated from Parti québécois, *Biographie des candidats, Élection 1976*, as cited in Milner, *Politics in the New Quebec*, 158.

68. Marcel Fournier, "La question nationale: enjeux et impasses," in Jean-François Léonard (ed.), *La chance au coureur* (Montréal: Éditions nouvelle optique, 1978), 177-92.

69. Pinard and Hamilton claim that: "*the top leadership of the movement* (its candidates, deputies, and cabinet ministers) *is not recruited from the new middle class or the new petty bourgeoisie as a whole, or even the state middle classes as a whole, but from a very specific and narrow segment of those classes, the intellectuals proper.*" Maurice Pinard and Richard Hamilton, "The Class Bases of the Quebec Independence Movement: conjectures and evidence," *Ethnic and Racial Studies*, 7, 1 (January, 1984), 41 (italics in original).

70. The teachers included: J-Y. Morin, L. Lessard, C. Charron, J. Garon, G. Tardiff, L. O'Neill. Also, there were two journalists: R. Lévesque and L. Payette.

As opposed to our figure of 33 per cent, Pinard and Hamilton claim that no less than fifteen (63 per cent) of the members of the first PQ cabinet were "intellectuals" (teachers or journalists). At least part of the explanation of the disparity lies in the fact that Pinard and Hamilton have "coded professionals who were university professors as professors" (Pinard and Hamilton, "The Class Bases," Table 5). We have sought to classify individuals in terms of the *primary* occupation. On this basis, individuals who may have taught at some point in their career may not meet the normal sense of "intellectual." Thus, we have categorized as "administrators" or technocrats" individuals Pinard and Hamilton apparently have classified as "intellectuals." Cases include: Claude Morin, who had taught at ENAP but had spent most of his career as an administrator; J. Parizeau and R. Tremblay, who had taught economics at university but also had been very active in advising governments on economic policy; and Jacques Leonard, an accountant by training who had spent most of his career as a university administrator.

Our figure more closely approximates the 29 per cent that emerges on the basis of the statements of occupation in the official report on the 1976 election. These statements are based on the individuals' own designation. Québec, *Rapport du président général des élections*, Appendice II.

On this basis, we have classified 42 per cent of the members of the first PQ cabinet as members of the new middle class, although not "intellectuals." When combined with "intellectuals" (33 per cent), the total new-middle-class membership in the first cabinet is 75 per cent.

71. C. Morin, B. Landry, M. Léger, J. Léonard, and D. de Belleval were the former; J. Parizeau and R. Tremblay were the latter.

72. In addition, Marcel Léger had administered a Catholic fund-raising organization.

73. They were Robert Burns and Pierre Marois, respectively. We have also included among these ten individuals Yves Bérubé, whose position as a professor at Laval University might qualify him as an "intellectual" but whose area of teaching and professional training, engineering, suggests that he be placed elsewhere in the new middle class.

74. Of these nine members, none of whom were "intellectuals," at least three had been based in large private corporations (G. Saint Pierre, B. Lachapelle, and G. Harvey). Two had been Liberal Party officials (R. Garneau and L. Bacon). Only two had been state administrators or government economic advisers (R. Bourassa and C. Forget).

75. These calculations are based upon data found in Rapport du président général des élections, *Élections: 1976*, Appendix II, supplemented by information in Pierre G. Normandin (ed.), *The Canadian Parliamentary Guide* (Ottawa). I am indebted to Lise Gotell for preparing these findings.

76. On the Ralliement pour l'indépendance nationale, see André d'Allemagne, *le R.I.N. de 1960 à 1963*; and Réjean Pelletier, *Les militants du R.I.N.* (Ottawa: Éditions de l'Université d'Ottawa, 1974).

77. See the discussion of the relationship between the Parti québécois and the Quebec unions in Julien Bauer, "Attitude des syndicats," *Études internationales*, 8 (juin, 1977), 307-19.

78. André Bernard, *Québec: élections 1976* (Montréal: Éditions Hurtubise HMH, 1976), 86.

79. John Saywell, *The Rise of the Parti Québécois, 1967-1976* (Toronto: University of Toronto Press, 1977), 140.

80. Milner, *Politics in the New Quebec*, 164.

81. These documents are analysed at length in Murray, *Le Parti québécois*. For an early analysis, see a special issue of *Maintenant*, entitled "L'avenir économique d'un Québec souverain," published in March, 1970.

82. Parti québécois, *Quand nous serons vraiment chez nous* (Montréal: Éditions du Parti québécois, 1972), 24 (our translation).

83. These various measures are outlined in *ibid.*, Chapter 3. They are all listed in the party program, with the interesting exception of the proposal for government ownership of one or two banks (Parti québécois, *Le programme*, Édition 1975, 11-14).

84. Parti québécois, *Le programme*, 14 (our translation).

85. Parti québécois, *Le programme*, 18 (our translation).

86. *Ibid.*; *Quand nous serons vraiment chez nous*, Chapters 3, 5.

87. Parti québécois, *Le programme*, 12-13; *Quand nous serons vraiment chez nous*, Chapter 4.

88. Parti québécois, *Le programme*, 12 (our translation).

89. *Ibid.* (our translation)

90. *Quand nous serons vraiment chez nous*, 93 (our translation).

91. Parti québécois, *Le programme*, 12.

92. Niosi, "La nouvelle bourgeoisie canadienne-française," 33 (our translation; italics in original deleted).

93. Bourque contends that: "the Québécois bourgeoisie is massively concentrated in enterprises of which the establishments count 500 employees or less. However, it has secured a significant presence in the banking and agricultural-food sectors, as well as certain large manufacturing enterprises which often are controlled or supported by the State." Bourque et Legaré, *le Québec*, 360 (our translation).

While admitting that "the private sector is the weak link in the chain for the Quebec bourgeosie," Fournier insists that the Quebec bourgeoisie has made important progress in transportation equipment, metal products, and chemicals as well as in the financial sector. He includes within the Quebec bourgeoisie such major firms as the National Bank, Bombardier, Provigo, Culinar, and Steinbergs – while placing Power Corporation and Rolland Paper within the "Canadian" bourgeoisie (see firms listed in Pierre Fournier *et al.*, *Capitalisme et politique au Québec* [Montréal: Éditions coopérative Albert Saint-Martin, 1981], Table 4).

94. Laurin-Frenette, *Production de l'État et formes de la nation*, 152 (our translation).

95. The term was, however, introduced to the party program in 1982.

96. René Lévesque, *La passion du Québec* (Montréal: Éditions Québec/Amérique, 1979), 48 (our translation).

97. See Anton Pelinka, *Social Democratic Practice in Europe* (New York: Praeger, 1983), 137.

98. See Ralph Miliband and Marcel Liebman, "Beyond Social Democracy," in Ralph Miliband *et al.* (eds.), *Socialist Register, 1985-86* (London: Merlin Press, 1986), 477.

99. This listing is adapted from James A. McAllister, *Democratic Socialism in Manitoba* (Kingston and Montreal: McGill-Queen's Press, 1984), 4-5.

100. See Adam Przeworski, *Capitalism and Social Democracy* (Cambridge: Cambridge University Press, 1985), 241, and Ian Gough, *The Political Economy*

of the Welfare State (London: Macmillan, 1979), 69-70. For a critique of such arrangements, see Leo Panitch, "A Social Contract or Socialism?" in John Richards and Don Kerr (eds.), *Canada, What's Left? a new social contract, pro and con* (Edmonton: NewWest Press, 1986), 13-23, and Leo Panitch, *Social Democracy and Industrial Militancy* (Cambridge: Cambridge University Press, 1976).

101. Parti québécois, *Le programme*, 19-24.

102. *Ibid.*, 17 (our translation).

103. René Lévesque, "Conduire à la victoire un parti populaire," *Le Devoir*, November 29, 1971 (our translation).

104. See note 84.

105. This list is adapted from John Richards, "Populism: a qualified defence," *Studies in Political Economy*, 5, (Spring, 1981), 5. See also Alvin Finkel, "Populism and the Proletariat: Social Credit and the Alberta working class," *Studies in Political Economy*, 13 (Spring, 1984), 109

106. C.-Raymond Laliberté, "Critique du nationalisme populaire," in Léonard (ed.), *La chance au coureur*, 92 (our translation).

107. See Murray, *Le Parti québécois*, 191-95.

108. Parti québécois, *Le programme*, 17 (our translation).

109. *Quand nous serons vraiment chez nous*, 135 (our translation).

110. *Ibid.*, 134 (our translation).

111. Coleman, *The Independence Movement in Quebec*, 211.

Chapter Eight

1. For a discussion of how these data were derived, see Chapter Seven, note 70.

2. These figures reflect gross provincial expenditures expressed in current dollars (Statistics Canada, *Provincial Government Finances*, 1970-1983, 68-205). Most of this growth was in fact a product of inflation. In constant dollars, growth had been only .03 per cent in 1974-75 and .06 per cent in 1975-76. See Blais and McRoberts, "Public Expenditure in Ontario and Quebec," Table 2.

3. He declared that "le sens pratique et l'élementaire prudence nous obligent à prendre des mesures sévères pour diminuer le coût croissant des dépenses publiques. . . ." (Québec, *Discours sur le Budget, 1976-77*, 21.)

4. Québec, *Discours sur le Budget, 1977-78*, 23.

5. With respect to the impact on spending patterns of the timing of elections in Quebec and Ontario, see André Blais, Kenneth McRoberts, and Richard Nadeau, "The 'Electoral Cycle' Thesis: Ontario and Quebec, 1950-1980," unpublished paper..

6. This point was carefully underlined by Lévesque in his address to the New York Economic Club (*Le Devoir*, January 26, 1977).

7. Québec, *Budget 1978-79*, Discours sur le budget, 30 (our translation).

8. See the discussion of these measures in Niosi, "le gouvernement du P.Q. deux ans après"; Jean-Marc Piotte, "le gouvernement Lévesque après 24 mois," *Le Devoir*, November 13, 14, 15, 1978.

9. Québec, *Budget 1979-80*, Discours sur le budget, 34 (our translation).

10. Yves Vaillancourt, *le P.Q. et le sociale* (Montréal: Éditions Saint-Martin, 1983), 43-51.

11. *Ibid.*, 54-58.

12. Quebec, *An Act to Amend the Labour Code* (received royal assent December 22, 1977).

13. See discussions of these provisions in Jean Boivin, "Labour Relations in Quebec," in John Anderson and Morley Gunderson, *Union-Management Relations in Canada* (Don Mills, Ontario: Addison-Wesley, 1982), 440-43; A. Brian Tanguay, "Recasting Labour Relations in Quebec, 1976-1985: towards a disciplinary state?" paper presented to annual meeting of Canadian Political Science Association, June 6-9, 1986, 12-16.

14. For a highly critical account of labour relations under the Lévesque government, see Jean-Marc Piotte, "La lutte des travailleurs de l'État," *Les Cahiers du socialisme*, 3 (printemps, 1979), 4-39.

15. As quoted in Tanguay, "Recasting Labour Relations in Quebec," 12-13.

16. D.D. Carter, "The Labour Code of Quebec: some reflections and comparisons," in Michel Brossard (ed.), *La loi et les rapports collectifs du travail*, 11.

17. Tanguay, "Recasting Labour Relations in Quebec," 14.

18. In his 1979 Budget Speech, Parizeau noted that "in general, workers in the public sector are higher paid than those in the private sector." He claimed that as a consequence: "four-fifths of the workers are now going to have to contribute to the salaries of the remaining fifth whose income is higher than theirs. It is remarkable in this respect that the unions, whose collective agreements terminate on June 30th, are demanding a minimum salary of $265 by week. This demand represents the equivalent of the mean industrial salary in Quebec in 1978. In sum, because one works in the public sector, one would like the minimal remuneration to be equivalent to the mean remuneration for workers in the private sector. There is here a surprising form of inequity which underlines once again the need to moderate appetites which no longer correspond to reality." Québec, *Budget 1979-1980*, Discours sur le budget, 23 (our translation).

19. These events are discussed in Jacques Rouillard, *Histoire de la CSN (1921-1981)* (Boréal Express/CSN, 1981), 291; Tanguay, "Recasting Labour Relations in Quebec," 18.

20. François Demers, *Chroniques impertinentes du 3ème Front commun syndical* (Montréal: Nouvelle optique, 1982), 136.

21. See the analysis of the relationship between the unions and the Parti québécois in Bauer, "Attitude des syndicats," 307-19.

22. Lévesque, *La passion du Québec*, 76 (our translation).

23. See the analysis in Gérard Bergeron, *Pratique de l'État au Québec* (Montréal: Éditions Québec/Amérique, 1984), 388-91.

24. See the development of this understanding of corporatism in Leo Panitch, "The Development of Corporatism in Liberal Democracies," *Comparative Political Studies*, 10, 1 (April, 1977), 61-90; and "Corporatism in Canada," *Studies in Political Economy*, 1 (Spring, 1979), 43-92.

25. See Québec, le Sécretariat permanent des conférences socio-économiques du Québec, *Le bilan des conférences socio-économiques de novembre 1979 à mai 1983*, Appendix I. Our assessment of the PQ's experience with *concertation* draws heavily on A. Brian Tanguay, "Concerted Action in Quebec, 1976-83: a dialogue of the deaf," Alain Gagnon (ed.), *Quebec: state and society* (Toronto: Methuen, 1984), 365-85.

26. Gilles Bourque and Anne Legaré have been especially active in developing this thesis. See Bourque et Legaré, *Le Québec: la question nationale*, Chapter Seven; Gilles Bourque, "La nouvelle trahison des clercs," *Le Devoir*, January 8, 9, 1979; Anne Legaré, "Les classes sociales et le gouvernement PQ à Québec," *Canadian Review of Sociology and Anthropology*, 15 (1978), 218-26. Also see

Pierre Fournier, "Projet national et affrontement des bourgeoisies québécoise et canadienne," in Léonard (ed.), *La chance au coureur*, 39-59; Pierre Fournier, "Vers une grande bourgeoisie canadienne-française?" unpublished paper.

27. These data on expenditure patterns directly contradict the affirmations in Bourque et Legaré, *Le Québec: la question nationale*, 208.

28. Calculations based on Québec, *Budget 1979-80*, Crédits, xii-xv.

29. *Ibid.*

30. *Ibid.*

31. *Le Devoir*, February 3, 1977.

32. *Le Devoir*, April 13, 1977.

33. *Le Devoir*, June 20, 1979.

34. See the discussion of these various measures in Arnaud Sales, "Vers une techno-bureaucratie d'État," in Léonard (ed.), *La chance au coureur*, 25-39; Fournier, "Projet national."

35. *Le Devoir*, January 14, 1978 (our translation).

36. Jorge Niosi, "le gouvernement du P.Q. deux ans après," *Les Cahiers du socialisme*, 2 (automne, 1978), 49 (our translation).

37. *Ibid.*

38. Fournier, "Projet national," 52-53.

39. See Fournier, "La question nationale: enjeux et impasses," 177-92. Also see the analysis of Bill 101 and its various provisions in François Vaillancourt, "La Charte de la Langue française du Québec," *Canadian Public Policy*, 4 (Summer, 1978), 284-308.

40. Québec, *Charte de la langue française*, Article 58.

41. *Ibid.*, Article 73.

42. René Lévesque claimed that he felt "torn" over this provision (*Le Devoir*, July 19, 1977).

43. See survey administered by crop/Selection, August, 1977. The survey showed that the majority of Quebec Francophones approved Bill 101 as a whole.

44. *Charte de la langue française*, Chapter iv.

45. Unlike municipal institutions, school boards and health and social service agencies were to be allowed to communicate internally in French and "une autre langue" (*ibid.*, Article 26). See the discussion in William Coleman, "From Bill 22 to Bill 101: The Politics of Language under the Parti Québécois," *Canadian Journal of Political Science*, xiv, 3 (September, 1981), 459-85.

46. *Charte de la langue française*, Article 73.

47. *Ibid.*, Chapter v.

48. The regulations appear in *Le Devoir*, July 21, 1978.

49. *Le Devoir*, December 18, 1976.

50. *Quebec's Policy on the French Language* (March, 1977), 98-99.

51. *Projet de loi no. 1*, Article 112 (as reproduced in *Le Devoir*, April 28, 1977, our translation).

52. *Ibid.*, preamble (our translation).

53. Yvan Allaire, "La nouvelle classe politique et les pouvoirs économiques," in Léonard (ed.), *La chance au coureur*, 63.

54. *Charte de la langue française*, Article 141.

55. *Le Devoir*, February 1, 1978.

56. *Ibid.*

57. *Ibid.*

58. *Ibid.*

59. Yvan Allaire and Roger E. Miller, *Canadian Business Response to the Legislation on Francization in the Workplace*, Accent Québec (Montreal: C.D. Howe Institute, 1980), 37.

60. This discussion of Bill 1 is drawn from William Coleman's analyses in "From Bill 22 to Bill 101" and "A Comparative Study of Language Policy in Quebec: a Political Economy Approach," in Michael M. Atkinson and Marsha A. Chandler (eds.), *The Politics of Canadian Public Policy* (Toronto: University of Toronto Press, 1983), 21-42.

61. *Financial Post*, January 28, 1978.

62. *Le Devoir*, May 23, 1978.

63. Rapport de la Commission d'enquête sur la situation de la langue française et sur les droits linguistiques au Québec, *Livre I: Langue de travail* (Québec: Gouvernement du Québec, 1972), 164-70.

64. Paul Bernard, Andrée Demers, Diane Grenier et Jean Renaud, *L'évolution de la situation socio-économique des francophones et des non-francophones au Québec (1971-1978)*, Collection Langues et sociétés (Montréal: Office de la langue française, 1979), 132.

65. Coleman, "A Comparative Study of Language Policy."

66. *Le Devoir*, March 30, 1977 (our translation).

67. *Le Devoir*, November 16, 1974 (our translation).

68. See the analysis by PQ sympathizer Pierre Drouilly, *Le Devoir*, May 5, 1979.

69. Lévesque, *La Passion du Québec*, 69 (our translation).

70. Jean-Pierre Charbonneau et Gilbert Paquette, *l'Option* (Montréal: Éditions de l'homme, 1978).

71. *D'égal à égal* was originally prepared by the Conseil executif national of the party, bearing the subtitle "Manifeste et propositions concernant la souveraineté-association." The *manifeste* was a long preamble written by veteran *indépendantiste* Pierre Vadeboncoeur. The various propositions were submitted in the form of resolutions to the Congrès national; in some cases, relatively minor modifications had been made. All these resolutions were adopted by overwhelming majorities at the Congrès national. Many of the other resolutions approved at the Congrès national amplified these various propositions of *D'égal à égal*.

72. Quebec economist Bernard Bonin was appointed as an assistant deputy minister in charge of *"planification."* He proceeded to commission approximately forty studies that dealt either with the present form of Quebec-Canada relations or with alternative forms suggested by general economic theory or by experiences in other settings.

73. From "Transcription du discours d'ouverture du président du Parti Monsieur René Lévesque, vendredi 1er juin 1979," p. 3. See the analyses of *étapisme* in Murray, *Le Parti québécois*, troisième partie; Yves Vaillancourt, "La position constitutionelle du MSA-PQ de 1969 à 1979," in Centre de formation populaire, *Au-delà du parti québécois* (Montréal: Éditions nouvelle optique, 1982), 69-124; Gilles Bourque, "Petite bourgeoisie envahissante et bourgeoisie ténébreuse," *les Cahiers du socialisme*, 3 (printemps, 1979), 122-61.

74. In the 1975 edition of the PQ program, a PQ government was committed to hold a referendum "In the case where it should have to proceed unilaterally" to sovereignty (*Le programme du Parti québécois*, Édition 1975, 5; our translation). At the 1977 Congrès national, approval was given to a change in the program that shifted reference to a referendum to a new provision. Under this provision, a PQ government is committed "to make certain, by means of a referendum at the

moment that it will judge oppportune, during the first mandate, of the support of Québécois for the sovereignty of Quebec" (*Le programme du Parti québécois*, Édition 1978, 7; our translation).

75. The text of the new commitment calls on the PQ government: "To ask the citizens of Quebec, in the eventuality that it appears impossible to arrive at a satisfactory arrangement with Canada, for the mandate to exercise without sharing the powers of a sovereign state" (Septième Congrès national, Résolutions adoptées en atelier, cahier no. 1, B-1, 1/2; our translation). Interestingly, the provision does not return to the more militant phraseology of the 1975 edition of the program with its notion of the PQ government proceeding "unilaterally" to sovereignty. The PQ government is simply committed to ask for a "mandate."

76. Based on author's notes taken at the Congrès national, 1979.

77. The document, entitled "L'accession démocratique à la souveraineté," was reproduced in *Le Jour*, September 26, 1974. Morin's thesis provoked a response from a pioneer of the *indépendantiste* movement, André d'Allemagne. It must be said that d'Allemagne's apprehensions were at least partly borne out by the PQ's experience in office: "One can guess with what ease the irreducible adversaries of our liberation would be able to exploit this period of uncertainty, even confusion, which elapses between the election and the referendum and in the course of which the new government would no longer be able to function as a provincial power without yet being in a position to function as a national power. It is then that one would have reason to fear the fomenting of political and social troubles as well as economic threats, all measures which would have hardly the same interest for the adversaries once the new power is firmly established and is determined to follow the route it has set for itself." (André d'Allemagne, "A propos de ce référendum," *Le Jour*, November 9, 1974; our translation.)

78. In fact, there is evidence that support for sovereignty-association fell slightly during the first two years of PQ government. Surveys administered in August and November of 1977 showed 40 per cent in favour of sovereignty-association; surveys administered in September, 1978, and February, 1979, showed 35 per cent in favour. (Confédération/référendum [an analysis conducted by Radio-Canada/CBC based largely on the results of a February, 1979, national survey], March, 1979, 59.) In the February, 1979, survey 49 per cent of the respondents were "satisfied" with the Quebec government – a full fourteen percentage points more than the proportion favouring sovereignty-association (*ibid.*, 14). Only 53 per cent of these satisfied respondents said they approved sovereignty-association (*ibid.*, 57). It should be noted, however, that 51 per cent of the respondents said that they were prepared to vote "Yes" in a referendum calling for a mandate to negotiate sovereignty-association; in August, 1977, 50 per cent were in favour (*ibid.*, 107).

79. Vincent Lemieux notes that surveys have shown that a full 50 per cent of Québécois were satisfied with the PQ government but only 35 per cent would be prepared to vote for its re-election. "The explanation of this difference probably lies in the low popularity of the PQ's constitutional option." (Vincent Lemieux, "Histoire de vingt électeurs," *Le Devoir*, June 1, 1979; our translation.)

80. *Le Devoir*, December 20, 1976 (our translation).

81. Jean-Claude Picard, "Le PQ après deux ans," *Le Devoir*, November 14, 1978.

82. Robert Barberis, "Redevinir militants," *Le Devoir*, May 15, 1979. See also Louise Thibauld, "Le PQ et le gouvernement," *Le Devoir*, May 31, 1979.

83. Based on author's notes taken at Congrès national, June, 1979.

84. See the reproduction of the Court's decision in *Le Devoir*, December 14, 1979.

85. *Le Devoir*, December 3, 1977.

86. *Le Devoir*, January 27, 1977.

87. *Le Devoir*, April 1, 1978.

88. *Ibid.*

89. *Le Devoir*, April 6, 1978.

90. *La Presse*, May 16, 1978.

91. *Le Devoir*, May 18, 1978.

92. *Le Devoir*, June 14, 1978.

93. *Le Devoir*, March 9, 1978.

94. *Le Devoir*, May 30, June 14, 1978.

95. This agreement and the two preceding ones are discussed in Kenneth McRoberts, "Unilateralism, Bilateralism and Multilateralism: Approaches to Canadian Federalism," in Richard Simeon (ed.), *Intergovernmental Relations*, Vol. 63, Collected Research Studies, Royal Commission on the Economic Union and Developmental Prospects for Canada (Toronto: University of Toronto Press, 1985), 86-87.

96. See the declaration of Jacques Parizeau, *Le Devoir*, April 18, 1978.

Chapter Nine

1. For detail on the origins of *D'égal à égal*, see note 71 of the previous chapter. In discussing *D'égal à égal* we will, in fact, be referring to the slightly modified version of the propositions of this document as they emerged from the 1979 Congrès national. Citations will be based on the Congrès national texts.

2. Citations from the White Paper will be based on the official English-language version, *Québec-Canada: A New Deal* (Québec, 1979), hereafter referred to as White Paper.

3. The differences between the two documents are detailed in the revised edition of this volume: (Toronto: McClelland and Stewart, 1980), Chapter 10.

4. Conseil exécutif national du Parti québécois, *D'égal à égal*, Manifeste et propositions concernant la souveraineté-association, 10.

5. See, for instance, Edmond Orban, *Un modèle de souveraineté-association?* (Montréal: Éditions Hurtubise нмн, 1978).

6. White Paper, 58.

7. *Ibid.*, 60.

8. *Ibid.*, 62.

9. *Ibid.*, 62.

10. *Ibid.*, 60.

11. In their discussion of a possible Quebec-Canada customs union, Charbonneau and Paquette acknowledge that "The problem of the real weight of Quebec in the common policy presents itself, even if there should be parity in decision-making and thus an improvement with respect to the present situation." (Charbonneau et Paquette, *L'option*, 418; our translation.)

12. See Lamonde, "Le contrôle étranger, ou la difficulté d'être Maîtres chez nous," in Latouche (ed.), *Premier mandat*, 42.

13. Murray, *Le Parti québécois*, 65 (our translation).

14. Jean-P. Vezina, "Le développement économique: les enjeux en cause," in Latouche (ed.), *Premier mandat*, 61 (our translation).

15. *Le Devoir,* July 15, 1978 (our translation).

16. See, in particular, Vaillancourt, "La position constitutionelle du MSA-PQ."

17. René Lévesque, *Option Québec* (Montréal: Les Éditions de l'homme, 1968).

18. Thus, in the 1978 interview in which he detailed the disadvantages of monetary union, Parizeau remarked that the PQ was proposing a common money with English Canada essentially to avoid the difficulties that might arise in establishing a Quebec money (*Le Devoir,* July 15, 1978).

19. In principle, the two parties could form a free trade area: they would agree to impose no tariffs against each other but, unlike a customs union, they would not maintain a common tariff structure against third countries. In the case of Quebec and Canada, however, this option is foreclosed by the massive problem of regulating the transshipment to the higher-tariff country. See the discussion in J.M. Treddenick, "Quebec and Canada: the Economics of Independence," *Journal of Canadian Studies,* 7 (November, 1973), 16-30. See also Charles Pentland, "Association after Sovereignty?" in Richard Simeon (ed.), *Must Canada Fail?* (Montreal: McGill-Queen's University Press, 1977), 234; Charbonneau et Paquette, *l'Option,* 418.

20. See Fortin, Paquet et Rabeau, "Coûts et bénéfices," 12. See Chapter One, note 28.

21. See Clarence Barber, "The Customs Union Issue," *Options Canada,* Proceedings of the Conference on the Future of the Canadian Federation (University of Toronto, October, 1977), 214-32.

22. See Carl E. Beigie and Judith Maxwell, *Quebec's Vulnerability in Energy,* Accent Quebec (Montreal: C.D. Howe Research Institute, 1977).

23. Carmine Nappi, "La souveraineté, la structure d'exportation et le choix d'une politique commerciale pour le Québec," in Luc-Normand Tellier (ed.), *Économie et indépendance* (Montréal: Quinze, 1977), 154-55, Table i.

24. This point has been made on several occasions by University of Western Ontario economist Thomas Courchene. See the report on discussions at the Conference on the Political Economy of Confederation, Kingston, Ontario, in *Le Devoir,* November 13, 1978.

25. See Pentland, "Association after Sovereignty?" 214.

26. Barber, "The Customs Union Issue," 224.

27. Richard Lipsey, "Parting is not such an Economic Wrench," *Financial Post,* December 15, 1978.

28. L. Auer and K. Mills, "Confederation and Some Regional Implications of the Tariffs on Manufacturers," Economic Council of Canada (paper presented to Workshop on the Political Economy of Confederation, Kingston, Ontario, November 8-10, 1978), 21, Table 11.

29. Léon Courville, Marcel Dagenais, Carmine Nappi et Alain Van Peetersen, *La sensibilité des industries au commerce interrégional: le cas du Québec, de l'Ontario et du reste du Canada,* Préparé pour le compte du Ministère des affaires intergouvernementales du Québec (Québec: Éditeur Officiel, 1979), Partie i, 30-31.

30. See Tredennick, "Quebec and Canada"; Pentland, "Association after Sovereignty?"

31. Tim Hazeldine, "The Costs and Benefits of the Canadian Customs Union," Economic Council of Canada (paper presented to Workshop on the Political Economy of Confederation, Kingston, Ontario, November 8-10, 1978), 15. The quotation is from *Globe and Mail* columnist William Johnson (*Globe and Mail,* November 13, 1978).

32. See Pentland, "Association after Sovereignty?" 237.

33. Bernard Fortin, *Les avantages et les coûts des différentes options moné-taires d'une petite économie ouverte: un cadre analytique*, préparé pour le compte du ministère des affaires intergouvernementales du Québec (Québec: Éditeur officiel, 1978), 15.

34. *Ibid.*, 23-25.

35. *Globe and Mail*, January 26, 1977.

36. This raises the spectre of "dynamic consequences," which receive great emphasis by Richard G. Lipsey in his critique of Clarence Barber's analysis. Lipsey contends that Barber has restricted his attention to "static" factors. See Lipsey, "The Relation between Economic and Political Separatism: A Pessimistic View," in *Options Canada*, 244-51. Lipsey's list of "dynamic consequences" is a long one: "Investment, entrepreneurial and inventive activity, and hence the growth rate, may be seriously retarded by changes in the tax structure, by rising political and economic uncertainty, by social attitudes hostile to private capitalism, and by threats – or even unfounded fears – of nationalization. Restrictive practices by labour unions may be encouraged and productivity, and hence living standards, be affected. Endemic inflations and repeated currency devaluations and/or foreign exchange controls may greatly upset forward planning and reduce incentives to make money through legitimate business activities" (*ibid.*, 250). If the pattern of policies of the PQ government over the first three and half years of its tenure could be taken as any indication of the probable behaviour of a sovereign Quebec state, then the possible "dynamic consequences" of accession to sovereignty listed by Lipsey would be fairly limited in effect. In fact, in a subsequent article, Lipsey acknowledged there also could be "dynamic" effects that would *benefit* Quebec (see Lipsey, "Parting is not such an Economic Wrench").

37. Michael D. Ornstein, H. Michael Stevenson, and A. Paul Williams, "Public Opinion and the Canadian Political Crisis," *Canadian Review of Sociology and Anthropology*, 15 (1978), Table IV.

38. Government of Saskatchewan News Release, Western Premiers' Response to Sovereignty-Association, November 7, 1979, as quoted in Institute of Intergovernmental Relations, *The Response to Quebec; the other provinces and the constitutional debate*, Documents of the Debate, 2 (Kingston, Ontario: Institute of Intergovernmental Relations, Queen's University, 1980).

39. Excerpt from a statement to Ontario Legislature on Quebec's White Paper on Sovereignty-Association, November 26, 1979 (as quoted in Institute of Intergovernmental Relations, *The Response to Quebec*, 16-17).

40. Halifax *Chronicle-Herald*, April 18, 1980 (as quoted in *Canadian Annual Review*, 1980, 51).

41. *Toronto Star*, May 2, 1980 (as quoted in *Canadian Annual Review*, 1980, 51).

42. Donald V. Smiley, *Canada in Question: Federalism in the Seventies*, second edition (Toronto: McGraw-Hill Ryerson, 1976), 218.

43. Abraham Rotstein, "Is There an English-Canadian Nationalism?" *Journal of Canadian Studies*, 13 (Summer, 1978), 109-18.

44. See Donald Smiley, "The Sovereignty-Association Alternative: An Analysis," text of lecture given at Ryerson Polytechnical Institute (November 22, 1978), 6.

45. See Frederick J. Fletcher, "The View from Upper Canada," in Simeon (ed.), *Must Canada Fail?*, 103-04. A 1977 survey of elite attitudes found that "federal politicians" were the second most hostile (one percentage point less than "small

business") of all thirteen elite categories to the notion of negotiating an economic agreement if Quebec becomes independent (51 per cent were opposed, 41 per cent in favour). This was not true, however, of federal civil servants who favoured it by 64 per cent to 30 per cent. (Michael D. Ornstein and H. Michael Stevenson, "Elite and Public Opinion Before the Quebec Referendum: A Commentary on the State in Canada," *Canadian Journal of Political Science*, XIV, 4 (December, 1981), 760, Table 2.

46. See the analysis of how different aspects of the PQ project of sovereignty-association would affect the interests of the English-Canadian financial bourgeoisie in Levasseur et Lacroix, "Rapports de classe," 88-121.

47. See Larry Pratt and John Richards, *Prairie Capitalism: Power and Influence in the New West* (Toronto: McClelland and Stewart, 1979). Also, see the comparison of Quebec and Alberta autonomism in Bourque et Legaré, *Le Québec*, Chapter Eight.

48. In a widely publicized interview with *Le Devoir* in April of 1977, Saskatchewan Premier Allan Blakeney contended that western Canadians had been ready to tolerate the costs imposed on them by tariff protection of central Canadian institutions because Confederation provided the assurance of federal financial support during economic difficulties. Given the cyclical nature of their resource-based economies, western Canadian provinces count heavily on this federal support. Under sovereignty-association, Quebec would be making no contribution to the federal programs yet it would expect western Canada to accept the tariff protection it requires. "We would then have the impression of obtaining nothing in return for the costs which we encounter in the form of tariffs. Such a proposition would have no interest for us." (*Le Devoir*, April 9, 1977; our translation.)

49. See Donald Smiley, "A New Look at Sovereignty-Association," unpublished paper, York University (July, 1978), 5-7.

50. The White Paper points to Luxembourg's status within the Benelux association as a precedent for Quebec: "In Benelux, the first contemporary model for association, tiny Luxembourg, with less than half a million inhabitants all told, deals on all essential questions as an equal of Belgium and Holland, whose populations are 25 or 30 times greater." Yet, surely Luxembourg's position relative to the two other partners was so weak that its parity status could have been no more than a formality. The other parties could give Luxembourg equal status because they could be certain that it would not seek to play an equal role. English Canada would not be able to count on Quebec to play a passive role. The more important lesson to be drawn from the Benelux experience is that the two active partners, Belgium and Holland, were roughly equal in demographic and economic strength.

The one instance of a two-party association in which the relationship between the two partners is at all comparable to the one between Quebec and Canada-without-Quebec is the association between Great Britain and Ireland. It should be noted that within this "pseudo monetary union" Ireland has no role in determining the value of the British pound, to which the Irish currency was permanently fixed. See Henri-Paul Rousseau, *Unions monétaires et monnaies nationales: une étude économique de quelques cas historiques*, Ministère des Affaires intergouvernementales, Gouvernement du Québec (Québec: l'Éditeur officiel, 1978), 81-168.

51. Auer and Mills, "Confederation and some Regional Implications," 21; Courville *et al.*, *La sensibilité des industries*, Partie I, 27-31.

52. Rotstein, "Is There an English-Canadian Nationalism?" 116.

53. See Levasseur et Lacroix, "Rapports de classe."

54. Negotiation of an economic association was narrowly rejected by small businessmen (48 per cent vs. 52 per cent). Ornstein and Stevenson, "Elite and Public Opinion," 760, Table 2. Apparently, each of these samples included some Quebec Francophone respondents.

55. "For most of the people interviewed, the only logical attitude for English Canada would be to form a common market or a customs union with the new State. It is even possible to think that Washington might exert pressure in this direction, although of course no one is insinuating this for the moment." (Louis Balthazar, "Le Québec d'après le 15 novembre vu de Washington," *Le Devoir*, March 5, 1977; our translation.)

56. Calculated from Courville *et al.*, *La sensibilité des industries*, Partie I, Table III.

57. Donald Smiley, "Quebec Independence and the Democratic Dilemma," *Canadian Forum*, 58 (February, 1979), 12.

58. The English-language version of the question, as reproduced in the *Globe and Mail*, December 21, 1979.

59. Fraser, *P.Q.*, 405, relates the results of a linguistic analysis of the question: "As a test, a Laval linguist, Conrad Bureau, gave the question to groups of students to memorize; none were able to do it. In a study of the question, he concluded that, although clear, it was more complex in one of its parts than Proust and almost twice as complex as Gide in its syntactical structure." See "Le référendum de mai au Québec: une analyse linguistique de 'la question,'" *Langues et Linguistique*, No. 10 (1984).

60. Marie-Hélène Bergeron, Douglas Brown, and Richard Simeon, eds., *The Question: The Debate on the Referendum Question, Quebec National Assembly, March 4-20, 1980* (Kingston, Ontario: Institute of Intergovernmental Relations, Queen's University, 1980), 65.

61. *Ibid.*, 9.

62. Le Directeur général des élections du Québec, *Référendum: Oui – Non* (1980), 2; our translation.

63. Bergeron *et al.*, *The Question*, 8.

64. *Ibid.*, 40.

65. Contrary to Coleman, *The Independence Movement*, Chapter VIII.

66. Directeur général, *Référendum*, 8.

67. As quoted in Denis Monière, "Deux discours pour le choix d'un pays: les propagandes," in En collaboration, *Une pays incertain: réflexions sur le Québec post-référendaire* (Montréal: Éditions Québec/Amérique, 1980), 95 (our translation).

68. Journalist Denise Bombardier claimed to have witnessed such statements ("Noir sur blanc," Radio-Canada, May 17, 1980). See also the citations in Gérald Bernier, "Les aspects économiques du débat: un dialogue de sourds," in En collaboration, *Québec: un pays incertain*, 123.

69. Ryan is quoted in *Le Devoir*, May 3, 1980 (our translation).

70. As reproduced from Prime Minister's Office transcripts by Fraser, *P.Q.*, 227.

71. Based on notes taken from televised version of National Assembly Debates, March 20, 1980.

72. *La Presse*, May 3, 1980 (our translation).

73. *La Presse*, March 13, 1980 (our translation).

74. See a series of articles by Pierre Drouilly in *La Presse*, May 24, 26, 27, 28, 1980.

75. See André Blais, "Le vote: ce que l'on sait . . . ce que l'on n'en sait pas," in En collaboration, *Québec: un pays incertain*, 170-72.

76. Blais, "Le vote," 171.

77. On the basis of their analysis, Blais and Nadeau concluded that "the hypothesis that the "Yes" clientele is less diversified than the *péquiste* clientele is thus confirmed." André Blais et Richard Nadeau," La clientèle du OUI," in Jean Crête (ed.), *Comportement électoral au Québec* (Chicoutimi: Gaetan Morin, 1984), 334.

78. *Ibid.*, 326.

79. *Ibid.*, 326-30.

80. Maurice Pinard et Richard Hamilton, "Les Québécois votent 'non': 2. Les assises de l'appui au régime et de son rejet," paper presented to Conference on Political Support in Canada, Duke University, November, 1980; and Maurice Pinard and Richard Hamilton, "The Class Bases of the Quebec Independence Movement: conjectures and evidence," *Ethnic and Racial Studies*, 7, 1 (January, 1984), 20-54.

81. Blais and Nadeau, commenting on the table on older voters furnished by Pinard and Hamilton in "Les Québécois votent 'non'," note that not only is the sample size small but variables such as level of education are not controlled (Blais et Nadeau, "La clientèle du OUI," 328).

82. In addition, their classification of occupations places "managers" in the same category as "proprietors" – a group we have argued has had little attraction to Quebec sovereignty (Pinard and Hamilton, "The Class Bases," Table 1).

83. Blais et Nadeau, "La clientèle du OUI," 327.

84. Monière traces this to the abstract, "rational" terms in which the government framed its campaign: "If one excludes the appeal to the collective pride of Québécois, the *souverainiste* discourse focused above all on cold, abstract, conceptual values which have no direct relationship to the concrete experience of individuals. Openness to this message is dependent on reasoning since it implies knowledge of the unequal relationship between the federal and provincial states, between the Anglophone majority and the Francophone minority and between the economic system and the political system. . . . Its persuasive power is conditioned by levels of schooling and of political education since it draws on historical, sociological, and economic knowledge to justify its conclusions and projects. Its *champ de mobilisation* encompasses the upwardly mobile *couches sociales*, which act collectively, which experience more directly the contradictions between their capacities and the limits the power structure imposes upon them, and which link their personal situation to that of the group to which they belong." (Denis Monière, "Deux discours pour le choix d'un pays: les propagandes," in En collaboration, *Québec un pays incertain*, 108; our translation.)

85. Jon H. Pammet, Jane Jenson, Harold D. Clarke et Lawrence LeDuc, "Soutien politique et comportement électoral lors du référendum québécois," in Crête (ed.), *Comportement électoral au Québec*, 397.

86. Radio-Canada, *Les Québécois et la question référendaire* (Montréal: Radio Canada, May 9, 1980), III-18 (as cited in Pammet *et al.*, "Soutien politique," 398, note 29; our translation). Pammet *et al.* also cite the responses to two statements that more closely approximate the Quebec government's position: "Quebec would issue passports": yes – 47 per cent, no – 33 per cent (the White Paper

indicated that with sovereignty Quebec citizens would have distinct passports, although it also evoked the possibility of a common Quebec-Canada passport [White Paper, 61]) and "Quebec would have its own army": yes – 43 per cent, no – 33 per cent (the White Paper indicated that Quebec would remain within Norad and NATO but seemed to imply that Quebec would have its own armed forces [*ibid.*, 62, 104-05]).

87. Pinard et Hamilton, "Les Québécois votent non," 360, note 40.

88. *Ibid.*, 362, note 44. This was the pattern among respondents Pinard and Hamilton classified as "neo-federalist yes" voters. The pattern was the opposite among "*souverainiste*-yes" voters. At the same time, they acknowledge that these data also reflected a reverse causality: one's constitutional option leading one to select "positive" information. This would conform with the Pammet *et al.* thesis that people's referendum options were determined less by technical considerations regarding the option of sovereignty-association itself than by higher concerns.

89. They adopt the Eastonian political community/regime/authorities distinction, associating sovereignty-association and federalism with the regime, and classifying questions of the Canada-Quebec linkage, *per se*, or cultural identity within political community category. They found that only 22 per cent of the respondents referred to matters that fall within the political authorities category. (Pammet *et al.*, "Soutien politique," 401.)

90. The other responses were: "to secure a better place for Quebec within Canada": 19 per cent; "to achieve Quebec sovereignty in an economic association with the rest of Canada": 32 per cent; and "don't know": 10 per cent (Pammet *et al.*, "Soutien politique," 395).

91. Pammet *et al.*, "Soutien politique," 400. They claim, unlike Pinard and Hamilton, that there was a major surge in support for sovereignty-association during the year leading up to the referendum. Thus, they see support going from 27 per cent in 1979 to 45 per cent just before the referendum (recalculated from Pammet *et al.*, "Soutien politique," Table 10.3); Pinard and Hamilton see support for sovereignty-association remaining around 32 per cent (Pinard et Hamilton, "Les Québécois votent non," 349). The Pammet *et al.* estimate includes individuals who also declare themselves favourable to "renewed federalism" (22 per cent of the total sample). Pinard and Hamilton would regard such individuals as falling within their category of "neo-federalist yes" voters, who vote "yes" not out of support for sovereignty-association but simply as a tactic to secure a "renewed federalism." They claim that over two-fifths of "yes" votes were of such a nature. Yet, Pinard and Hamilton may be too quick to place individuals in such a category. Within their own data, most individuals classified as "neo-federalist yes" do not actually reject sovereignty-association: 55 per cent would give Quebec a mandate to *establish* sovereignty-association (31 per cent would not). By the same token, 58 per cent reject the proposition that the federal system permits Quebec to satisfy its aspirations (*ibid.*, Tables 9.8, 9.9).

92. See the summary of survey results on the referendum question in *Canadian Annual Review, 1980*, 54, Table 6. Two polls taken during or just after the National Assembly debate (IQOP – March 16 and Sorecom – April) show the highest scores (47 per cent and 46 per cent) in the table. They are almost matched by the 44 per cent obtained by CROP – March 26-April 7, according to a summary of survey results in Ronald James Zukowsky, *Struggle over the Constitution from the Quebec Referendum to the Supreme Court* (Kingston, Ontario: Institute of Intergovernmental Relations, 1981), 30, Table 2.1. See also the summary of PQ

internal polls in Fraser, *P.Q.*, 234. It was only at this point that support for the "Yes" recovered from the slump during the fall of 1979 from the high of 54 per cent registered in a CROP-Cloutier poll taken in June, 1979. (Zukowsky does note a 46 per cent obtained in an internal PQ poll held in January, before the National Assembly debate.) See also *Dimanche-matin*, May 12, 1980.

This, moreover, is the pattern observed by Monière: "In June, 1979, the Cloutier survey demonstrated that a majority were favourable to the government's question. In February, 1980, after the federal election that returned the Liberals to power, the first CROP survey revealed a strong majority for the 'No.' Then after the National Assembly debate, the pendulum swung to the 'Yes' side. Then, after the intensification of the propaganda effort for the 'No' vote and the entry of federal spokesmen who used federal public funds to promote Canada, the 'No' regained the lead, conserving and then enlarging its advantage." (Monière, "Deux discours," 90; our translation.)

93. The 25 per cent figure appears in Pammet *et al.*, "Soutien politique," 399, Table 10.3, panel B. The proportion of 27 per cent of Quebec Francophones is the result of the Pinard-Hamilton survey as reported by Peter Regenstreif in *Toronto Star*, May 16, 1980. This is the highest percentage ever to be recorded for Quebec independence. (See the summary of past results in Maurice Pinard, "A House Divided," *Report* [May, 1980].)

94. Michael D. Ornstein and H. Michael Stevenson, "Elite and Public Opinion Before the Quebec Referendum: A Commentary on the State in Canada," *Canadian Journal of Political Science*, XIV, 4 (December, 1981), 774. For analyses of the "Yvette" phenomenon, see Susan Mann Trofimenkoff, *The Dream of Nation* (Toronto: Gage, 1983), 329-31; Michèle Jean et Marie Lavigne, "Le phénomène des Yvettes: analyse externe," *Atlantis*, 6 (1981), 17-23; Jacqueline Lamothe et Jennifer Stoddart, "Les Yvettes ou: Comment un parti politique traditionnel se sert encore des femmes," *ibid.*, 10-16. For their part, Blais and Nadeau find that gender and the "Yvette" episode had little influence on the referendum vote. (Blais et Nadeau, "La clientèle du OUI," 332.)

95. See Pinard, "A House Divided," 24.

96. *Ibid.* To be sure, Pammet *et al.* suggest otherwise. See note 91.

97. See note 93.

98. As Graham Fraser says of Lévesque himself, "His instinct – characteristic of all his gestures since becoming premier – was caution: no hasty decisions, no snap judgements." (Fraser, *P.Q.*, 237.) See the analysis of *étapisme* and the PQ's approach to the national question in Marc Henry Soulet, *Le silence des intellectuels* (Montréal: Éditions Saint-Martin, 1987), 83-85.

99. Carol Levasseur et Jean-Guy Lacroix, "Rapports de classes et obstacles économiques à l'association," *Cahiers du socialisme*, 2 (automne, 1978), 112-13 (our translation).

100. Fournier, "La question nationale: enjeux et impasses," in Léonard (ed.), *La chance au coureur*, 191 (our translation).

101. Laurin-Frenette, *Production de l'État*, 150 (our translation).

102. Lévesque, *La passion du Québec*, 60-61 (our translation).

Chapter Ten

1. See the analysis of the electoral campaign in Claude-V. Marsolais, "Lévesque parle surtout d'économie," *La Presse*, March 28, 1981, A-11. This is also the conclusion of André Bernard and Bernard Descôteaux, *Québec: élections 1981*

(Montréal: Hurtubise ʜᴍʜ, 1981), 199-200. Bernard and Descôteaux also note that the commitment not to hold a referendum on sovereignty-association during a new term in office had already been approved by the National Council and the expanded National Council of the party. The latter body, however, had stipulated that the *next* election would have to focus on sovereignty. *Ibid.*, 100-01.

2. See Bernard et Descôteaux, *Québec: élections 1981,* Chapter 11. See also William Johnson, "Timid Liberals seem to have missed the boat," *Globe and Mail,* April 6, 1981.

3. The results of a ᴄʀᴏᴘ-administered survey are analysed in *La Presse,* March 28, 1981. These results are compared with those of a Sorecom survey in *Le Devoir,* March 30, 1981, 2.

4. *La Presse,* March 28, 1981, ᴀ-8.

5. *Ibid.*

6. *Le Devoir,* March 30, 1981, 2.

7. André Blais, "L'élection de 1981," unpublished paper, 12.

8. Bernard et Descôteaux, *Québec: élections 1981,* 61-64.

9. *Ibid.*, 110-14.

10. *Ibid.*

11. Canada, *House of Commons Debates,* May 21, 1980, 1263.

12. The Task Force on Canadian Unity, *A Future Together* (Ottawa: Supply and Services, 1979); La Commission constitutionnelle du Parti libéral du Québec, *Une nouvelle fédération canadienne* (Montréal: le Parti libéral du Québec, 1980).

13. "The new constitution could include, if the people so wish, several provisions in our present organic laws, but it will also have to contain new elements reflecting the most innovative proposals emerging from our consultations or from the numerous analyses and considered opinions that have flowed in the last few years from the will to change of Canadians. I am referring, of course, to the many proposals made by the Canadian government since 1968, *but also to the Pépin-Robarts report,* to the policy papers issued by the governments of British Columbia, Ontario, Alberta and by almost every province but Quebec, *to the constitutional proposals of the Liberal Party of Quebec, many elements of which could orient the renewal of our constitution if they were put forward by the political authorities of that province.*" (Canada, *House of Commons Debates,* May 21, 1980, 1264 [emphasis added].)

14. The Beige Paper does call for the creation of a "dualist committee" within its Federal Council, which would have jurisdiction over matters "affecting Canadian duality." It would be composed equally of Francophones and Anglophones. This parity would involve not Quebec and the rest of Canada but the two linguistic collectivities. In fact, the provision stipulates that no more than 80 per cent of the Francophone members could be from Quebec. (La commission constitutionnelle, *Une nouvelle fédération,* 56.)

15. Canada, *A Time for Action* (Ottawa: Supply and Services, 1978). The proposal for a House of the Federation is elaborated in Canada, *Constitutional Reform: House of the Federation* (Ottawa: Canadian Unity Information Office, 1978).

16. The proposed resolution is reproduced in Edward McWhinney, *Canada and the Constitution, 1979-82* (Toronto: University of Toronto Press, 1982), 141-48.

17. This listing of items is drawn from Allan C. Cairns, "The Politics of Constitutional Conservatism," in Keith Banting and Richard Simeon, *And No*

One Cheered: federalism, democracy and the Constitution Act (Toronto: Methuen, 1983), 29. Cairns analyses at length the processes through which an agreement of such limited scope emerged.

18. Canada, *Constitution Act, 1982*. The Act does clarify provincial jurisdiction over most natural resources. This was a response to western Canadian concerns.

19. *Ibid.*, Section 23.

20. *Ibid.*, Section 6.

21. *Ibid.*, Part v.

22. See Donald Smiley, "A Dangerous Deed: The Constitution Act, 1982," in Banting and Simeon, *And No One Cheered*, 74-95.

23. The Fulton-Favreau formula and the Victoria Charter, the major past attempts at repatriation, had both afforded Quebec a veto over all forms of constitutional change. *A New Canadian Federation* adopted the Victoria Charter formula. Within the federal government's own proposed resolution of October, 1980, all amendments would have to be approved by the Quebec National Assembly. In the case of the Task Force on National Unity's *A Future Together*, Quebec representatives in the Council of the Federation would not have a veto over constititional amendment (only a majority was necessary) but a majority of Quebec electors voting in a Canada-wide referendum would have to ratify the proposed amendment.

24. Fraser, *P.Q.*, 239.

25. This new approach of the federal government to dealings with the provinces is documented and analysed at much greater length in Kenneth McRoberts, "Unilateralism, Bilateralism and Multilateralism: approaches to Canadian federalism," in Richard Simeon (ed.), *Intergovernmental Relations*, Vol. 63, Collected Research Studies of the Royal Commission on the Economic Union and Development Prospects for Canada (Toronto: University of Toronto Press, 1985), 71-129.

26. This shift in policy is analysed in Michael Jenkin, *The Challenge of Diversity: Industrial Policy in the Canadian Federation*, Science Council of Canada, Background Study 50 (Ottawa: Supply and Services Canada, 1983); and Peter Aucoin and Herman Bakvis, "Organizational Differentiation and Integration: the case of regional economic development policy in Canada," paper presented to the Canadian Political Science Association, June, 1983.

27. See *Globe and Mail*, June 24, 1981; *Le Devoir*, June 26, 1981; plus the analysis by Marc Laurendeau, *La Presse*, June 27, 1981.

28. This initiative is examined at length in Allan Tupper, *Bill S-31 and Federalism of State Capitalism* (Kingston: Queen's University, Institute of Intergovernmental Relations, 1983).

29. Accounts of these measures appear in *Globe and Mail*, May 7, 1983; *Le Devoir*, June 5, 1984.

30. See J. Stefan Dupré, "Reflections on the Workability of Executive Federalism," in Simeon (ed.), *Intergovernmental Relations*, 1-31. Donald Smiley has taken this argument one step further, contending that central agencies responsible for managing and co-ordinating intergovernmental relations have had an especially deleterious effect (Donald V. Smiley, *Canada in Question*, third edition. [Toronto: McGraw-Hill Ryerson, 1980], 113). Nonetheless, a study of the federal government's Federal-Provincial Relations Office found that during the 1970s personnel were divided in their conception of the agency's role, with some seeing it as one of facilitating federal-provincial collaboration (Timothy B. Woolstencroft, "Organizing Intergovermental Relations," Discussion Paper 12

[Kingston: Queen's University, Institute of Intergovernmental Relations, 1982], 52). To be sure, by the 1980s the agency had clearly moved to an openly adversarial role.

31. On this basis, Gillespie and Maslove contend that the publicly stated concern with the deficit was "more smokescreen than substance." W. Irwin Gillespie and Allan M. Maslove, "Volatility and Visibility: The Federal Revenue and Expenditure Plan," in G. Bruce Doern (ed.), *How Ottawa Spends Your Tax Dollars, 1982* (Toronto: James Lorimer, 1982), 56.

32. *Globe and Mail*, November 25, 1981.

33. As quoted in Sharon Dunn, "Federalism, Constitutional Reform and the Economy: the Canadian experience," *Publius*, 13, 2 (Spring, 1983), 134.

34. R.M. Burns recounts that in 1945 Louis St. Laurent feared that Duplessis, recently returned to power, would seek aggressively to mobilize public support behind the Quebec government. Feeling that the provinces had the advantage in such a campaign since they provided more services directly to the people than did Ottawa, he advocated new federal programs such as family allowances. (R.M. Burns, *The Acceptable Mean: the Tax Rental Agreements, 1941-1962*, Financing Canadian Federation 3 [Toronto: Canadian Tax Foundation, 1980], 46-47.) For an account of the role that fear of Quebec separatism played in stimulating the federal government's concern with visibility in the 1960s, see Anthony Careless, *Initiative and Response* (Montreal: McGill-Queen's University Press, 1977), 177.

35. The Quebec government's position was reproduced in a two-page ad in *La Presse*, August 21, 1980.

36. This interpretation is advanced in Fraser, *P.Q.*, 283. See also René Lévesque, *Attendez que je me rappelle* (Montréal; Québec/Amérique, 1986), 436. Yet, the actual impact of this should be minor. As Lévesque himself wrote of the set of revisions: "The only truly serious worry that it created for us is that Ottawa would now have the power to reduce the scope of Bill 101, to the benefit of Anglo-Québécois. However, in no way to the point of endangering our fundamental position. Much more than the content, it was the procedure which was intolerable." *Ibid.*, 448 (our translation).

37. The provision does go beyond the "Canada clause" to the extent that in addition to children whose parents were educated in English in Canada it also covers children who have received, or have a sibling who has received, education in English anywhere in Canada - whatever the status of the parent. Lévesque recounted that even Quebec public opinion was beginning to respond to the federal argument that it was intolerable that constitutional amendment should depend on the British Parliament. As for Quebec's loss of a veto, Lévesque contended that in the hands of other provinces a veto could be used to frustrate Quebec's own development. If Quebec is to have one, then Ontario and the other provinces would insist on one, too. Yet, he also acknowledged that in extremely serious instances, a veto would indeed be necessary. *Ibid.*, 440.

38. Quebec, *Draft Agreement on the Constitution: Proposals by the Government of Quebec*, May, 1985.

39. Both documents called for the changes in federal powers and in the division of powers. The Task Force study, but not the Liberal document, had called for full control over language matters within provincial jurisdiction. The Liberal document would have given Quebec a total veto over constitutional change, while the Task Force provided for a provincial referendum. The Task Force report proposed that a new constitutional preamble should include recognition of Quebec as a "distinct society"; the Liberal document did not propose a preamble.

40. See the analysis of the Mitterand experience in Mark Kesselman, "Lyrical Illusions of a Socialism of Governance: whither French socialism?" in Ralph Miliband *et al.* (eds.), *Socialist Register, 1985/86* (London: Merlin Press, 1986), 233-48.

41. Luc Bureau, *Entre l'éden et l'utopie: les fondements imaginaires de l'espace québécois* (Montréal: Éditions Québec/Amérique, 1984). Reaction against state dominance has also permeated the Quebec left, as is demonstrated in Soulet, *Le silence des intellectuels*, 103-09.

42. The figures are drawn from James A. McAllister, "Fiscal Capacity and Tax Effort: explaining public expenditures in the Ten Canadian Provinces," unpublished paper presented to Canadian Political Science Association, June, 1984, Table 5.

43. Fraser, *Quebec, Inc.*, 158.

44. *Ibid.*, 172, 177.

45. *Ibid.*, 107 (emphasis in original).

46. Québec, Assemblée nationale, *Journal des débats*, le mardi 29 mai 1981 (our translation).

47. *Ibid.*

48. *Ibid.*

49. While the Conseil was eliminated, the government did maintain the regularly threatened research organism: l'Office de planification et de développement du Québec.

50. *Journal des débats*, 16 octobre 1984 (our translation).

51. These percentages reflect the increase in gross provincial expenditures expressed in current dollars (Statistics Canada, *Provincial Government Finance*, 1970-1983, 68-205).

52. Calculated from Statistics Canada, *Provincial Government Finance, Revenues and Expenditures*, cs 68-205, 1970-83, and Statistics Canada, *System of National Accounts: Provincial Economic Accounts*, 1969-1984, 13-213.

53. McAllister, "Fiscal Capacity and Tax Effort."

54. Québec, *Discours sur le budget, 1981-82*, 29 (our translation).

55. Québec, *Budget Speech, 1982-83*, 15. The same point was stressed by Treasury Board President Yves Bérubé in his presentation of the 1982-83 credits (Québec, *Budget, 1982-83*, renseignements supplémentaires, crédits, 5-9).

56. See note 51.

57. See note 52.

58. Gouvernement du Québec, *Bâtir le Québec: énoncé de politique économique* (Québec: Éditeur officiel du Québec, 1979), 137-39.

59. Québec, *Budget, 1981-82, Discours sur le budget*, 10 mars 1981, 23.

60. *Le Devoir*, May 26, 1978.

61. The statute has a provision guaranteeing that Hydro-Québec could retain at least 25 per cent of its financial needs. *Le Devoir*, June 13, 1981.

62. *La Presse*, November 9, 1983.

63. *Le Devoir*, October 13, 1984. See also Jean-Claude Leclerc, "De Gagnon à Sidbec," *Le Devoir*, October 15, 1984.

64. See the account in Pierre Fournier, "The National Asbestos Corporation of Quebec," in Allan Tupper and G. Bruce Doern (eds.), *Public Corporations and Public Policy in Canada* (Montreal: Institute for Research on Public Policy), 353-64.

65. *La Presse*, May 15, 1984, April 1, 1985; *Le Devoir*, May 10, 1984.

66. Québec, *1985-86 Budget: Budget Speech*, 24.

67. *Ibid.*, 26.

68. *Le Devoir*, April 24, 1985; *La Presse*, August 2, 1986. Under the law, the Quebec government was to sell no more than 10 per cent of its shares. This provision was designed both to ensure government control of Hydro-Québec and to spare the enterprise from taxation.

69. In this fashion, the SGF would in fact return to the "mixed" format with which it was founded, but the formula would not be the same. (*Le Devoir* and *La Presse*, May 3, 1985.)

70. In February, 1982, Transport Minister Michel Clair had declared that his government had no intention of creating a state enterprise; the government's investment in Québecair was purely "defensive," intended to maintain it as a Quebec-based enterprise (*La Presse*, February 17, 1982).

71. *Le Devoir*, December 18, 1982.

72. *Ibid.*, February 3, June 22, 1983.

73. See, for instance, Michel Nadeau, "Pour une caisse plus active," *Le Devoir*, February 7, 1980.

74. *La Presse*, February 21, 1980; *Le Devoir*, September 6, 1980.

75. Stephen Brooks and A. Brian Tanguay, "Quebec's Caisse de dépôt et de placement: tool of nationalism?" *Canadian Public Administration*, 28, 1 (Spring, 1985), 99-119.

76. *Le Devoir*, August 19, 1981.

77. *Ibid.*, March 17, 1982.

78. *La Presse*, February 26, 1982.

79. *Le Devoir*, May 5, 1983.

80. *Ibid.*, December 3, 1982.

81. Brooks and Tanguay, "Quebec's Caisse."

82. *The Financial Post*, July 26, 1986.

83. These findings are drawn from Québec, *Budget 1981-82*, renseignements supplémentaires: crédits. They are also discussed in André Blais et Kenneth McRoberts, "Dynamique et contraintes des finances publiques," *Politique*, No. 3 (1983), 57-60.

84. *Ibid.*, 54.

85. These figures were calculated from the statements of "Budgétisation par missions, domaines et secteurs," reproduced in issues of Québec, *Budget: Crédits*, Conseil du trésor. I am grateful to Lise Gotell for performing the calculations.

86. See the discussion of PQ policy with respect to the minimum wage in Yves Vaillancourt, *le P.Q. et le sociale* (Montréal: Éditions Saint-Martin, 1983), 43-51.

87. *Le Devoir*, August 1, October 25, 1985.

88. Québec, *Budget Speech, 1982-83*, 15.

89. For an elaboration of these criticisms, as well as bibliographical detail on the government studies, see Blais and McRoberts, " Public Expenditure in Ontario and Quebec," 44-45.

90. Fraser, *P.Q.*, 324.

91. While there were two previous instances in which back-to-work measures had contained provisions making the Quebec Charter inoperable, the clauses were restricted to a single feature of the Charter: the presumption of innocence (*Globe and Mail*, March 15, 1983).

92. Gérard Bergeron, *Pratique de l'État du Québec*, 158, note 38; "la Fédération internationale des droits condamne la loi 111," *Le Devoir*, March 16, 1983. Bergeron also notes the isolated defence of the measure by past civil liberties activist Maurice Champagne-Gilbert.

93. Bergeron, *Pratique de l'État du Québec*, 158.

94. As quoted in Lise Bissonnette, "De la légitimité," *Le Devoir*, February 16, 1983. There was a deep irony in people such as Laurin, who had vigorously attacked Pierre Trudeau's 1970 invocation of the War Measures Act, defending the right of the state to defend itself.

95. *Le Devoir*, March 7, 1983 (Lévesque's phrase was "normaux et ordinaires").

96. *Ibid.*, February 17, 1983.

97. Quebec, *An Act Respecting the Process of Negotiation of the Collective Agreements in the Public and Parapublic Sectors*. Given Royal Assent June 19, 1985.

98. Quebec, *An Act to Amend the Labour Code and various Legislation*.

99. Quebec, *An Act to establish the Fonds de solidarité des travailleurs du Québec (F.T.Q.)*.

100. Calculated from Québec, Secrétariat permanent des conférences socio-économiques du Québec, *Le bilan des conférences socio-économiques de novembre 1979 à mai 1983* (Québec, 1983), 120; *Le bilan des conférences socio-économiques 1981-1985* (Québec, 1985).

101. Tanguay, "Concerted Action in Quebec, 1976-1983: Dialogue of the Deaf," in Gagnon (ed.), *Quebec: State and Society* (Toronto: Methuen, 1984), 380.

102. As proof that the Parti québécois was attacking its own clientele, André Blais *et al.* have found that "29 per cent of those who voted Parti québécois in 1981 suffered a salary decrease compared to only 19 per cent among supporters of other parties" (André Blais, Jean Crête, and Richard Johnston, "Can a Party Punish its Faith Supporters? The Parti québécois and Public Sector Employees," unpublished paper, 4).

103. Thomas J. Courchene, "Market Nationalism," *Policy Options*, 7, 8 (October, 1986), 7.

104. Fraser, *Quebec, Inc.*, 95.

105. *Ibid.*, 96.

106. This account is drawn from *ibid.*, 97, 101-02, and from Courchene, "Market Nationalism," 7. Apparently, Castonguay himself suggested the measure to Parizeau (Fraser, *Quebec, Inc.*, 102).

107. "Some veterans of Wall Street credit rating from outside Quebec argued convincingly that Bill 70 was responsible, single-handedly, for Quebec's loss of its AA credit rating. Wall Street, the argument went, disliked instability, and unilaterally taking back salary increases was asking for trouble. Since the whole purpose of the exercise was to keep Quebec's deficit fixed at the arbitrary figure of $3 billion which the government had decided was acceptable to public opinion, the operation was hardly a success." (Fraser, *P.Q.*, 329.)

108. *Témoignage de Camille Laurin: pourquoi je suis souverainiste*, quoted by Jean Provencher, *René Lévesque: Portrait of a Quebecer*, trans. David Ellis, 263-64 – as quoted in Fraser, *P.Q.*, 14.

109. Burns declared, "Look, I am a socialist, and the Parti Québécois is not always socialist." (Fraser, *P.Q.*, 180-82.)

110. Fraser, *P.Q.*, 344.

111. Twenty PQ members, including six ministers, absented themselves from the vote on Bill 105; Louise Harel abstained. In the case of Bill 111 Louise Harel abstained once again; Gilbert Paquette, Robert Dean, Marcel Léger, and Jérôme Proulx absented themselves. (Bergeron, *Pratique de l'État*, 154, note 25 and 158, note 42.)

112. "Les entreprises demandent au gouvernement provincial de leur donner

les moyens de résister aux syndicats," *La Presse*, March 3, 1983. Also, see the denunciation of the amendment by Ghislain Dufour of the Conseil du patronat. He cites in particular its effect on small and medium-sized enterprises. (Le Devoir, May 19, 1983.)

113. *Le Devoir*, February 10, 1982. See also Lévesque, *Memoirs*, 334-37.

114. *Le Devoir*, September 24, 1984 (our translation).

115. *Le Devoir*, November 20, 1984.

116. Lévesque, *Memoirs*, 18-25.

117. Pierre O'Neil, "Pierre-Marc Johnson n'a pas su personnifier le changement," *Le Devoir*, December 2, 1986.

118. Jean Crête, "Pas de clivage majeur entre les clientèles du Parti libéral et du Parti québécois," *Le Devoir*, November 23, 1985. Only on the PQ government's cutback of public-sector salaries did a major difference appear.

119. André Blais, "Le PQ attire encore les jeunes," *Le Devoir*, November 22, 1985. Blais *et al.* calculate that the public-sector salary cuts cost the PQ a loss of seven percentage points among public-sector employees. Conversely, the measure brought minor gains among voters outside the public sector. The total net loss to the party was one percentage point. (Blais *et al.*, "Can a Party Punish?" 8.)

120. *Le Devoir*, November 29, 1985.

121. Crête, "Pas de clivage."

122. Gilles Lesage, "Johnson inspire plus confiance," *Le Devoir*, November 22, 1985.

123. These figures, secured from Conseil scolaire de l'Île de Montréal, are reproduced in Marc V. Levine, "Language Policy, Education and Cultural Survival: Bill 101 and the Transformation of Anglophone Montreal, 1977-1985," unpublished paper, 18.

124. Conseil de l'Île de Montréal, *Prévision des populations scolaires francophones et anglophones de l'Île de Montréal* (Montréal: CSIM, 1980), 89 (as quoted in Levine, "Language Policy, Education and Cultural Survival," 18). See also Matthews, *Le choc démographique*, Chapter Five.

Chapter Eleven

1. The findings are drawn from André Blais et Jean Crête, "La clientèle péquiste en 1985: caractéristiques et évolution," *Politique*, 10, 5-29. Their analysis is framed in terms of a comparison of PQ supporters with supporters of "other parties," rather than just the Liberal Party. Nonetheless, the level of support for parties other than the Liberals, and the PQ, was so negligible that for our purposes we have equated the non-PQ vote with support of the Liberal Party.

2. Daniel Johnson, Paul Gobeil, Pierre MacDonald, and Pierre Fortier, respectively.

3. Richard French; Herbert Marx and Gil Remillard.

4. André Vallerand.

5. These calculations are based on the occupational designations appearing in Québec, *Rapport du directeur général des élections, 1985*, 35-40, supplemented primarily by the accounts in *Le Devoir*, December 13, 1985. Yvon Picotte was excluded from the calculations since no information was available on his previous occupation.

6. *Le Devoir*, December 13, 1985 (our translation).

7. *Ibid.*, December 17, 1985.

8. Our discussion will be based on the text reproduced in *Globe and Mail*, June 4, 1987.

9. These various passages are drawn from Section 2 of the proposed amendment to the Constitution Act, 1867.

10. "Nothing in this section derogates from the powers, rights or privileges of Parliament or the Government of Canada, or of the legislatures or governments of the provinces, including any powers, rights or privileges relating to language." (Section 4, proposed amendment to Constitution Act, 1867.) According to Peter W. Hogg, the new Section 2 "will have no significant impact on the distribution of powers between the federal parliament and the provincial legislatures." (Hogg, *Meech Lake Constitutional Accord Annotated* [Toronto: Carswell, 1988], 14.)

11. A final provision of the Charter not subject to the notwithstanding clause is the mobility of labour provision. Here Quebec is "protected" by the stipulation that the provision does not apply in provinces whose levels of employment fall below the national average.

12. Section 2 of the preamble of Constitution Act, 1987.

13. Section 106a (1) of the proposed amendment to Constitution Act, 1867. In point of fact, the provision would not affect the Canada Health Act since it is already on the books. See Hogg, *Meech Lake*, 41.

14. Pierre Elliott Trudeau, "Say Goodbye to the Dream of One Canada," *Toronto Star*, May 27, 1987.

15. Section 25 of the proposed amendment to the Constitution Act, 1867.

16. Sections 40 and 41 of proposed amendment to Constitution Act, 1982.

17. Section 50 of proposed amendment to Constitution Act, 1982.

18. Unlike the Langevin accord, the Victoria Charter did not include provisions for Senate nomination nor did it deal with the spending power or the provincial role in immigration. However, it did eliminate the federal powers of disallowance and reservation – which the Langevin accord does not deal with – and it provided Quebec with a blanket veto over *all* forms of amendment, unlike Langevin. As for the selection of Supreme Court justices, it called for federal consultation of the provinces, but did not assign the provinces the actual task of drawing up the lists of nominees. Like the Langevin accord, it guaranteed that three of the nine justices be from the bar of Quebec. Unlike Langevin, it also included safeguards that a case involving Quebec civil law be heard by justices of whom a majority were trained in that law. Also, the Victoria Charter called for an annual first ministers' conference, a measure included in the Constitution Act, 1982; the Langevin accord goes the added step of specifying that the conference be on the constitution. (Also, the Charter included an entrenchment of certain human rights and an amendment formula – provisions already incorporated in the Constitution Act, 1982.) In effect, the Victoria Charter dealt with the same range of matters as did the Langevin accord, excluding in the process any expansion of Quebec's jurisdictions. Thus, in finally rejecting the Victoria Charter, Bourassa pointed to its failure to specify clearly an enhanced role for Quebec in income security. (See the analysis of the Victoria Charter in Smiley, *Canada in Question*, 75-79.)

19. Trudeau, "Say Goodbye."

20. Robert Fulford, "Surrendering Canada," *Saturday Night* (August, 1987), 5-7.

21. "Meech Lake Accord Attacked by Head of Calgary Group," *Globe and Mail*, August 7, 1987, A5.

22. "Meech Lake Accord Gains General Support Polls Show," *Toronto Star*, June 1, 1987. A survey taken just after the Langevin version was reached suggests less concern that too much power had been given to the provinces. In each region, respondents were most likely to agree that the provinces would have the "right amount" of power. ("Voice of the People," *Maclean's*, June 15, 1987, 12-13.)

23. "Voice of the People," 12.

24. La Commission constitutionnelle du Parti libéral du Québec, *Une nouvelle fédération canadienne* (Montréal: le Parti libéral du Québec, 1980).

25. Task Force on Canadian Unity, *A Future Together*.

26. *Le Devoir*, May 20, 1987.

27. *Ibid.*, May 15, 1987.

28. *Ibid.*, May 4, 1987 (our translation).

29. "Voice of the People," 13. The figure includes Anglophone respondents. Given the evident unease of Quebec Anglophones with the Accord, in all likelihood the approval rate would have been even higher among Quebec Francophones alone.

30. Solange Chaput-Rolland, member of the Pépin-Robarts Task Force, declared that the agreement "largely exceeds our hopes" ("Il n'y pas de monstre au lac Meech," *Le Devoir*, May 8, 1987, 11). For his part, Claude Ryan issued a spirited defence of the agreement in response to Pierre Trudeau's attack ("L'accord du lac Meech permettra au Québec de faire des gains importants et incontestables," *La Presse*, May 30, 1987, A-11).

31. *Le Devoir*, February 28, 1987.

32. *Ibid.*, June 12, 1987.

33. For his part, Claude Morin published an analysis of the Accord in mid-May ("l'entente du lac Meech: le bon, le relatif et l'inquiétant," *Le Devoir*, May 16, 1987, A-ll). After voicing his approval of the amendment formula, he voiced concern about four matters: nominees to the three Supreme Court positions guaranteed for civil law jurists need not be from Quebec (this was corrected in the Langevin version); Quebec's powers over immigration might be generalized to all the provinces; the spending power provision may facilitate undue federal intervention; and the "distinct society" provision has insufficient teeth. Like Lévesque, he made no reference to the *additional* jurisdictions the Quebec government had sought for so long.

34. The Gobeil Report is presented and analysed in *Le Devoir*, July 8, 9, 14, 1987.

35. See the critique of this aspect of the Gobeil Report in Pierre Sormay, "Le rapport Gobeil dégraissage ou concentration?", *Le Devoir*, July 21, 1986.

36. *Le Devoir*, July 3, 1986 (our translation).

37. *Ibid.*

38. *Ibid.*, July 5, 1986 (our translation).

39. As quoted in Jean Francoeur, "Le pari de Reed Scowen," *Le Devoir*, July 9, 1986 (our translation). The article is the first of three insightful analyses of the report by Francoeur (see also *Le Devoir*, July 10, 11, 1986).

40. *Ibid.*, July 5, 1986.

41. *Ibid.*, December 15, 1986 (our translation).

42. André Blais et Stéphane Dion, "Trop d'État? Un baromètre de l'opinion," unpublished paper.

43. The results of the CROP survey are cited in Léo-Paul Lauzon, "Les prétendues visées de Power sur Domtar," *Le Devoir*, October 2, 1986.

44. *Le Devoir*, July 9, 1986 (our translation).
45. *The Financial Post*, July 19, 1986.
46. *Le Devoir*, September 26, 1986.
47. *Ibid.*, December 19, 1985.
48. *Ibid.*, February 11, 1986.
49. Québec, *Débats de l'Assemblée nationale*, May 1, 1986, 1093.
50. Québec, *Débats de l'Assemblée nationale*, May 1, 1987, 7038.
51. See Jacques Parizeau's comments to this effect in *Le Devoir*, December 15, 1986. Also, see the Graph of Tax Tables, projecting the reform, in the last PQ budget: Québec, *Budget, 1985-86*, 16.
52. The 1985-86 budget had indeed coupled the proposed reduction in the marginal tax rate with the introduction of tax exemptions for dependent children and increases in the child-care allowance for *young* children – although a reduction for older children and abolition for children over twelve years of age (Québec, *Budget, 1985-86*, 14-15).
53. *Le Devoir*, December 19, 1986.
54. Québec, *Débats de l'Assemblée nationale*, May 1, 1986, 1093.
55. *Ibid.*, 1096 (our translation).
56. Gouvernement du Québec, Ministère des finances, *Privatisation de sociétés d'État*, February, 1986.
57. "La mine de sel des Îles pourrait bien être privatisée cet automne," *Le Devoir*, July 9, 1987.
58. *Ibid.*, July 31, 1986.
59. See the accounts in *Le Devoir*, August 1, 1986, and Lise Bissonnette, "Quebec's 'Private' Concern," *Globe and Mail*, November 29, 1986.
60. This account is drawn from Bissonnette, "Quebec's 'Private' Concern."
61. *Le Devoir*, February 13, 1987.
62. See the analysis by Gilles Lesage, "Des encans pour l'épicerie," *ibid.*, October 4, 1986.
63. *Ibid.*, September 22, 1986.
64. *Ibid.*, October 2, 1986.
65. *Ibid.*, February 23, 1987.
66. *Ibid.*, April 11, 1987.
67. In announcing the new policy, Ministre délégué aux Finances et à la Privatisation, Pierre Fortier, and Ministre de l'Industrie et du Commerce, Daniel Johnson, declared that the SGF no longer needed to play the role of a conglomerate seeking to ensure a Québécois presence in the economy, since "les objectifs de la *Révolution tranquille*, soit l'implantation dans le secteur industriel et la création d'emplois pour les cadres francophones, ont été dans une grande mesure atteints." (*Le Devoir*, October 1, 1986.)
68. *Ibid.*, October 19, 1986 (our translation).
69. Bissonnette, "Quebec's 'Private' Concern."
70. *Le Devoir*, October 9, 1986.
71. See, for instance, Clément Trudel, "Le président de la FTQ y voit un danger pour tous les 'corps démocratiques,' " *Le Devoir*, June 12, 1987.
72. See, for instance, the critique by Gilles Lesage, "Privé du coffre d'outils?", *ibid.*, October 29, 1986.
73. Québec, *Débats de l'Assemblée nationale*, April 30, 1987, 7031-033.
74. Gilles Lesage, "L'intendance Bourassa," *Le Devoir*, December 2, 1986. Apparently, a primary reason for the delay was the need to prepare for the immense administrative change that would be involved in classifying welfare

recipients in terms of such categories as availability for work. (Gilbert Brunet, "Paradis apprend que réformer l'aide sociale, ce n'est pas simple," *La Presse*, August 30, 1986.)

75. For a preliminary assessment of the proposed reform, see Jean Francoeur, "Le Québec, province pilote?", *Le Devoir*, May 27, 1987.

76. *Ibid.*, May 2, 1987.

77. This account draws on Lise Bissonnette, "Bourassa's 'Revolution' Quietly Stalled," *Globe and Mail*, August 15, 1987.

78. "Les gens d'affaires se disent très satisfaits du gouvernement Bourassa, selon le CPQ," *Le Devoir*, July 10, 1987.

79. The FTQ did give its "tacit support" to the bill, while opposing it publicly. (*Le Devoir*, December 17, 24, 1987.)

80. See, for instance, Paul-André Comeau, "Et un pas en arrière," *ibid.*, November 15, 1986.

81. See Jean-Pierre Proulx, "Anglais par référendum," *Le Devoir*, December 8, 1986 (our translation).

82. *Ibid.*

83. *Ibid.*, December 1, 1986 (our translation).

84. *Ibid.*, January 22, 1987.

85. *Ibid.*, December 23, 1987.

86. *Ibid.*, February 28, 1987 (our translation).

87. *Ibid.*, June 12, 1987.

88. Gilles Lesage, "Un an après les sages," *ibid.*, July 23, 1987, 6.

Chapter Twelve

1. Statistics Canada, *Provincial Economic Accounts, 1961-1976* (Ottawa, 1978), as cited in Judith Maxwell and Gérard Bélanger, *Taxes and Expenditures in Québec and Ontario: a comparison*, Accent Québec Series (Montreal: C.D. Howe Institute, 1978), 3.

2. Québec, Développement économique, *Bâtir le Québec: énoncé de politique économique* (Québec: Éditeur officiel du Québec, 1979), 125. The greater importance of the Quebec public sector, compared to those of other provinces, is explored in detail by Jean Vézina, "Les gouvernements," Annexe 11 of *Prospective socio-économique du Québec, Première étape*, "Sous-système économique (2)," Collection Études et recherches (Québec: Office de planification et de développement du Québec, 1977). See also Marc Renaud, "Réforme ou illusion? Une analyse des interventions de l'État québécois dans le domaine de la santé," *Sociologie et sociétés*, 9 (avril, 1977), 127-52; Levasseur et Lacroix, "Rapports de classe," 88-94.

3. Courchene situates these moves within a general strategy of "market nationalism." (Courchene, "Market Nationalism.")

4. Fraser, *Quebec, Inc.*, 238. The data in the preceding paragraph are taken from *The Financial Post 500* (Toronto: Maclean Hunter, 1985). See also Jorge Niosi, "The Rise of French-Canadian Capitalism," in Gagnon, *Québec: State and Society*, 186-200; Niosi, "La multinationalisation des firmes Canadiennes-françaises," *Recherches sociographiques*, 24, 1 (1983), 55-74.

5. *Ibid.*, 100-01.

6. *Ibid.*, 114

7. *Ibid.*, 189.

8. *Le Devoir*, September 9, 1987.

9. Alain G. Gagnon and Khayam Z. Paltiel, "Toward *Maîtres chez nous*: the ascendancy of a Balzacian Bourgeoisie in Quebec," *Queen's Quarterly*, 93, 4 (Winter, 1986), 739.

10. *Ibid.*

11. *Ibid.*; Fraser, *Quebec, Inc.*, 164

12. Gagnon and Paltiel, "Toward *Maîtres chez nous*," 740.

13. Data on the increase in Francophone presence in management and on the decline in income disparities appear in Francois Vaillencourt, "Le français sur le marché du travail du Québec: 1970-1980," Centre de recherche et développement en économique, Université de Montréal, unpublished paper. See also D.M. Shapiro and M. Stelcner, "Earnings Disparities among Linguistic Groups in Quebec, 1970-1980," *Canadian Public Policy*, 13, 1 (1987), 97-104.

14. For surveys of this phenomenon, see Edward Tiryakian and Ronald Rogowski (eds.), *New Nationalism of the Developed West* (Boston: Allen & Unwin, 1985); "After the Referenda: the future of ethnic nationalism in Britain and Canada," theme issue of *Ethnic and Racial Studies*, 7, 1 (January, 1984); Anthony D. Smith, *The Ethnic Revival* (Cambridge: Cambridge University Press, 1981); and Mary Beth Montcalm, "Quebec Nationalism in a Comparative Perspective," *Quebec: state and society*, 48-58. See also Katherine O'Sullivan See, *First World Nationalisms: class and ethnic politics in Northern Ireland and Quebec* (Chicago: University of Chicago Press, 1986).

15. Michael Hechter, *Internal Colonialism* (Berkeley: University of California Press, 1975). For a survey of possible applications of the model, see *Ethnic and Racial Studies*, 2, 3 (July, 1979). The applicability of the model to Quebec is assessed in Kenneth McRoberts, "Internal Colonialism: the case of Quebec," *ibid.*, 296-318.

16. Tom Nairn, *The Break-up of Britain: crisis and neo-nationalism* (London: New Left Books, 1977), 203. Within one analysis, only these "overdeveloped" regions can produce serious nationalist movements. See Peter Gourevitch, "Politics, Economics, and Nationalism: some comparative speculations," *Comparative Studies in Society and History*, 21, 303-22. These approaches are assessed in McRoberts, "The Sources of Neo-nationalism in Quebec."

17. Dominique Clift et Sheila McLeod Arnopoulos, *Le fait anglais au Québec* (Montréal: Libre Expression, 1979), 153-54.

18. See Alain G. Gagnon and Mary Beth Montcalm, "Economic Peripheralization and Quebec Unrest," *Journal of Canadian Studies*, 17, 2, 32-42.

19. Coleman, *The Independence Movement*, 211.

20. *Ibid.*

21. To be sure, one *indépendantiste* activist, François-Albert Angers, did seek to reserve membership in the Quebec nation to "authentic" French Canadians. In a remarkable intervention after the referendum defeat, he blamed the Quebec government for allowing non-French Canadians to vote in the referendum (Angers, "Notre réferendum: Les dangers d'une opération mal engagée et mal conduite," *Le Devoir*, September 19, 1980, 17). Yet, no other Quebec intellectuals took up the theme. Rather, it was seen as one more bit of evidence of the degree to which Angers, well advanced in his years, was simply out of touch with contemporary Quebec political thought. (See the response of *indépendantiste* historian René Durocher, who criticized Angers both for his faulty notion of democracy and for his misunderstanding of Quebec's historical development: Durocher, "En réponse à François-Albert Angers," *Le Devoir*, October 2, 3, 1980.) A driving force behind the Tremblay Commission and a harsh critic of the Parent Commis-

sion's report, Angers may well represent an instance of *indépendantisme* that is partly fuelled by reaction to the changes engendered by the Quiet Revolution. Yet his singularity only underscores the degree to which the *indépendantiste* movement cannot be properly understood in these terms.

22. Coleman, *The Independence Movement*, 228.

23. *Ibid.*, 209.

24. Léon Dion, *A la recherche du Québec* (Québec: Presses de l'Université Laval, 1987). Also, on the continuing bases for a Quebec national identity, see Gilles Bourque, "À propos du mouvement indépendantiste," *Canadian Journal of Political and Social Theory*, 10, 3 (Fall, 1986), 163.

25. Jacques Henripin, *l'Immigration et le déséquilibre linguistique* (Ottawa: Main-d'oeuvre et immigration, 1974), 22.

26. This is the estimate by demographer Jacques Henripin of the proportion using French at home ("Les anglophones pourraient ne représenter que 10.4% de la population du Québec en 2001," *Le Devoir*, November 28, 1984).

27. Matthews, *Le choc démographique*, 149-51.

28. In the survey, which was administered by SORECOM, respondents were asked to choose among these three options. The percentages selecting the other two are unavailable. (*La Presse*, November 30, 1987, B1.) The 44 per cent may partially reflect the impact of René Lévesque's recent death. However, surveys in the fall of 1985 produced a figure of 35 per cent for sovereignty-association. (Balthazar, *Bilan du nationalisme* [Montréal: l'Hexagone, 1986], 197.)

29. "Parizeau laisse les syndiqués froids," *Le Devoir*, January 9, 1988.

Works Cited

"After the Referenda: the future of ethnic nationalism in Britain and Canada," theme issue of *Ethnic and Racial Studies*, 7, 1 (January, 1984).

Ajzenstat, Janet. "Liberalism and Nationality," *Canadian Journal of Political Science*, 14, 3 (September, 1981), 588-609.

Allaire, Yvan. "La nouvelle classe politique et les pouvoirs économiques," in Léonard (ed.), *La chance au coureur*, 60-69.

———, and Roger E. Miller. *Canadian Business Response to the Legislation on Francization in the Workplace*. Accent Québec. Montreal: C.D. Howe Institute, 1980.

Amin, Samir. *Le développement inégal*. Paris: Éditions de Minuit, 1973.

Arès, Richard. *Les positions ethniques, linguistiques et religieuses des Canadiens français à la suite du recensement de 1971*. Montréal: Éditions Bellarmin, 1975.

Armstrong, Christopher, and H.V. Nelles. "Contrasting Development of the Hydro-Electric Industry in the Montreal and Toronto Regions, 1900-1930," *Journal of Canadian Studies*, 18, 1 (Spring, 1983), 5-27.

Aucoin, Peter, and Herman Bakvis. "Regional Responsiveness and Government Organization: the case of regional economic development policy in Canada," in Aucoin (ed.), *Regional Responsiveness and the National Administrative State*. Collected Research Studies of the Royal Commission on the Economic Union and Development Prospects for Canada, Vol. 38. Ottawa: Supply and Services Canada, 1985, 51-118.

Audet, Louis-Philip. *Histoire de l'enseignement au Québec 1840-1971*. Montréal: Holt, Rinehart & Winston, 1971.

Auer, L., and K. Mills. "Confederation and Some Regional Implications of the Tariffs on Manufacturers," Economic Council of Canada (paper presented to Workshop on the Political Economy of Confederation, Kingston, Ontario, November 8-10, 1978).

Balthazar, Louis. *Bilan du nationalisme au Québec*. Montréal: Hexagone, 1986.

Banting, Keith, and Richard Simeon (eds.). *And No One Cheered: federalism, democracy and the Constitution Act*. Toronto: Methuen, 1983.

Barber, Clarence. "The Customs Union Issue," *Options Canada*, Proceedings of the Conference on the Future of the Canadian Federation (University of Toronto, October, 1977), 214-32.

Bauer, Julien. "Attitude des syndicats," *Études internationales*, 8 (juin, 1977), 307-19.

Beattie, Christopher. *Minority Men in a Majority Setting: middle-level*

Francophones in the Canadian public service. Toronto: McClelland and Stewart, 1975.

Behiels, Michael D. *Prelude to Quebec's Quiet Revolution*. Montreal: McGill-Queen's University Press, 1985.

Beigie, Carl E., and Judith Maxwell. *Quebec's Vulnerability in Energy*. Accent Québec. Montreal: C.D. Howe Research Institute, 1977.

Bélanger, André J. *L'apolitisme des idéologies québécoises: le grand tournant de 1934-36*. Québec: Les Presses de l'Université Laval, 1974.

———. *Ruptures et constantes: idéologies du Québec en éclatement, La Relève, La JEC, Cité libre, Parti pris*. Montreal: Hurtubise HMH, 1977.

Bercuson, David Jay. *The Burden of Unity*. Toronto: Macmillan, 1977.

Bergeron, Gérard. *Le Canada français: après deux siècles de patience*. Paris: Éditions du Seuil, 1967.

———. *Pratique de l'État au Québec*. Montréal: Éditions Québec/Amérique, 1984.

Bergeron, Léandre. "Pour une langue québécoise," *Chroniques*, 1 (mars, 1975).

Bergeron, Marie-Hélène, Douglas Brown, and Richard Simeon (eds.). *The Question: the debate on the referendum question, Quebec National Assembly, March 4-20, 1980*. Kingston, Ontario: Institute of Intergovernmental Relations, Queen's University, 1980.

Bernard, André. *Québec: élections 1976*. Montréal: Hurtubise HMH, 1976.

———, and Bernard Descôteaux. *Québec: élections 1981*. Montréal: Hurtubise HMH, 1981.

Bernard, Paul, André Demers, Diane Grenier et Jean Renaud. *L'évolution de la situation socio-économique des francophones et des non-francophones au Québec (1971-1978)*. Collection Langues et sociétés. Montréal: Office de la langue française, 1979.

Bernier, Gérald. "Le cas québécois et les théories de développement et la dépendance," in Orban, *La modernisation politique du Québec*, 19-54.

———. "Les aspects économiques du débat: un dialogue de sourds," in En collaboration," *Québec: un pays incertain*, 111-34.

Bill, J.A., and Robert Hardgrave, Jr. *Comparative Politics: the quest for theory*. Columbus, Ohio: Charles E. Merrill, 1973.

Bilodeau, J.C. "Canada: Quebec," *Yearbook of Education 1951*. London, 1951.

Binder, Leonard, *et al. Crises and Sequences in Political Development*. Princeton, N.J.: Princeton University Press, 1971.

Black, C.E. *The Dynamics of Modernization*. New York: Harper, 1967.

Black, Conrad. *Duplessis*. Toronto: McClelland and Stewart, 1976.

Blais, André. "L'élection de 1981," unpublished paper.

———. "Le vote: ce que l'on sait . . . ce que l'on n'en sait pas," in En collaboration, *Québec: un pays incertain*, 157-82.

———. , et Jean Crête. "La clientèle péquiste en 1985: caractéristiques et évolution," *Politique*, 10, 5-29.

———. , Jean Crête, and Richard Johnston. "Can a Party Punish its Faithful Supporters? The Parti québécois and Public Sector Employees," unpublished paper.

———. , et Kenneth McRoberts. "Dynamique et contraintes des finances publiques," *Politique*, No. 3 (1983), 57-60.

———. , and Kenneth McRoberts. "Public Expenditure in Ontario and Quebec, 1950-1980: explaining the differences," *Journal of Canadian Studies*, 18, 1 (Spring, 1983), 28-53.

———, and Philippe Faucher. Review

of Jobin, *Les enjeux économiques de la nationalisation de l'électricité,* in *Revue canadienne de science politique,* 12, 4 (décembre, 1979), 809-16.

_____, et Richard Nadeau. "La clientèle du OUI," in Crête, *Comportement électoral au Québec,* 321-34.

_____, et Stéphane Dion. "Trop d'État? Un baromètre de l'opinion," unpublished paper.

Block, Fred. "The Ruling Class Does Not Rule," *Socialist Revolution,* 7, 3 (1977), 6-28.

Boily, Robert. "Les hommes politiques du Québec, 1867-1967," *Revue d'histoire de l'Amérique française,* 21, 3a (décembre, 1967), 599-636.

_____. "Montréal, une forteresse libérale," *Socialisme,* 66 (1966), 138-60.

Boismenu, Gérard. *Le duplessisme: politique économique et rapports de force, 1944-1960.* Montréal: Presses de l'Université de Montréal, 1981.

Boivin, Jean. "Labour Relations in Quebec," in Hugh Anderson and Morley Gunderson (eds.), *Union-Management Relations in Canada* (Don Mills, Ont.: Addison-Wesley, 1982), 422-56.

Bolduc, Roch. "Le recrutement et la sélection dans la fonction publique au Québec," *Administration publique du Canada,* 7 (1964), 205-14.

Bonin, Bernard, et Mario Polése. *À propos de l'association Canada-Québec.* Québec: École nationale d'administration publique, 1980.

Borins, Sanford F. *Language of the Skies: the bilingual air traffic control conflict in Canada.* Montréal: McGill-Queen's University Press, 1983.

Borris, Val. "Capital Accumulation and the Rise of the New Middle Class," *The Review of Radical Political Economics,* 12, 1 (Spring, 1980), 17-34.

Bourque, Gilles. "Class, Nation and the Parti québécois," in Gagnon, *Quebec: State and Society,* 124-47.

_____. *Classes sociales et question nationale au Québec, 1760-1840.* Montréal: Parti pris, 1970.

_____. *L'État capitaliste et la question nationale.* Montréal: Presses de l'Université de Montréal, 1977.

_____. "Petite bourgeoisie envahissante et bourgeoisie ténébreuse," *Cahiers du socialisme,* 3 (printemps, 1979), 122-61.

_____. "À propos du mouvement indépendantiste," *Revue canadienne de théorie politique et sociale,* 10, 3 (automne, 1986), 153-64.

_____, et Anne Legaré. *Le Québec: la question nationale.* Paris: Maspero, 1979.

_____, et Nicole Laurin-Frenette. "Classes sociales et idéologies nationalistes au Québec (1760-1970)," *Socialisme québécois,* No. 20 (avril-mai-juin, 1970), 13-55.

Brazeau, Jacques. "Language Differences and Occupational Experience," *Canadian Journal of Economics and Political Science,* 24 (November, 1958), 532-40.

Brooks, Stephen, and A. Brian Tanguay. "Quebec's Caisse de dépôt et de placement: tool of nationalism?" *Canadian Public Administration,* 28, 1 (Spring, 1985), 99-119.

Brunelle, Dorval. *La désillusion tranquille.* Montréal: Hurtubise HMH, 1978.

Brunelle, Richard, et Pierre Papineau. "Le gouvernement du capital," *Socialisme québécois,* no. 23 (1972).

Brunet, Michel. *La présence anglaise et les Canadiens.* Montréal: Beauchemin, 1964.

Bureau, Conrad. "Le référendum de mai au Québec: une analyse linguistique de 'la question'," *Langues et linguistique,* 10 (1984).

Bureau, Luc. *Entre l'éden et l'utopie: les fondements imaginaires de l'espace québécois.* Montréal: Éditions Québec/Amérique, 1984.

Burns, R.M. *The Acceptable Mean: the Tax Rental Agreements, 1941-1962*. Financing Canadian Federation 3. Toronto: Canadian Tax Foundation, 1980.

Cairns, Allan C. "The Politics of Constitutional Conservatism," in Banting and Simeon, *And No One Cheered*, 28-58.

Campbell, Colin, and George Szablowski. *The Superbureaucrats*. Toronto: Macmillan, 1979.

Canada. *A Time for Action*. Ottawa: Supply and Services, 1978.

_____. *Annual Report, 1978: Commissioner of Official Languages*. Ottawa: Supply and Services, 1979.

_____. *Constitutional Reform: House of the Federation*. Ottawa: Canadian Unity Information Office, 1978.

_____. *Foreign Direct Investment in Canada*. Ottawa: Information Canada, 1972.

_____. *Working Paper on Social Security in Canada* (April, 1973).

_____, Royal Commission on Bilingualism and Biculturalism. *Report*. Ottawa: Queen's Printer, various volumes.

_____, Statistics Canada. *Provincial Economic Accounts, 1961-1976*. Ottawa, 1978.

_____, Statistics Canada. *Provincial Government Finance, 1970-1983*, 68-205.

_____, Statistics Canada. *System of National Accounts: provincial economic accounts, 1969-1984*, 13-213.

_____, The Task Force on Canadian Unity. *A Future Together*. Ottawa: Supply and Services, 1979.

Cappon, Paul. *Conflit entre les Néo-Canadians et les francophones de Montréal*. Québec: Presses de l'Université Laval, 1974.

Cardechi, G. "On the Economic Identification of the New Middle Class," *Economy and Society*, 4, 1 (1975), 1-86.

Careless, Anthony. *Initiative and Response*. Montreal: McGill-Queen's University Press, 1977.

Carlos, Serge, Edouard Cloutier et Daniel Latouche. "Le choix des électeurs en 1973: caractéristiques sociales et orientation nationale," in Daniel Latouche, Guy Lord et Jean-Guy Vaillancourt (eds.), *Le processus électoral au Québec: les élections provinciales de 1970 et 1973* (Montréal: Hurtubise HMH, 1976), 213-34.

Carrier, André. "L'idéologie politique de la revue Cité libre," *Revue canadienne de science politique*, 1, 4 (décembre, 1968), 414-28.

Carroll, William K. "Dependency, Imperialism, and the Capitalist Class in Canada," in Robert J. Brym (ed.), *The Structure of the Canadian Capitalist Class* (Toronto: Garamond Press, 1985), 21-52.

Carter, D.D. "The Labour Code of Quebec," in *La loi et les rapports collectifs du travail*, 14ième Colloque de l'École des relations industrielles, Université de Montréal, 1984.

CBC-90 Minutes Live. "Hamilton-Pinard Study" [opinion survey results], unpublished paper, October, 1977.

Chaloult, René. *Mémoires politiques*. Montréal: Éditions du Jour, 1969.

Chamberland, Paul. "De la damnation à la liberté," in Parti pris, *Les Québécois* (Paris: Maspero, 1967), 75-113.

Charbonneau, Hubert, Jacques Henripin et Jacques Légaré. "L'avenir démographique des francophones au Québec et à Montréal en l'absence de politiques adéquates," *Revue de géographie de Montréal*, 24 (1974), 199-202.

Charbonneau, Jean-Pierre, et Gilbert Paquette. *L'Option*. Montréal: Éditions de l'Homme, 1978.

Chorney, Harold. "Regional Underdevelopment and Cultural Decay," in

Marxist Institute of Toronto, *Imperialism, Nationalism, and Canada* (Toronto: New Hogtown Press, 1977), 108-41.

Clement, Wallace. *The Canadian Corporate Elite: an analysis of economic Power*. Carleton Library No. 89. Toronto: McClelland and Stewart, 1975.

Clift, Dominique, et Sheila McLeod Arnopolous. *Le fait anglais au Québec*. Montréal: Libre Expression, 1979.

Cobban, Alfred. *The Nation State and National Self-Determination*. London: Collins, 1969.

Coleman, William. "A Comparative Study of Language Policy in Quebec: a political economy approach," in Michael M. Atkinson and Marsha A. Chandler (eds.), *The Politics of Canadian Public Policy* (Toronto: University of Toronto Press, 1983), 21-42.

———. "From Bill 22 to Bill 101: The Politics of Language under the Parti Québécois," *Canadian Journal of Political Science*, 14, 3 (September, 1981), 459-85.

———. *The Independence Movement in Quebec, 1945-1980*. Toronto: University of Toronto Press, 1984.

———. "Quebec Nationalism and the Organization of Business Interests," paper presented to the Conference on the Regional Organization of Business Interests and Public Policy, McMaster University, May 22-24, 1985.

La Collection Choix. *Le nationalisme québécois à la croisée des chemins*. Québec: Centre québécois de relations internationales, 1975.

La Commission constitutionelle du Parti libéral du Québec. *Une nouvelle fédération canadienne*. Montréal: le Parti libéral du Québec, 1980.

Cook, Ramsay. *Canada and the French-Canadian Question*. Toronto: Macmillan, 1967.

———. "French-Canadian Interpretations of Canadian History," *Journal of Canadian Studies*, 2 (May, 1967), 3-18.

———. *The Maple Leaf Forever*. Toronto: Macmillan, 1971.

Cooper, C.J. "The Social Structure of Montreal in the 1850s," *Canadian Historical Association Annual Report* (1956), 66-72.

Courchene, Thomas J. "Market Nationalism," *Policy Options*, 7, 8 (October, 1986), 7-12.

Courville, Léon, Marcel Dagenais, Carmine Nappi et Alain Van Peetersen. *La sensibilité des industries au commerce interrégional: le cas du Québec, de l'Ontario et du reste du Canada*. Préparé pour le compte du Ministère des affaires intergouvernementales du Québec. Québec: Éditeur Officiel, 1979.

Cox, Robert. "Employment, Labour and Future Political Structures," in R.B. Byers and Robert W. Reford (eds.), *Canada Challenged* (Toronto: Canadian Institute for International Affairs, 1979), 262-92.

Crête, Jean (ed.). *Comportement électoral au Québec*. Chicoutimi: Gaetan Morin, 1984.

Cuneo, Carl J., and James E. Curtis. "Quebec Separatism: an analysis of determinants within social-class levels," *Canadian Review of Sociology and Anthropology*, 2 (1974), 1-29.

Cutright, Phillips. "National Political Development: measurement and analysis," *American Sociological Review*, 28 (1963), 253-64.

Dagenais, Pierre. "Le mythe de la vocation agricole du Québec," in *Mélanges géographiques canadiens offerts à Raoul Blanchard* (Québec: Presses de l'Université Laval, 1959), 193-201.

Dales, John H. "A Comparison of Manufacturing Industry in Quebec and Ontario, 1952," in Mason Wade (ed.), *Canadian Dualism* (Québec:

Presses de l'Université Laval, 1960), 203-21.

d'Allemagne, André. *Le R.I.N. de 1960 à 1963: étude d'un groupe de pression au Québec.* Montréal: Éditions l'étincelle, 1974.

David, Hélène. "L'état des rapports de classe au Québec de 1945 à 1967," *Sociologie et sociétés*, 7, 2 (novembre, 1975), 33-66.

―――. "La grève et le bon Dieu: la grève de l'amiante au Québec," *Sociologie et sociétés*, 1, 2 (novembre, 1969), 249-76.

Dechêne, Louise. *Habitants et marchands de Montréal au XVIIe siècle.* Paris: Plon, 1974.

Demers, François. *Chroniques impertinentes du 3ème Front commun syndical.* Montréal: Nouvelle Optique, 1982.

Denis, Roch. *Luttes de classes et question nationale au Québec, 1948-1968.* Montréal: Presses Socialistes Internationales, 1979.

Derbyshire, E. "Notes on the Social Structure of a Canadian Pioneer Town," *Sociological Review*, 8 (July, 1960), 63-75.

Deutsch, Karl. "Social Mobilization and Political Development," *American Political Science Review*, 55 (September, 1961), 493-514.

Dion, Gérard. "Les relations patronales-ouvrières sous la 'révolution tranquille'," *Relations*, 344 (décembre, 1969).

Dion, Léon. *Le Bill 60 et la société québécoise.* Montréal: Hurtubise HMH, 1967.

―――. "Genèse et caractères du nationalisme de croissance," in Congrès des affaires canadiennes, *Les nouveaux Québécois* (Québec: Presses de l'Université Laval, 1964), 59-76.

―――. *Nationalismes et politique au Québec.* Montréal: Hurtubise HMH, 1975.

―――. "La polarité des idéologies: conservatisme et progressisme," in Dumont et Montminy, *Le pouvoir*

dans la société canadienne-française*, 25-35.

―――. *La prochaine révolution.* Québec: Éditions Lémeac, 1973.

―――. *À la recherche du Québec.* Québec: Presses de l'Université Laval, 1987.

Djwa, Sandra. *The Politics of the Imagination: A Life of F.R. Scott.* Toronto: McClelland and Stewart, 1987.

Drache, Daniel (ed.). *Quebec – Only the Beginning: the manifestoes of the Common Front.* Toronto: New Press, 1972.

Duchesne, Raymond. "D'intérêt public et d'intérêt privé: l'institutionnalisation de l'enseignement et de la recherche scientifiques au Québec (1920-1940)," in Yvan Lamonde et Esther Trépanier (eds.), *L'avènement de la modernité culturelle au Québec* (Québec: Institut québécois de recherche sur la culture, 1986), 195-202.

―――. *La science et le pouvoir au Québec (1920-1965).* La documentation québécoise. Québec: Éditeur Officiel du Québec, 1978.

Dumas, Evelyn. "The Two Faces of the Revolution," *Canadian Forum* (December, 1984), 31-32.

Dumont, Fernand. "Idéologie et conscience historique," in Jean-Paul Bernard (ed.), *Les idéologies québécoises au 19e siècle* (Montréal: Boréal Express, 1973), 61-82.

―――, et Jean-Paul Montiminy (eds.). *Le pouvoir dans la société canadienne-française.* Québec: Presses de l'Université Laval, 1966.

Dunn, Sharon. "Federalism, Constitutional Reform and the Economy: the Canadien experience," *Publius*, 13, 2 (Spring, 1983), 129-42.

Dupont, Antonin. "Louis-Alexandre Taschereau et la législation sociale au Québec, 1920-1936," *Revue d'histoire de l'Amérique française*, 26, 3 (décembre, 1972), 397-426.

―――. *Les relations entre l'Église et*

l'*État sous Louis-Alexandre Tasche-reau, 1920-1936*. Montréal: Guerin, 1973.

Dupré, J. Stefan. "Reflections on the Workability of Executive Federalism," in Richard Simeon (ed.), *Intergovernmental Relations*, Collected Research Studies of the Royal Commission on the Economic Union and Development Prospects for Canada, Vol. 63 (Ottawa: Supply and Services Canada, 1985), 1-31.

Durocher, René. "Maurice Duplessis et sa conception de l'autonomie provinciale au début de sa carrière politique," *Revue d'histoire de l'Amérique française*, 23, 1 (juin, 1969), 13-34.

———, et Michèle Jean. "Duplessis et la Commission royale d'enquête sur les problèmes constitutionnels, 1953-1956," *Revue d'histoire de l'Amérique française*, 25, 3 (décembre, 1971), 337-64.

L'École sociale populaire. *Pour la restauration sociale au Canada*. Montréal: L'École sociale populaire, 1933.

Economic Council of Canada. *Living Together*. Ottawa, 1977.

En collaboration. *Québec: un pays incertain, réflexions sur le Québec post-référendaire*. Montréal: Québec/Amérique, 1980.

Falardeau, Jean-Charles. "The Role and Importance of the Church in French Canada," in Rioux and Martin, (eds.), *French-Canadian Society*, 342-57.

Faucher, Albert. "Pouvoir politique et pouvoir économique dans l'évolution du Canada français," in Dumont et Montiminy, *Le pouvoir dans la société canadienne-française*, 61-79.

———, and Maurice Lamontagne. "History of Industrial Development," in Rioux and Martin (eds.), *French-Canadian Society*, 257-71.

Finkel, Alvin. "Populism and the Proletariat: Social Credit and the Alberta working class," *Studies in Political Economy*, 13 (Spring, 1984), 109-35.

Fletcher, Frederick J. "The View from Upper Canada," in Simeon, *Must Canada Fail?*, 28-41.

Fortin, Bernard. *Les avantages et les coûts des différentes options monétaires d'une petite économie ouverte: un cadre analytique*, préparé pour le compte du ministère des affaires intergouvernementales du Québec. Québec: Éditeur Officiel, 1978.

Fortin, Gérald. "Une classification socio-économique des municipalités agricoles du Québec," *Recherches sociographiques*, 1 (avril-juin, 1960), 207-16.

———. "L'étude du milieu rural," in F. Dumont (ed.), *Situation de la recherche sur le Canada français* (Québec: Presses de l'Université Laval, 1962), 106-09.

———. "Le nationalisme canadien-français et les classes sociales," *Revue d'histoire de l'Amérique française*, 22, 4 (mars, 1969), 525-34.

———. "Le Québec: une ville à inventer," *Recherches sociographiques*, 9 (janvier-août, 1968), 11-21.

Fortin, Pierre, Gilles Paquet et Yves Rabeau. "Coûts et bénéfices de l'appartenance du Québec à la Confédération canadienne: analyse préliminaire," préparé à la demande de Radio-Canada pour l'émission l'Économthèque du 21 Mai 1977; published as "Quebec in the Canadian Federation: a provisional evaluative framework," *Canadian Public Administration*, 21 (1978), 558-83.

Fournier, Marcel. *L'entrée dans la modernité: science, culture et société au Québec*. Montréal: Éditions Saint-Martin, 1986.

———. "L'institutionnalisation des sciences sociales au Québec," *Sociologie et sociétés*, 5, 1 (mai, 1973), 27-58.

_____. "La question nationale," *Possibles*, 1 (hiver, 1977).

_____. "La question nationale: enjeux et impasses," in Léonard (ed.), *La chance au coureur*, 177-92.

Fournier, Pierre. "The National Asbestos Corporation of Quebec," in Allan Tupper and G. Bruce Doern (eds.), *Public Corporations and Public Policy in Canada* (Montreal: Institute for Research on Public Policy), 353-64.

_____. "Les nouveaux paramètres de la bourgeoisie québécoise," in Pierre Fournier (ed.), *Le Capitalisme au Québec* (Montréal: Éditions Coopératives Albert Saint-Martin, 1978), 135-81.

_____. "Projet national et affrontement des bourgeoisies québécoise et canadienne," in Léonard (ed.), *La chance au coureur*, 39-59.

_____. *The Quebec Establishment*. Montreal: Black Rose Books, 1976.

_____. "Vers une grande bourgeoisie canadienne-française?" Département de science politique, Université du Québec à Montréal (juin, 1976).

Fraser, Graham. *PQ: René Lévesque and the Parti Québécois in power*. Toronto: Macmillan of Canada, 1984.

Fraser, Matthew. *Quebec, Inc.* Toronto: Key Porter Books, 1987.

Frechette, Pierre. "L'économie de la Confédération: un point de vue québécois," *Analyse de politiques*, 3, 4 (1977), 431-39.

Fulford, Robert. "Surrendering Canada," *Saturday Night* (August, 1987), 5-7.

Fullerton, Douglas H. *The Dangerous Delusion*. Toronto: McClelland and Stewart, 1978.

_____ (ed.). *Quebec's Access to Financial Markets*. Understanding Canada Series. Ottawa: Supply and Services, 1979.

Gagnon, Alain G. "The Development and Nationalization of Social Sciences in Quebec," *Quebec Studies*, 1, 4 (1986), 71-89.

_____. *Quebec: State and Society*. Toronto: Methuen, 1984.

_____, and Khayam Z. Paltiel. "Toward *Maître chez nous*: the ascendancy of a Balzacian Bourgeoisie in Quebec," *Queen's Quarterly*, 93, 4 (Winter, 1986), 731-49.

_____, and Mary Beth Montcalm. "Economic Peripheralization and Quebec Unrest," *Journal of Canadian Studies*, 17, 2 (1982), 32-42.

Gagnon, Serge. "The Historiography of New France, 1960-1974," *Journal of Canadian Studies*, 13 (Spring, 1978), 80-99.

Garigue, Philip. "Une enquête sur l'industrialisation de la province de Québec: Schefferville," *L'actualité économique*, 33 (octobre-décembre, 1957), 419-36.

Genest, Jean-Guy. "Aspects de l'administration Duplessis," *Revue d'histoire de l'Amérique française*, 25, 3 (décembre, 1971), 389-92.

Gérin, Léon. "The French-Canadian Family – its Strengths and Weaknesses," in Rioux and Martin (eds.), *French-Canadian Society*, 32-56.

Gerrard, Ted. "Quebec/Ontario Access to Capital Markets, 1867-1980," unpublished paper, York University.

Gibson, Frederick W. (ed.). "Cabinet Formation and Bicultural Relations," *Studies of the Royal Commission on Bilingualism and Biculturalism*, No. 6 (Ottawa: Queen's Printer, 1970).

Giddens, Anthony. *The Class Structure of Advanced Societies*, second edition. London: Hutchison, 1981.

Gillespie, W. Irwin, and Allan M. Maslove. "Volatility and Visibility: the federal revenue and expenditure plan," in G. Bruce Doern (ed.), *How Ottawa Spends Your Tax Dollars, 1982* (Toronto: James Lorimer, 1982), 37-62.

Gingras, François-Pierre, et Neil Nevitte. "La révolution en plan et le paradigme en cause," *Revue canadienne de science politique*, 16, 4 (décembre, 1983), 691-716.

Godin, Pierre. *Daniel Johnson: 1946-1964, la passion du pouvoir*. Montréal: Éditions de l'Homme, 1980.

Gough, Ian. *The Political Economy of the Welfare State*. London: Macmillan, 1979.

Gourevitch, Peter. "Politics, Economics, and Nationalism: some comparative speculations," *Comparative Studies in Society and History*, 21, 303-22.

Gow, James I. "L'histoire de l'administration publique québécoise," *Recherches sociographiques*, 16, 3 (septembre-décembre, 1975), 385-412.

_____. *Histoire de l'administration publique québécoise, 1867-1970*. Montréal: Presses de l'Université de Montréal, 1986.

_____. "Modernisation et administration publique," in Orban (ed.), *La modernisation politique du Québec*, 157-85.

Guermond, Bernard. "Evolution des investissements du Québec de 1961 à 1970," *L'actualité économique*, 47 (avril-juin, 1971), 162-75.

Guindon, Hubert. "Two Cultures: an essay on nationalism, class and ethnic tension," in Richard H. Leach (ed.), *Contemporary Canada* (Durham, N.C.: Duke University Press, 1967), 33-59.

_____. "The Social Evolution of Quebec Reconsidered," in Rioux and Martin (eds.), *French-Canadian Society*, 157-61.

Haggart, Ronald, and Aubrey E. Golden. *Rumors of War*. Toronto: New Press, 1971.

Hah, Chong-Do, and Jeffrey Martin. "Toward a Synthesis of Conflict and Integration Theories of Nationalism," *World Politics*, 27, 3 (April, 1975), 361-86.

Hamelin, Jean. *Économie et société en Nouvelle-France, 1729-1748*. Montréal: Fides, 1960.

_____, et al. *Aperçu de la politique canadienne au XIXe siècle*. Québec: Culture, 1965.

_____, et Louise Beaudoin. "Les cabinets provinciaux, 1867-1967," *Recherches sociographiques*, 8, 3 (september-décembre, 1967), 299-318.

_____, et Yves Roby. "L'évolution économique et sociale du Québec 1851-1896," *Recherches sociographiques*, 10 (mai-décembre, 1969), 157-69.

_____, Jacques Letarte et Marcel Hamelin. "Les élections provinciales dans le Québec," *Cahiers de Géographie du Québec*, 4, 7 (octobre, 1959-mars, 1960), 5-207.

Harvey, Pierre. "Nous sommes tous des sous-développés," *Interprétation*, 4, 3 (juillet-septembre, 1970), 85-96.

_____. "La perception du capitalisme chez les Canadiens français: une hypothèse pour la recherche," in Jean-Luc Migué (ed.), *Le Québec d'aujourd'hui* (Montréal: Hurtubise HMH, 1971), 129-38.

_____. "Pourquoi le Québec et les Canadiens français occupent-ils une place inférieure sur le plan économique?" in René Durocher et Paul-André Linteau (eds.), *Le "retard" du Québec et l'infériorité économique des Canadiens français* (Montréal: Boréal Express, 1971), 113-27.

Hazeldine, Tim. "The Costs and Benefits of the Canadian Customs Union," Economic Council of Canada (paper presented to Workshop on the Political Economy of Confederation, Kingston, Ontario, November 8-10, 1978).

Hechter, Michael. "Group Formation and the Cultural Division of Labor," *American Journal of Sociology*, 84, 2 (September, 1978), 293-318.

_____. *Internal Colonialism: The Cel-*

tic Fringe in British National Development, 1536-1966. Berkeley: University of California Press, 1975.

Heintzman, Ralph R. "The Struggle for Life: The French Daily Press of Montreal and the Problem of Economic Growth in the Age of Laurier, 1896-1911." Ph.D. dissertation, York University, 1977.

Henripin, Jacques. L'immigration et le déséquilibre linguistique. Ottawa: Main-d'oeuvre et immigration, 1974.

Hogg, Peter. Meech Lake Constitutional Accord Annotated. Toronto: Carswell, 1988.

Hughes, Everett. French Canada in Transition. Chicago: University of Chicago Press, 1963.

Hutcheson, John. Dominance and Dependency: liberalism and national policies in the North Atlantic triangle. Toronto: McClelland and Stewart, 1978.

Institut canadien des affaires publiques. Le rôle de l'État. Montréal: Éditions du Jour, 1962.

Institute of Intergovernmental Relations. The Response to Quebec: the other provinces and the constitutional debate. Documents of the Debate, 2. Kingston, Ontario: Institute of Intergovernmental Relations, Queen's University, 1980.

Jean, Michèle, et Marie Lavigne. "Le phénomène des Yvettes: analyse externe," Atlantis, 6 (1981), 17-23.

Jenkin, Michael. The Challenge of Diversity: industrial policy in the Canadian federation. Science Council of Canada, Background Study 50. Ottawa: Supply and Services Canada, 1983.

Jobin, Carol. Les enjeux économiques de la nationalisation de l'électricité (1962-1963). Montréal: Éditions Coopératives Albert Saint-Martin, 1978.

Johnson, Daniel. Égalité ou indépendance. Montréal: Éditions de l'Homme, 1965.

Jones, Richard. Community in Crisis: French-Canadian nationalism in perspective. Carleton Library No. 59. Toronto: McClelland and Stewart, 1972.

Joy, Richard J. Languages in Conflict. Toronto: McClelland and Stewart, 1972.

Kernaghan, Kenneth. "Representative Bureaucracy: the Canadian perspective," Canadian Public Administration, 21, 4 (Winter, 1978), 489-512.

Kerr, Donald. "Metropolitan Dominance in Canada," in W.E. Mann (ed.), Canada: A Sociological Profile (Toronto: Copp Clark, 1968), 225-43.

Kesselman, Mark. "Lyrical Illusions of a Socialism of Governance: whither French socialism?" in Miliband et al. (eds.), Socialist Register, 233-48.

Keyfitz, Nathan. "Canadians and Canadiens," Queen's Quarterly, 70 (Winter, 1963), 163-82.

Laliberté, C.-Raymond. "Critique du nationalisme populaire," in Léonard (ed.), La chance au coureur, 82-92.

Lamonde, Pierre. "Le contrôle étranger, ou la difficulté d'être maîtres chez nous," in Latouche (ed.), Premier mandat, I, 19-48.

Lamothe, Jacqueline, et Jennifer Stoddart. "Les Yvette ou: comment un parti politique traditionnel se sert encore une fois des femmes," Atlantis, 6 (1981), 10-16.

Lapalme, Georges-Émile. Le Paradis du pouvoir. Montréal: Lémeac, 1973.

Laporte, Pierre. The True Face of Duplessis. Montreal: Harvest House, 1960.

Latouche, Daniel (ed.). Premier mandat. Montréal: L'Aurore, 1977.

———. "Le Québec et l'Amérique du Nord: une comparaison à partir d'un scénario," in Choix, Le nationalisme québécois à la croisée des chemins, 92-106.

———. "Violence, politique et crise dans la société québécoise," in Laurier Lapierre *et al.* (eds.), *Essays on the Left* (Toronto: McClelland and Stewart, 1971), 177-99.

———. "La vraie nature de . . . la Révolution tranquille," *Revue canadienne de science politique*, 7, 3 (septembre, 1974), 525-36.

Laurendeau, Marc. *Les Québécois violents*. Montréal: Boréal Express, 1974.

Laxer, R.M. (ed.). *Canada (Ltd.): the political economy of dependency*. Toronto: McClelland and Stewart, 1973.

Lefebvre, Gilles-R. "L'étude de la culture: la linguistique," in Fernand Dumont et Yves Martin (eds.), *Situation de la recherche sur le Canada français* (Québec: Les Presses de l'Université Laval, 1965), 233-49.

Legaré, Anne. "Les classes sociales et le gouvernement PQ à Québec," *Revue canadienne de sociologie et d'anthropologie*, 15, 2 (1978), 218-26.

Léger, Jean-Marc. "Commentaire: paradoxes d'une révolution ou le temps des illusions," in Dumont et Montiminy (eds.), *Le pouvoir dans la société canadienne-français*, 36-38.

———. "Le néo-nationalisme, ou conduit-il?," in Congrès des affaires canadiennes, *Les nouveaux Québécois* (Québec: Presses de l'Université Laval, 1964), 41-48.

Lemieux, Vincent. *Parenté et politique: l'organisation sociale dans l'Ile d'Orléans*. Québec: Les Presses de l'Université Laval, 1971.

———. "Les partis et leurs contradictions," in Jean-Luc Migué (ed.), *Le Québec d'aujourd'hui* (Montréal: Hurtubise HMH, 1971), 153-72.

———. "Les partis provinciaux du Québec," in Réjean Pelletier (ed.), *Partis politiques au Québec* (Montréal: Hurtubise HMH, Cahiers du Québec, 1976), 53-68.

———. "Quebec: heaven is blue and hell is red," in Martin Robin (ed.), *Canadian Provincial Politics: the party systems of the ten provinces* (Scarborough: Prentice-Hall, 1972), 262-89.

———. *Le quotient politique vrai: le vote provincial et fédéral au Québec*. Québec: Les Presses de l'Université Laval, 1973.

———, et Raymond Hudon. *Patronage et politique au Québec, 1944-1972*. Montréal: Boréal Express, 1975.

Léonard, Jean-François (ed.). *La chance au coureur*. Montréal: Éditions Nouvelle Optique, 1978.

Lernier, Daniel. "Towards a Communication Theory of Modernization: a set of considerations," in Lucian Pye (ed.), *Communications and Political Development* (Princeton, N.J.: Princeton University Press, 1963), 327-50.

Lesemann, Frédéric. *Services and Circuses: community and the welfare state*. Montreal: Black Rose Books, 1984. Translation of *Du pain et des services*.

Levasseur, Carol. "De l'État-providence à l'État-disciplinaire," in Gérard Bergeron et Réjean Pelletier (eds.), *l'État du Québec en devenir* (Montréal: Boréal Express, 1980), 284-328.

———, et Jean-Guy Lacroix. "Rapports de classes et obstacles économiques à l'association," *Cahiers du socialisme*, 2 (automne, 1978), 87-121.

Lévesque, Georges-Henri. "La première décennie de la Faculté des sciences sociales à l'Université Laval," in Georges-Henri Lévesque *et al.* (eds.), *Continuité et rupture: les sciences sociales au Québec*, Vol. I (Montréal: Presses de l'Université de Montréal, 1984), 51-63.

Lévesque, René. *Attendez que je me rappelle*. Montréal: Éditions Québec/Amérique, 1986.

———. *Memoirs*. Toronto: McClelland and Stewart, 1986.

_____. *Option Québec*. Montréal: Les Editions de l'Homme, 1968.

_____. *La passion du Québec*. Montréal: Éditions Québec/Amérique, 1979.

Levine, Marc V. "Language Policy, Education and Cultural Survival: Bill 101 and the transformation of Anglophone Montreal, 1977-1985," *Québec Studies*, 4 (1986), 3-27.

Levitt, Kari. *Silent Surrender*. Toronto: Macmillan, 1970.

Lijphart, Arend. *Democracy in Plural Societies: a comparative exploration*. New Haven: Yale University Press, 1977.

_____. *The Politics of Accommodation*. Berkeley: University of California Press, 1968.

Lindberg, Leon (ed.). *Stress and Contradiction in Modern Capitalism*. Lexington, Mass: Heath, 1975.

Linteau, Paul-André. "Quelques réflexions autour de la bourgeoisie québécoise 1850-1914," *Revue d'histoire de l'Amérique française*, 30, 1 (juin, 1976), 55-66.

_____, René Durocher et Jean-Claude Robert. *Histoire du Québec contemporain: de la Confédération à la crise (1867-1929)*. Montréal: Boréal Express, 1979.

_____, René Durocher, Jean-Claude Robert et François Ricard. *Histoire du Québec contemporain: le Québec depuis 1930*. Montréal: Boréal Express, 1986.

Lipsey, Richard G. "The Relation between Economic and Political Separatism: A Pessimistic View," in *Options Canada*, Proceedings of the Conference on the Future of the Canadian Federation (University of Toronto, October, 1977), 244-51.

Lipsig-Mummé, Carla. "The Web of Dependence: Quebec unions in politics before 1976," in Gagnon, *Quebec: State and Society*, 286-313.

Macpherson, C.B. *Democracy in Alberta: Social Credit and the Party System*, second edition. Toronto: University of Toronto Press, 1962.

Maheu, Louis. "La conjoncture des luttes nationales au Québec: mode d'intervention étatique des classes moyennes et enjeux d'un mouvement social de rupture," *Sociologie et sociétés*, 11, 2 (1979), 125-44.

Mahon, Rianne. "Canadian Public Policy: the unequal structure of Representation," in Leo Panitch (ed.), *The Canadian State: political economy and political power* (Toronto: University of Toronto Press, 1977), 167-98.

Mascotto, Jacques, et Pierre-Yves Soucy. *Sociologie politique de la question nationale*. Montréal: Éditions Coopératives Albert Saint-Martin, 1979.

Matthews, George. *Le choc démographique*. Montréal: Boréal Express, 1984.

Maxwell, Judith, and Gérard Bélanger. *Taxes and Expenditures in Québec and Ontario: a comparison*. Accent Québec Series. Montreal: C.D. Howe Institute, 1978.

Mayer, L.C. *Comparative Political Inquiry*. Homewood, Ill.: Dorsey Press, 1972.

McAllister, James A. "Fiscal Capacity and Tax Effort: explaining public expenditures in the ten Canadian provinces," paper presented to Canadian Political Science Association, June, 1984.

_____. *Democratic Socialism in Manitoba*. Montreal: McGill-Queen's University Press, 1984.

McCallum, John. *Unequal Beginnings: agriculture and economic development in Quebec and Ontario until 1870*. Toronto: University of Toronto Press, 1980.

McRae, Kenneth. "Consociationalism and the Canadian Political System," in McRae (ed.), *Consociational Democracy: political accommodation in segmented societies* (Toronto: McClelland and Stewart, 1974), 238-61.

_____. "The Structure of Canadian History," in Louis Hartz et al., The Founding of New Societies (New York: Harcourt Brace & World, 1964), 219-74.

McRoberts, Kenneth. "Internal Colonialism: The Case of Quebec," Ethnic and Racial Studies, 2, 3 (July, 1979), 293-318.

_____. "Mass Acquisition of a Nationalist Ideology: Quebec Prior to the Quiet Revolution." Ph.D. dissertation, University of Chicago, 1975.

_____. "The Sources of Neo-nationalism in Quebec," Ethnic and Racial Studies, 7, 1 (January, 1984), 55-85.

_____. "The Study of English-French Relations in Canada," unpublished paper.

_____. "Unilateralism, Bilateralism and Multilateralism," in Richard Simeon (ed.), Intergovernmental Relations, Collected Research Studies of the Royal Commission on the Economic Union and Development Prospects for Canada, Vol. 63 (Ottawa: Supply and Services Canada, 1985), 71-129.

McWhinney, Edward. Canada and the Constitution, 1979-82. Toronto: University of Toronto Press, 1982.

Memmi, Albert. Portrait du colonisé. Montréal: Les Éditions l'Etincelle, 1972.

Miliband, Ralph, and Marcel Liebman. "Beyond Social Democracy," in Miliband et al., Socialist Register, 476-89.

_____, et al. (eds.). Socialist Register, 1985/86. London: Merlin Press, 1986.

Milner, Henry. "The Decline and Fall of the Quebec Liberal Regime: contradictions in the modern Quebec state," in Panitch (ed.), The Canadian State: political economy and political power, 101-32.

_____. Politics in the New Quebec. Toronto: McClelland and Stewart, 1978.

Milner, Sheilagh Hodgins, and Henry Milner. The Decolonization of Quebec. Toronto: McClelland and Stewart, 1973.

Miner, Horace. "Changes in French-Canadian Rural Culture," in Rioux and Martin (eds.), French-Canadian Society, 64-70.

Monière, Denis. "Deux discours pour le choix d'un pays: les propagandes," in En collaboration, Québec: un pays incertain, 87-110.

_____. Le développement des idéologies au Québec des origines à nos jours. Montréal: Éditions Québec/Amérique, 1977.

Montcalm, Mary Beth. "Quebec Nationalism in a Comparative Perspective," in Gagnon, Quebec: State and Society, 45-58.

Moreux, Colette. Fin d'une religion? monographie d'une paroisse canadienne-française. Montréal: Presses de l'Université de Montréal, 1969.

Morf, Mustave. Le terrorisme québécois. Montréal: Éditions de l'Homme, 1970.

Morin, Claude. Le pouvoir québécois . . . en négociation. Montréal: Boréal Express, 1972.

Murray, Vera. Le Parti québécois. Montréal: Hurtubise HMH, 1977.

Nairn, Tom. The Break-up of Britain: crisis and neo-nationalism. London: New Left Books, 1977.

Nappi, Carmine. "La souveraineté, la structure d'exportation et le choix d'une politique commerciale pour le Québec," in Luc-Normand Tellier (ed.), Économie et indépendance (Montréal: Quinze, 1977), 154-55.

Nash, Paul. "Quality and Inequality in Canadian Education," Comparative Education Review, 5, 2 (October, 1961), 118-35.

Niosi, Jorge. La bourgeoisie canadienne: la formation et le développement d'une classe dominante. Montréal: Boréal Express, 1980.

———. "Le gouvernement du P.Q. deux ans après," *Cahiers du socialisme*, 2 (automne, 1978), 32-71.

———. "La multinationalisation des firmes canadiennes-françaises," *Recherches sociographiques*, 23, 1 (hiver, 1983), 55-73.

———. "La nouvelle bourgeoisie canadienne-française," *Cahiers du Socialisme*, 1 (printemps, 1978), 5-50.

———. "The Rise of French-Canadian Capitalism," in Gagnon, *Quebec: State and Society*, 186-200.

Nish, Cameron. *Les bourgeois gentilshommes de la Nouvelle-France, 1729-1748*. Montréal: Fides, 1968.

Noel, S.J.R. "Political Parties and Elite Accommodation: interpretations of Canadian federalism," in J. Peter Meekison (ed.), *Canadian Federalism: myth or reality*, second edition (Toronto: Methuen, 1971), 121-40.

Normandin, Pierre G. (ed.), *The Canadian Parliamentary Guide*. Ottawa.

O'Connor, James. *The Fiscal Crisis of the State*. New York: St. Martin's Press, 1973.

Orban, Edmond (ed.). *La modernisation politique du Québec*. Sillery, Québec: Boréal Express, 1976.

———. *Un modèle de souveraineté-association?* Montréal: Hurtubise HMH, 1978.

Organski, A.F.K. *The Stages of Political Development*, New York: Alfred Knopf, 1965.

Ornstein, Michael D., and H. Michael Stevenson. "Elite and Public Opinion Before the Quebec Referendum: a commentary on the state in Canada," *Canadian Journal of Political Science*, 14, 4 (December, 1981), 715-74.

———, H. Michael Stevenson, and A. Paul Williams. "Public Opinion and the Canadian Political Crisis," *Canadian Journal of Sociology and Anthropology*, 15 (1978), 158-205.

Ossenberg, Richard J. "The Conquest Revisited: Another Look at Canadian Dualism," *Canadian Review of Sociology and Anthropology*, 4, 4 (November, 1967), 201-18.

O'Sullivan, Katherine. *First World Nationalisms: class and ethnic politics in Northern Ireland and Quebec*. Chicago: University of Chicago Press, 1986.

Pammet, Jon H., Jane Jenson, Harold D. Clarke et Lawrence LeDuc. "Soutien politique et comportement électoral lors du référendum québécois," in Crête (ed.), *Comportement électoral au Québec*, 387-419.

Panitch, Leo. "Corporatism in Canada," *Studies in Political Economy*, 1 (Spring, 1979), 43-92.

———. "The Development of Corporatism in Liberal Democracies," *Comparative Political Studies*, 10, 1 (April, 1977), 61-90.

———. "A Social Contract or Socialism?" in John Richards and Don Kerr (eds.), *Canada, What's Left? a new social contract, pro and con* (Edmonton: New West Press, 1986), 13-23.

———. *Social Democracy and Industrial Militancy*. Cambridge: Cambridge University Press, 1976.

Paquet, Gilles, et Jean-Pierre Wallot. *Patronage et pouvoir dans le Bas-Canada (1794-1812)*. Montréal: Presses de l'Université du Québec, 1973.

Parenteau, Roland. "L'expérience de la planification au Québec (1960-1969)," *L'actualité économique*, No. 4 (janvier-février, 1970), 679-96.

Parti pris. "Manifeste 1965-1966," in Parti pris, *Les Québécois*, 249-80.

Parti québécois. *Le Programme*, various editions.

———. *Quand nous serons vraiment chez nous*. Montréal: Éditions du Parti québécois, 1972.

———, Conseil exécutif national. *D'égal à égal*. Manifeste de propositions concernant la souveraineté-association, 1978.

Pelinka, Anton. *Social Democratic Practice in Europe*. New York: Praeger, 1983.

Pelletier, Gérard. *La crise d'octobre*. Montréal: Éditions du Jour, 1971.

Pelletier, Réjean. *Les militants du R.I.N.* Ottawa: Éditions de l'Université d'Ottawa, 1974.

Pelletier-Baillargeon, Hélène. "L'exode vers les collèges privés," *Maintenant*, No. 123 (février, 1973).

Pentland, Charles. "Association after Sovereignty?" in Simeon, *Must Canada Fail?*, 223-42.

Pinard, Maurice. "La dualité des loyautés et les options constitutionnelles des Québécois francophones," in *Le nationalisme québécois à la croisée des chemins* (Québec: Centre québécois de relations internationales, La Collection Choix, 1975), 63-91.

_____. "La rationalité de l'électorat: le cas de 1962," in Vincent Lemieux (ed.), *Quatre élections provinciales au Québec: 1956-1966* (Québec: Presses de l'Université Laval, 1969), 179-96.

_____. "Working Class Politics: An Interpretation of the Quebec Case," *Canadian Review of Sociology and Anthropology*, 7, 2 (1970), 87-109.

_____, and Richard Hamilton. "The Class Bases of the Quebec Independence Movement: conjectures and evidence," *Ethnic and Racial Studies*, 7, 1 (January, 1984), 20-54.

_____. "The Independence Issue and the Polarization of the Electorate: The 1973 Quebec Election," *Canadian Journal of Political Science*, 10, 2 (June, 1977), 215-59.

_____. "The Parti Québécois Comes to Power: the 1976 election," *Canadian Journal of Political Science*, 11 (December, 1978), 739-75.

_____. "Les Québécois votent 'non': 2. Les assises de l'appui au régime et de son rejet," paper presented to

Conference on Political Support in Canada, Duke University, November, 1980.

Piotte, Jean-Marc. "La lutte des travailleurs de l'État," *Cahiers du socialisme*, 3 (printemps, 1979), 4-39.

_____. "Le syndicalisme au Québec depuis 1960," in Diane Ethier, Jean-Marc Piotte et Jean Reynolds, *Les travailleurs contre l'État bourgeois* (Montréal: L'Aurore, 1975), 17-48.

Porter, John. *The Vertical Mosaic*. Toronto: University of Toronto Press, 1965.

Posgate, W. Dale. "Social Mobilization and Political Change in Quebec." Ph.D. dissertation, State University of New York at Buffalo, 1972.

Pratt, Larry, and John Richards. *Prairie Capitalism: Power and Influence in the New West*. Toronto: McClelland and Stewart, 1979.

Presthus, Robert. *Elite Accommodation in Canadian Politics*. Cambridge: Cambridge University Press, 1973.

Przeworski, Adam. *Capitalism and Social Democracy*. Cambridge: Cambridge University Press, 1985.

Québec. *Annuaire du Québec*, various years.

_____. *Bâtir le Québec: énoncé de politique économique*. Québec: Éditeur Officiel du Québec, 1979.

_____. *Discours sur le budget*, various years.

_____. *Draft Agreement on the Constitution: Proposals by the Government of Quebec*, May, 1985.

_____. *Le Québec: maître d'oeuvre de la politique des communications sur son territoire*. Québec: Éditeur Officiel, n.d.

_____. *Québec-Canada: A New Deal*. Québec, 1979.

_____, Comité interministériel sur les investissements étrangers. *Le cadre et les moyens d'une politique québécoise concernant les investis-*

sements étrangers. Québec, septembre, 1973. Texte revisé de mars à juin, 1974; Québec: Éditeur Officiel du Québec.

——, Commission d'enquête sur la santé et le bien-être social, *Rapport*, 7 vols., 1967-1972.

——, Commission d'enquête sur la situation de la langue française et sur les droits linguistiques au Québec. *Livre I: Langue de travail*. Gouvernement du Québec, 1972.

——, Commission royale d'enquête sur les problèmes constitutionnels. *Rapport*, 4 vols., 1956.

——, Directeur général des élections. *Rapport: élection*, various years.

——, Directeur général des élections. *Référendum: Oui-Non*. 1980.

——, Ministère des finances. *Privatisation de sociétés d'État*. February, 1986.

——, Ministère de l'industrie et du commerce. *Une politique économique québécoise*. Québec, 1974.

Quinn, Herbert. *The Union Nationale: A Study in Quebec Nationalism*. Toronto: University of Toronto Press, 1963.

Rabeau, Yves. "Les relations économiques Québec-Ontario," background paper presented to colloquium on Quebec-Ontario relations, Toronto, January, 1978.

Racine, Luc, et Roch Denis. "La conjoncture politique québécoise depuis 1960," *Socialisme québécois*, 21-22 (avril, 1971), 17-79.

Ray, D.M. "The Location of American Subsidiaries in Canada," *Economic Geography*, 47, 3 (1971), 389-400.

Raymond, Maxime. *Programme fédéral du Bloc*. Document No. 10. Montréal: Imprimerie Populaire, 1943.

Raynauld, André. *Croissance et structure économique de la Province de Québec*. Québec: Ministère de l'industrie et du commerce, 1961.

——, Gérald Marion et Richard Béland. "La répartition des revenus selon les groupes ethniques au Canada," Research Report submitted to the Royal Commission on Bilingualism and Biculturalism.

Rempel, Henry David. "The Practice and Theory of the Fragile State: Trudeau's conception of authority," *Journal of Canadian Studies*, 10, 4 (November, 1975), 24-38.

Renaud, Gilbert. *A l'ombre du rationalisme: la société québécoise, de sa dépendance à sa quotidienneté*. Montréal: Éditions Saint-Martin, 1984.

——. *L'éclatement de la profession en service social*. Montréal: Éditions Coopératives Albert St-Martin, 1978.

Renaud, Marc. "Quebec New Middle Class in the Search of Local Hegemony," *International Review of Community Development*, 39-40 (1978), 1-36.

——. "Réforme ou illusion? Une analyse des interventions de l'État québécois dans le domaine de la santé," *Sociologie et sociétés*, 9, 1 (avril, 1977), 127-52.

Richards, John. "Populism: a qualified defence," *Studies in Political Economy*, 5 (Spring, 1981), 5-27.

Rioux, Marcel. *La question du Québec*. Paris: Seghers, 1969.

——. "Sur l'évolution des idéologies au Québec," *Revue de l'Institut de sociologie*, 1 (1968), 95-124.

——, and Yves Martin (eds.). *French-Canadian Society*, Vol. I. Toronto: McClelland and Stewart, 1964.

Rose, Richard (ed.). *The Dynamics of Public Policy: a comparative analysis*. Beverly Hills: Sage, 1976.

Ross, George. "Marxism and the New Middle Classes," *Theory and Society*, 5, 2 (1978), 163-90.

——, and Jane Jenson. "Post-War Class Struggles and the Crisis of Left Politics," in Miliband *et al.*, *Socialist Register*, 23-49.

Rotstein, Abraham. "Is There an

English-Canadian Nationalism?" *Journal of Canadian Studies*, 13, 2 (Summer, 1978), 109-18.

Rouillard, Jacques. *Histoire de la CSN, 1921-1981*. Montréal: Boréal Express et CSN, 1981.

Rousseau, Henri-Paul. *Unions monétaires et monnaies nationales: une étude économique de quelques cas historiques*. Ministère des affaires intergouvernementales, Gouvernement du Québec. Québec: l'Éditeur Officiel, 1978.

Rumilly, Robert. *Histoire de la Province de Québec*, XXXVI. Montréal: Fides, 1966.

———. *Histoire de la Province de Québec*, XL. Montréal: Fides 1966.

———. *Maurice Duplessis et son temps*. Montréal: Fides, 1973, vol. II.

Rustow, Dankwart. *A World of Nations*. Washington, D.C.: Brookings Institution, 1967.

Ryerson, Stanley B. "Quebec: Concepts of Class and Nation," in Gary Teeple (ed.), *Capitalism and the National Question in Canada* (Toronto: University of Toronto, 1972), 221-28.

———. *Unequal Union*. Toronto: Progress Books, 1968.

Saint-Germain, Maurice. *Une économie à libérer: le Québec analysé dans ses structures économiques*. Montréal: Presses de l'Université de Montréal, 1973.

Sales, Arnaud. *La bourgeoisie industrielle au Québec*. Montréal: Presses de l'Université de Montréal, 1979.

———. "Vers une techno-bureaucratie d'État," in Léonard (ed.), *La chance au coureur*, 25-39.

Savaria, Jules. "Le Québec est-il une société périphérique?" *Sociologie et sociétés*, 7, 2 (novembre, 1975), 115-28.

Saywell, John. *The Rise of the Parti québécois, 1967-1976*. Toronto: University of Toronto Press, 1977.

———. *Quebec, 70: A Documentary Narrative*. Toronto: University of Toronto Press, 1971.

Seton-Watson, Hugh. *Nationalism Old and New*. Sydney: Sydney University Press, 1964.

Shapiro, D.M., and M. Stelcner. "Earnings Disparities among Linguistic Groups in Quebec, 1970-1980", *Canadian Public Policy*, 13, 1 (1987), 97-104.

Simard, Jean-Jacques. *La longue marche des technocrates*. Montréal: Éditions Coopératives Albert Saint-Martin, 1979.

Simeon, Richard. "The 'Overload' Thesis and Canadian Government," *Canadian Public Policy* (Autumn, 1976), 541-52.

——— (ed.). *Must Canada Fail?* Montreal: McGill-Queen's University Press, 1977.

Smiley, Donald V. *Canada in Question*, third edition. Toronto: McGraw-Hill Ryerson, 1980.

———. "Constitutional Adaptation and Canadian Federalism since 1945," *Documents of the Royal Commission on Bilingualism and Biculturalism*, No. 4 (Ottawa: Queen's Printer, 1970).

———. "A Dangerous Deed: The Constitution Act 1982," in Banting and Simeon (eds.), *And No One Cheered*, 74-95.

———. "French-English Relations and Consociational Democracy," in Milton J. Esman (ed.), *Ethnic Conflict in the Western World* (Ithaca: Cornell University Press, 1977), 179-203.

———. "A New Look at Sovereignty-Association," unpublished paper, York University (July, 1978).

———. "Quebec Independence and the Democratic Dilemma," *Canadian Forum*, 58 (February, 1979), 11-12.

———. "The Sovereignty-Association Alternative: an analysis," text of lecture given at Ryerson Polytechnical Institute (November 22, 1978).

Smith, Denis. *Bleeding Hearts . . . Bleeding Country*. Edmonton:

Hurtig, 1971.

Smith, Anthony D. *The Ethnic Revival*. Cambridge: Cambridge University Press, 1981.

———. *Theories of Nationalism*. New York: Harper and Row, 1972.

Société Radio-Canada. "Confédération/Référendum" (opinion survey results), unpublished paper, March, 1979.

———. "Le gouvernement Lévesque, un an après" (opinion survey results), unpublished paper, 1977.

———. "Les Québécois et la dualité fédérale-provinciale" (opinion survey results), unpublished paper, June, 1978.

Sorecom. "Opinions et attitudes des Québécois au sujet de la situation politique au Québec" (opinion survey results), unpublished paper, 1977.

Soulet, Marc Henry. *Le silence des intellectuels: radioscopie de l'intellectuel québécois*. Montréal: Éditions Saint-Martin, 1987.

Stein, Michael. "Le Bill 22 et la population non-francophone au Québec: une étude de cas sur les attitudes du groupe minoritaire face à la législation de la langue," *Choix*, 7 (1975), 127-59.

Tanguay, A. Brian. "Concerted Action in Quebec, 1976-83: a dialogue of the deaf," in Gagnon, *Quebec: State and Society*, 365-85.

———. "Recasting Labour Relations in Quebec, 1976-1985: towards a disciplinary state?" paper presented to annual meeting of Canadian Political Science Association, June 6-9, 1986.

Taylor, Charles. "Nationalism and the Political Intelligentsia: A Case Study," *Queen's Quarterly*, 72, 1 (Spring, 1965), 150-68.

Taylor, Norman W. "The Effects of Industrialization, its Opportunities and Consequences Upon French-Canadian Society," *Journal of Economic History*, 20 (December, 1960), 638-47.

Thomson, Dale C. *Jean Lesage and the Quiet Revolution*. Toronto: Macmillan, 1984.

Tilly, Charles. "Western State-Making and Theories of Political Transformation," in Tilly (ed.), *The Formation of National States in Western Europe* (Princeton, N.J.: Princeton University Press, 1975), 601-38.

Tiryakian, Edward, and Ronald Rogowski (eds.). *New Nationalism of the Developed West*. Boston: Allen & Unwin, 1985.

Travailleurs québécois et lutte nationale. Montréal, 1974.

Tredenick, J.M. "Quebec and Canada: some economic aspects of independence," *Journal of Canadian Studies*, 8, 4 (November, 1973), 16-30.

Tremblay, Louis-Marie. *Idéologies de la C.S.N. et de la F.T.Q.: 1940-1970*. Montréal: Presses de l'Université de Montréal, 1972.

Tremblay, M.A., and W.J. Anderson. *Rural Canada in Transition*. Agricultural Economics Research Council of Canada, Publication No. 6.

Trofimenkoff, Susan Mann. *Action française: French-Canadian nationalism in the twenties*. Toronto: University of Toronto Press, 1975.

———. *The Dream of Nation: a social and intellectual history of Quebec*. Toronto: Gage, 1983.

Trudeau, Pierre Elliott. *Federalism and the French Canadians*. Toronto: Macmillan, 1968.

———. *Approaches to Politics*. Toronto: Oxford University Press, 1970.

——— (ed.). *La grève de l'amiante*. Montréal: Cité libre, 1956.

Tupper, Allan. *Bill S-31 and Federalism of State Capitalism*. Kingston: Queen's University, Institute of Intergovernmental Relations, 1983.

Vaillancourt, François. "La Charte de la Langue française du Québec," *Analyse de politiques*, 4, 3 (été,

1978), 284-308.

_____. "La situation démographique et socio-économique des Francophones du Québec: une revue," Cahier 7940, Département de science politique, Université de Montréal (mai, 1979).

Vaillancourt, Yves. "La position constitutionelle du MSA-PQ de 1969 à 1979," in Centre de formation populaire, *Au-delà du Parti québécois* (Montréal: Éditions nouvelle optique, 1982), 69-124.

_____. *Le P.Q. et le sociale.* Montréal: Éditions Saint-Martin, 1983.

Vallières, Pierre. *Nègres blancs d'Amérique.* Montréal: Éditions parti pris, 1969.

Van Schendel, Michel. "Impérialisme et classe ouvrière au Québec," *Socialisme québécois*, 21-22 (avril, 1971), 156-209.

Vaugeois, D., et J. Lacoursière (eds.). *Histoire 1534-1968.* Montréal: Éditions du renouveau pédagogique, 1968.

Veltmeyer, Henry. "Dependency and Underdevelopment," *Canadian Journal of Political and Social Theory*, 2, 2 (Spring, 1978), 55-71.

Vezina, Jean-P. "Le développement économique: les enjeux en cause," in Latouche, *Premier mandat*, I, 49-61.

Vézina, Jean. "Les gouvernements," Annexe 11 of *Prospective socio-économique du Québec, première étape*, "Sous-système économique (2)," Collection études et recherches (Québec: Office de planification et de développement du Québec, 1977).

Vigod, Bernard L. *Quebec Before Duplessis; the political career of Louis-Alexandre Taschereau.* Montreal: McGill-Queen's University Press, 1986.

Wade, Mason. *The French Canadians, 1760-1976*, revised edition, vols. I & II. Toronto: Macmillan, 1968.

Wallot, Jean-Pierre. *Un Québec qui bougeait.* Montréal: Boréal Express, 1973.

_____. "Religion and French-Canadian Mores in the Early Nineteenth Century," *Canadian Historical Review*, 52, 1 (March, 1971), 51-94.

Whitaker, Reg. "Reason, Passion and Interest: Trudeau's eternal liberal triangle," *Canadian Journal of Political and Social Theory*, 4, 1 (Winter, 1980), 5-31.

Williams, Glen. "The National Policy Tariffs," *Canadian Journal of Political Science*, 12, 2 (1979), 333-68.

Winn, Conrad, and John McMenemy (eds.). *Political Parties in Canada.* Toronto: McGraw-Hill Ryerson, 1976.

Woolstencroft, Timothy B. "Organizing Intergovernmental Relations," Discussion Paper 12 (Kingston: Queen's University, Institute of Intergovernmental Relations, 1982).

Wright, Erik Olin. *Class, Crisis and the State.* London: Verso, 1979.

Zukowsky, Ronald James. *Struggle over the Constitution from the Quebec Referendum to the Supreme Court.* Kingston, Ontario: Institute of Intergovernmental Relations, 1981.

Index

government
Cappon, Paul, 183
Cardinal, Jean-Guy, 216
Carter, D.D., 269
Cascades, Inc., 429
Castonguay, Claude, 159, 222, 361-62, 406
Catalonia, 433
Catholic Church in Quebec, 26, 38, 39, 41, 44, 51, 53-59, 70, 77, 82, 87, 90, 92, 95, 97, 103, 105-06, 126, 129, 132, 137-39, 149-56, 153-55, 193, 434
CCF, 290
Centrale des syndicats démocratiques (CSD), 193, 241, 333
Centre des intellectuels catholiques canadiens, 98
Chaloult, René, 89, 111
Chamberland, Paul, 197
Chambre de commerce de Montréal, 111, 124, 162, 163, 381, 392, 419
Chambre de commerce du Québec, 101, 165, 333, 366, 381
Charbonneau, Archbishop Joseph, 103, 106
Charbonneau, Yvon, 409
Charpentier, Alfred, 103
Charter of Rights and Freedoms, 292, 349, 356-57, 373, 388-89, 395, 397, 429
Choquette, Jérôme, 229, 235
Cité libre, 95, 98-99, 103, 144
Class alignments in Quebec, 27-29; impact on Quebec's development, 425; working class and new middle class, 28-29, 167, 204
Classes in French Quebec, see Francophone business class, Intellectuals, New middle class, Petty bourgeoisie, Working class
Clement, Pierre, 407
Clement, Wallace, 177
Cliche Commission, 193, 230
Cloutier, François, 222
CLSC (Centre locaux de services communautaires), 416, 422
Cobban, Alfred, 30
Coleman, William, 151-53, 168, 281, 435-36
Collèges d'enseignement général et professionnel (CEGEPs), 131, 211, 222

Comité constitutionnel du Parti libéral, see A New Canadian Federation
Common Front Strike, 191-95, 205
Confederation, 24, 26, 36, 53, 125
Confédération des travailleurs catholiques du Canada (CTCC), 102, 105, 120, 144, 159
Confédération des syndicats nationaux (CSN), 159-61, 170, 190-92, 204-07, 245, 279-70, 359, 374, 376, 414, 417, 426
Conquest, 25, 44, 71, 87, 88, 89
Conscription, during world wars, 35, 58, 86
Conseil de la langue française, 418
Conseil de l'instruction publique, 54, 82, 106, 131
Conseil de planification et de développement du Québec, 363
Conseil d'orientation économique du Québec, 157, 162-63, 167
Conseil du patronat du Québec, 207-08, 330, 371, 417
Conseil supérieur du travail, 162
Conservative Party, Quebec, 85-86, 89
Conservative Party, federal, 53, 58, 118
Consociationalism, 35-36
Constitution Act (1982), 387, 394; contents of, 292, 349-50; processes leading up to, 350-58
Constitutional Act (1791), 46-47
Corporation des enseignants du Québec (CEQ), also named Centrale de l'enseignement du Québec (CEQ), 192, 204-07, 217, 245, 269-71, 333, 359, 374, 381, 409, 417, 426, 436
Corporation des travailleurs sociaux professionnels de la Province du Québec, 155
Corvée-habitation, 371
Couture, Jacques, 380
Cross, James, 200, 201
Culinar, Inc., 175, 360-61, 431
Cullen-Couture agreement, 295, 333, 389, 397-98
Cultural division of labour, concept of, 25
Cultural division of labour in Quebec, 43, 46, 65, 231, 430, 434; historical importance, 25-27;

impact on Quebec's development, 24, 425; in federal government, 35; persistence in 1970s of, 174-81; sources of, 27, 70-71

Cutright, Phillips, 16

Cyr, J.V. Raymond, 406

Dales, John, 21, 24

David, Hélène, 80

Davis, William, 312

Decolonization movements in Asia and Africa, 146

Demography, *see* Population

Denis, Roch, 164-65

Dependence, theory of, 17-19

Dependence of Quebec economy: compared with other regions of Canada, 20-21; future importance, 431; and Quebec's development, 425; and Quebec nationalism, 146, 432-34; sources of, 21-25

Depuis Frères, 103

Descoteaux Report, 221

Desmarais, Paul, 428-29

de Tocqueville, Alexis, 78

Development, components of, 11-17

Diefenbaker, John, 118, 145

Dion, Gérard, 269

Dion, Léon, 31, 130, 171, 186, 439

Dofor, Inc., 367, 413, 414

Domtar, 368, 413

Donohue, Inc., 413

Duchesne, Raymond, 92

Dufour, Ghislain, 417

Duhaime, Yves, 367

Duplessis, Maurice, 120, 124-25, 143, 153, 170, 217, 289, 297; control of Union nationale, 112; fear of public borrowing, 111-12; and Quebec nationalism, 89, 111, 117-22; resistance to political modernization, 110-13; and intellectuals, 94; and the Church, 105-06; and Anglophone business, 107-10

Duplessis administrations (1936-1939, 1944-1959), 171; economic policy, 80-81, 101-02, 109-10; education policy, 82; electoral support, 115-22; and federal government, 102, 123-26, 140, 142, 145; health and welfare policy, 82; and Quebec nationalism, 89, 117-22; and trade unions, 103-05, 374

Durham, Lord, 51

Durocher, René, 111

Dussault, René, 407

Le Devoir, 59, 89, 99, 103, 144, 186, 221, 226

Eaton, Cyrus, 109

École des hautes études commerciales, 55, 95, 96, 99, 429

École polytechnique, 55, 95-96

École sociale populaire, 85

Economic Council of Canada, 309

Economic elites, *see* Anglophone business class, Francophone business class

Education in Quebec, 54-55, 58, 76-78, 82-83, 99, 106-07, 131-32, 135, 154, 159, 178, 426

D'égal à égul, 286, 300, 313

Elections: federal, 58; provincial, 85-86, 115-22, 143-44, 169-72, 212-13, 233-34, 237, 243, 342-44, 385-87

Elgin, Lord, 49

English Canada: attachment to federal government, 401; and constitutional revision, 395; definitions of collective identity, 312-14; economic and political elites and Quebec sovereignty, 310-21, 336; public opinion and Quebec sovereignty, 311

En lutte, 203

Étapisme, *see* Lévesque administration, strategy for securing sovereignty

European Economic Community, 301, 306

Faculté des sciences sociales, Université Laval, 93-95

Faculté des sciences sociales, Université de Montréal, 93

Falardeau, Jean-Charles, 42

Fanon, Frantz, 196, 203

Faucher, Albert, 21-22

Federal government, 312; and Anglophone corporate elites, 165; economic policy, 23, 165; French Canadians in, 26, 35-36, 126, 145, 185-86, 430; language policy, 185-87, 236;

and October Crisis, 200-01; proposals for constitutional reform, 346-49; relations with Quebec government, 89, 123-26, 135, 139-43, 144-45, 214-15, 223-27, 293-97, 351-56, 383-84, 394-404

Federalism, Canadian: Francophone attitudes toward, 32, 53, 401; general impact of, 33-35; structure of, 53, 126, 185; proposals for "renewal" of, 346-49, 402; *see also* Constitution Act (1982), Meech Lake Accord

Fédération des travailleurs du Québec (FTQ), 159-61, 190-93, 204-07, 245, 269, 333, 375, 386

Fédération des unions industrielles du Québec (FUIQ), 104, 120, 144

Fédération provinciale du travail du Québec (FPTQ), 104-05, 120

Filion, Gérard, 99

Flanders, 433

Fonds de solidarité des travailleurs du Québec, 375

Ford Motors, 275

Fortier, Pierre, 404, 411

Fortin, Gérald, 75

Fournier, Marcel, 94, 157, 204, 243, 338

Fournier, Pierre, 252-53

Francophone business class (bourgeoisie), 28; and Duplessis's Union nationale, 100-02; and economic reforms of Quiet Revolution, 162-64; growth in 1960s and 1970s, 360-61; impact of Conquest, 44-45; and Parti québécois, 245, 381; and political modernization, 101-02; present strength, 427-28; role in New France, 43-44; weakness before 1960s, 100-01

Frégault, Guy, 101

French language: federal policy, 187, 236, 348, 430; strength outside Quebec, 32-33, 145, 185-87, 430; in workplace, 178-80, 205-06, 229-30, 388-89; *see also* Assemblée nationale, Québec: Bill 63, Bill 22, Bill 101

Frère Untel, 177

Front de libération du Québec, 200-02

Fulford, Robert, 400

Fuller, J.A., 158, 166

Garneau, Raymond, 265

Gazette, Montreal, 108

Gendron Commission, 177-80, 217

General Dynamics, 266

General Motors, 274

Gérin-Lajoie, Jean, 245

Gérin-Lajoie, Paul, 143, 216, 218

Gobeil, Paul, 405, 410, 414, 416, 422

Godbout, Adélard, 107-08

Godbout administration (1939-1944), 80, 96, 97, 102, 105, 107-08, 110, 163, 387

Godin, Gérald, 388

Gordon, Donald, 156

Gouin, Lomer, 105

Gray Report, 221

Groulx, Abbé, Lionel, 59

Guindon, Hubert, 153

Hamel, Alfred, 367-68

Hamelin, Jean, 43-44

Hamilton, Richard, 233, 243, 328-29, 330

Harel, Louise, 291, 385

Hartz, Louis, "fragment culture" theory of, 39, 87

Harvey, Pierre, 88

Hatfield, Richard, 351

Hazeldine, Tim, 308

Hechter, Michael, 25

Henripin, Jacques, 182, 187

Hudon, Raymond, 115, 120

Hughes, Everett, 68, 94, 183

Hydro-Québec, 62, 80-81, 97, 110, 132-34, 138, 158, 163, 166, 167, 168, 170, 174, 175, 188, 220, 252, 323, 352, 366, 367-68, 406, 408, 413, 430, 433

Immigrants in Quebec: access to English-language schools, 216-17, 228-29, 276-77, 388-89; Anglicization of, 74-75, 181-82, 206; Francophone reaction to Anglicization of immigrants, 182-84, 200, 210

Independence of Quebec, *see* Quebec *indépendantisme*, Parti québécois, Rassemblement pour l'indépendance nationale, Ralliement national, Lévesque administration, Sovereignty-association

Institut canadien des affaires publiques, 95, 98, 144

Intellectuals in French Quebec: juxtaposition of class and nation, 195-203, 234; liberalism among, 89-90; and Parti québécois, 242-45; and traditional nationalism, 86-90

Internal colony: concept of, 433; Quebec as, 433

James Bay Project, 220, 361
Jean, Michèle, 111
Jean Coutu Group, 429
Jeunesse étudiante catholique, 99
Johns-Manville Corporation, 103
Johnson, Daniel, 213, 215, 224, 289
Johnson, Pierre-Marc, 385-86, 402
Johnson administration (1966-68), 211-29; and bureaucracy, 212; economic policy, 211-12; education policy, 211; electoral support, 212; and federal government, 214-15; and unions, 217

Joron, Guy, 245, 264

Keyfitz, Nathan, 178
Kierans, Eric, 216, 218
King, Mackenzie, 59, 124, 125

Laberge, Louis, 204
Labrador, 52
Laliberté, Raymond, 257
L'Allier, Jean-Paul, 226
Lamontagne, Maurice, 21-22
Landry, Bernard, 324
Langlois, Charles, 380
Langlois, Reynold, 407
Lapalme, Georges-Émile, 218
Laporte, Pierre, 200-01, 216
Latouche, Daniel, 137, 351
Laurendeau, André, 86, 99
Laurentian Group, 360-61, 428-29
Laurier, Wilfrid, 53, 58-59, 125
Laurin, Camille, 278-79, 292, 374, 385
Laurin-Frenette, Nicole, 253
Laval, Mgr. de, 41
Laval, Université, 55, 91, 92, 95, 96, 154, 159, 269
Lavalin Corporation, 360-62, 429, 431

Lavoie-Roux, Thérèse, 416, 422
Lazure, Denis, 380, 385
Leblanc-Bantey, Denise, 385
Legaré, Anne, 22, 30, 164, 165
Léger, Jean-Marc, 171
Legislation, of Quebec, see Assemblée nationale, Québec
Lemieux, Vincent, 115, 120, 188, 213
Léonard, Jacques, 385
Lesage, Jean, 140, 143, 158-62, 168, 170, 188, 215-18, 226, 289, 335
Lesage administration (1960-1966), 131-43, 171, 173; and bureaucracy, 137; economic policy, 132-35, 138, 156; electoral bases, 143-44, 169-70; education policy, 131-32, 137, 159; and federal government, 124, 139-44, 224; health and welfare policy, 132, 137, 156; and unions, 159-62, 189-90
Lesemann, Frédéric, 154
Lessard, Jean, 158
Lévesque, Father Georges-Henri, 94
Lévesque, Gérard-D., 326, 410, 411
Lévesque, René, 78, 143, 147, 157-59, 173, 216, 218, 253, 271, 274, 284, 287, 291, 304, 309, 323, 340, 343, 358, 362, 374, 379, 380, 383-85, 389, 403-04
Lévesque administration (1976-1985): compared with Lesage administration, 335-36; composition of cabinet, 244, 264; concertation, 272-73, 375-77; constitutional revision, 345-57; constraints upon, 282-85, 334-40, 378; economic policy, 264-67, 273-75, 362-69; and federal government, 293-97, 351-56, 383-84; and Francophone business class, 273-75, 377, 381; labour relations, 268-71, 282, 371-75, 378; and language policy, 275-82, 387-89; and "nationalist populism," 282, 381-82; and PQ organization, 358; public expenditures, 264-66, 273, 364-65, 369-71, 410; referendum on sovereignty-association, 271, 284-85; relations with unions, 268-71, 282, 371-75; as "social democratic," 267-68, 271-72, 282, 358-59, 378-80; social measures, 267-68; sovereignty-association, as

defined by, 301-10, 378; and state
enterprises, 266-67, 365-69; strategy
for securing sovereignty (*étapisme*),
285-93, 322, 331-40, 378-79, 383-85;
tax policy, 273, 360, 364-65, 377, 411
Levitt, Kari, 221
Liberal Party, federal, 53, 54, 58-59,
118, 145, 346
Liberal Party, Quebec, 110, 160, 217-
18, 243, 325, 346-47, 357, 419-20;
and elections, 116-21, 143-44, 169-
74, 233-34, 342-44, 385-86; leadership, 216, 218; and patronage, 115;
see also Lesage administration,
Bourassa administration
Liberal professionals, *see* Petty bourgeoisie
Ligue communiste (M-L), 203
Ligue nationaliste, 60
Linteau, Paul-André, 100
Lipsey, Richard, 307
Lortie, Pierre, 405

Mackasey, Bryce, 236
Madelipêche, 412
Malenfant, Raymond, 412, 414
Manicouaguan-Outardes ("Manic"),
109, 130, 133, 158, 220
Manitoba, 146, 411
Manoir Richelieu, 412, 414, 423
Marcellin-Laurin, Diane, 406
Marchand, Jean, 98, 103, 161-62, 236
Marcoux, Yvan, 405, 414
Marier, André, 157-59
Marie-Victorin, Brother, 92
Marine Industries, 133, 162, 222
Marler, George, 168-69
Marois, Pauline, 386
Marois, Pierre, 322, 380
Martin, Jean-Marie, 94
Marx, Herbert, 410
McCallum, John, 22
McConnell, J.W., 108-09
McGill University, 55, 73, 154
Meech Lake Accord (Langevin
accord), 396-404, 430; content of,
396-400; reaction to, 400-04
Memmi, Albert, 203
Mercier, Honoré, 36, 125
Migué, Jean-Luc, 407
Miller, Roger E., 279

Mills, K., 318
Milner, Henry, 236
Miner, Horace, 75-76
Mitterand, François, 359
Modernization, concept of, 12-17;
political, 14-17
Monopoly capitalism and political
modernization, 17; in Quebec,
164-67
Montpetit, Edouard, 93
Montreal, 24, 39, 46, 56, 69, 73, 116,
139, 144, 172, 181-83, 212, 237, 241,
272, 292, 315, 361, 389, 419
Montréal, Université de, 43, 55, 91-92,
93, 100, 154, 178
Montreal Light, Heat and Power, 96,
110
Moreux, Colette, 43
Morin, Claude, 156-59, 219, 287-88,
379, 403-04
Morin, Jacques-Yvan, 198, 402, 404
Mountain, Jacob, 54
Mouvement Desjardins, 175, 252, 367,
429
Mouvement laïque de langue fran-
çaise, 154, 159
Mouvement Québec français, 419
Mouvement souveraineté-association,
216, 219, 245, 274, 304, 360, 361
Mulroney, Brian, 383, 396

Nadeau, Richard, 328
Nation, concept of, 29-31
National Cablevision, 175
National consciousness, approaches
to, 29-31; *see also* Quebec national-
ism
National Energy Policy, 352-53
National Policy, 314
Nationalism, concept of, 29-31
New Brunswick, 430
New Democratic Party, 246, 346, 358
Newfoundland, 81, 352, 364, 399
New France, 40-44
New middle class, concept of 90-91
New middle class in French Quebec,
28, 209-10, 231; administrators and
bureaucrats, 95-97; compared with
western Canadian elites, 315; emer-
gence of, 90-100, 154-59; in
Lévesque cabinet, 244; and neo-